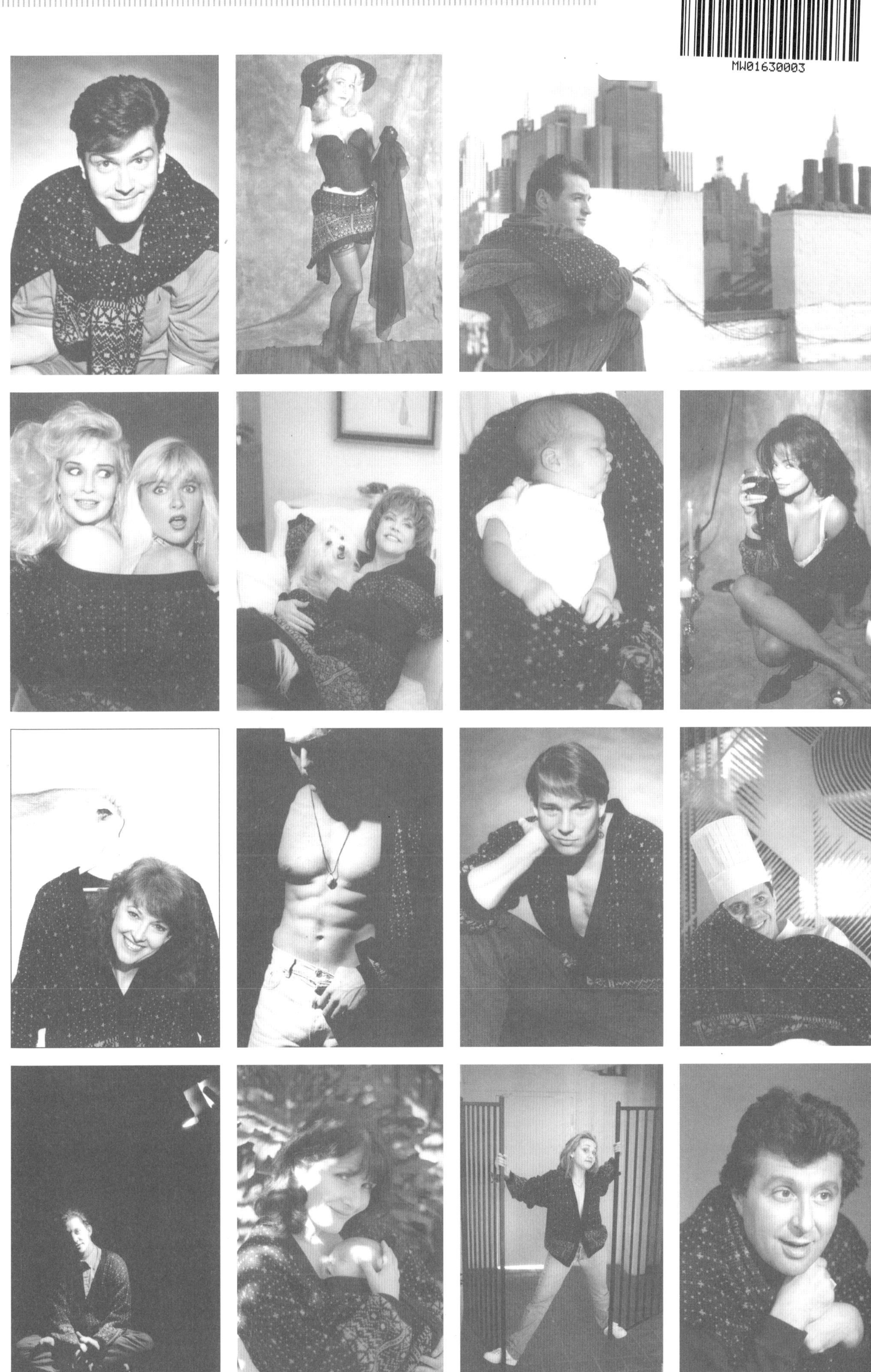

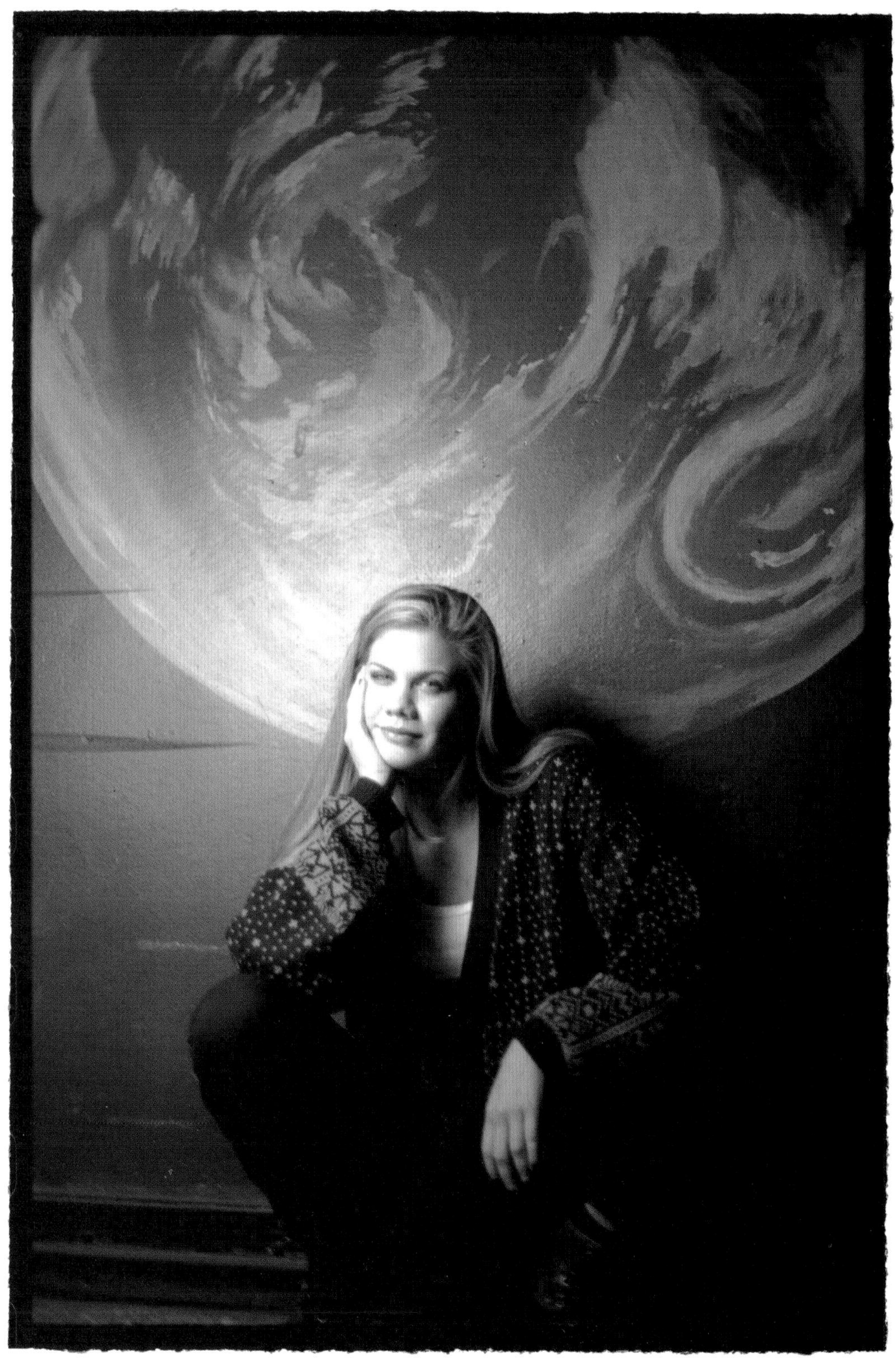

THE SWEATER BOOK

Hundreds of People ✦ One Common Thread

Stephen Mosher

Thomas Dunne Books
St. Martin's Press
New York

Endpaper photographs:
Front: *Left page from left to right:* Rodney Adams, Tom Dillon, Joyce Van Patten and Spike, Tamara Adams, Michael Whaley and son, Ricky and Willy Smithline, Rich Affanato, Jeff Feringa, Maryann Keleher, Wendye Clarendon, J. Paul Boehmer, Neil Sedaka, Faye Lane, Darren Doane, Jim Stanek and Demo. *Right page from left to right:* Ricky Pope, Carmen Thomas, Mark Tissot, Christine Stinson and Suellen Sharp, Rita McKenzie, Matthew England, Alex Datcher, Andi Allen, Todd Terry, Chris Gilbert, Arnauld Briand, Tom Wood, Mary Gordon Murray, Nicole Sullivan, Jerry Hadley.
Back: *Left page from left to right:* Elizabeth Hope, Don Dellair, Renee Humphrey, William Ivey Long, Dana Gillespie, Isai Cazares, Scott Winant and Hallie, Stephen Mosher, Pamela Payton Wright, Jeremy Schwartz, Melody Holland, Carolyn Freeman, Sean, Liam and Terry Johnston, Vince Gatton, Steve Lovett. *Right page from left to right:* Jimmy Cummings, Keven Kilner and Jordan Baker, Neil Foley, Marsha Mason, Shannon Bailey, Ted Casablanca, Alison Fraser, David Salih, Leslie Alexander, Mitchell Lichtenstein, Dolores Rivellino, Gene and Amy Connor, Brady Schwind, David Gianopoulos, Jeff Zubik.

Frontispiece photograph: Kristen Johnston

THOMAS DUNNE BOOKS.
An imprint of St. Martin's Press.

www.stmartins.com

Design by Susan Walsh

ISBN 0-312-31166-4

First Edition: October 2003

10 9 8 7 6 5 4 3 2 1

As I have pledged to donate a substantial portion of my royalties to the charities Broadway Cares/Equity Fights AIDS and Cassidy's Place, clearly my work on this project is dedicated to the fight to end AIDS and to the sustenance of people living with HIV and AIDS. This project, though, and all of my work is also dedicated to the making proud of four people: my grandmother, who taught me about art; my mother, who taught me about dignity; my father, who taught me about integrity; and Pat Dwyer, who taught me about harmony.

Without them I am nothing.

THERE WAS THIS SWEATER...

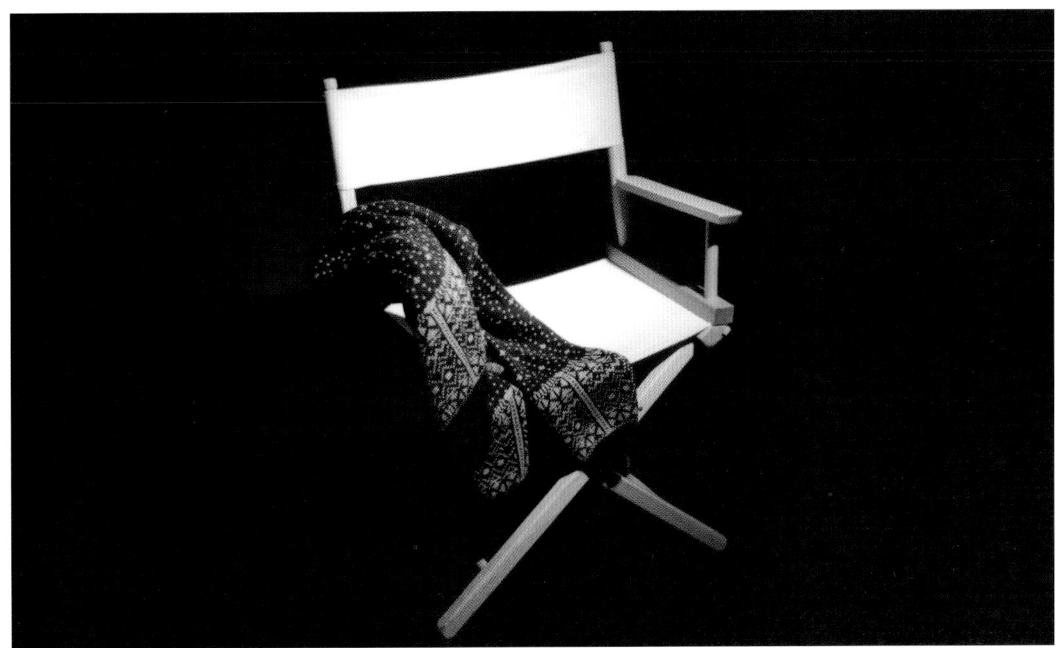

In a department store, on a December day in Denton, Texas; it called out to me, "Choose me. Buy me," it said; "Take me home," it said; "I would be a great Christmas present for Pat Dwyer," it said. Two, three times I passed the garment while doing my holiday shopping. Each glance caused a pause to feel the material, to examine the cut, to consider a purchase. The fourth pause found me headed to the cashier, credit card in one hand, sweater in the other. It did make a great gift for Pat Dwyer.

Pat Dwyer

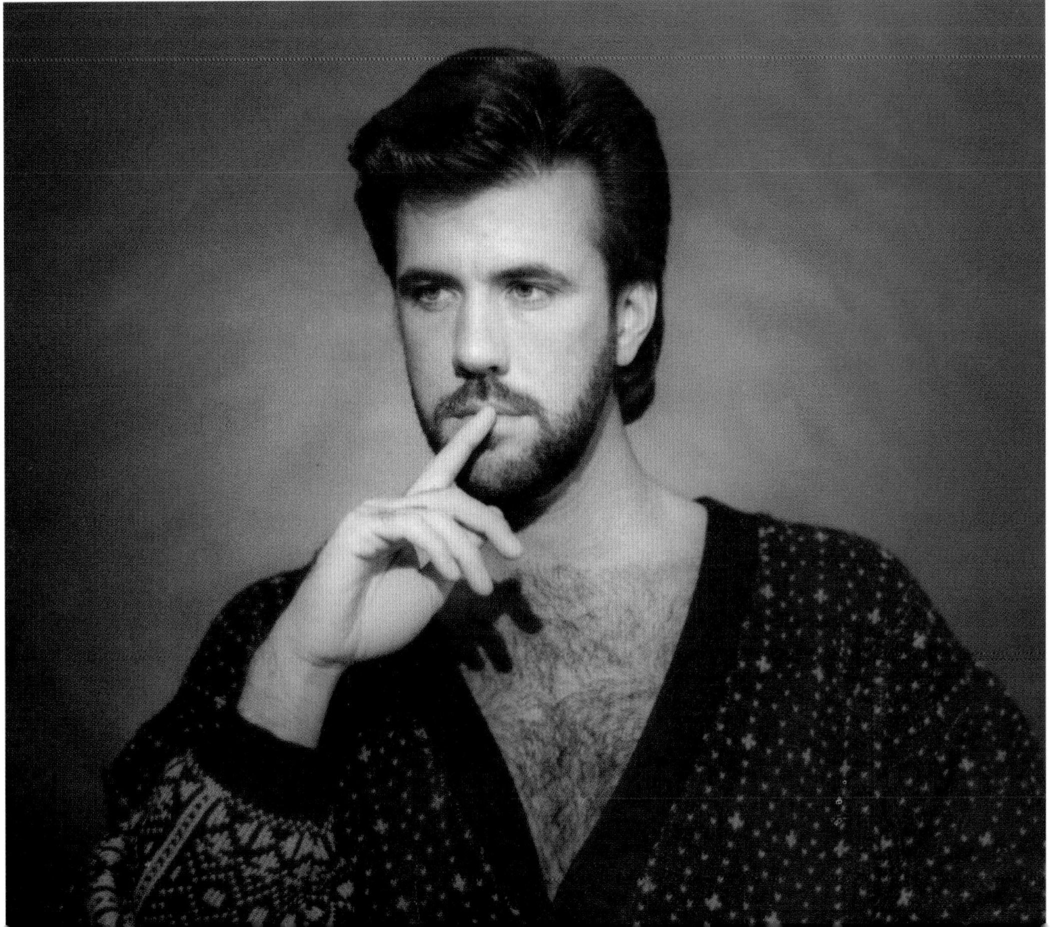

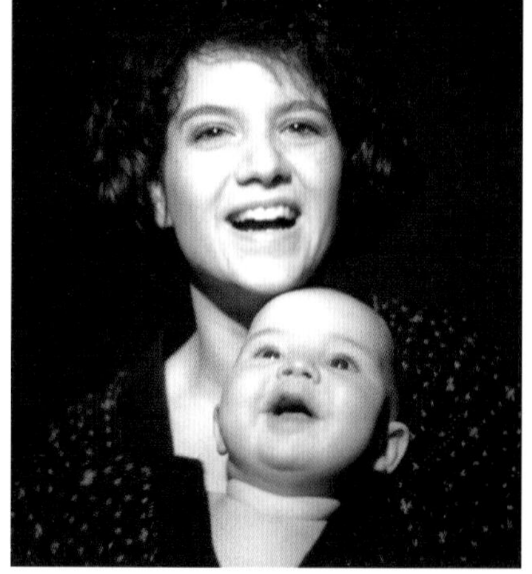

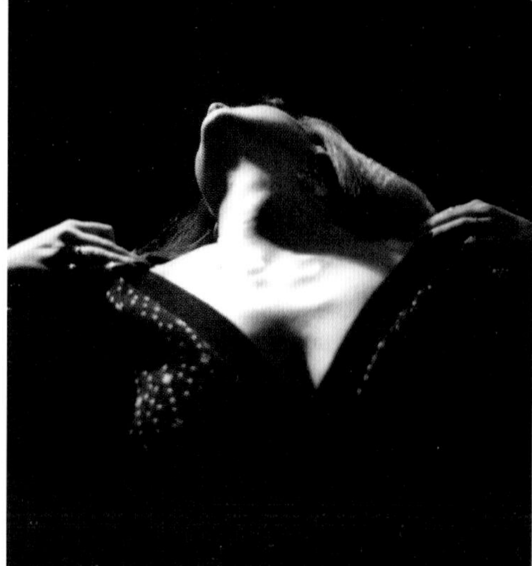

Clockwise from top left: Linda Ford with Timothy England; Amy Raynes; Paul Tigue; Laura Wells; Martha E. Weatherford; *(left to right)* Lisa Gabrielle Greene, Brigitte Bavousett, Morgana Shaw and Mary-Margaret Pyeatt; Ellen Locy; Jane Titus.

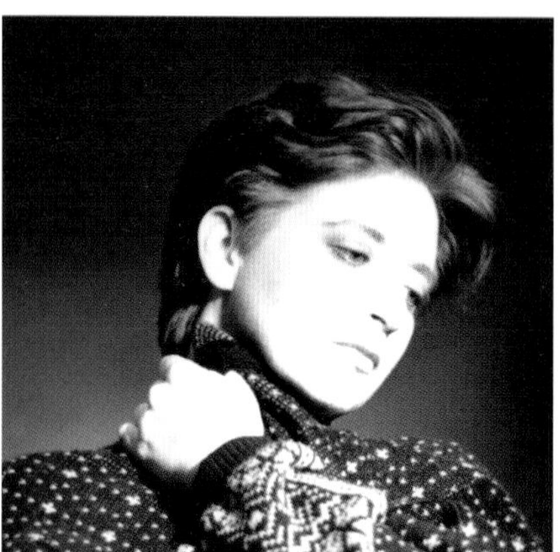

Sometimes the sweater hung in the closet. Othertimes, Pat wore the sweater. Most of the time, though, I wore the garment. It became my favorite article of clothing and was frequently on my back when I worked. No surprise that I was wearing it when Amy Raynes arrived for her head-shot sitting. A fair-skinned blond beauty, Amy had chosen a pink turtleneck for her shot. Worried the choice would render her ghostlike, I peeled off the sweater and she wore it instead. A few rolls of traditional head shots and one roll of portraits yielded stunning results.

Oddly, in a short space of time the same scenario occurred with other actors. Seeing the photos of these people wearing the same garment in varying ways surprised me: different people, same lighting, same garment, same photographer. What stood out in each photo was the individuality of each person. Fascinated, I began asking others to wear the sweater. The journey to study as many different personalities as possible that the sweater and I set out on resulted in a collection of more than eight hundred photos intended as a benefit for AIDS-related organizations. We were welcomed into many homes and many lives, but all along it was really the sweater's journey. I'm just glad that I was along for the ride.

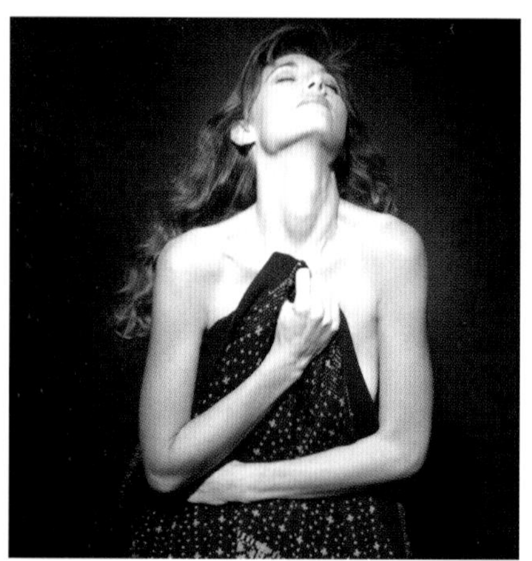

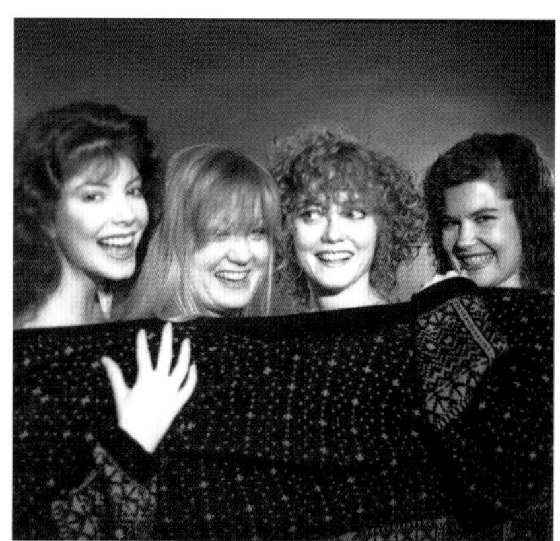

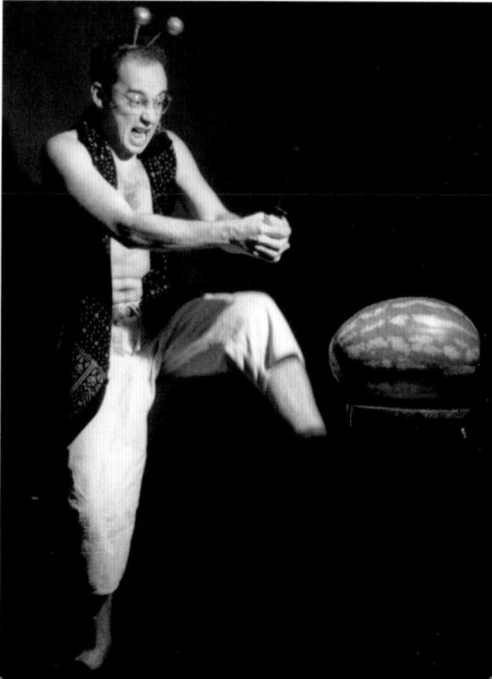

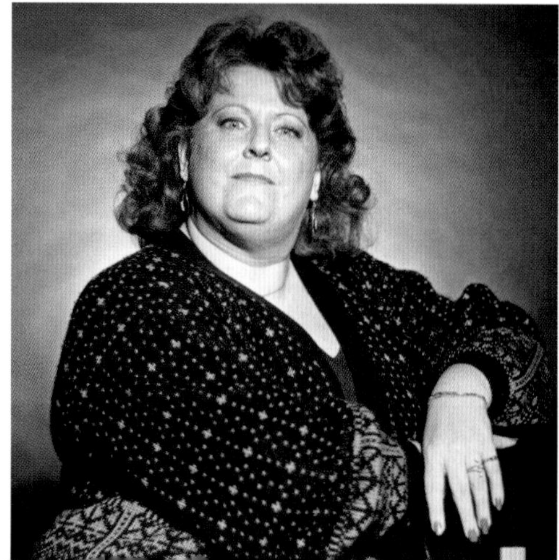

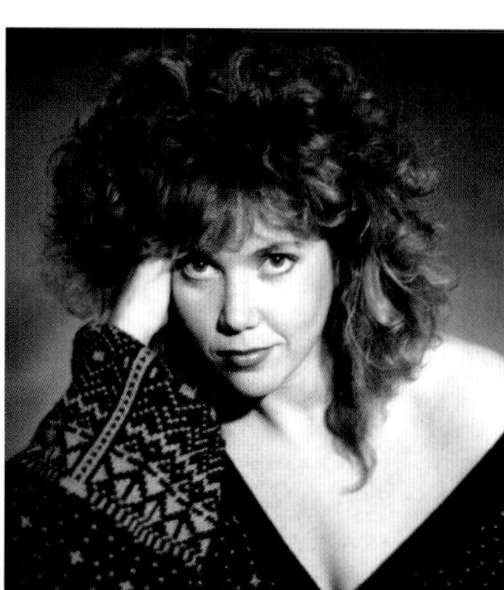

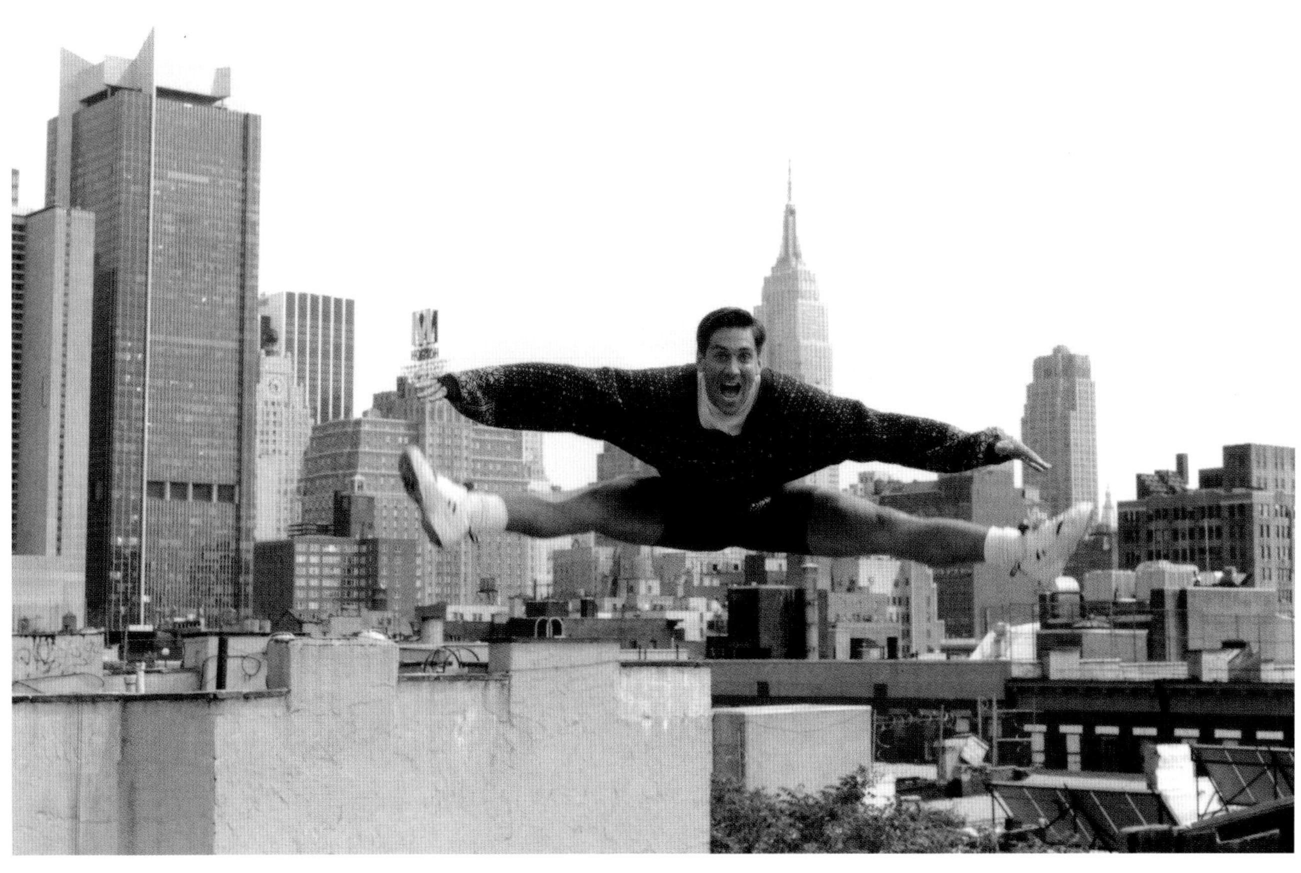

THE SWEATER IN NEW YORK—*in which the sweater wakes up in the city that never sleeps*

Michael Berresse and Suzanna Keller against the Manhattan skyline

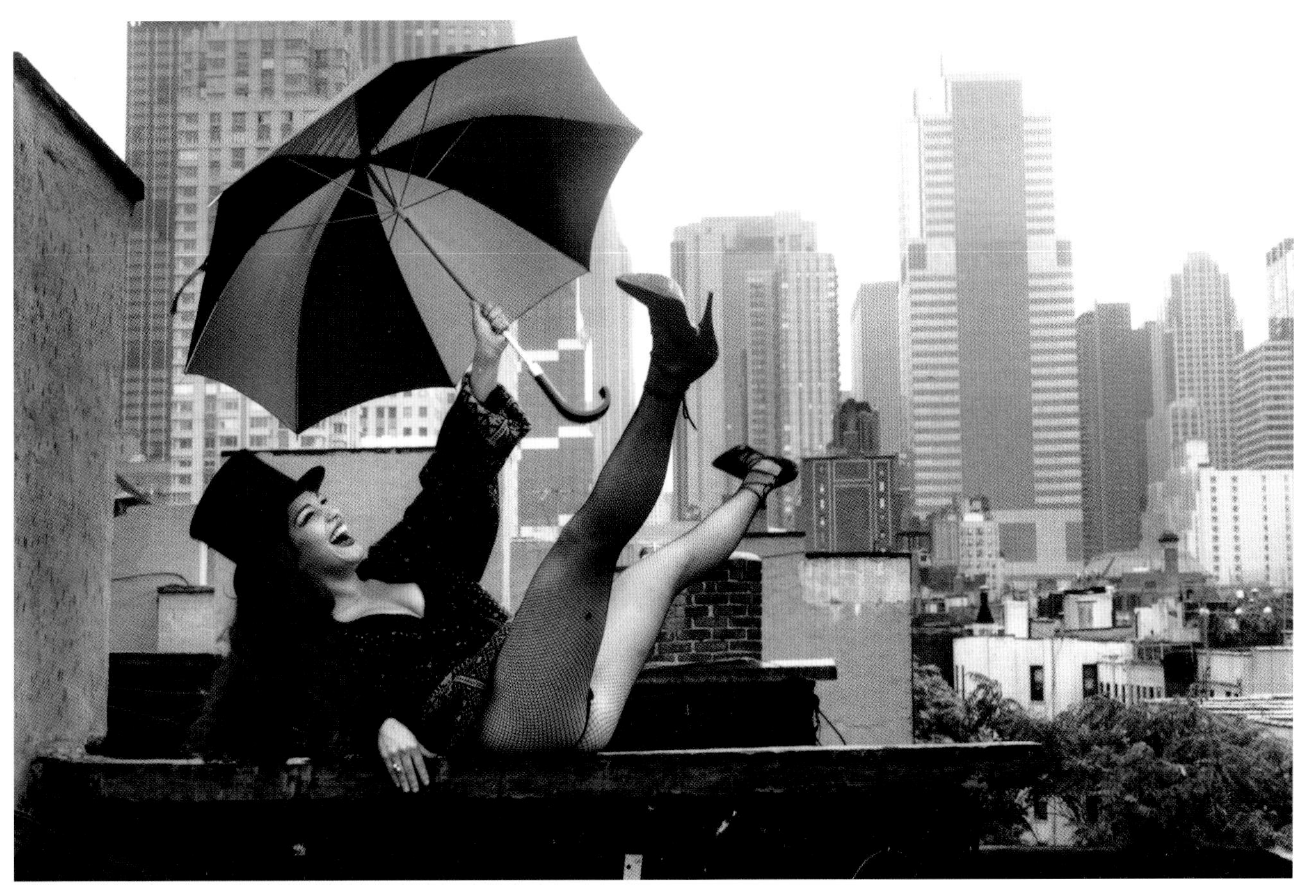

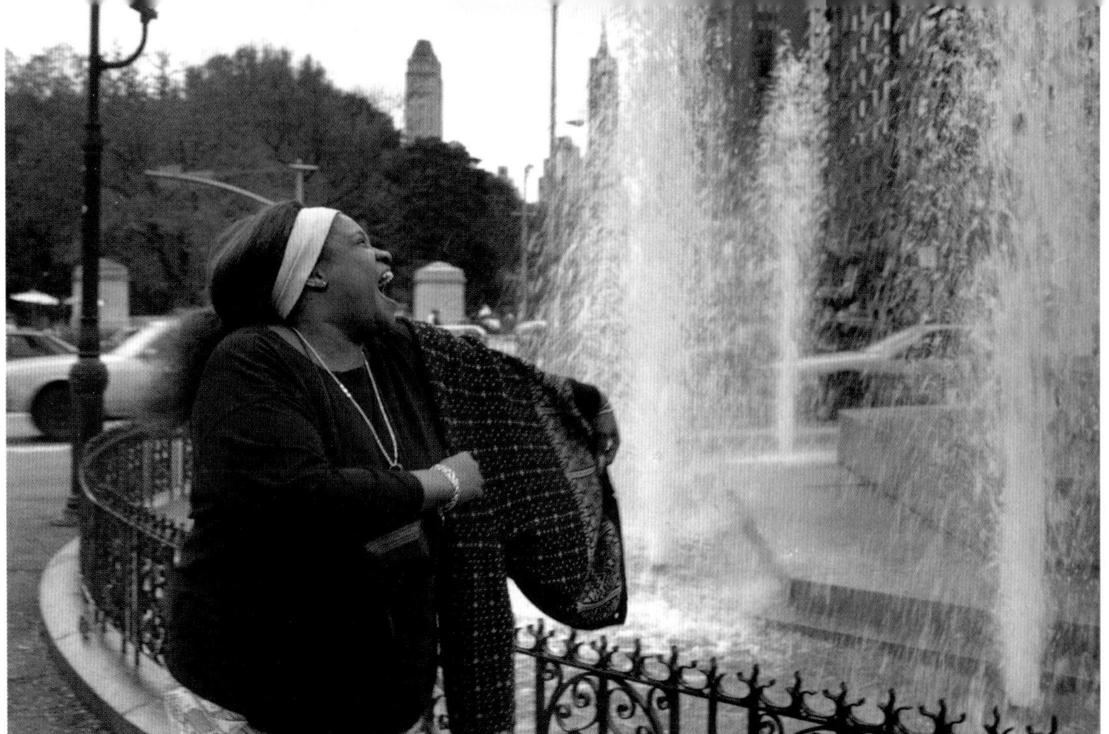

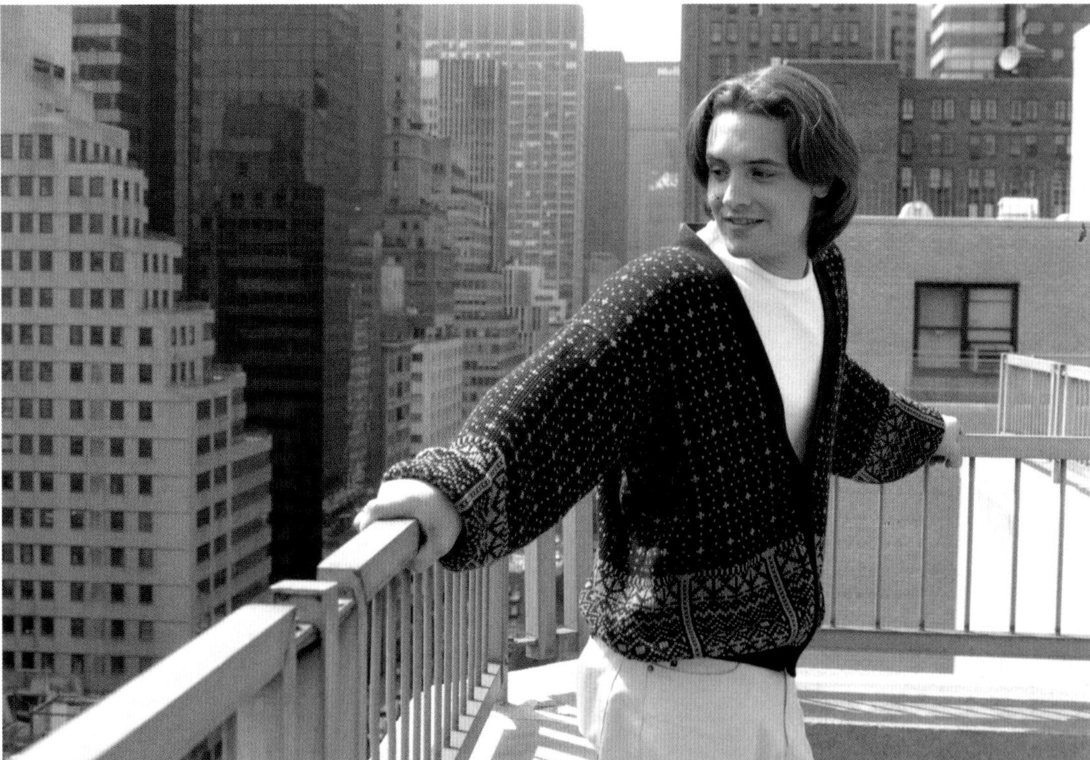

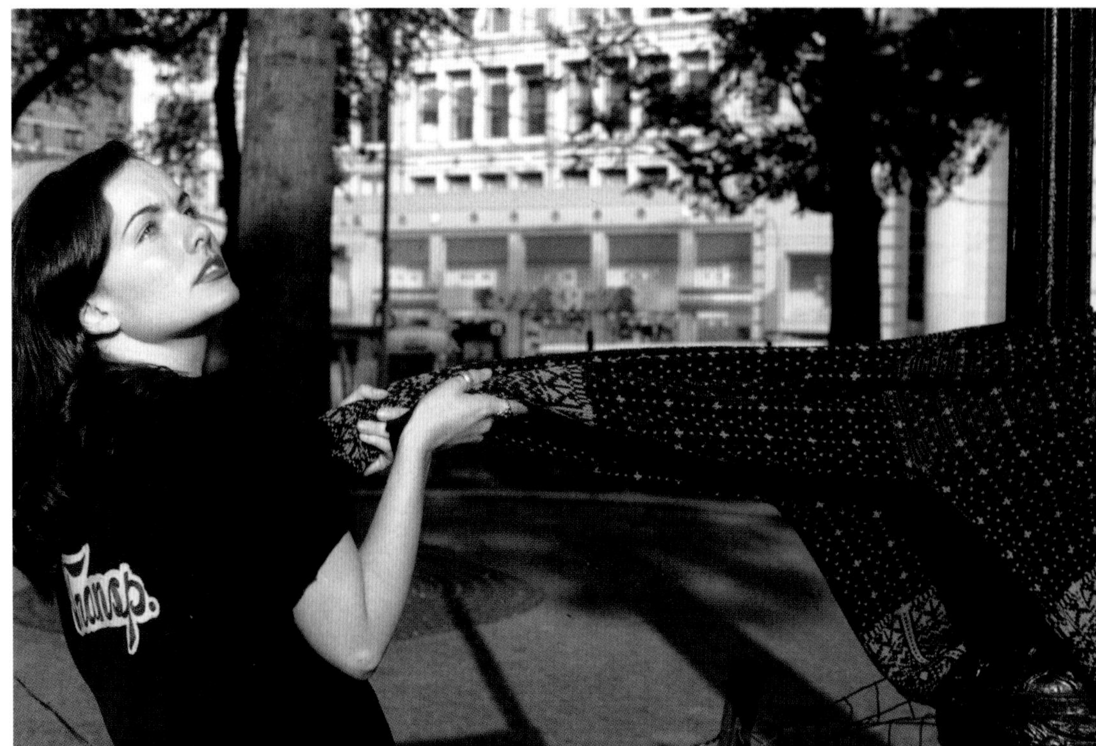

This page:

Thea Vidale in Columbus Circle

Will Freidle above Park Avenue

Gwin Turner in Union Square Park

Opposite, clockwise from top left:

Judy Kaye against the New York skyline

Lindsay Duncan on the East River

Maxwell Caulfield in Times Square

Jessica Hecht in Washington Square Park

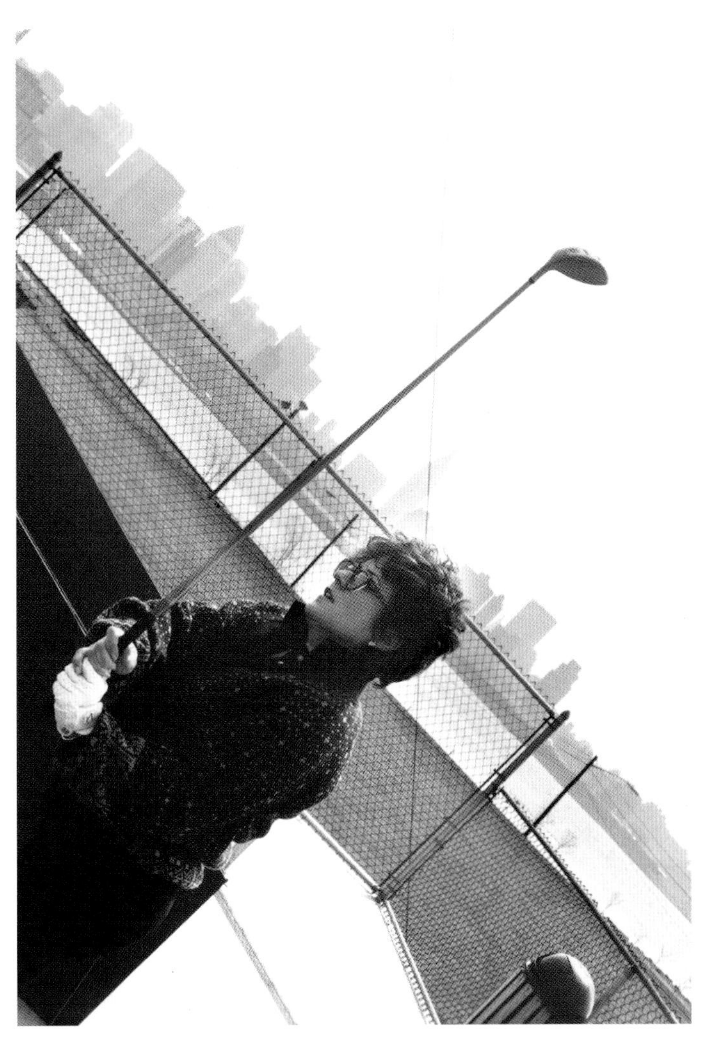

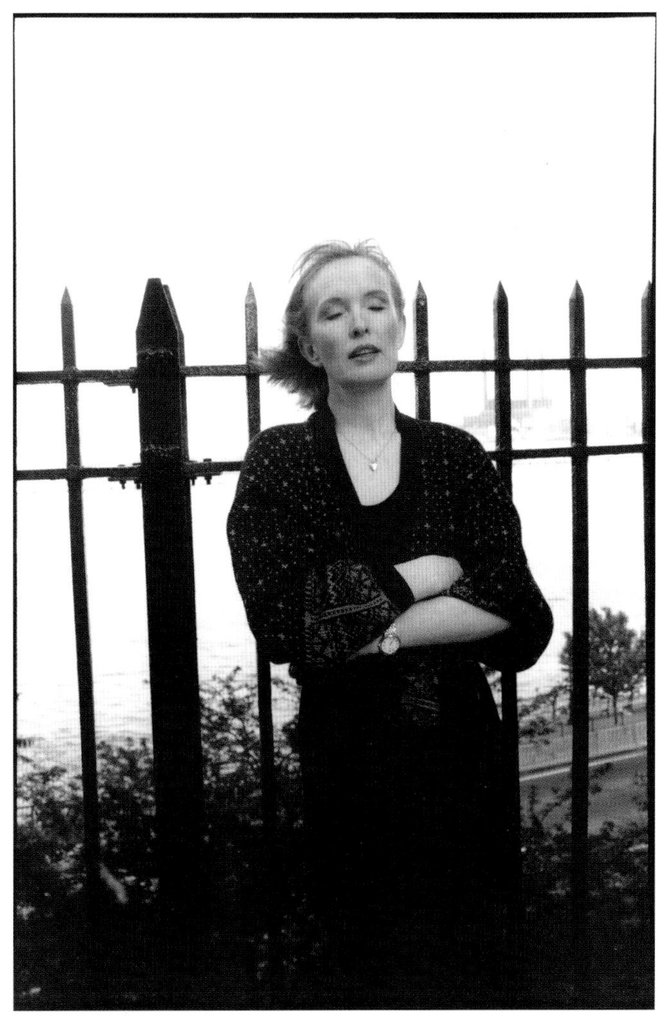

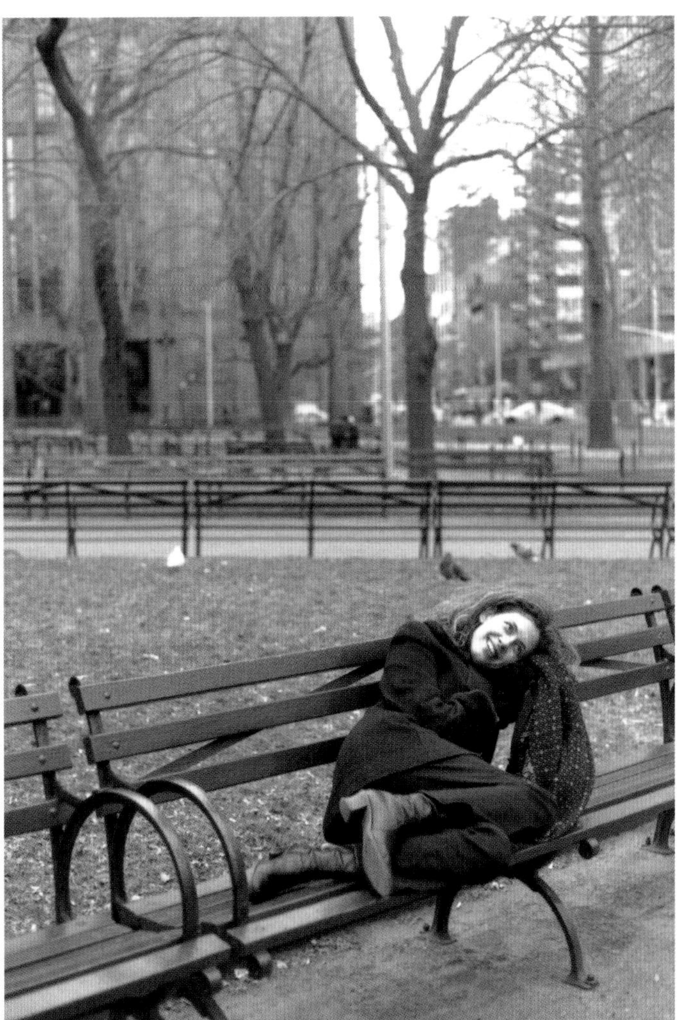

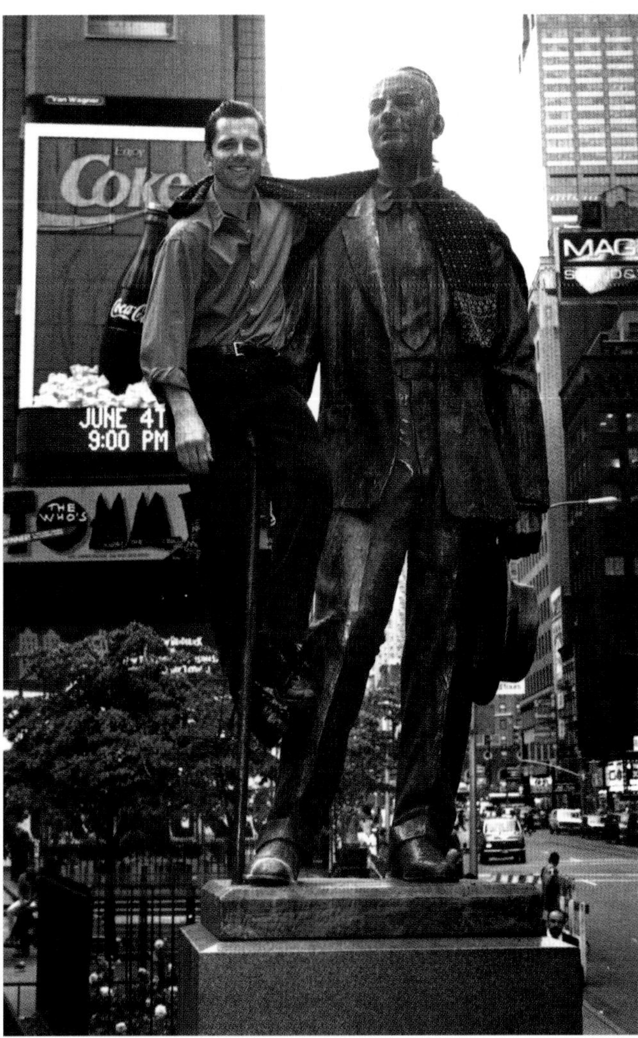
Coke
JUNE 4T
9:00 PM
THE WHO'S

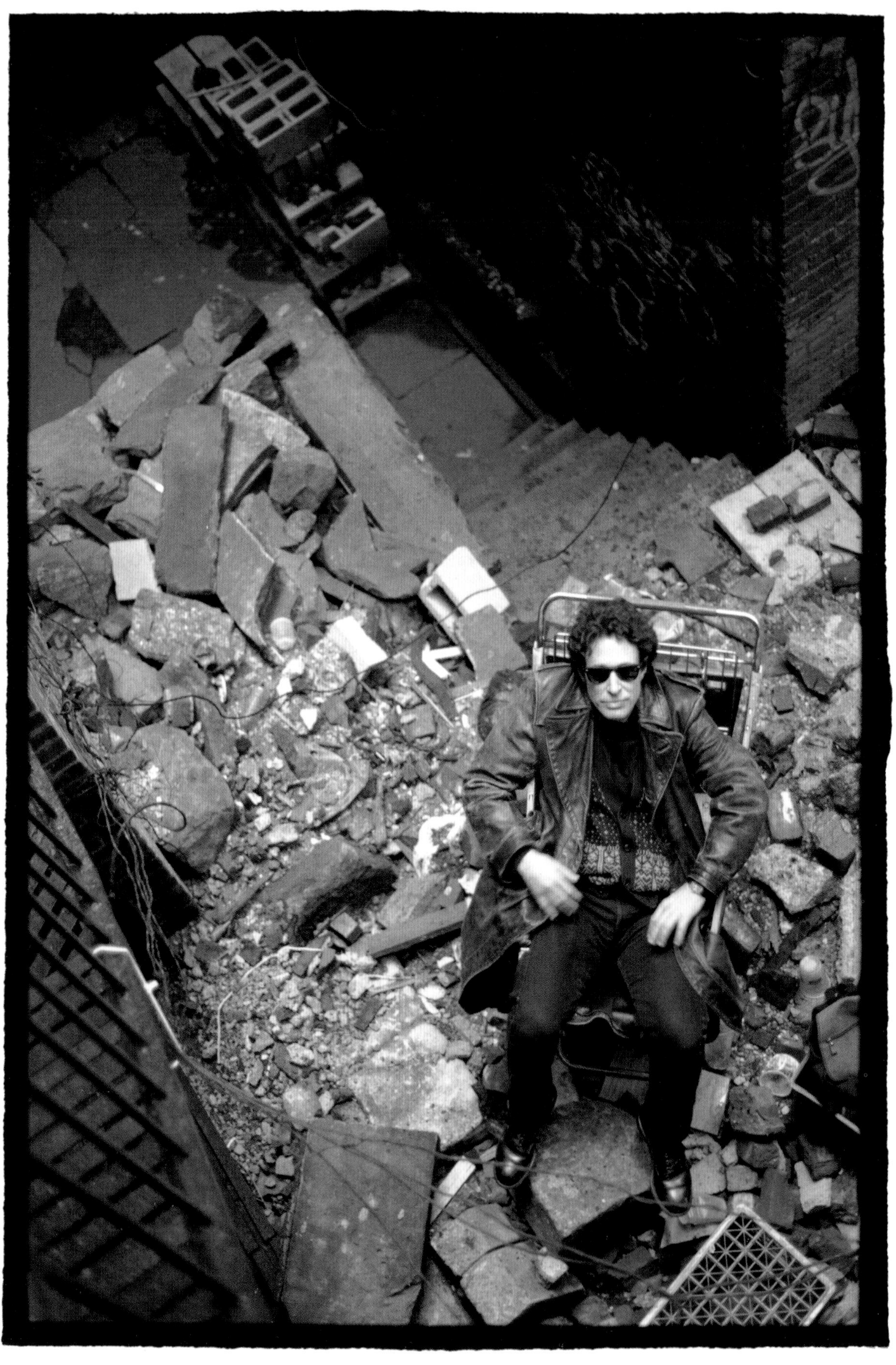

John Shea on 20th Street behind the Limelight

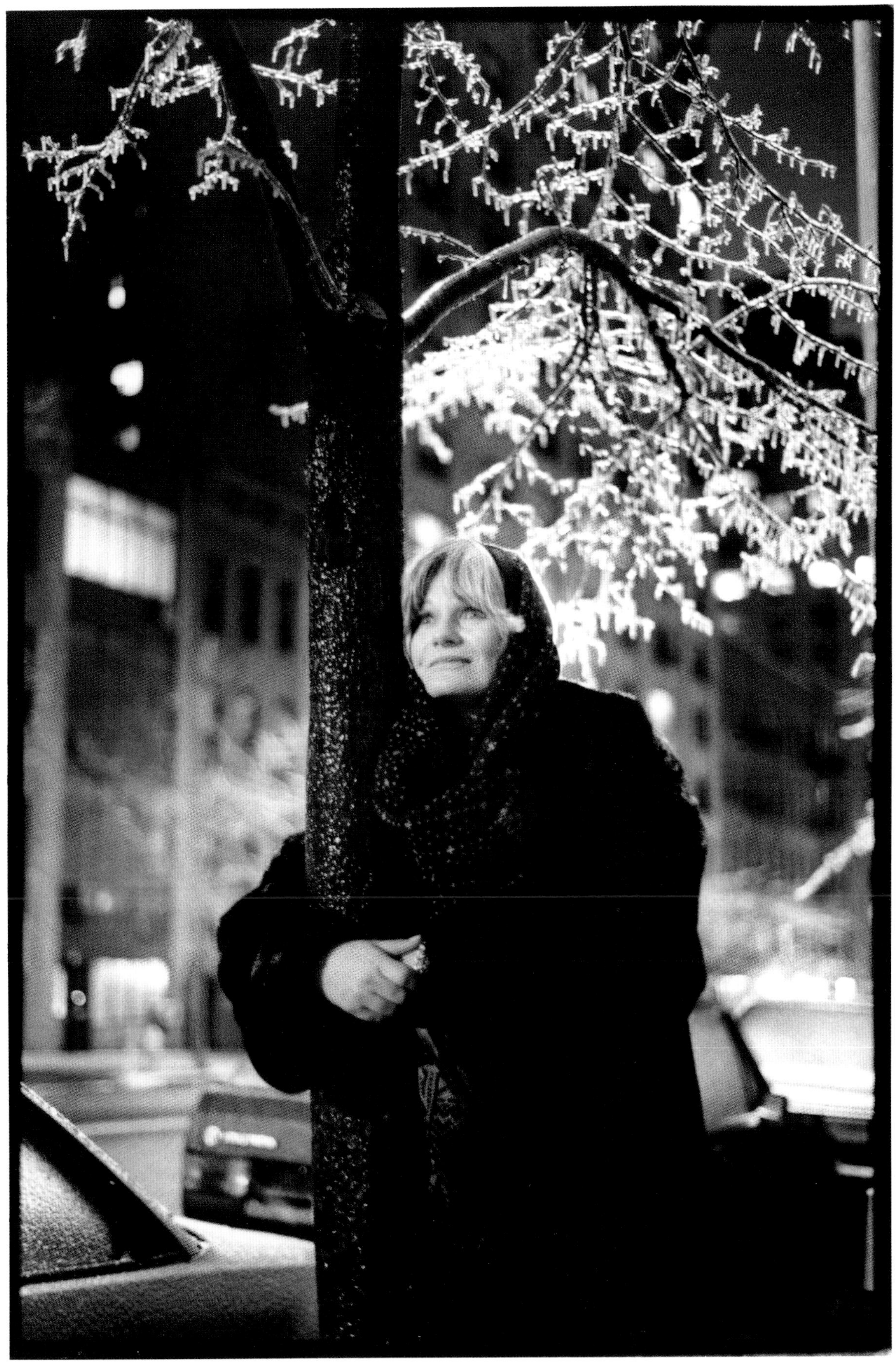

Valerie Perrine

It was dark, after an ice storm, but Valerie Perrine was anxious to be photographed outside with the beauty she insisted was God. I was worried about the lack of light but, as though from within, Valerie created all the light we needed to work.

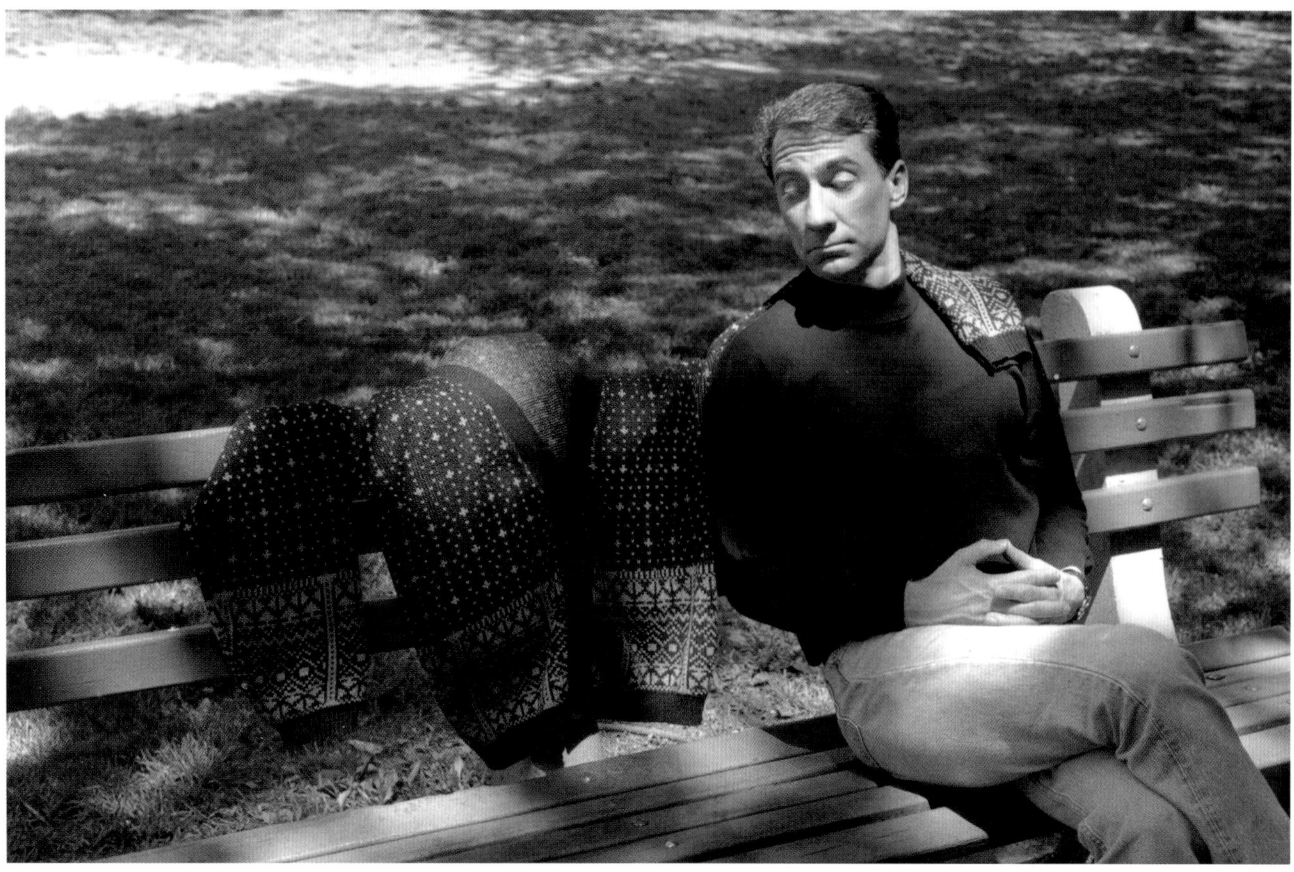

David Garrison in Riverside Drive Park

Mary Beth Hurt in the Riverside Drive Park boat basin

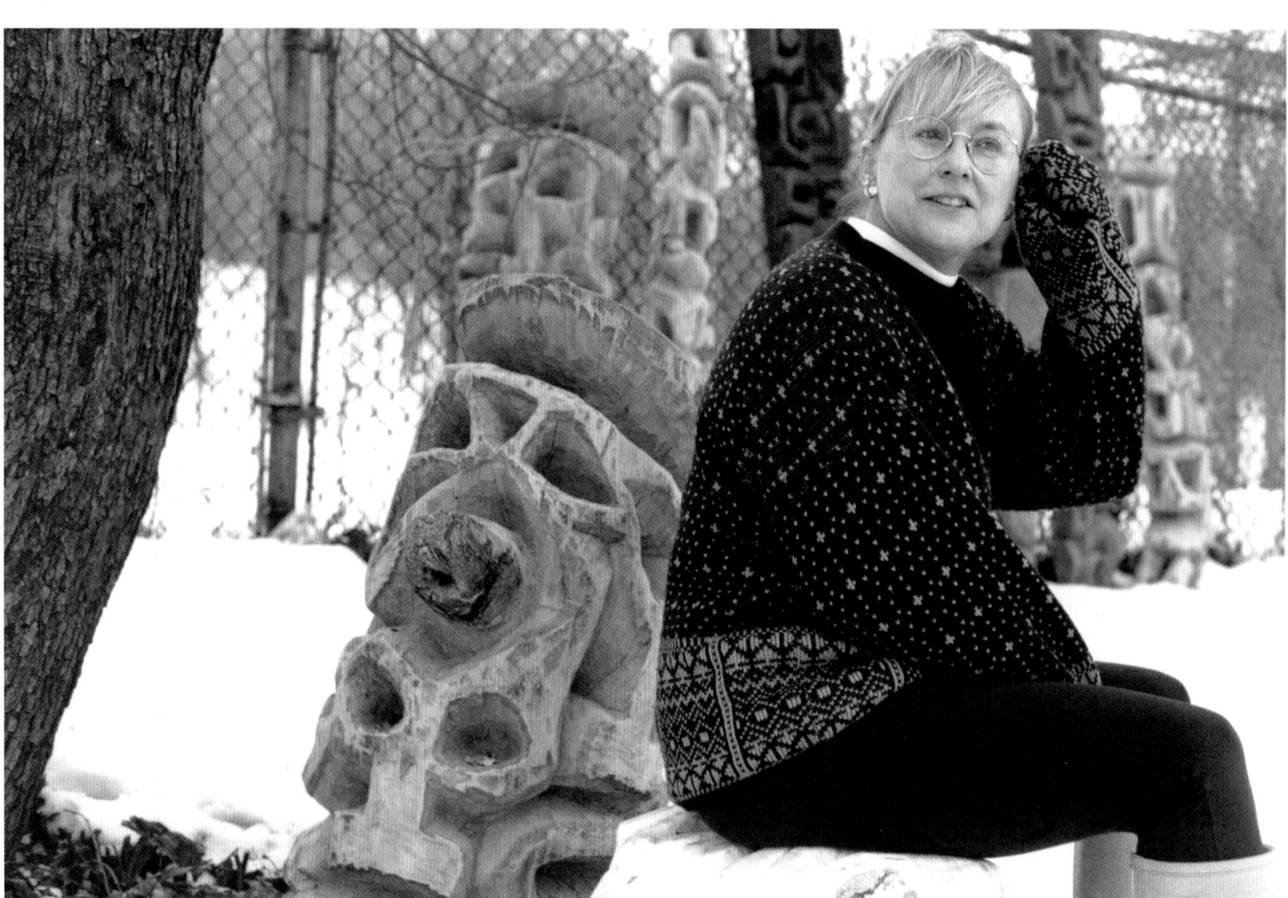

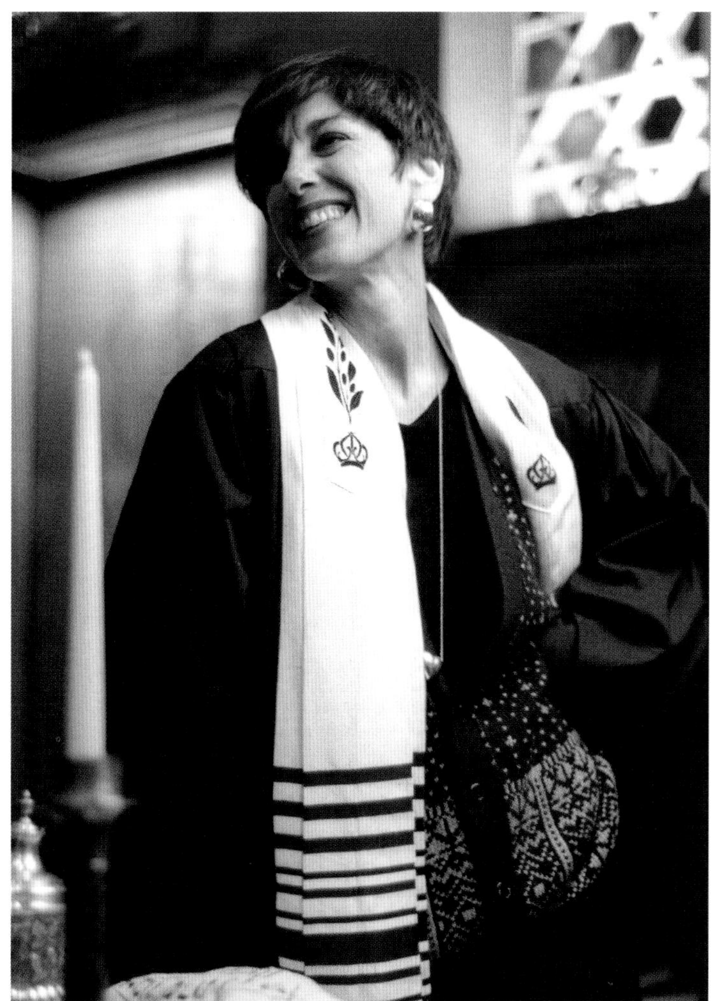

Cantor Ellen Stettner
at the Stephen Wise
Free Synagogue

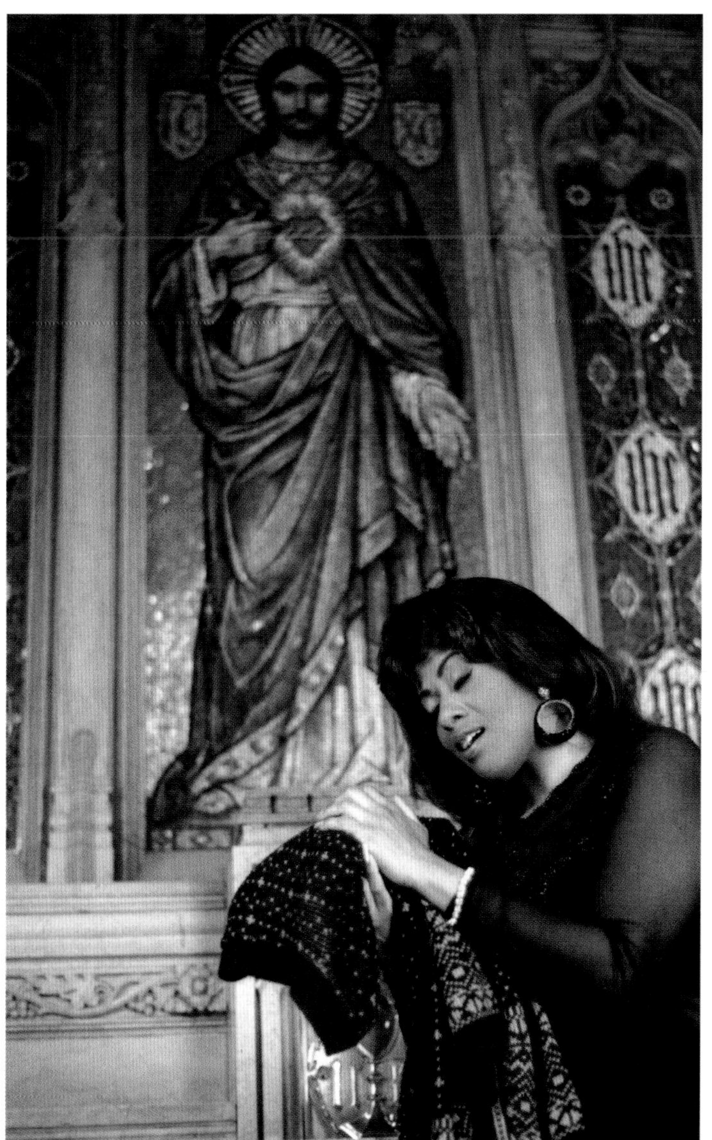

Jennifer Holiday
at St. Malachy's,
the Actor's Chapel

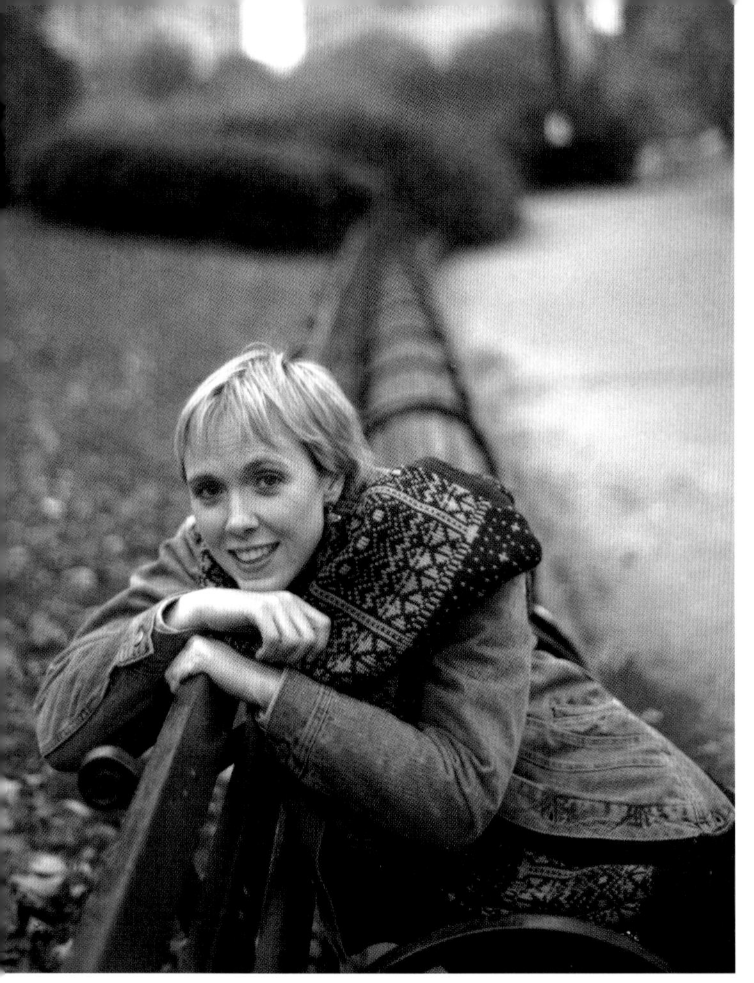

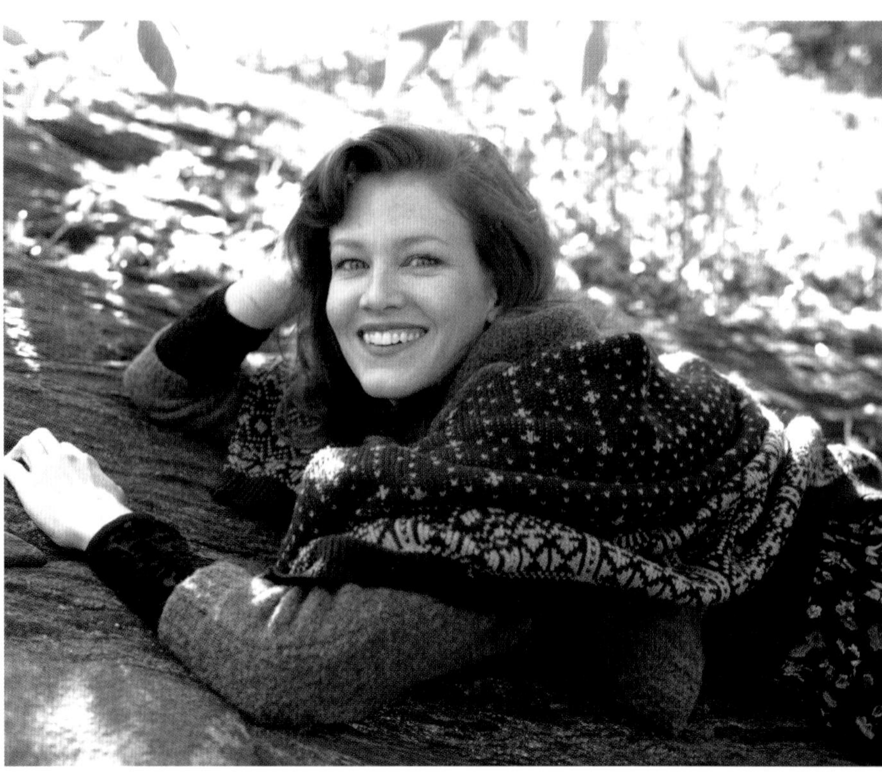

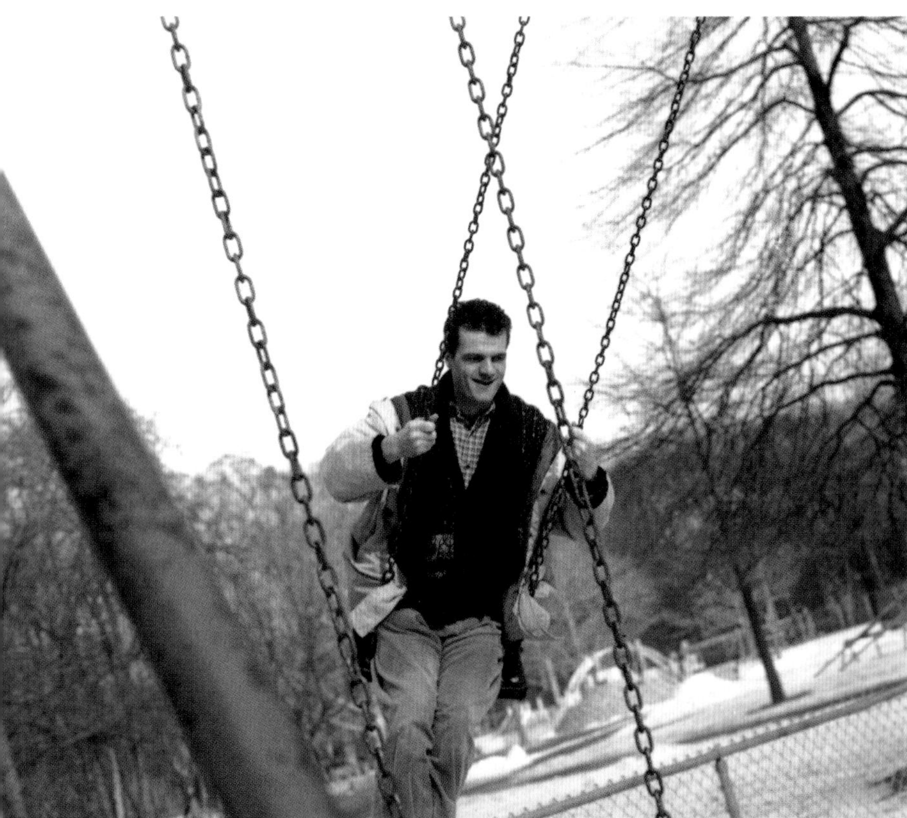

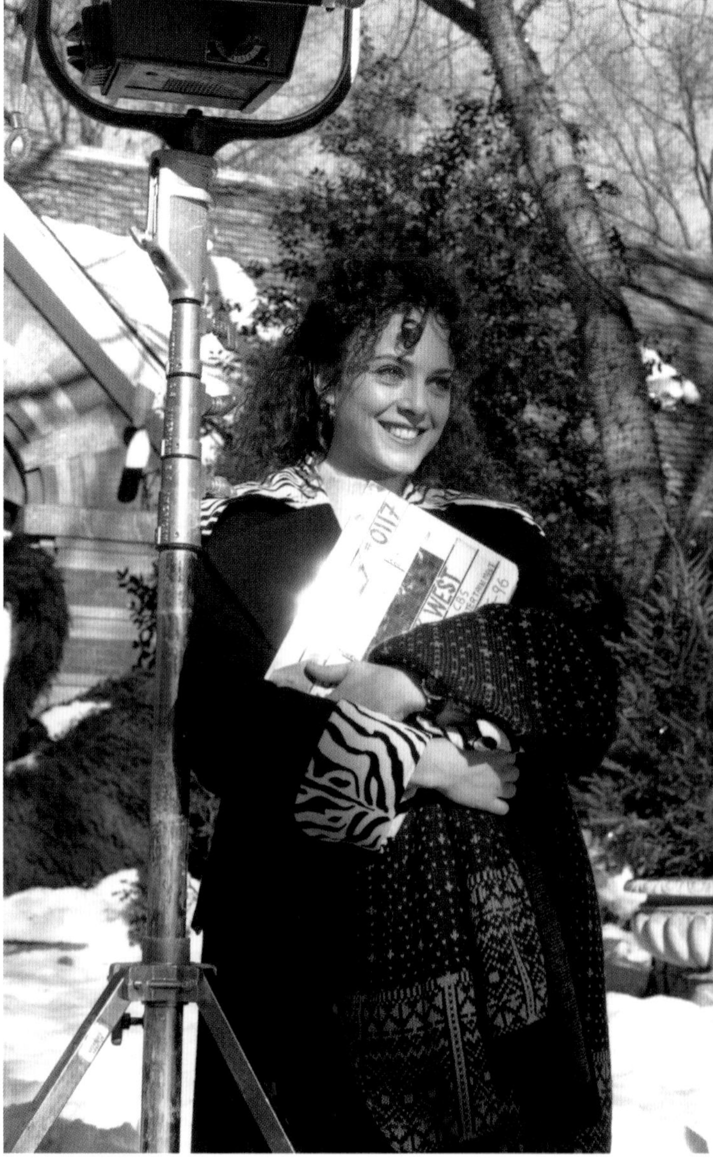

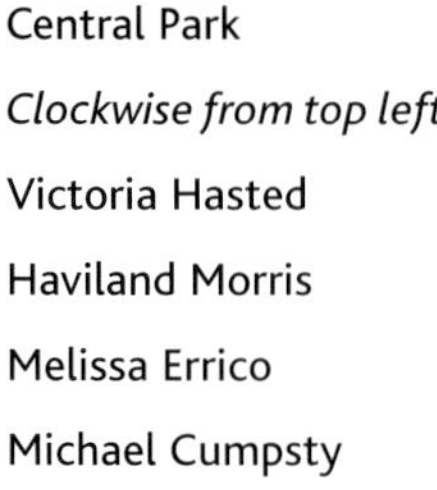

Central Park

Clockwise from top left:

Victoria Hasted

Haviland Morris

Melissa Errico

Michael Cumpsty

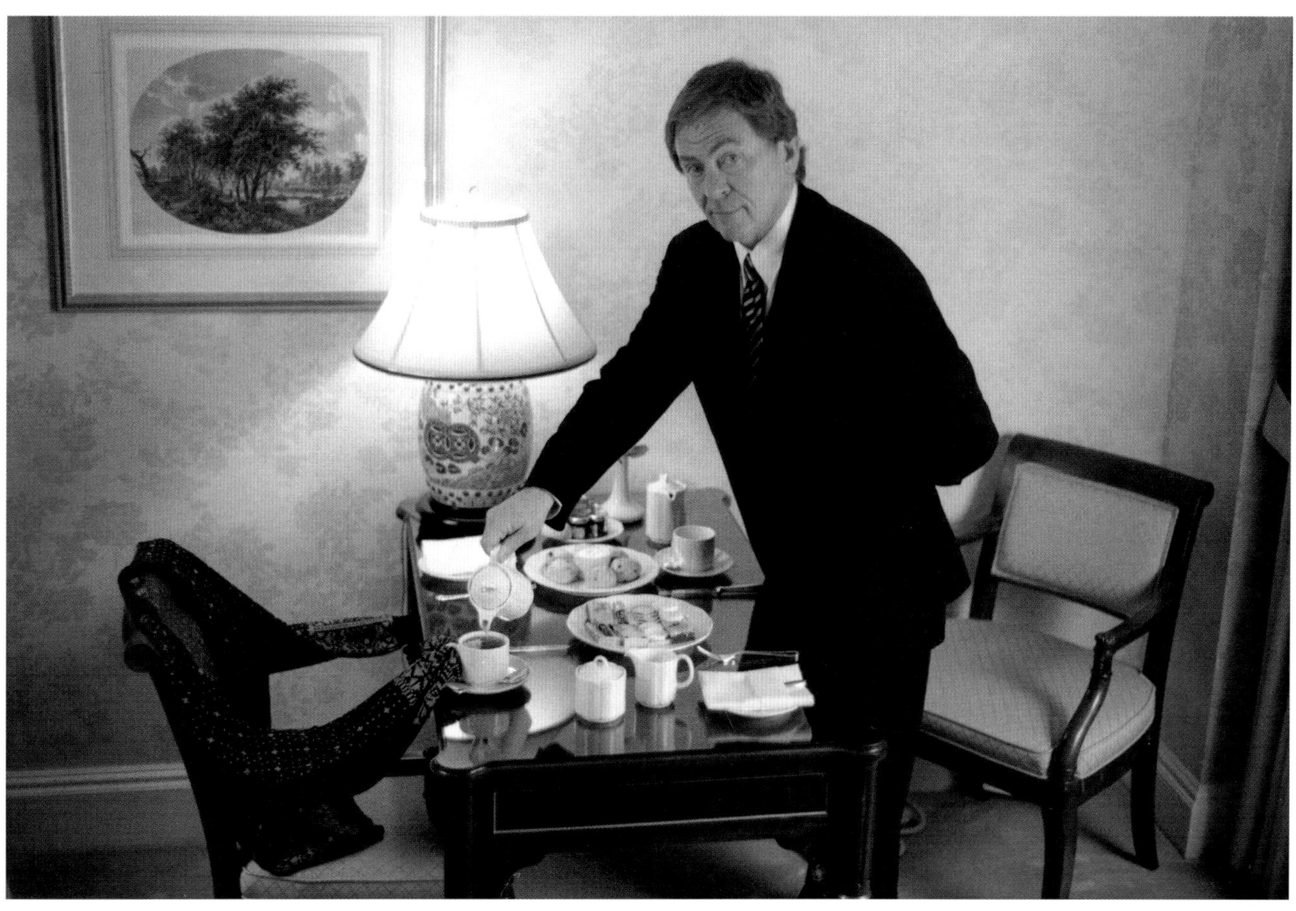

Daniel Davis at the Ritz-Carlton on Central Park South

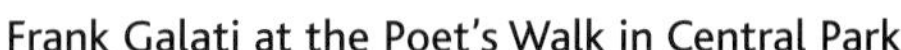
Frank Galati at the Poet's Walk in Central Park

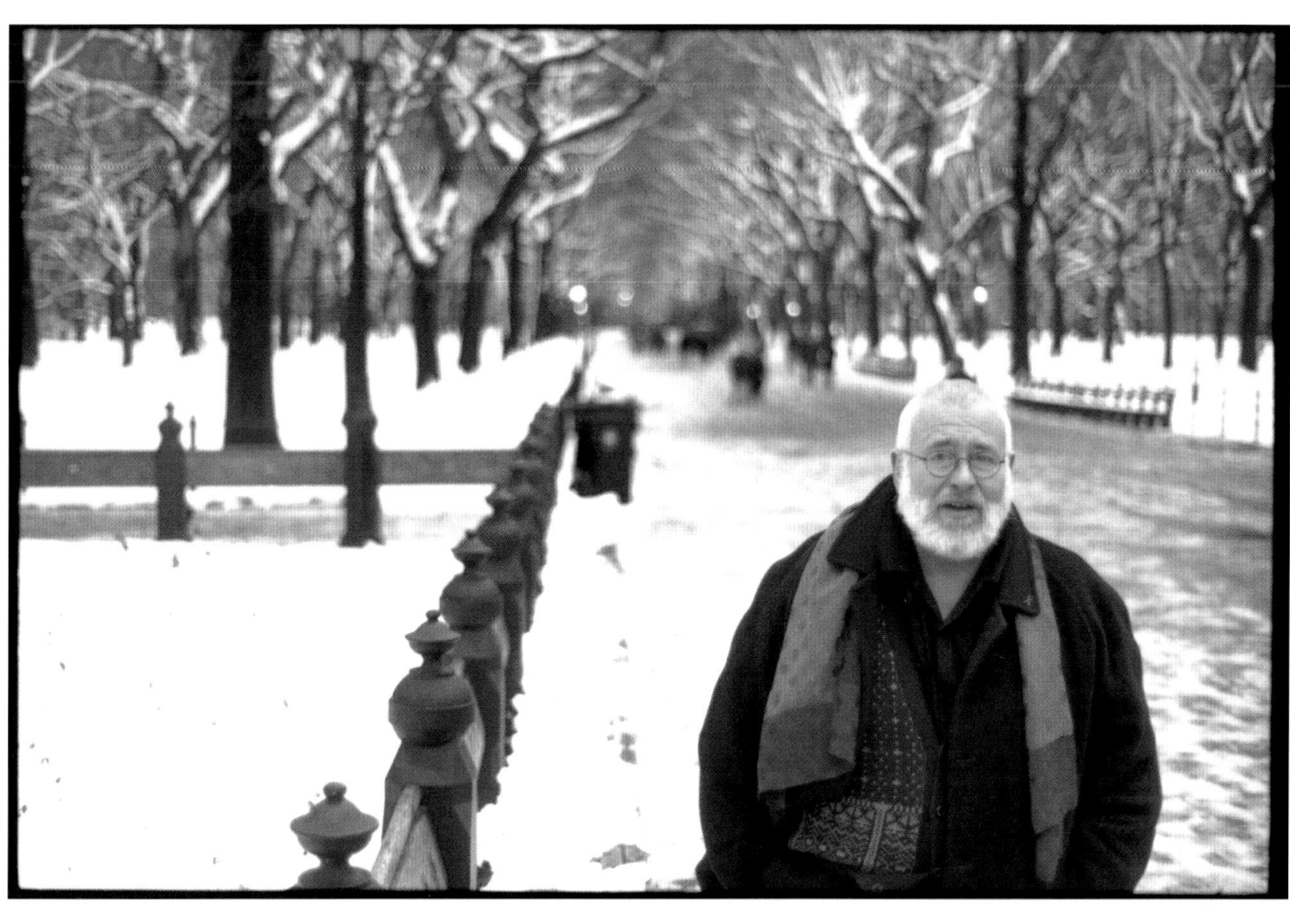

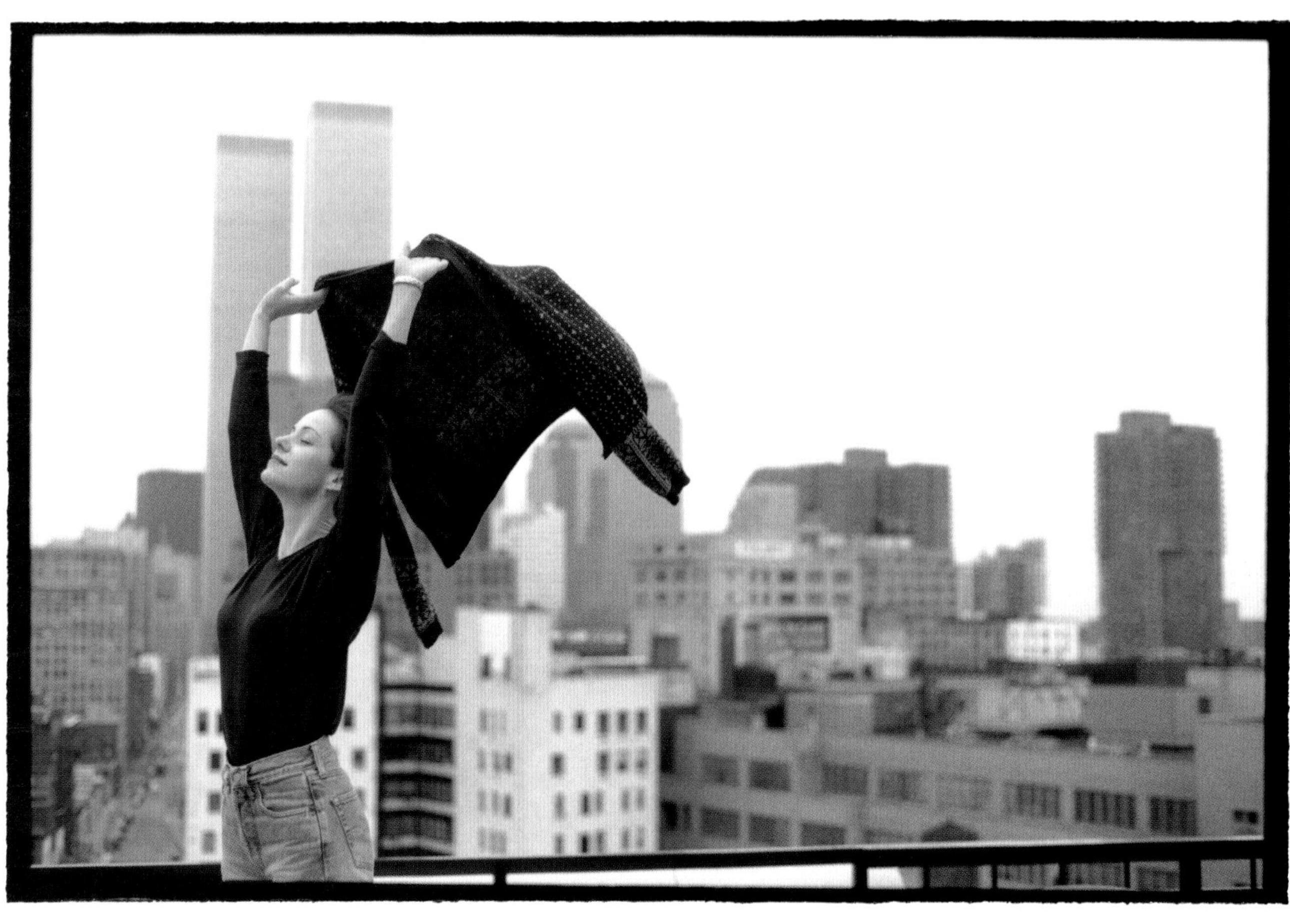

Susan Egan atop the Soho Grand in downtown Manhattan

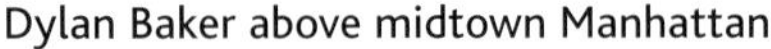

Dylan Baker above midtown Manhattan

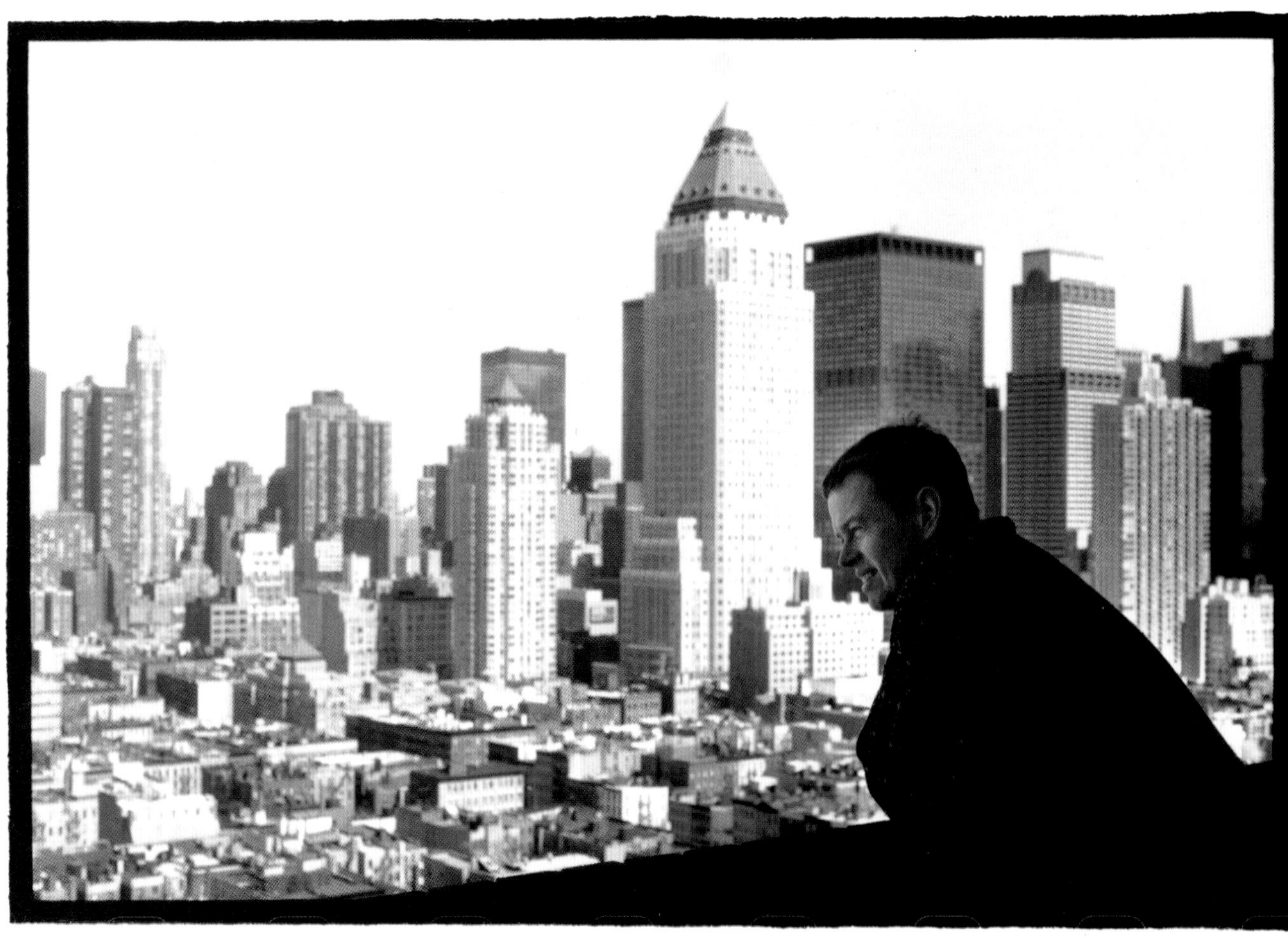

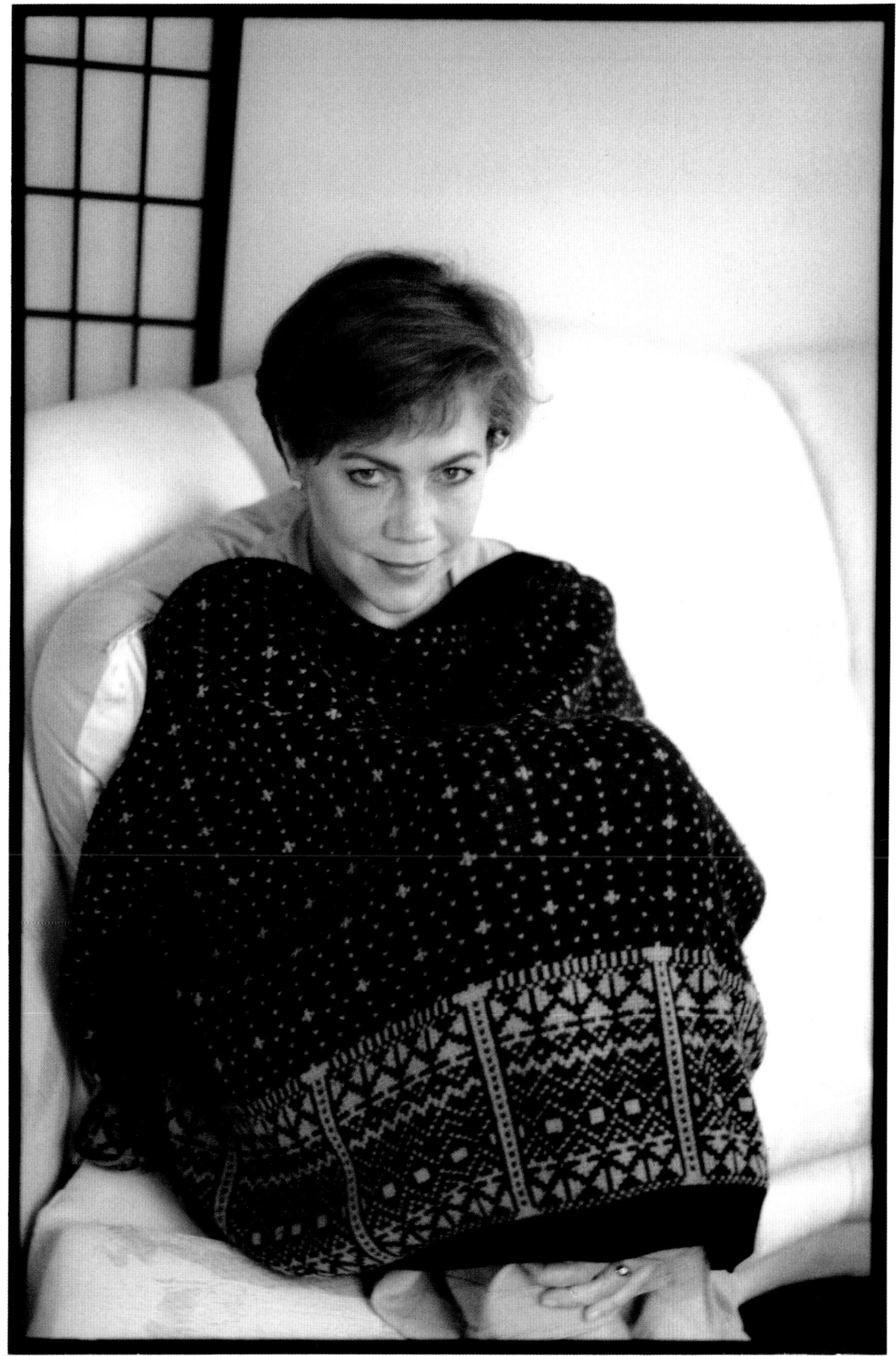

Kathleen Turner backstage at the Barrymore during *Indiscretions*

At the end of our time together, Kathleen said, "I'm so warm now. I want to keep this sweater." As she had been so warm and friendly a hostess, I found myself perilously close to saying, "Keep it. I want you to have it."

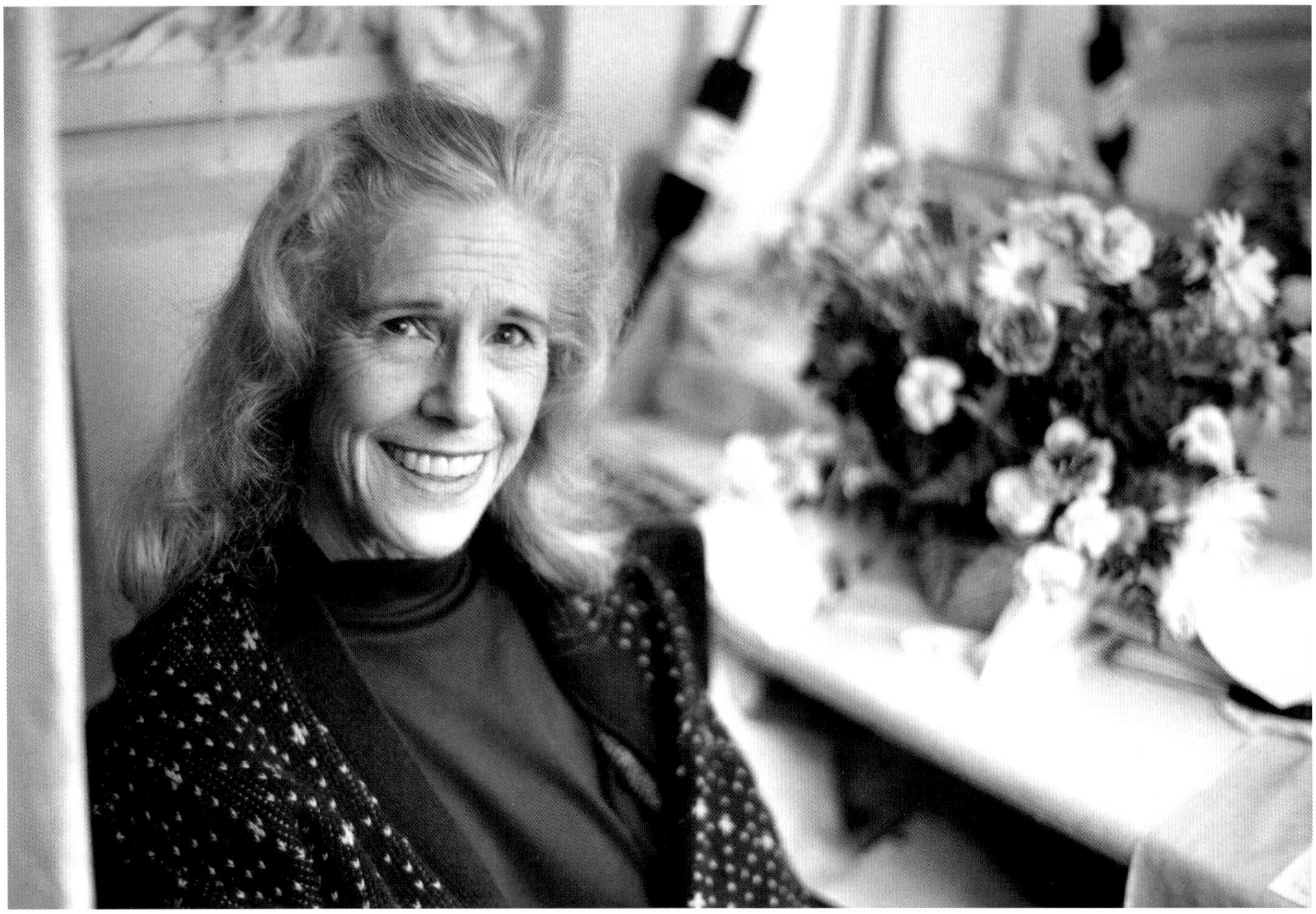

Frances Sternhagen and Donald Moffat backstage at the Cort during *The Heiress*

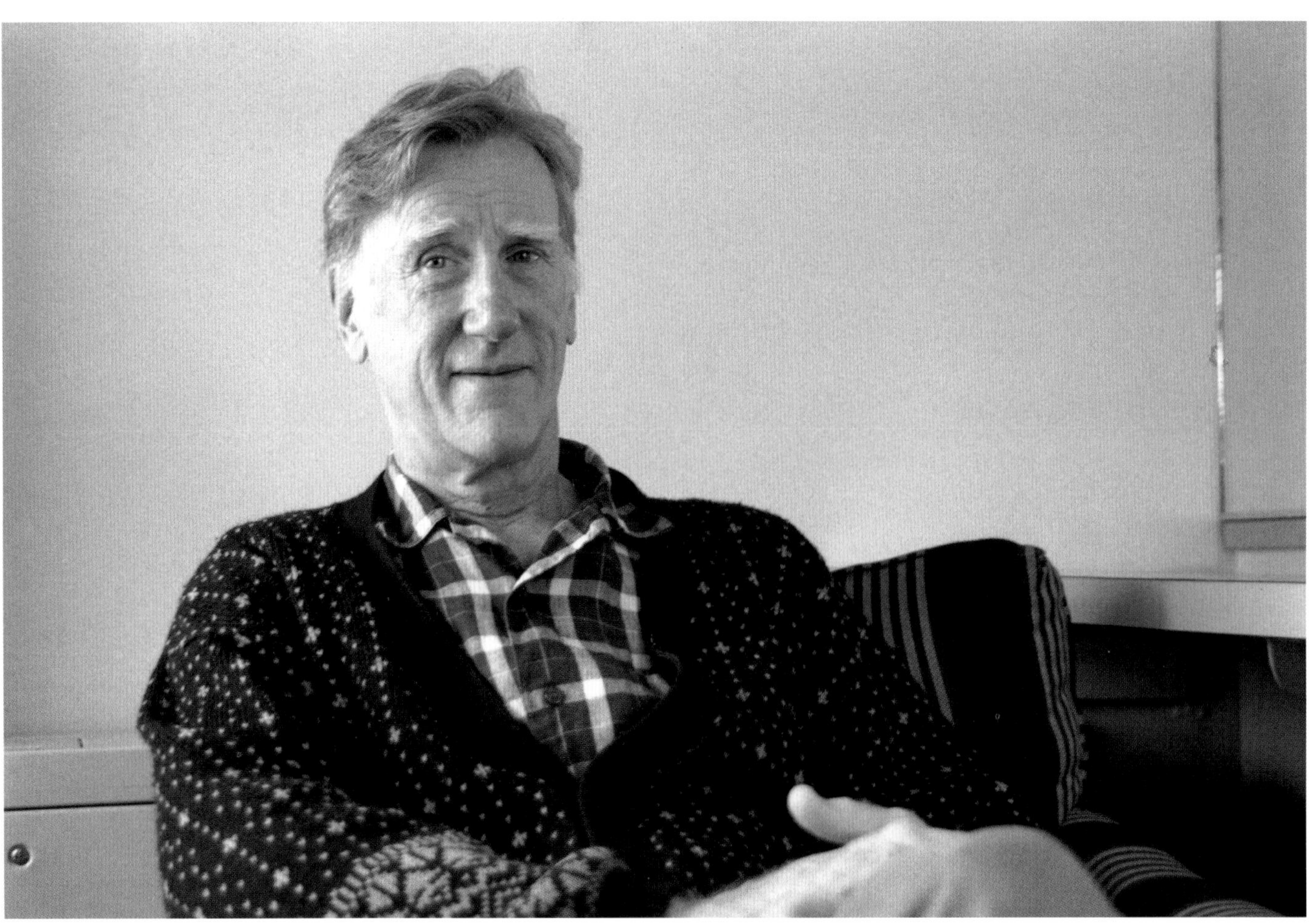

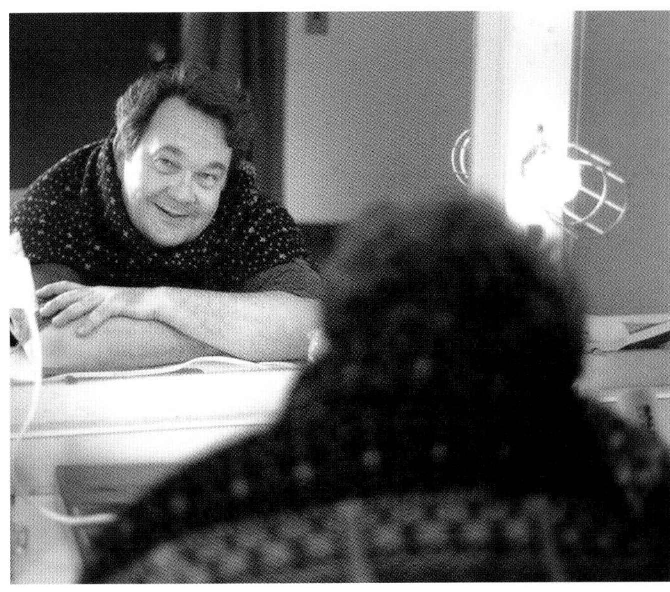

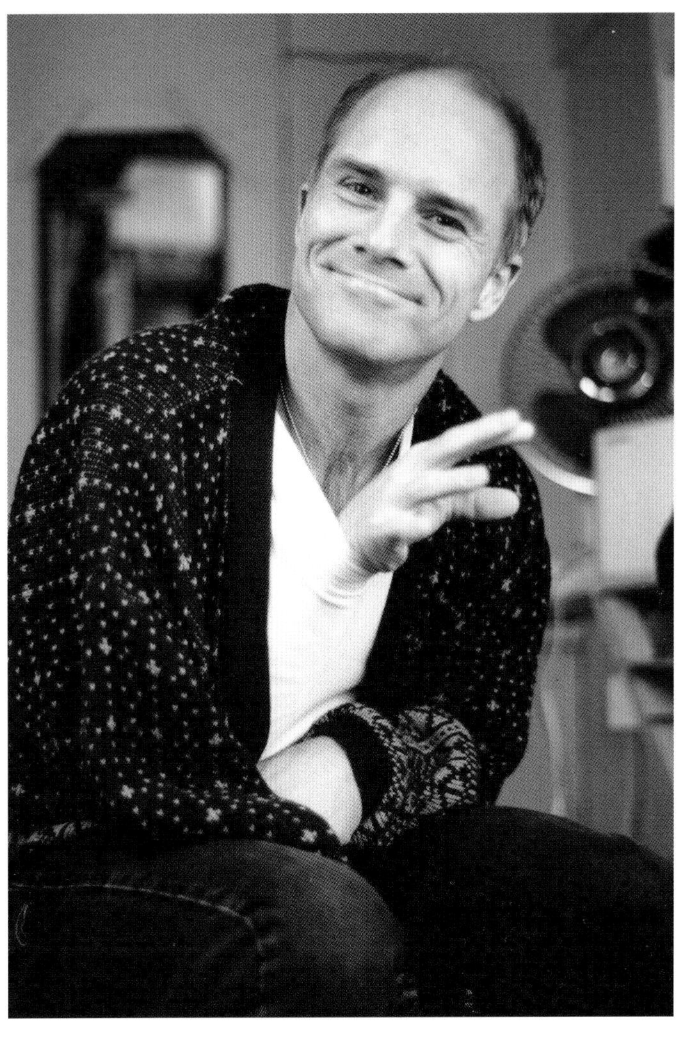

David Schramm backstage at Circle in the Square during *Tartuffe!*

Dan Butler backstage at the Actor's Playhouse during *The Only Thing Worse You Could Have Told Me...*

Joely Fisher backstage at the Eugene O'Neill during *Grease!*

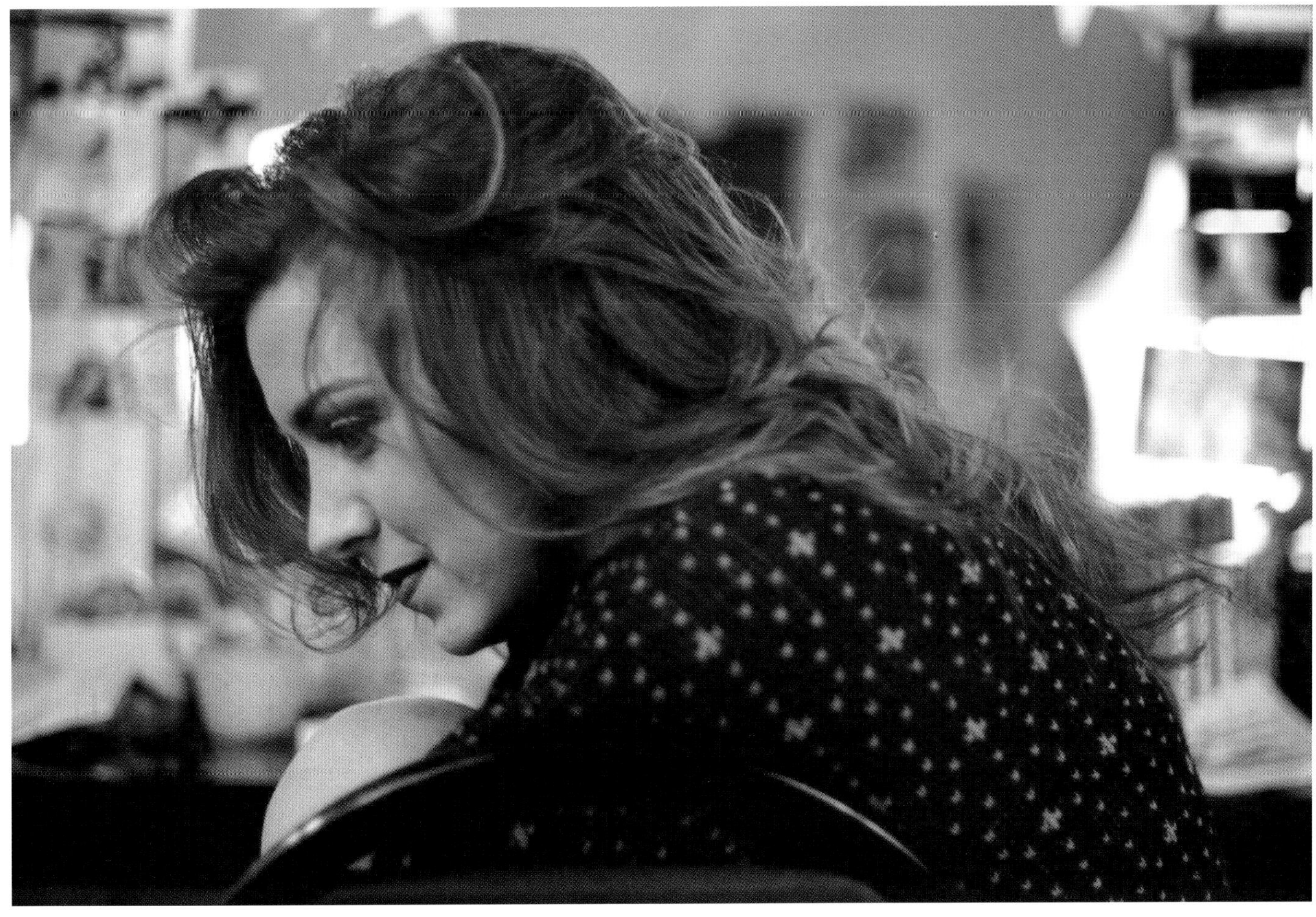

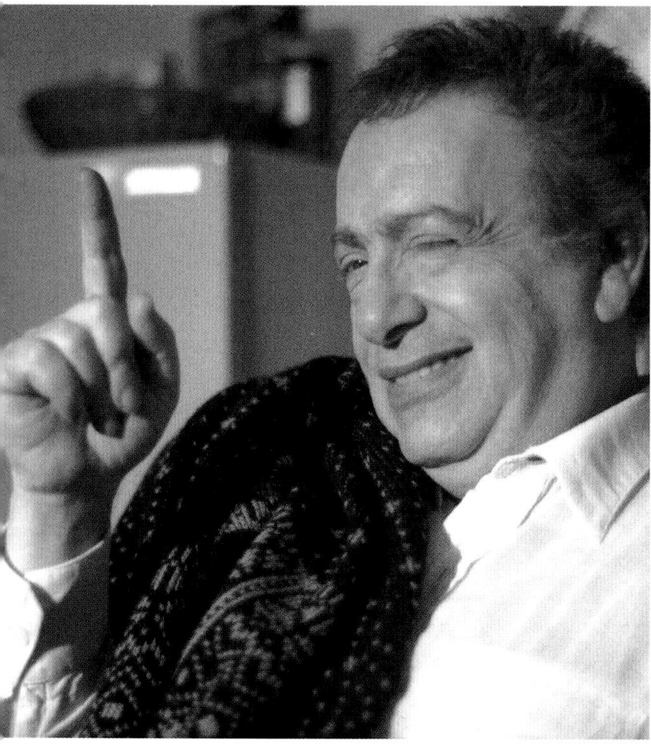

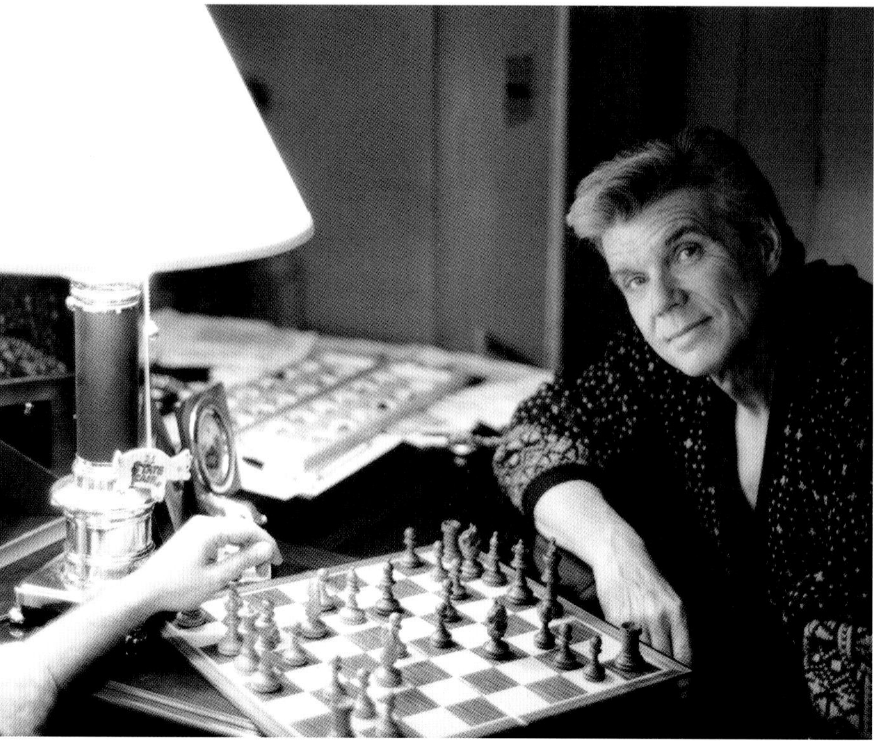

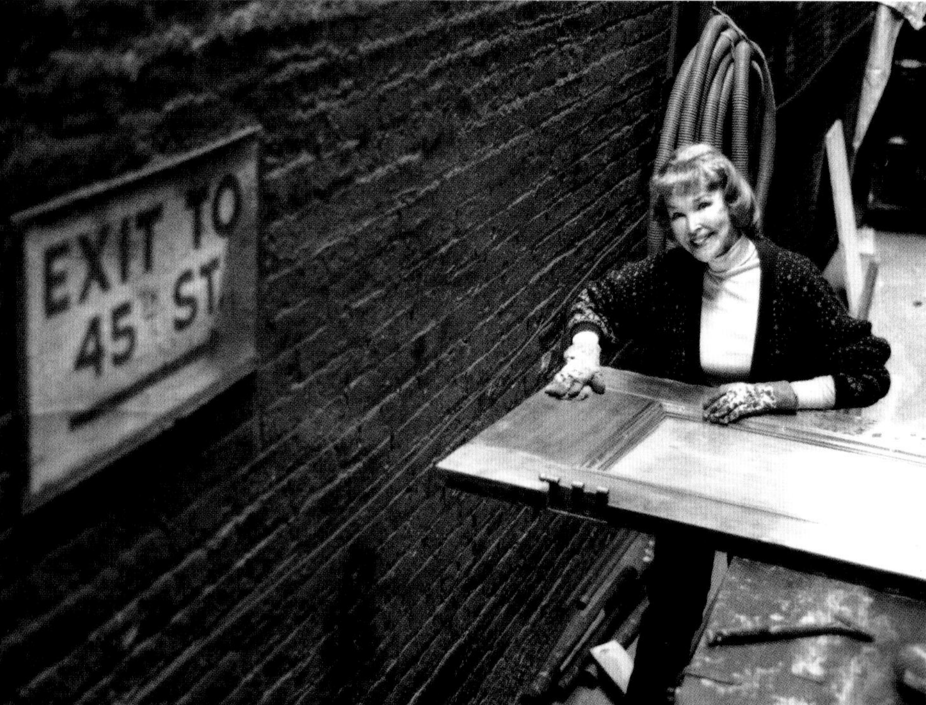

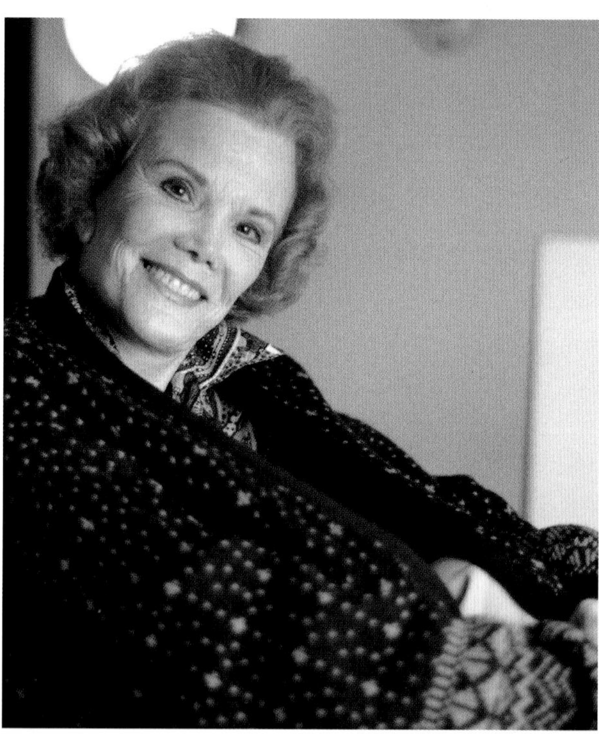

Clockwise from top left:

Jackie Mason backstage at the Golden during *Politically Incorrect*

John Davidson backstage at the Music Box during *State Fair*

Nanette Fabray backstage at the Promenade during
Curse of the Bermuda Avenue Triangle

Kathryn Crosby backstage at the Music Box during *State Fair*

Theatrical trivia, oh so interesting. In 1979, Carole Shelley *(top)* originated the role of Mrs. Kendall in *The Elephant Man*, winning a Tony Award for best actress. In 2002, Kate Burton *(bottom)* played Mrs. Kendall in the first revival of the play on Broadway, garnering a Tony nomination (one of two nominations she received that year, the other for *Hedda Gabler*). These two distinguished actresses have worked on film and in television, but here in New York they are revered as two of the greatest actresses to work on stage. These pictures were taken on the same day in the same dressing room, which they shared, at the Union Square Theatre, where they played mother and daughter in Neil Simon's *London Suite*. We in the business are all connected; and if we are lucky, we get to be family, onstage and off. Nothing trivial about that.

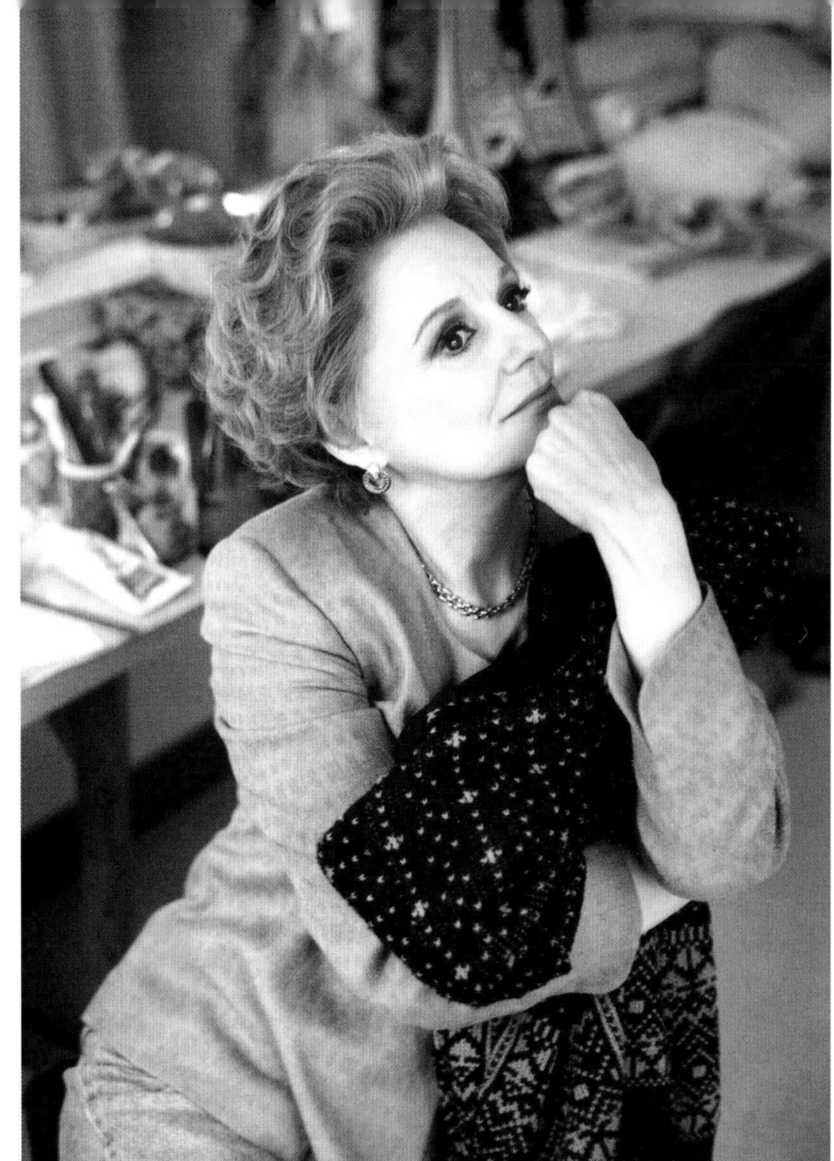

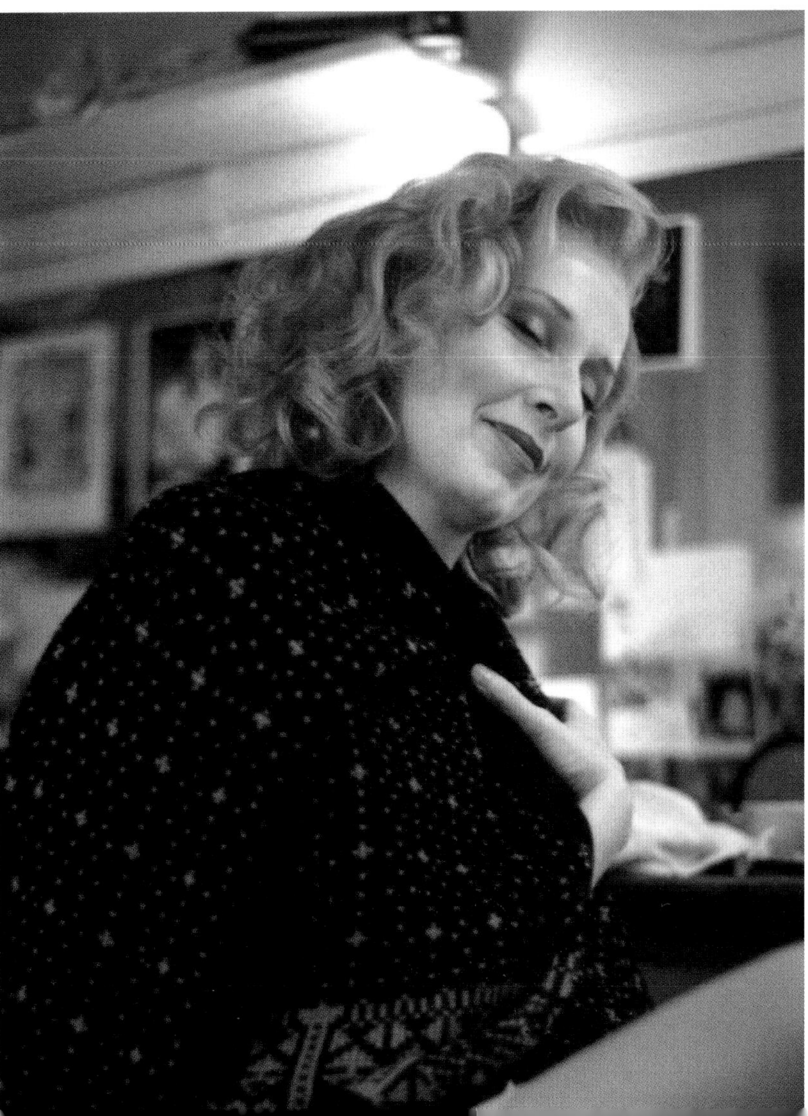

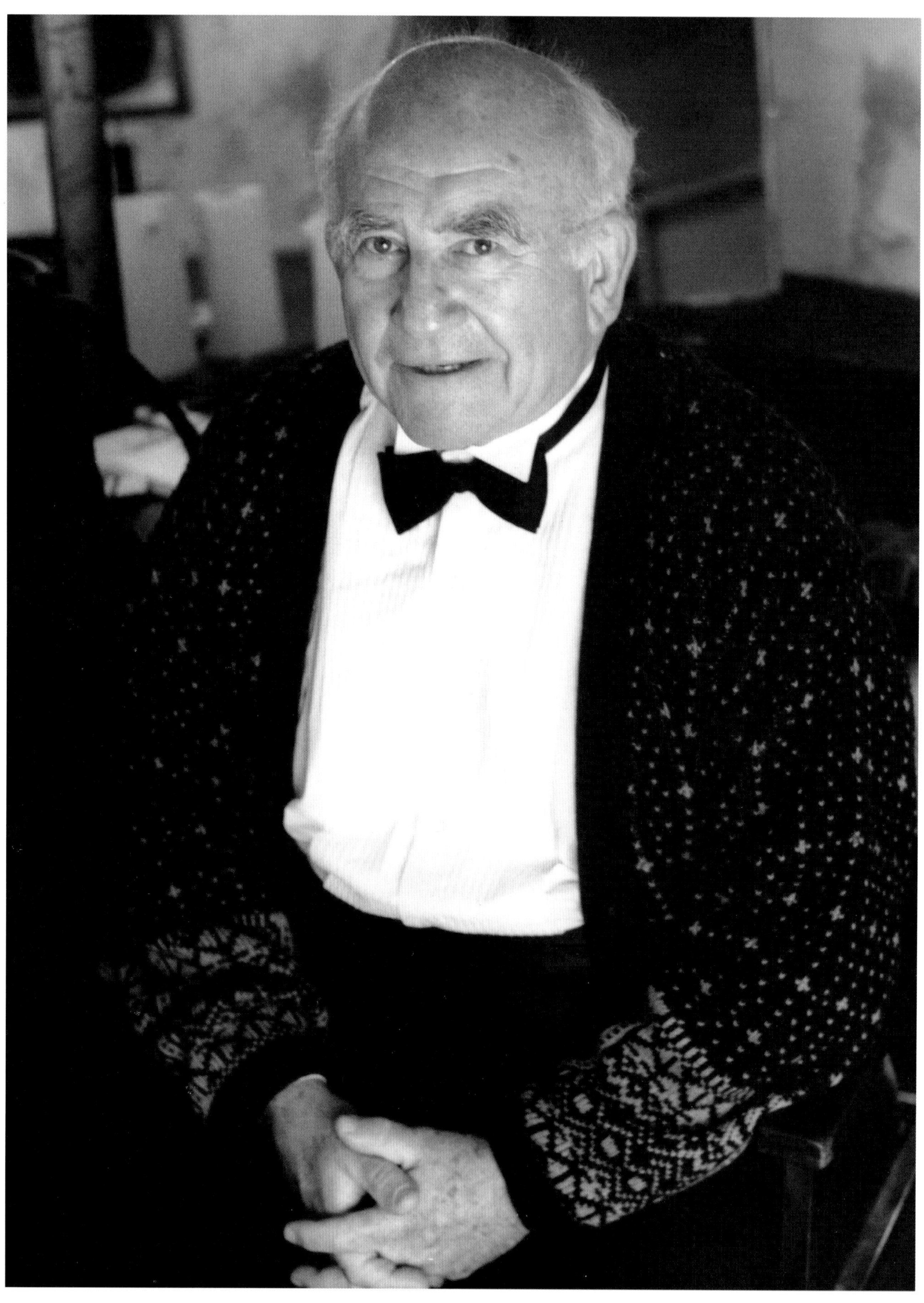

Edward Asner backstage at the Symphony Space during *Don Juan in Hell*

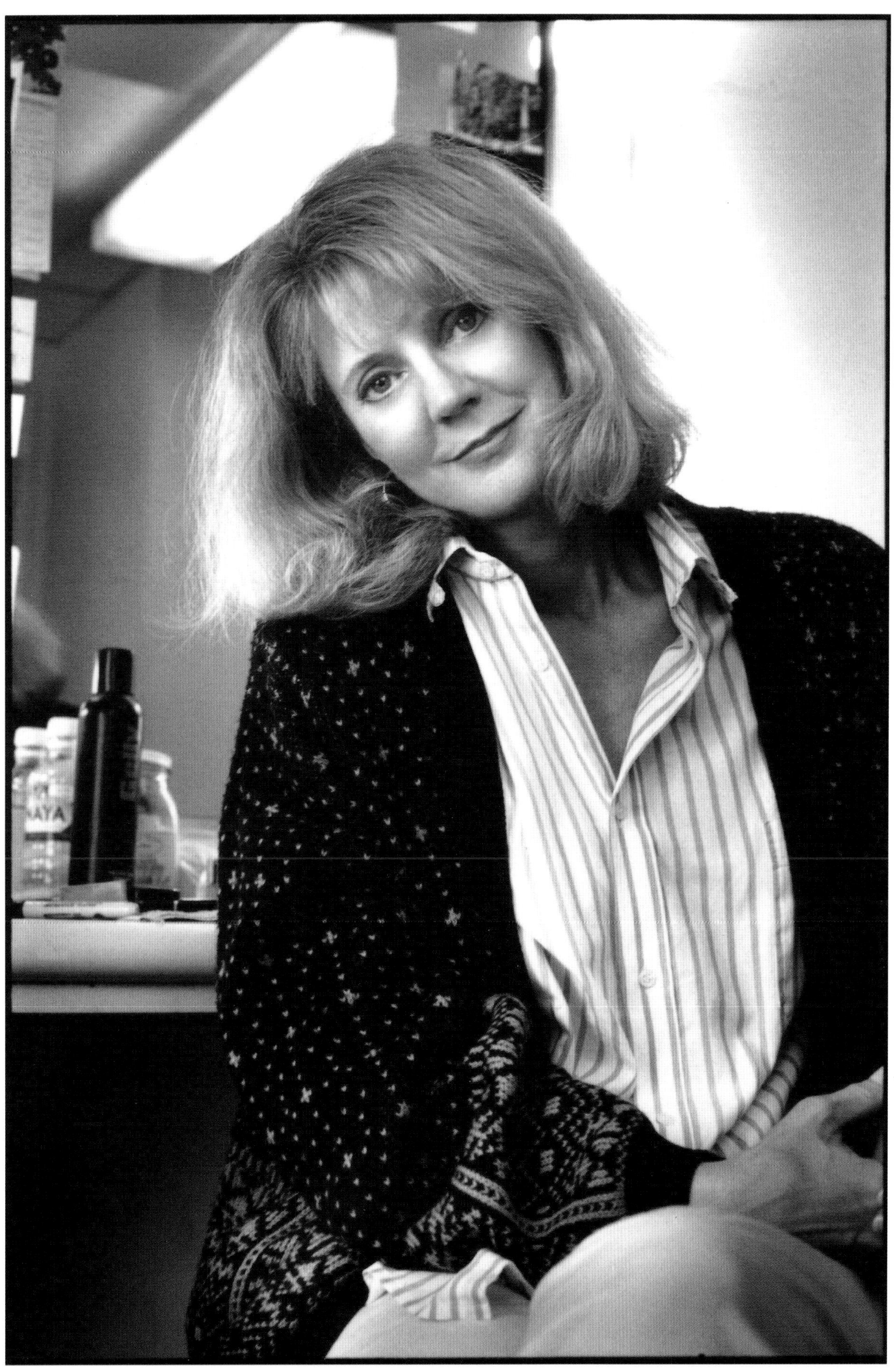

Blythe Danner backstage at the Manhattan Theatre Club during *Sylvia*

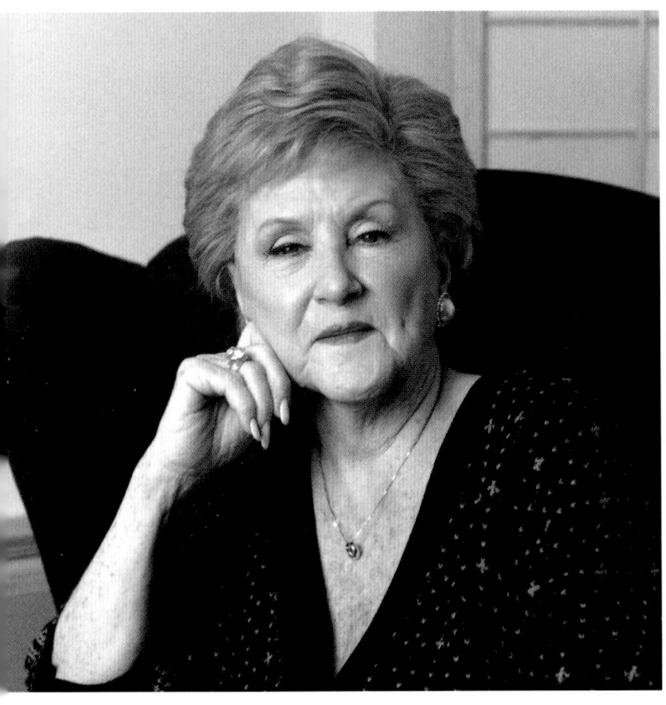

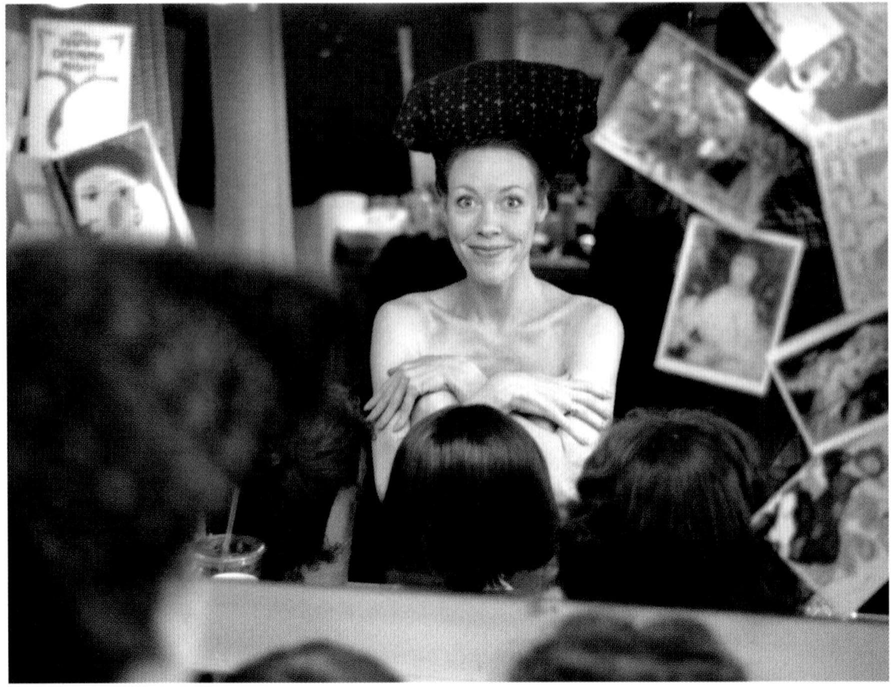

Clockwise from top left:

Margaret Whiting backstage at the Royale during *Dream*

Veanne Cox backstage at the Vineyard during *The Waiting Room*

Liz Callaway backstage at the Winter Garden during *Cats*

Crista Moore backstage at the Shubert during *Big*

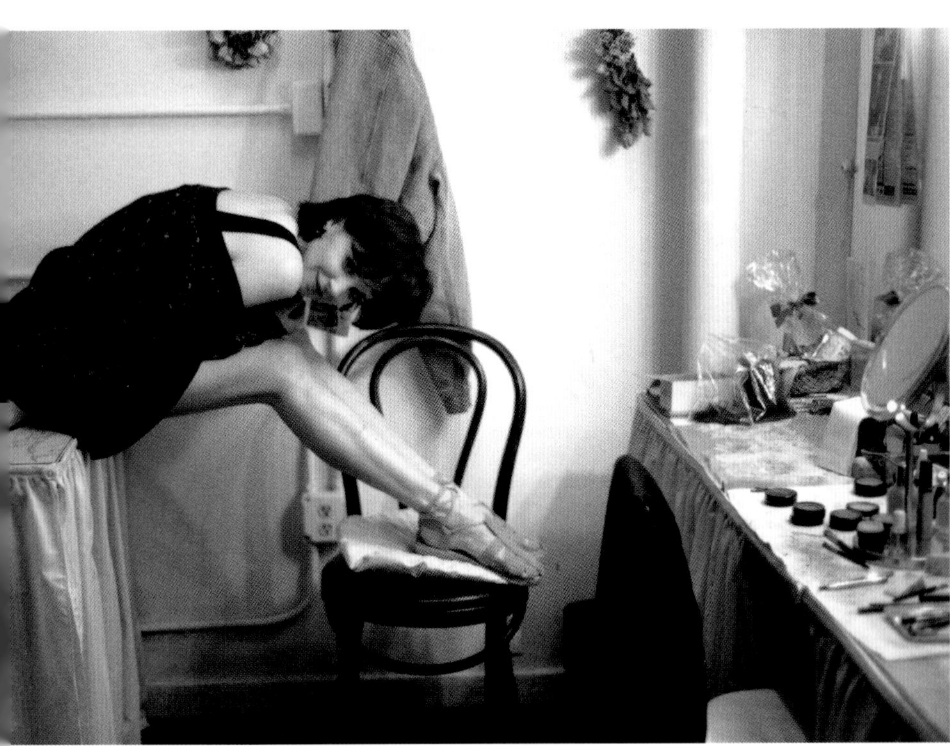

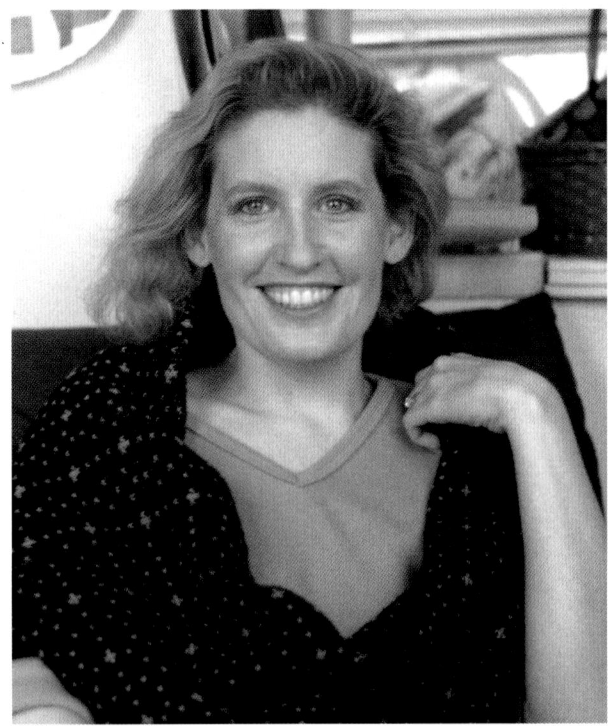

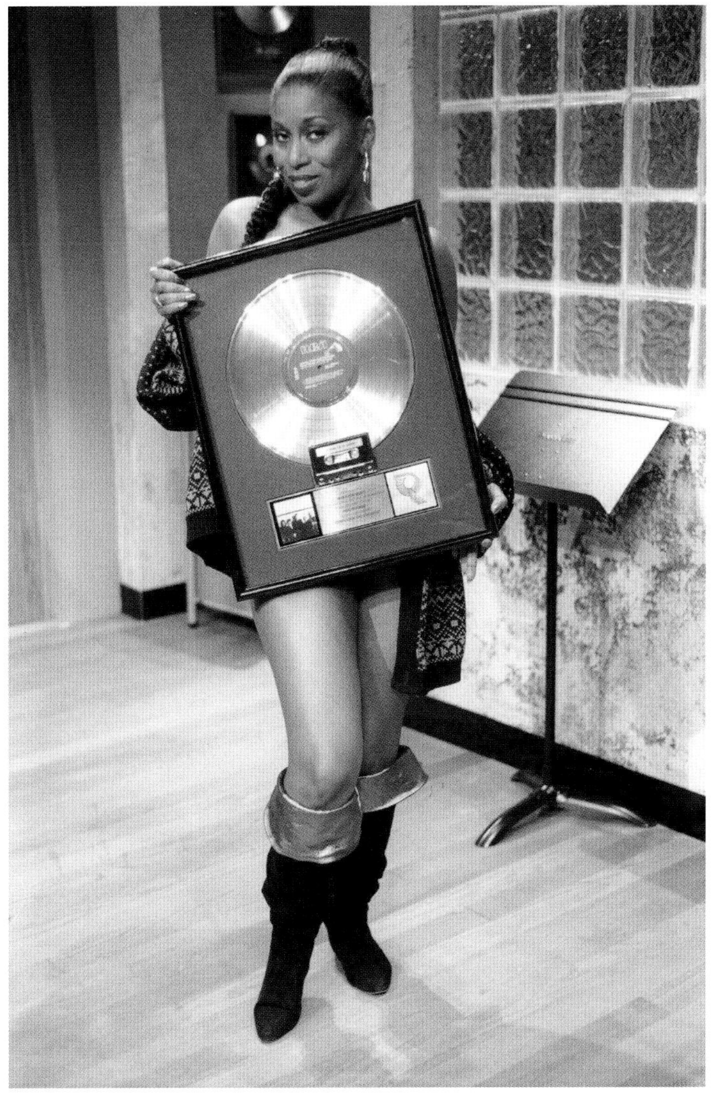

Grace Garland onstage at the 47th Street Theatre during *The Last Session*

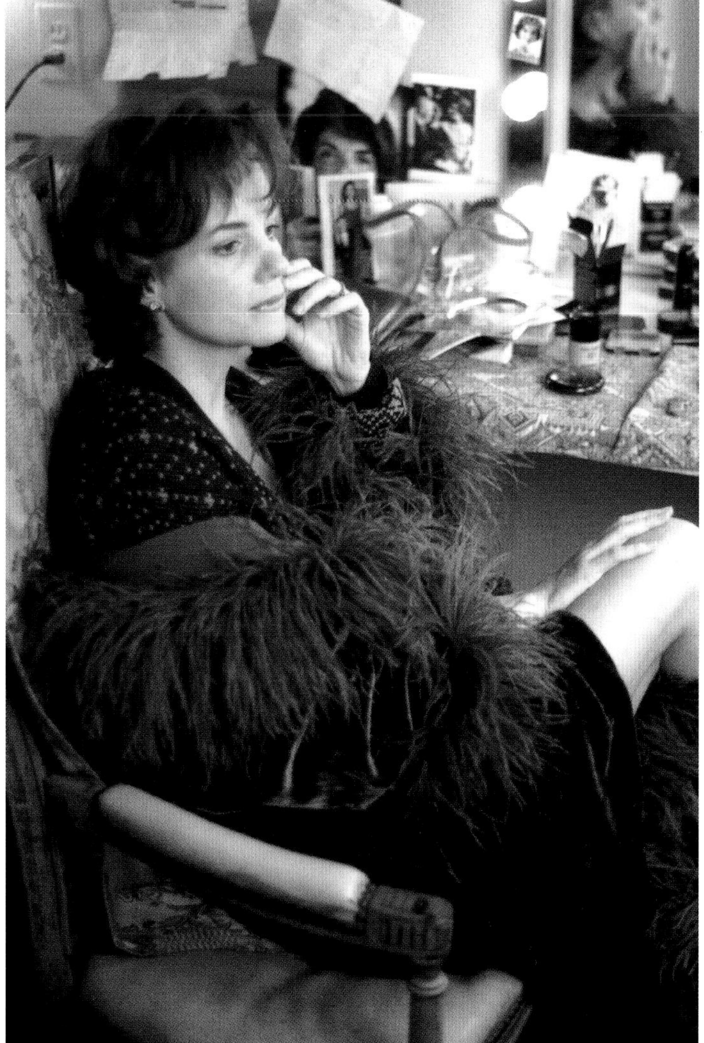

Margaret Colin backstage at the Belasco during *Jackie*

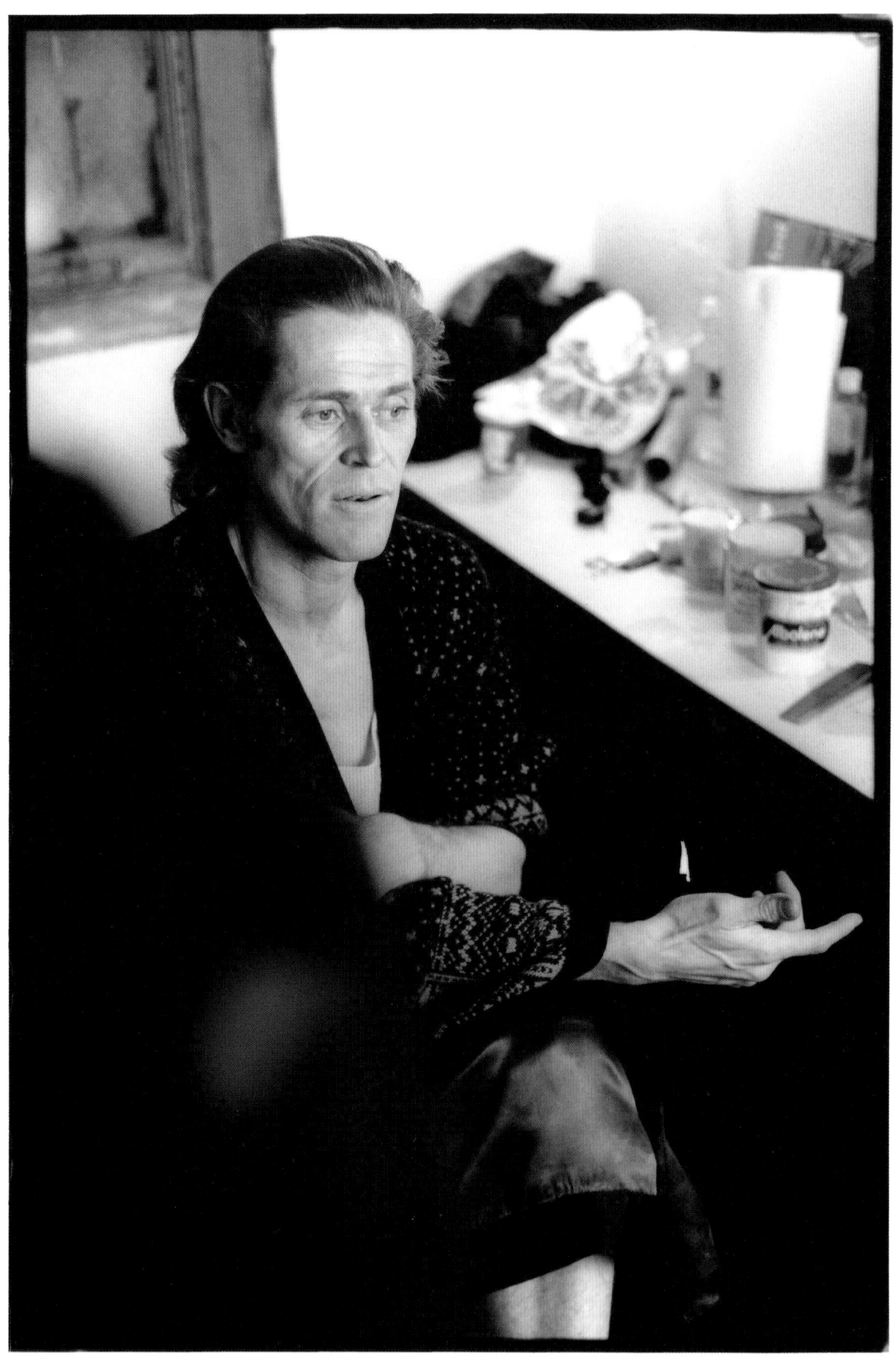

Willem Dafoe backstage at the Selwyn during *The Hairy Ape*

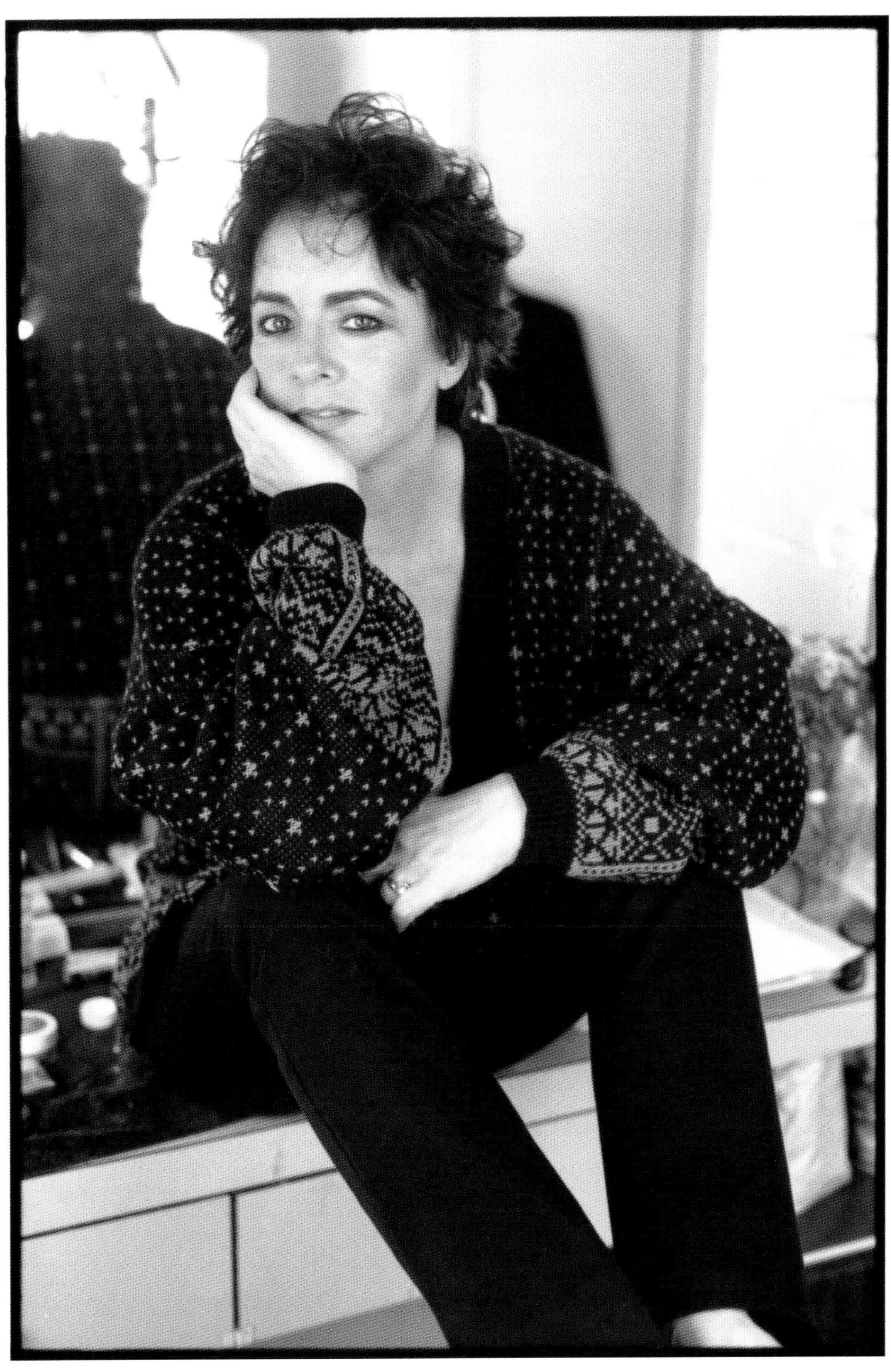

Stockard Channing backstage at the Lincoln Center Theater during *The Little Foxes*

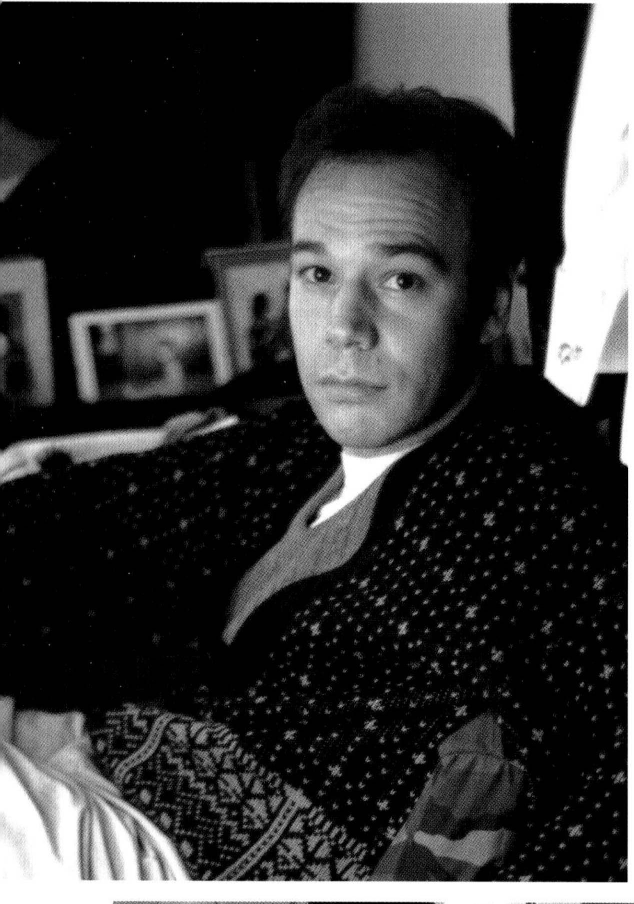

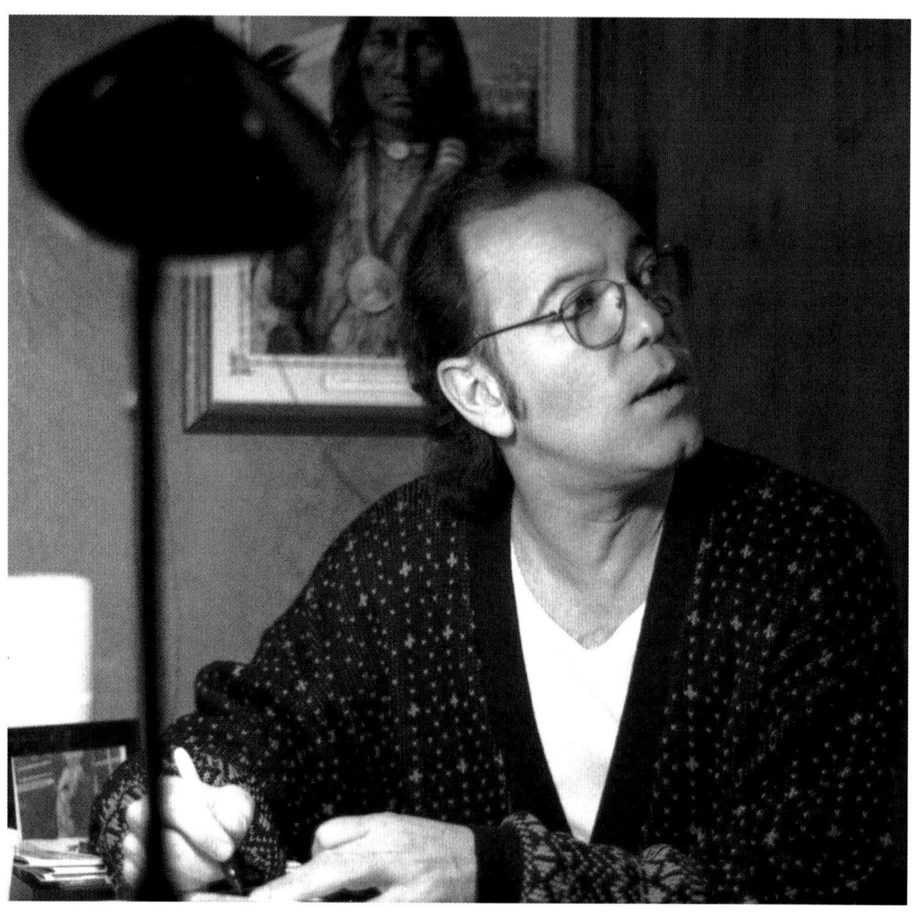

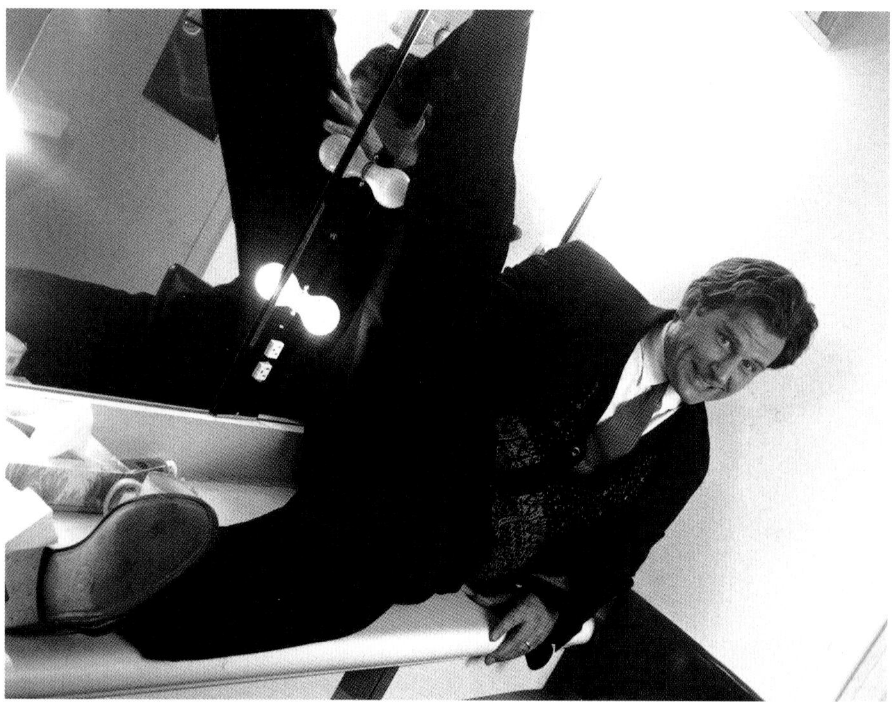

Clockwise from top left:

Danny Burstein backstage at the Roundabout during *Company*

Rubén Blades backstage at the Marquis during *The Capeman*

Timothy Carhart backstage at the Manhattan Theatre Club during *By the Sea, by the Sea, by the Beautiful Sea*

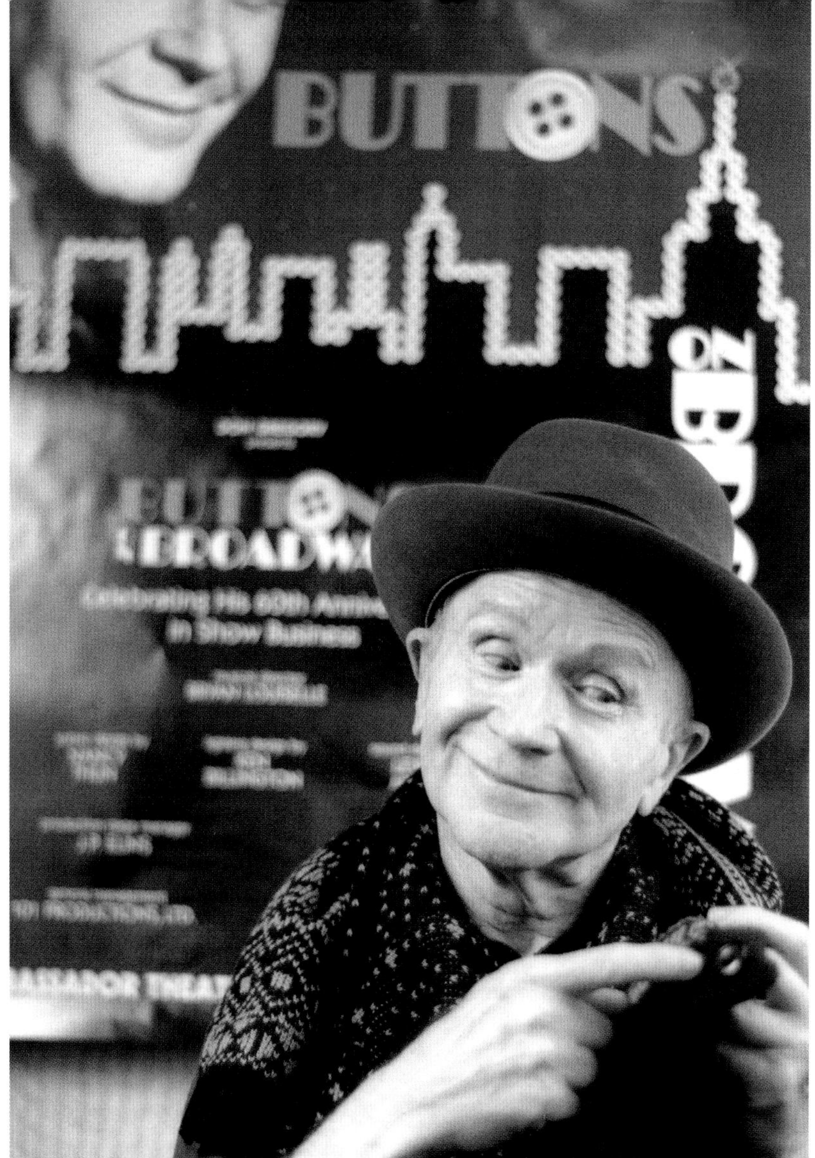

Red Buttons backstage at the Ambassador during *Buttons on Broadway*

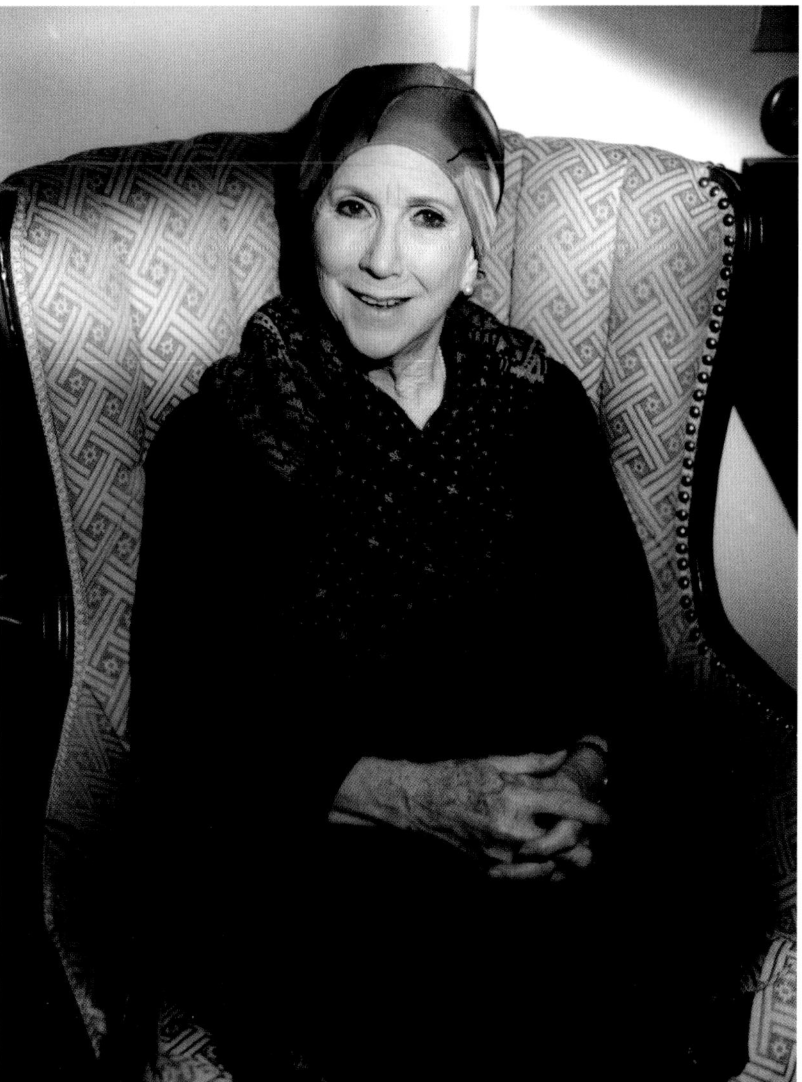

Miss Julie Harris backstage at the Roundabout during *Glass Menagerie*

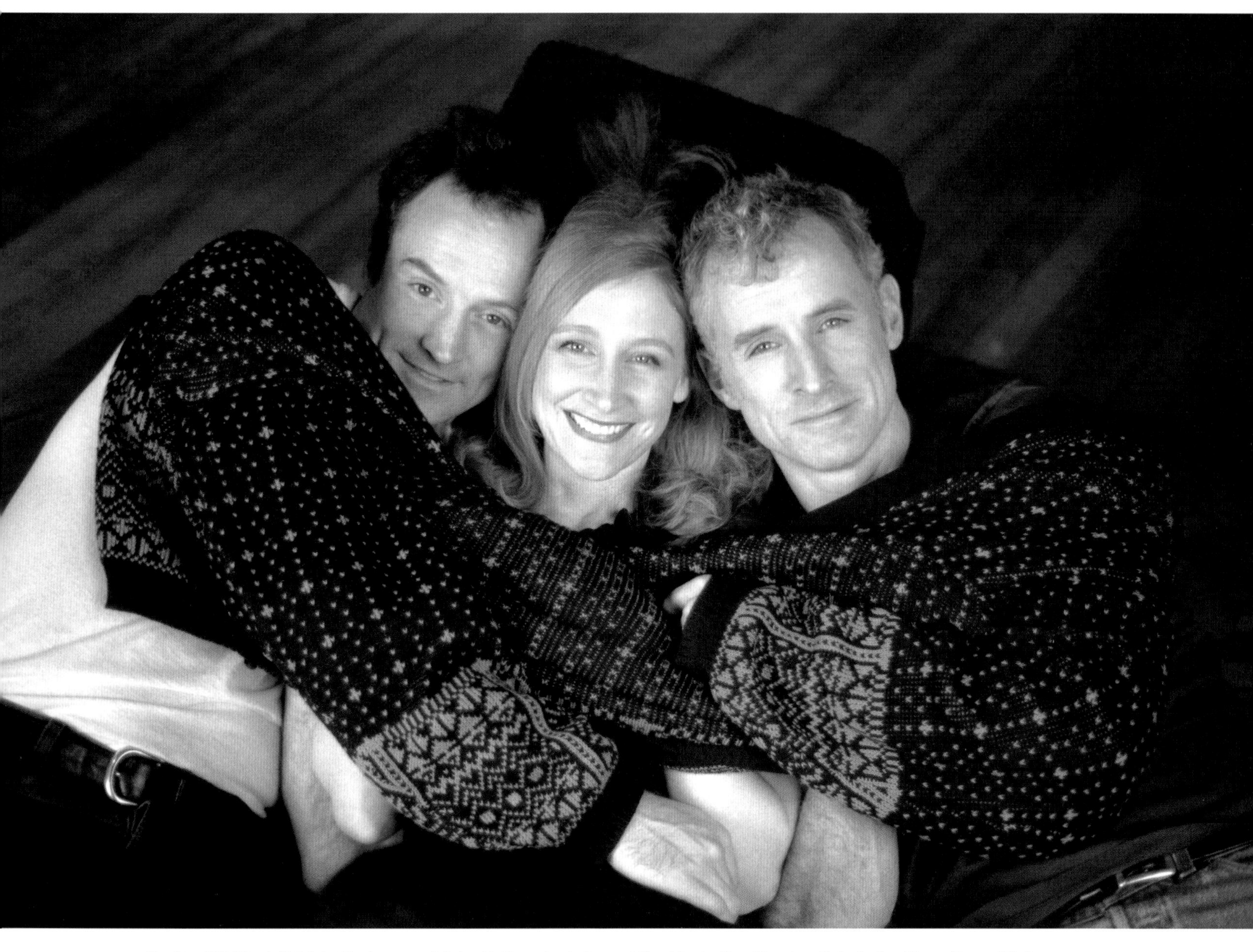

Bradley Whitford, Patricia Clarkson, and John Slattery backstage at the Manhattan Theatre Club during *Three Days of Rain*

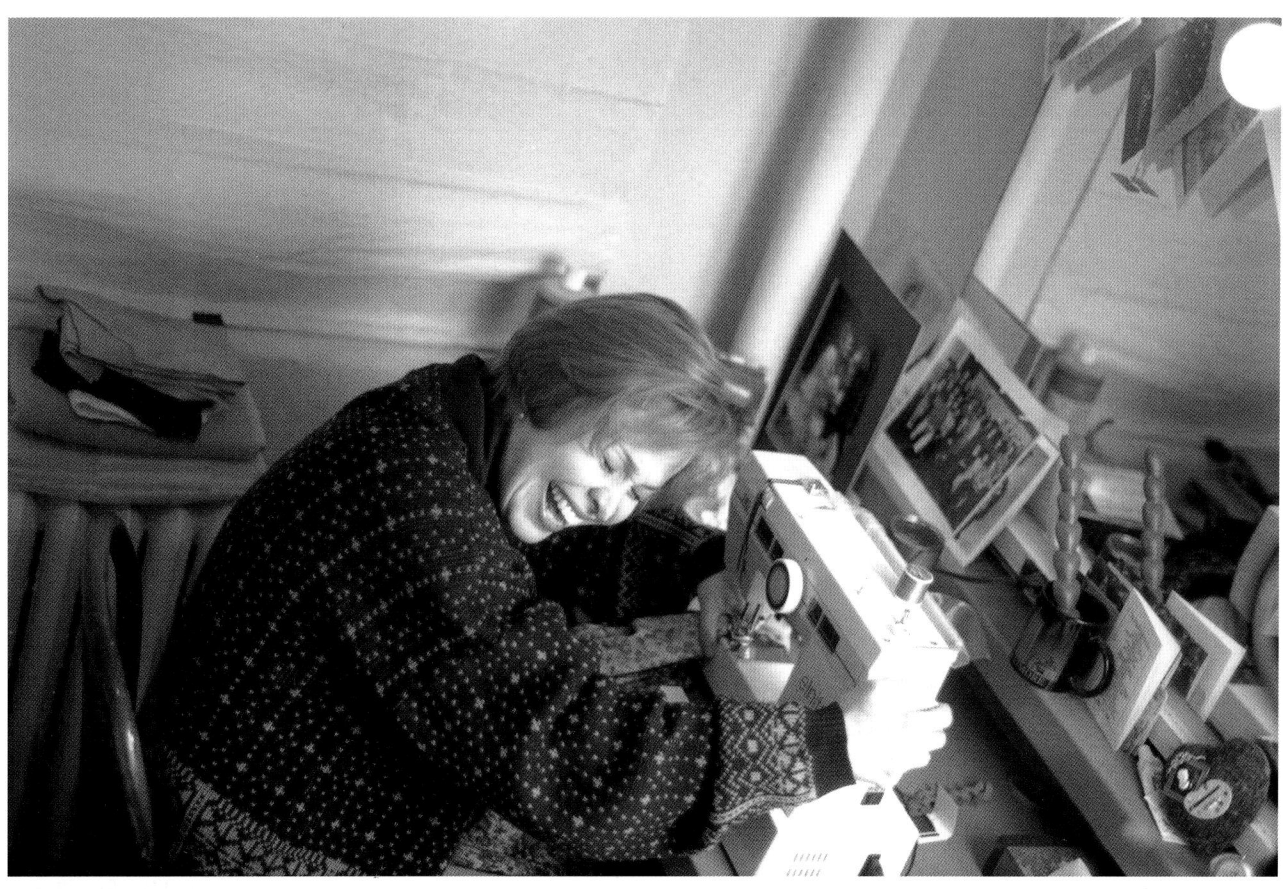

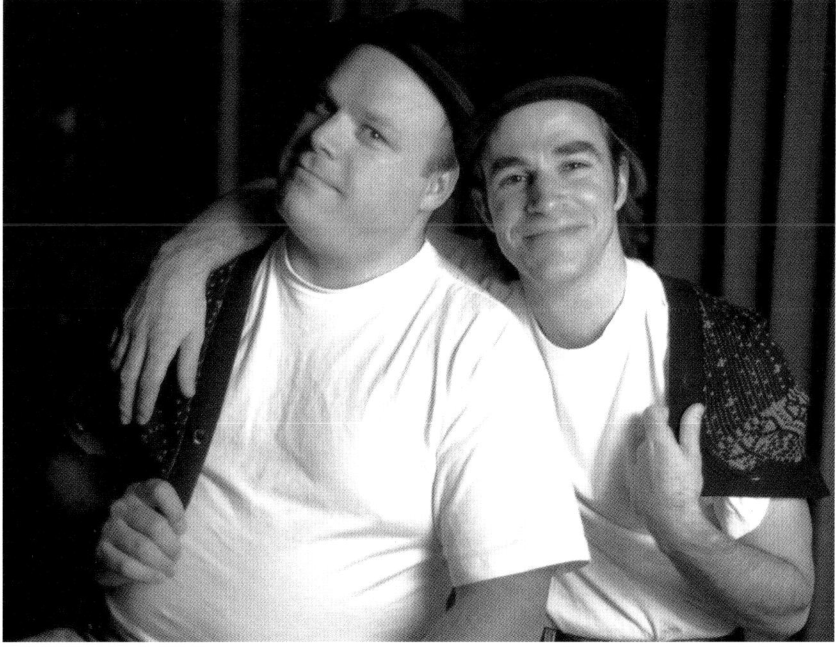

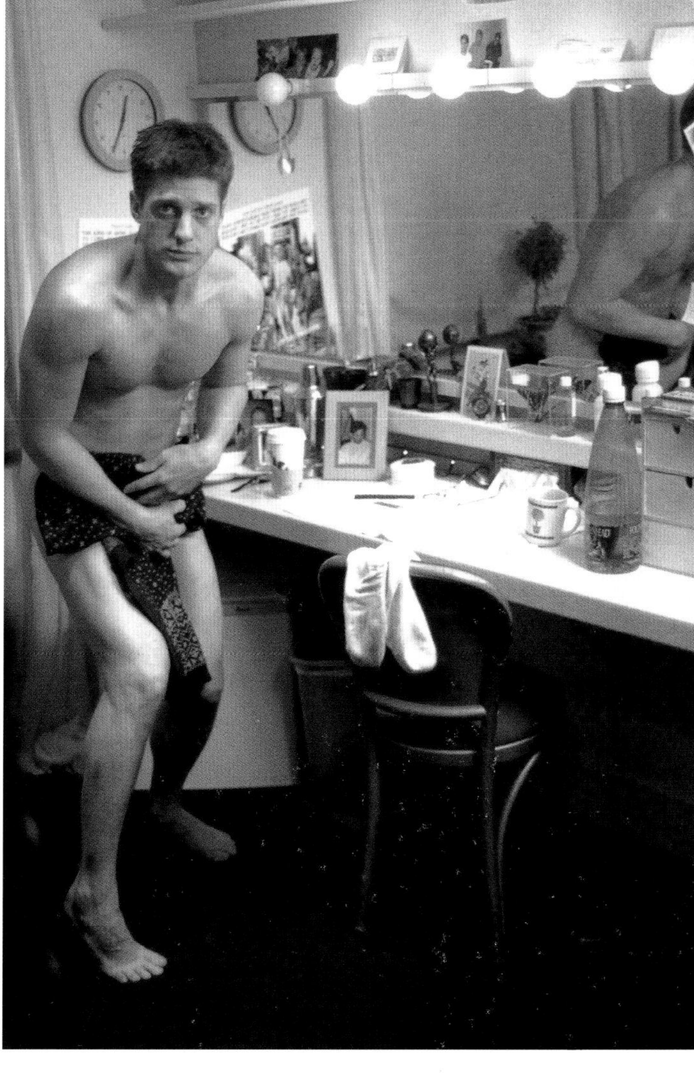

Clockwise:

Nancy Opel in her dressing room

Christopher Sieber in his dressing room

Roger Bart and Kevin Chamberlin in the box seats at the Royale during *Triumph of Love*

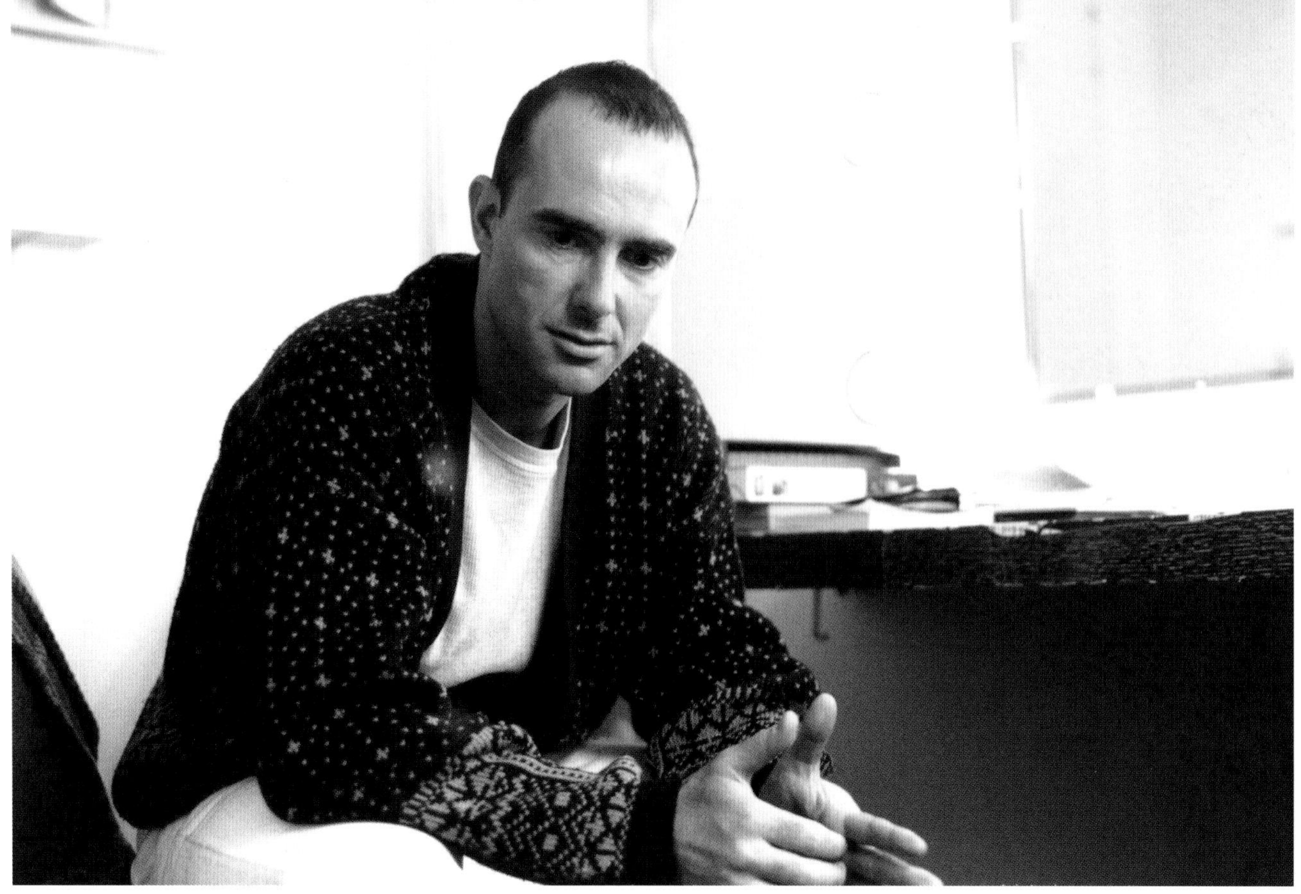

Finbar Lynch *(above)* and Alex Jennings *(below)* backstage at the Lunt-Fontanne during *Midsummer Night's Dream*

How cool is this? In the New York theatrical community we get to have the members of the British theatrical community visit us and share with us their talents. During the time I have lived in New York City, Broadway has been treated to Diana Rigg in *Medea,* Ralph Fiennes in *Hamlet*, Judi Dench in *Amy's View*, Janet McTeer in *A Doll's House*. Before I arrived here, Maggie Smith had been doing *Lettuce and Lovage*. It is always a treat and a pleasure to welcome these gifted performers from across the pond. Frequently the New York theater public does not instantly recognize British actors' names. After an extraordinary few hours seeing how it is done on the other side of the Atlantic, theatergoers leave with these actors' names and faces emblazoned on their minds.

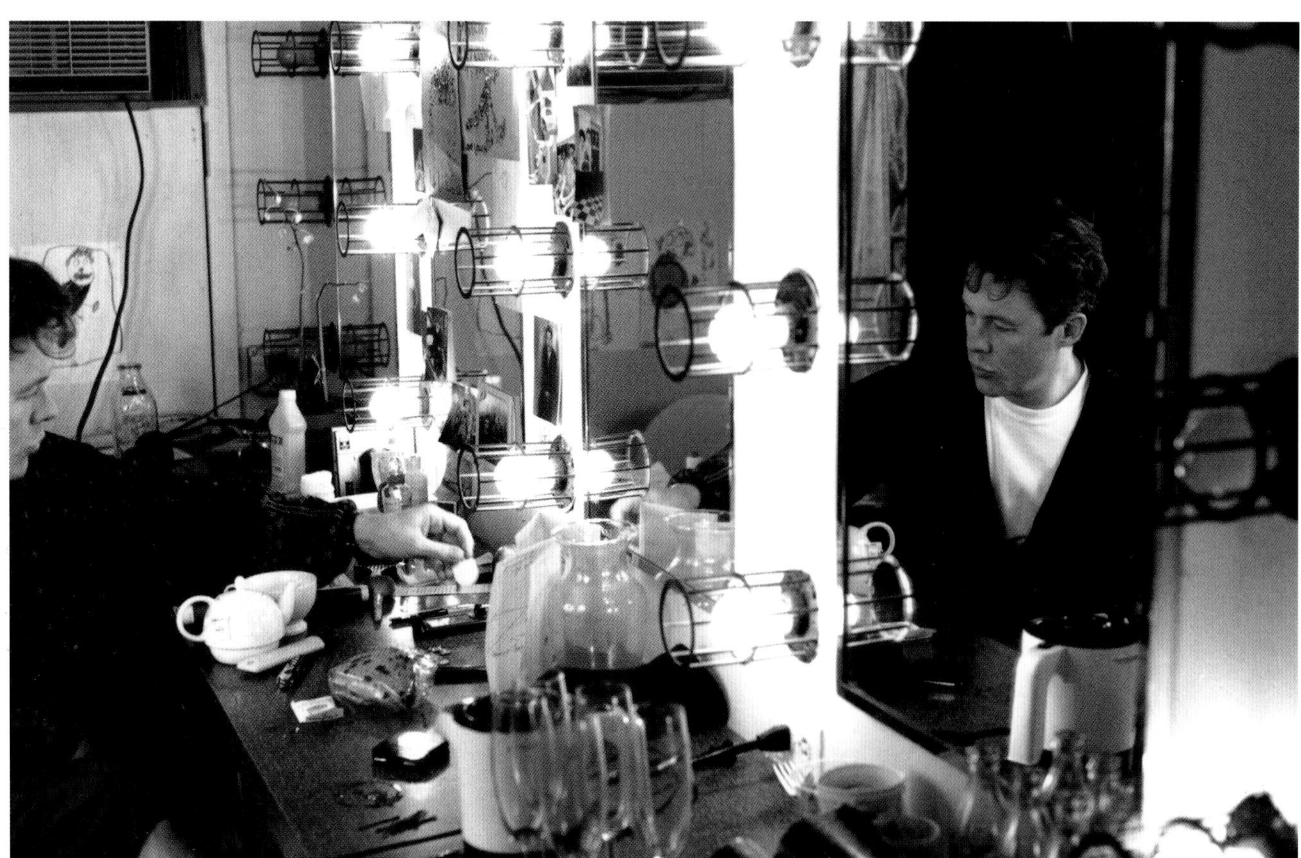

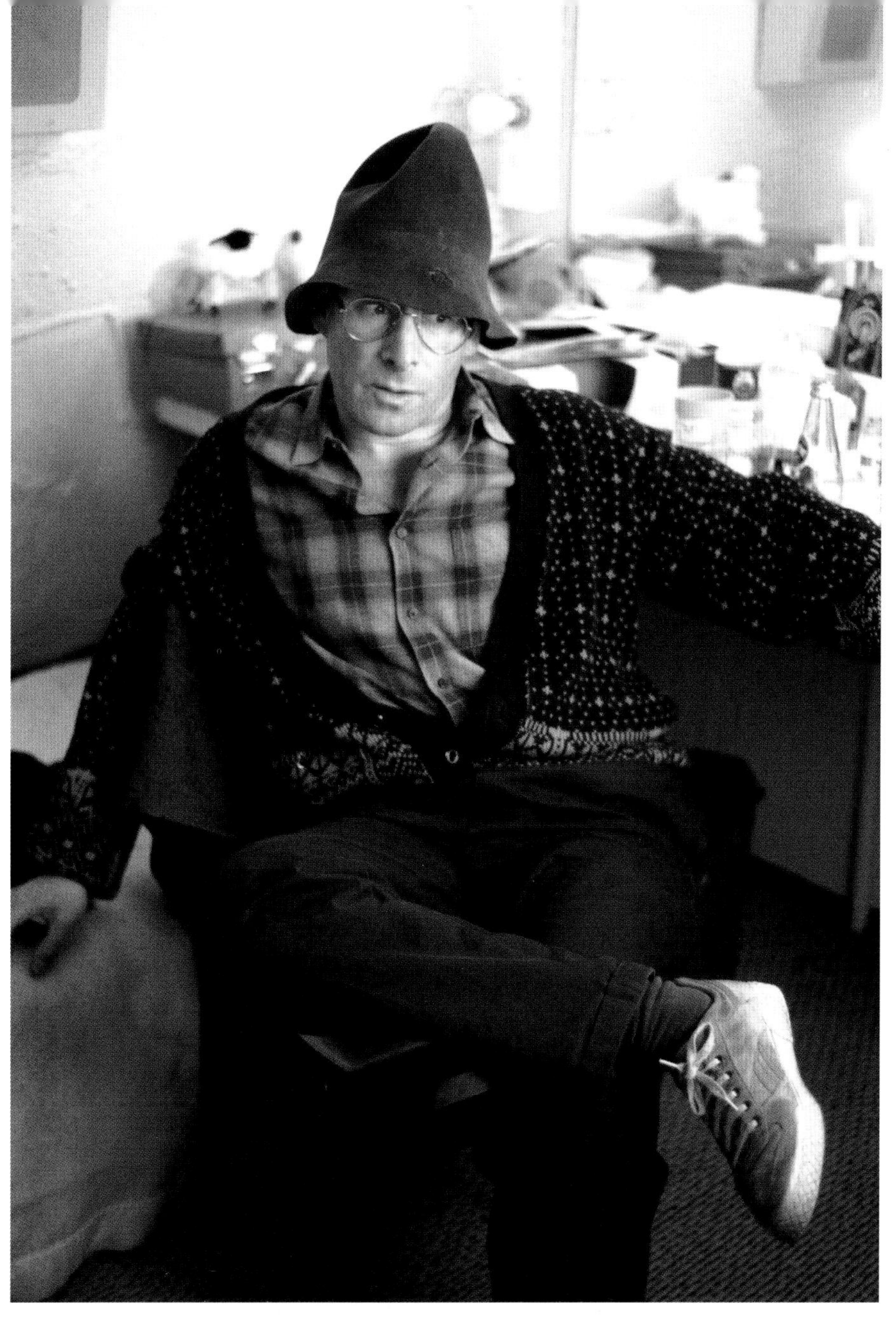

Antony Sher backstage at Circle in the Square during *Stanley*

Dulcie Gray and Michael Denison backstage at the Barrymore during *An Ideal Husband*

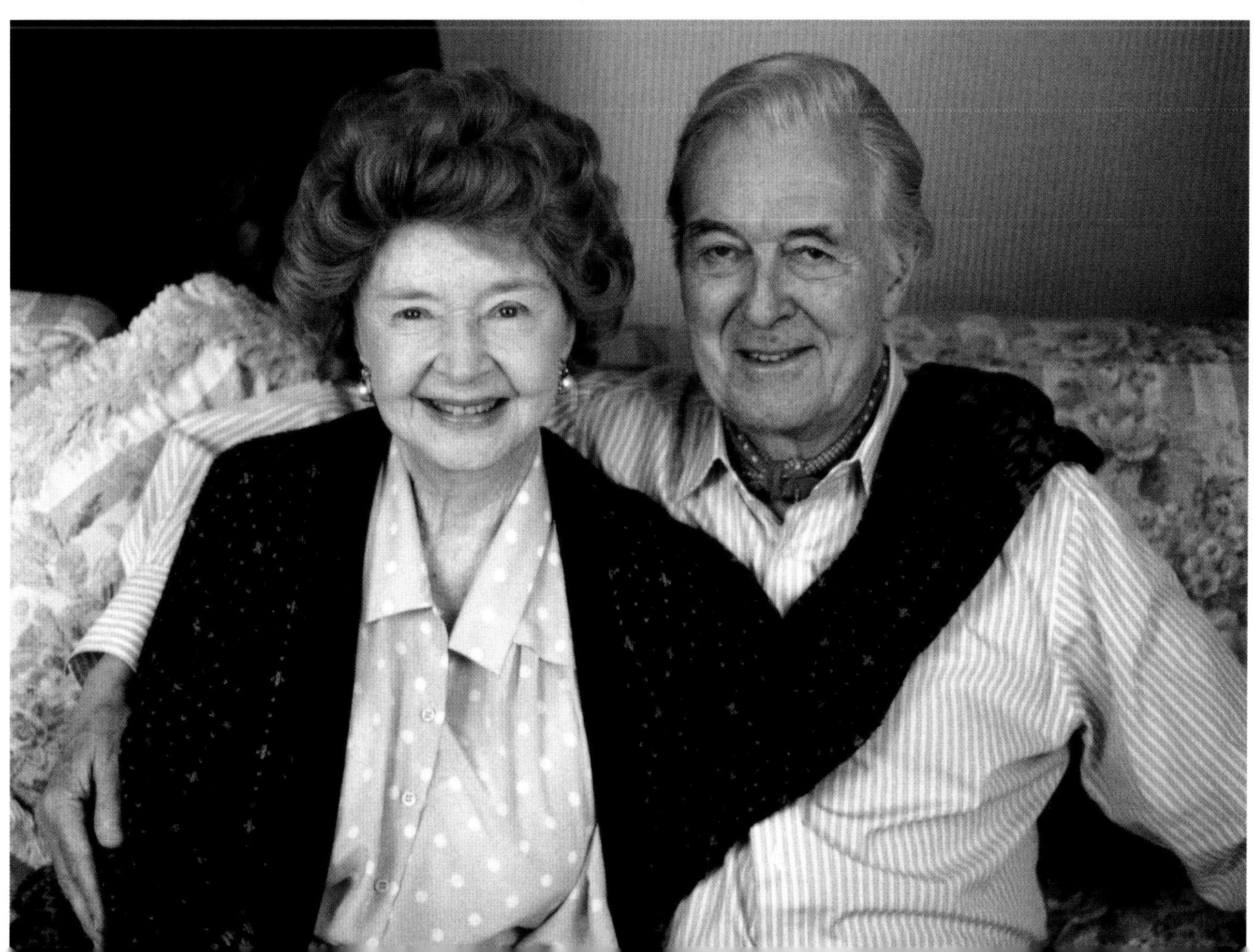

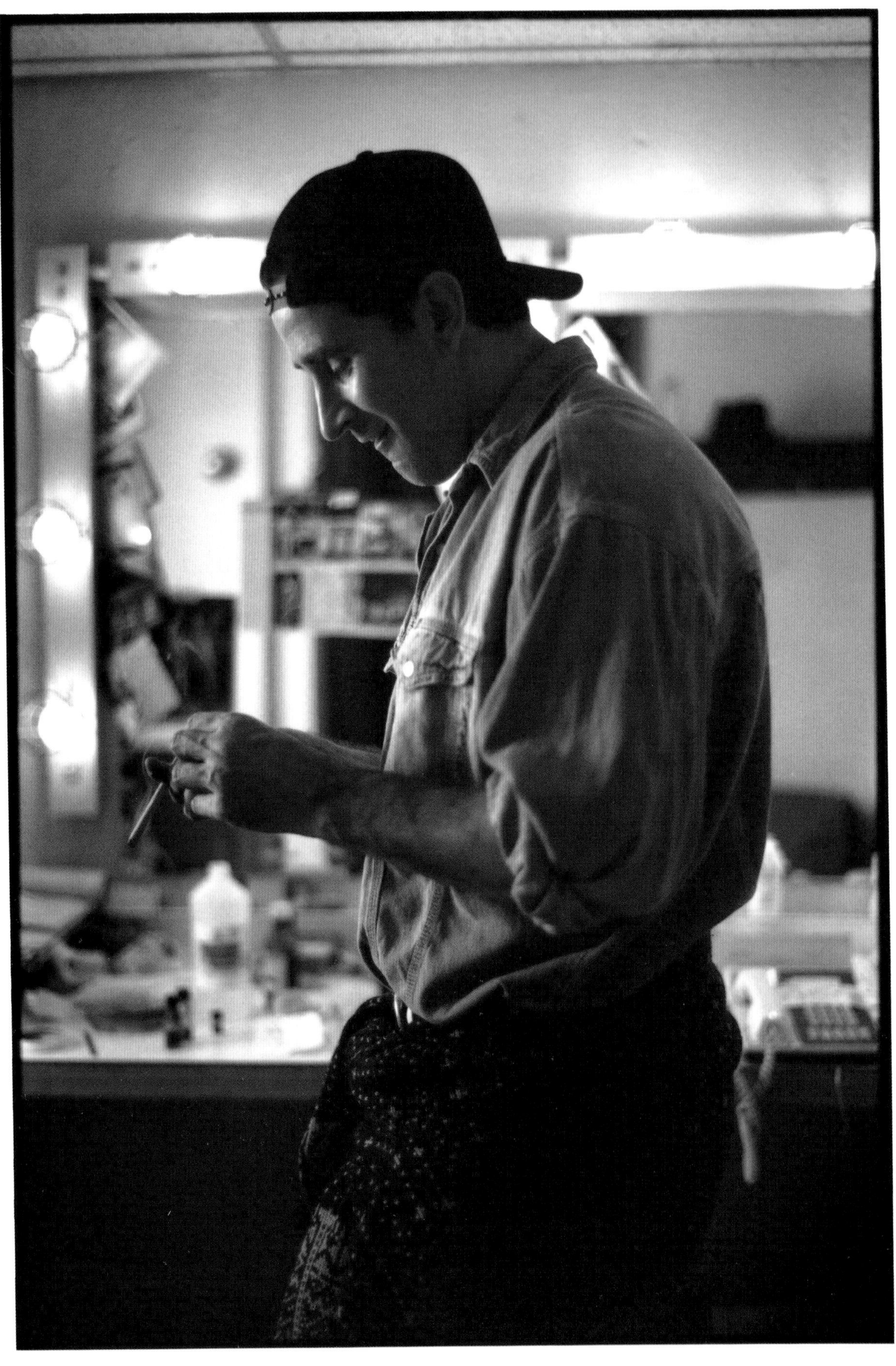

Anthony LaPaglia backstage at Circle in the Square during *The Rose Tattoo*

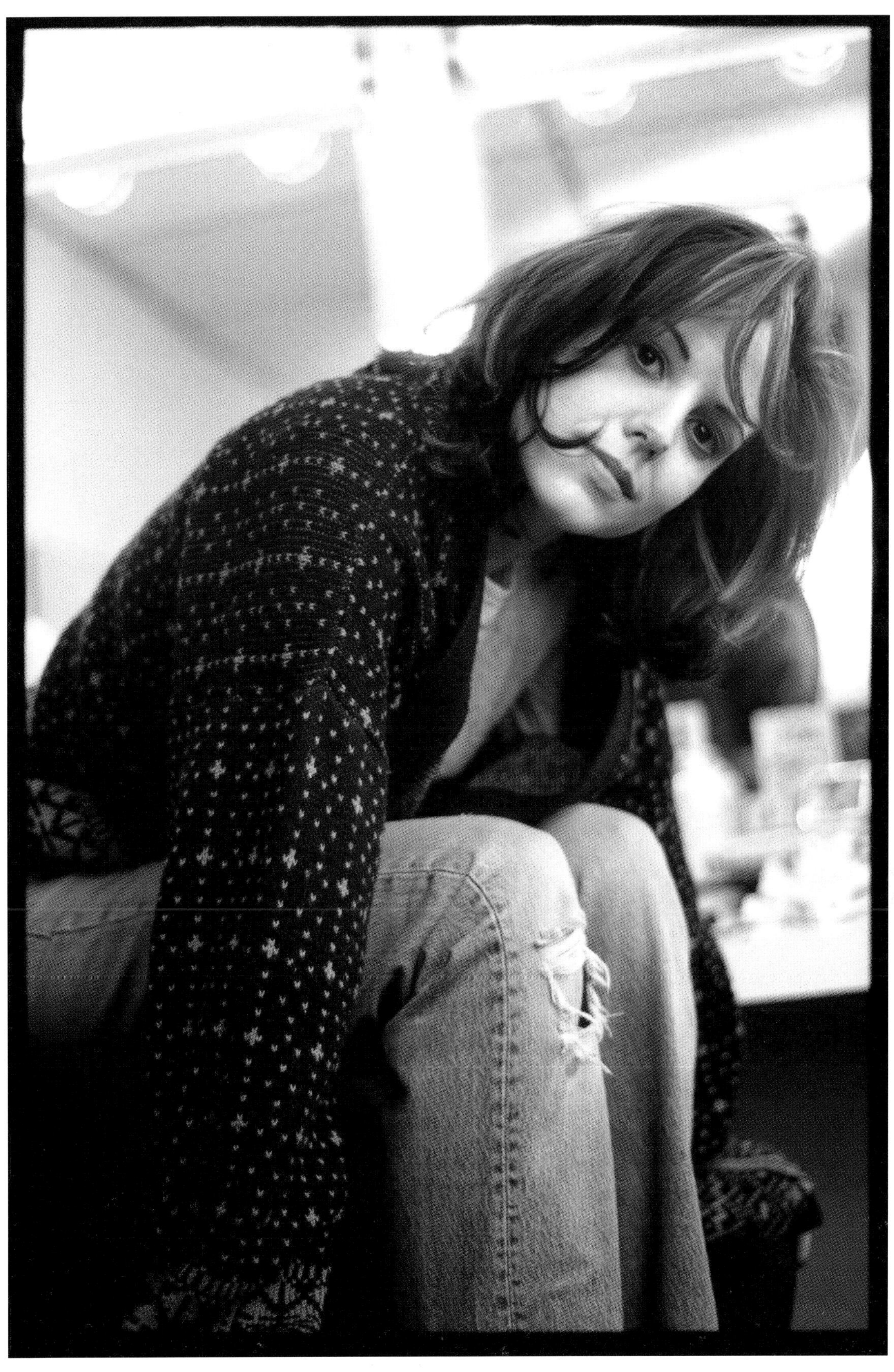

Mary Louise Parker backstage at Circle in the Square during *Bus Stop*

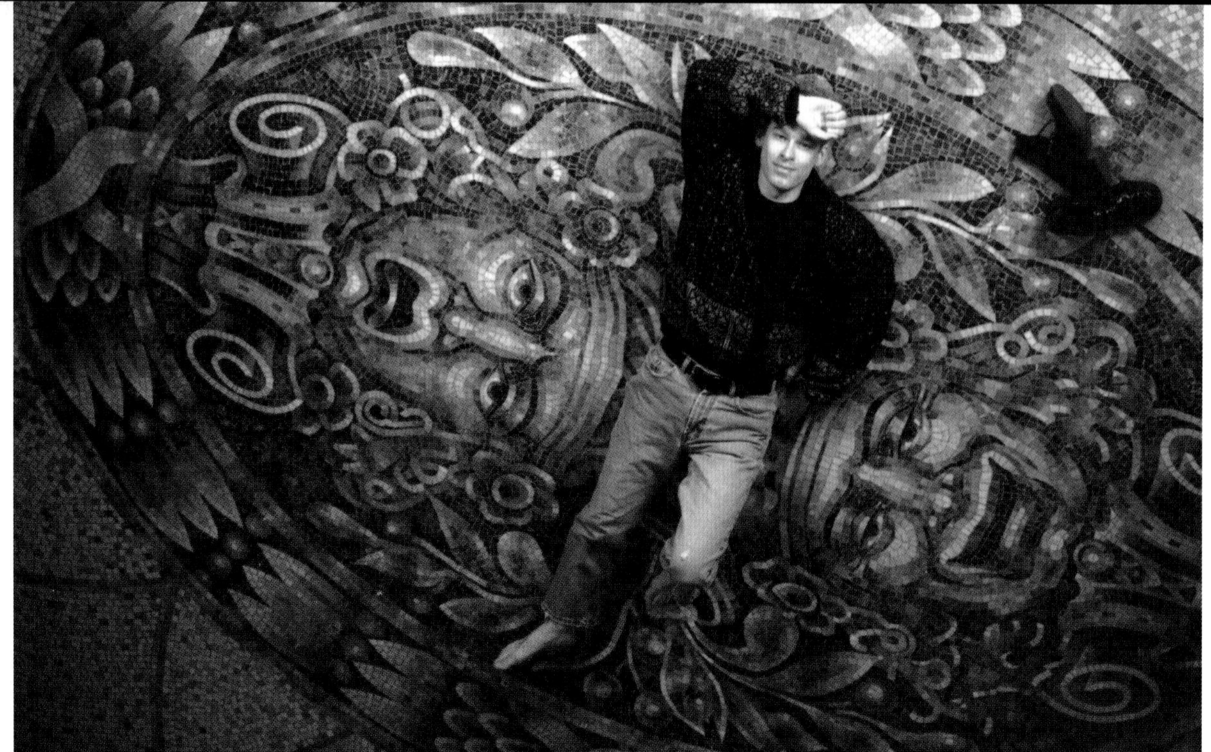

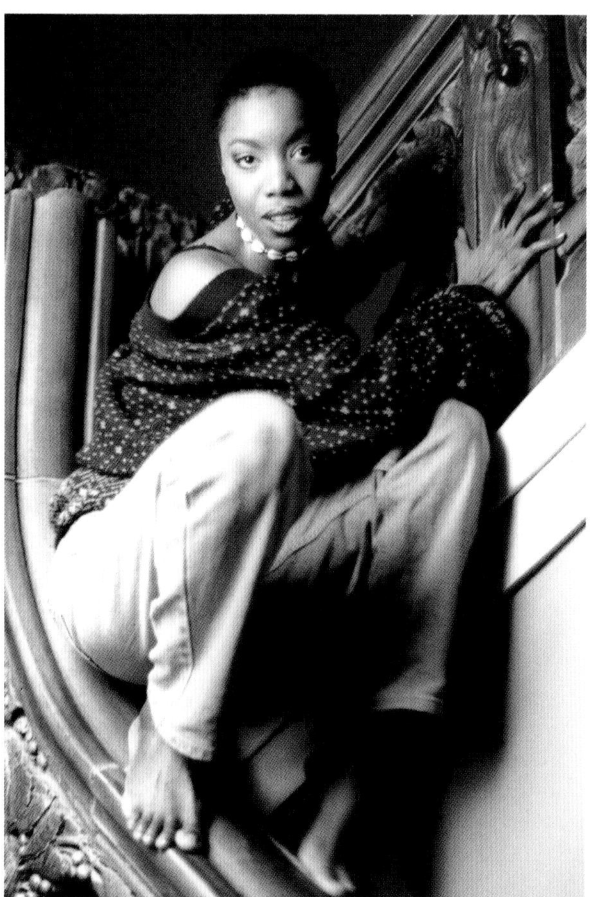

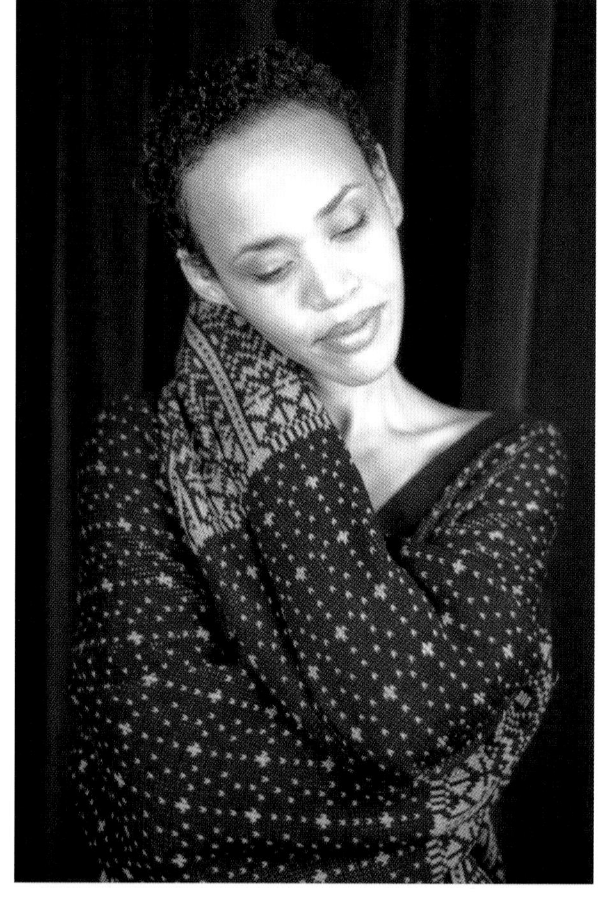

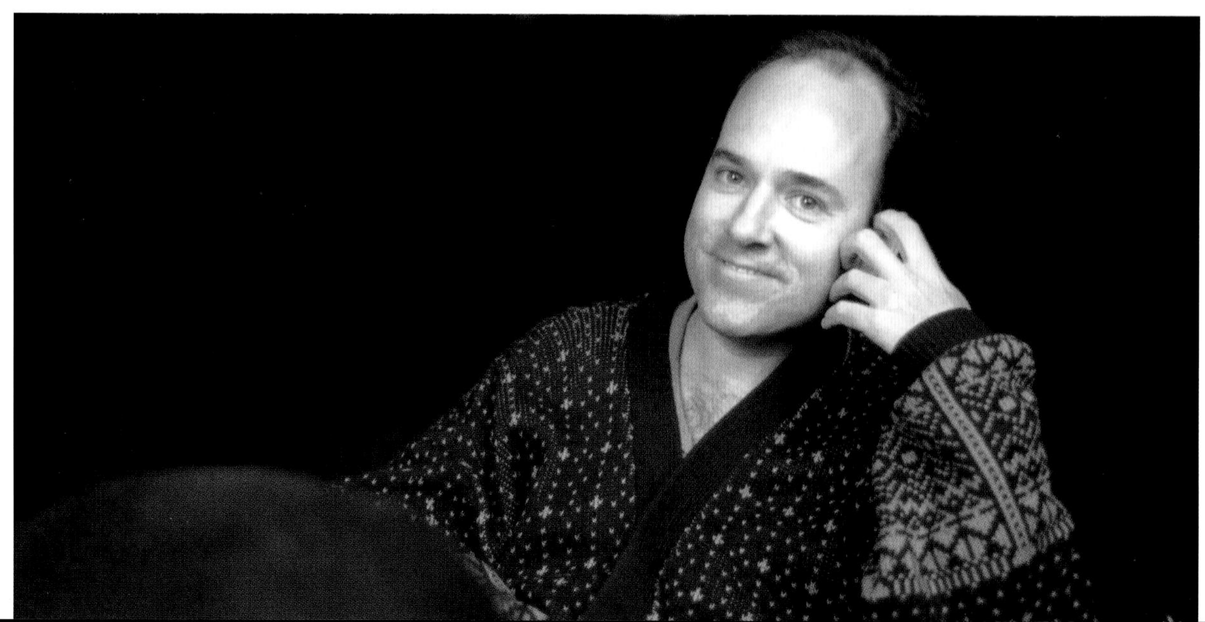

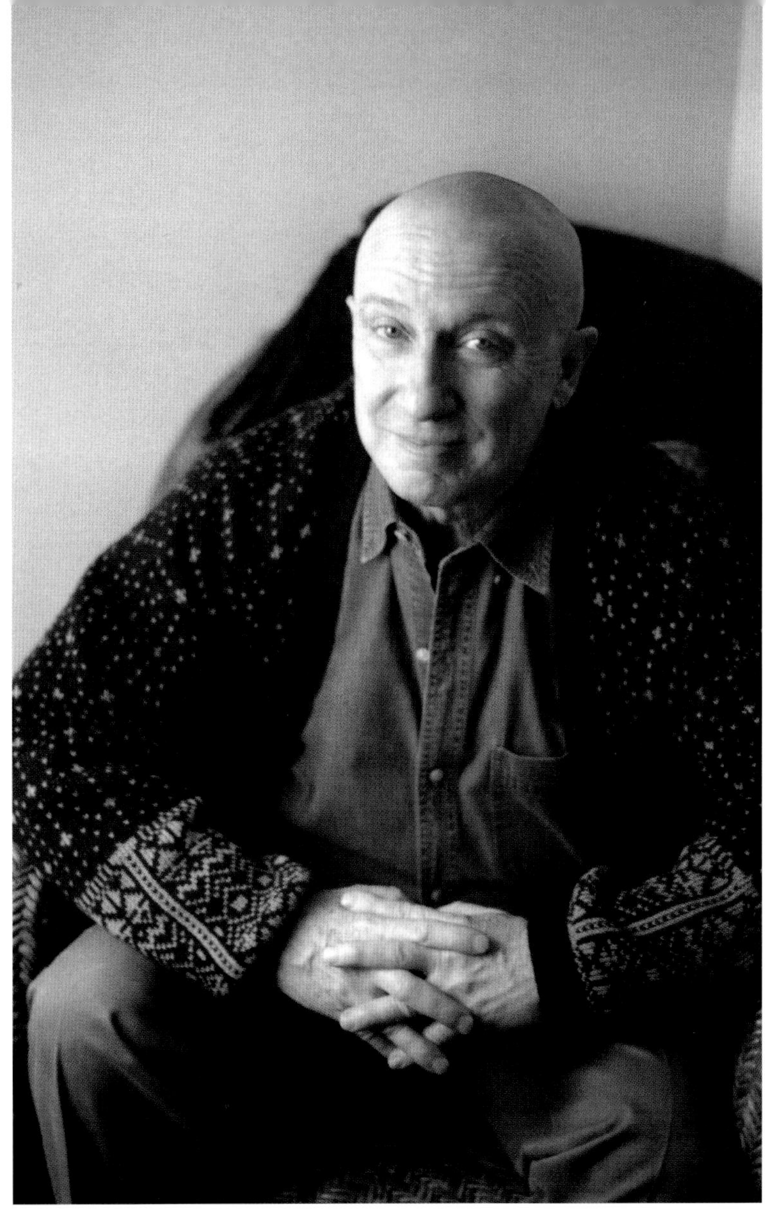

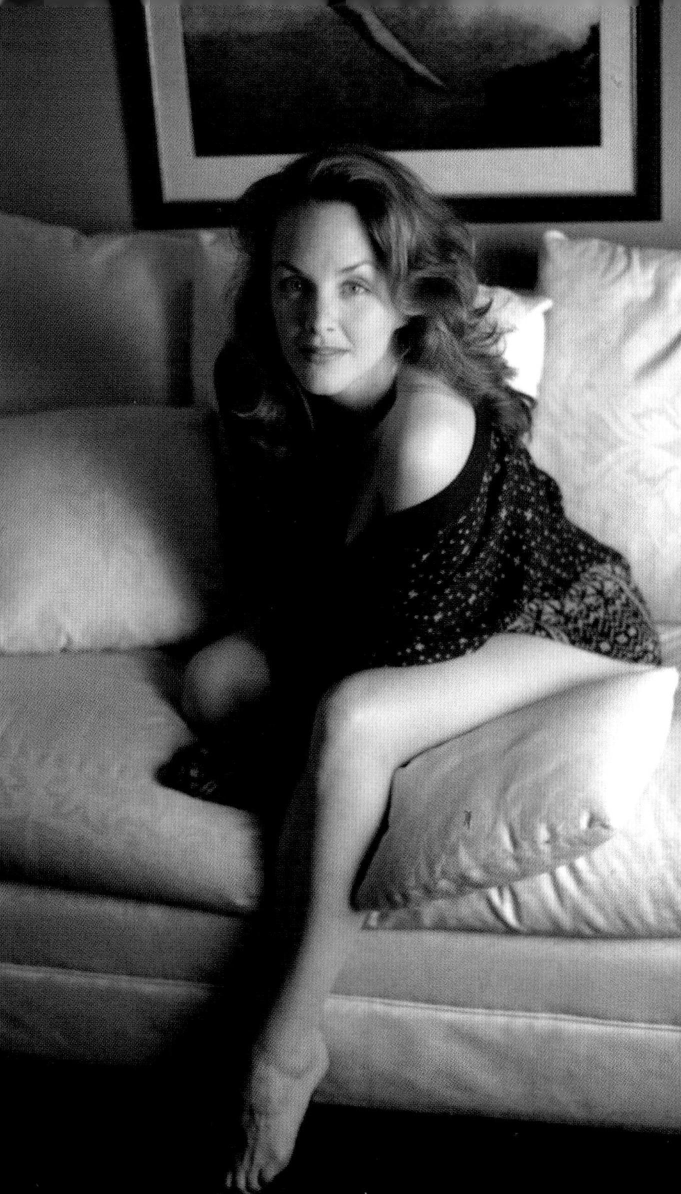

Opposite: The boys: Steven Sutcliffe on the lobby floor and
Stephen Flaherty (*bottom*) in the auditorium of the Ford Center during *Ragtime*
The girls: Heather Headley and Gina Breedlove in the lobby of the New Amsterdam during *The Lion King*

This page and next: George Hearn, Alice Ripley, Alan Campbell, and Glenn Close (page 34) in their dressing rooms at the Marquis during *Sunset Boulevard*

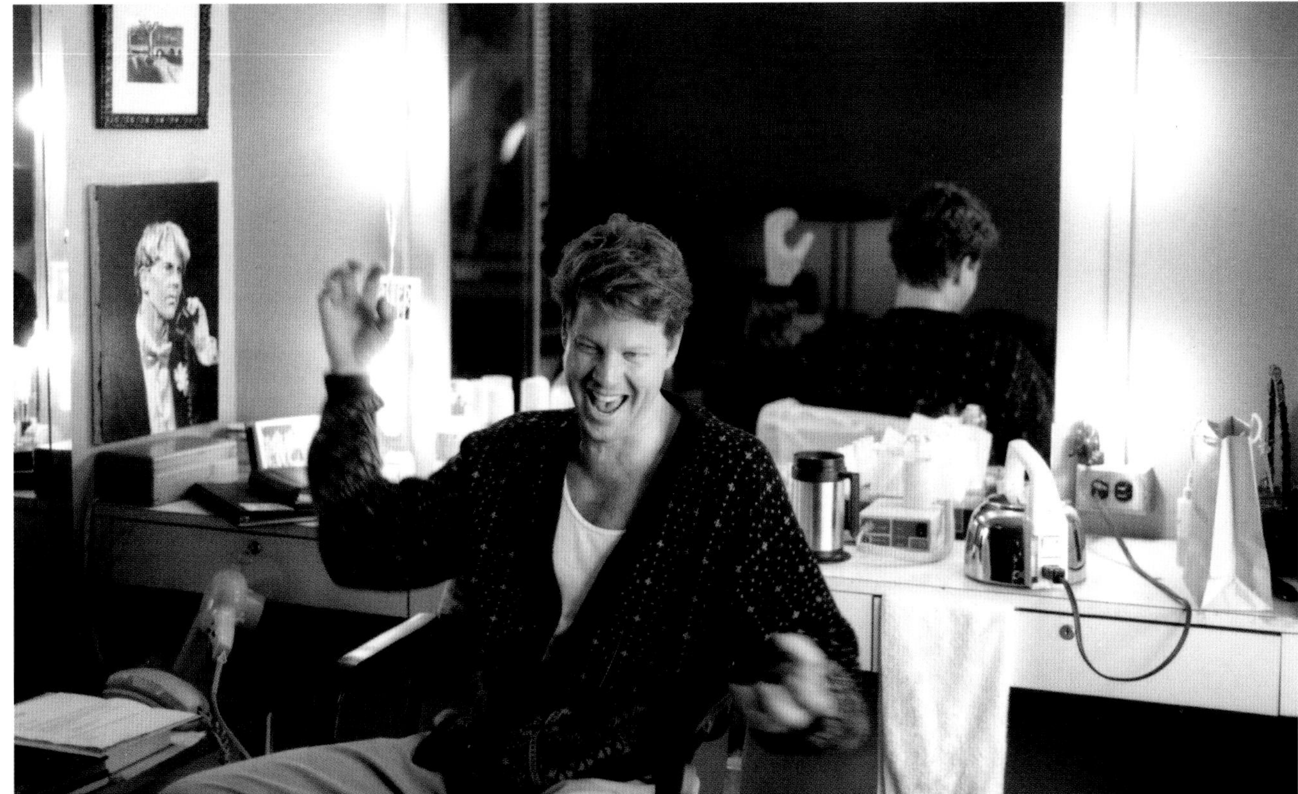

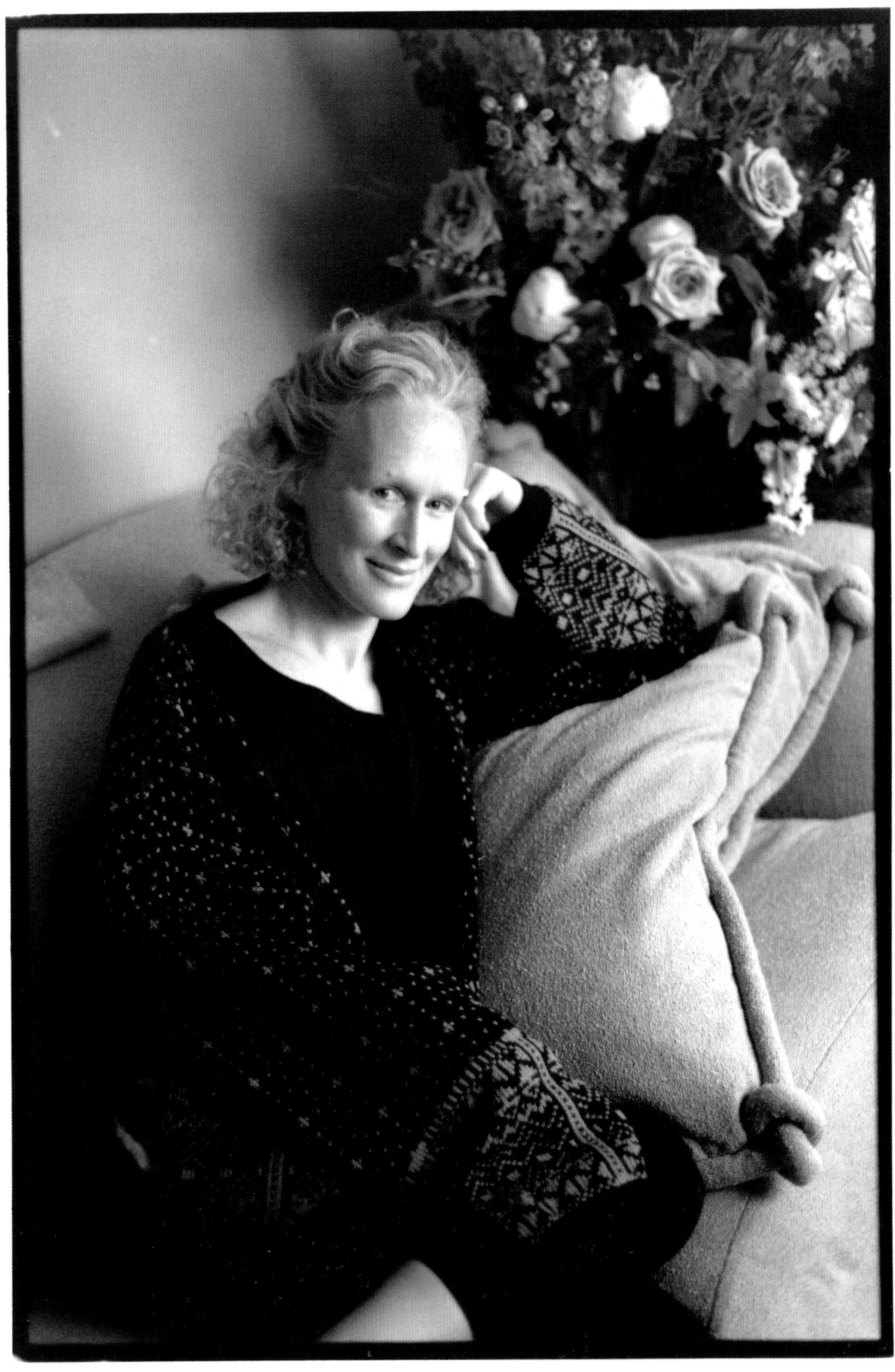

Glenn Close

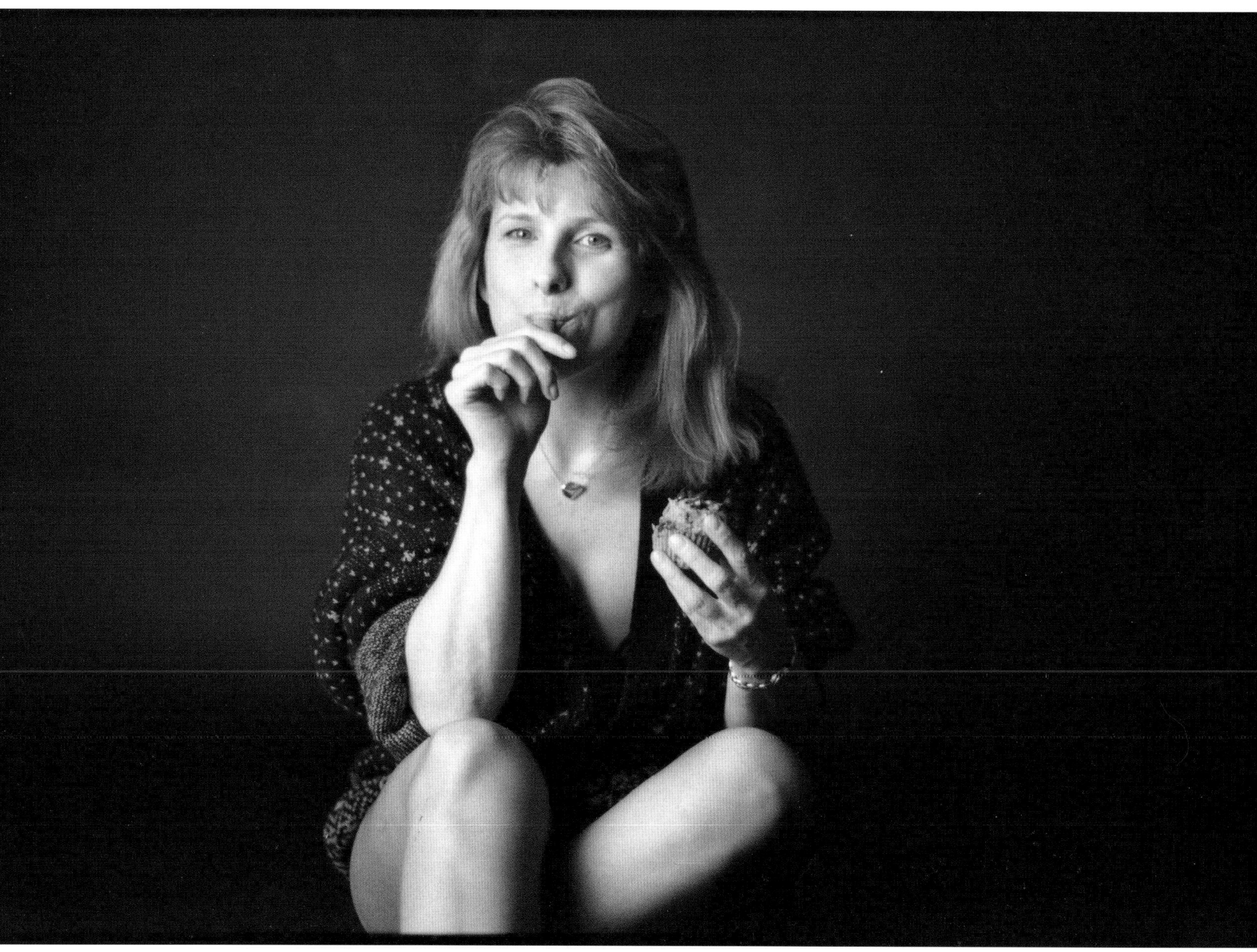

Miss Nancy LaMott

"I just made some pumpkin chocolate chip muffins. Would you like one?"
"There is no food that I will turn away."

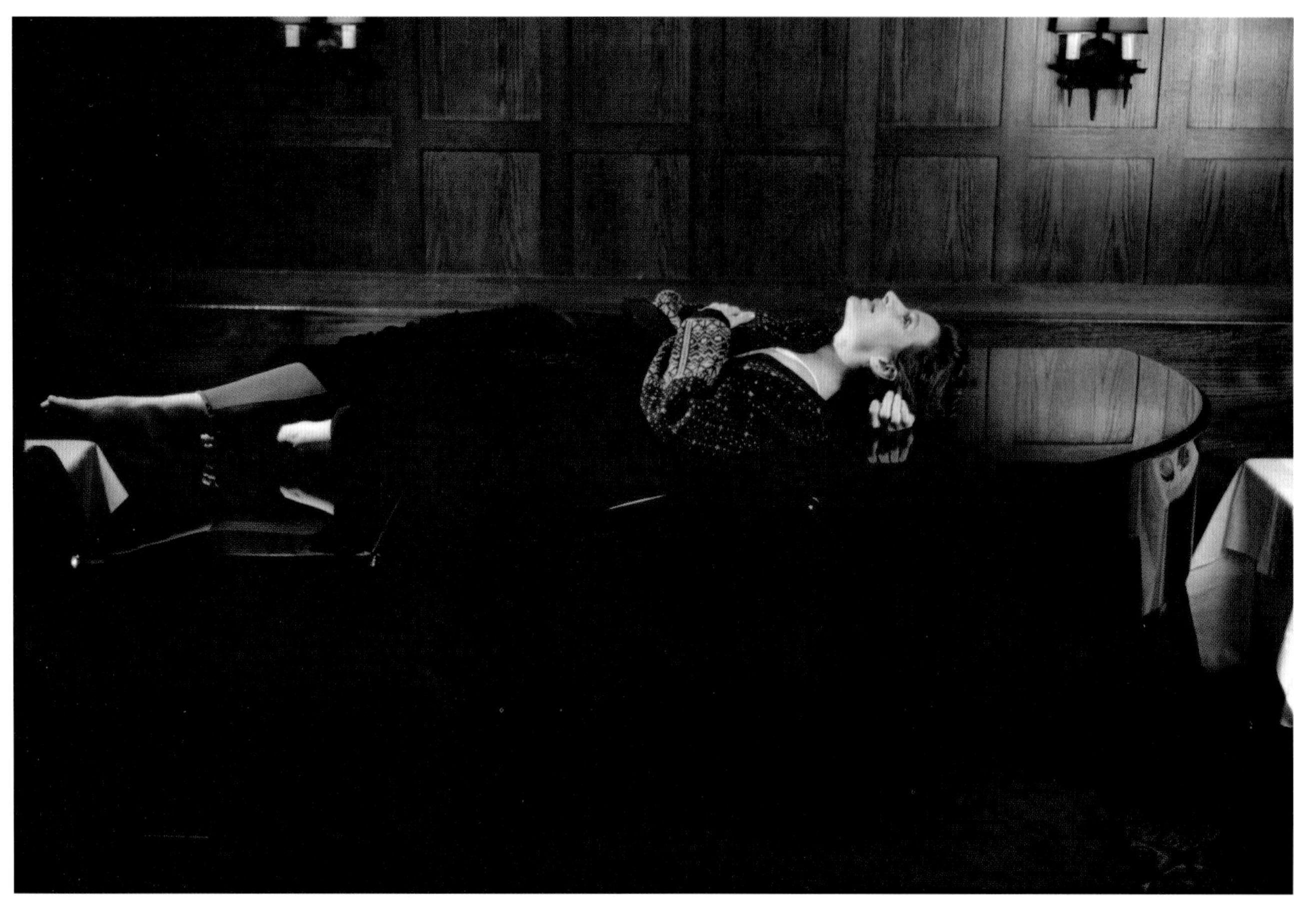

Andrea Marcovicci

Tony Cointreau

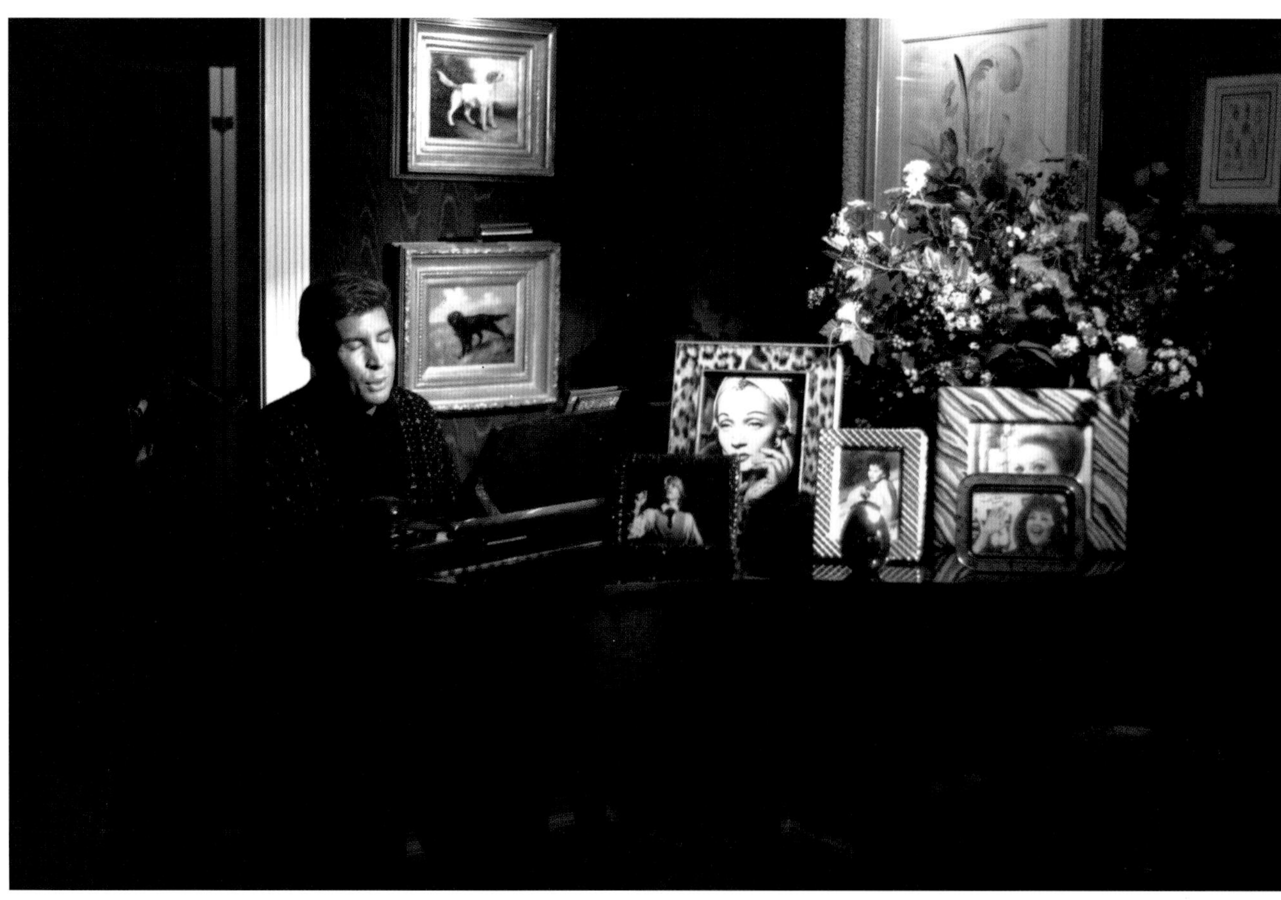

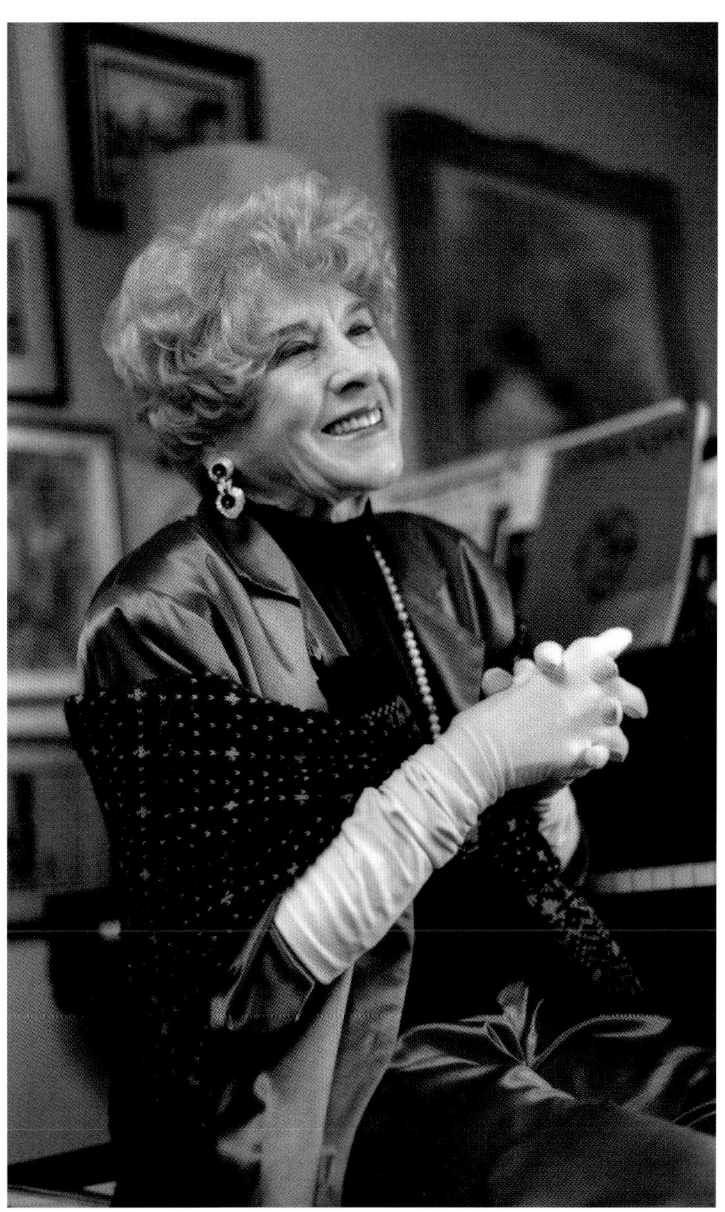

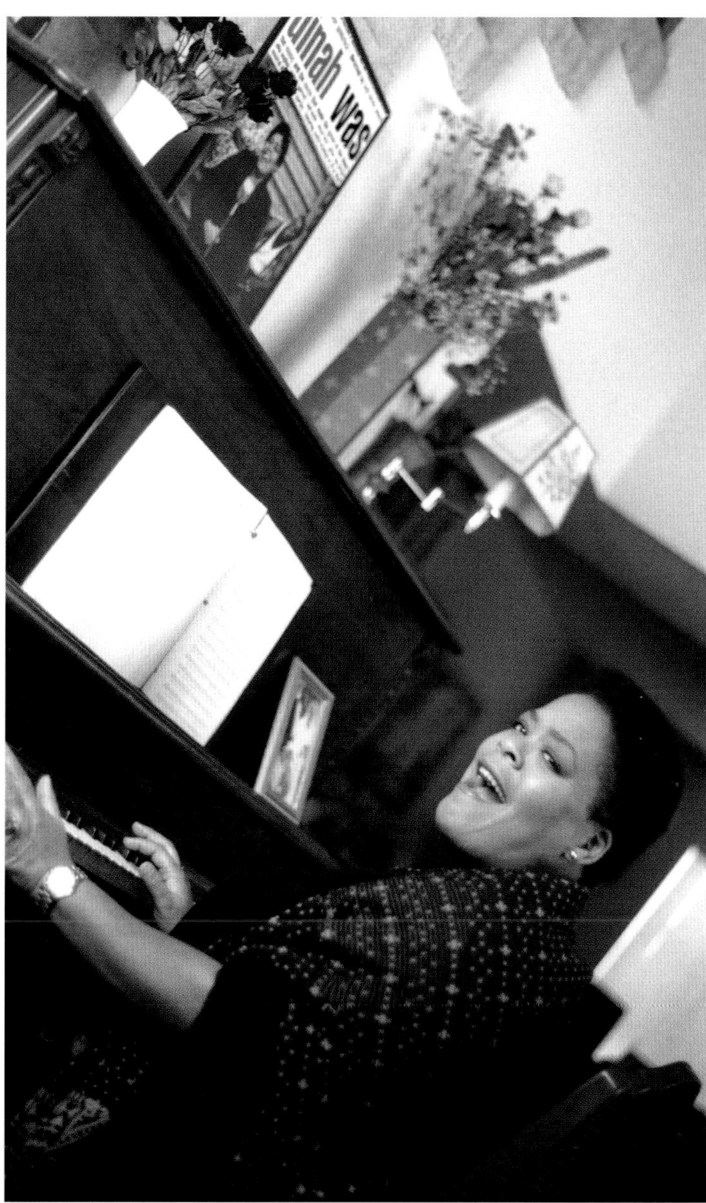

The Incomparable Hildegarde

Yvette Freeman

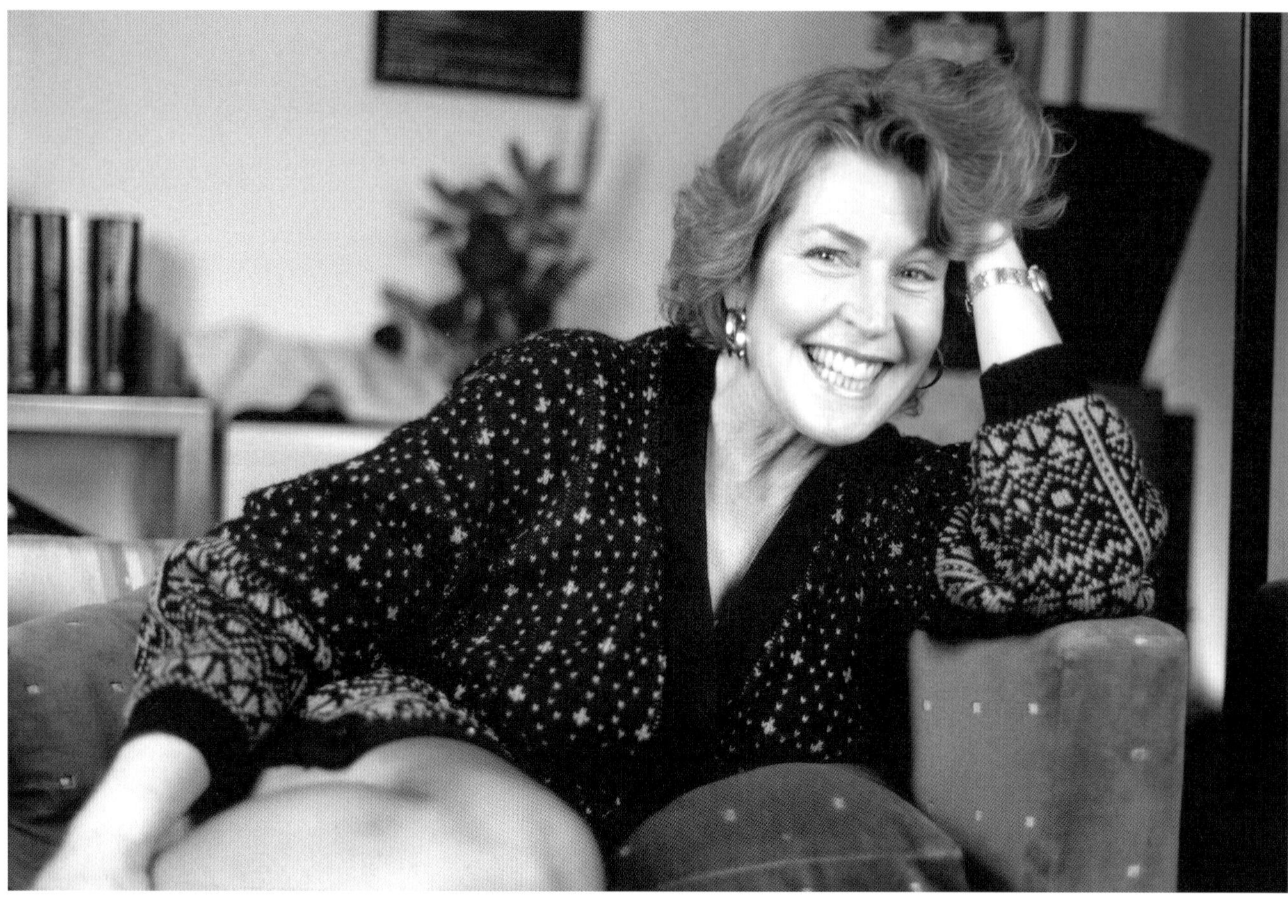

Helen Reddy

She is friendly, she is funny, she is intelligent, she is sexy, she is vulnerable, she is mysterious, she is strong, and she is professional. She is childlike, she is nurturing, she is excitable, she is calming, she is ambitious, she is grounded, she is playful, she is shapely, she is studious, and she is spiritual. She is the singer I have loved longer than any other. She is more than woman, she is a lady.

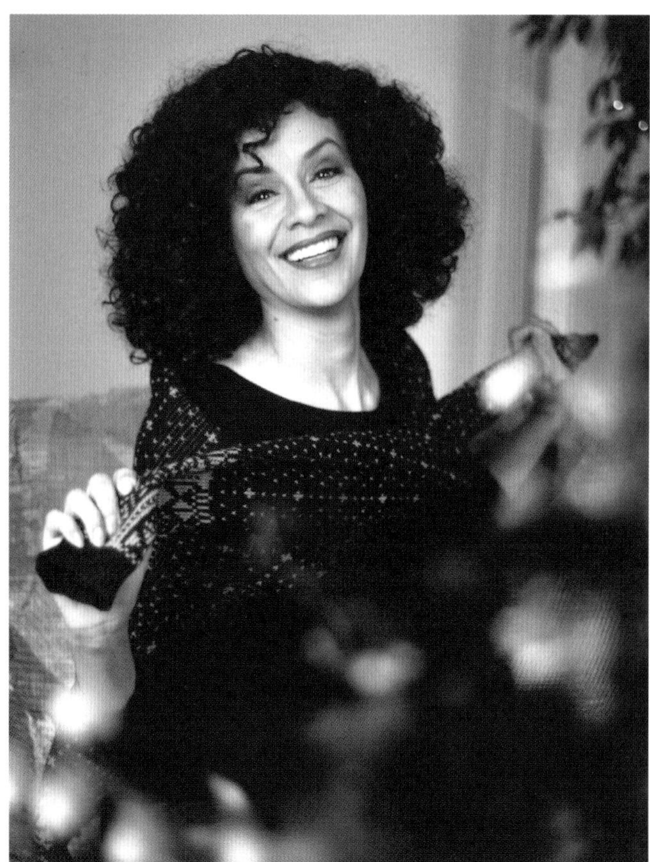

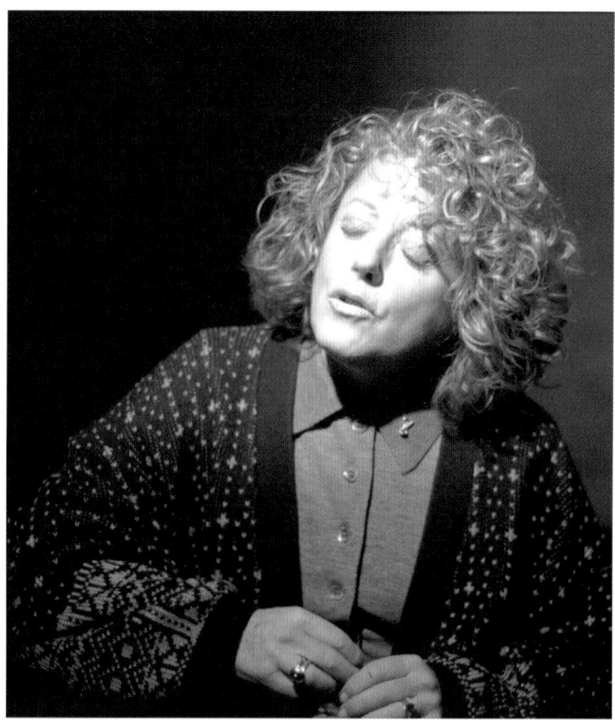

Lesley Gore

Left: Marilyn McCoo

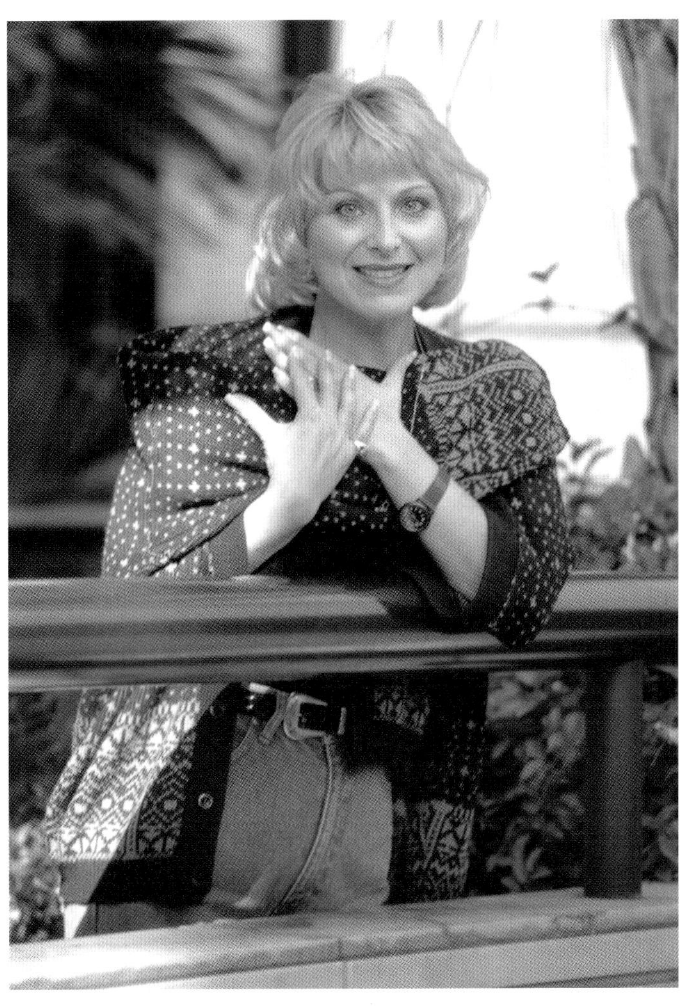

Rosalind Kind

Marilyn Lovell Matz

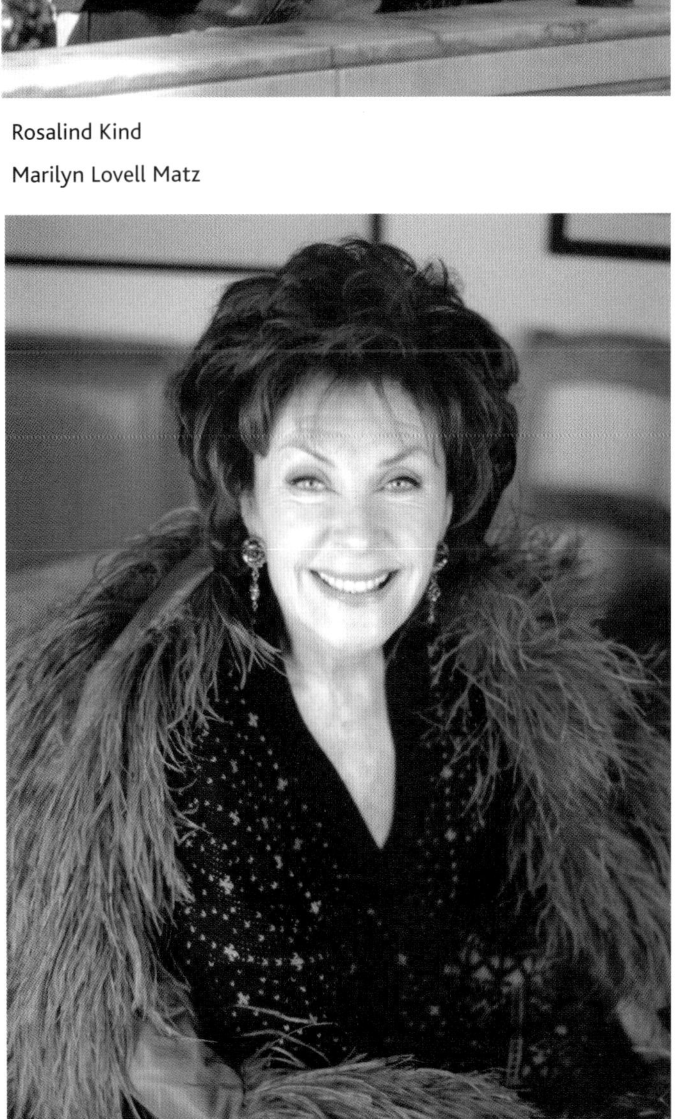

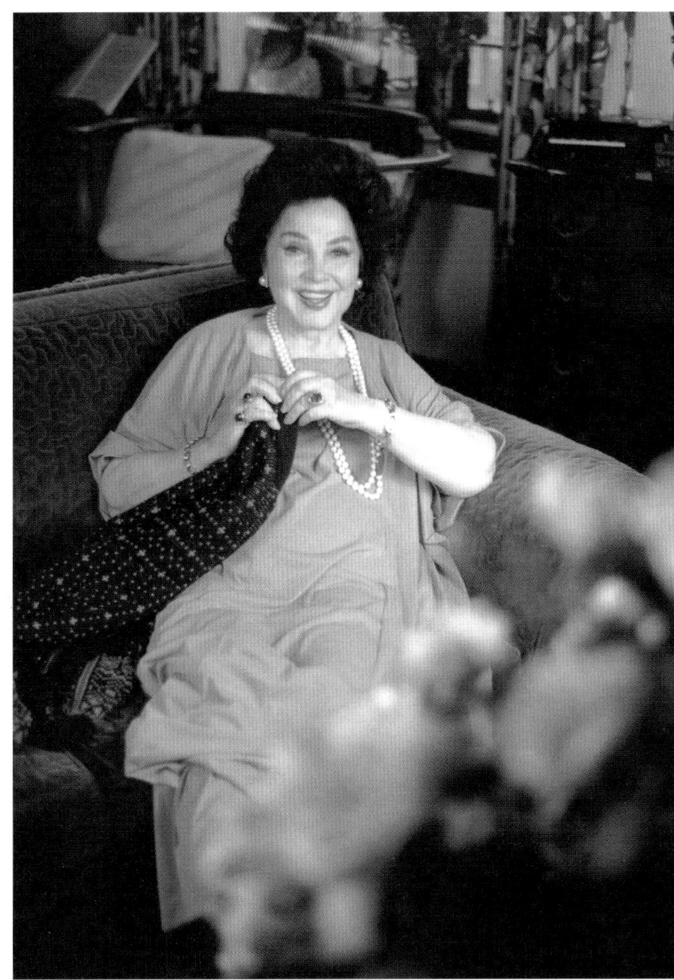

Kathryn Grayson

Karen Morrow

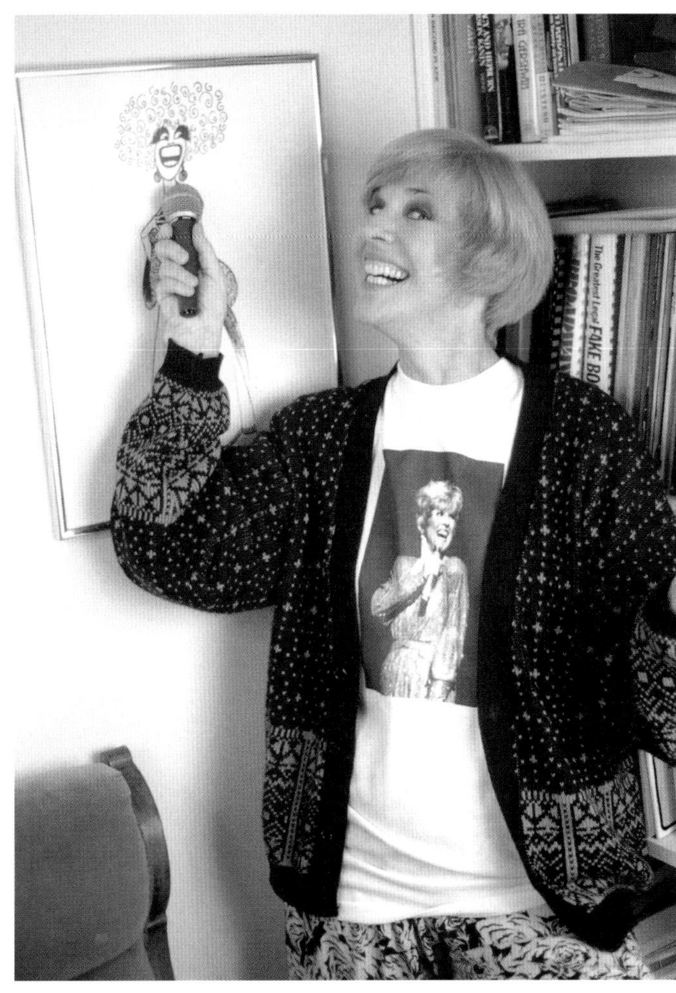

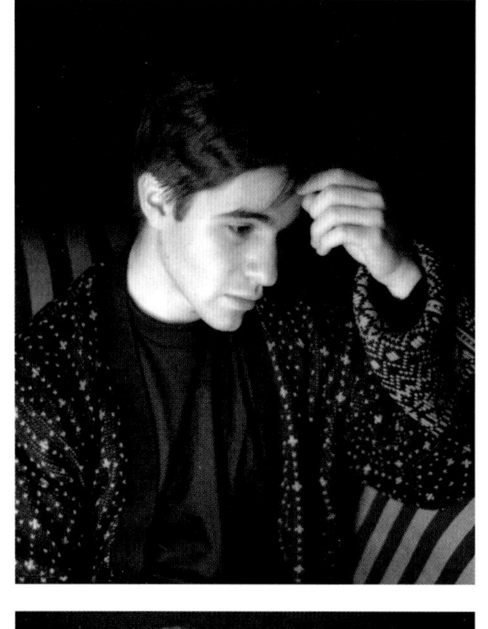
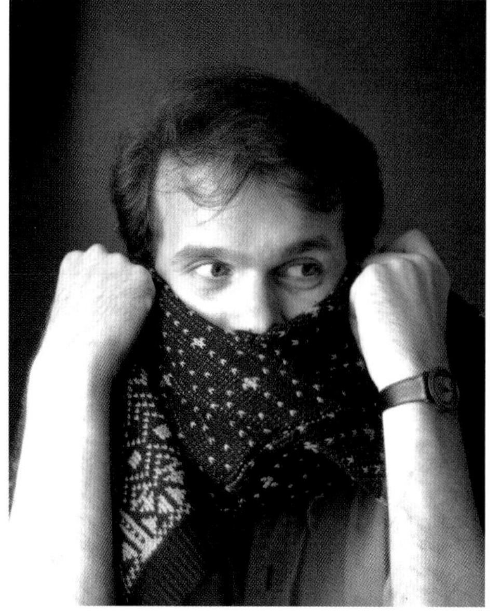
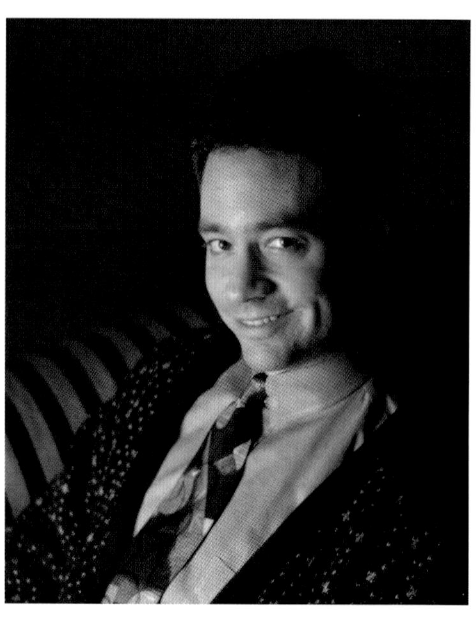
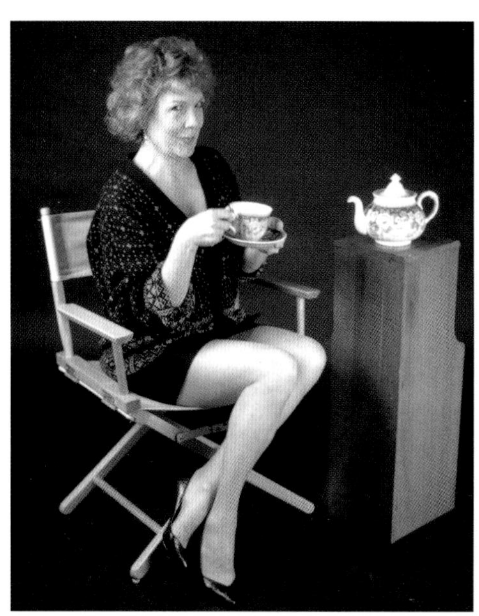
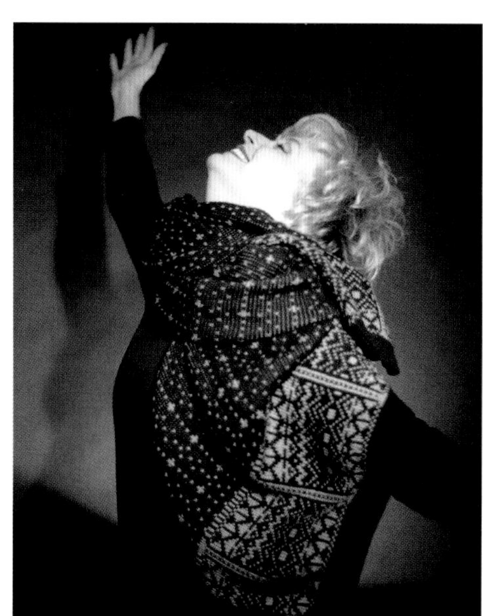
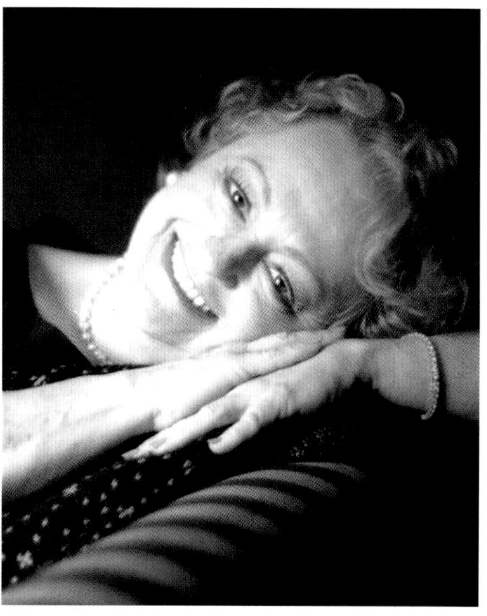
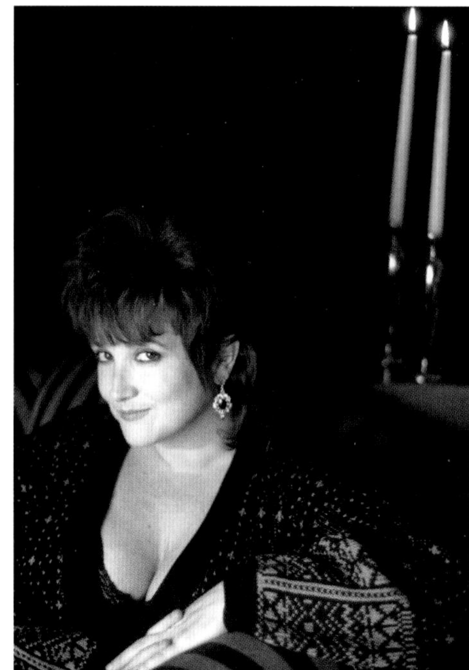
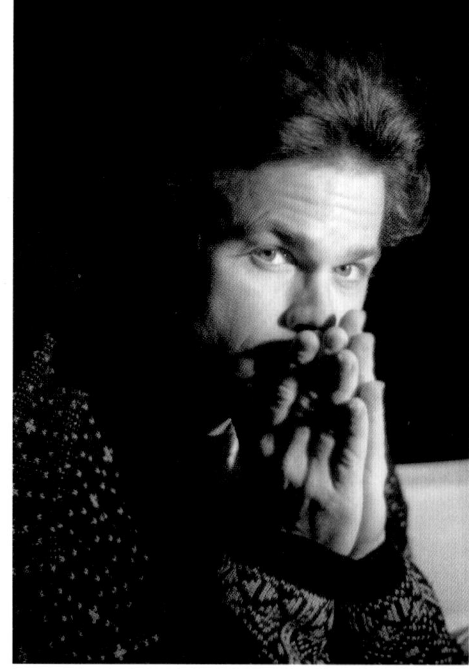

From left to right:

Brad Kane

George Dvorsky

Mark Sendroff

Beth Fowler

Sally Mayes

Marcia Lewis

Julie Johnson

Sam Harris

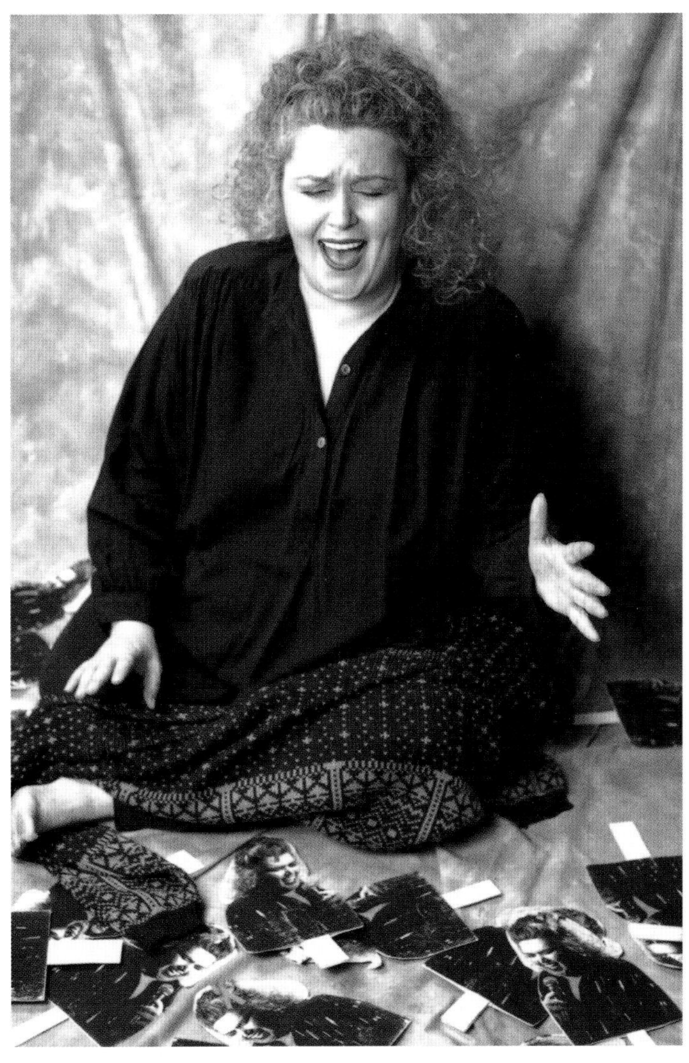

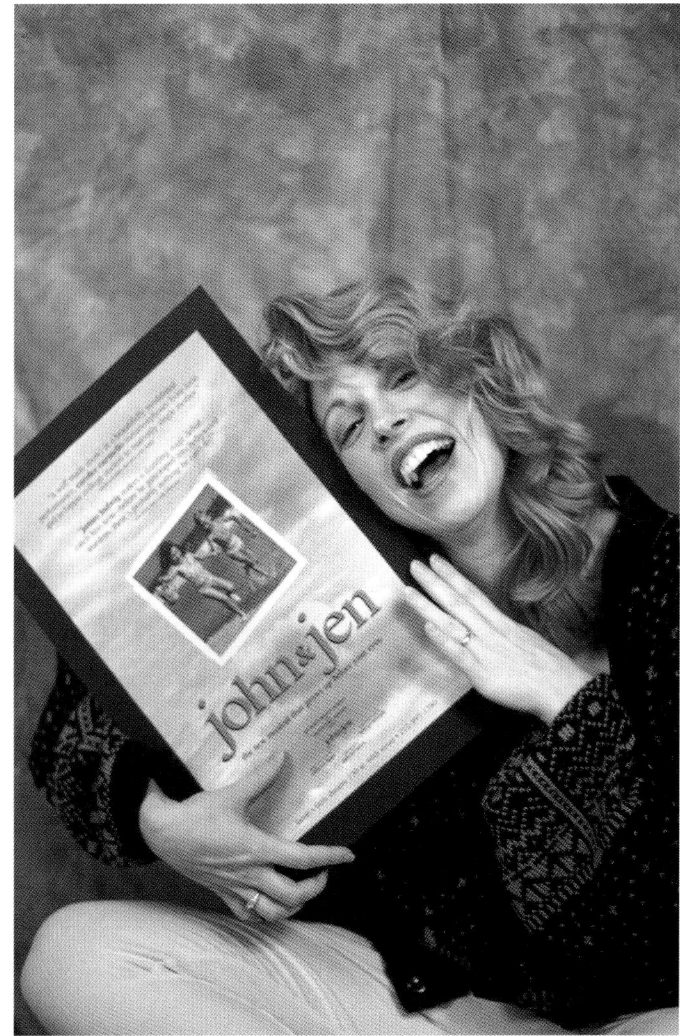

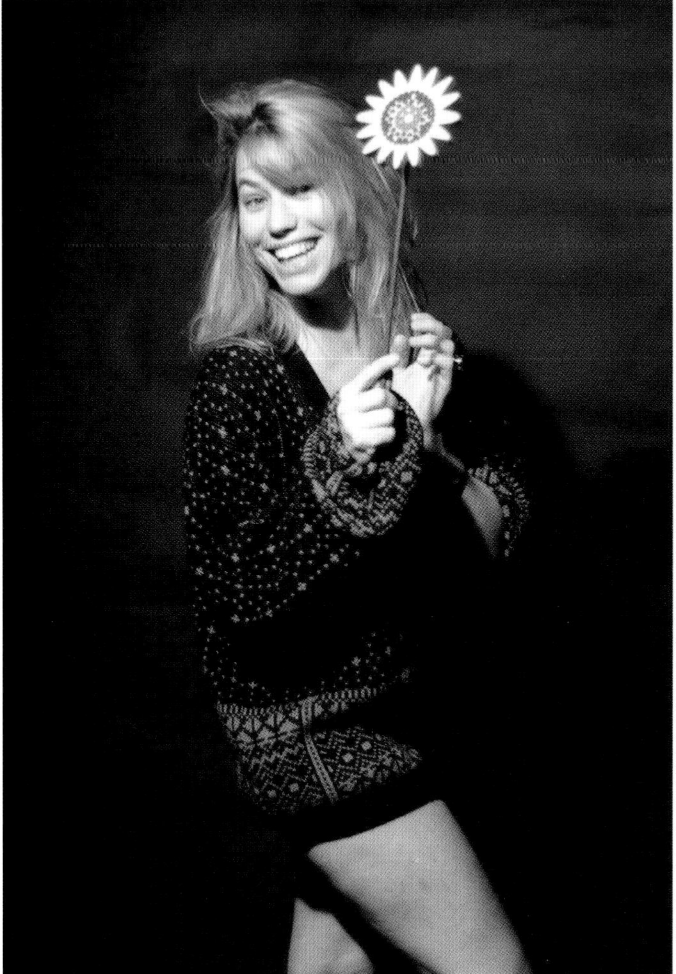

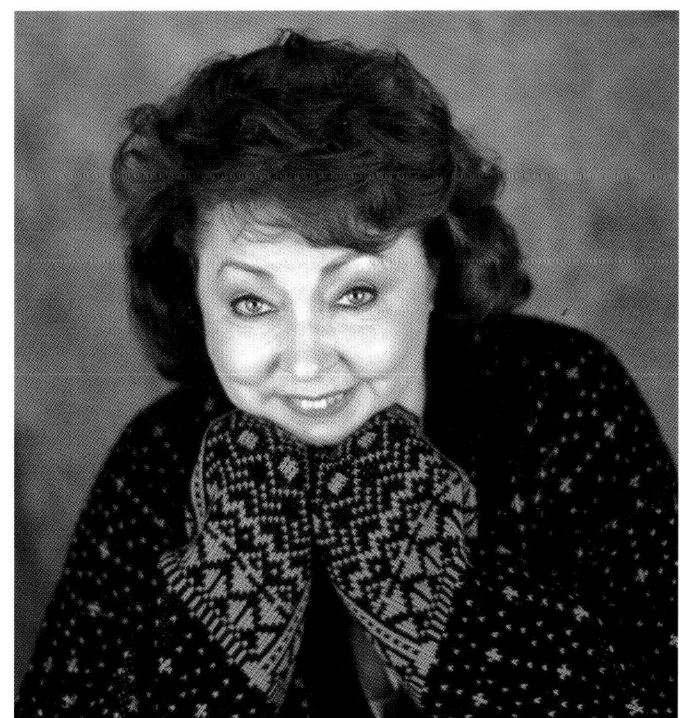

Clockwise from top left:

Baby Jane Dexter

Carolee Carmello

Mimi Hines

Sarah Hickman

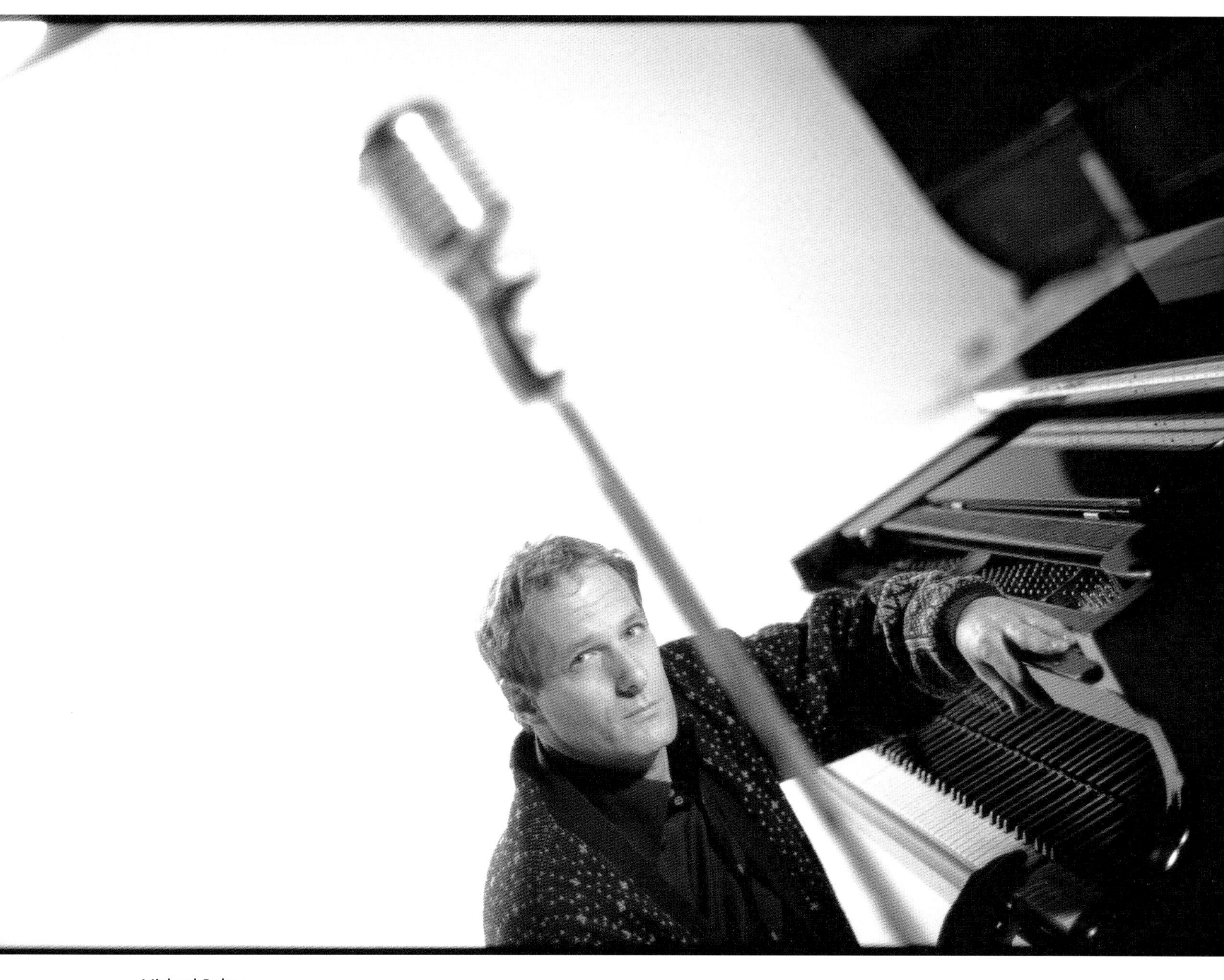

Michael Bolton

Sometimes when I work, I am not allowed the luxury of spending time with the people with whom I work. The celebrated are in great demand and it is not unusual for me to be with someone for less than five minutes, only one of which is spent actually taking pictures. I was given an opportunity to work with Michael Bolton while he was filming a commercial spot for a concert he was doing on television. Having been told that I would have to wait around until a convenient break in filming, at which time I would be rushed in to do the photo with the sweater, I came prepared, magazine in hand. I arrived on set and was introduced to Michael, who was very friendly and really handsome, and then I sat down to read and wait.

I did not get to read my magazine because Michael Bolton came and sat nearby and asked me questions about my work. He talked to me and asked questions and gave me advice. He didn't have to do that; he could have been doing any number of other things at that time, but instead, he showed an interest in the work of a struggling young artist trying to find his way in a crazy world and a crazier business.

Since that day, I have told anyone who asks that Michael Bolton is on my list of the five nicest celebrities who posed for *The Sweater Book*.

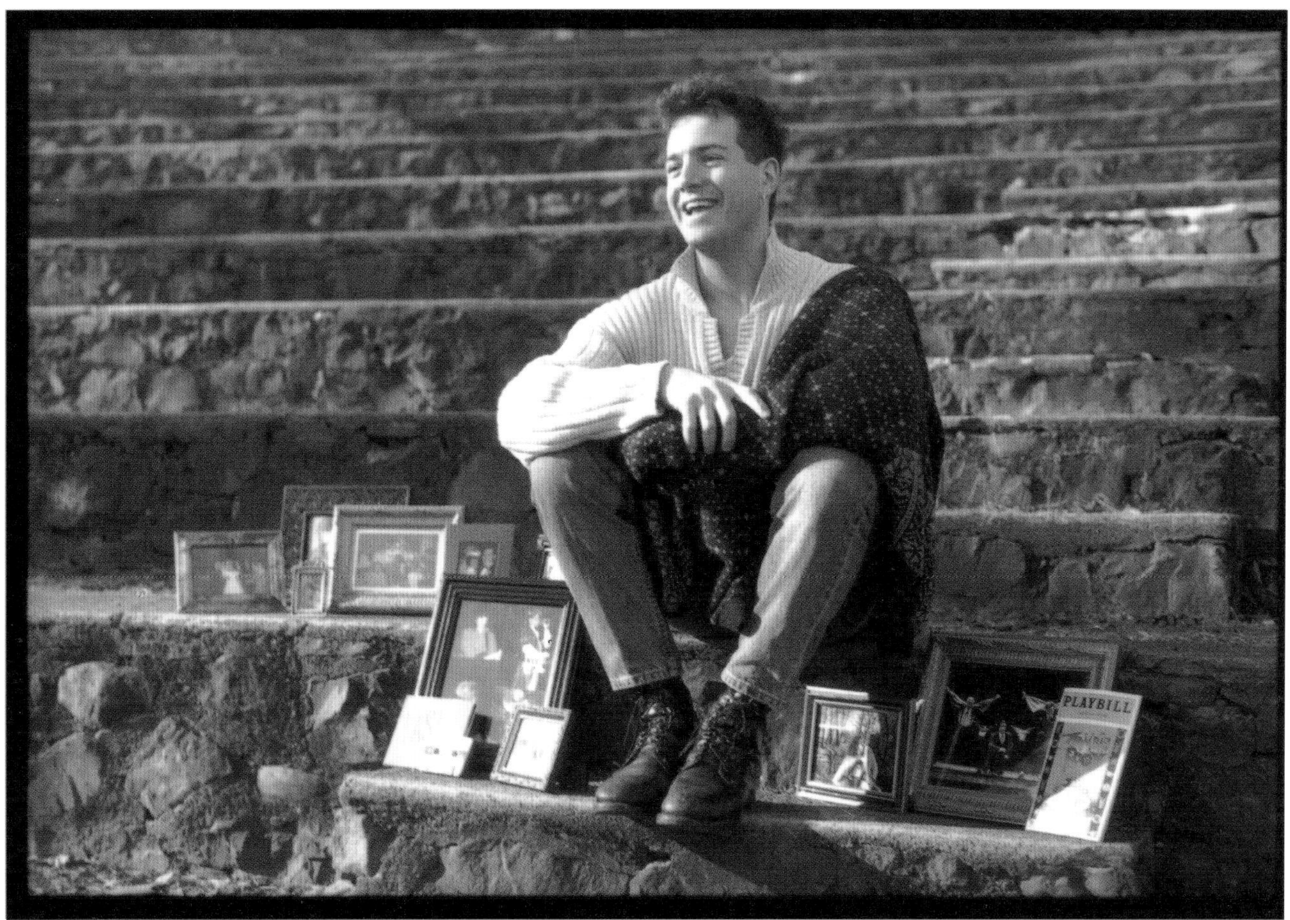

Stephen Bienskie

David Campbell

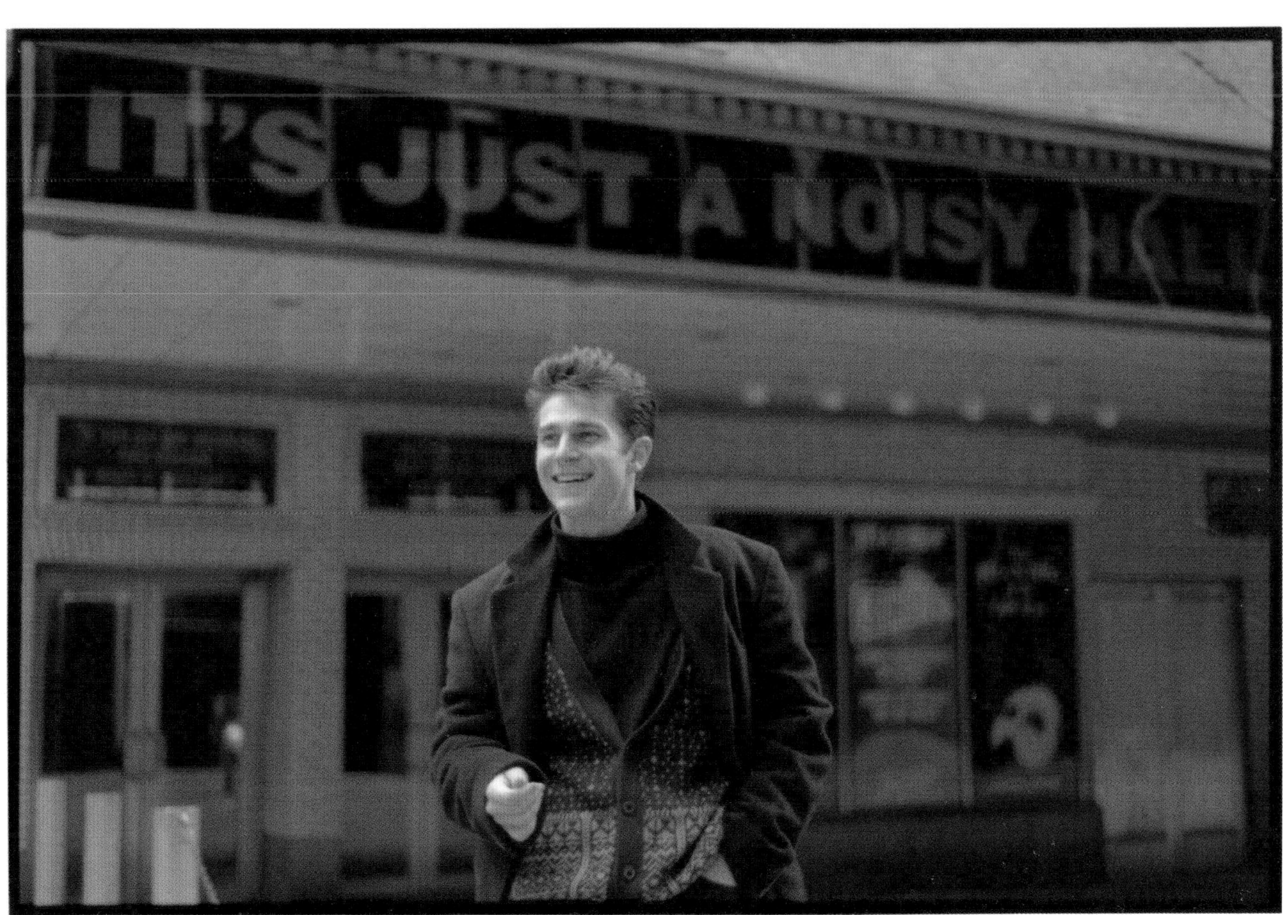

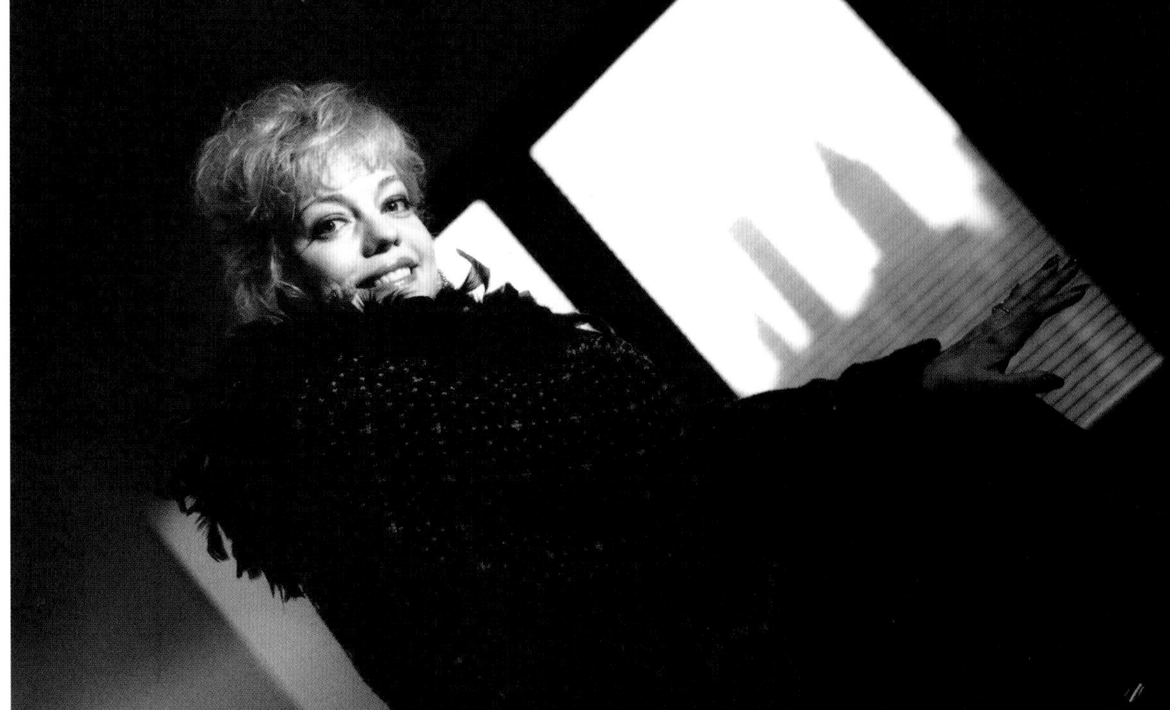

KT Sullivan

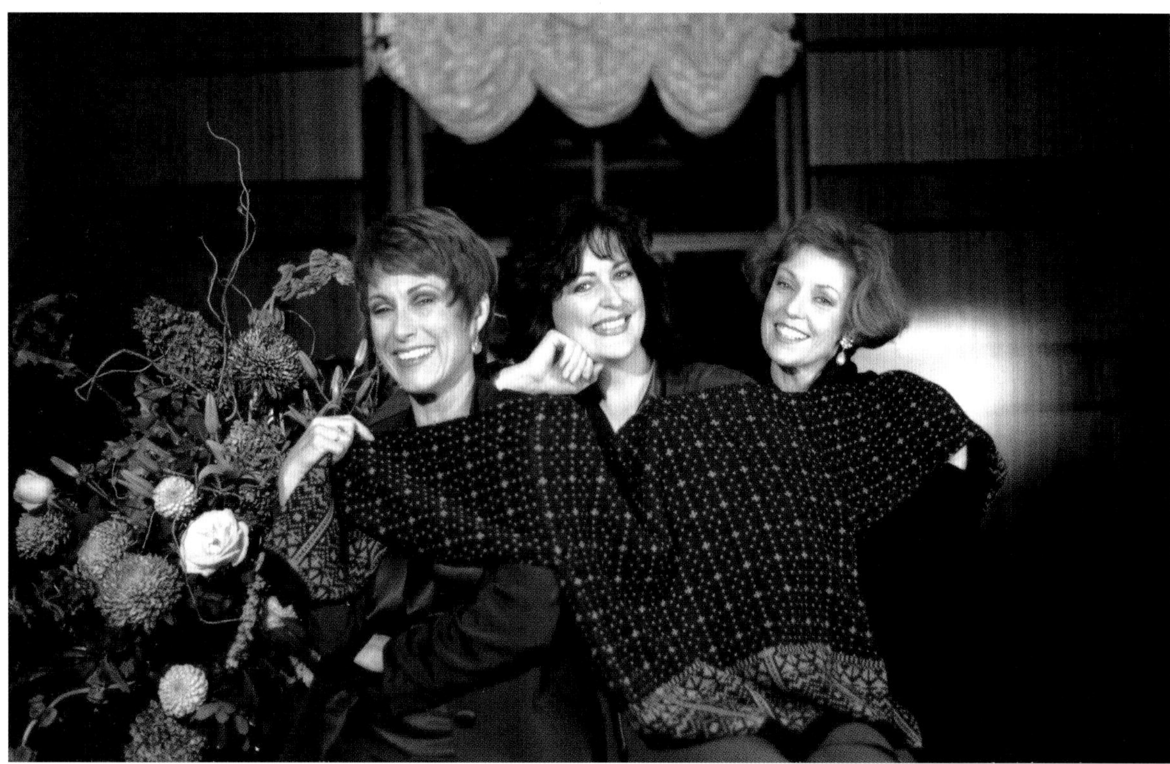

Left to right: Amanda McBroom, Ann Hampton Callaway, Mary Cleere Haran

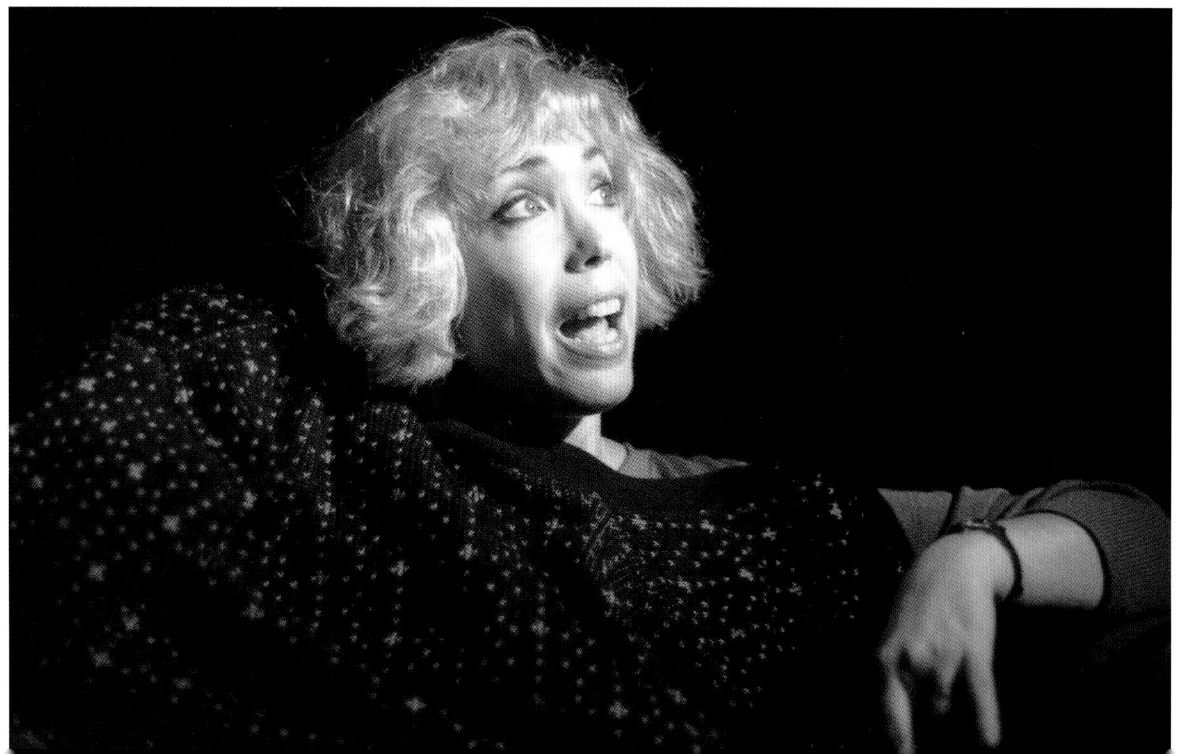

Alix Korey

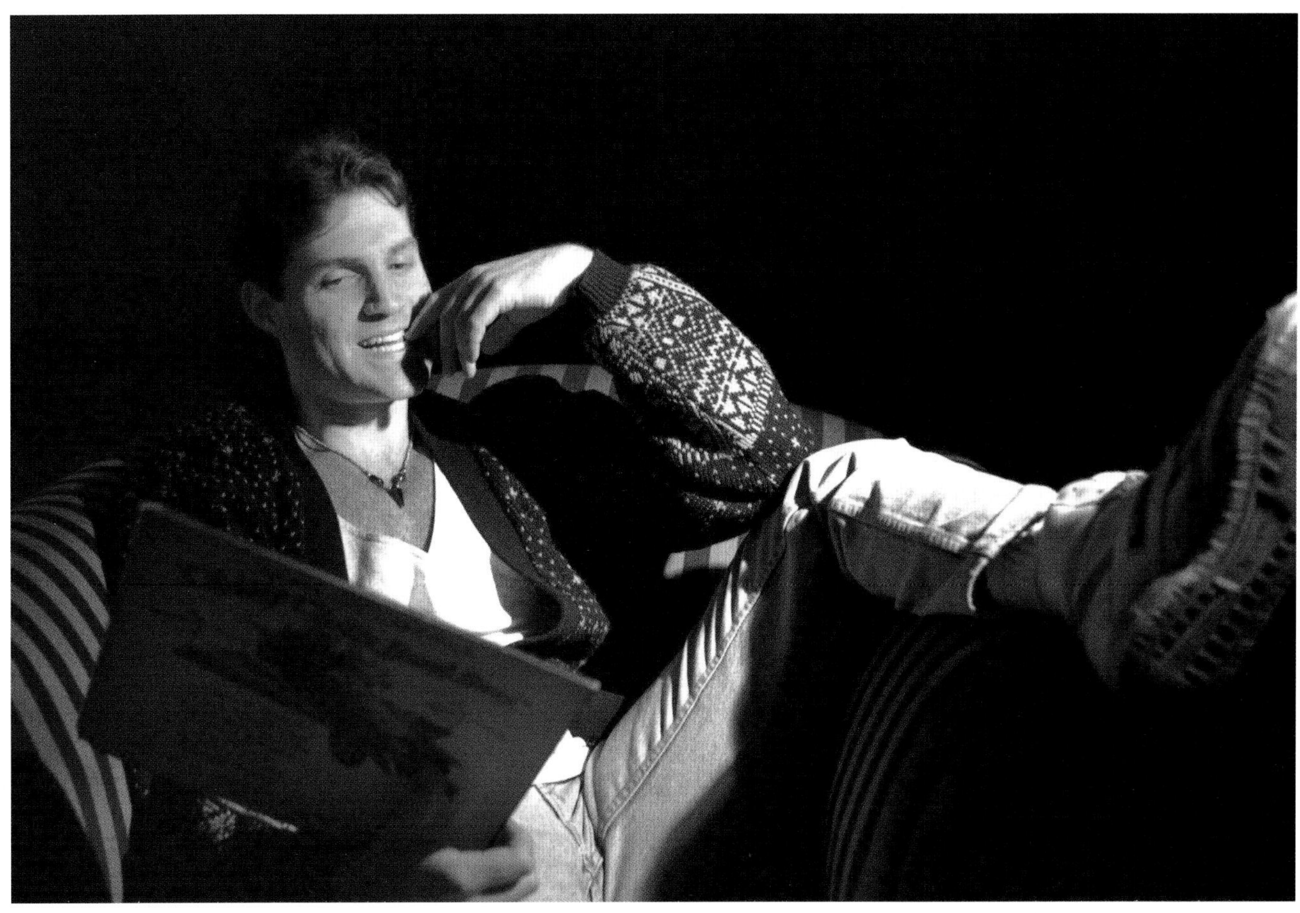

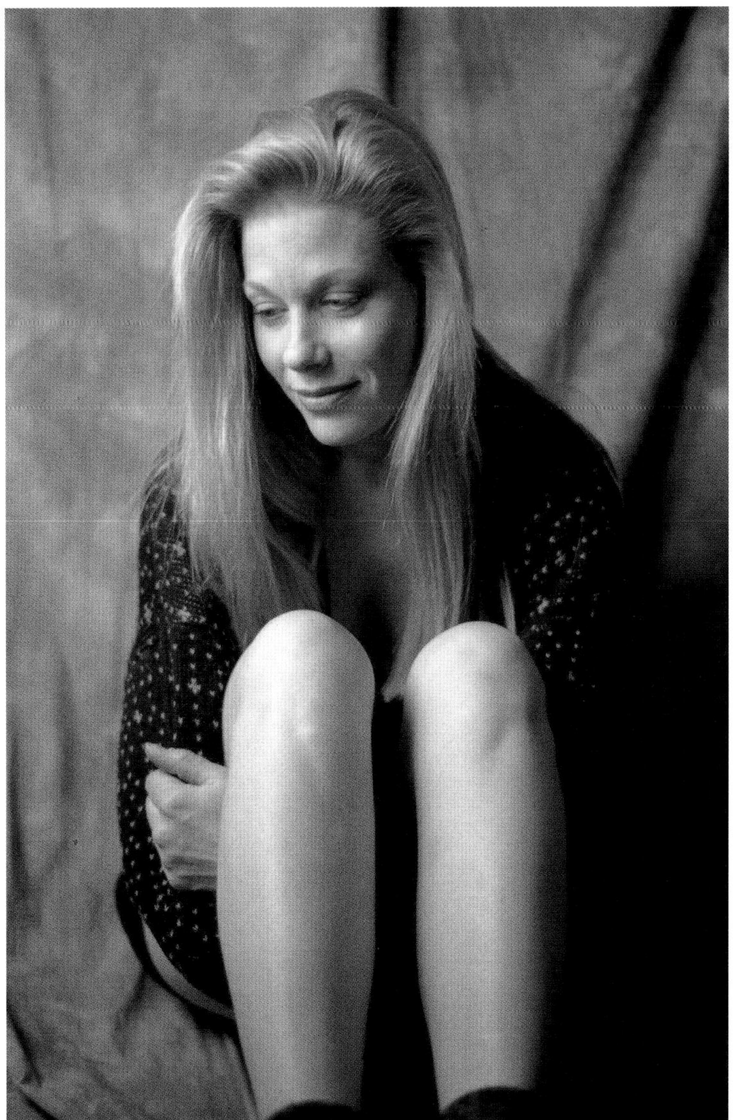

"You have the soundtrack to Chitty Chitty Bang Bang*?!"*

"Yes."

"Oh my God! That was my favorite movie. Can I have it in my picture?"

"Certainly."

"I have the toy. You know, the car with the wings that pop out."

"No way! Really? You still have it?"

The many wonderful things people bond over...

Above: Marc Kudisch

Marin Mazzie

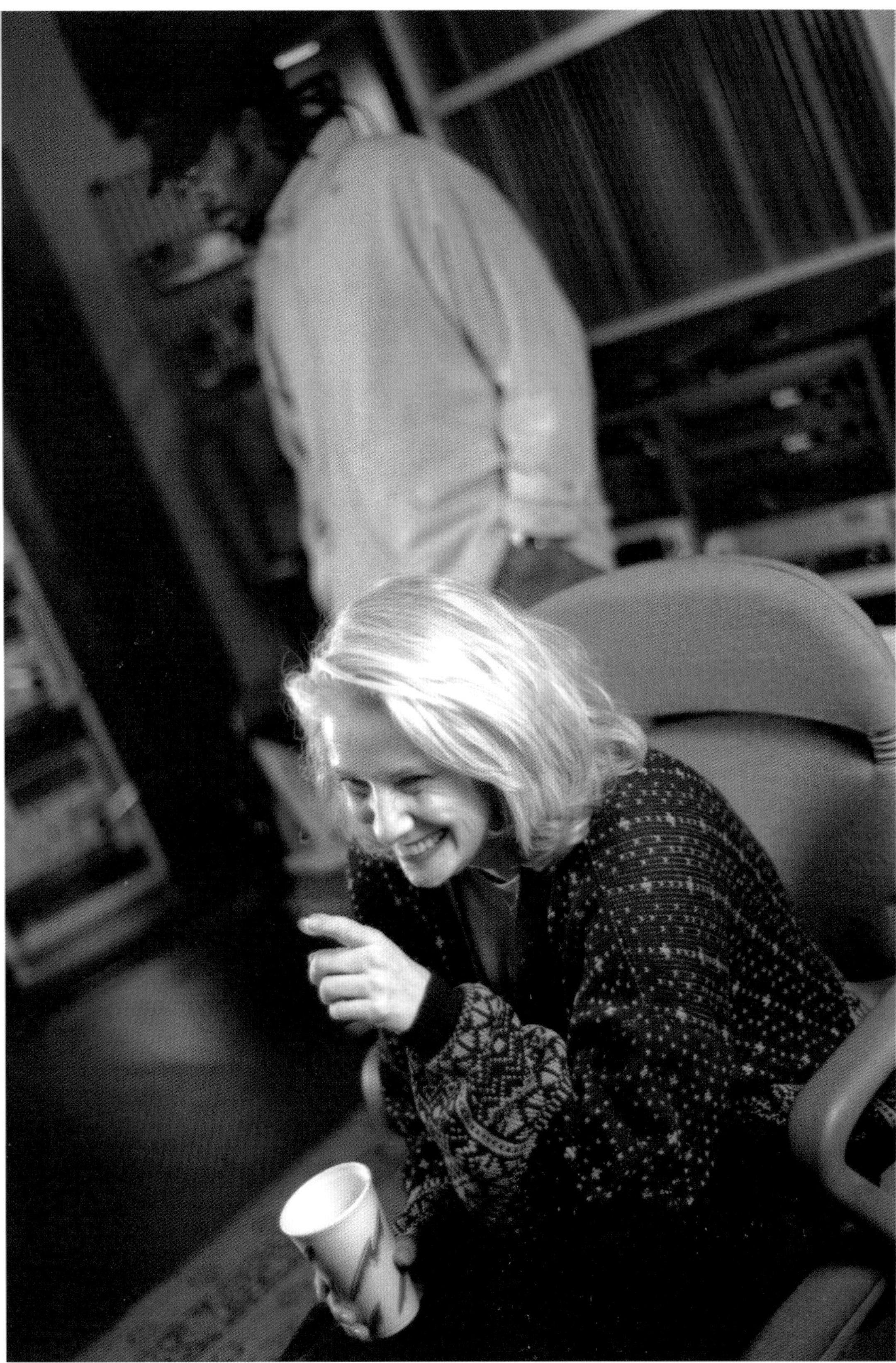

Betty Buckley

I frequently watch a talk show in which the interviewer ends with the same set of questions. One of the questions, "What turns you on?" always fascinates me. My favorite answer to date has been "Absolute honesty." I have wondered, though, what my answer would be.

Watching Betty Buckley record her showstopper from *Triumph of Love*, seeing the respect with which she treats the instrumentalists and technicians, hearing the precision with which she communicates her interpretation of the song, I found my answer.

What turns me on?

Knowledgeable and Reverent Craftsmanship.

THE SWEATER IN THE FAMILY WAY—*in which the sweater meets the kids*

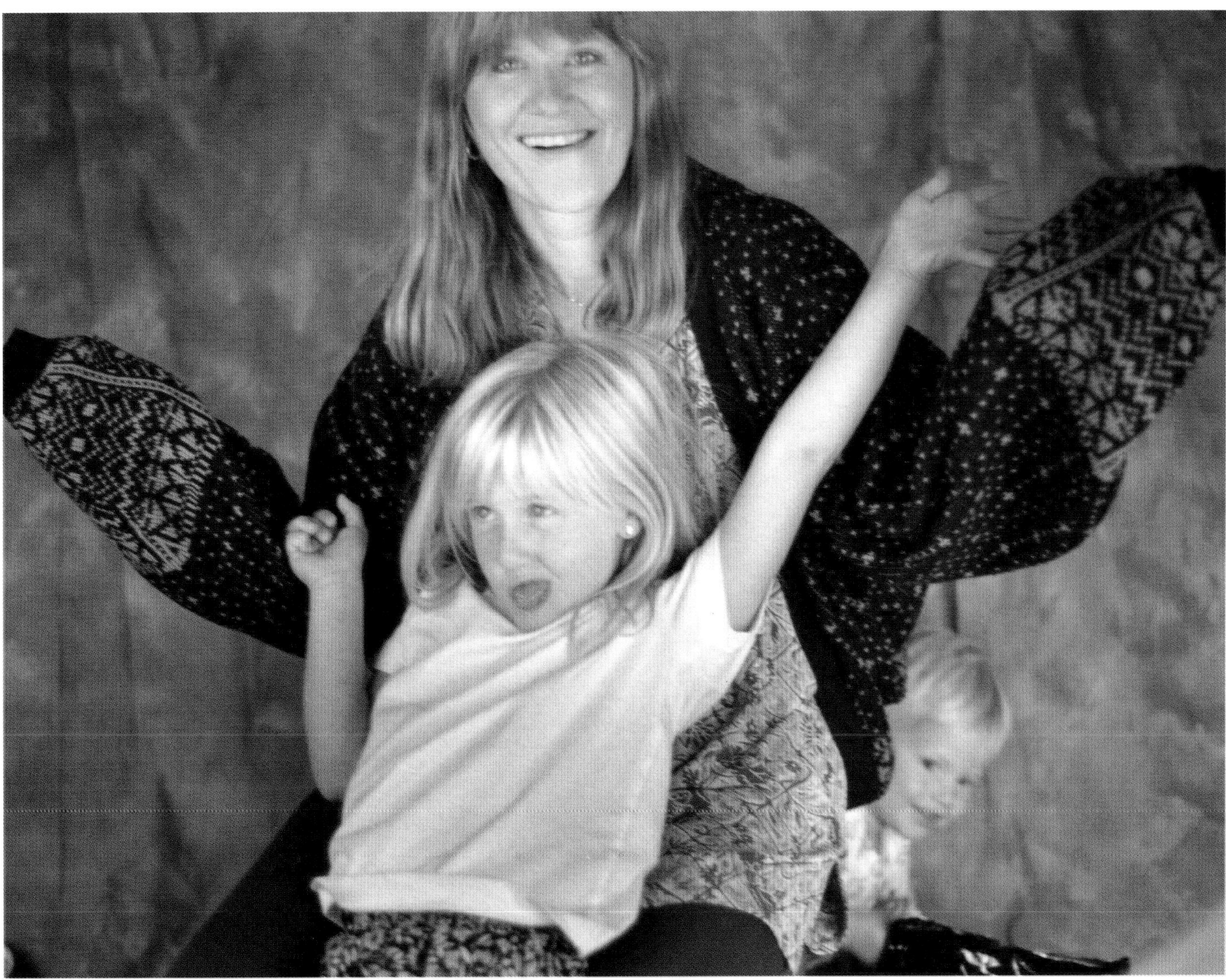

Judith Ivey with Maggie and Tom

There is something so intimate about doing a family portrait. People become so simple, so vulnerable, so honest when they are with a child or children they love, whether the photo is loving, humorous, or downright silly. The child becomes the focal point of the shoot and the resulting photos always show that most intimate emotion. Pure love. It is a thrill for me each time a person is willing not only to let me in but to permit me to record that love. The gift that the family members share with one another becomes a gift they share with me. How can this not become addictive?

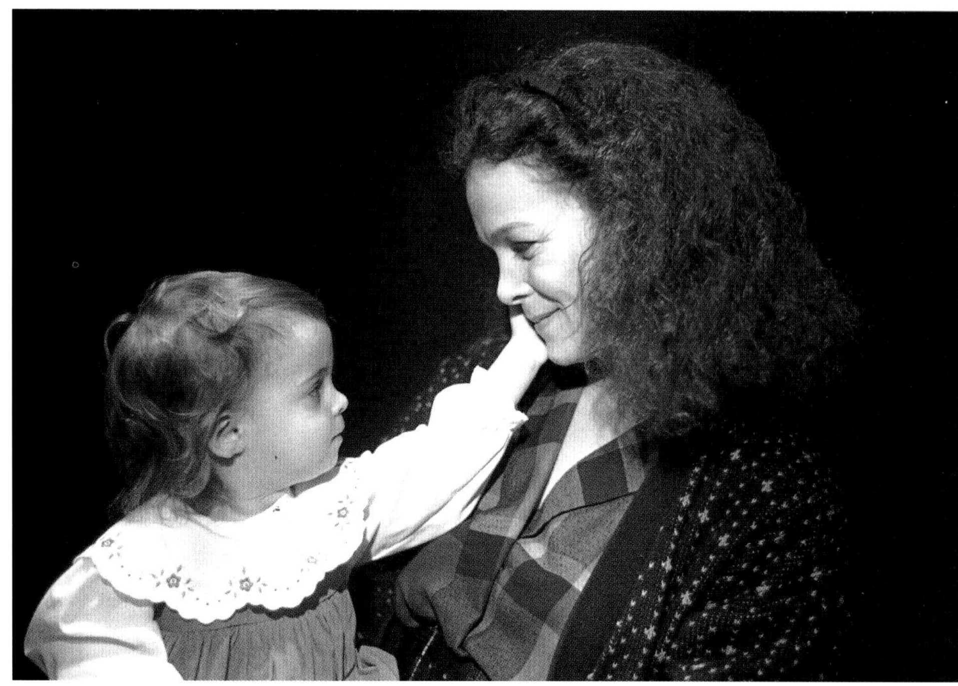

Clockwise from top:

Stephanie Dunnam with Elena

Siân Phillips with Kate O'Toole

Jo Sullivan Loesser with Emily Loesser

Russ and Jackie Cusick with Joan

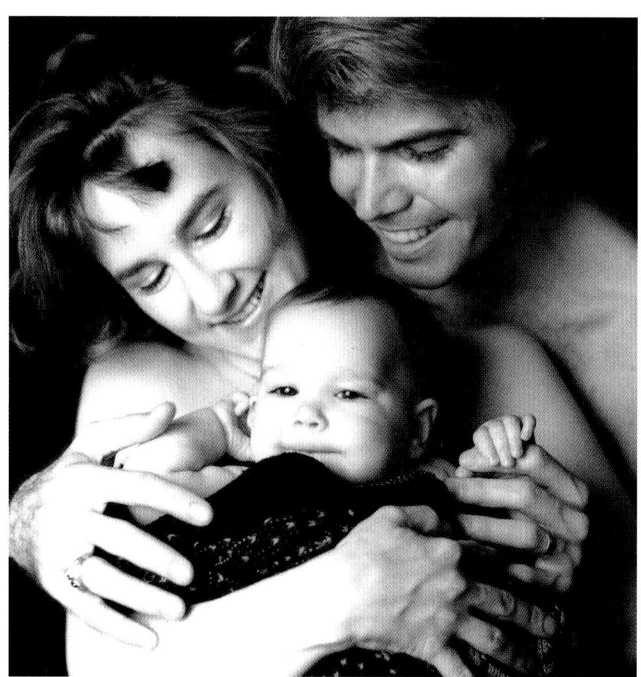

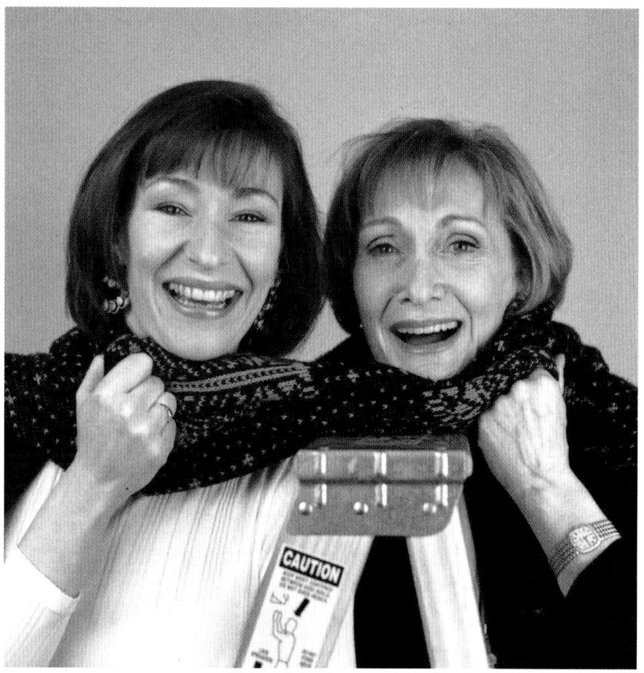

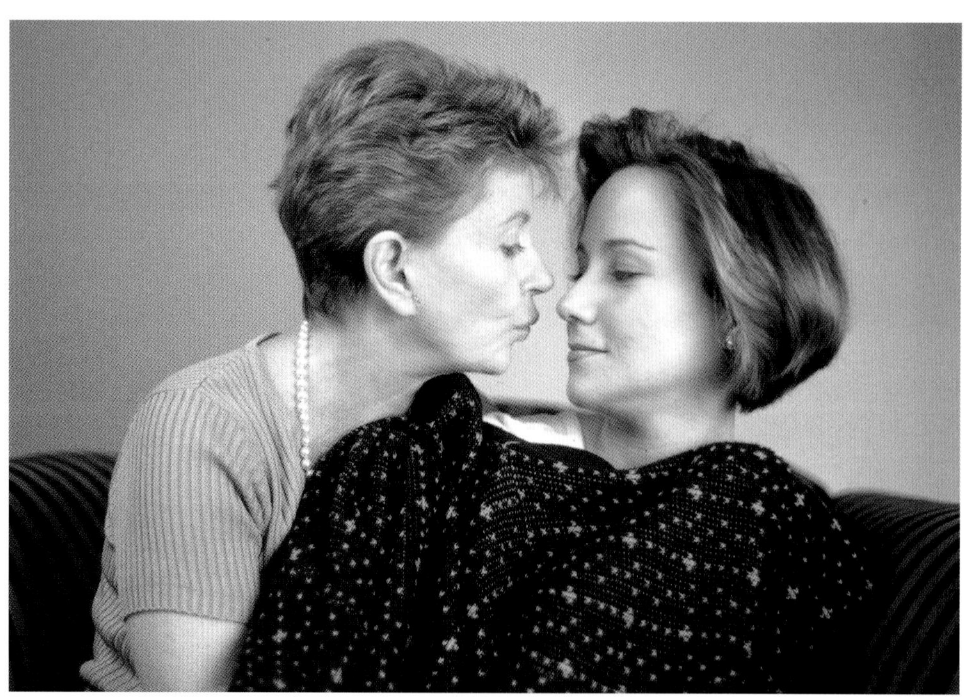

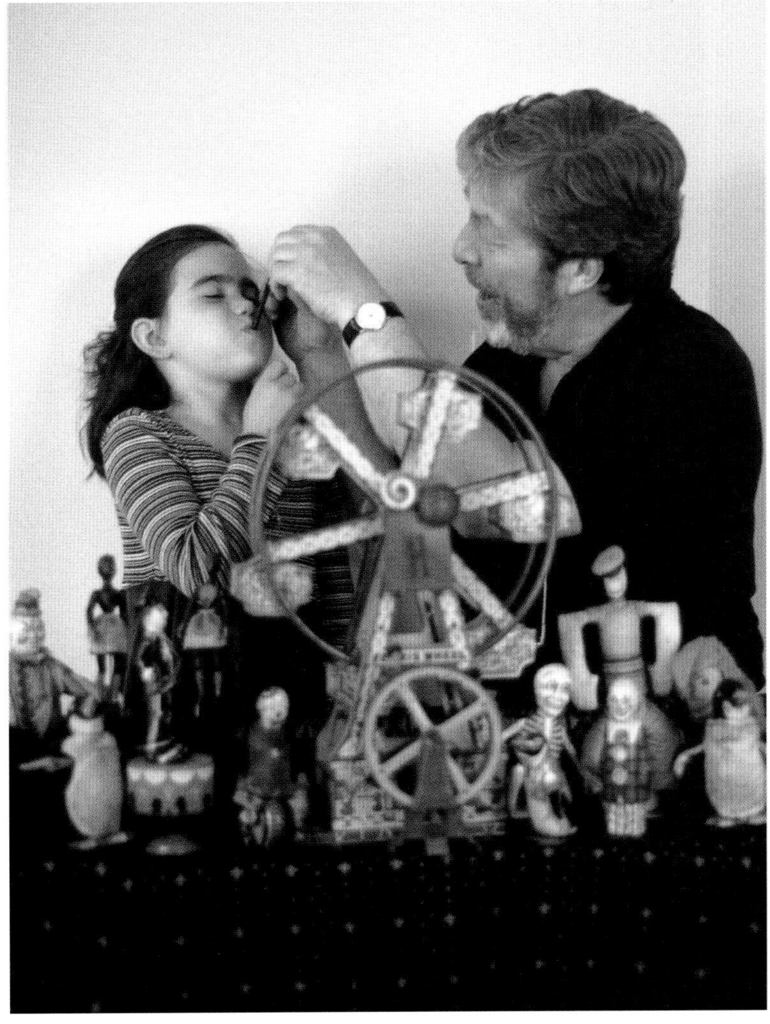

Tony Walton with granddaughter Georgie

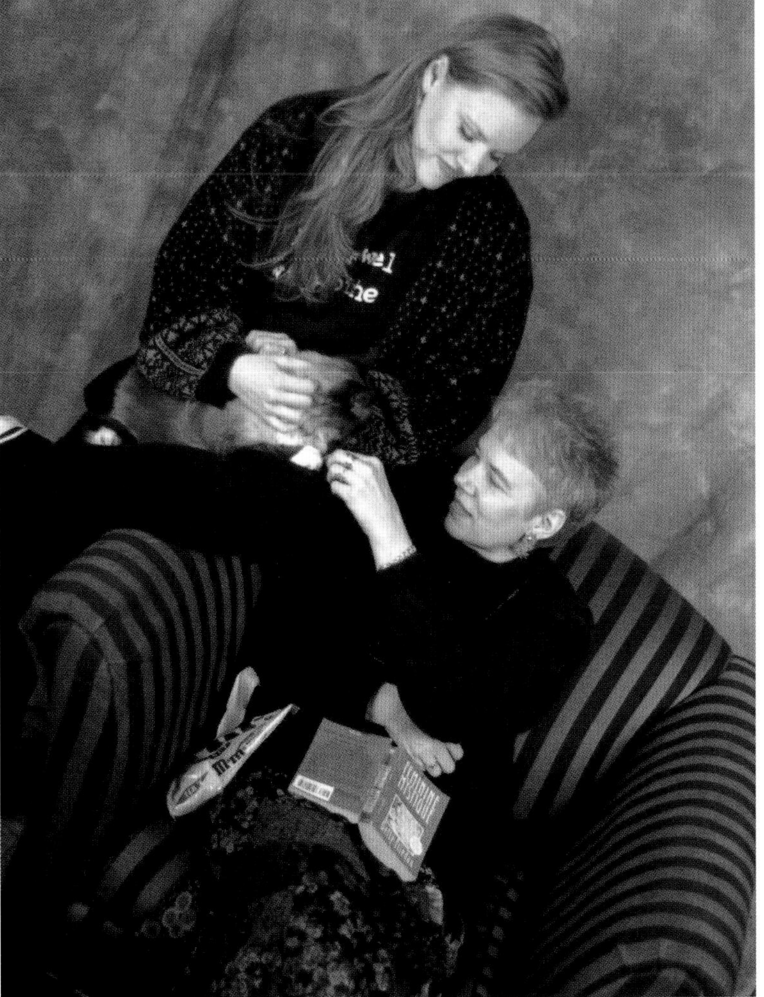

Emily Skinner with all her favorites: a good book, yummy treats, her mom, and her cat

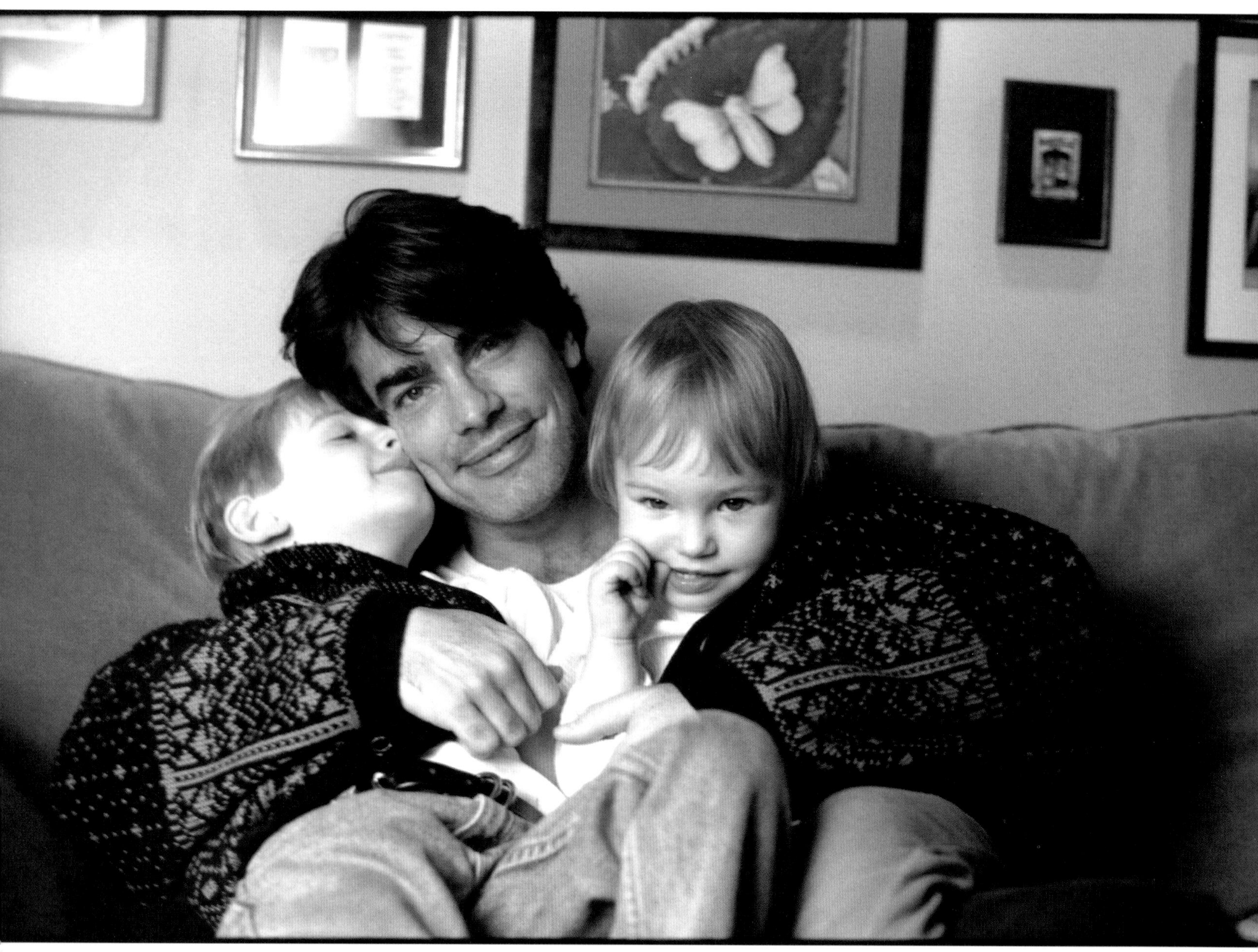

Peter Gallagher with Kathryn and Jamey

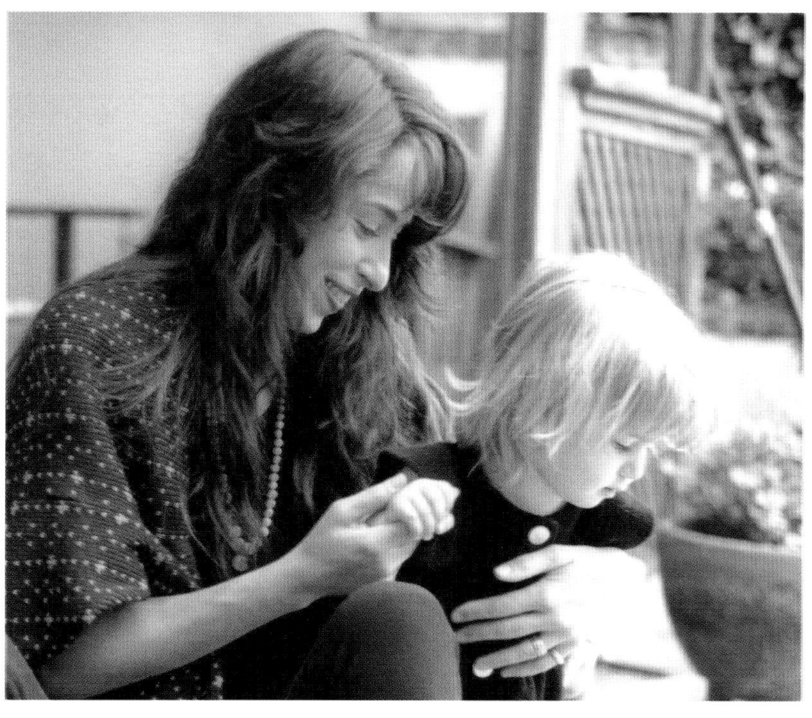

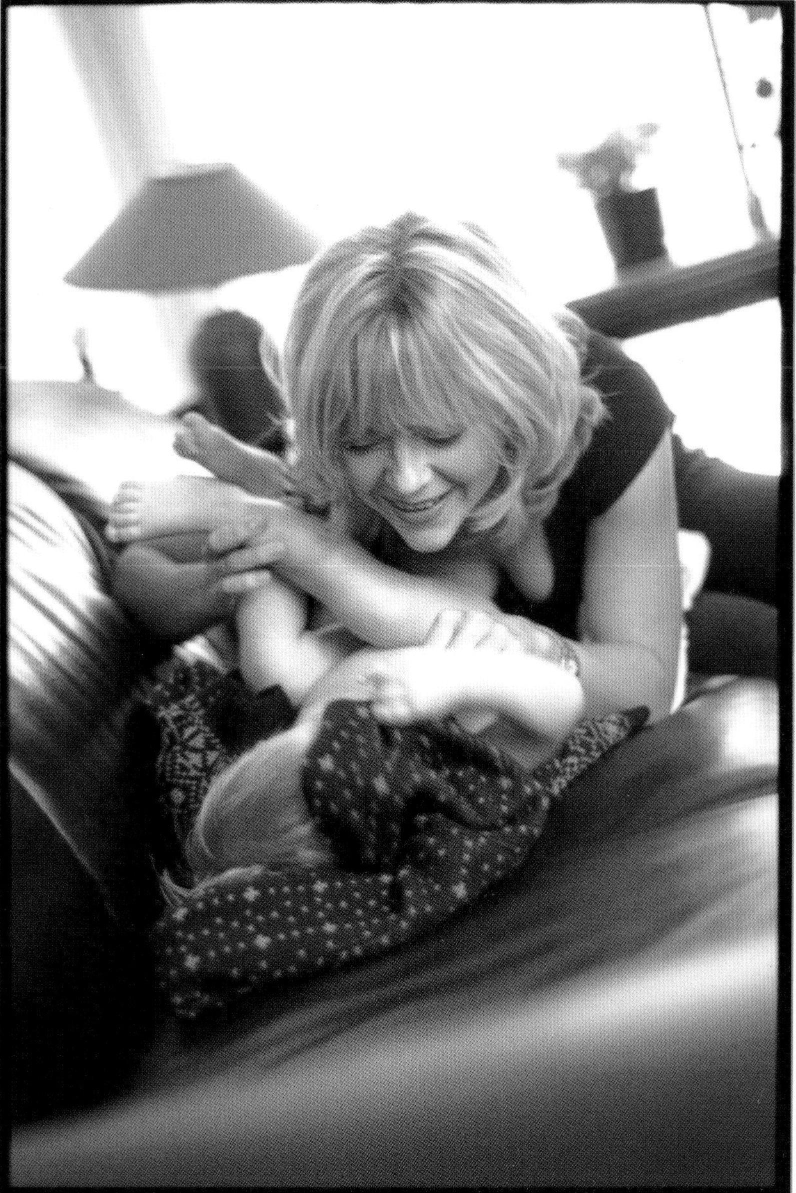

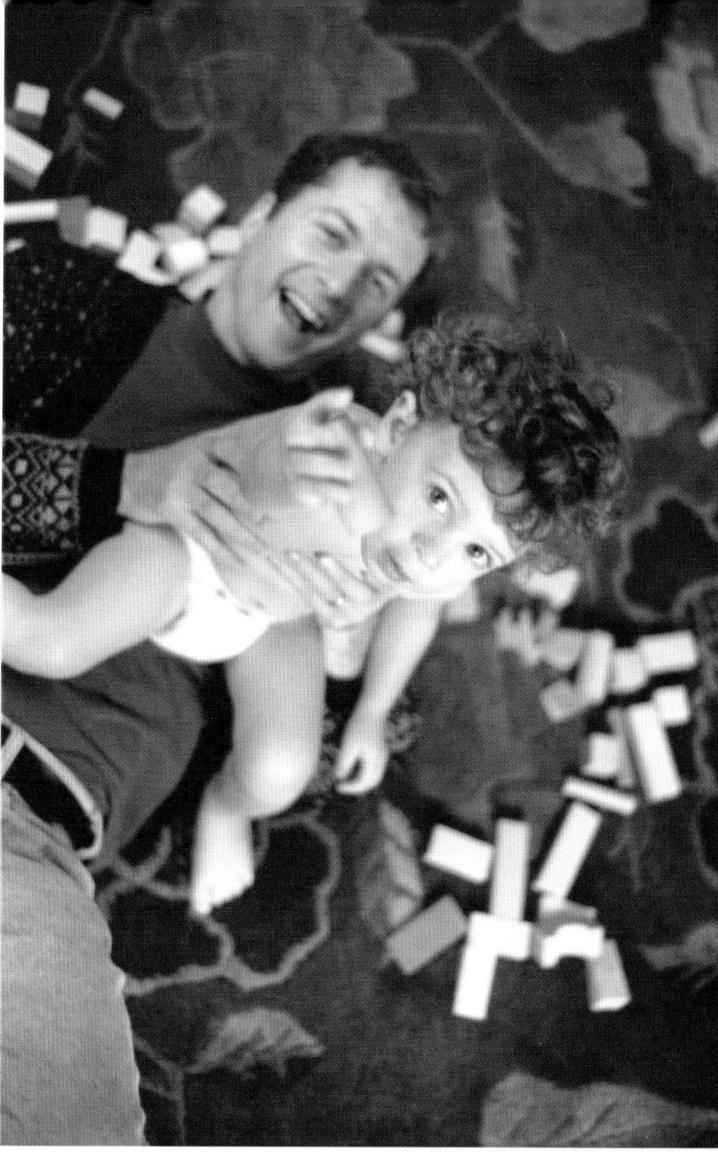

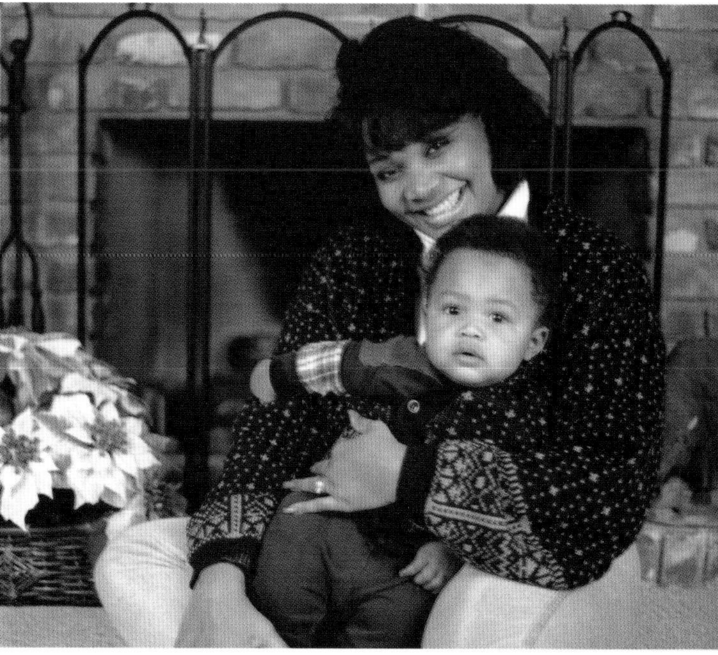

From left to right:
Maggie Wheeler with Juno
Daniel Jenkins with Jack
Jill Whelan with Harrison
Arnetia Walker with Trevor

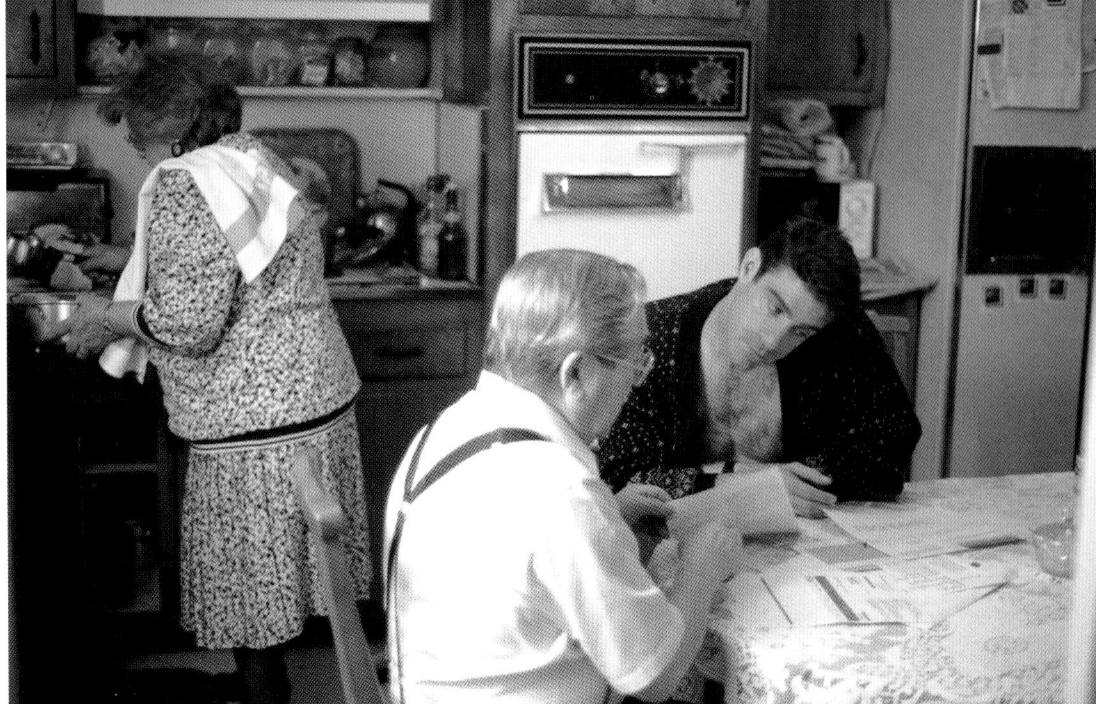

Lou Liberatore
with Mom and Dad

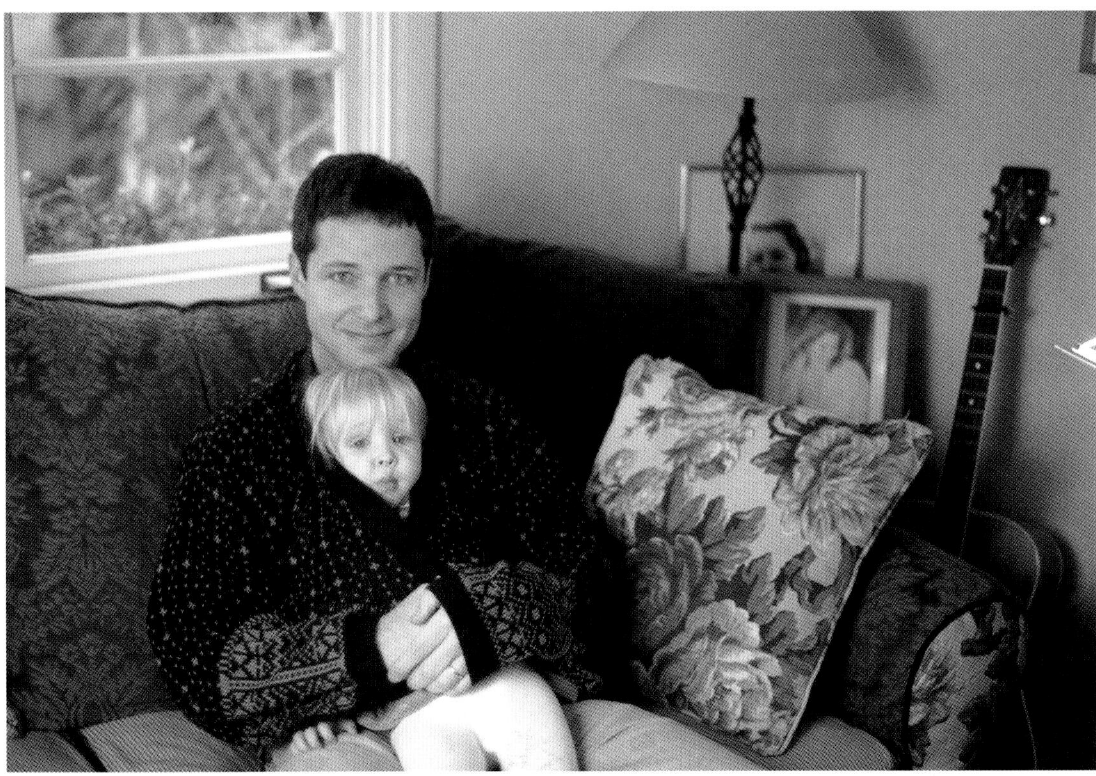

George Newbern
with Emma

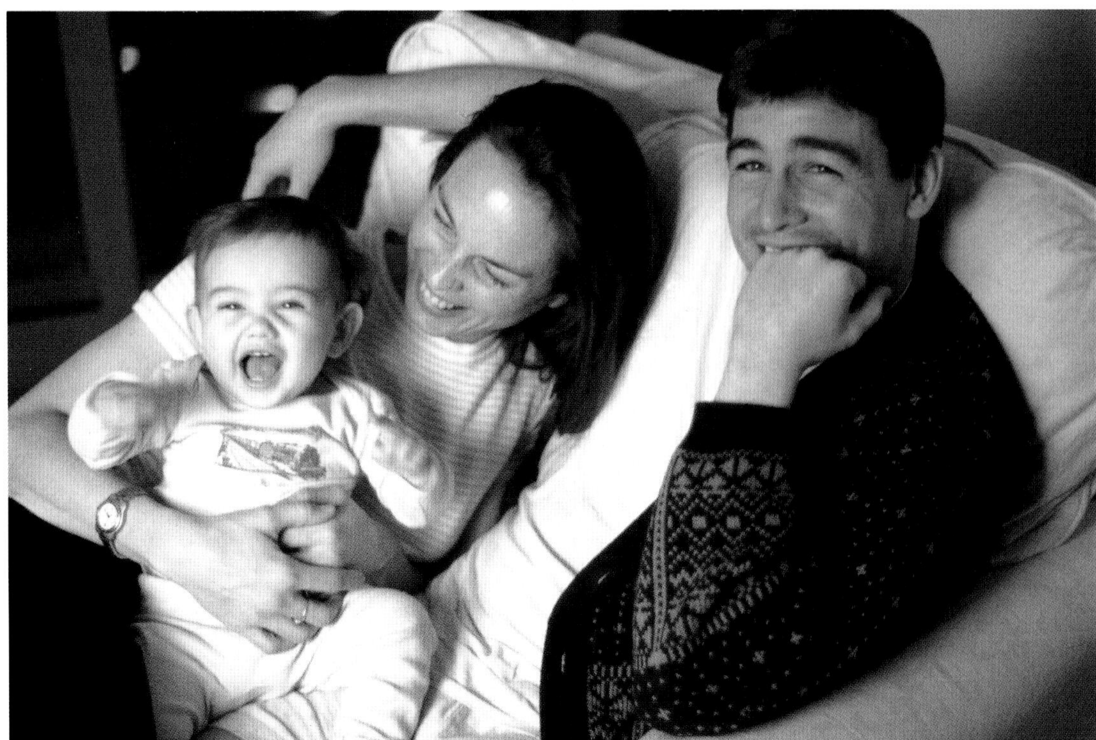

Kyle and
Kathryn Chandler
with Sidney

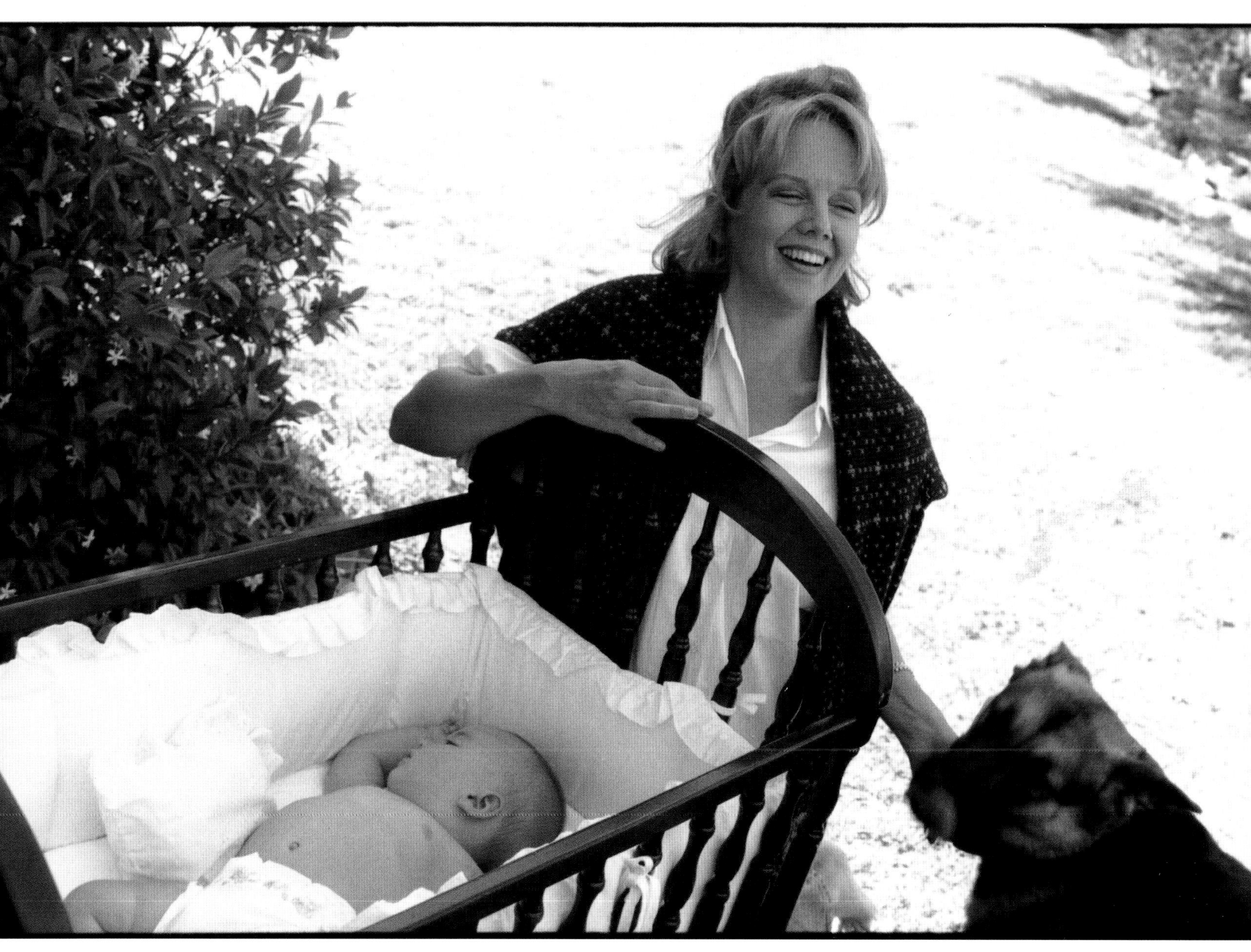

Linda Purl with Lucien (in the crib) and Cass (woof)

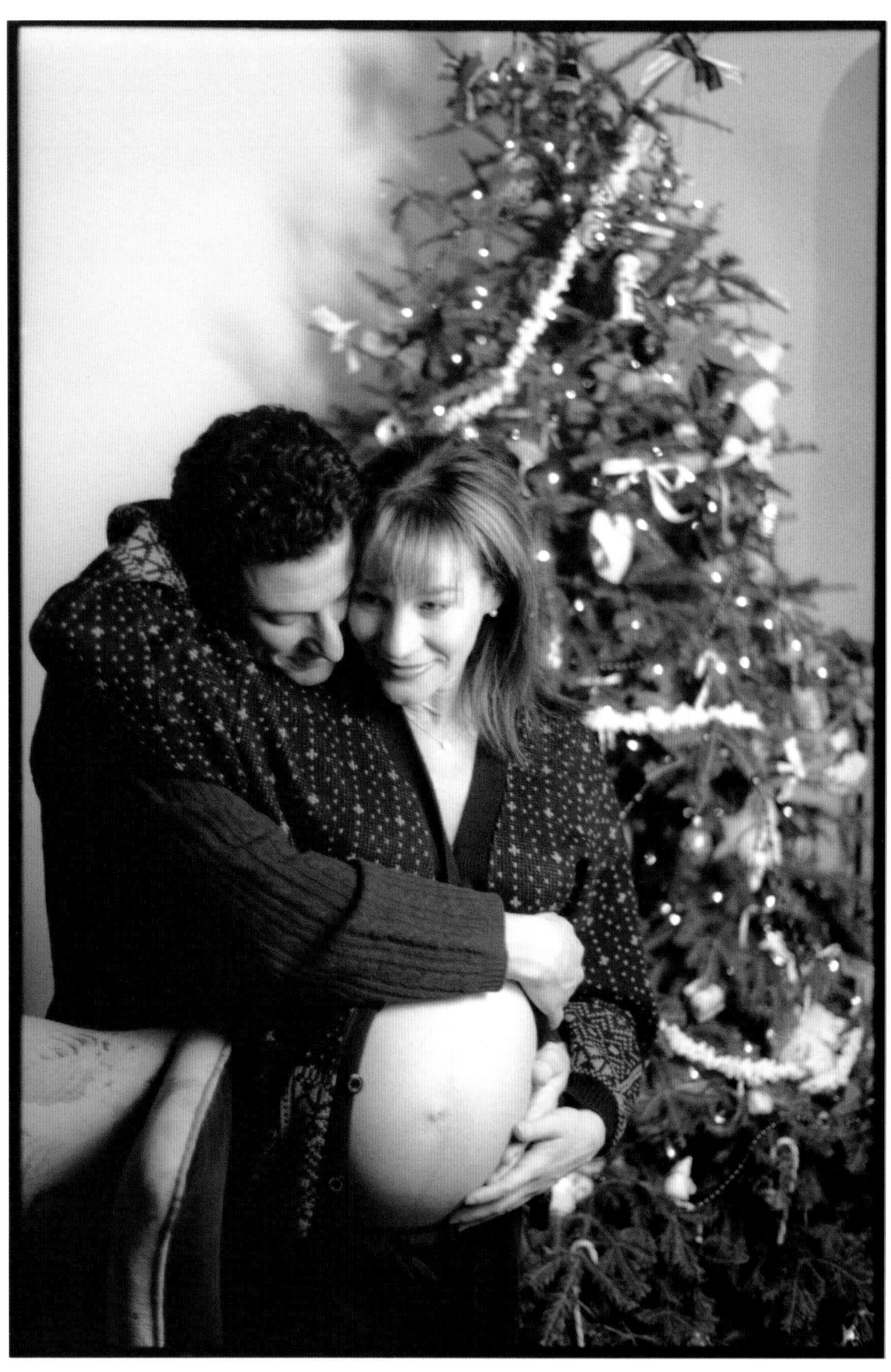

John Pizzarelli and wife, Jessica Molaskey

THE SWEATER GETS PETTED — *in which the sweater goes to the dogs*

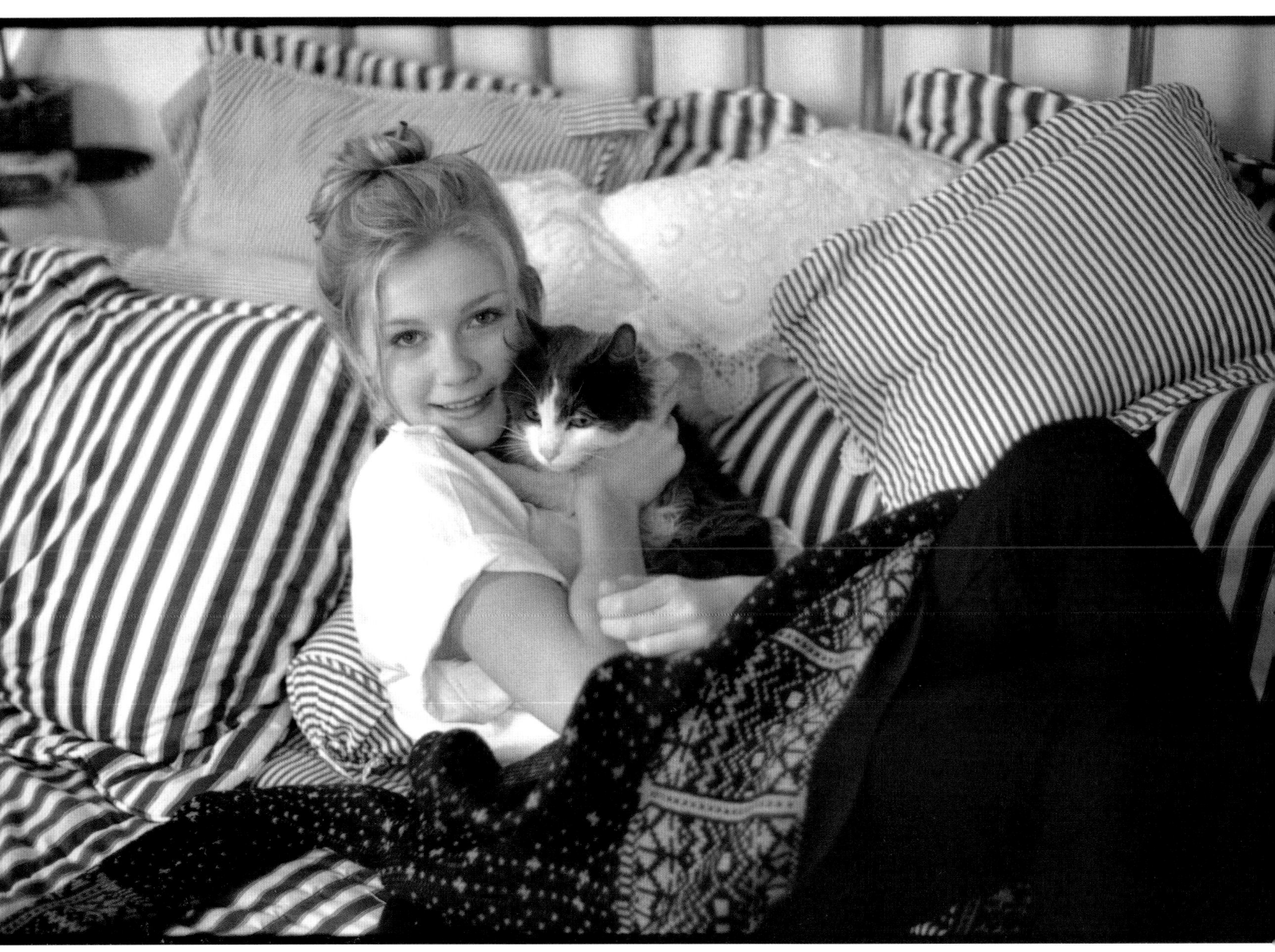

Kirsten Dunst

She's done a lot of work. She's played a variety of roles. Nevertheless, my frame of reference for Kirsten Dunst was a famous blood drinker named Claudia.

How long was I to hang on to that image once she began to search the garden for her cat, calling, "Here, baby!! Come on, sweetie! Heeeeere, baaaaaaabeeeeeeee!"

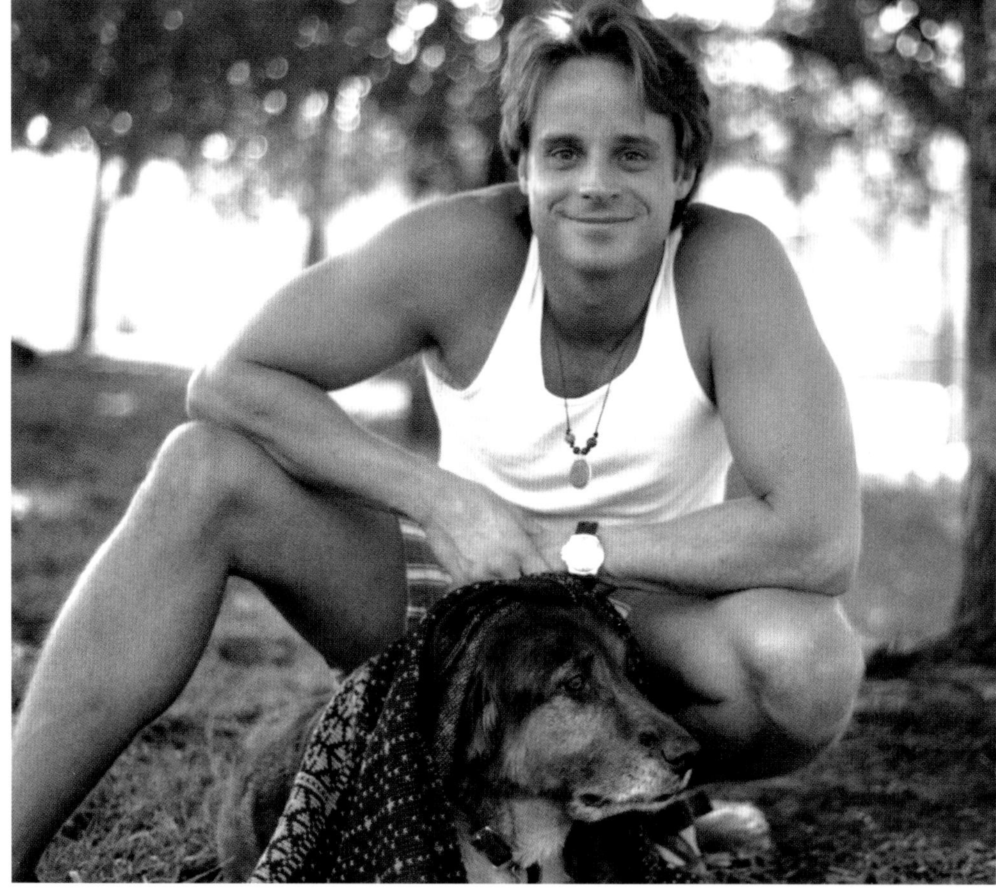

Clockwise from top:
Mitchell Anderson with Caliban
Lauren Lane with Atticus
Aaron Jackson with Coco
Merle Louise with Snakey

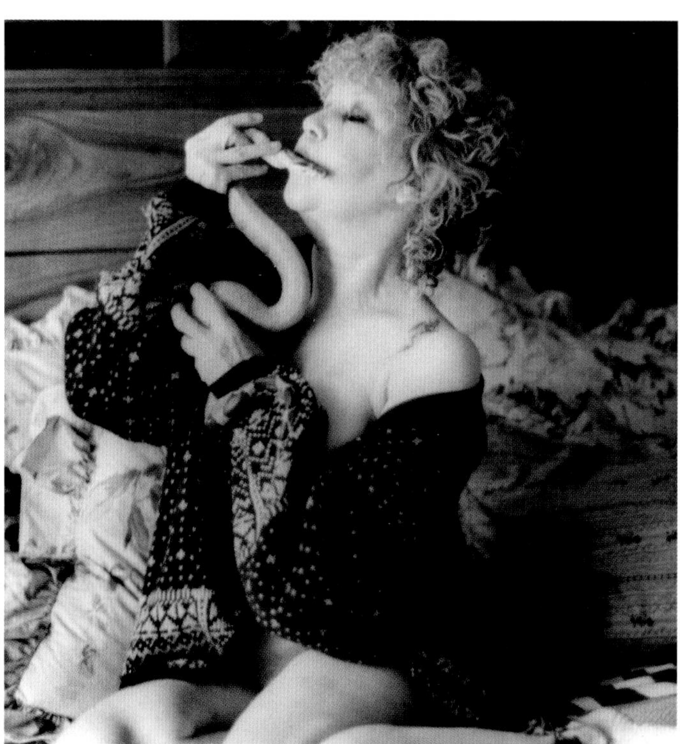

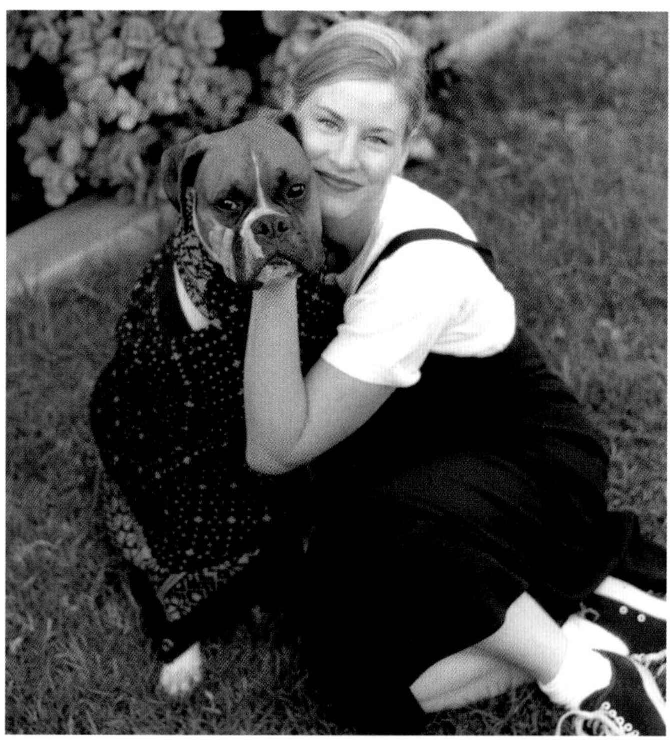

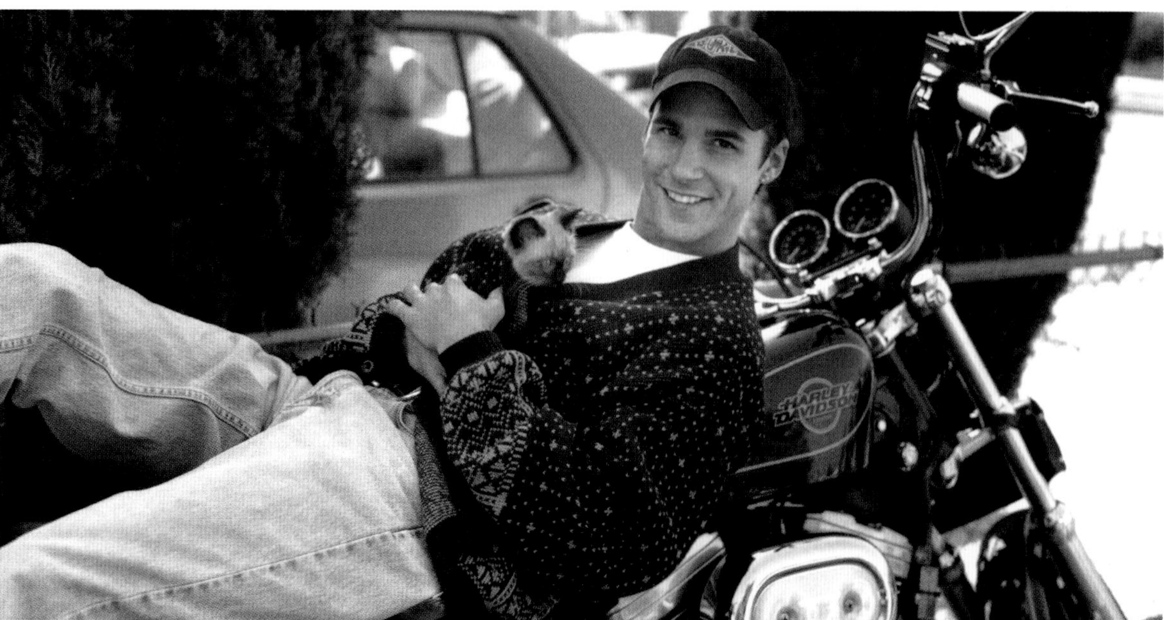

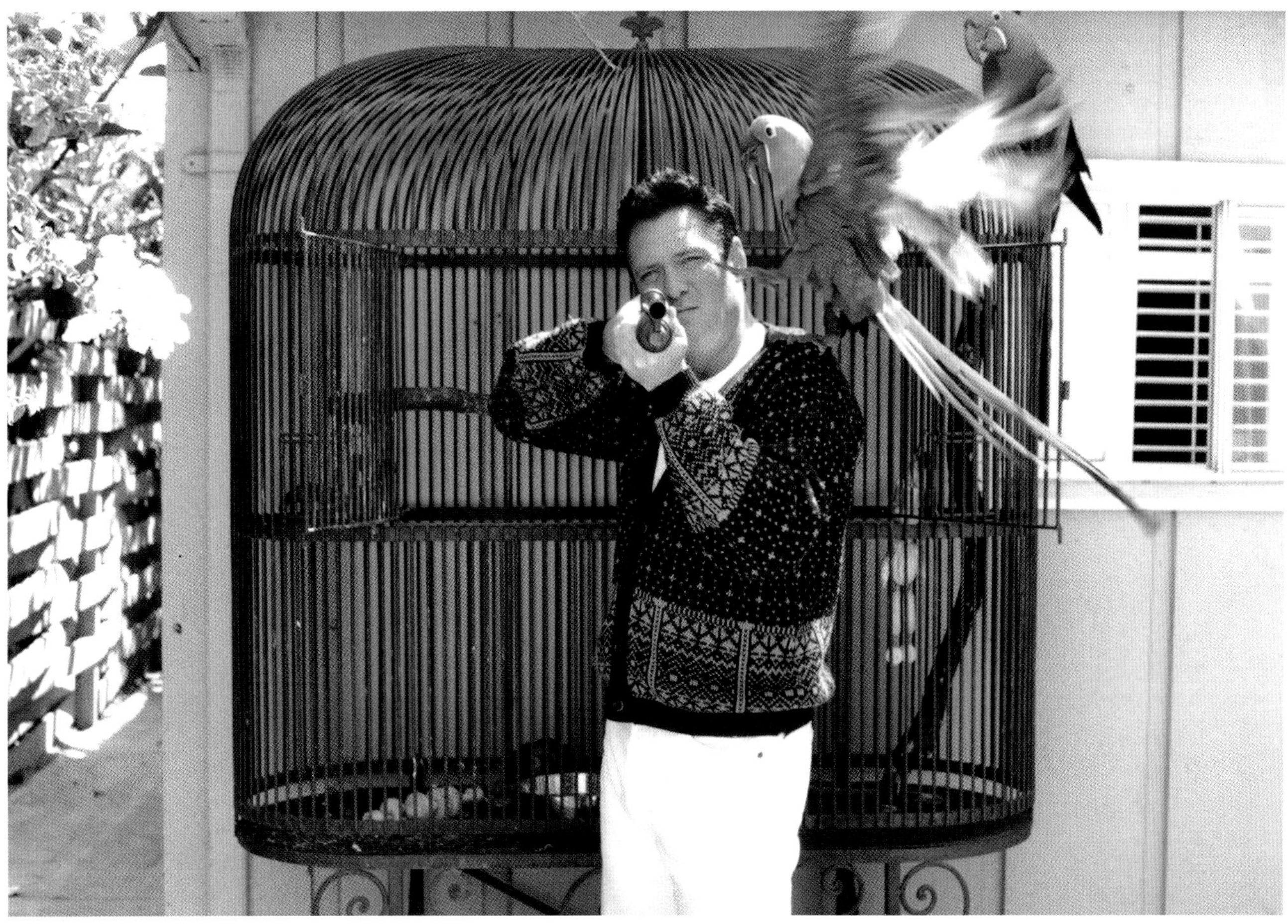

Michael Madsen with Bonnie and Clyde

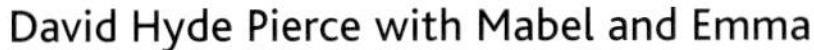

David Hyde Pierce with Mabel and Emma

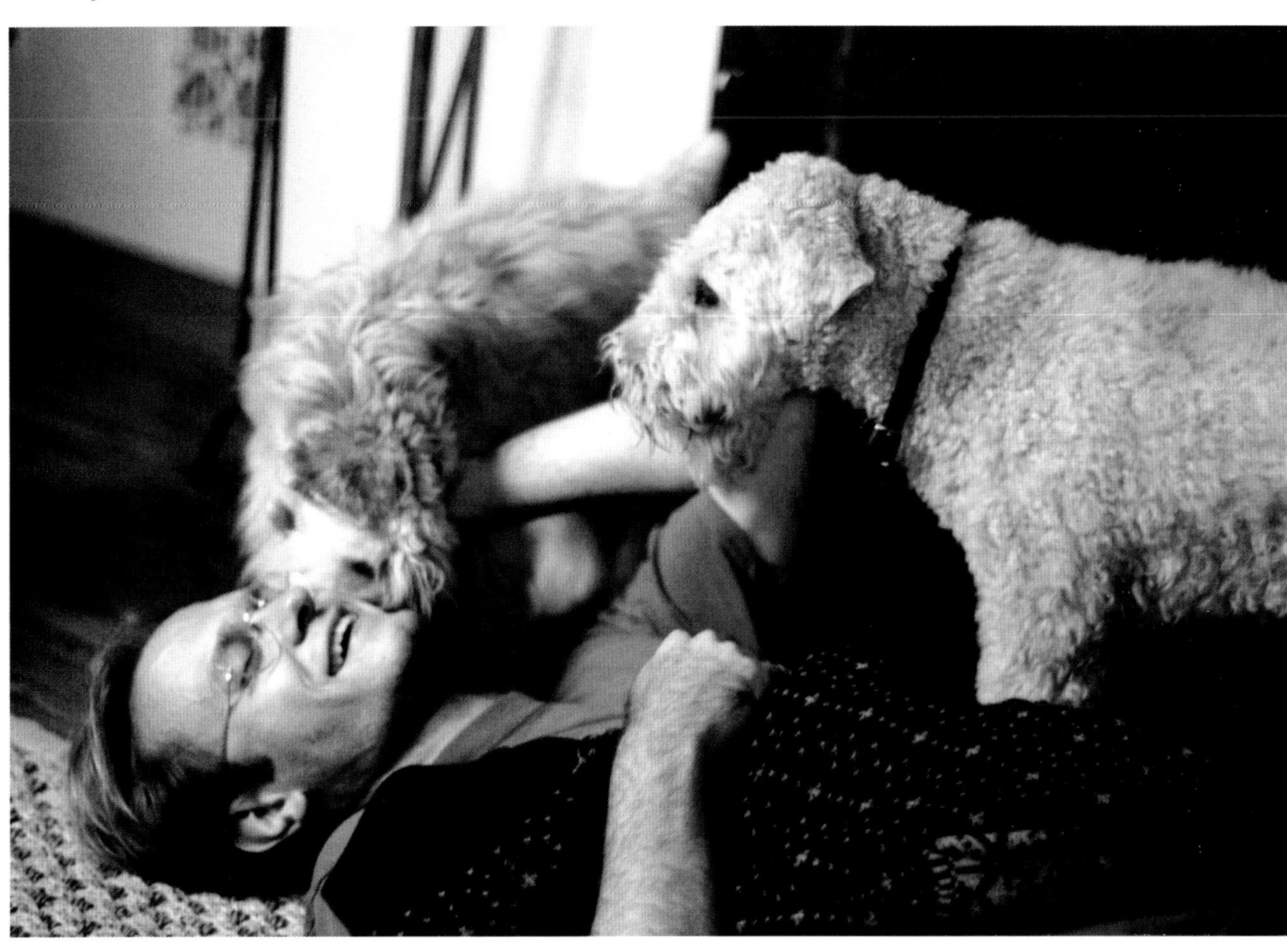

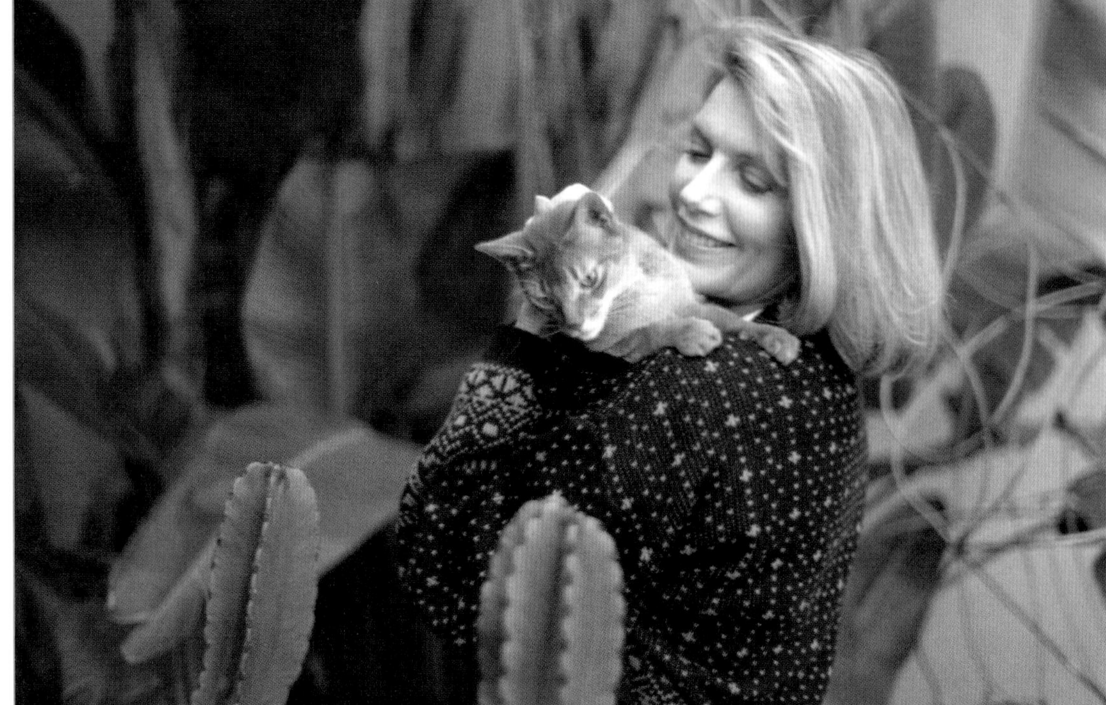

Susan Sullivan with Fred

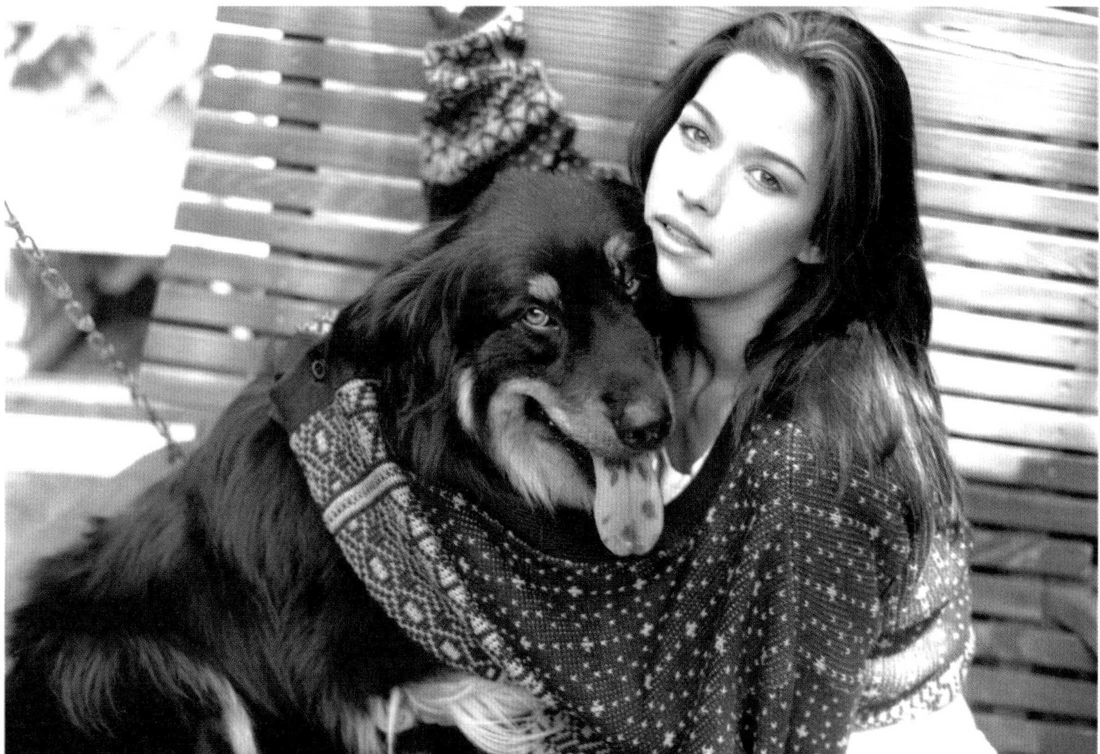

Brooke Langton with Riley

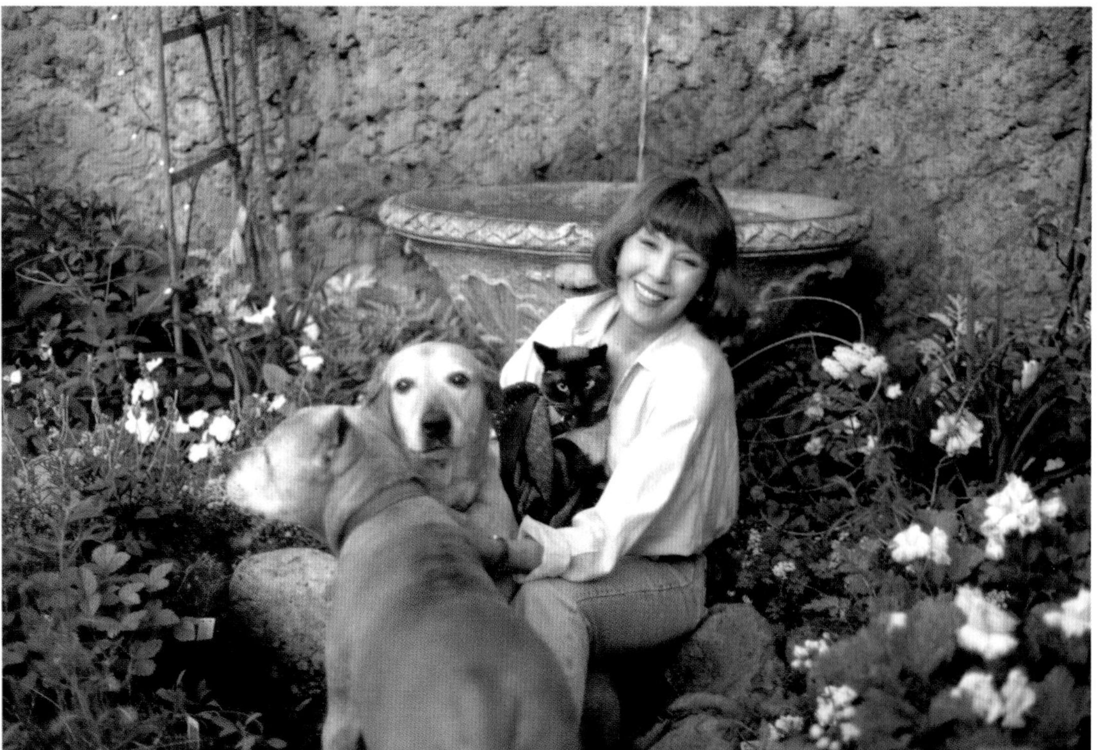

France Nuyen and menagerie

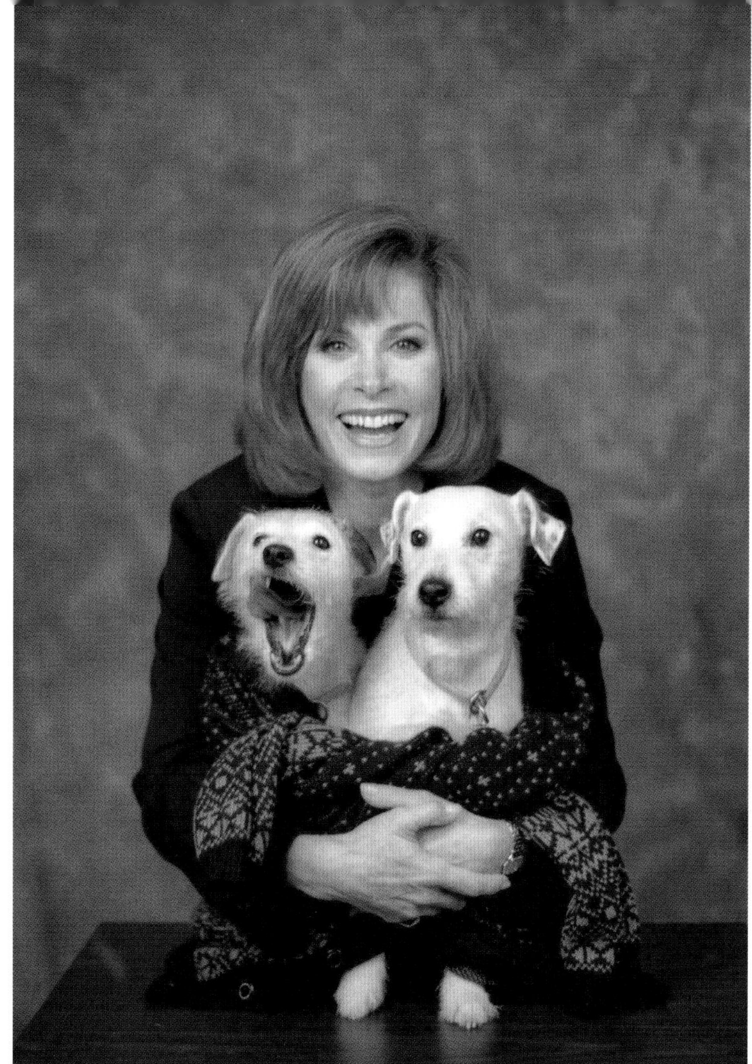

Stefanie Powers
with Jackie and Russell

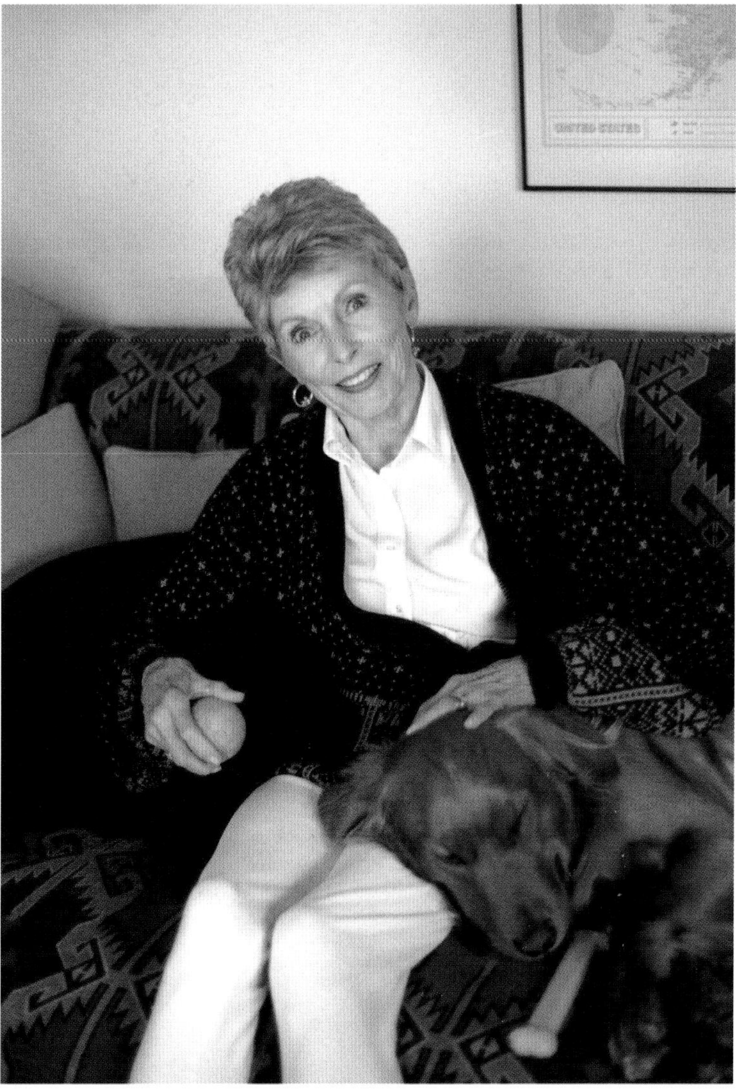

Janet Leigh
with Sara and Joe

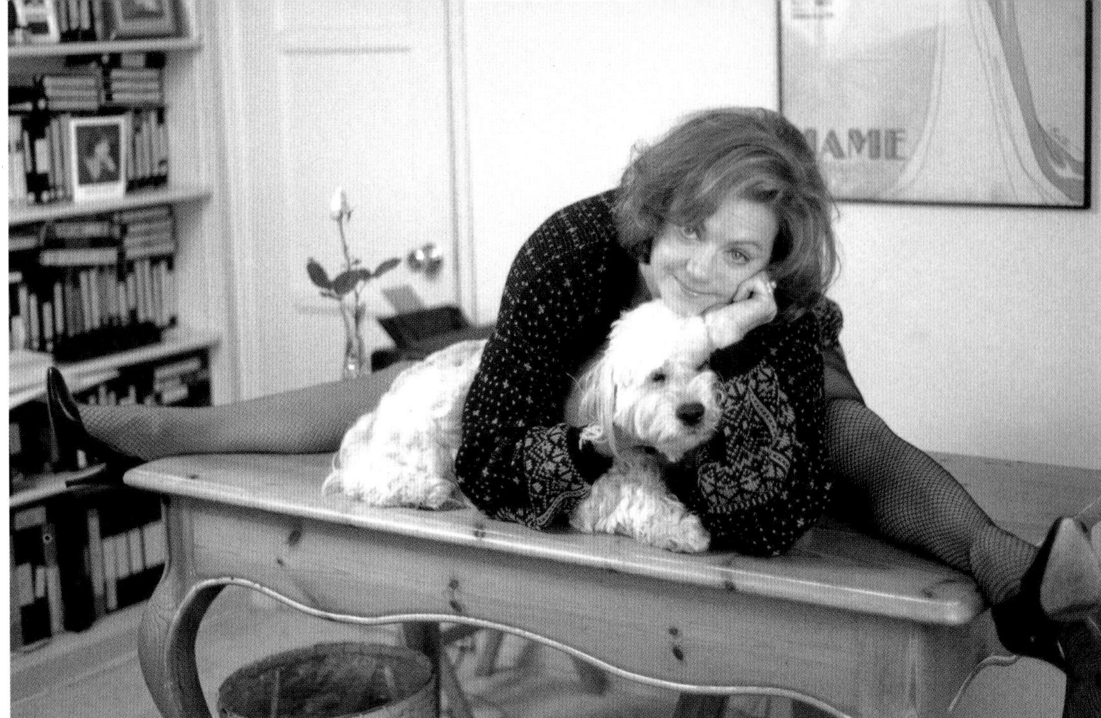

Janet Carroll
with Molly

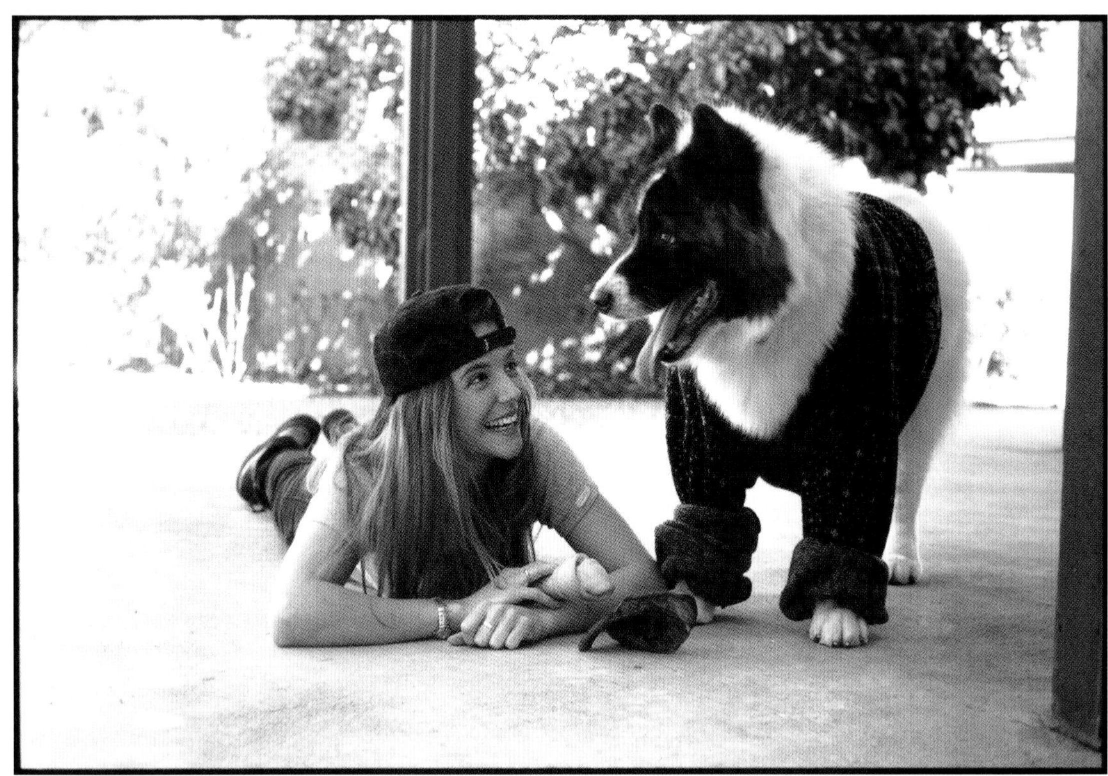

AJ Langer
with Bear

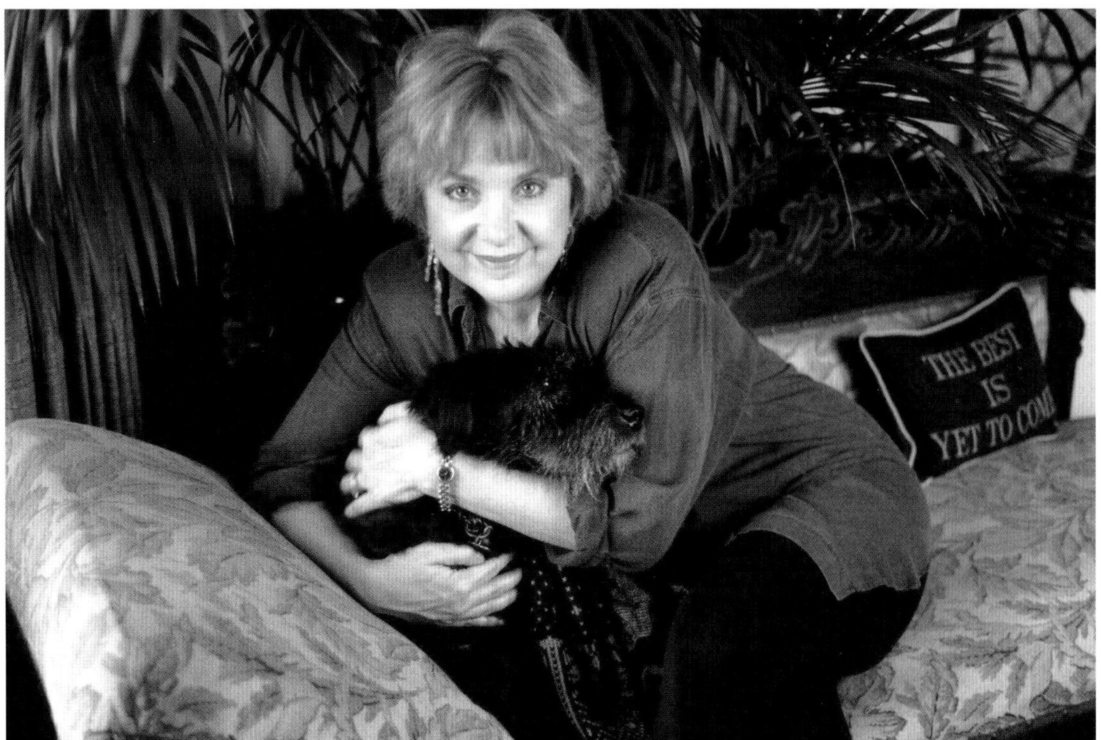

Lee Garlington
with Ida

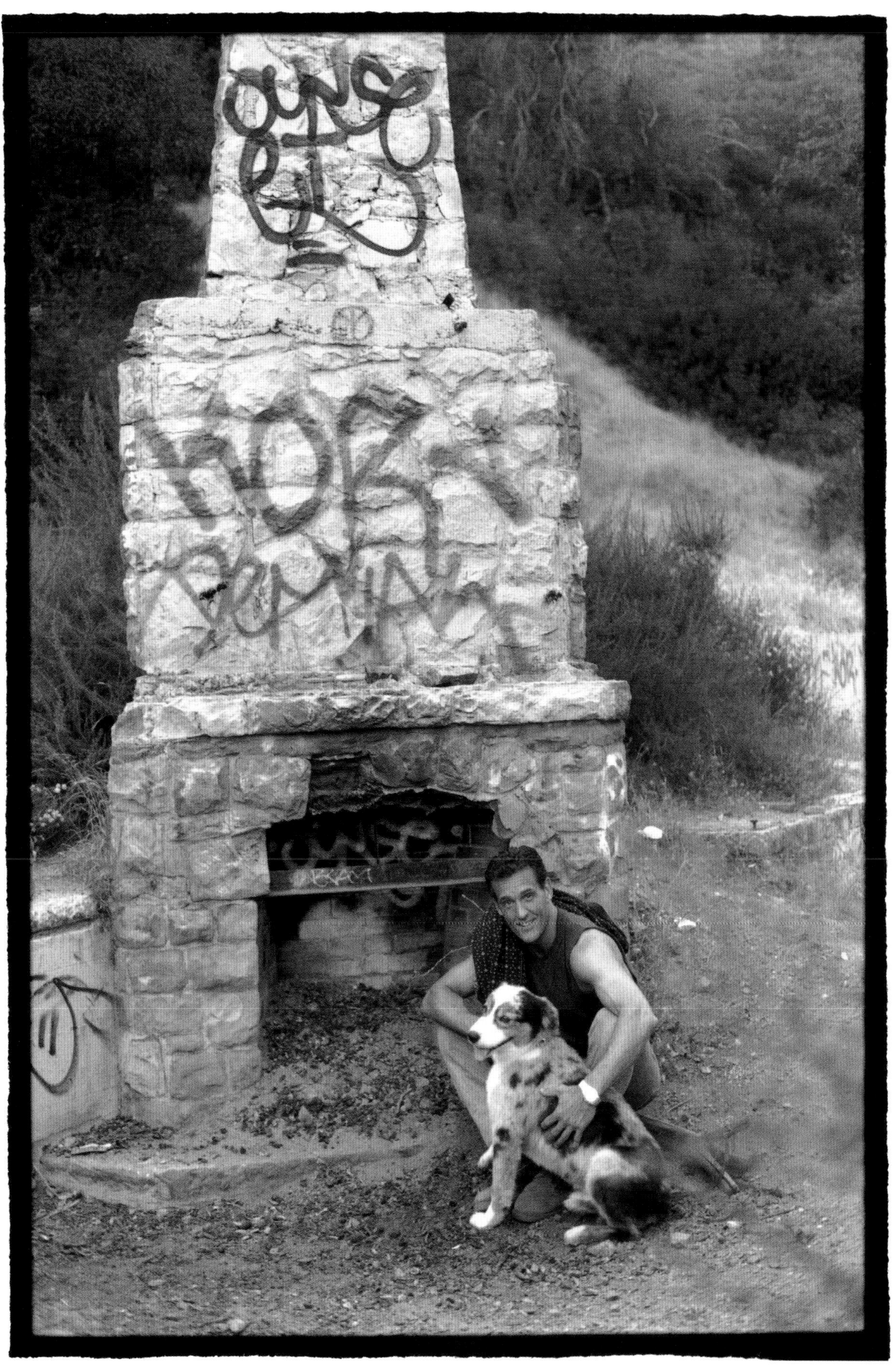

John Wesley Shipp with Mo

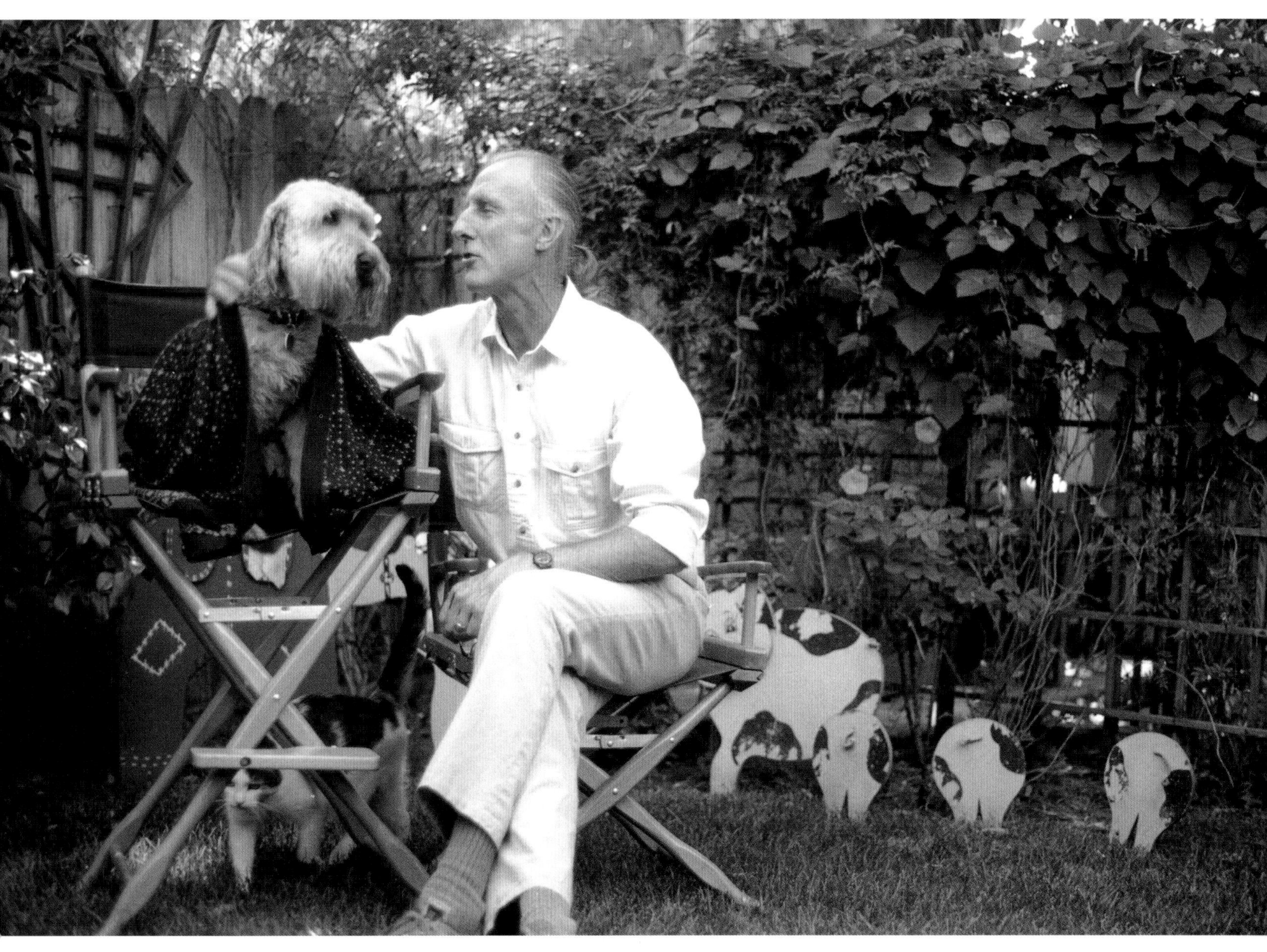

James Cromwell in his own backyard with Colin, Little John, and plywood pigs.

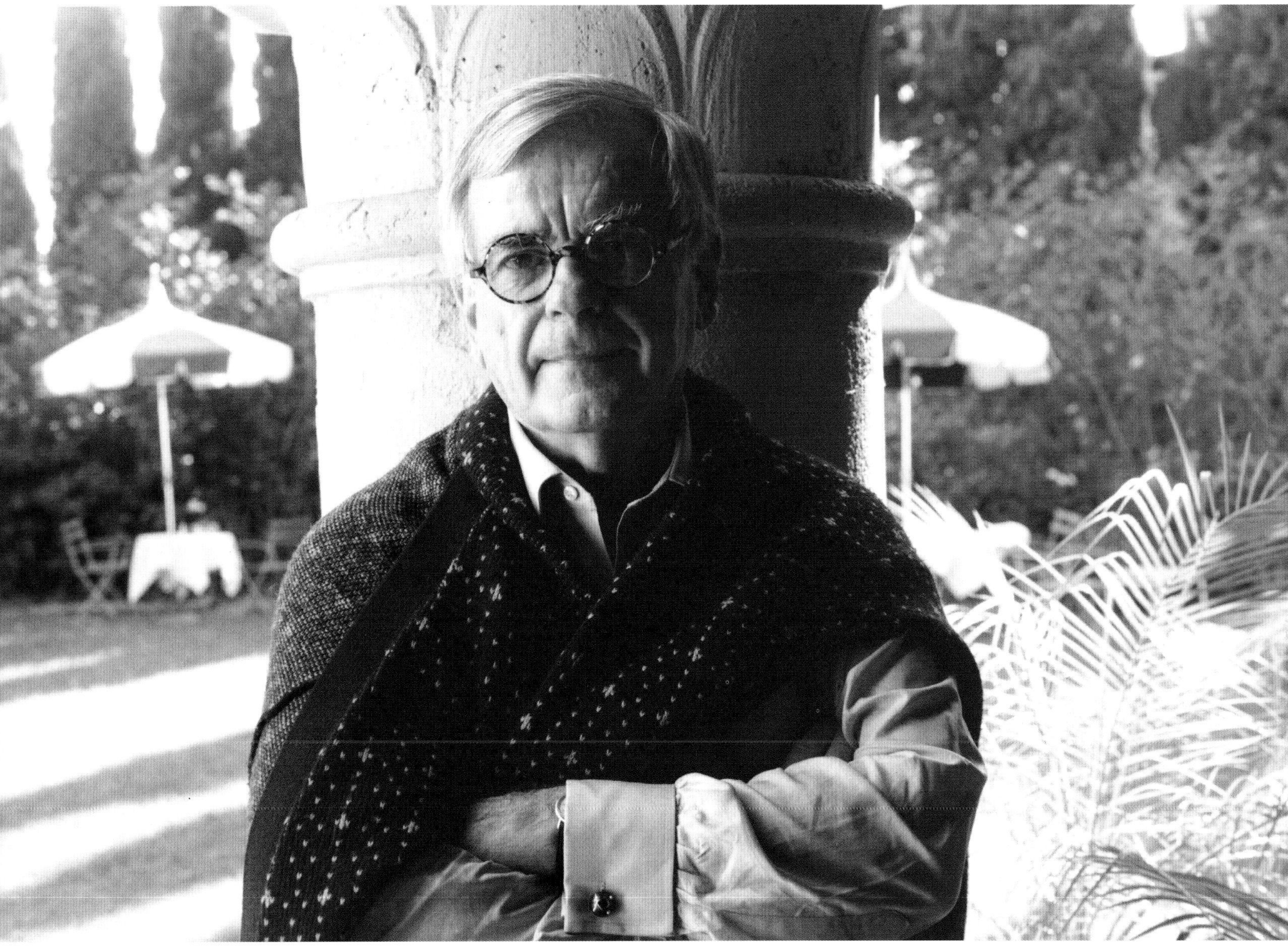

Dominick Dunne

We had to leave Dominick Dunne's room at the Château Marmont and go into the garden to do his picture, if only to escape from the continual ringing of the telephone. You see, at the time he was covering an internationally watched murder trial for an internationally read magazine and everyone was calling and calling. He was a good sport about the whole thing and chuckled when he suggested we flee the room for the safe haven downstairs. I didn't hear him the first time he said it, though; I was looking at a wall on which was taped *While You Were Out* messages from the people I read about in the press, notes for articles, thoughts on the trial.

History taped to the wall of the Château Marmont.

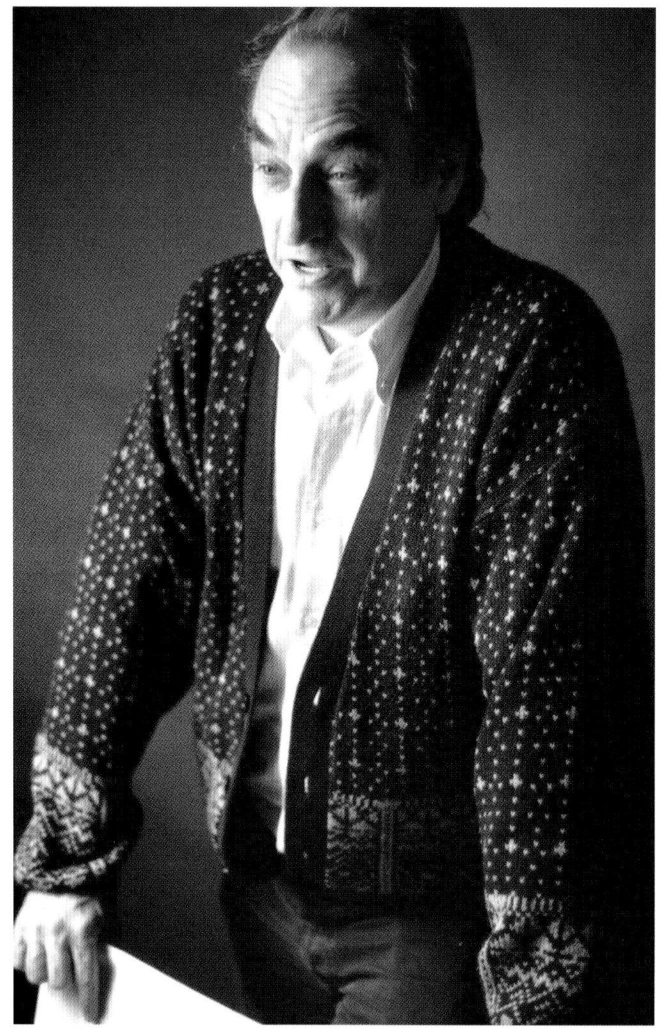

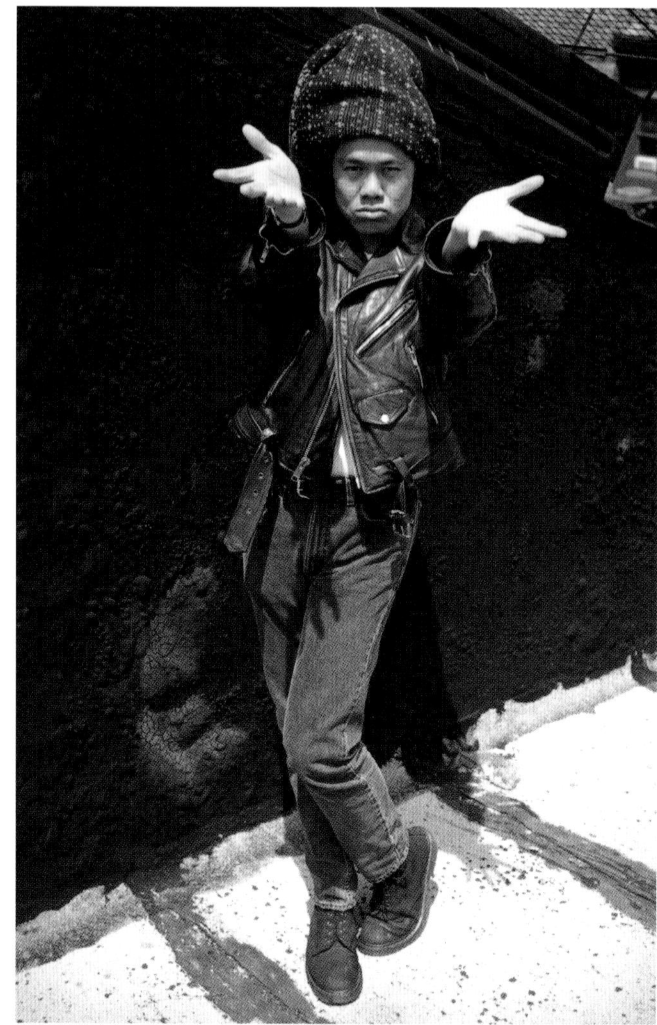

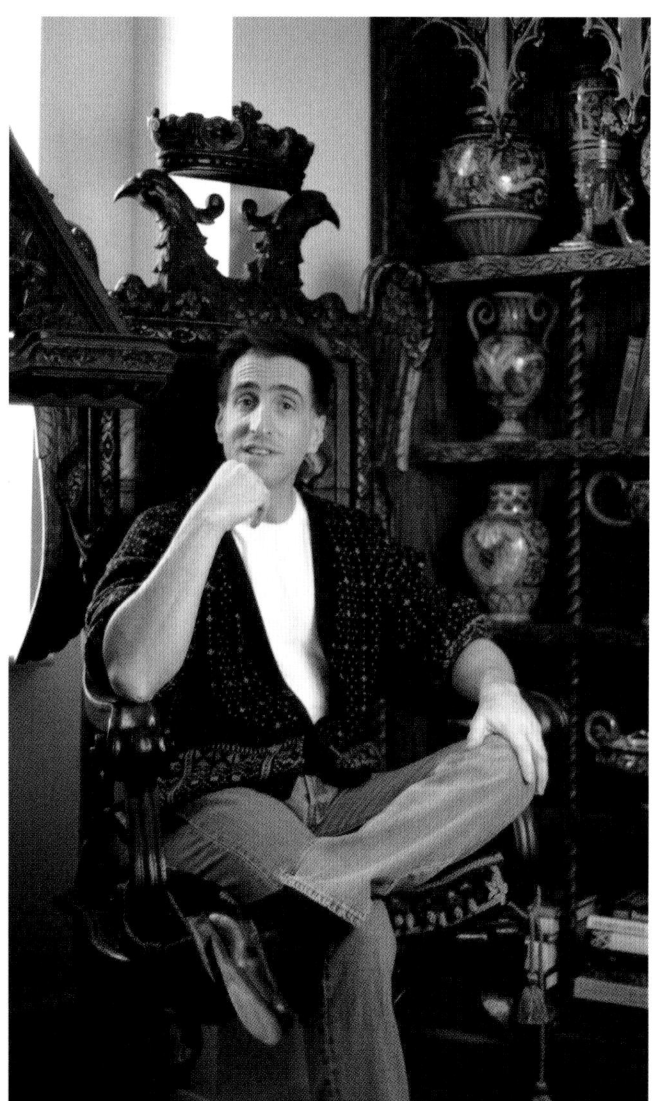

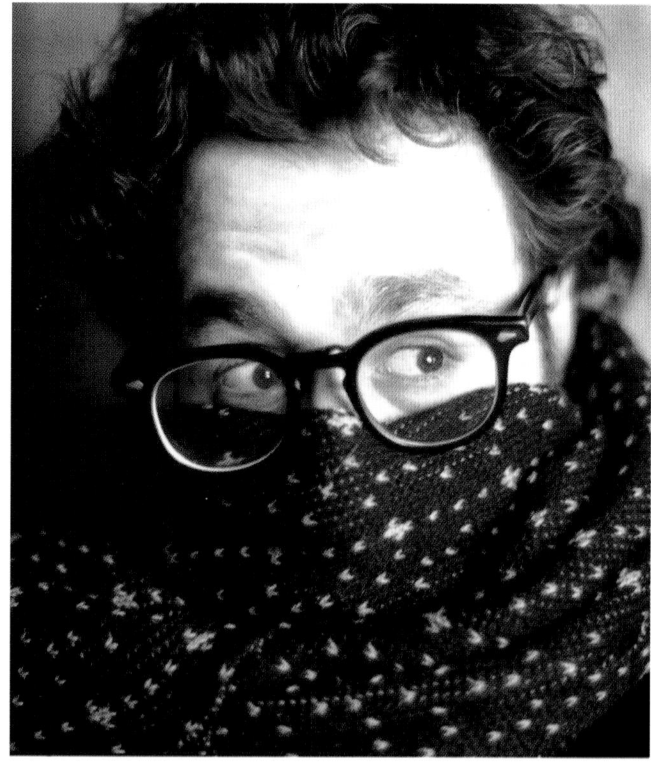

The Playwrights

Clockwise from top left:

Lanford Wilson

Chay Yew

Nicky Silver

Paul Rudnick

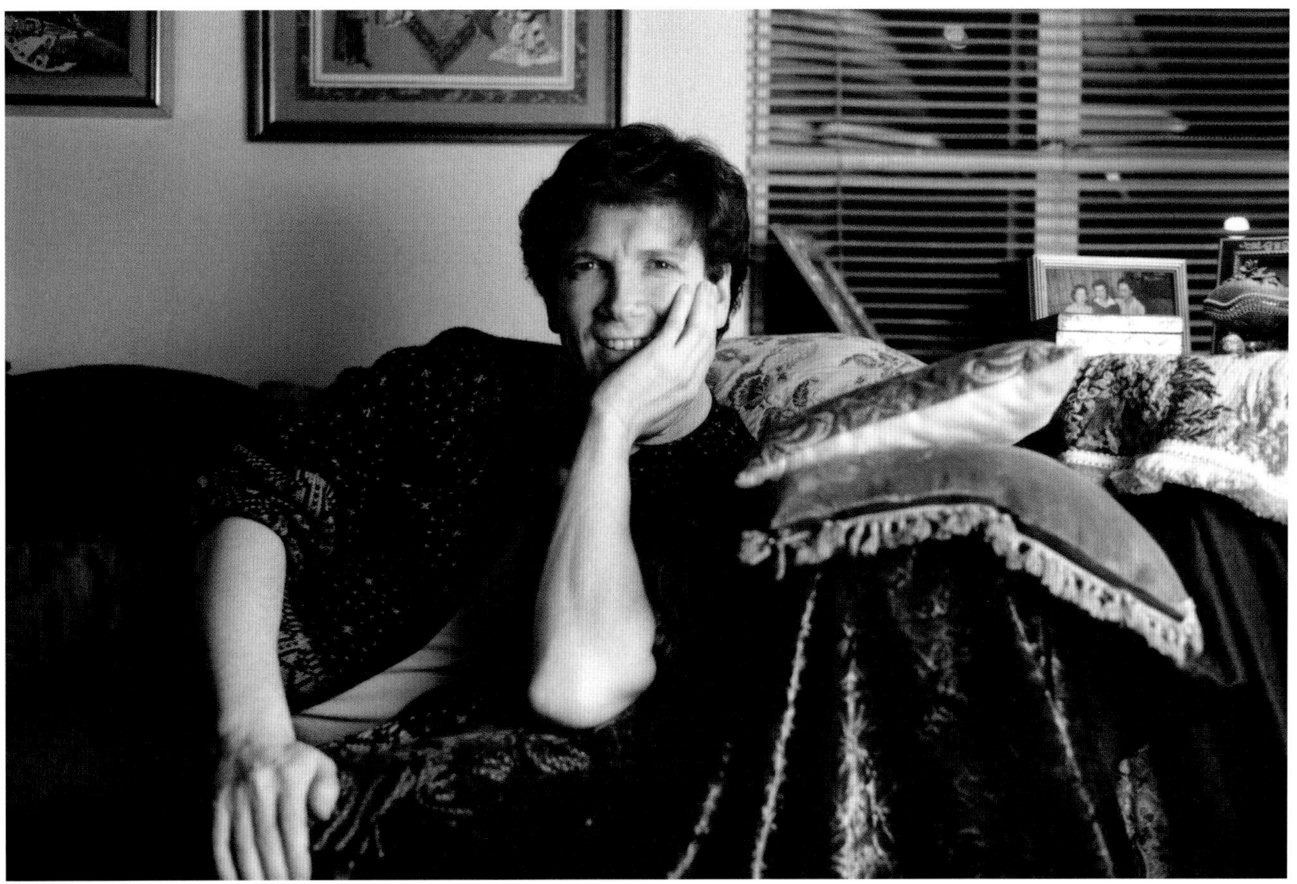

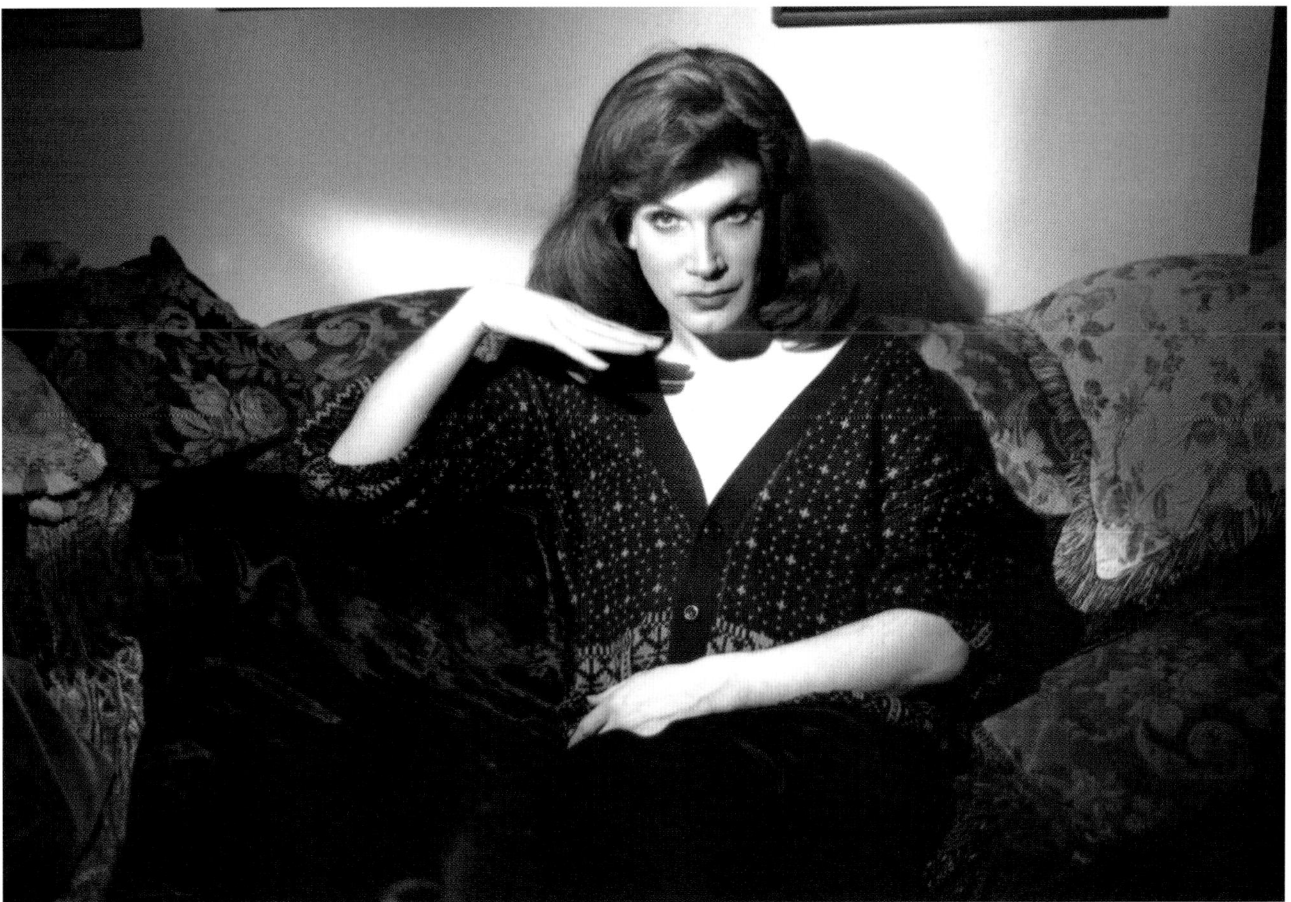

Two of the many faces of Charles Busch

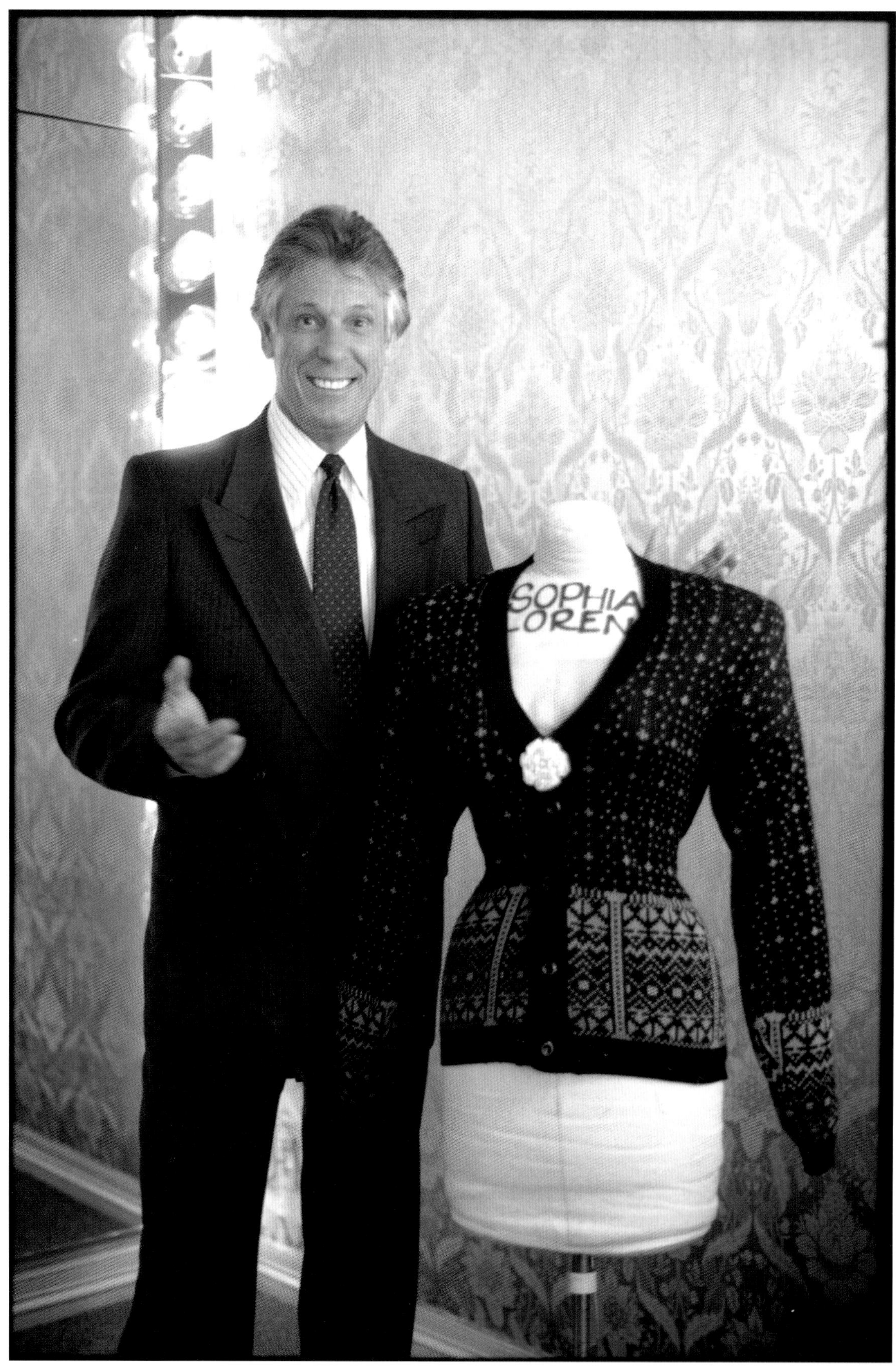

Nolan Miller

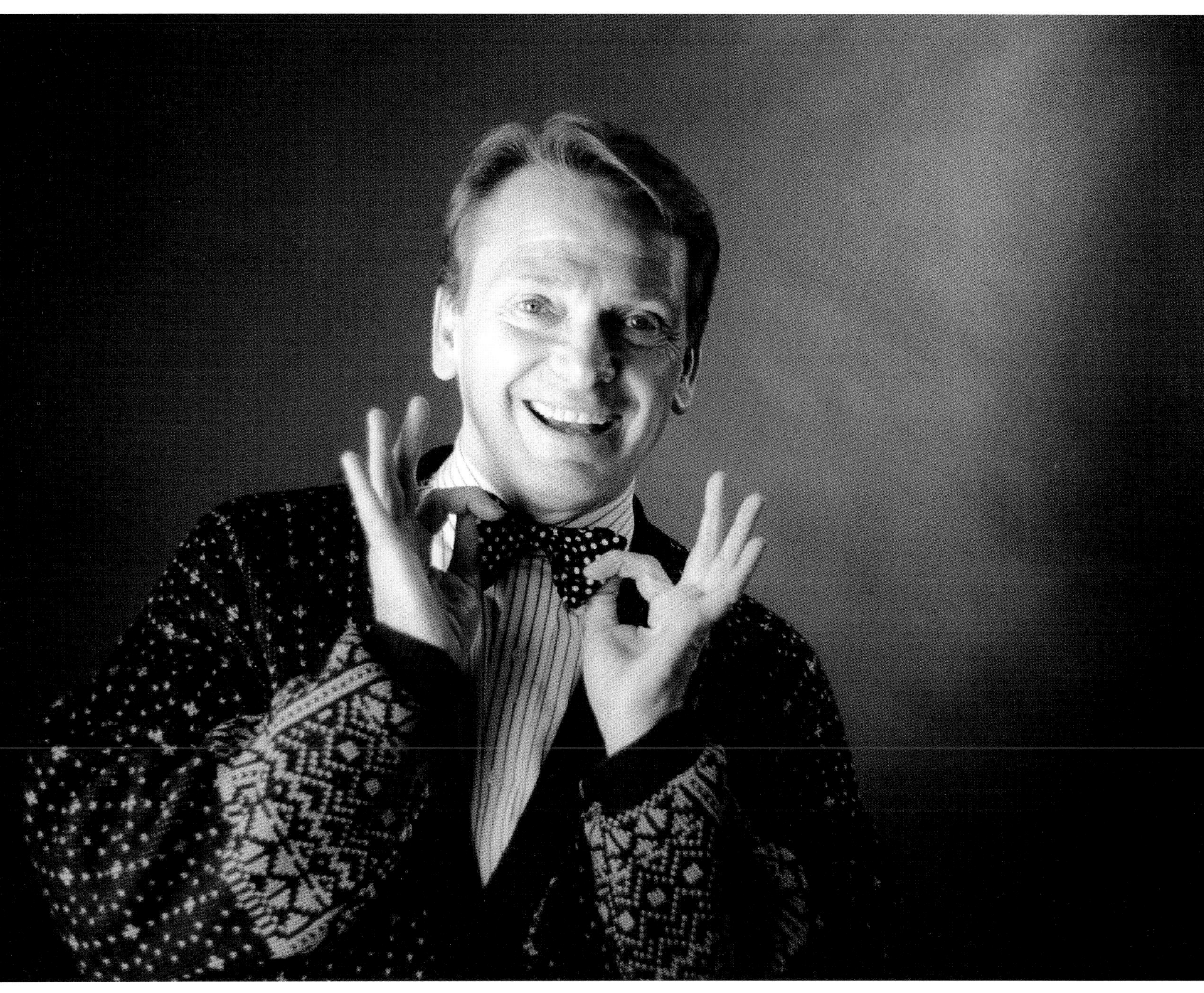

Bob Mackie

My grandmother and grandfather worked in the Hollywood studio system, she for Edith Head and he for Mae West. I was raised with Grandmother's views on fashion and glamour, for she designed and made clothing. Aside from the great Misses Head and Chanel, the two designers she mentioned most often were Nolan Miller (*opposite*) and Bob Mackie (*above*). I could listen to her talk at length about their individual styles and genius, complete with examples and photographs. Naturally, I have felt during my life that I had a good knowledge, a handle on fashion—at least that of a certain kind. On the days that I worked with these two men who had become personal heroes of my own, I felt comfortable and at home, for the love and admiration I have for them is not only my own but that passed on to me by Grandmother, who unlike me, really knew about what's good and what goes. Misters Mackie and Miller may be responsible for high fashion, but as men, they could not have been more down-to-earth and friendly, and for me, that is high class. I think that knowledge would have made Grandmother so happy.

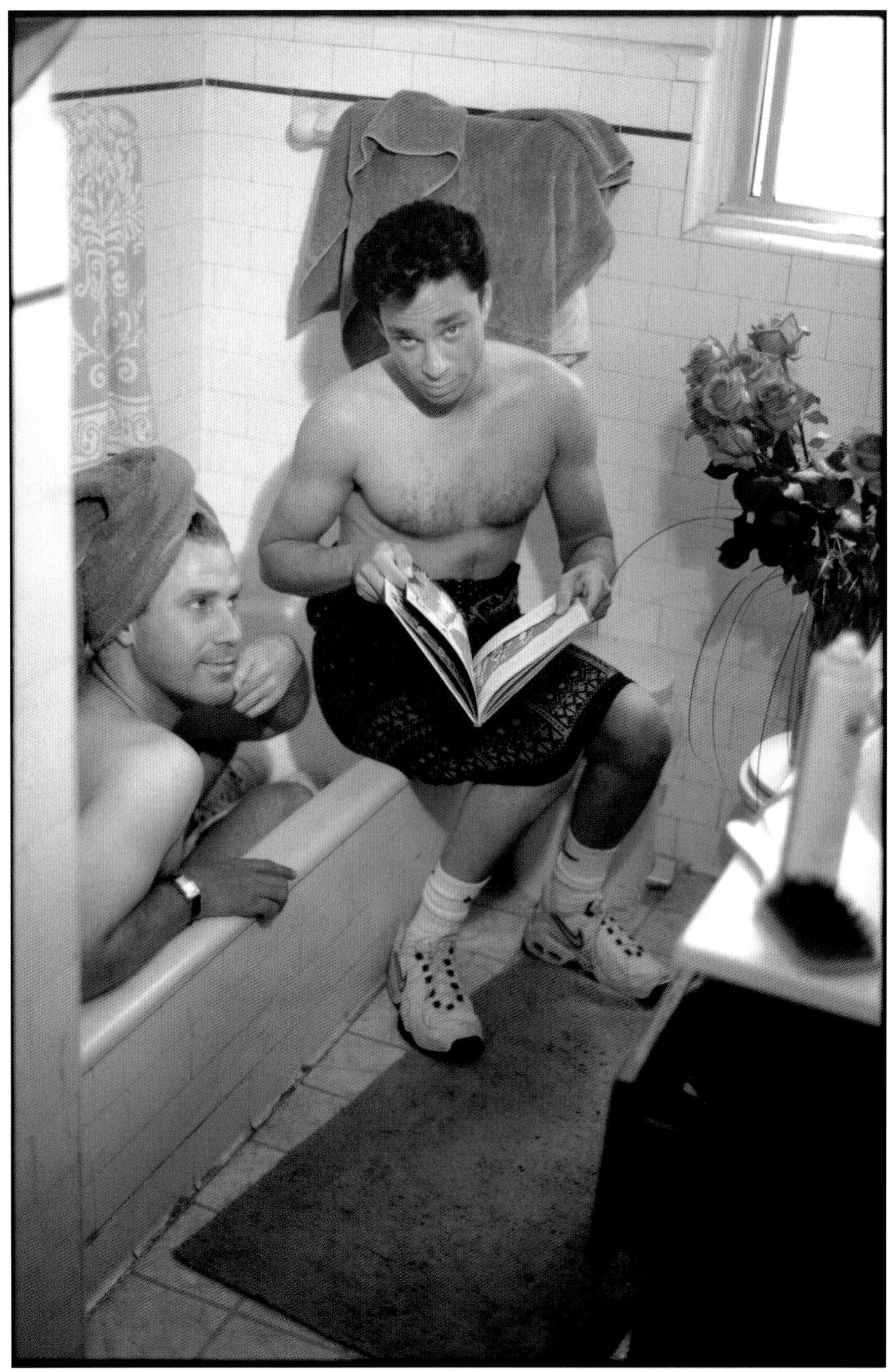

Will Ferrell and Chris Kattan

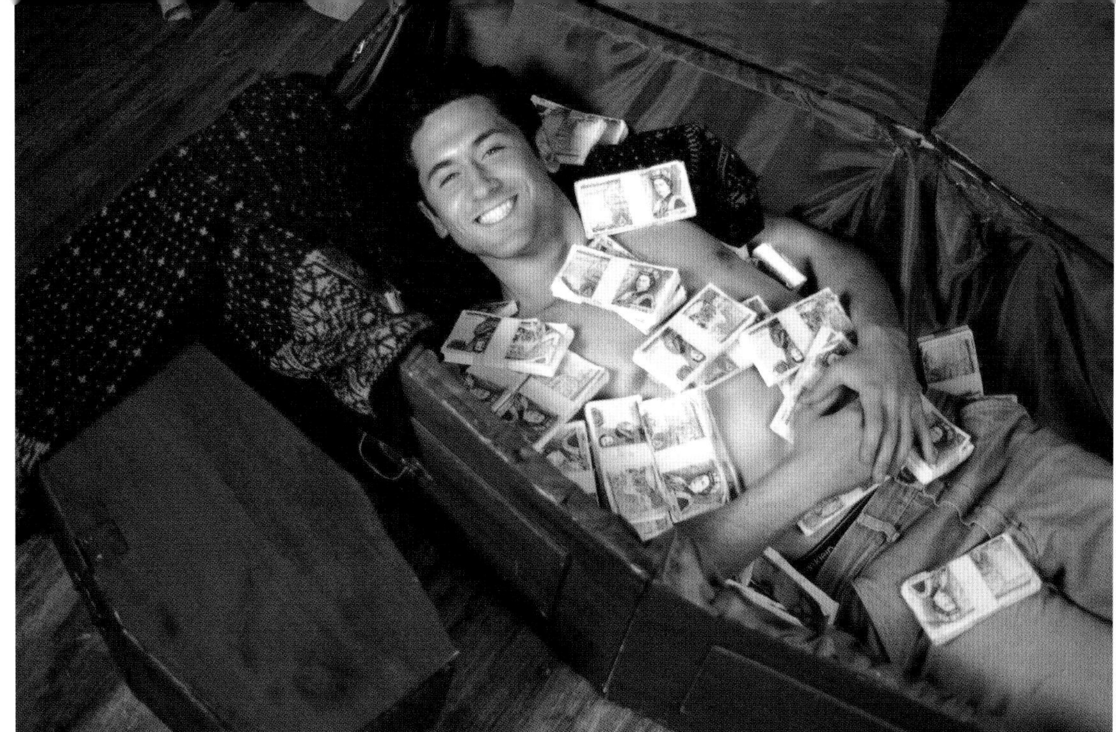

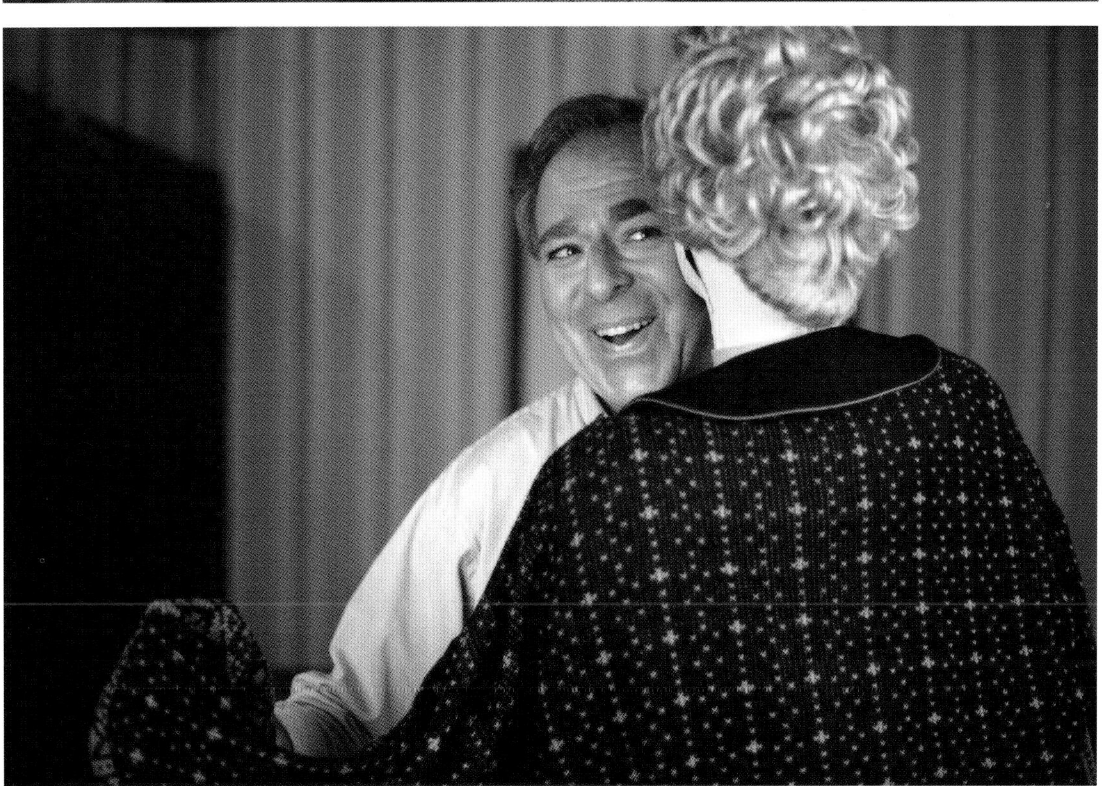

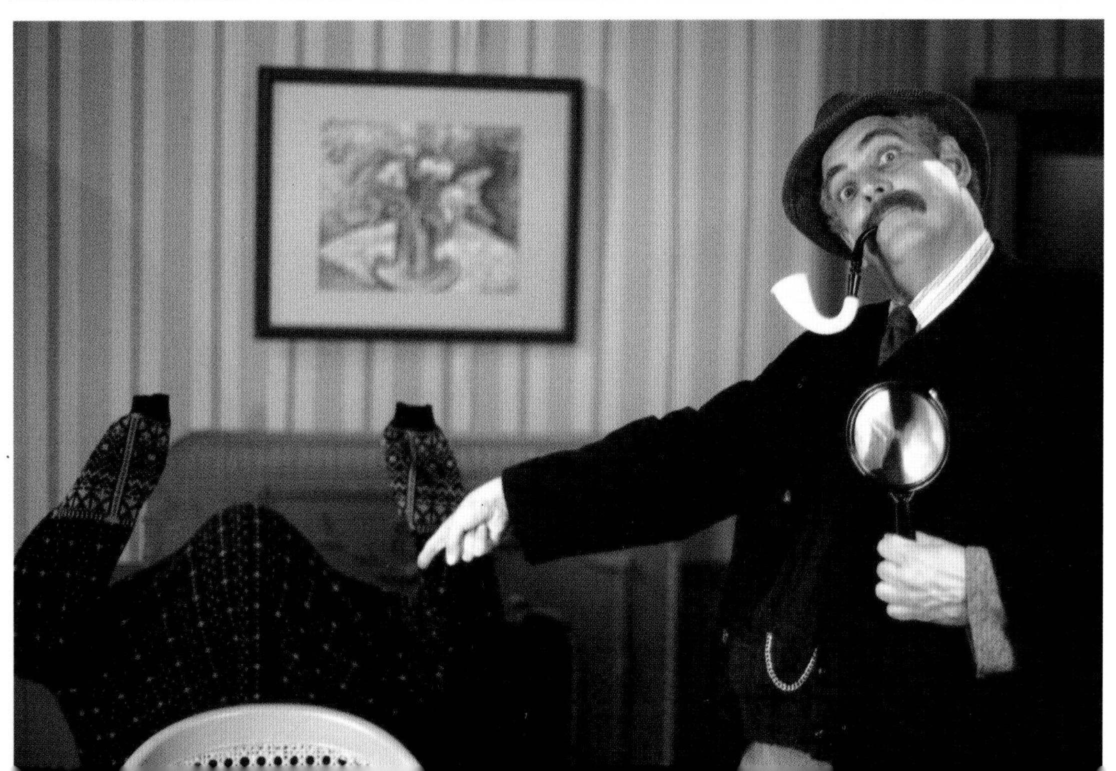

David O'Donnell
Lenny Wolpe
Peter Van Norden
Shot during a rehearsal of *Loot* at L.A.'s Blank Theatre Company

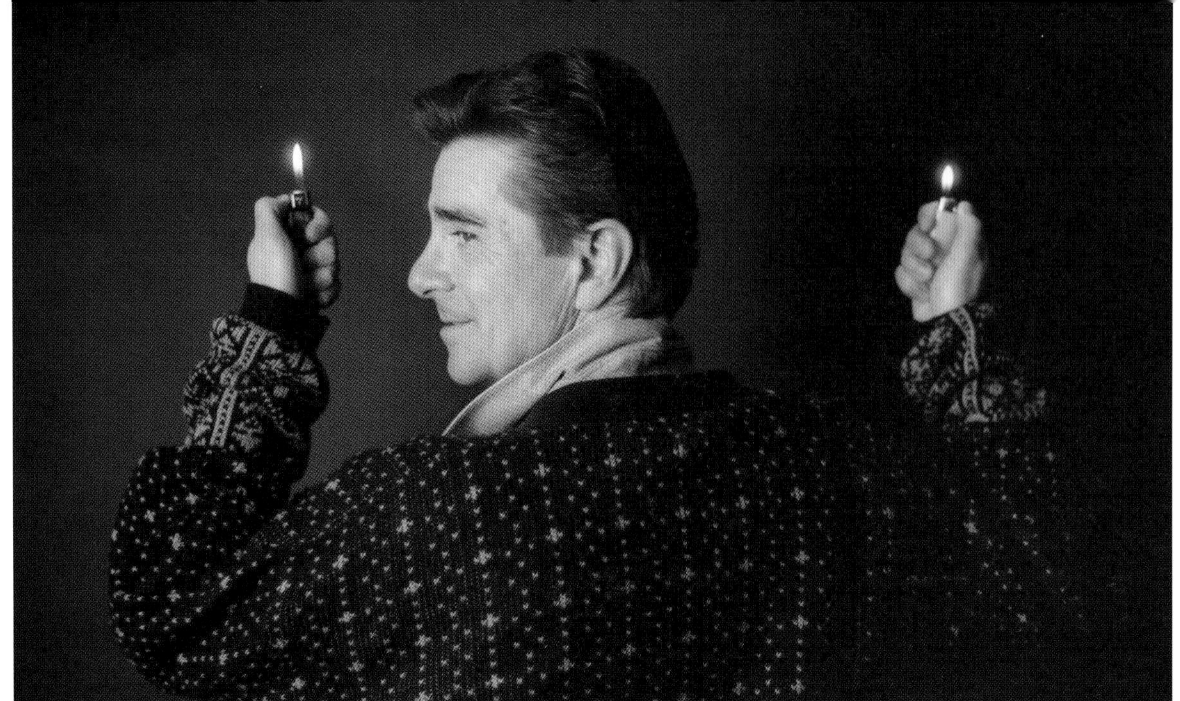

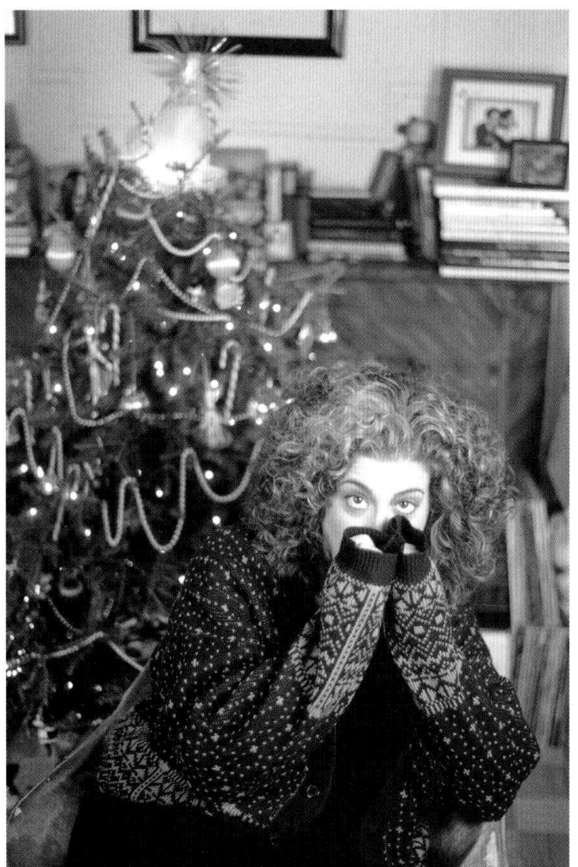

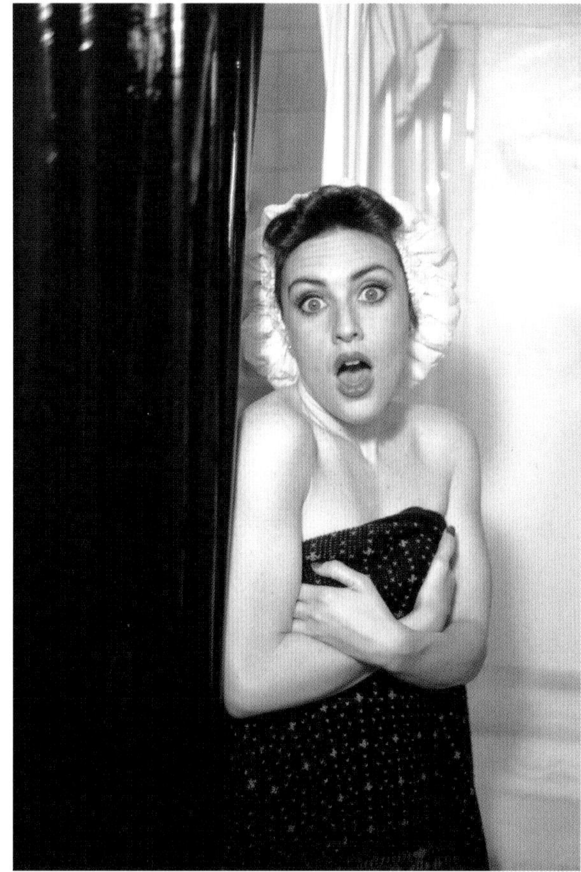

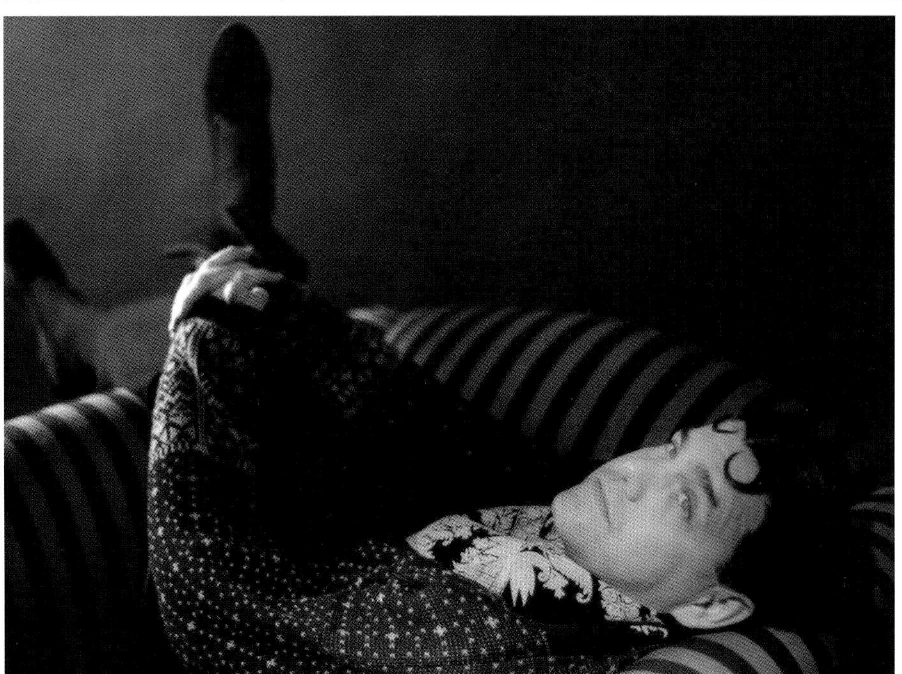

Clockwise from top:
Gary Beach
Justine Rossi
Jonathan Freeman
Mary Testa

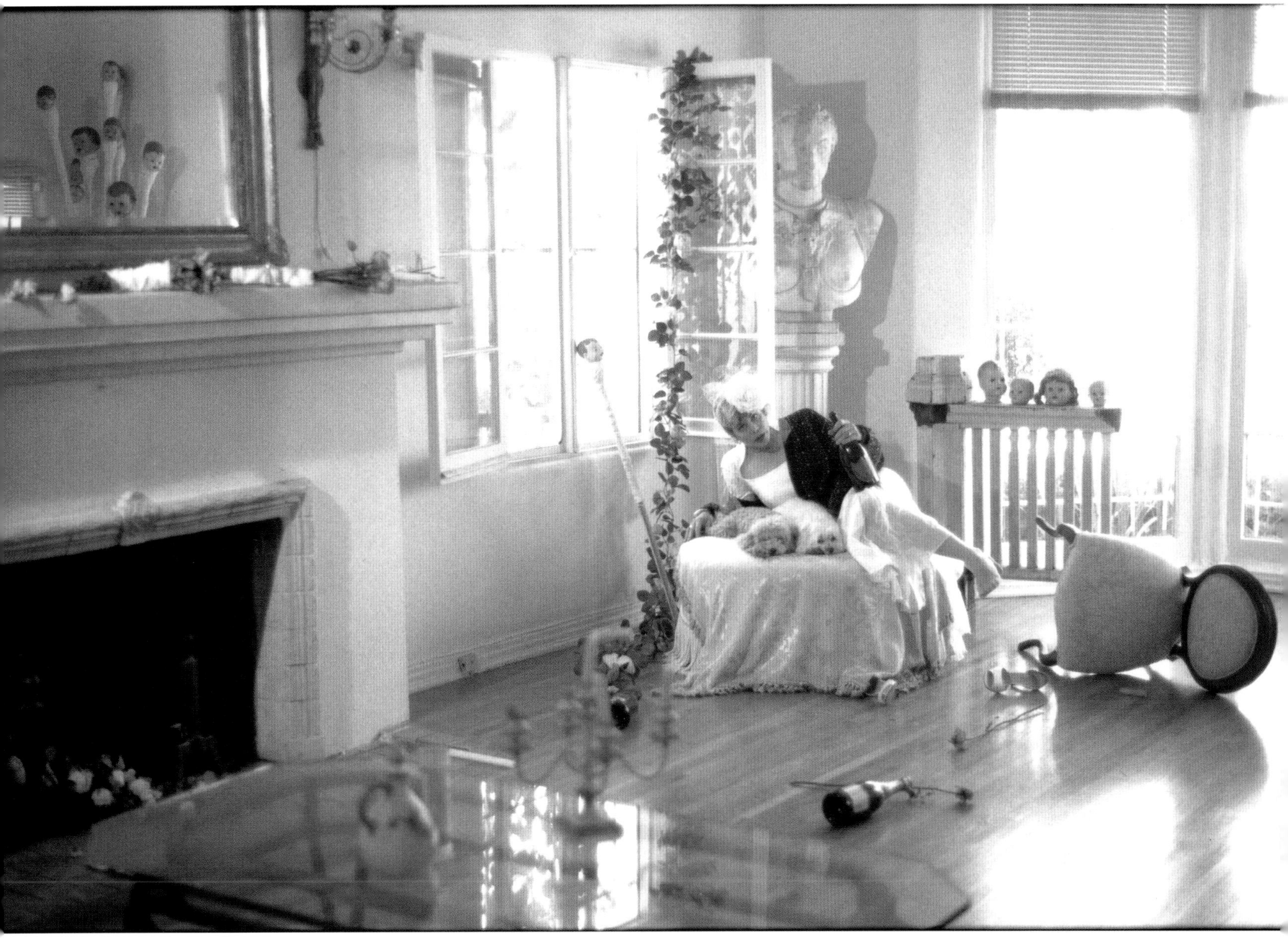

Twink Kaplan

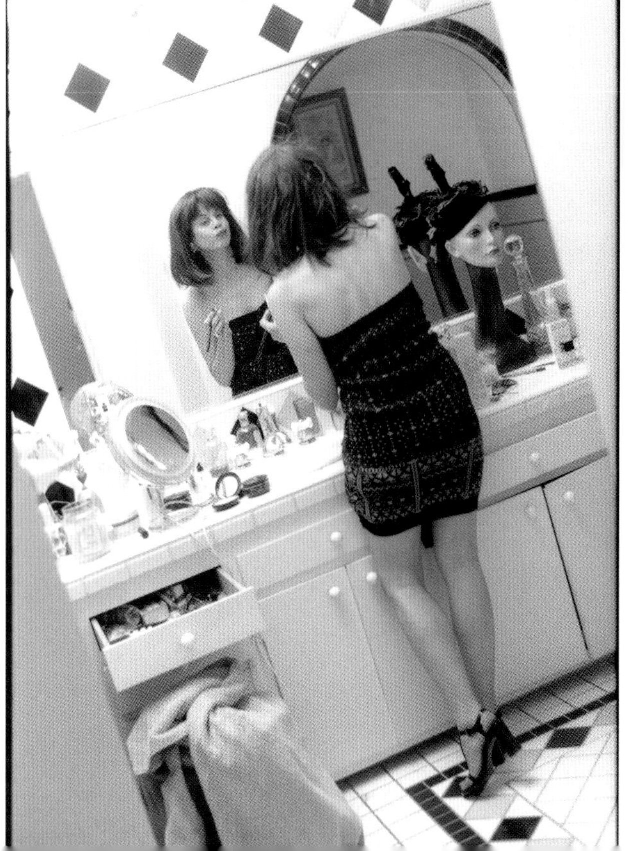

I love character actors and comedians, love watching them work, and love working with them. You never know what you are going to get with them, so it is always fun. Most of the time I like to let the photo do the work; every now and then, there is a story to tell, along with the photos. With character actors, though, the story *must* come out of the photo!

Here are two different photos that came out of my time with Twink Kaplan. The photo above is her with her dogs, Leon and Nathan. The photo to the left was taken in her powder room. Separately, each photo tells a story, but together they tell a different tale: the story of why I love character actors.

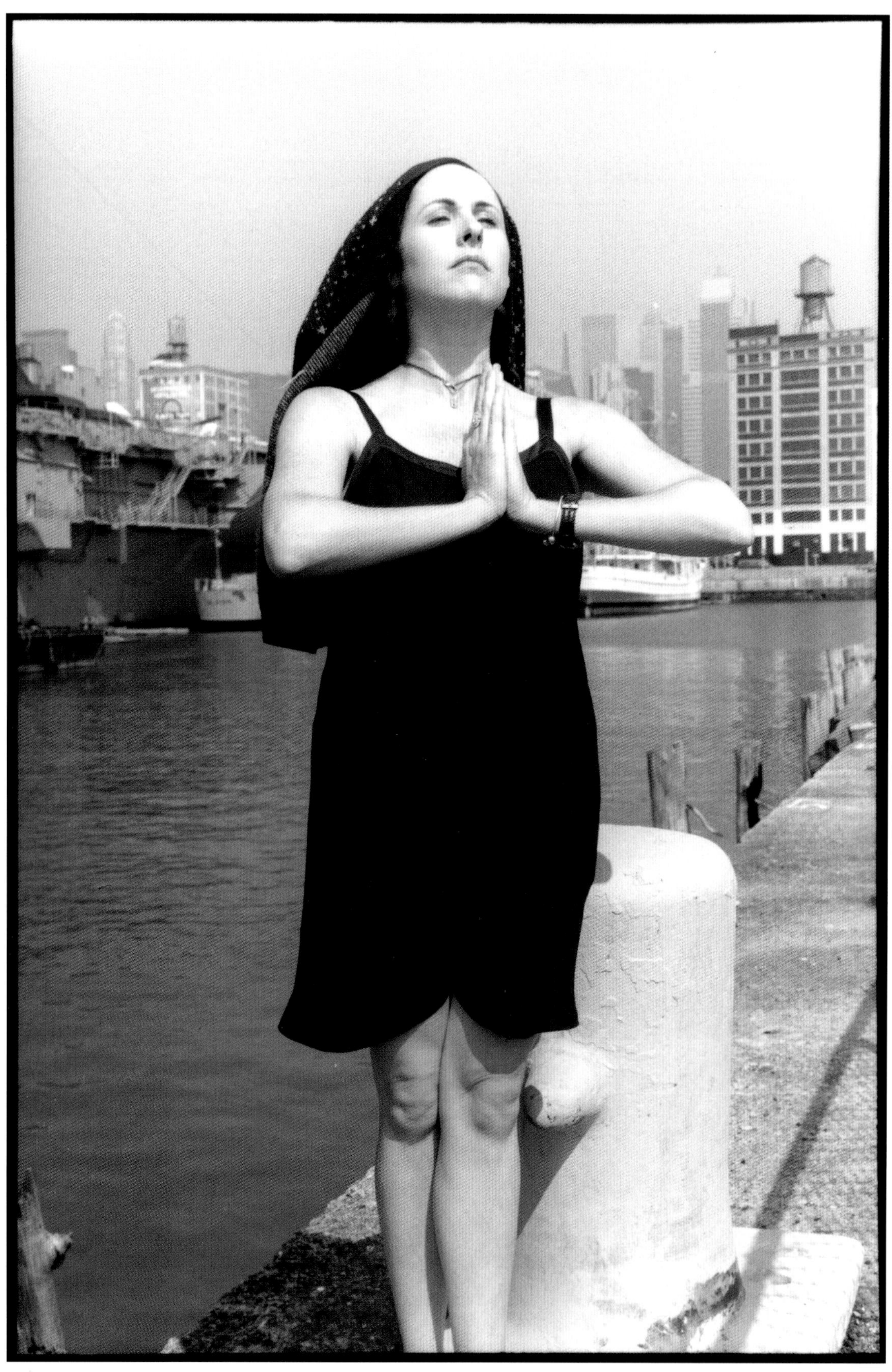

Molly Shannon

Opposite, from left to right:

Amy Hill, John Glover, Michael Chiklis, and Joan Van Ark

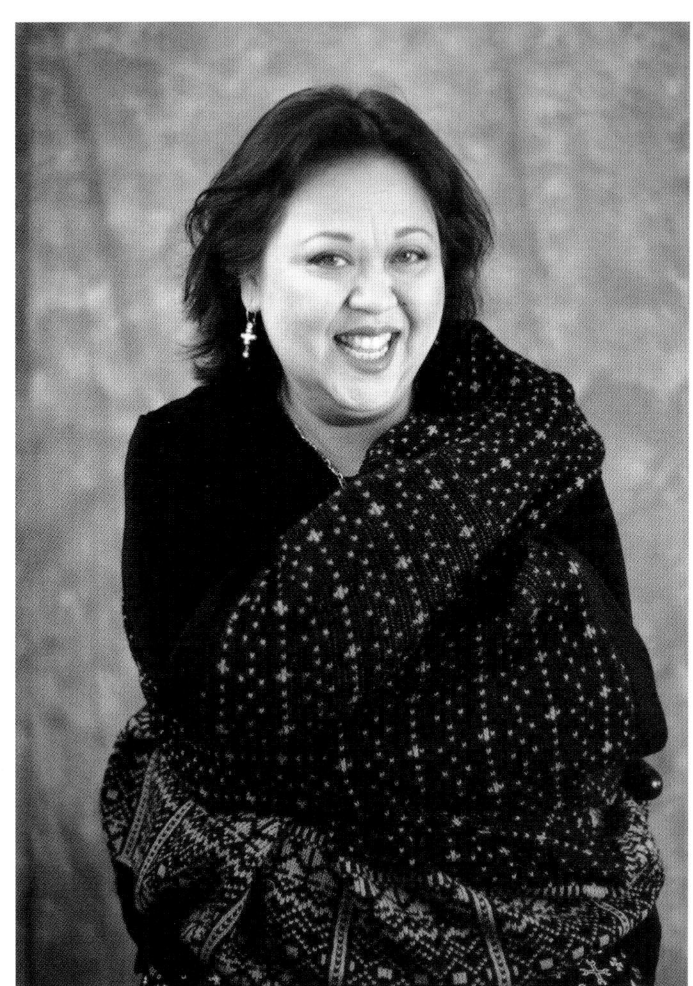

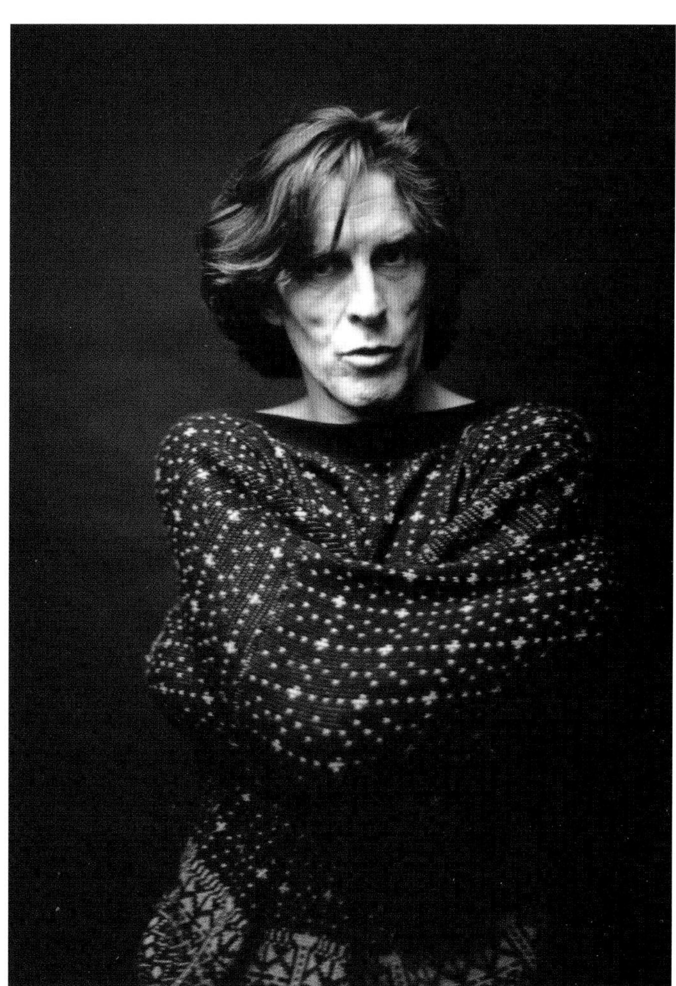

THE SWEATER ON THE EDGE—*in which the sweater is fit to be tied*

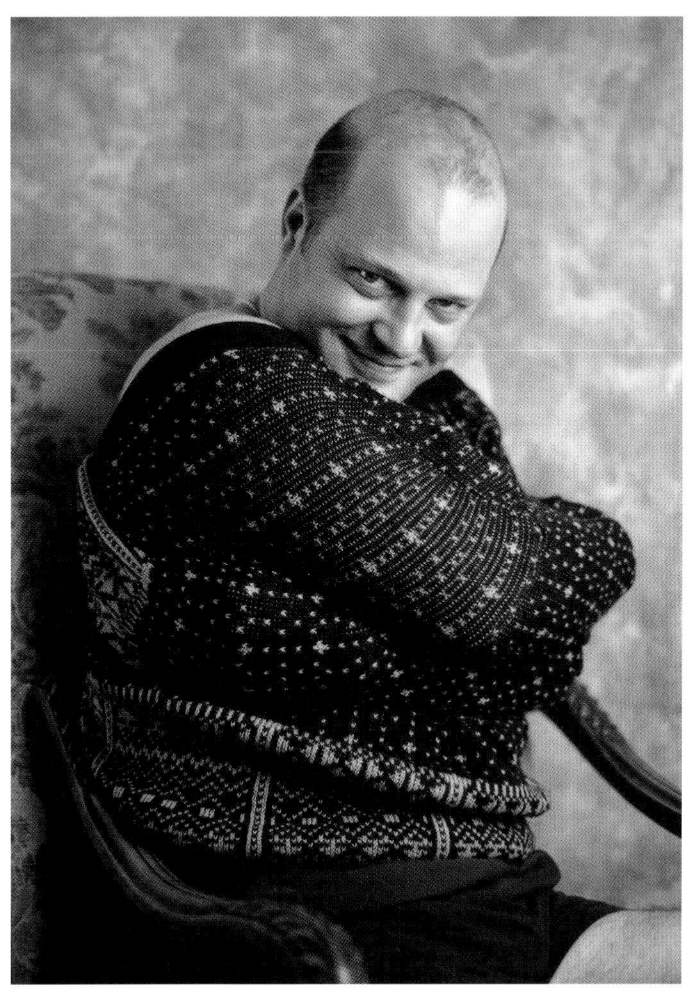

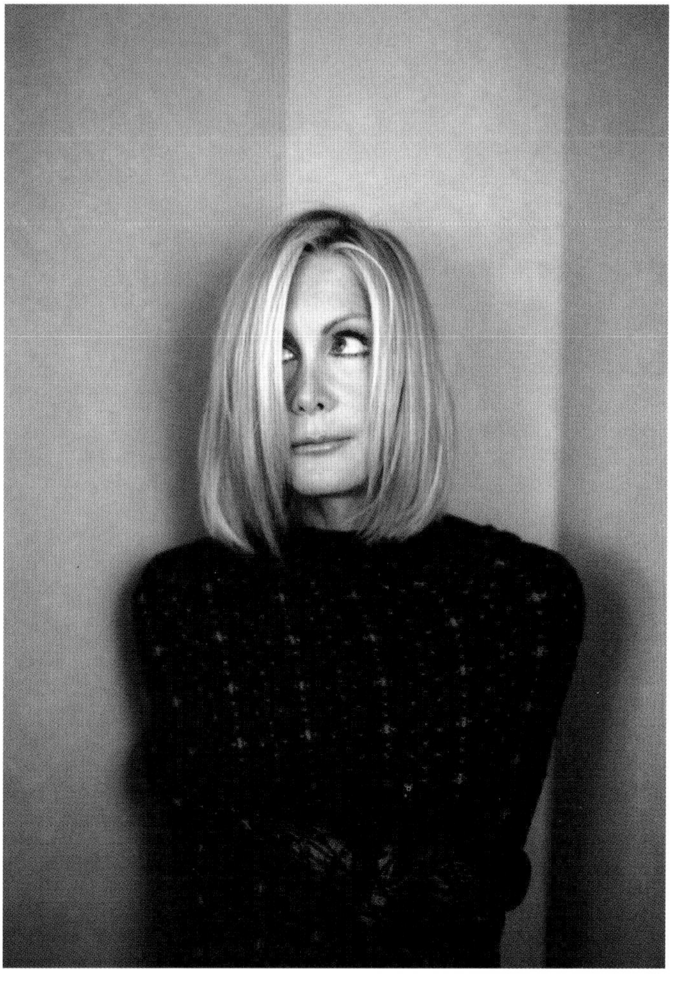

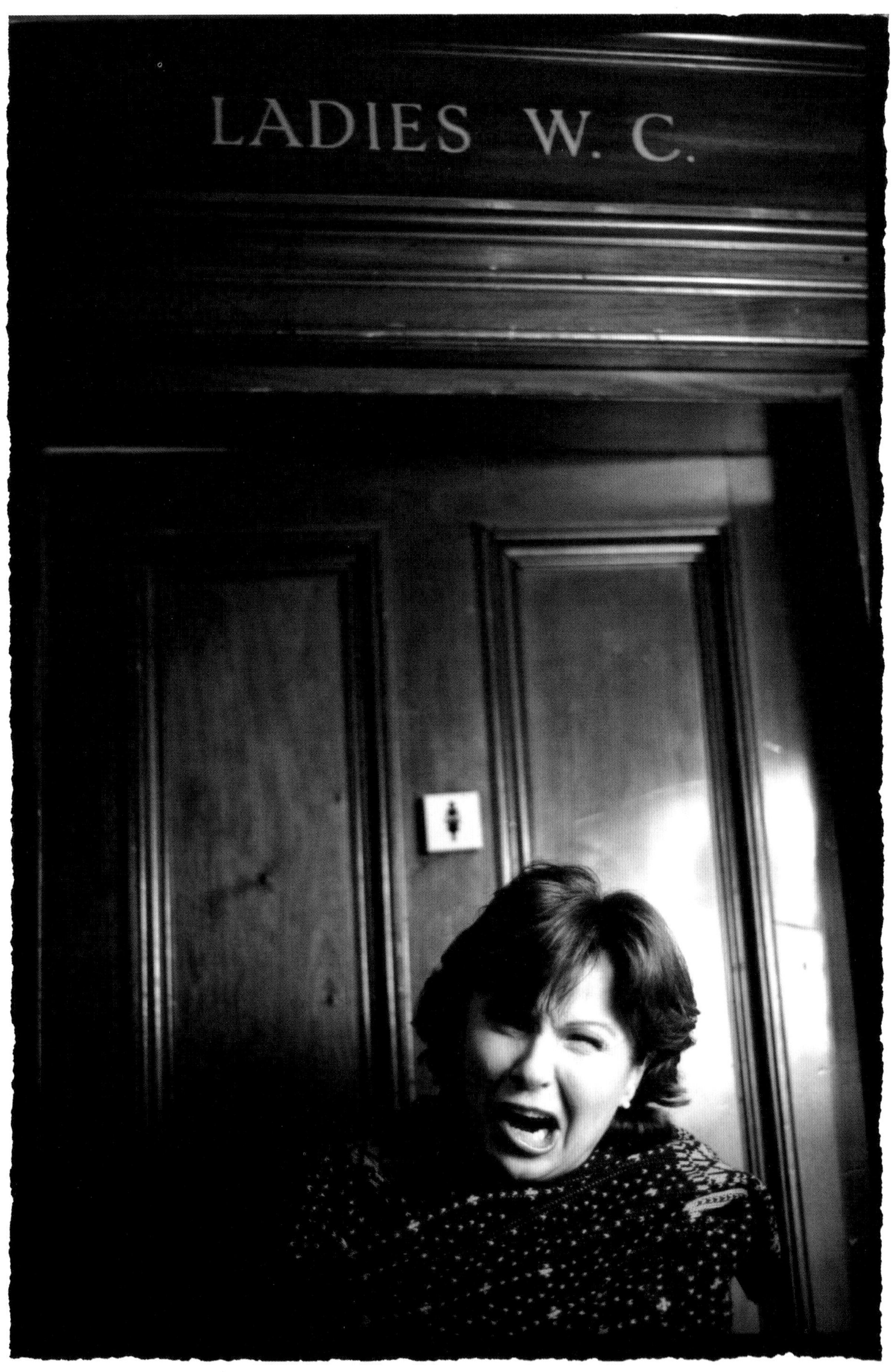

Julie Walters

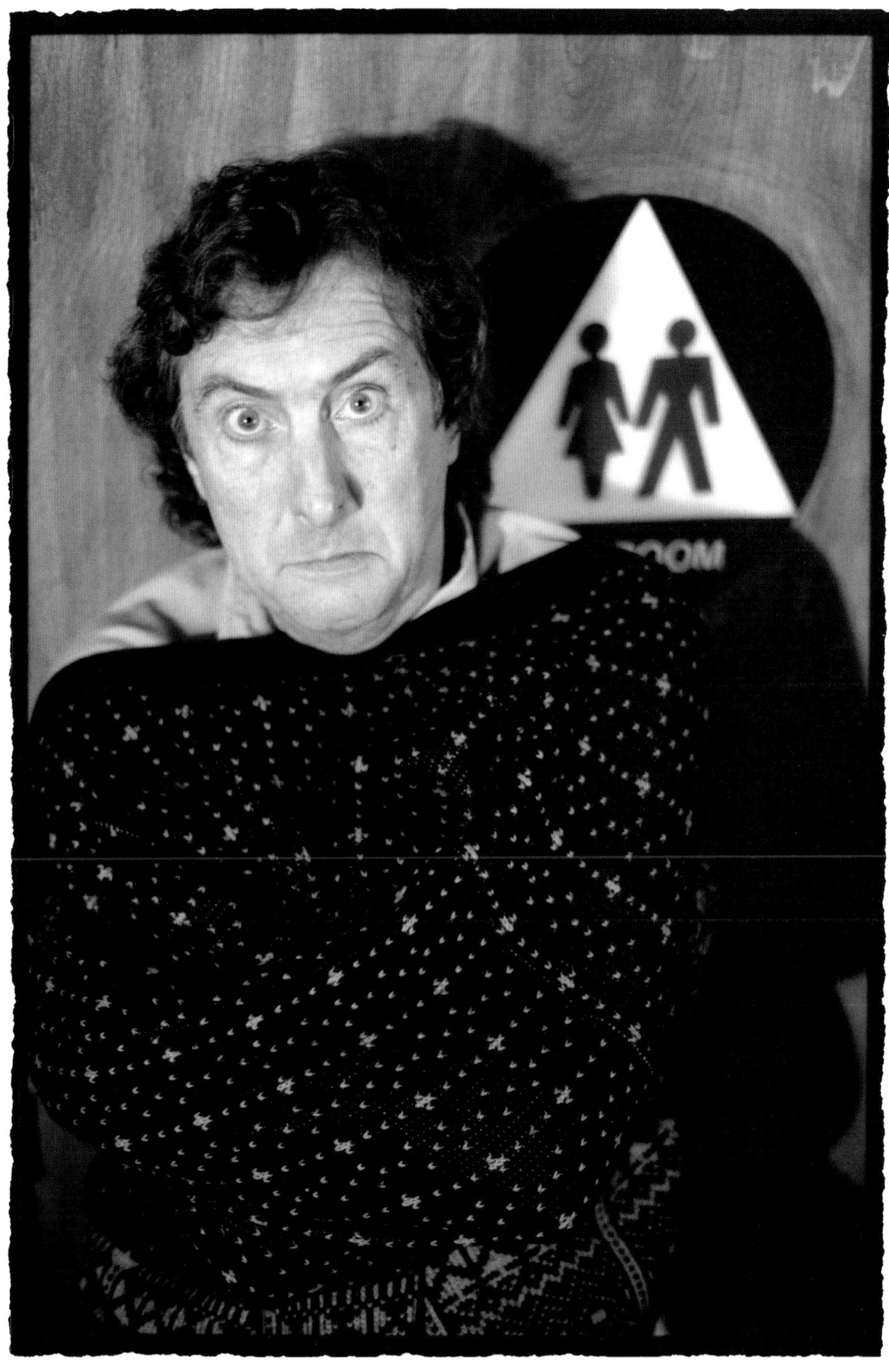

Eric Idle

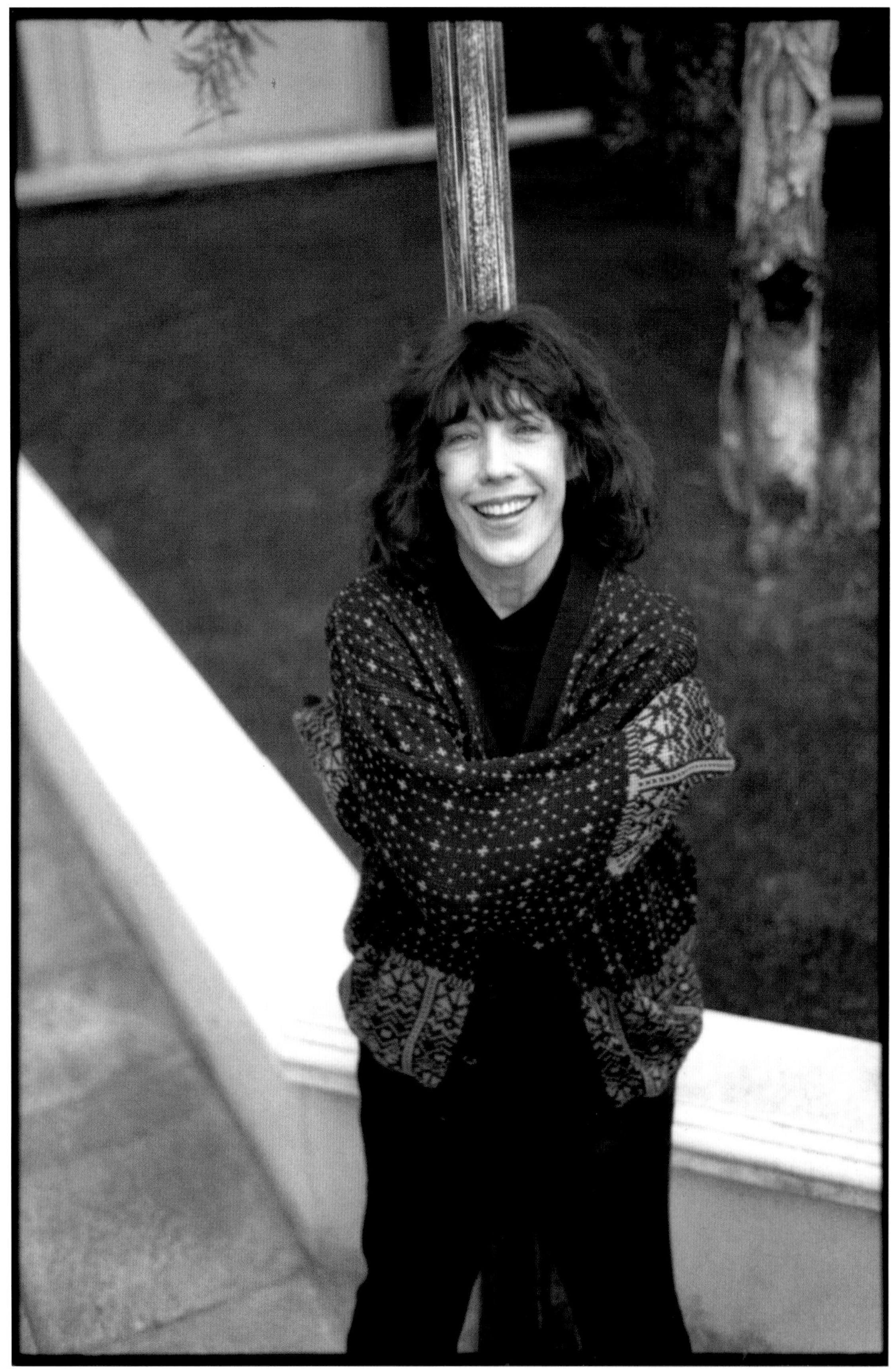

Lily Tomlin

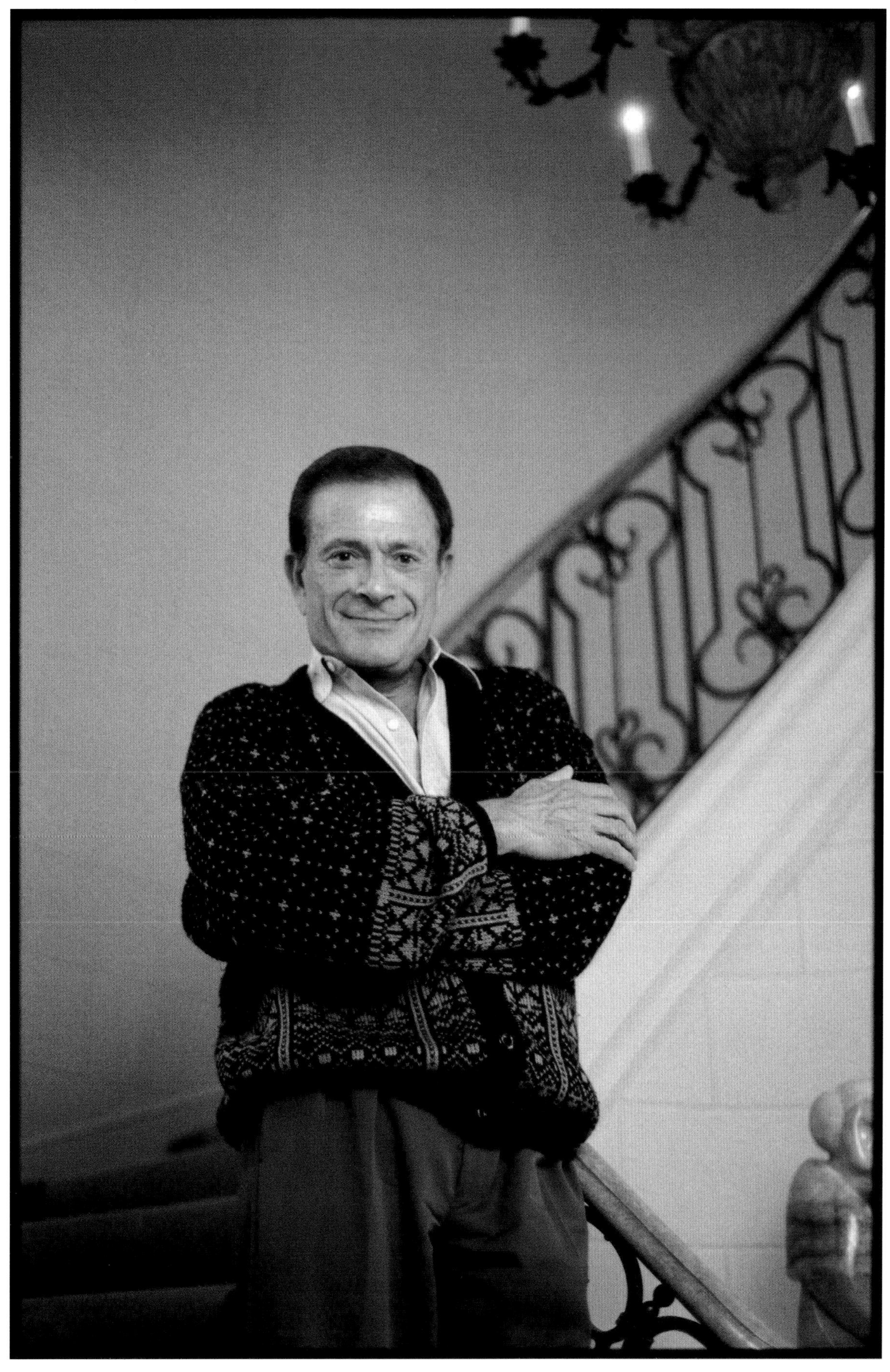

Jerry Herman

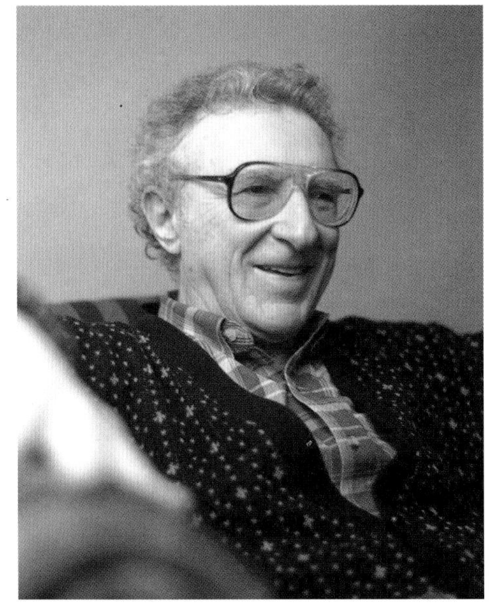

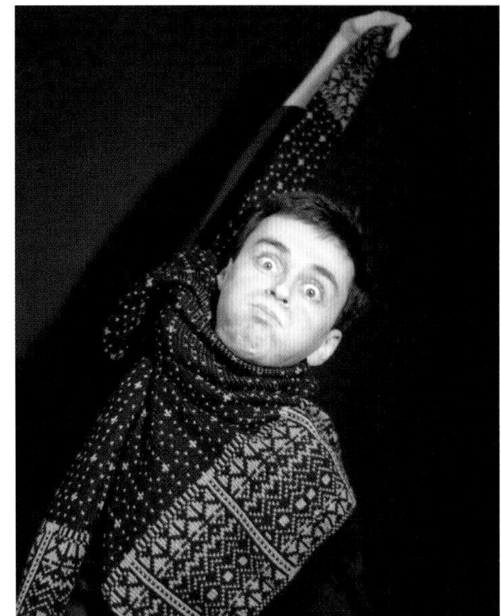

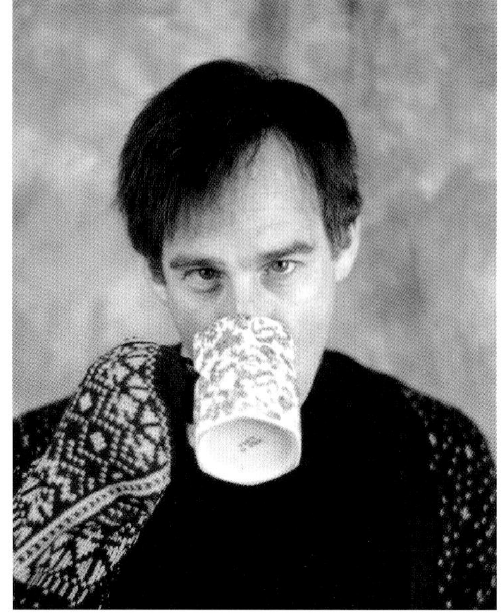

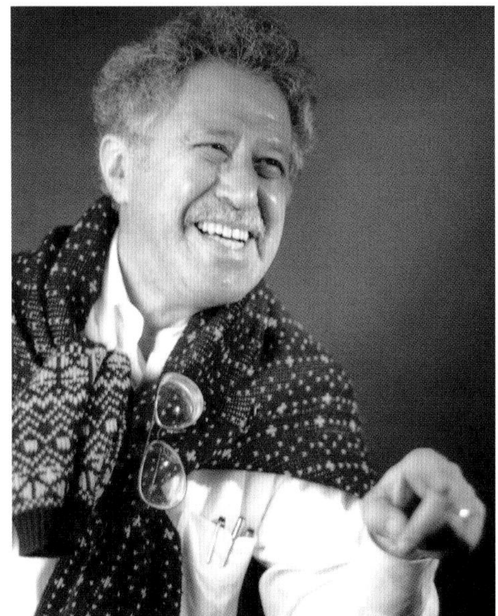

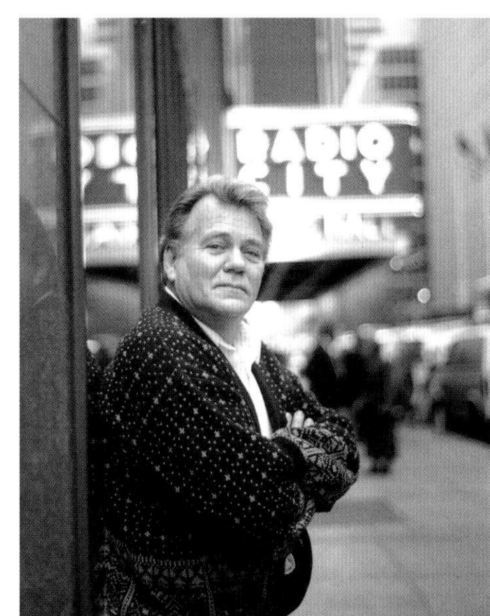

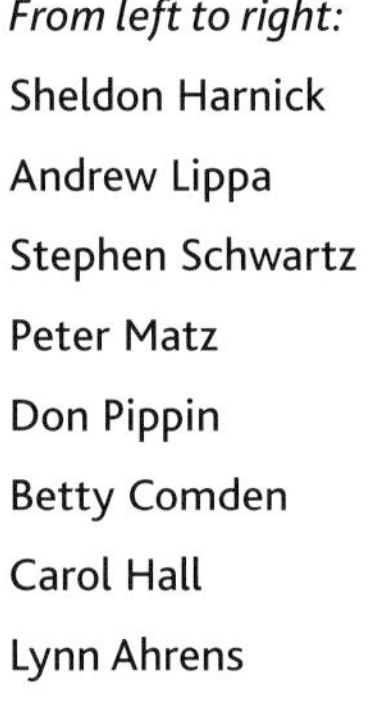

From left to right:
Sheldon Harnick
Andrew Lippa
Stephen Schwartz
Peter Matz
Don Pippin
Betty Comden
Carol Hall
Lynn Ahrens

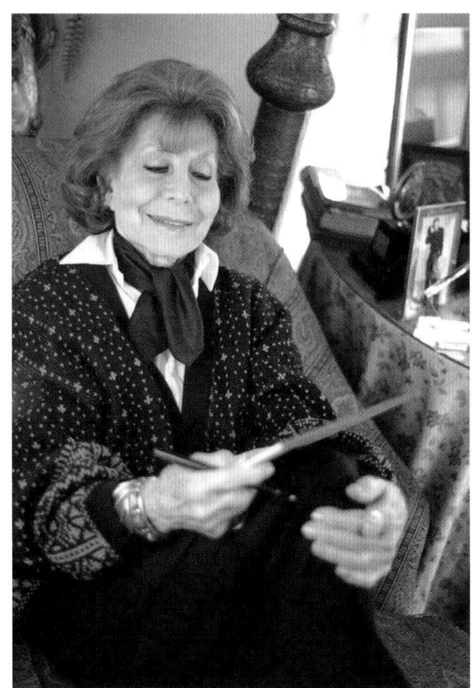

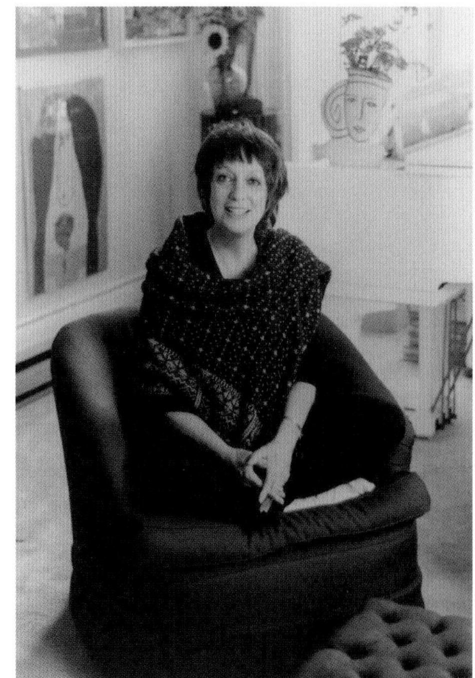

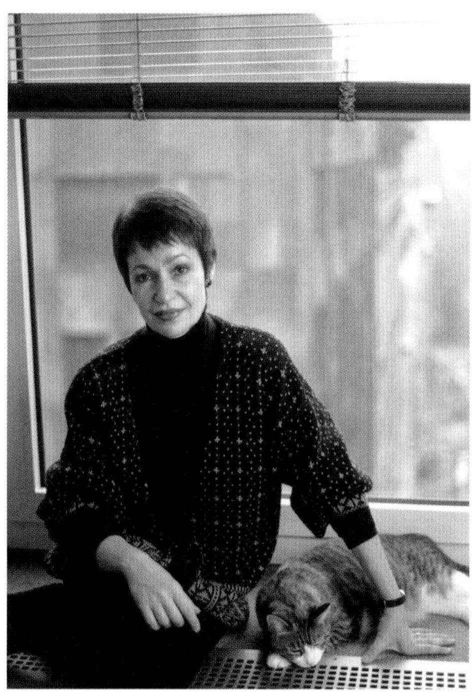

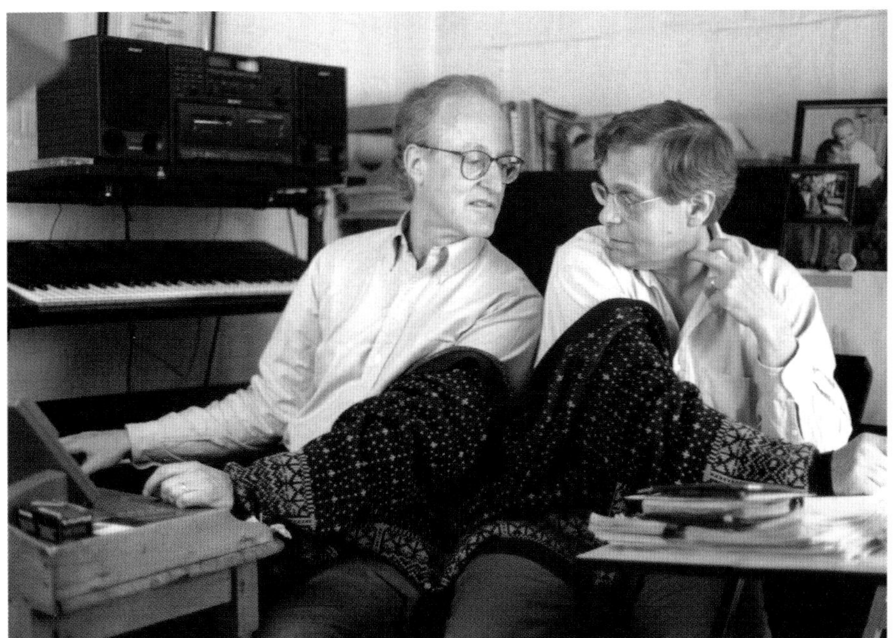

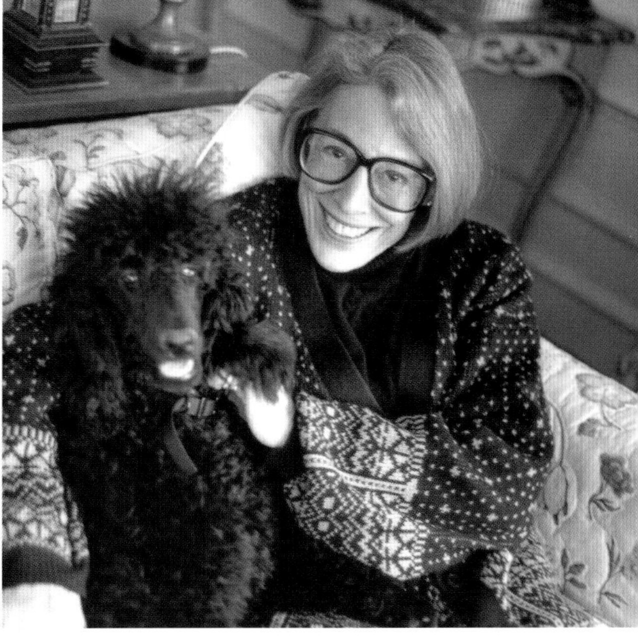

From left to right:
David Shire and Richard Maltby
Mary Rodgers
John Bucchino
Bill Russel with Bruce Bossard
David Zippel

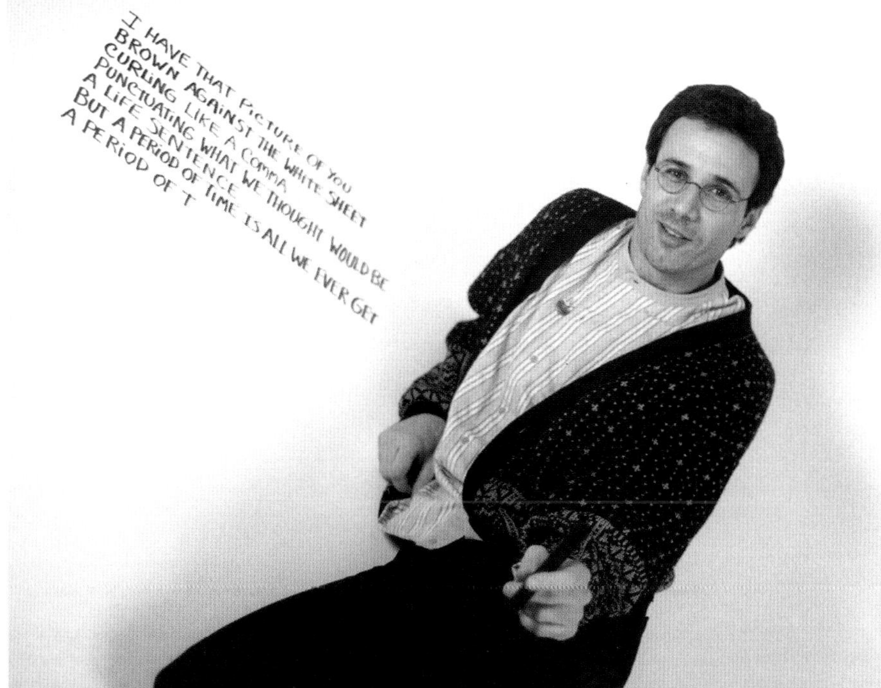

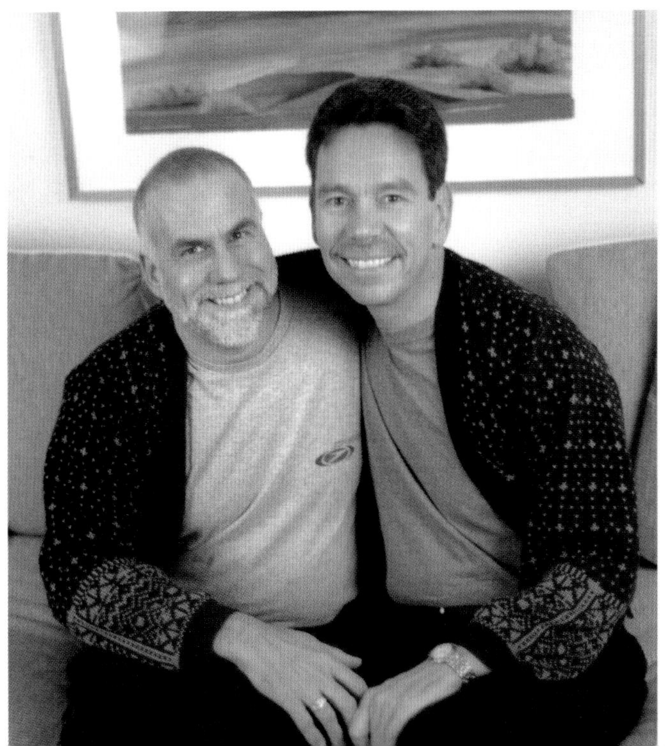

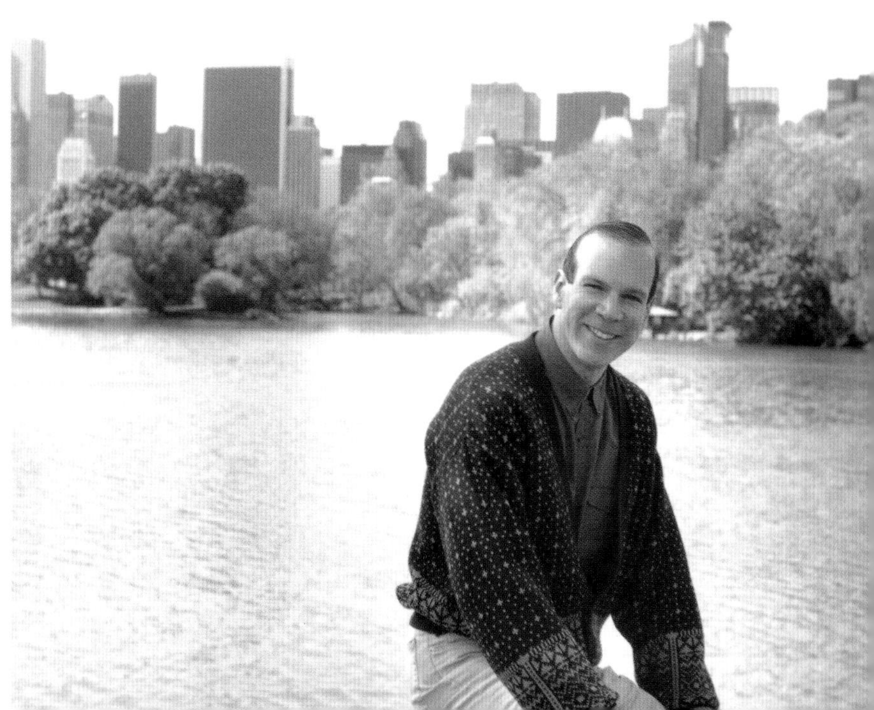

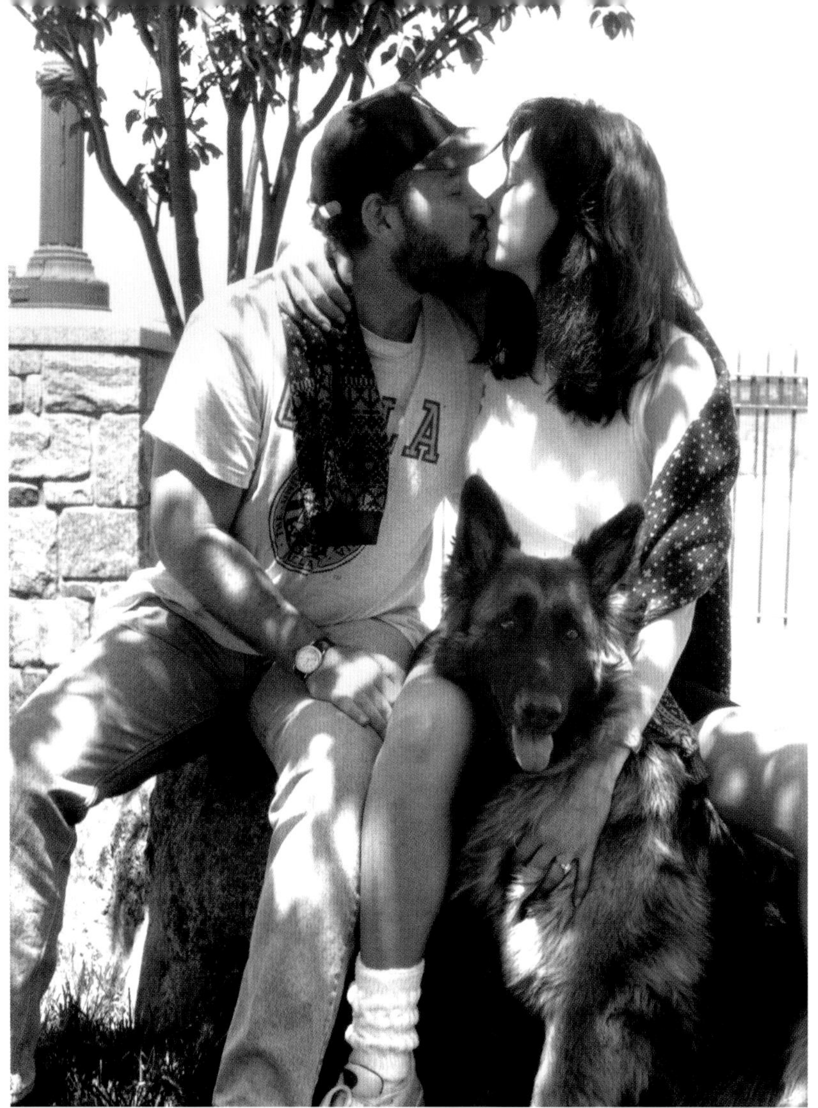

Frank Wildhorn with
Linda Eder Wildhorn

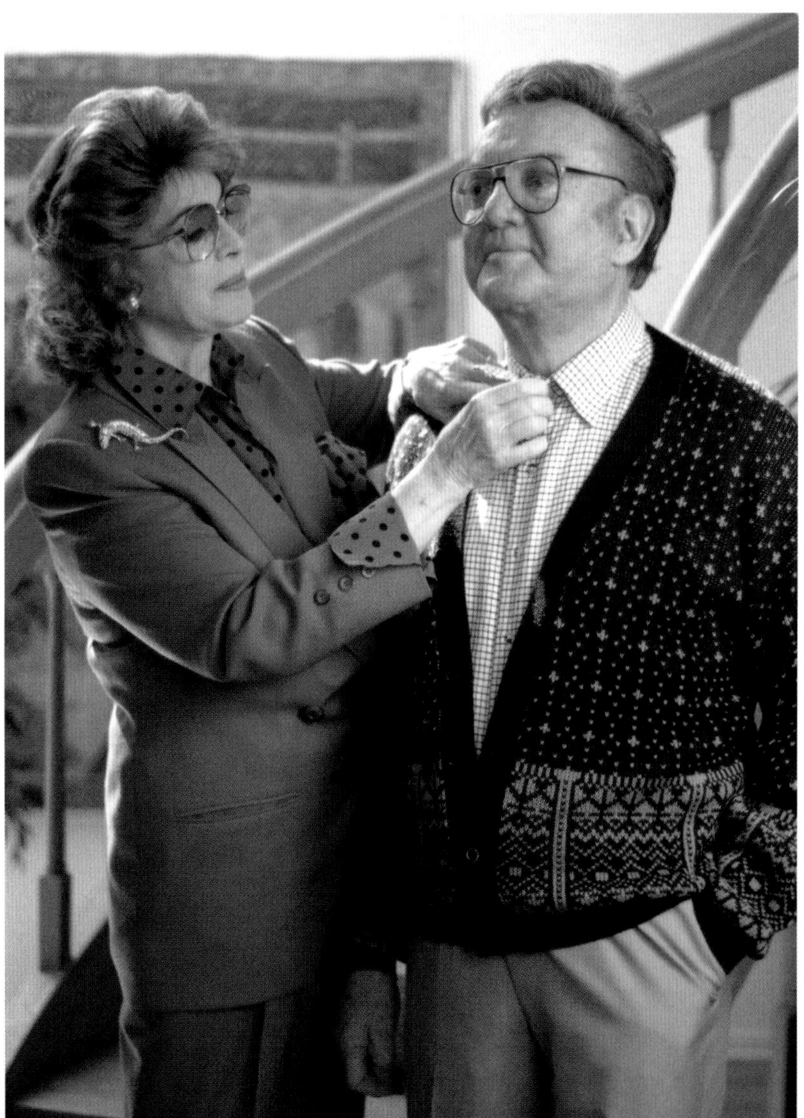

Steve Allen with
Jayne Meadows Allen

THE SWEATER IN LOVE—*in which the sweater gets some sex in the city*

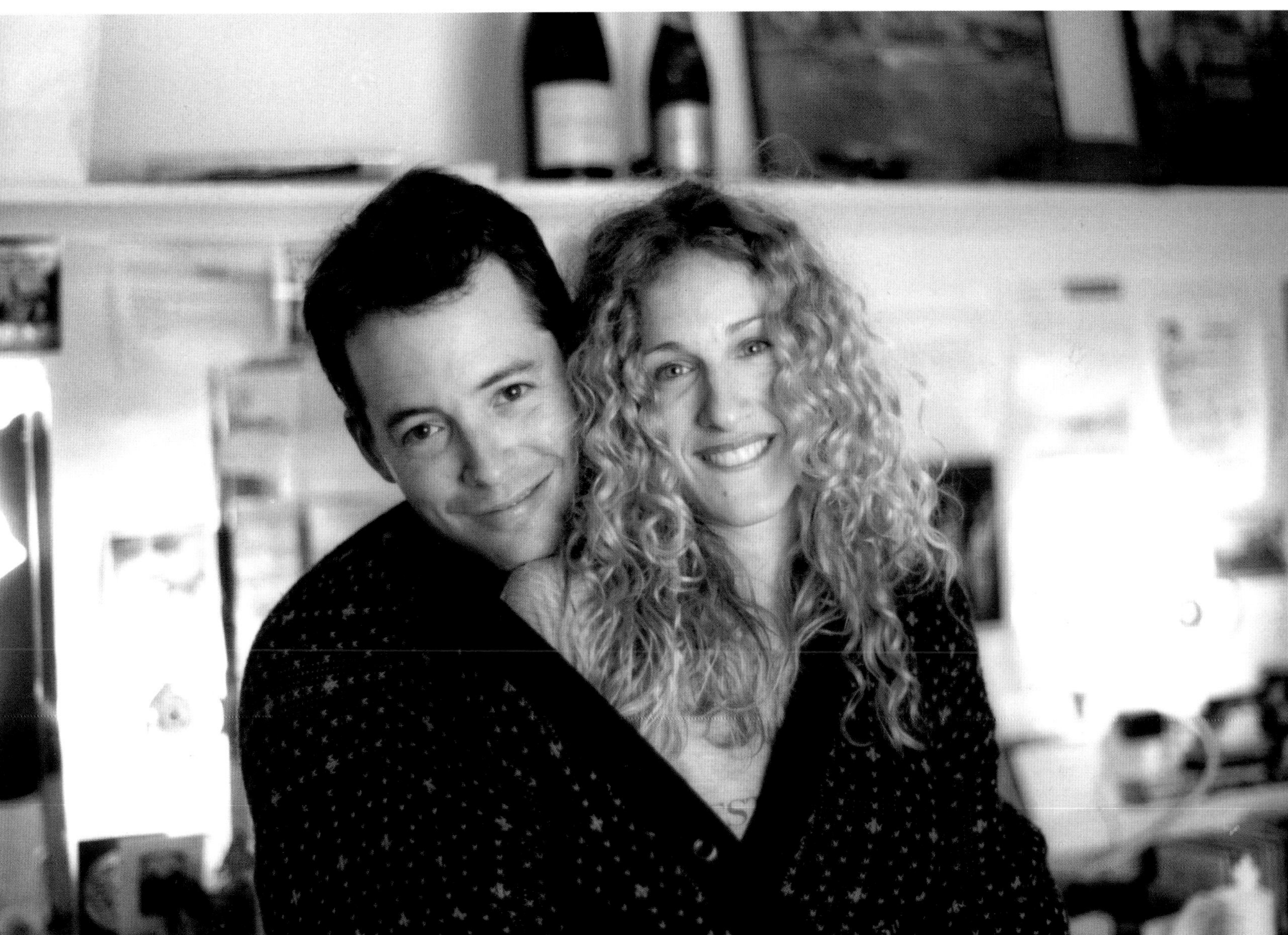

Matthew Broderick and Sarah Jessica Parker

A friend of mine who saw this picture said, "You can tell how Matthew and Sarah Jessica feel about each other when you look at the expression on her face."

Then he pointed out that their heads and the neckline of the sweater make a heart shape.

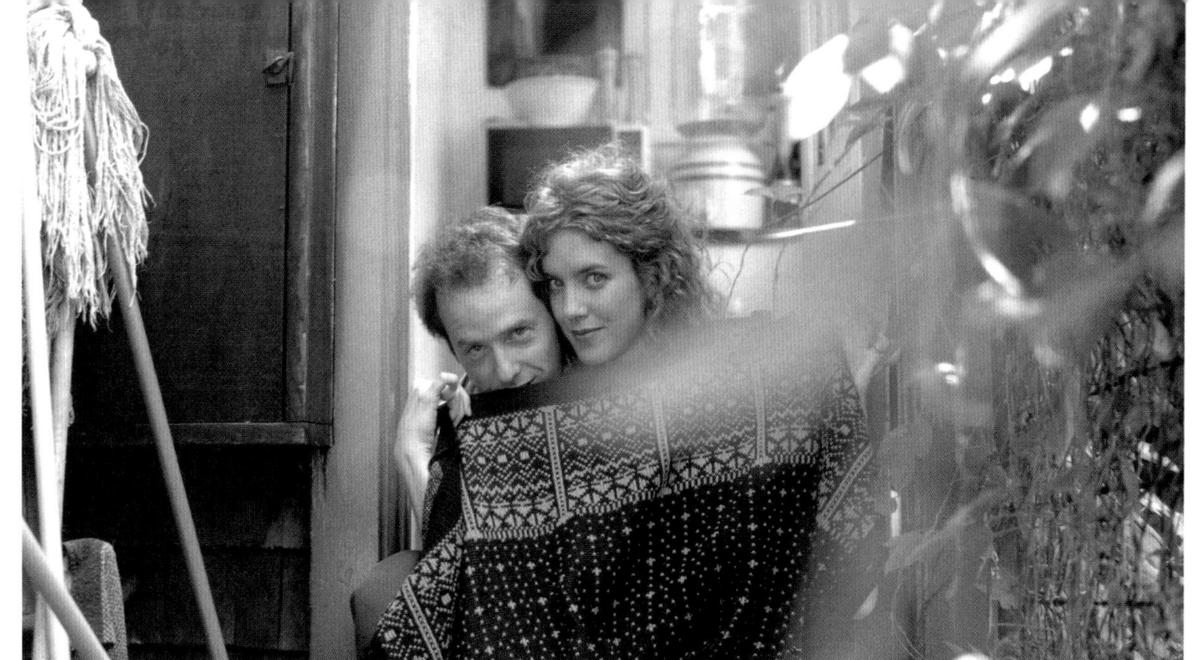
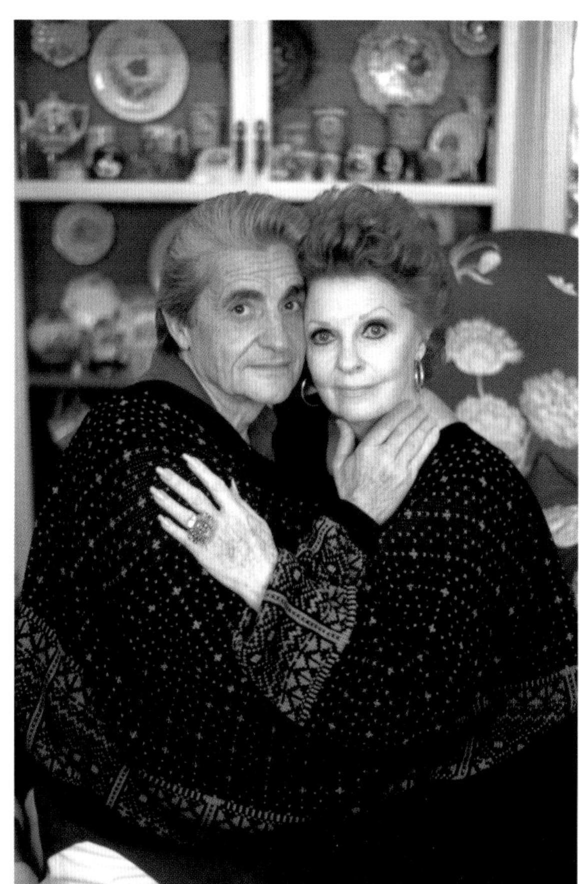
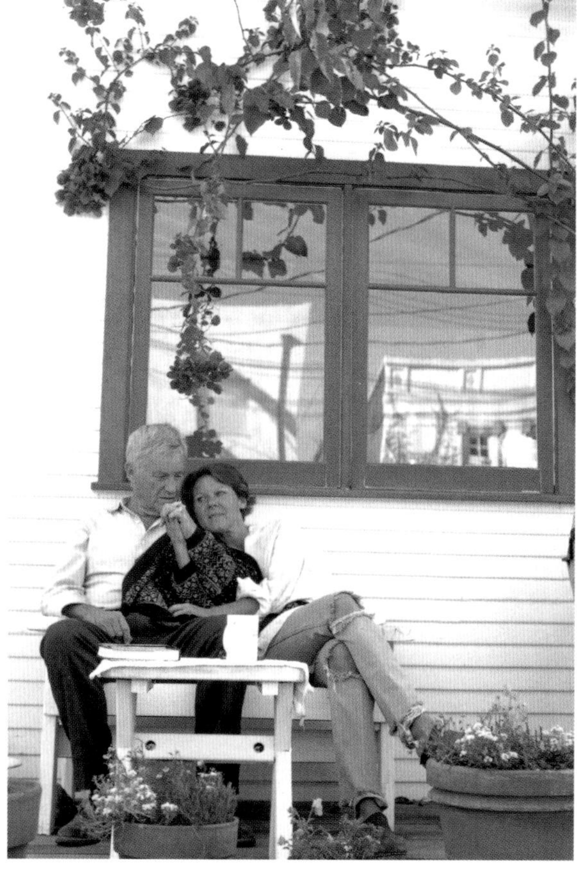
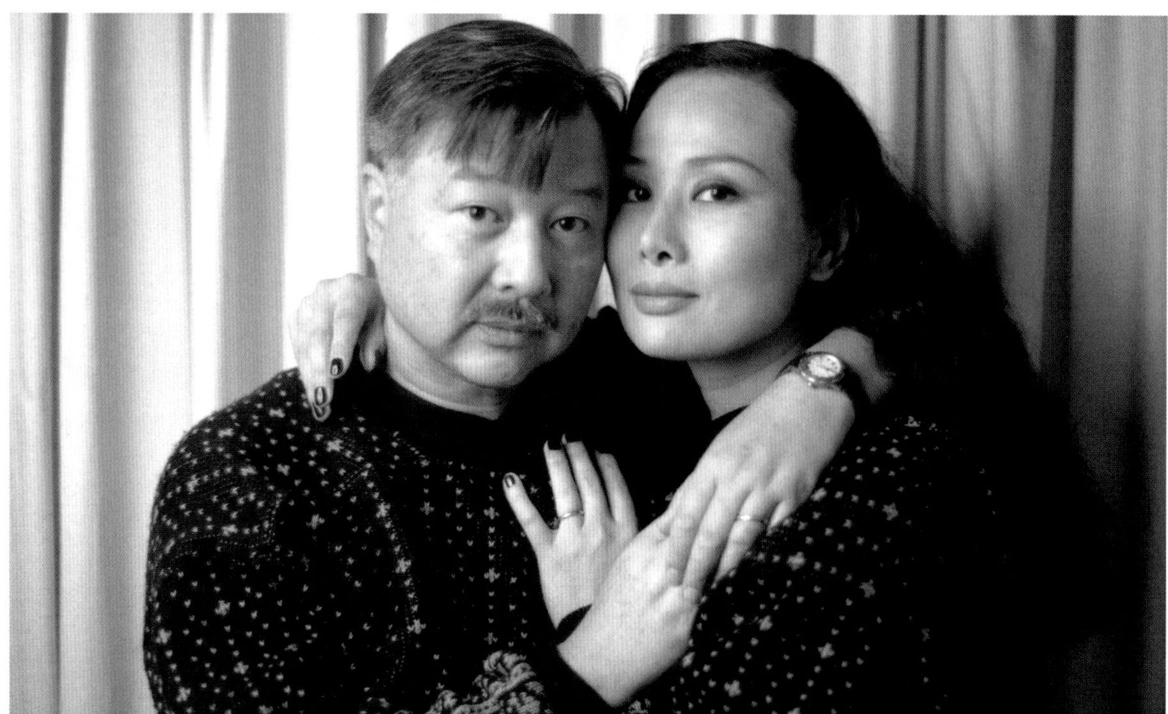

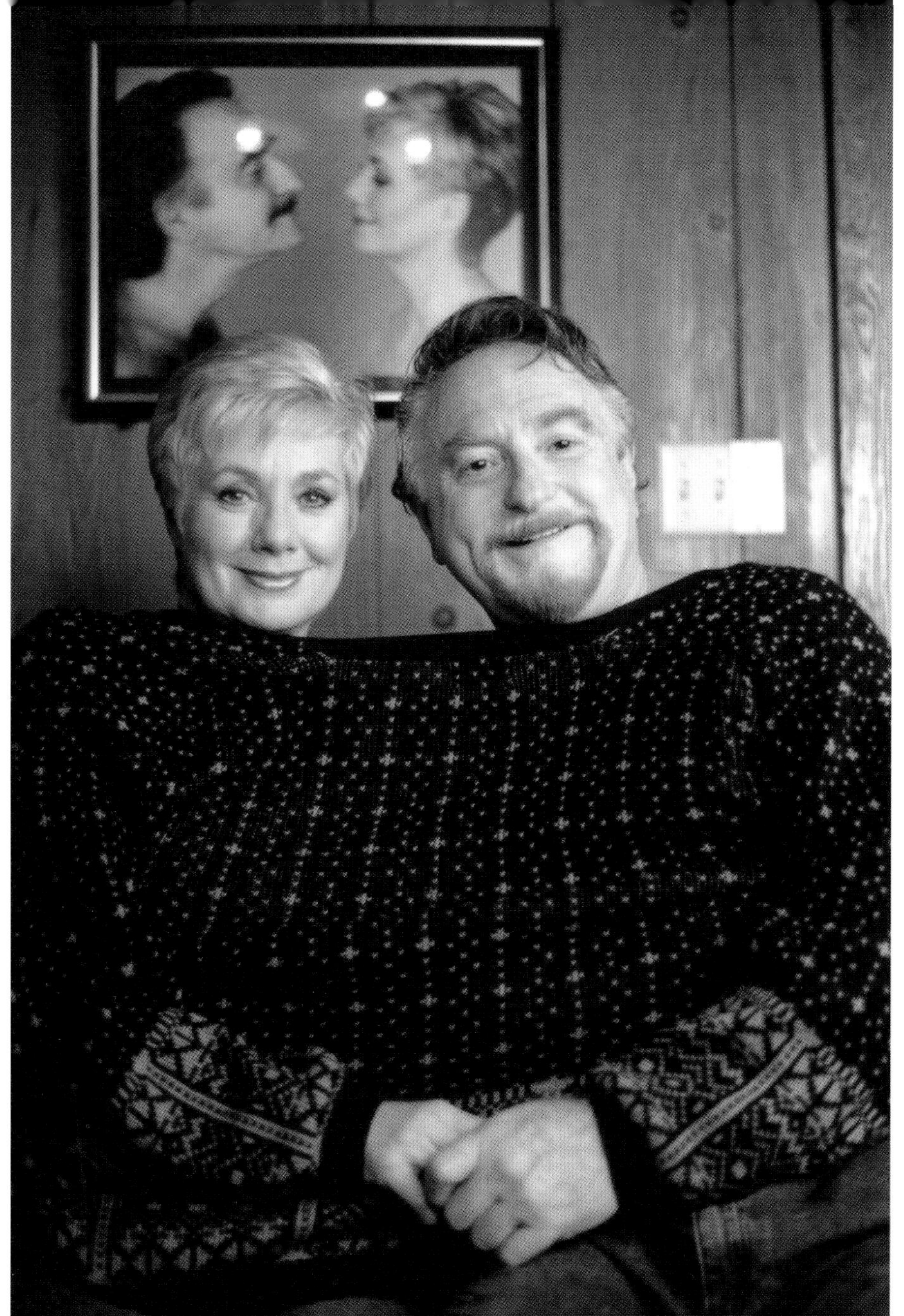

Opposite, clockwise from top:
Raphael Sbarge and wife, Lisa Akey
Orson Bean and wife, Ally Mills
Michael Chow and wife, Eva Chun
Tom Troupe and wife, Carole Cooke

This page:
Shirley Jones and Marty Ingels
Milo O'Shea and Kitty Sullivan O'Shea

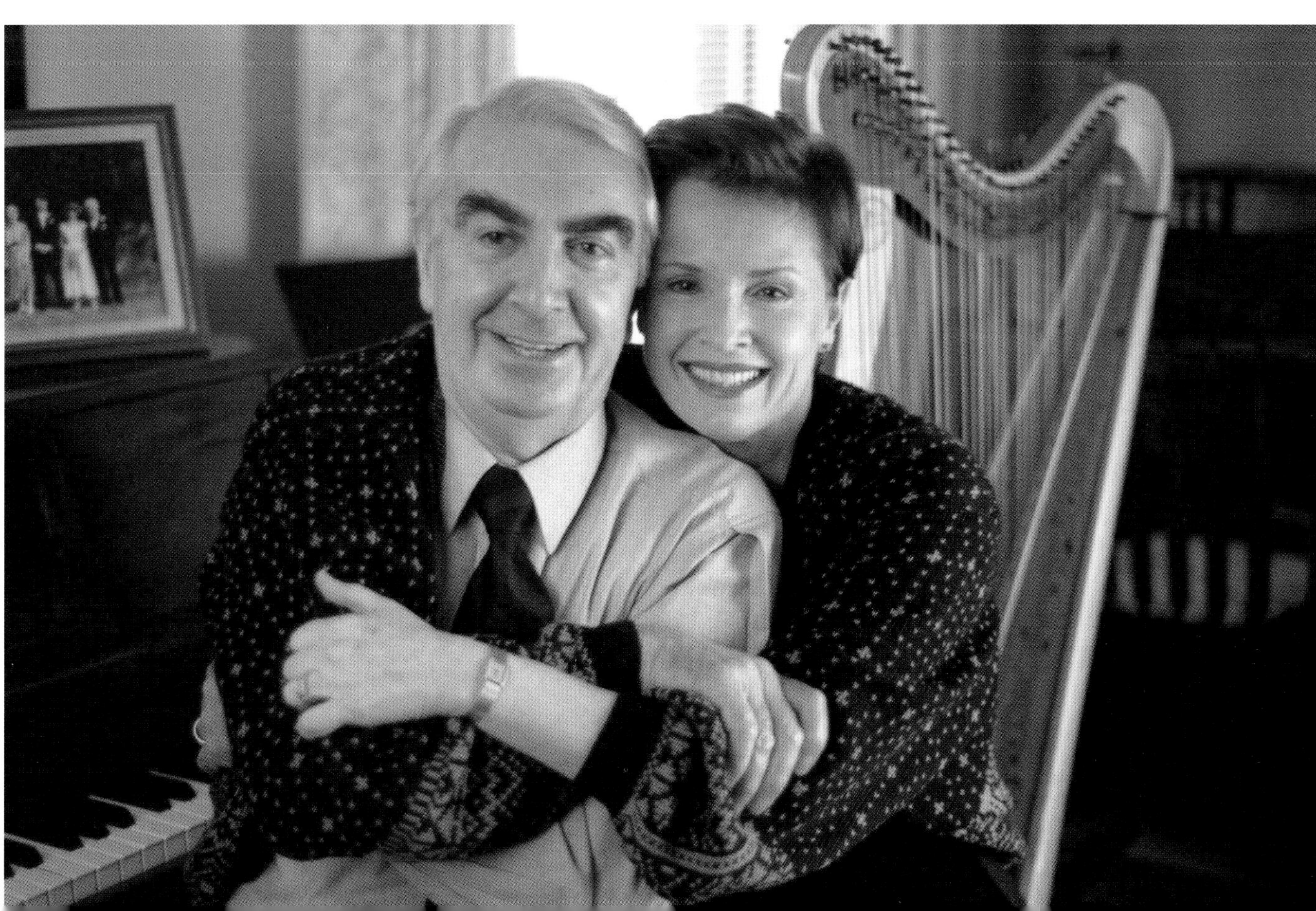

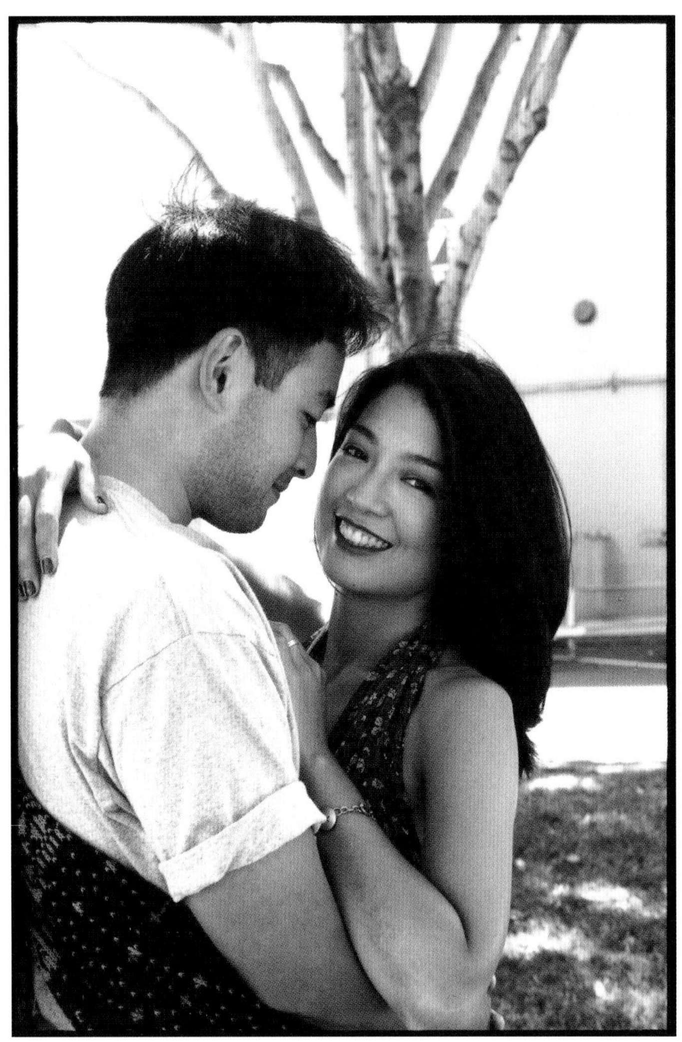

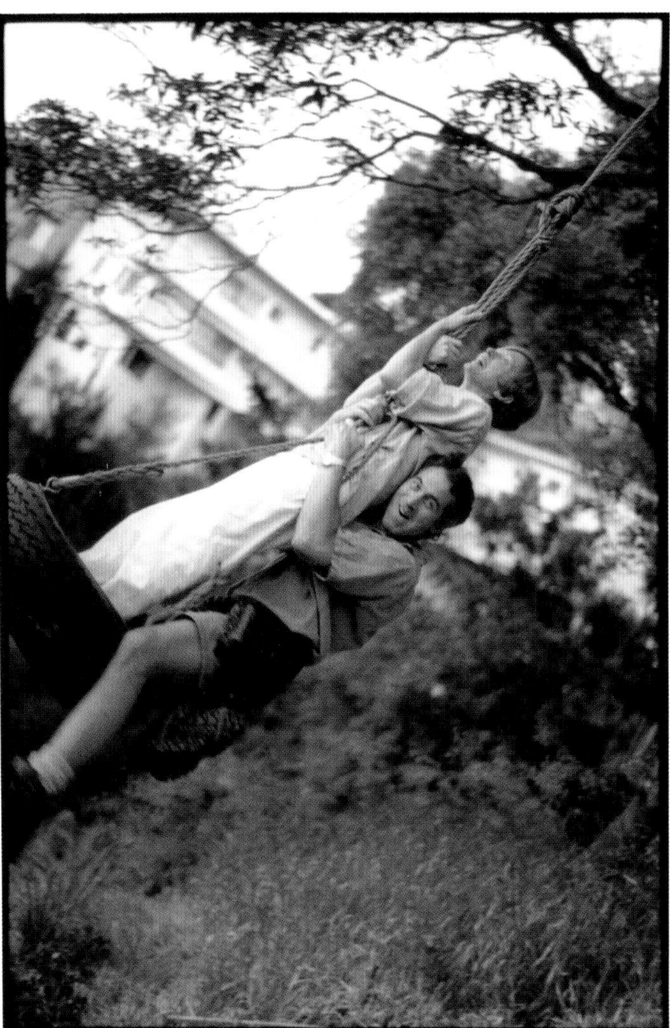

Ming-Na Wen and husband, Eric Michael Zee
Nancy Everhard and husband, Tom Amandes
Alex Deboe and Tracy Zahorian

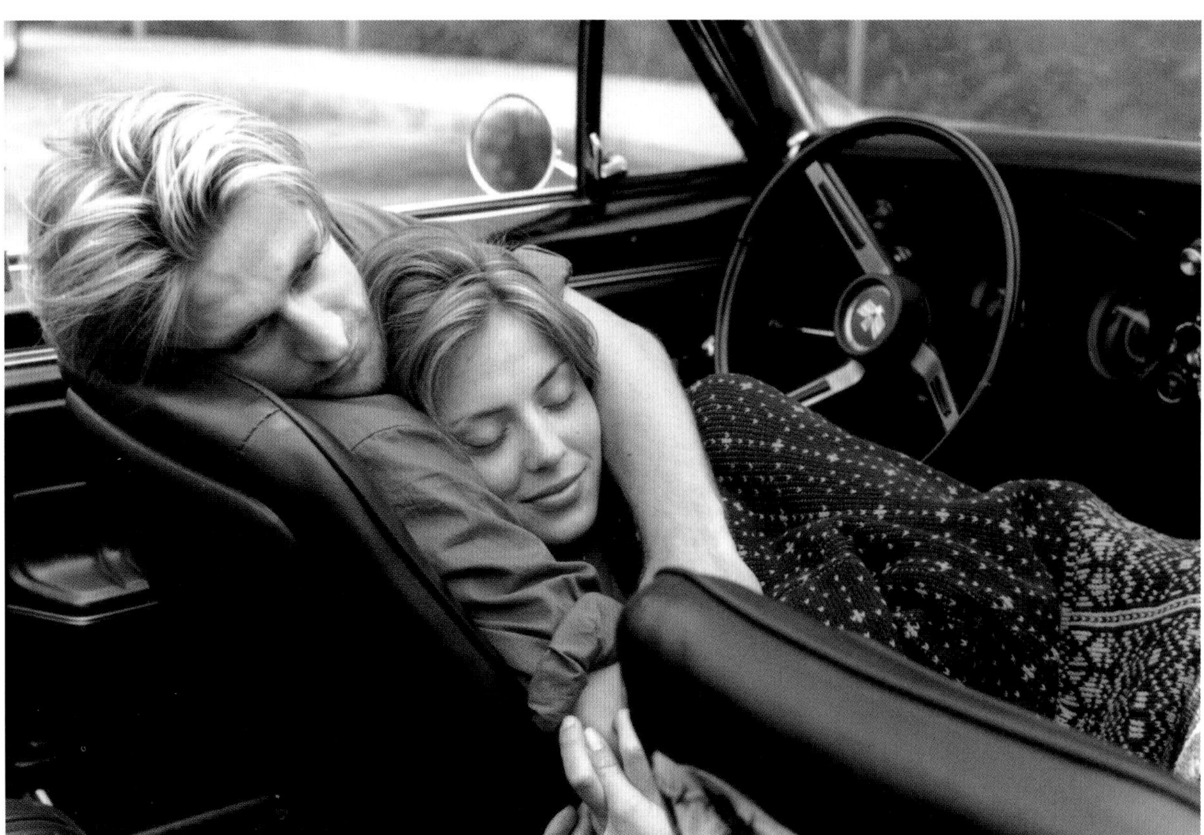

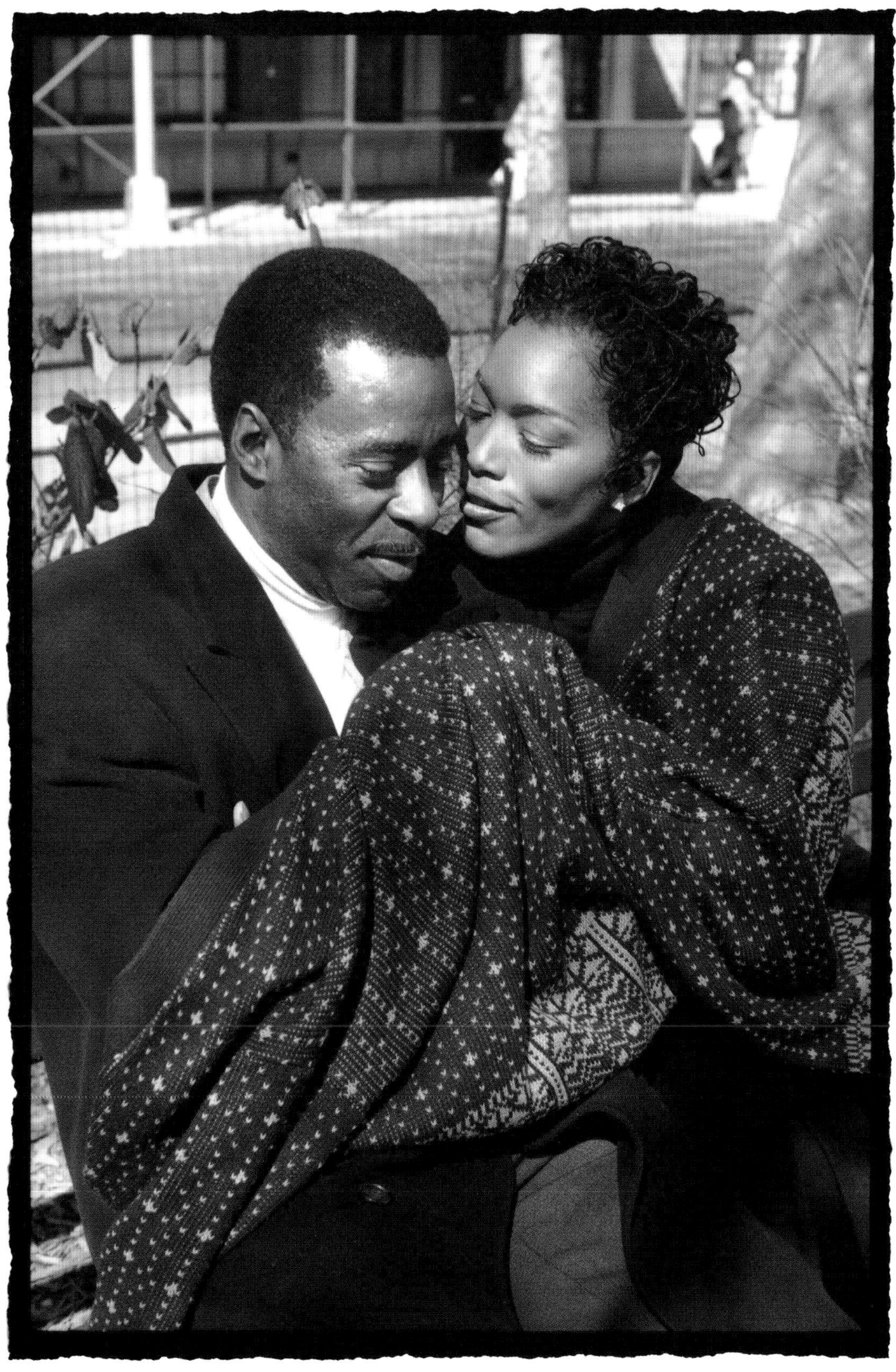

Courtney B. Vance and Angela Bassett

It was a cold winter day in New York when Courtney B. Vance and Angela Bassett posed for me in Washington Square Park. I was struck by the peace and calm strength that surrounded this couple. It was as if they were perfectly matched, as though they had always been destined to be together. I felt that they communicated without speaking, something you must know a person very well to do. I was also filled with respect for how he communicated with me man to man, silently, with gestures and facial expressions, letting me know how the shoot was going, when it had been running too long, and when his lady needed to go. I admire the way he protected her and what it says about love and couples and true partnership.

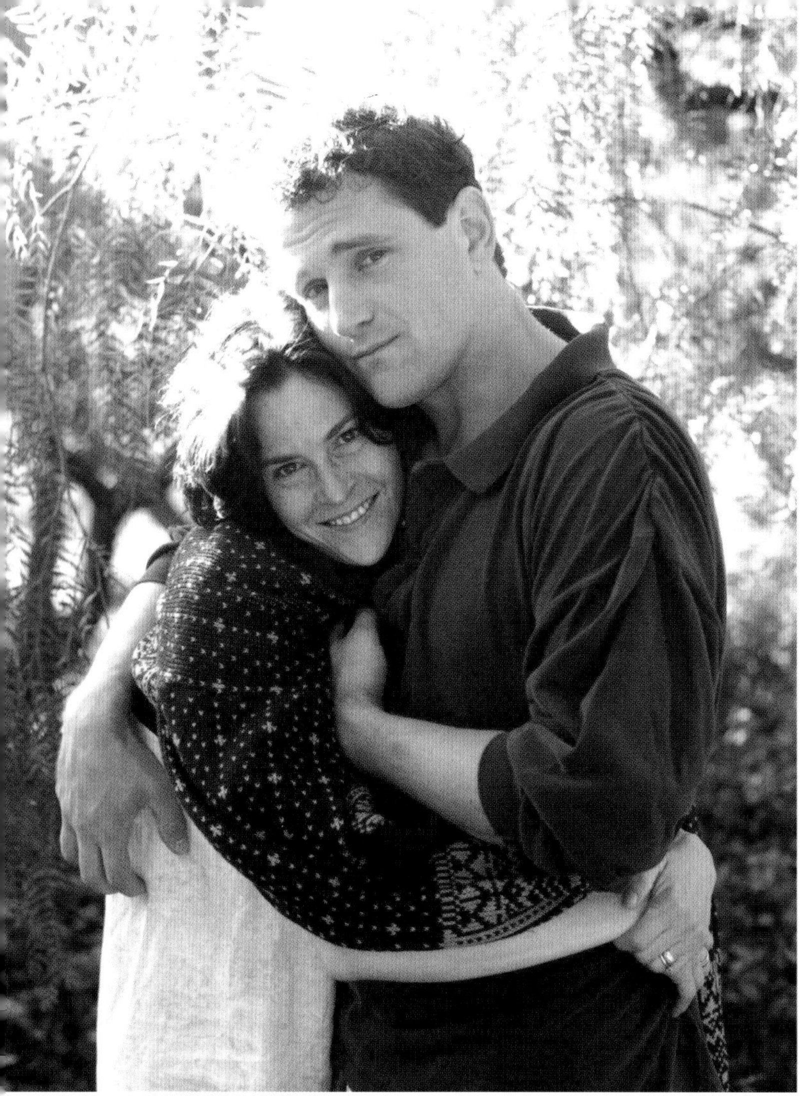

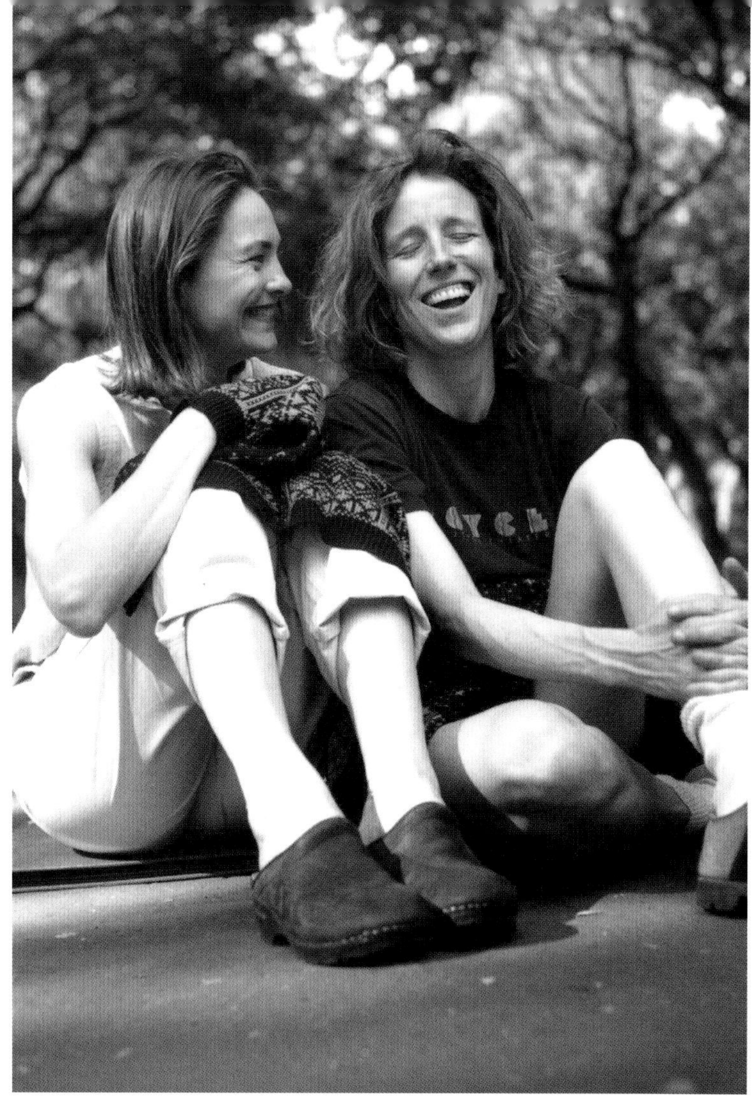

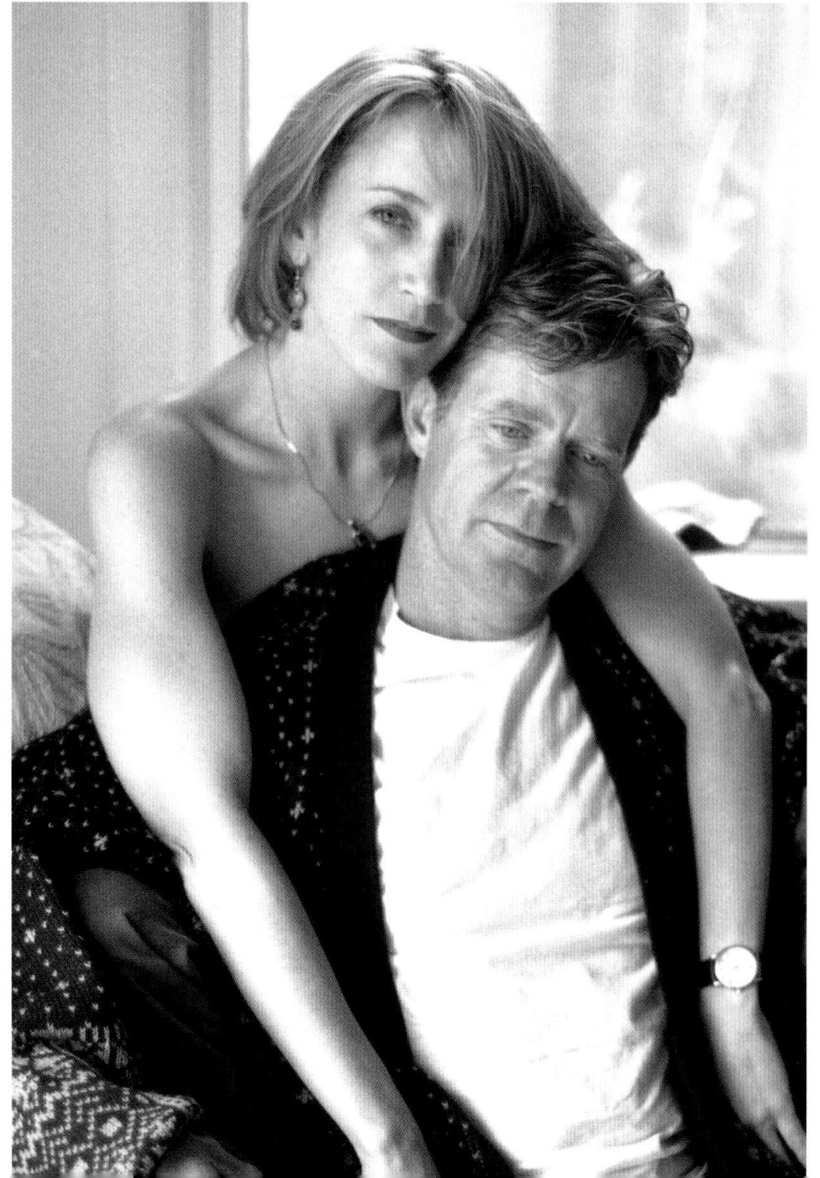

I am always amazed by the feeling I see in each photo that I do of a new couple. It is always powerful in its intimacy but it is never quite the same. Here, though, are three couples that I have ranked as the sexiest with whom I have ever worked. Ally Sheedy and David Lansbury were sexy because of the longevity of their relationship and the way she leaned on him; William H. Macy and Felicity Huffman were sexy because they were about to be married and could not keep their hands off each other; Cherry Jones and Mary O'Connor were celebrating ten years at about the same time that Pat and I were celebrating our ten-year anniversary, and when they looked at each other I could see that they were still as in love as we were. Sexy is as sexy does.

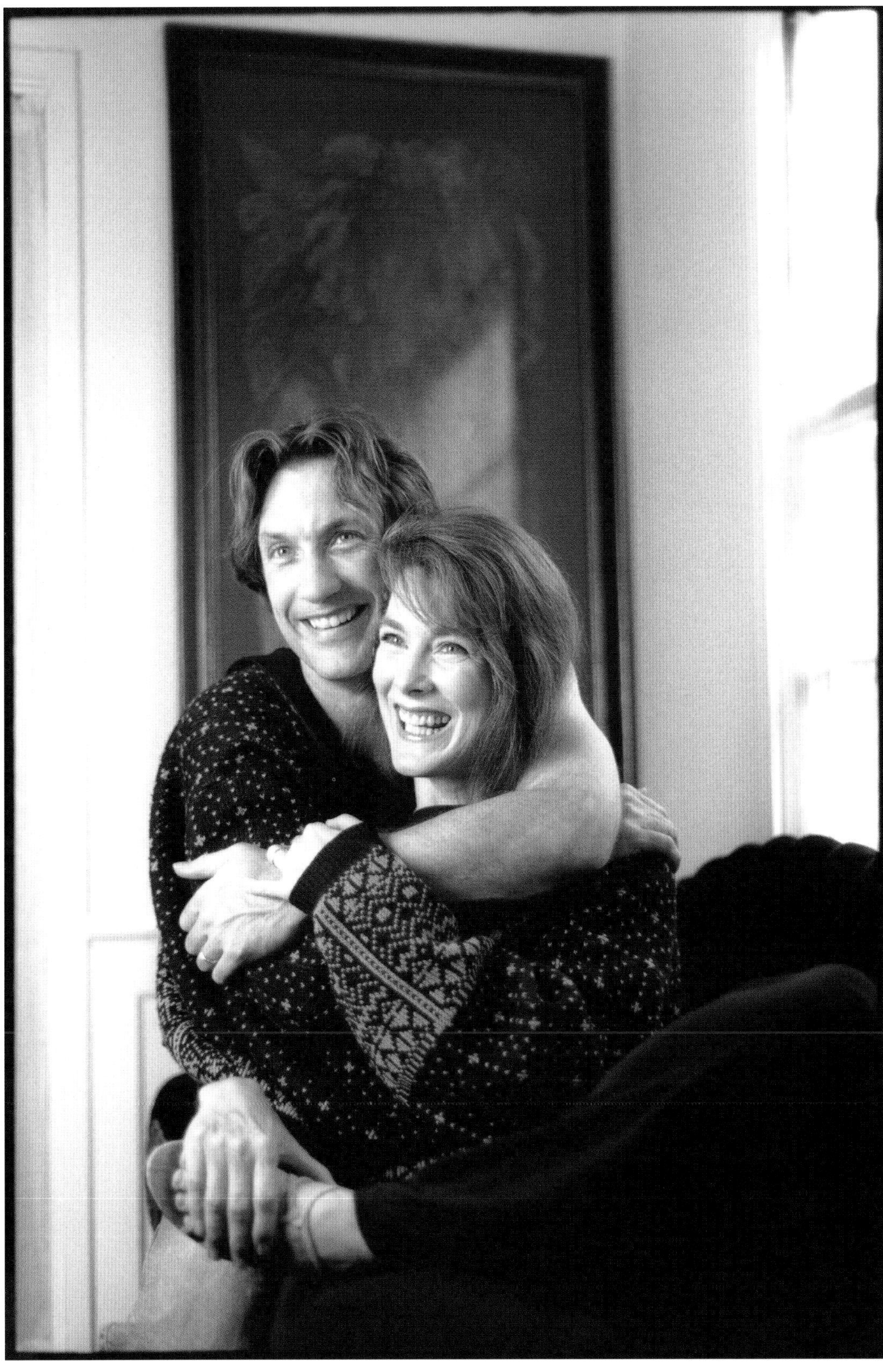

Opposite, clockwise from top left:
Ally Sheedy and David Lansbury
Cherry Jones and Mary O'Connor
William H. Macy and Felicity Huffman

This page:
Joe Kell and Valerie Mahaffey

Joe Kell and Valerie Mahaffey invited me to spend an afternoon and a night with them. They invited their friend Rebecca Staab over, and we all had this great meal and hung out and laughed. I felt like I had made these great friends. It was one of those truly satisfying photo shoots. What I remember primarily about the shoot was how radiant Valerie was, and I was proud when I found that the photographs I took reflected that. It was incredibly eye-opening when my new friends notified me that they were pregnant, and according to the math done by the doctor, the baby had possibly been conceived the night before our photo shoot. I have always loved this photo and the miracle of their first pregnancy.

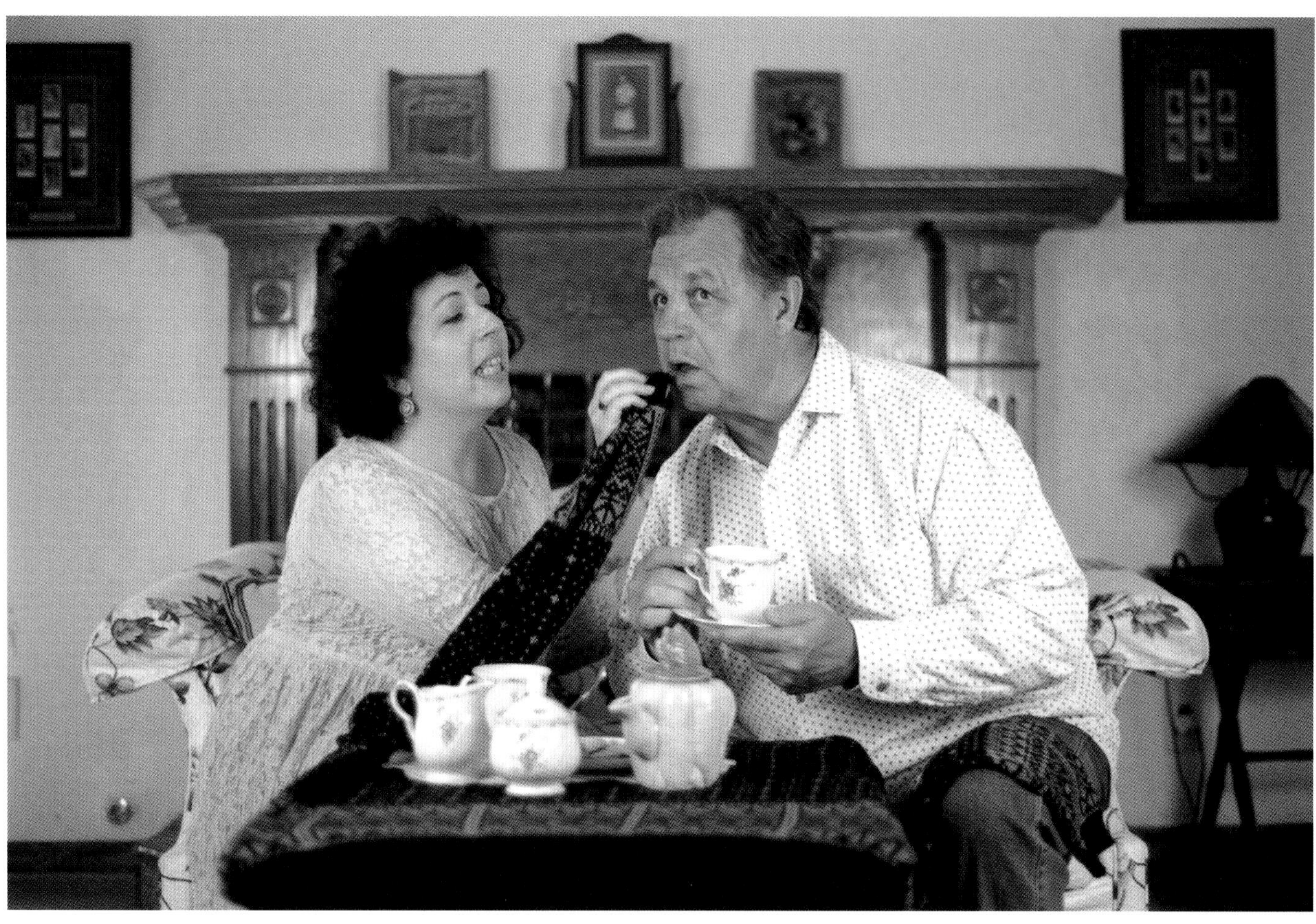

Above: Winnie Holzman with husband, Paul Dooley; *below:* Dan Lipman and spouse, Ron Cowen

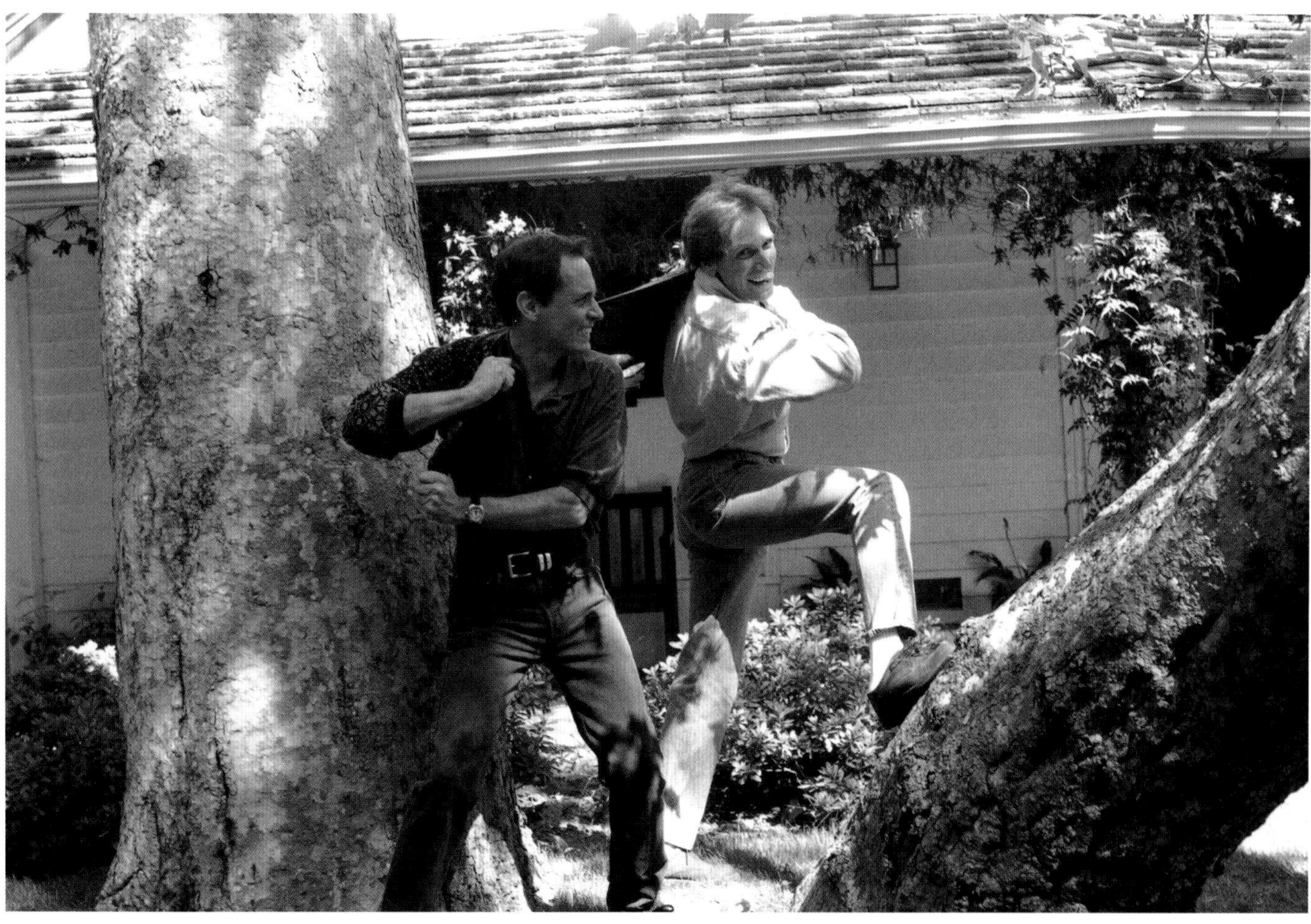

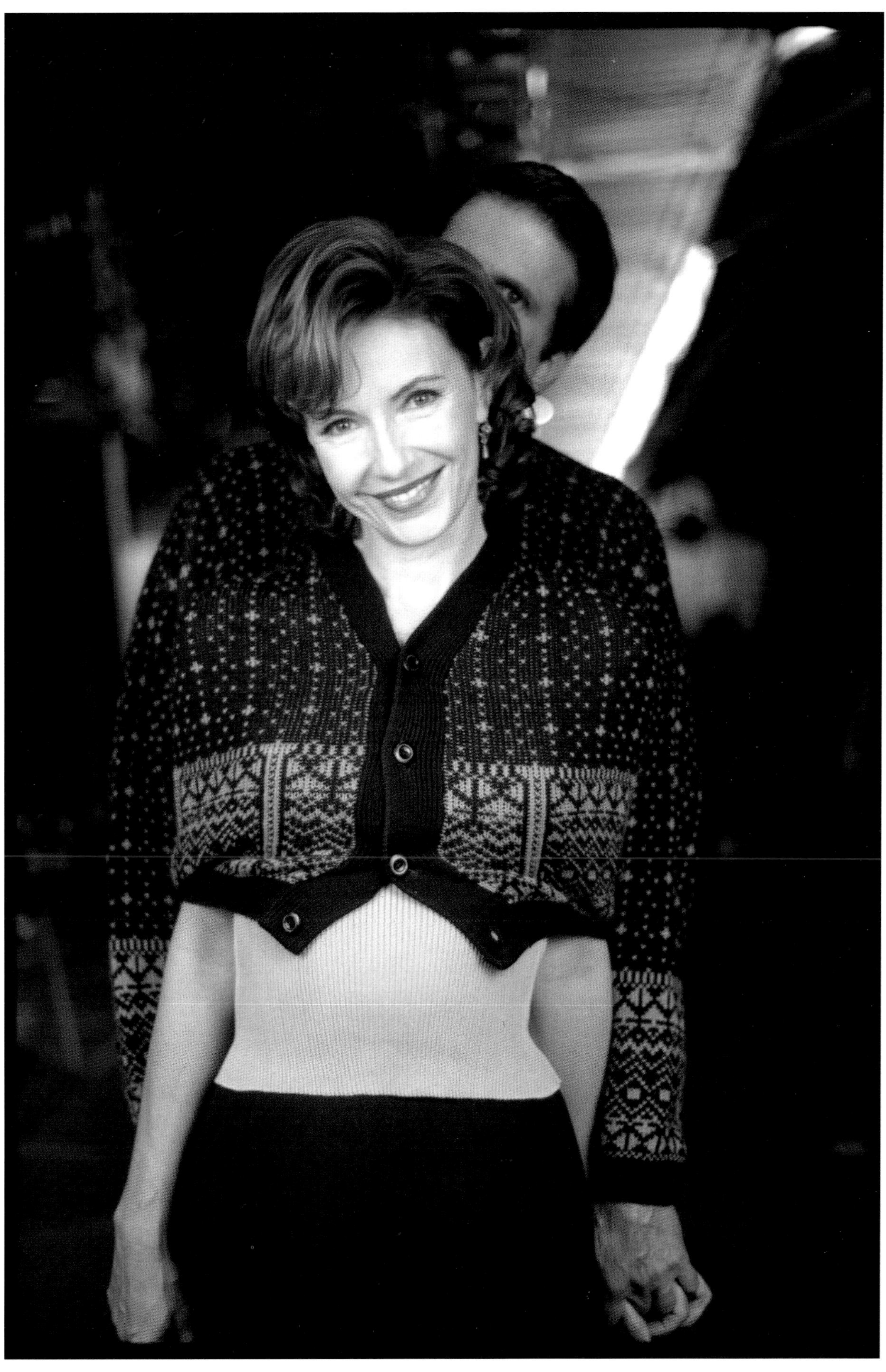

Mary Steenburgen with husband and full-time cutup, Ted Danson

THE SWEATER AT PLAY—*in which the sweater explores the child within*

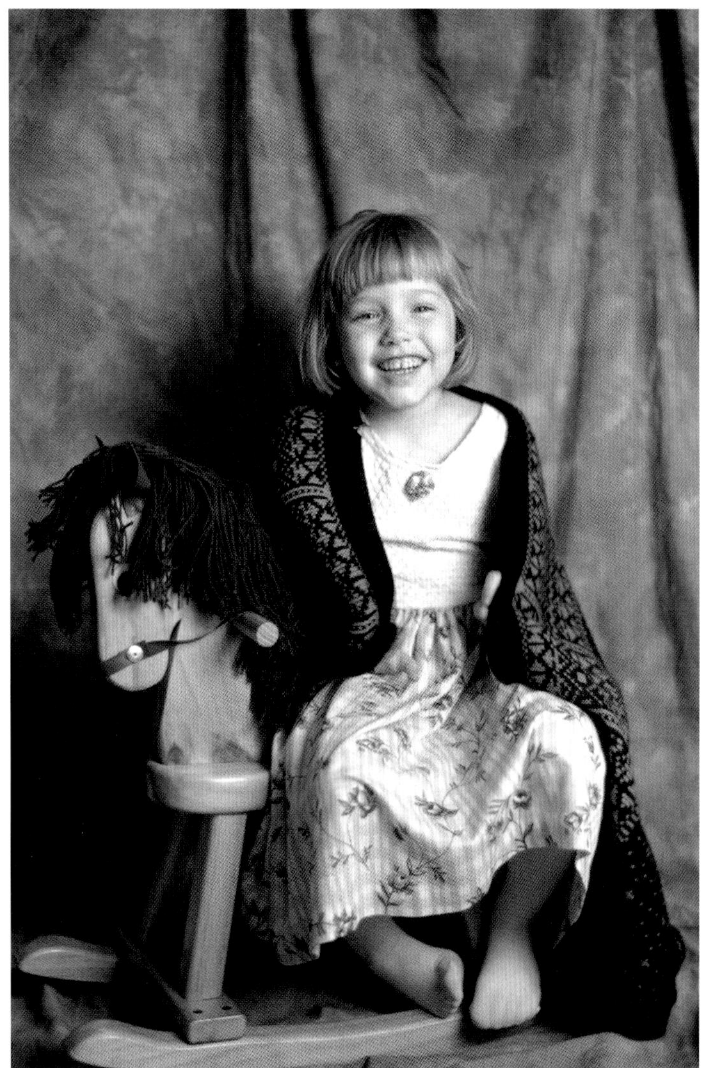

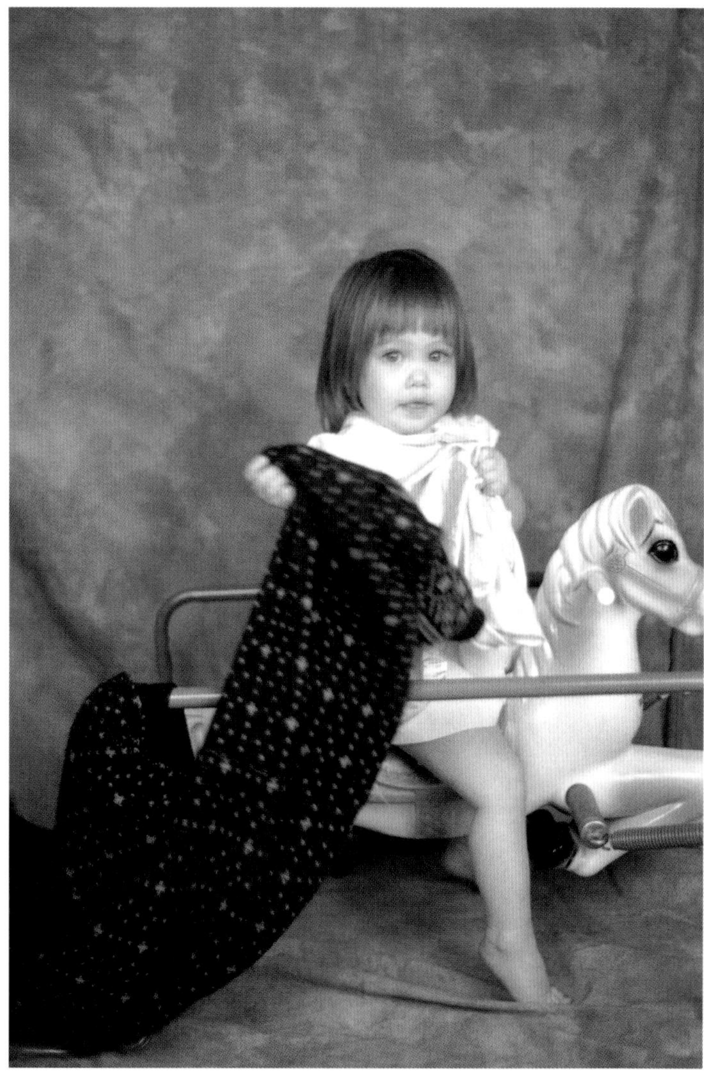

Erin and Alex—yes, they are sisters

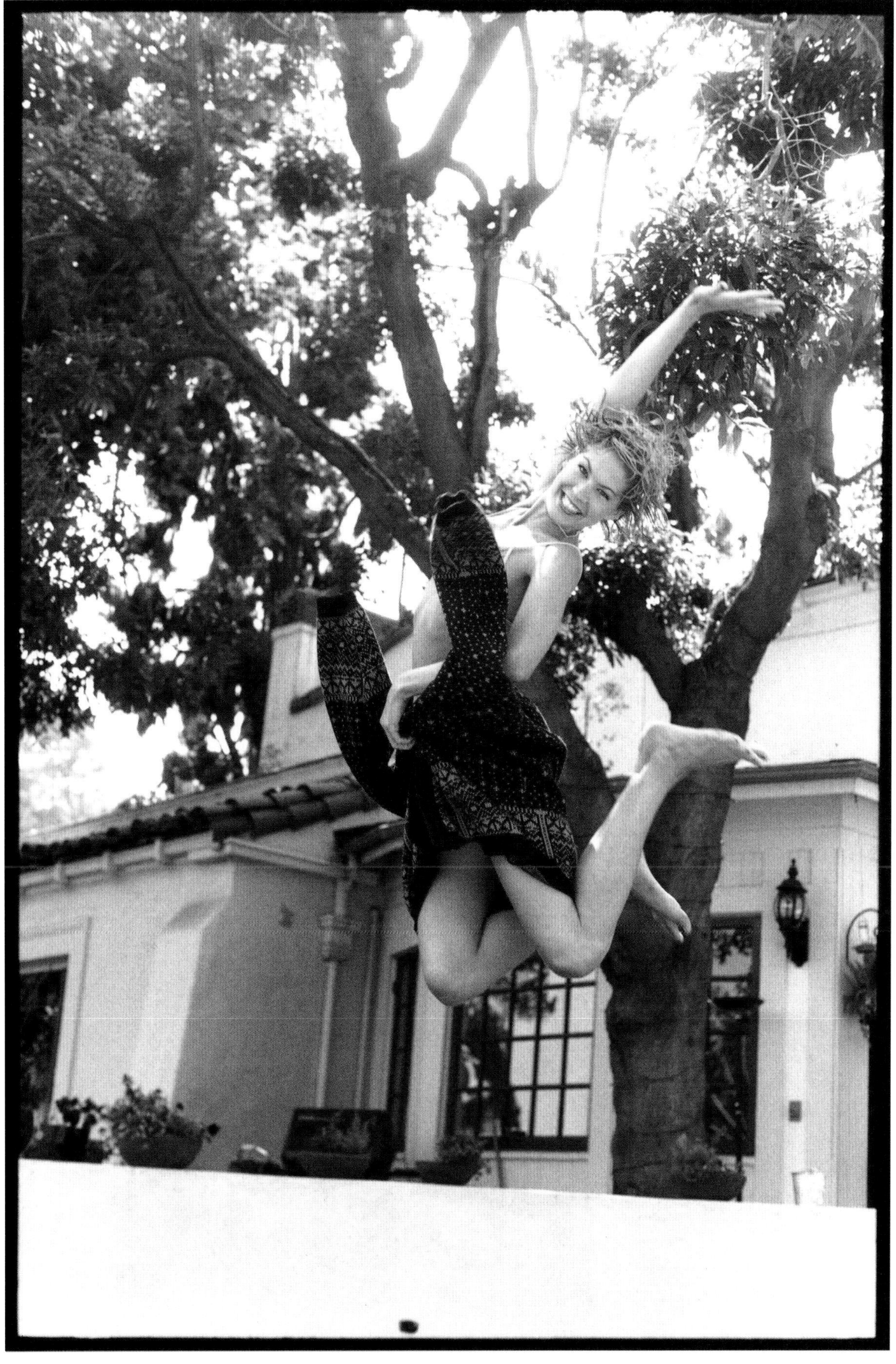

Jenna Elfman

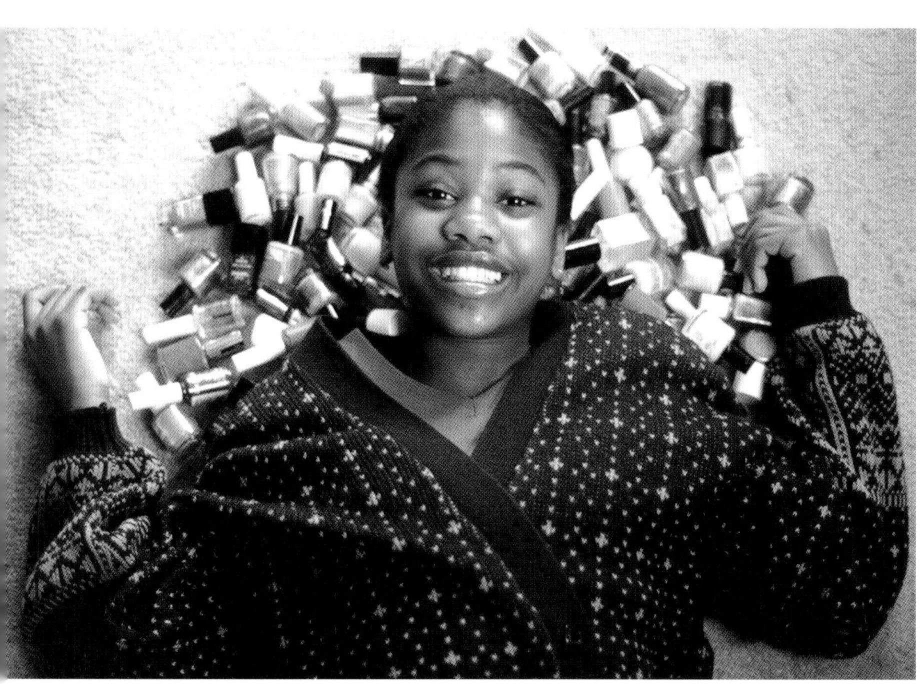

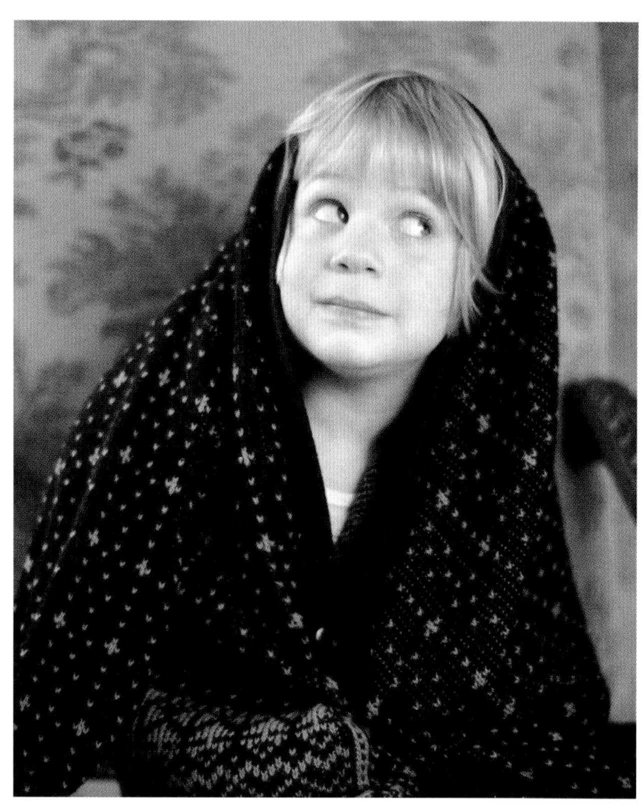

Clockwise from top left:
Vanessa Lee Chester
Autumn
Two Amandas
Madylin Sweetin

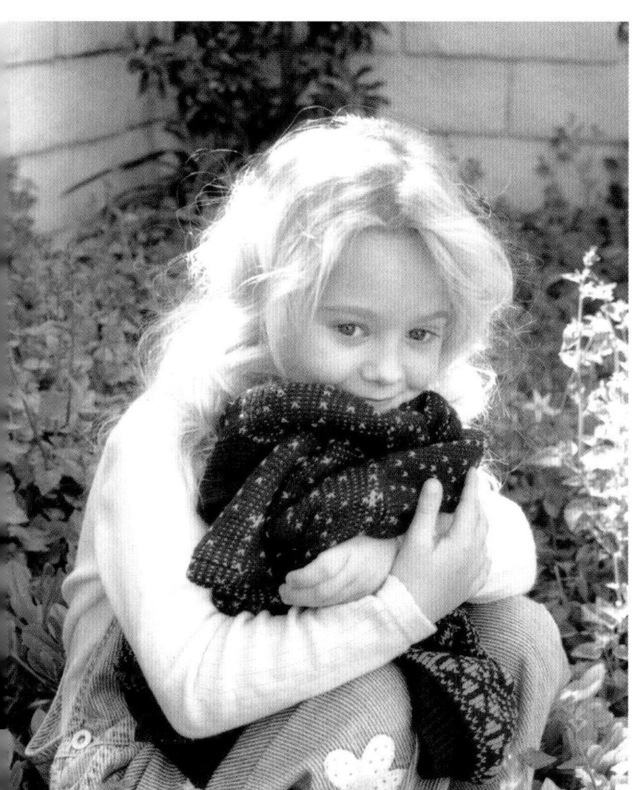

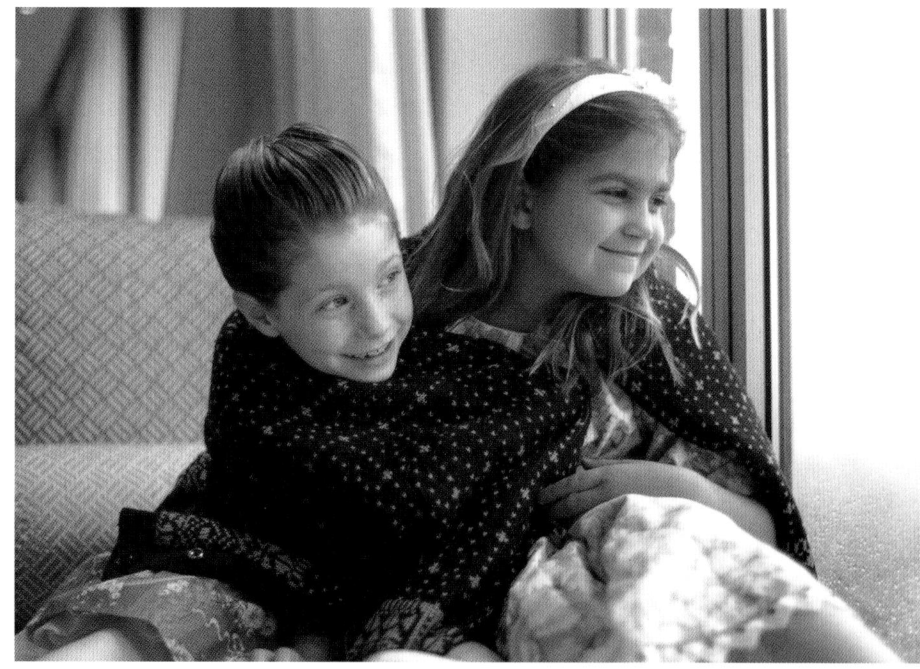

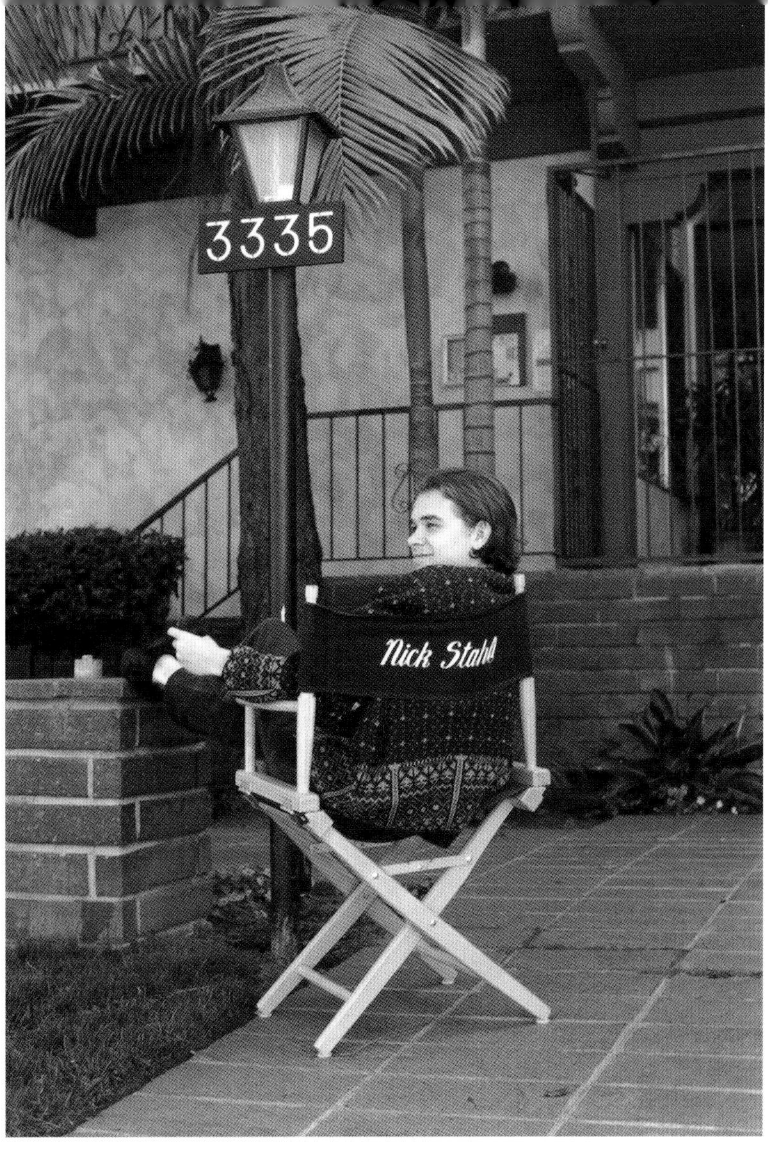

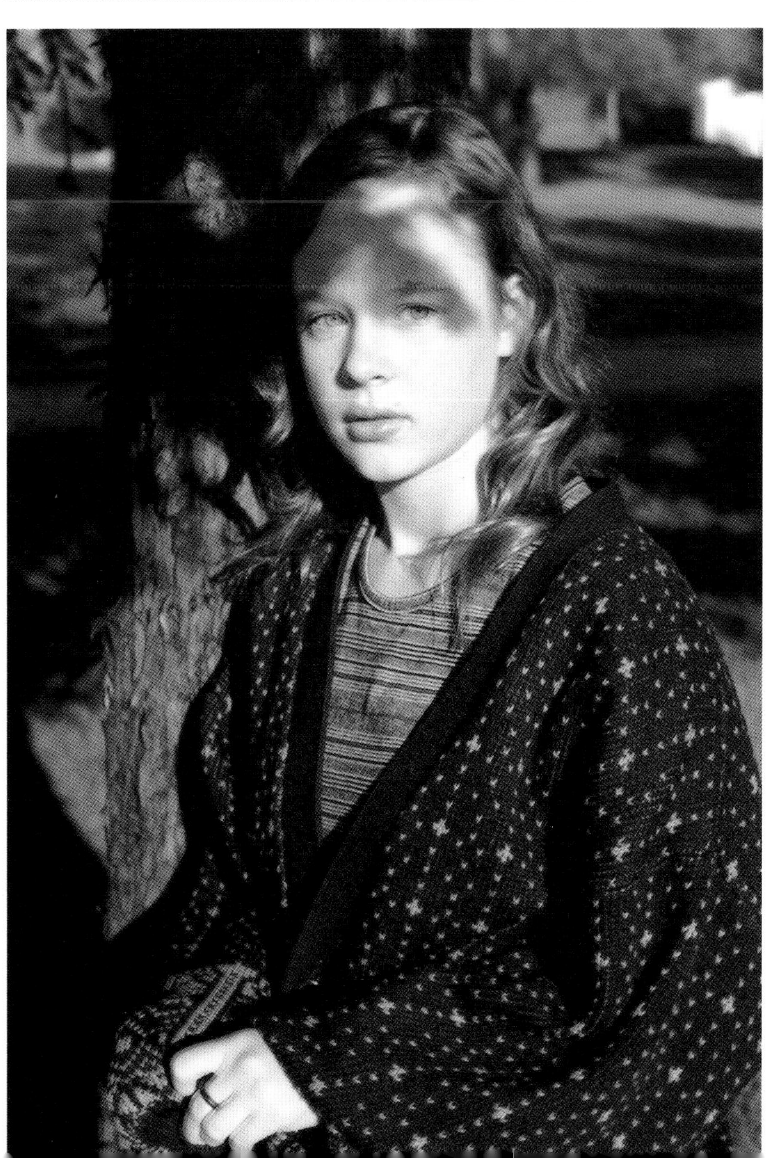

Nick Stahl

Thora Birch

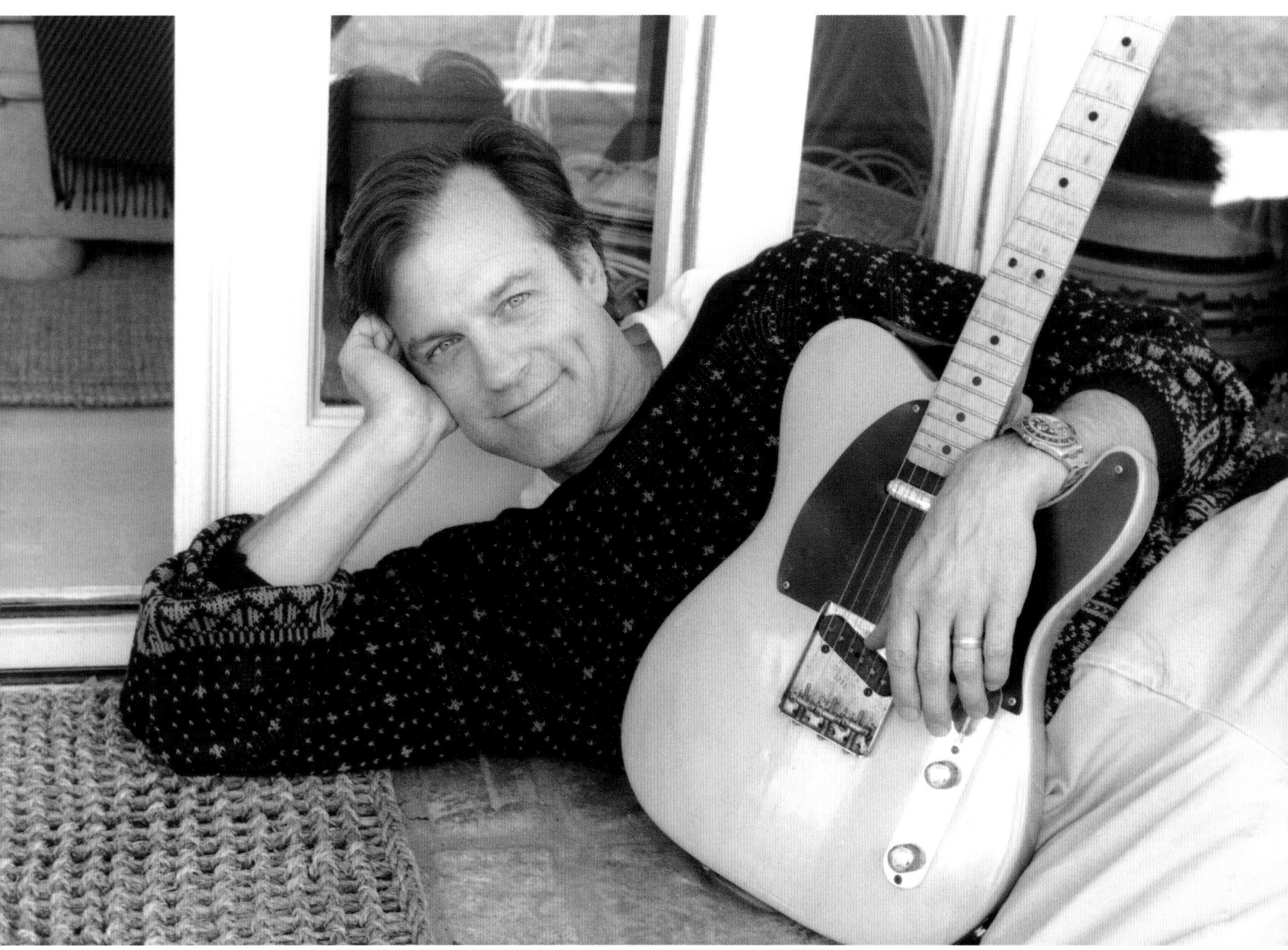

Stephen Collins

A friend avowed to me that Stephen Collins was the most attractive man in Hollywood—a town that boasts a high population of babes. Okay, she couldn't have been more right. Know what, though?

It all comes from within.

Almost.

 Opposite, clockwise from top left: Scott Patterson, Stephen Tobolowski, Nate Richert, John Austin Miller

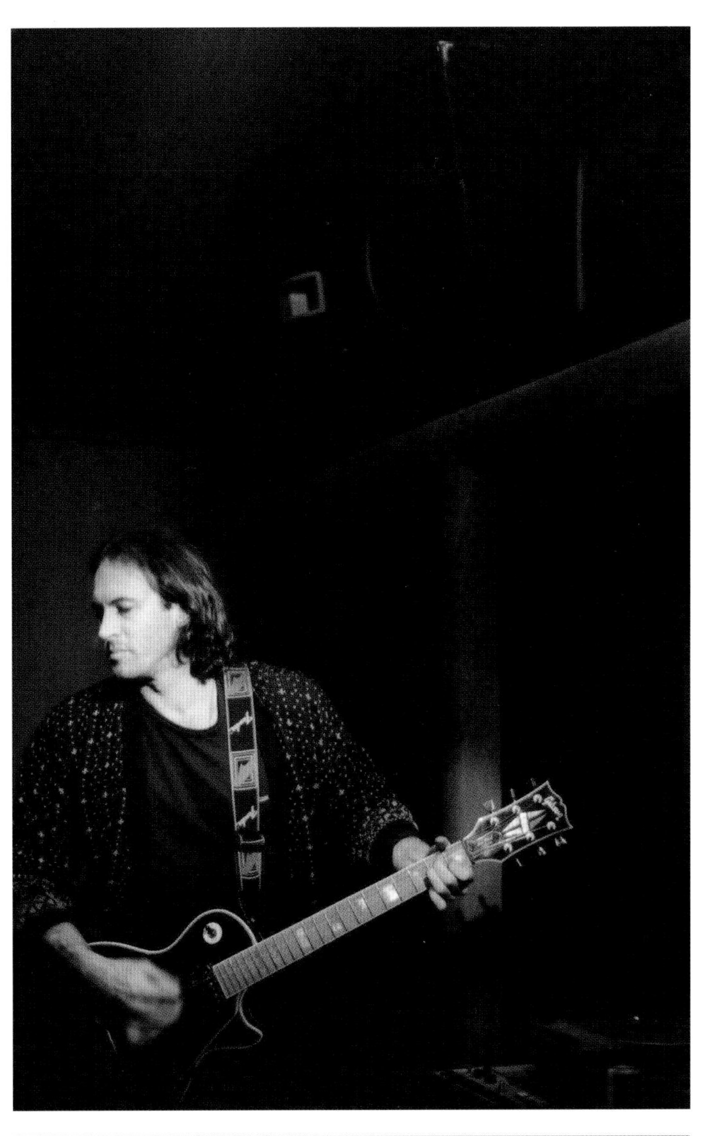
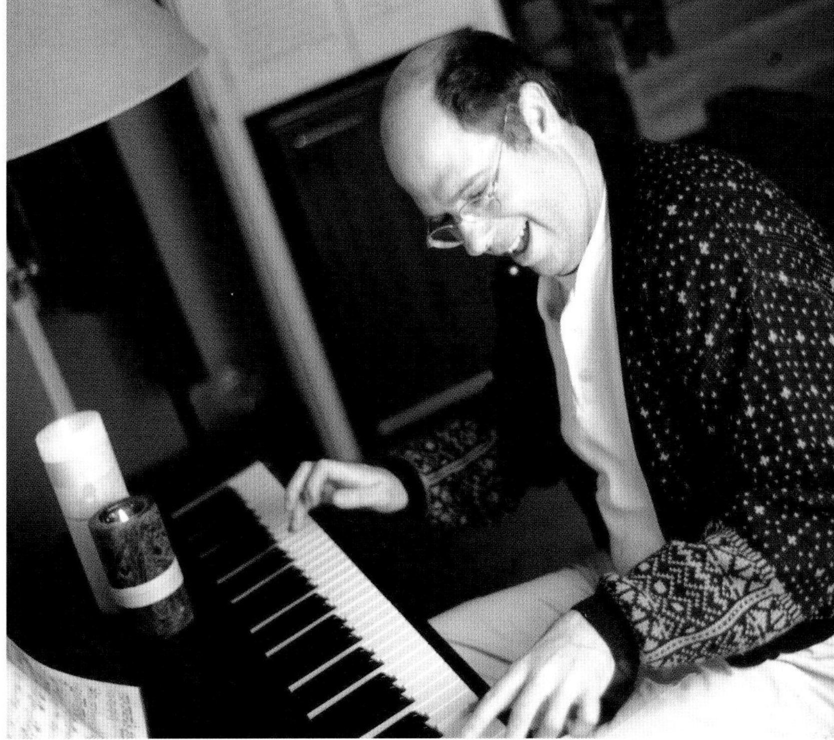
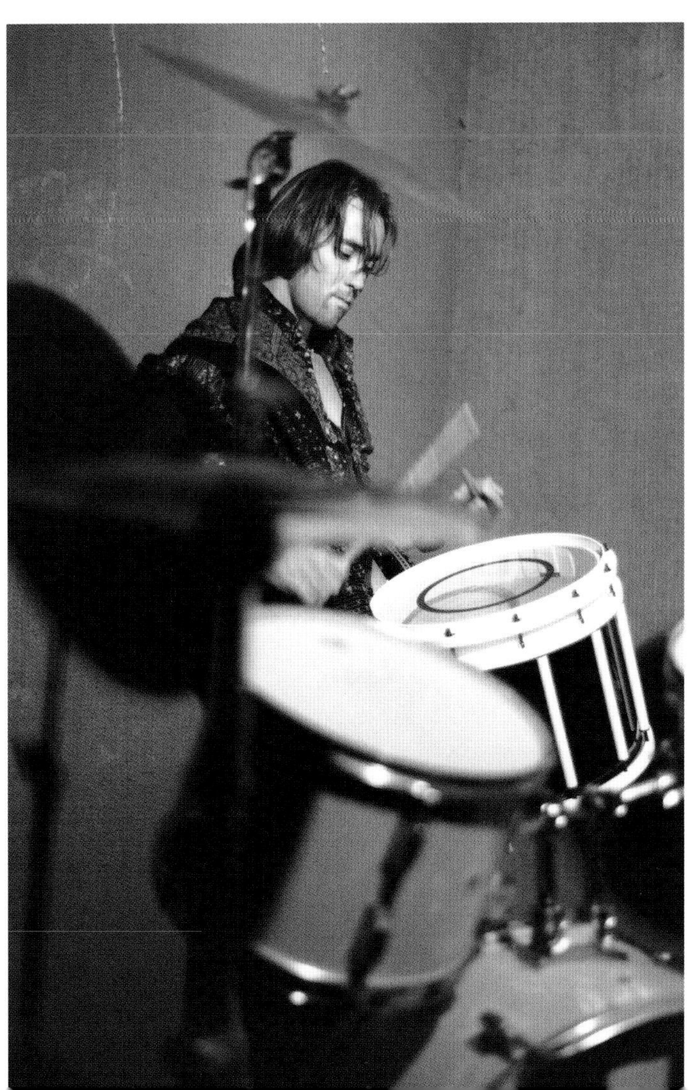
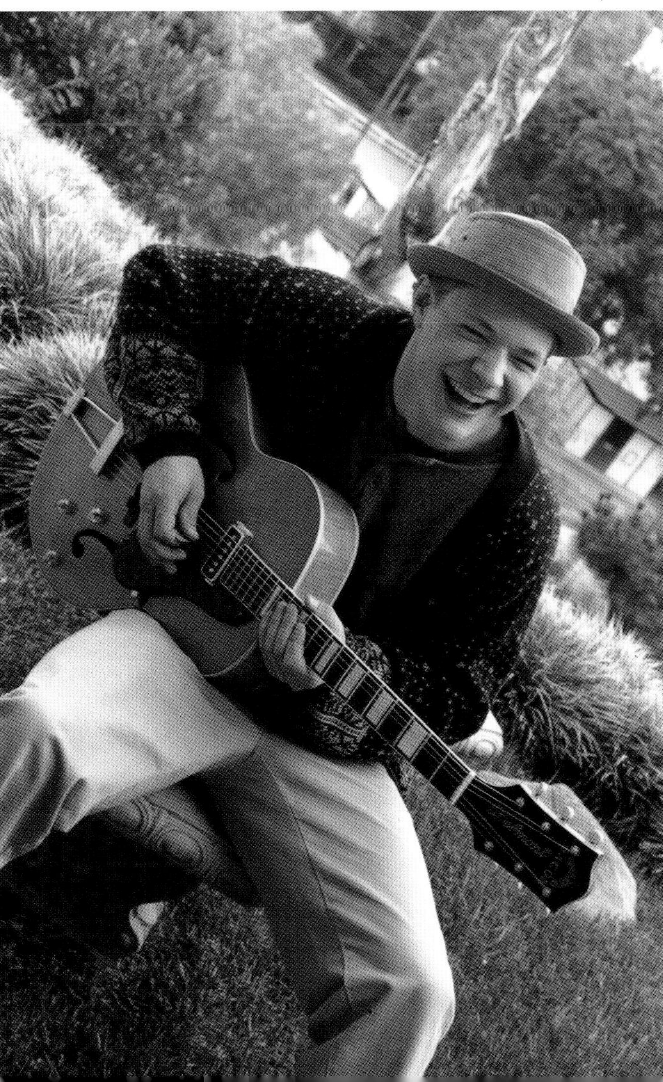

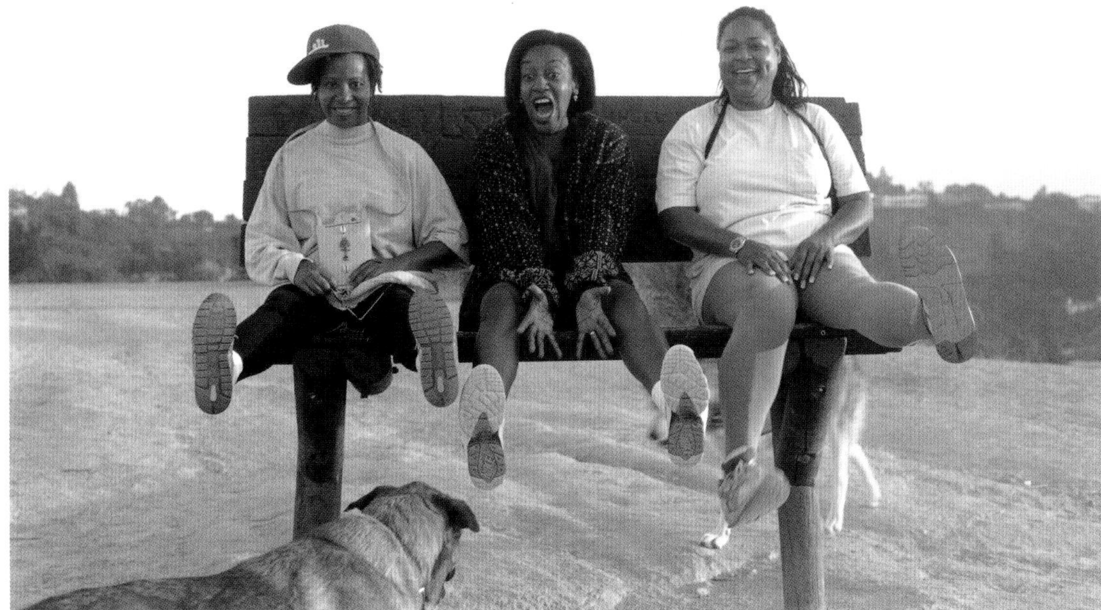

Conni Marie Brazelton, CCH Pounder, Francesca Roberts hiking in Runyon Canyon

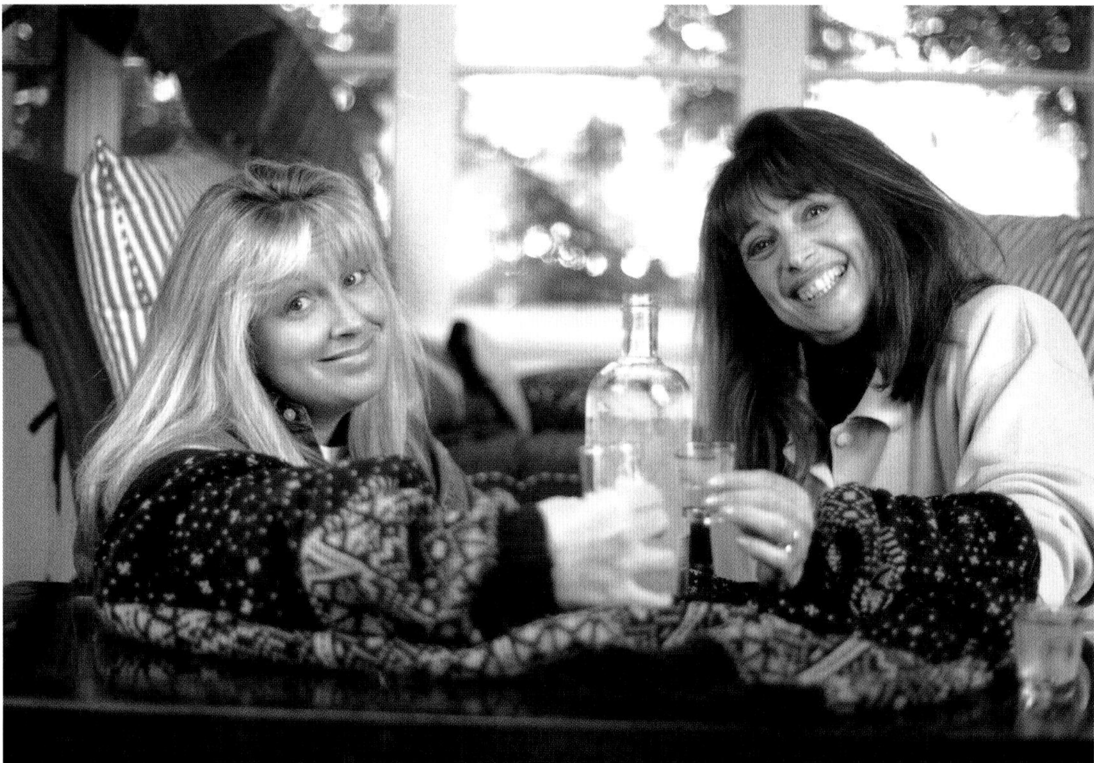

The Mommies: Marilyn Kentz and Caryl Kristensen

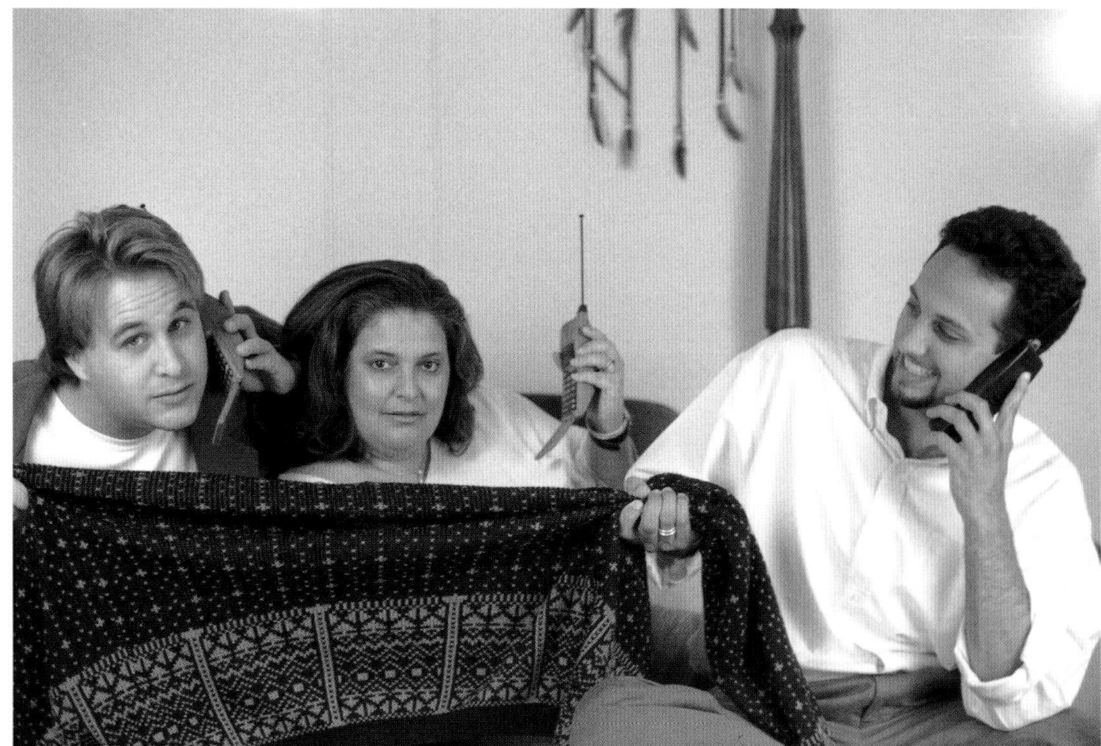

Steven Simon, Hillary Sachs, and Mark Armstrong

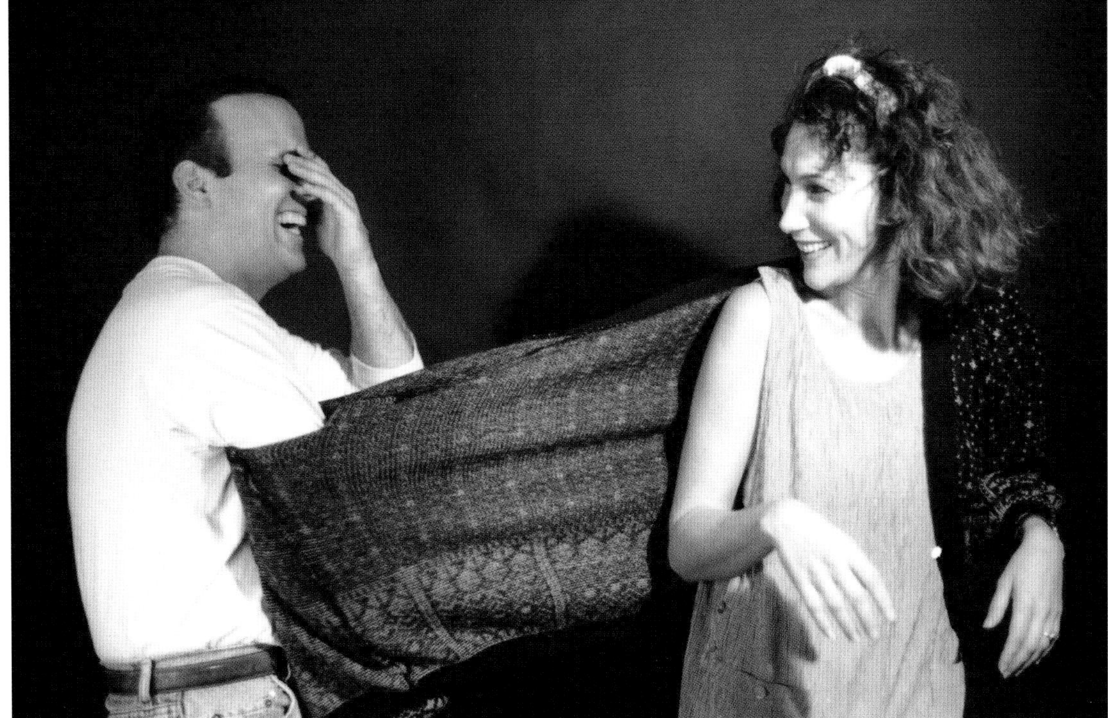

Scott Ellis
and Randy Graff

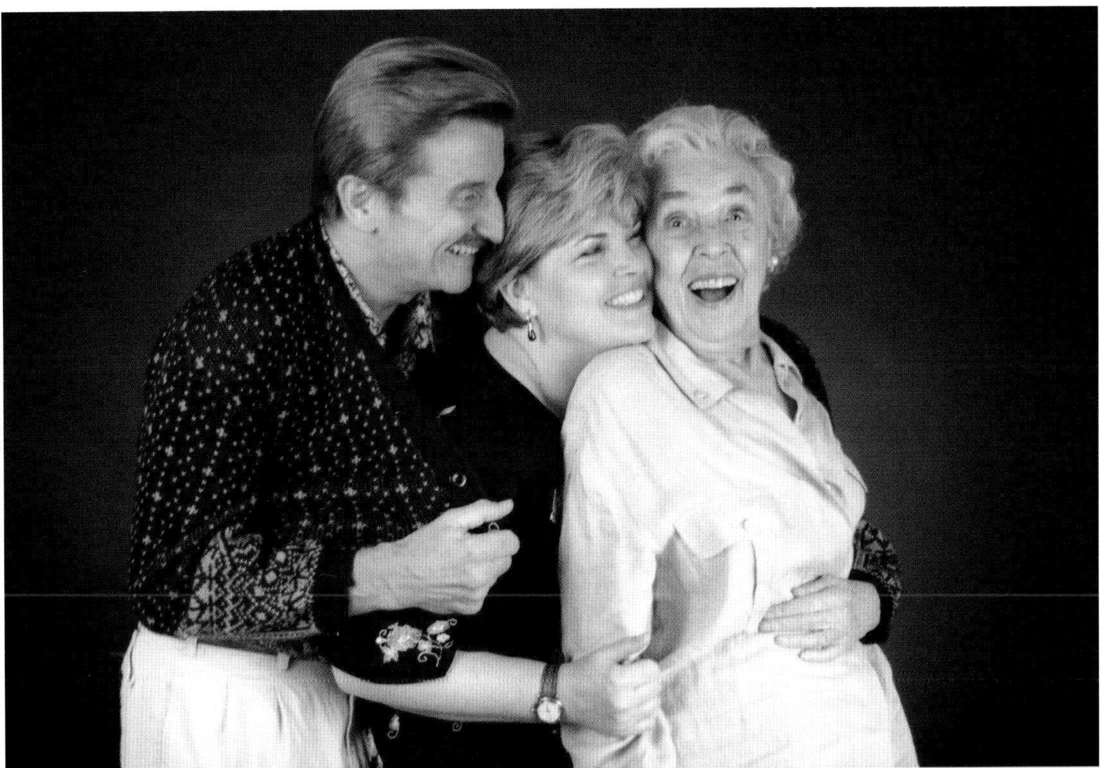

Larry Bryggman,
Debra Monk,
Anne Pitoniak

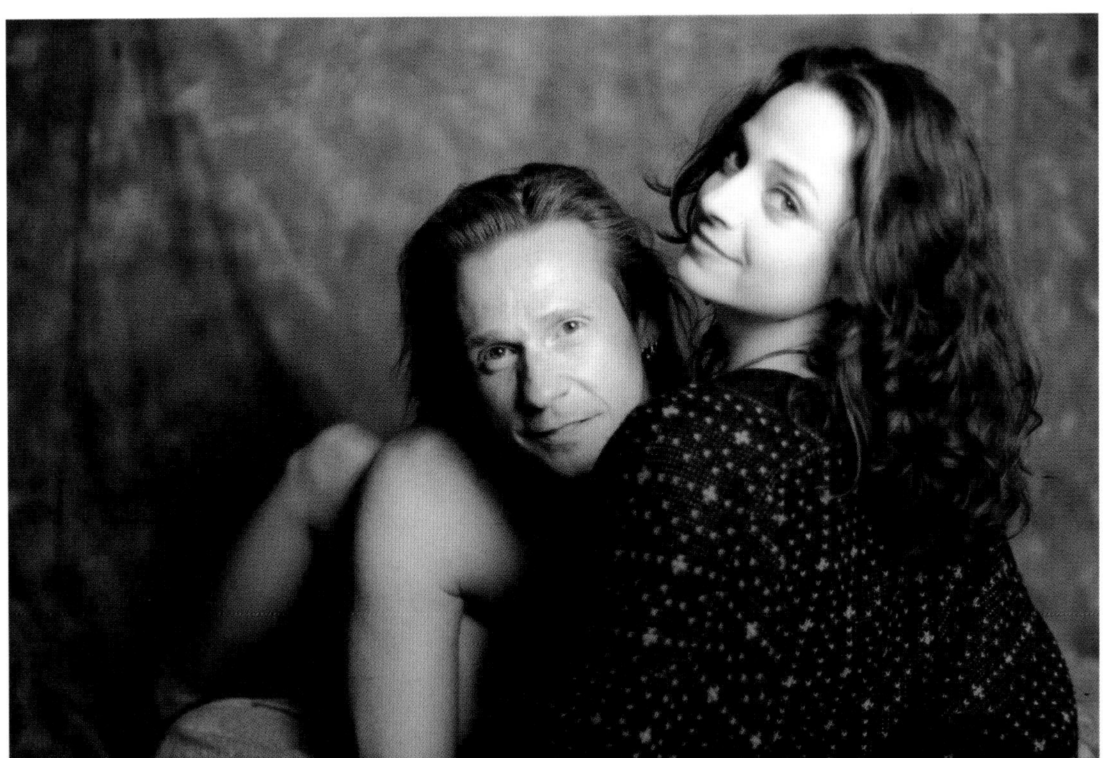

Dennis Christopher
and Katy Selverstone

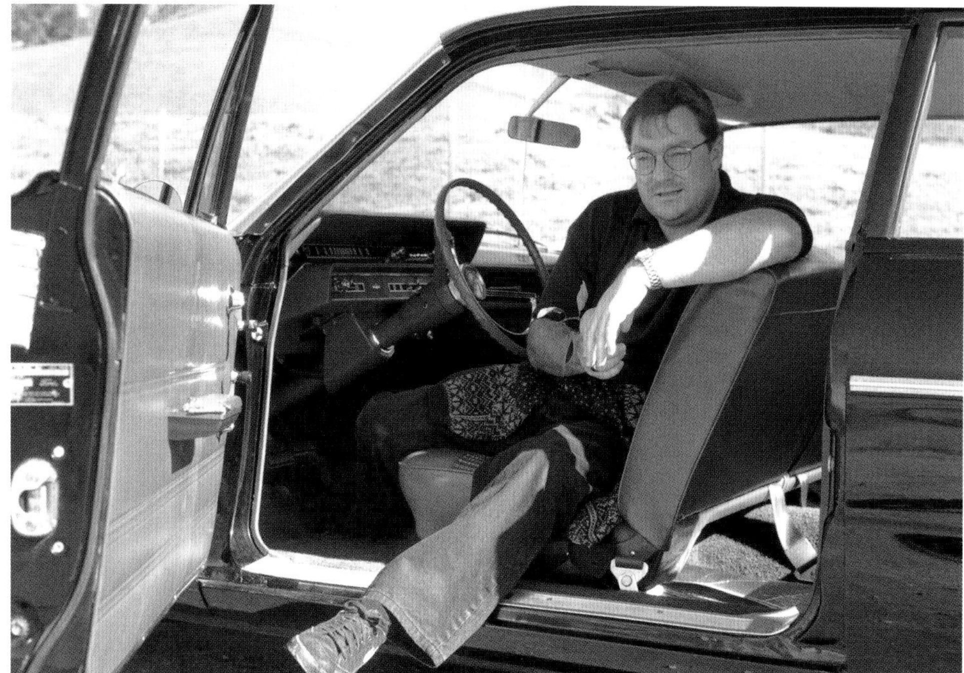

Stephen Root

Perry King

Scott Vickaryous

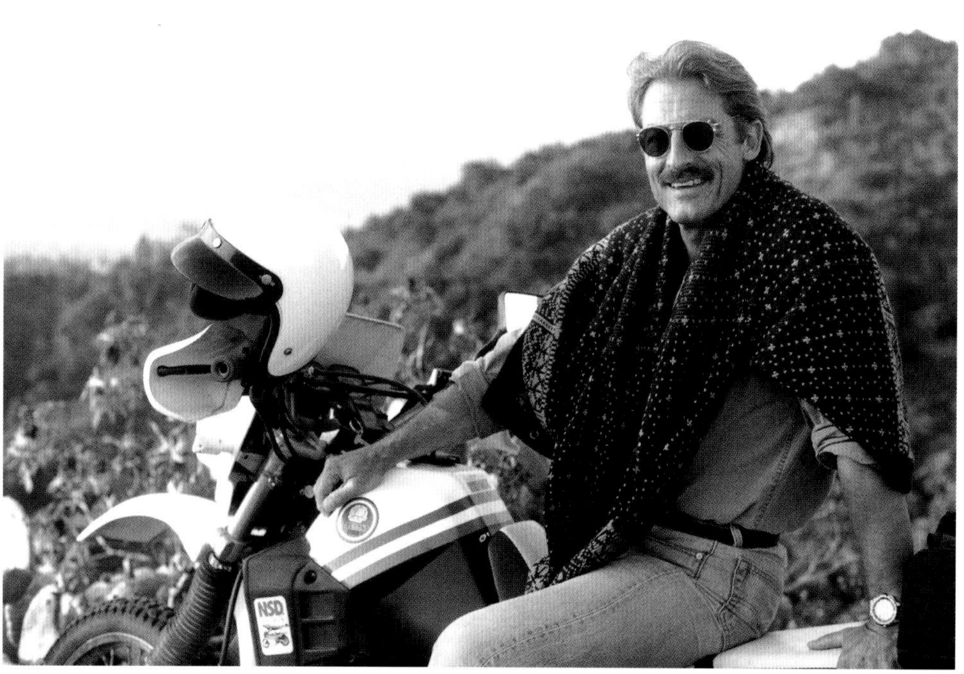

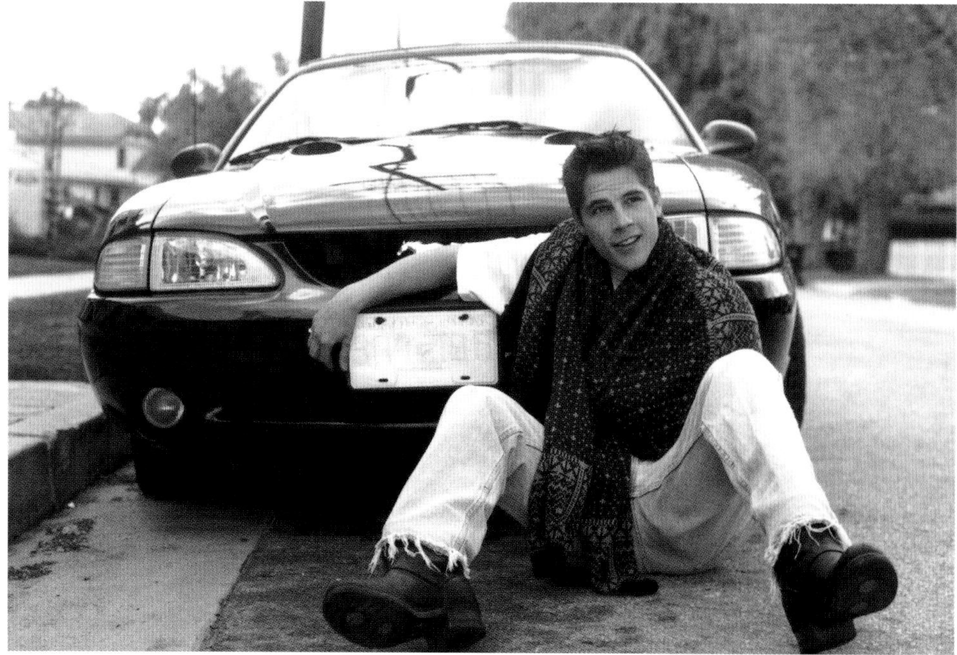

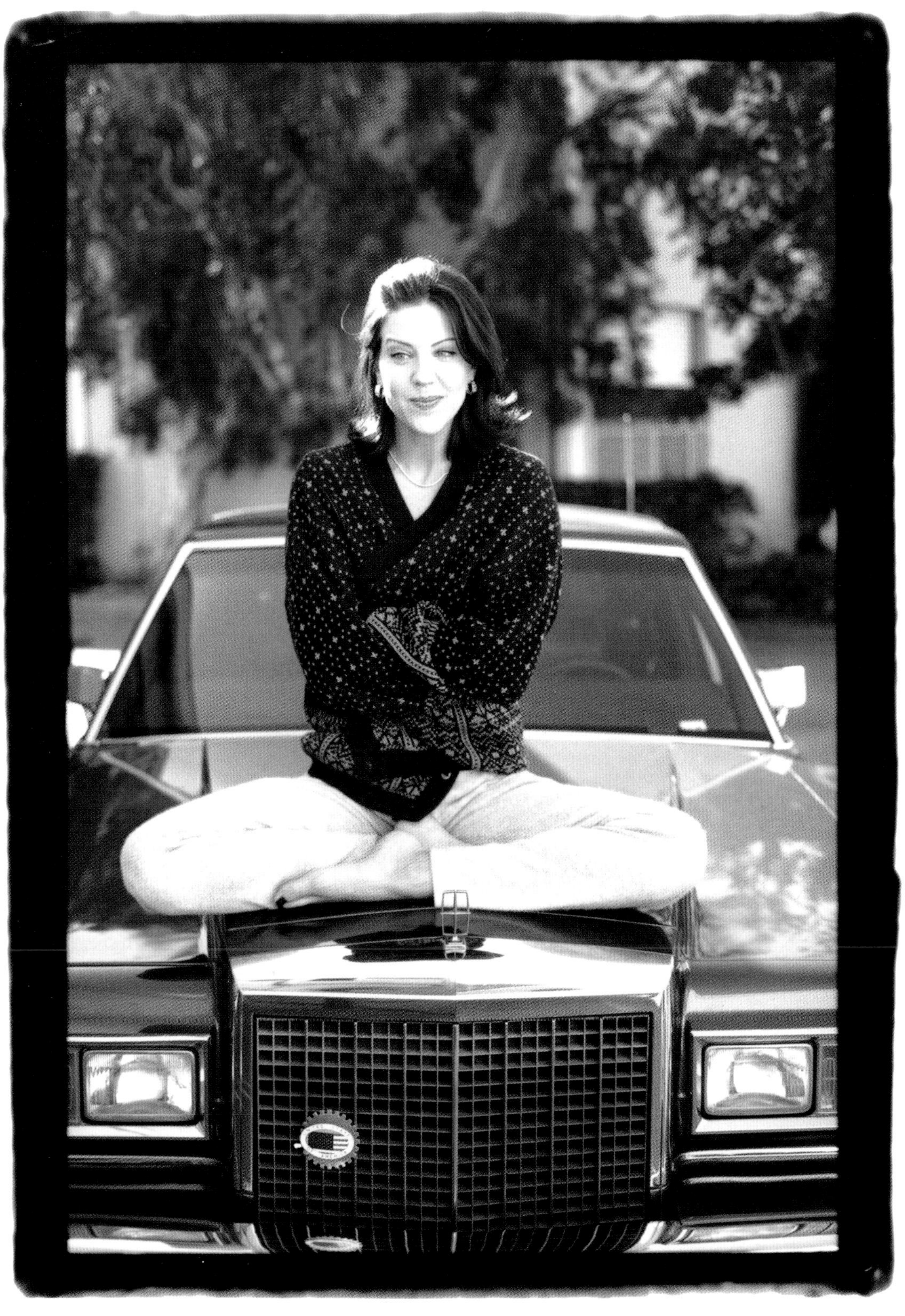

Andrea Parker

When she appeared flattered and slightly baffled by my invitation to be in this book, I was unable to explain why I am so drawn to her that I have followed her career from one show to another. Or why, off screen, I would go anywhere to photograph her. I did tell her that in my home, her TV show was called "The Miss Parker Show."

My instincts about her must be right, though, because not only did we laugh—and laugh a lot—I discovered that Andrea Parker and I are both former dancers who love to drive *fast*!

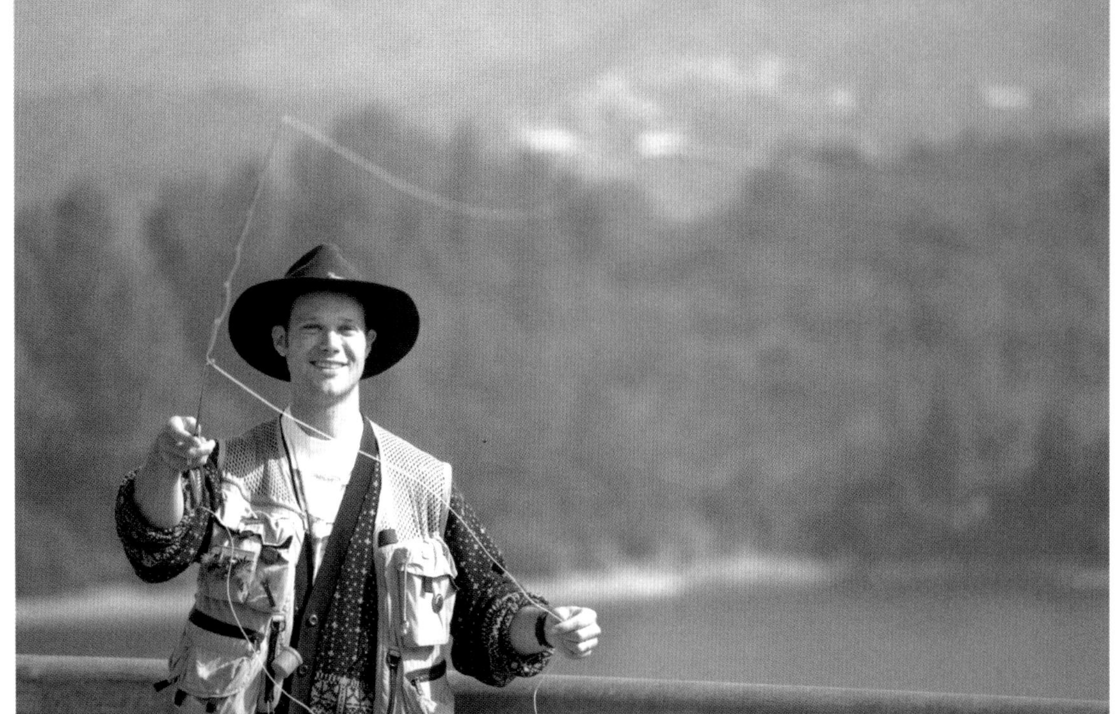

Jay Underwood

Chris Demetral

Jim Pirri

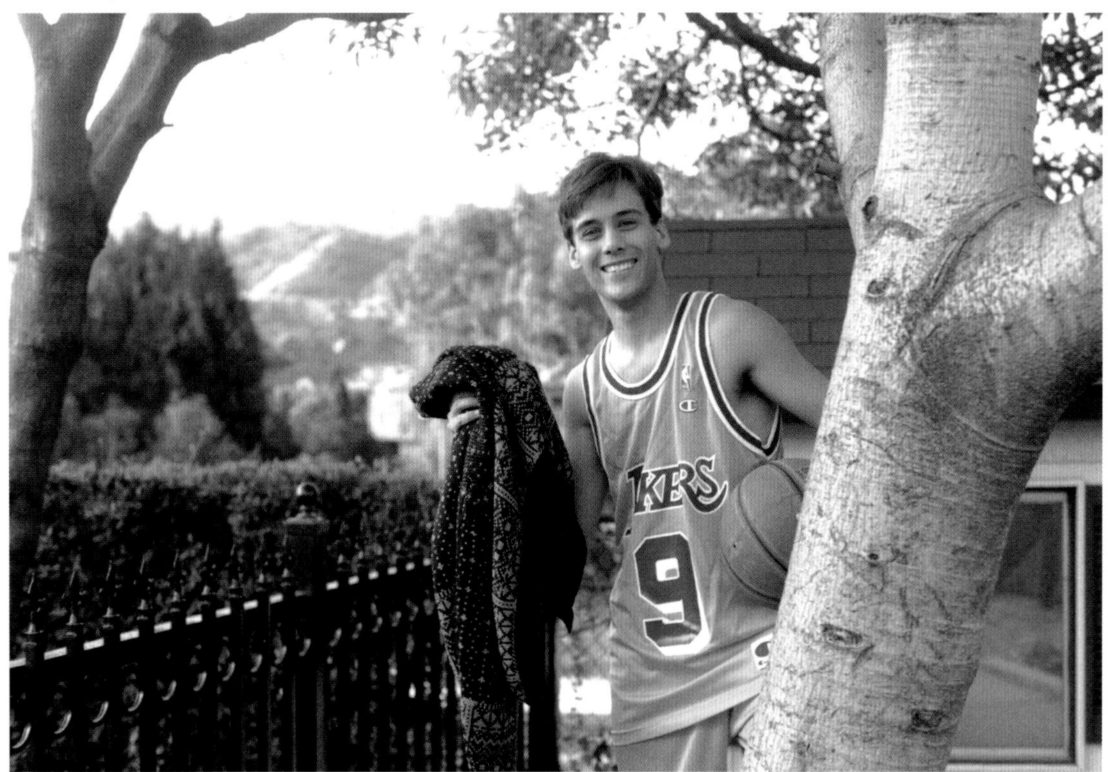

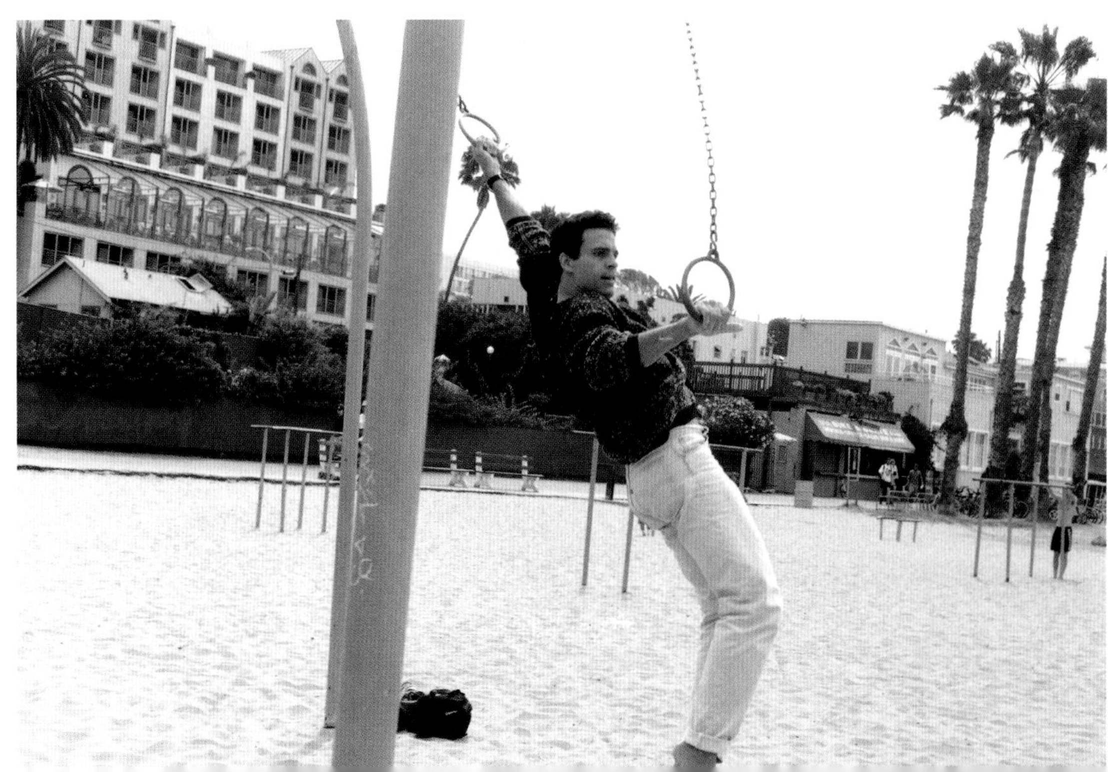

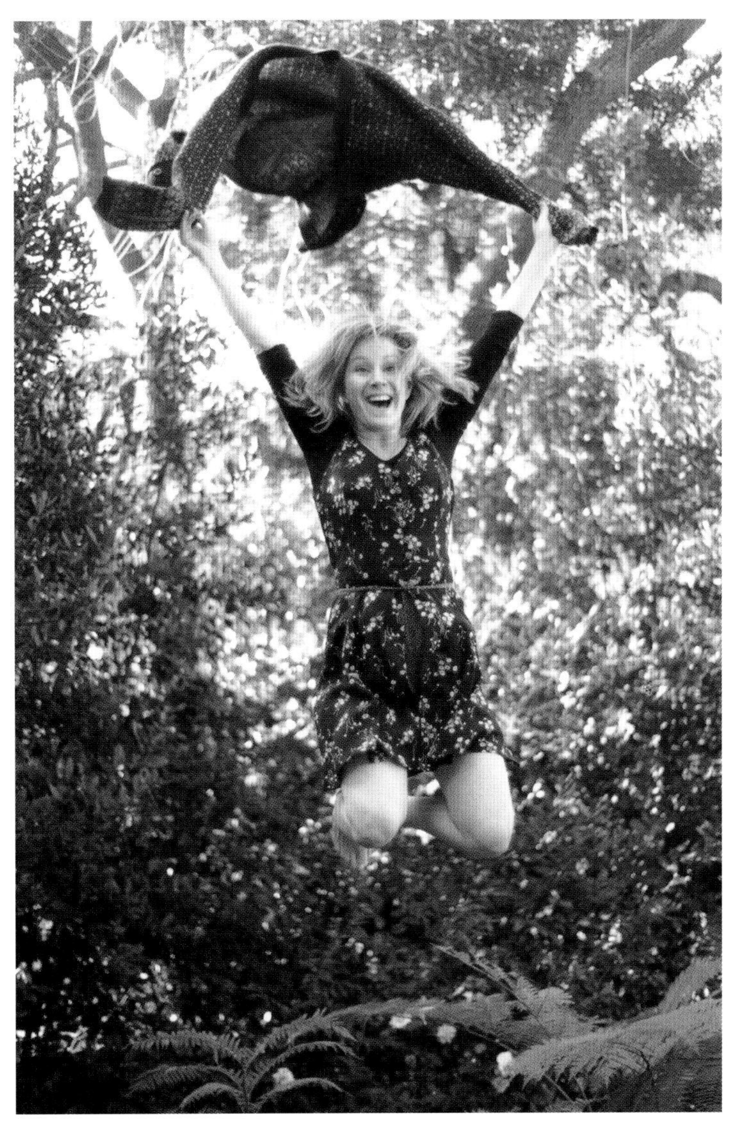

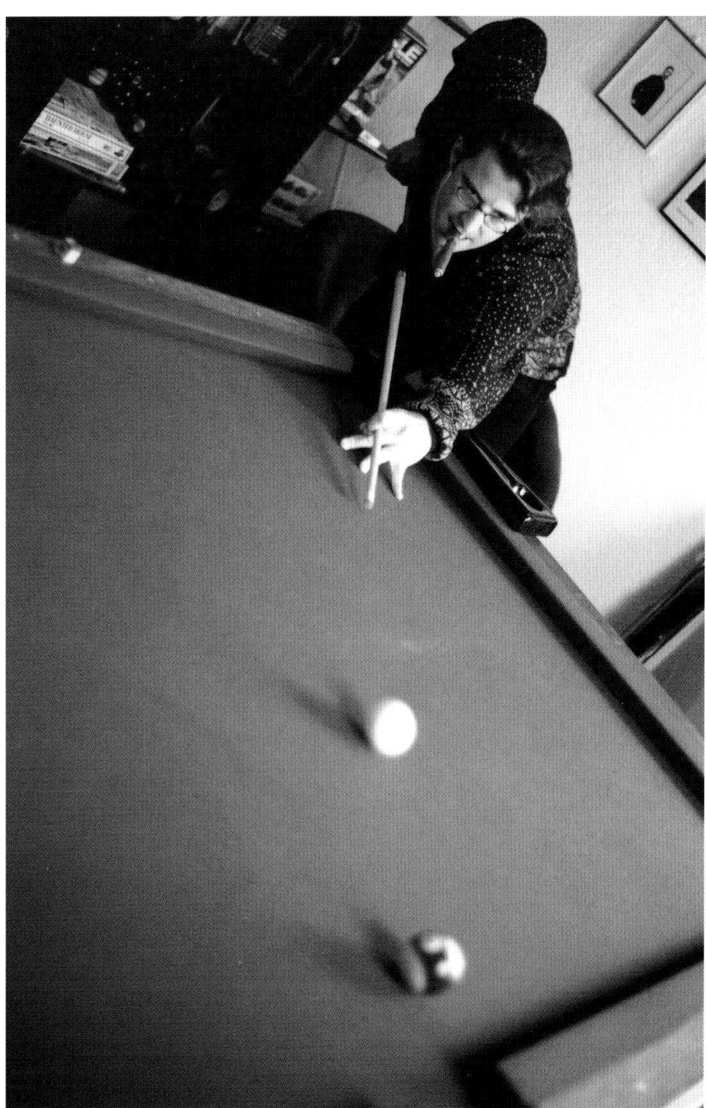

Chloe Webb, Eric Lutes

Sheree J. Wilson with Luke

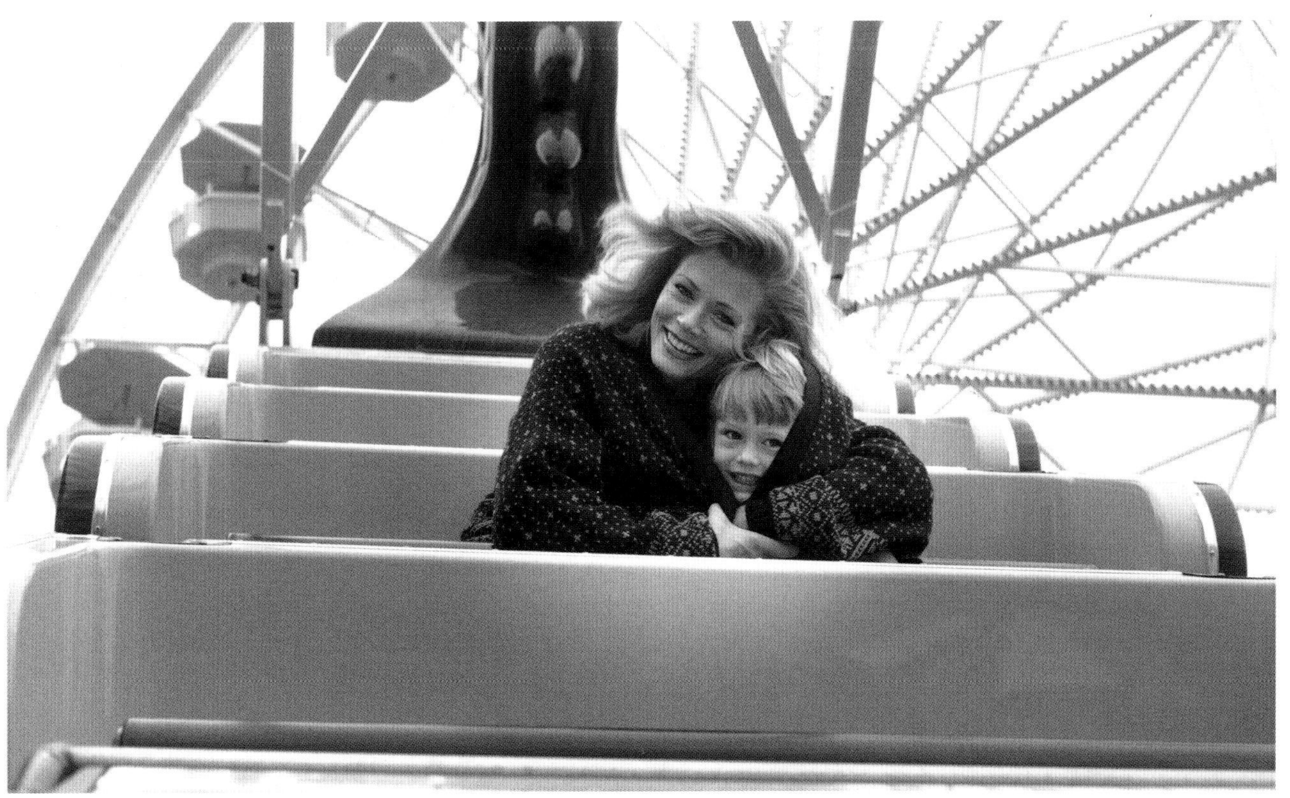

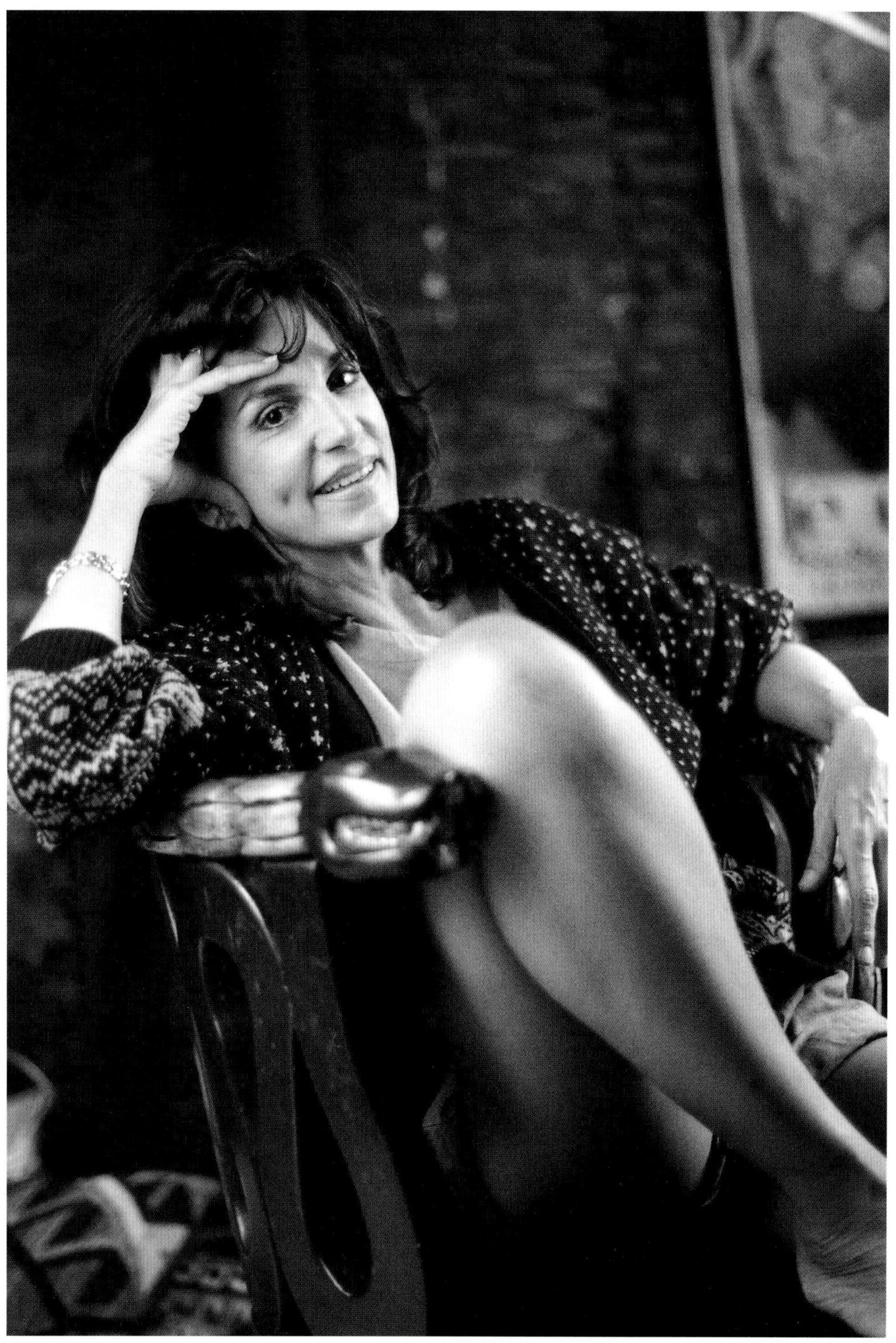

Mercedes Ruehl

A lot of stories came out of the extended visit we had in Mercedes Ruehl's home: stories about her work, stories about her family, stories about her closet space—and Pat's favorite story about a little gold statue that he almost tripped over. My favorite story, though, is the one she told about her home and its historical significance. Often she would look out the window to see NYU professors pointing to her building and lecturing their class about it, about Aaron Burr and about slave smuggling. So often did she see this particular sight that one day she decided to sneak up behind the group and hide among the students, just to listen to the history of the place where every night she lay her head to sleep.

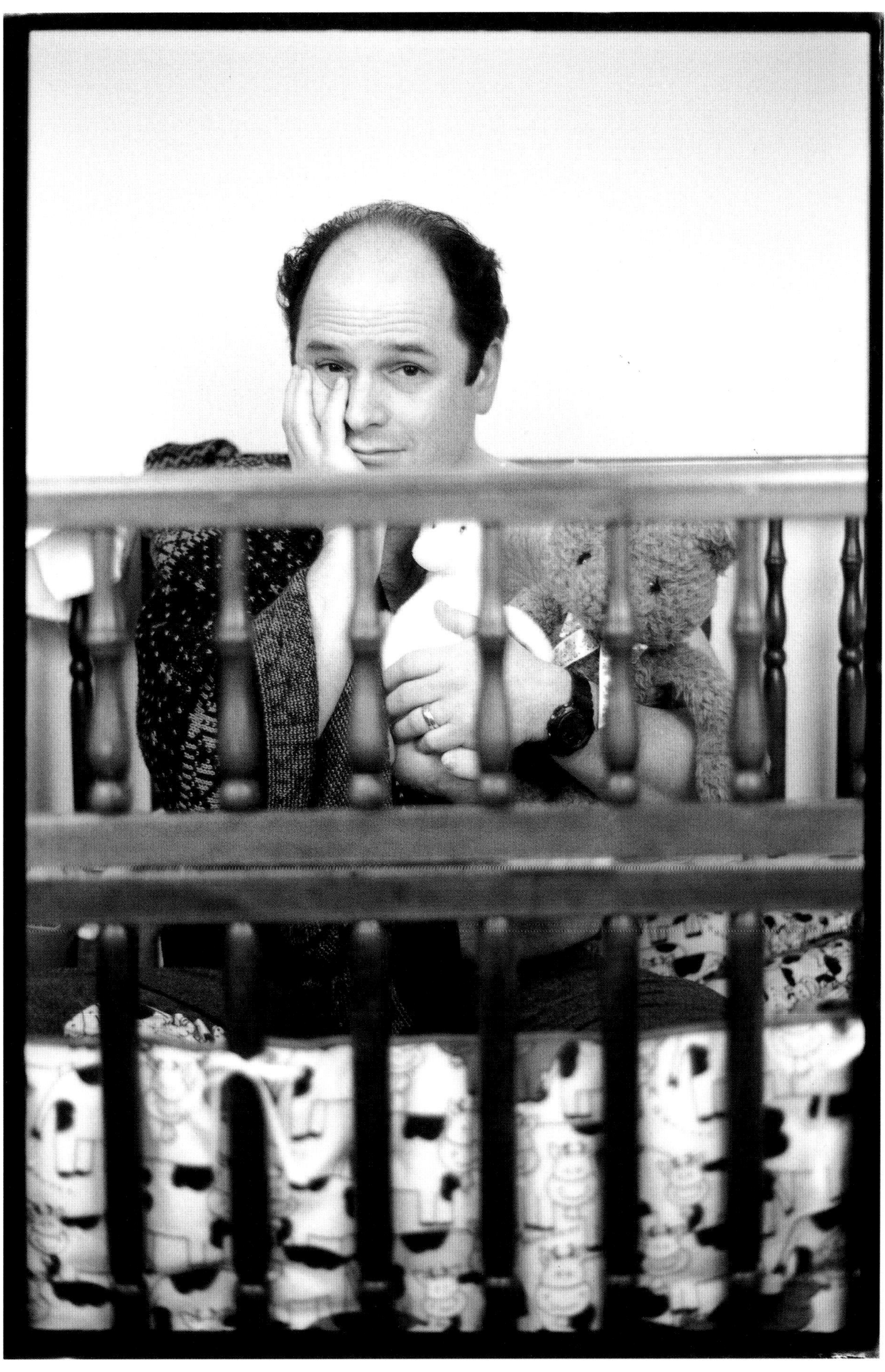

Jason Alexander

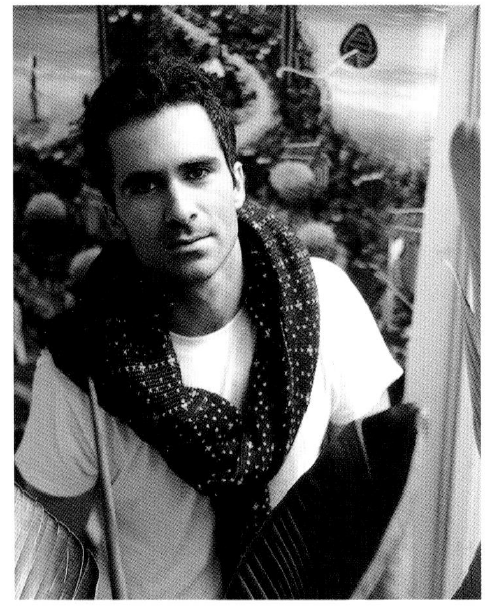
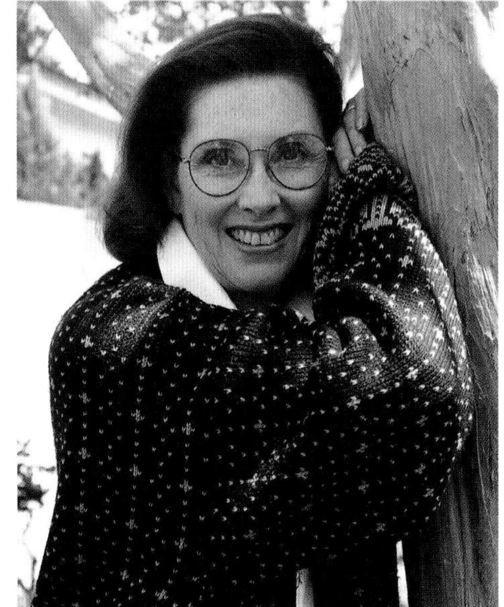
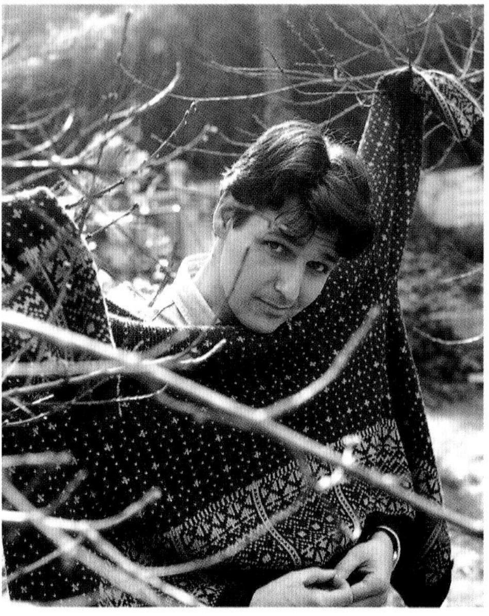
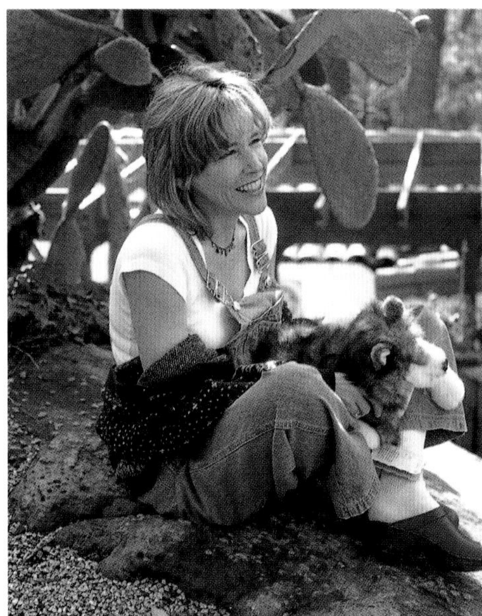
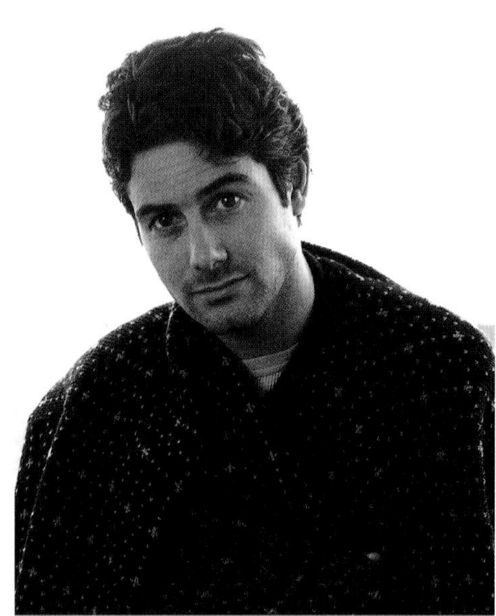

From left to right:
Nestor Carbonell
Elinor Donahue
Maurice Godin
Betsy Randle
Zach Galligan
Mark Harelik
Rain Phoenix
Jodi Long

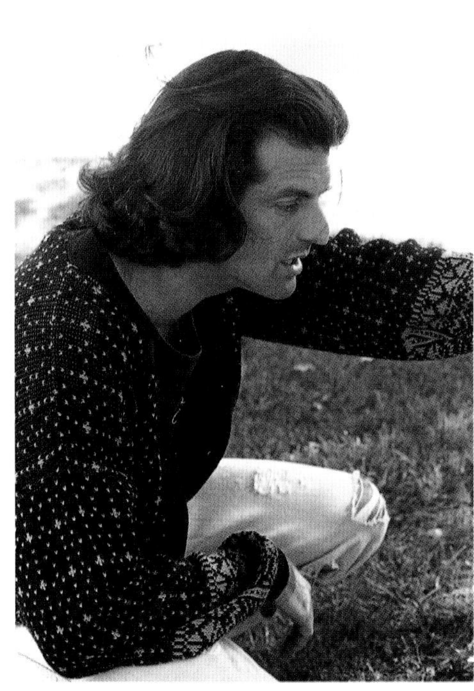
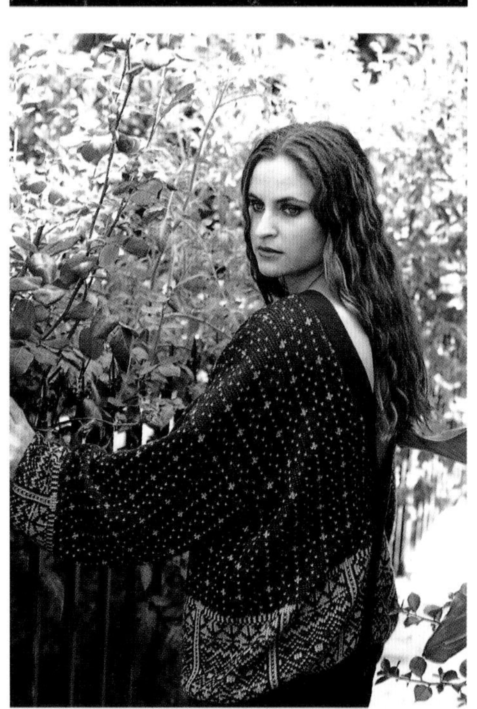
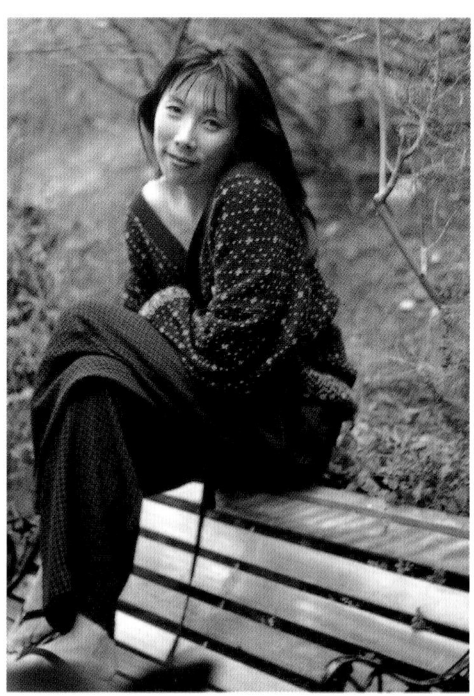

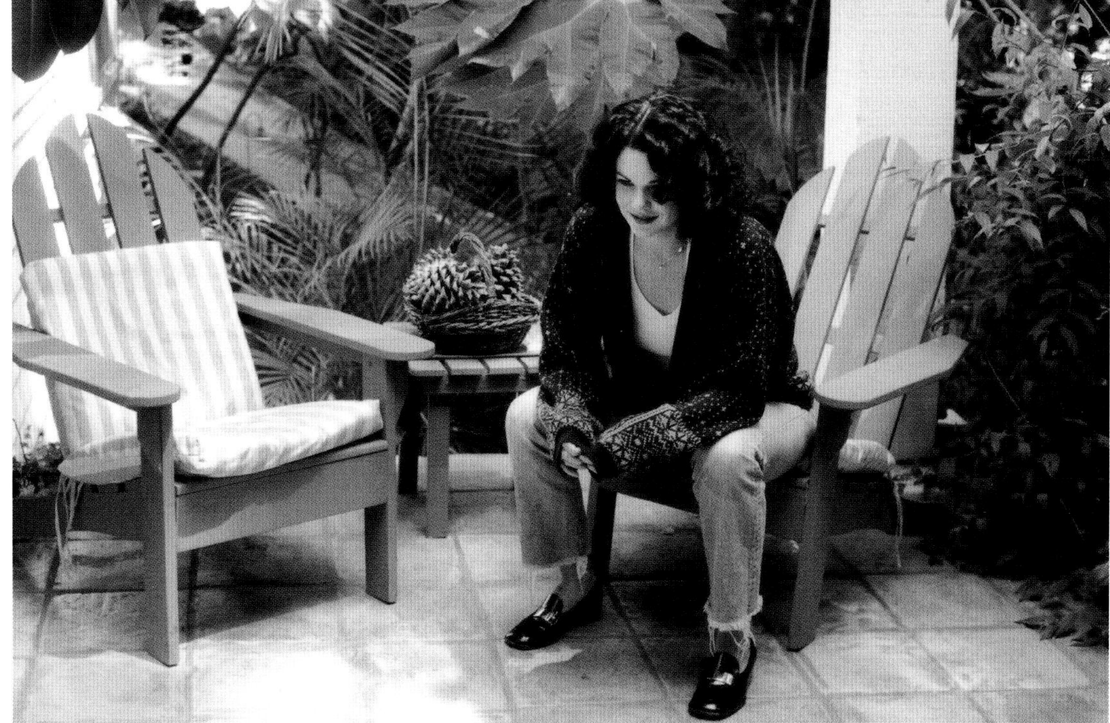

Lauren Graham
Cynthia Sikes
Lori Laughlin

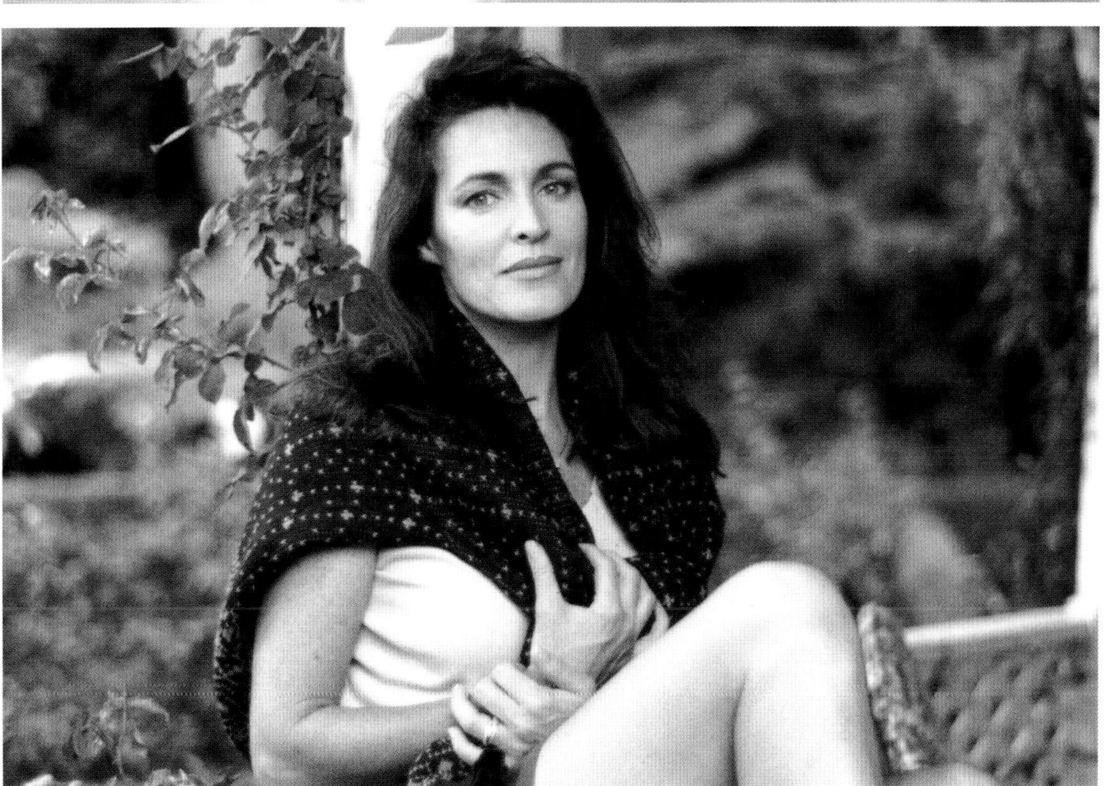

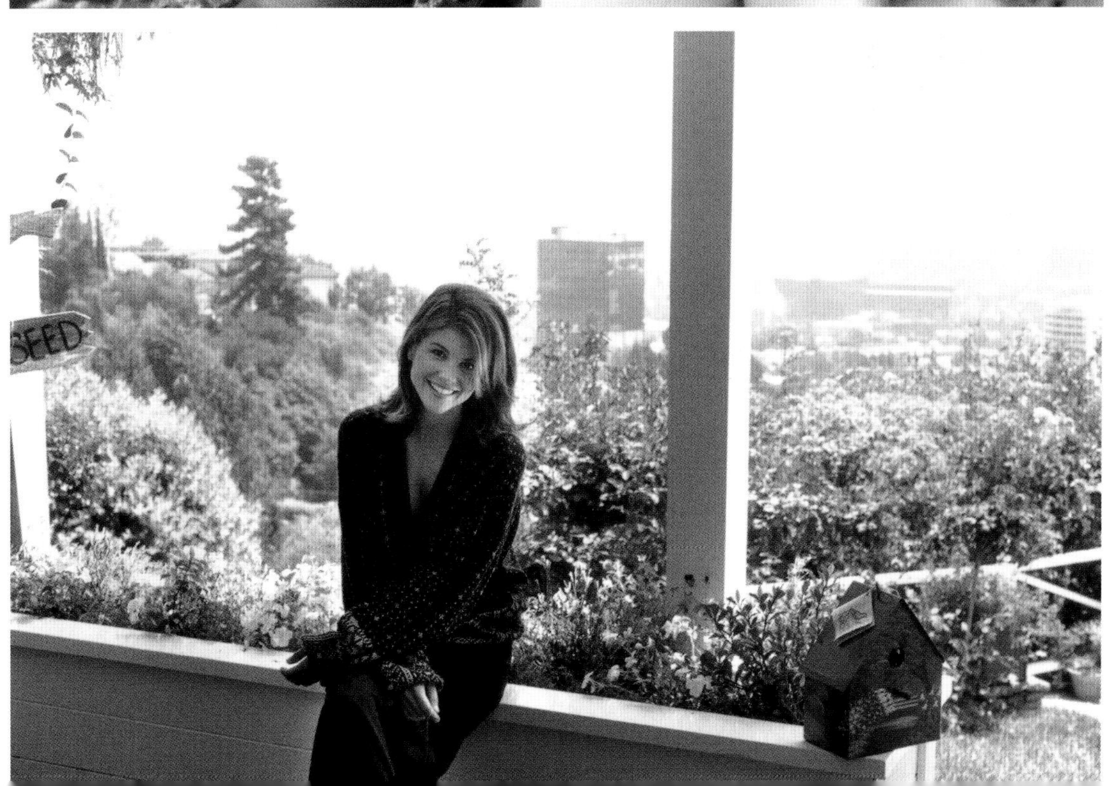

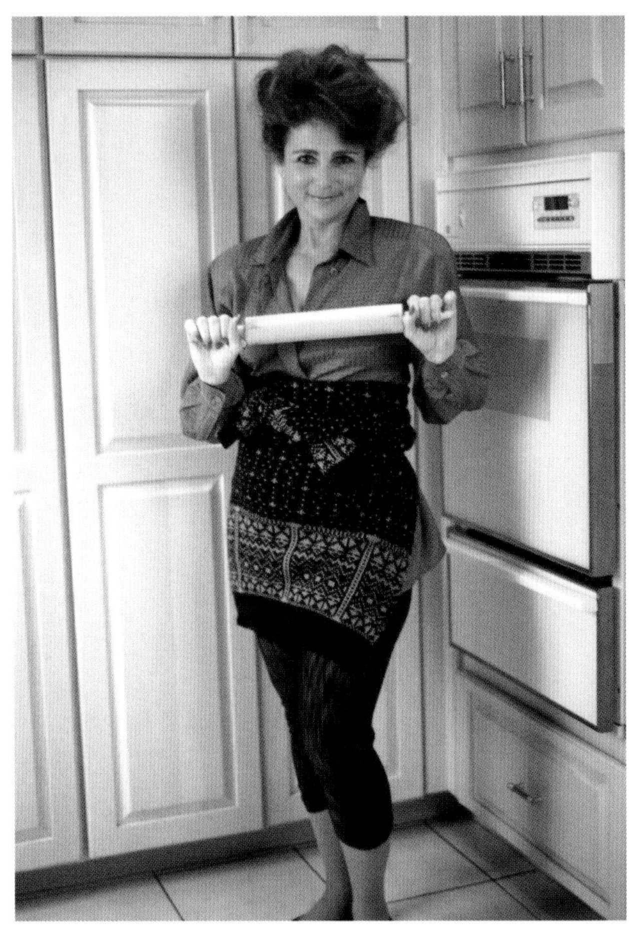
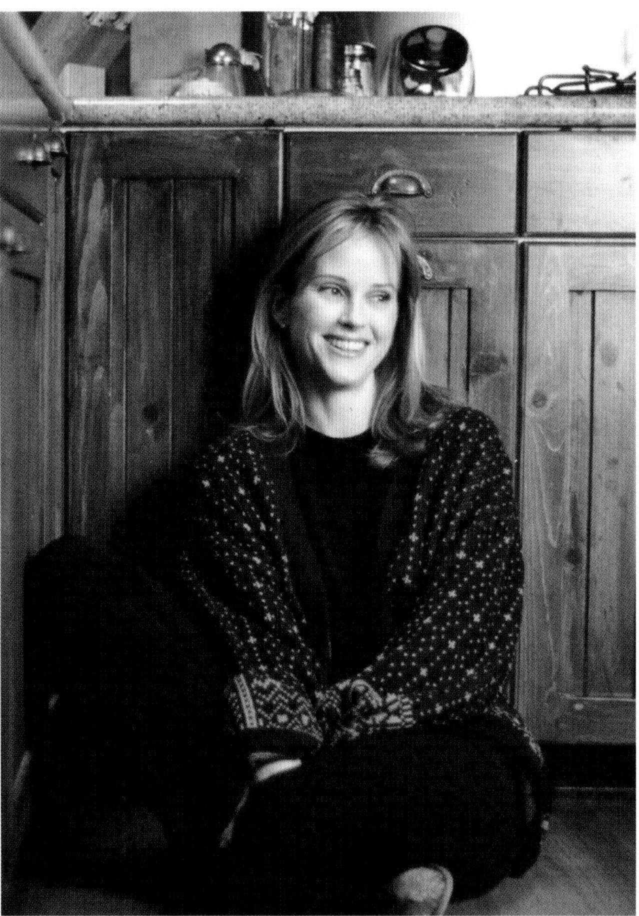
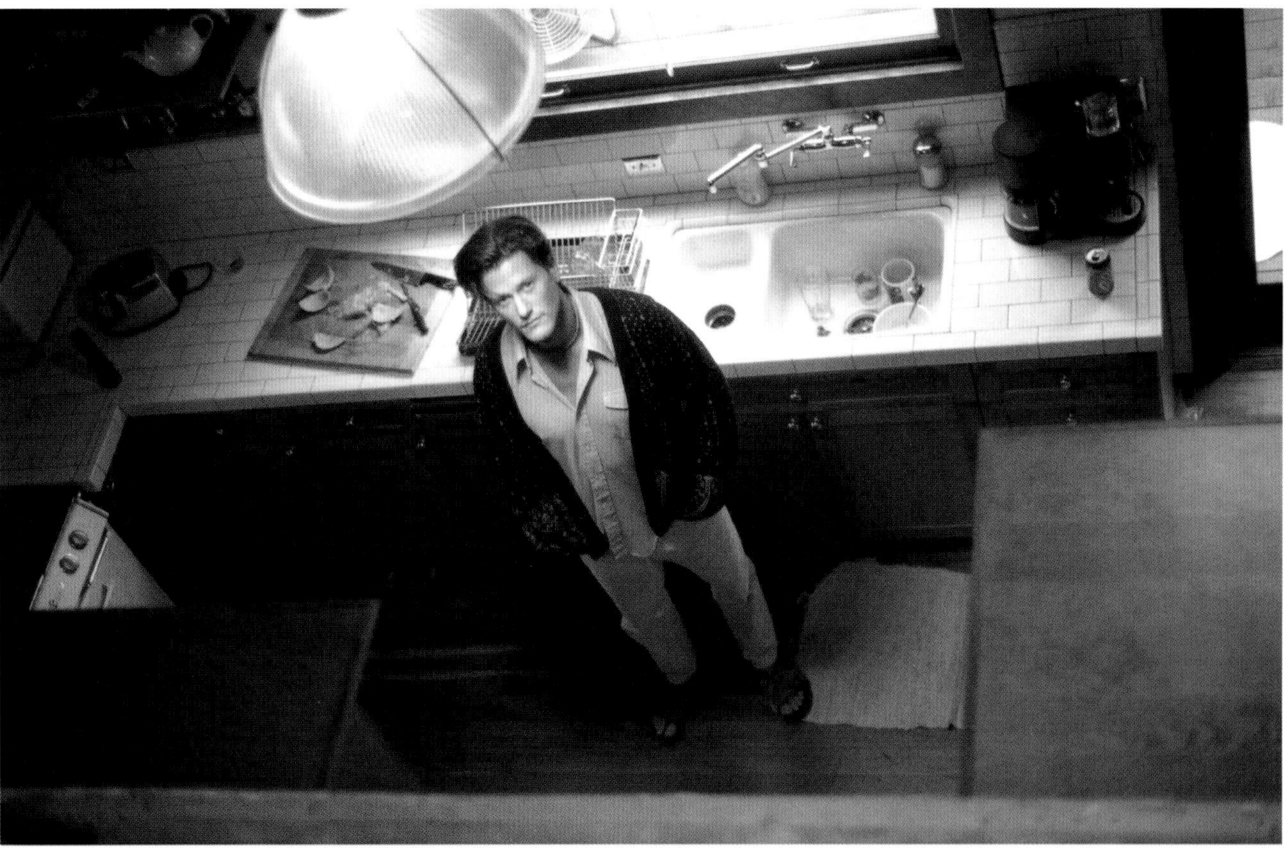

Clockwise from top left: Tovah Feldshuh, Rebecca Staab, Vincent Ventresca

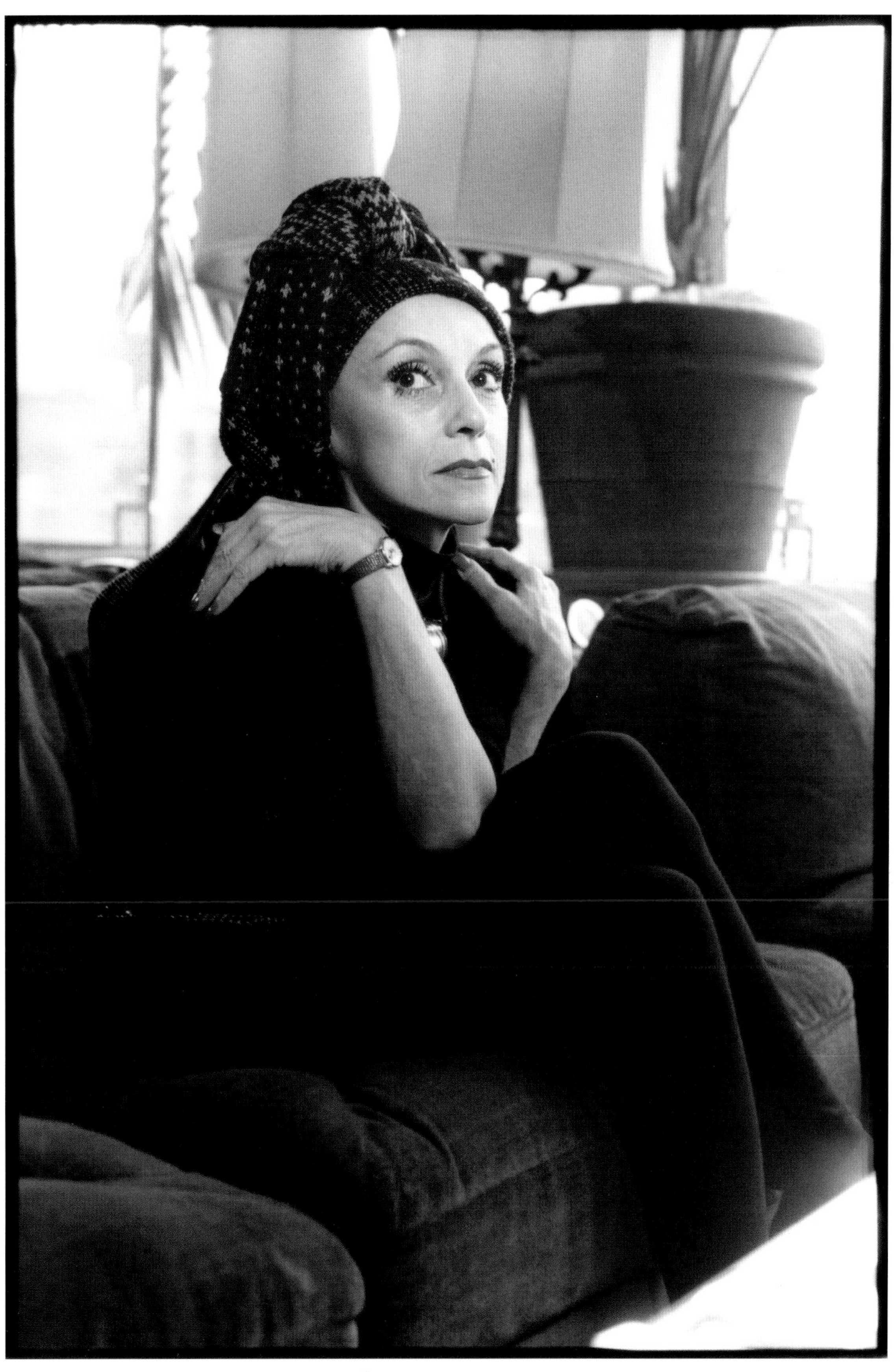

Liliane Montevecchi

"You have such long eyelashes."
"Merci. They are all mine, you know."

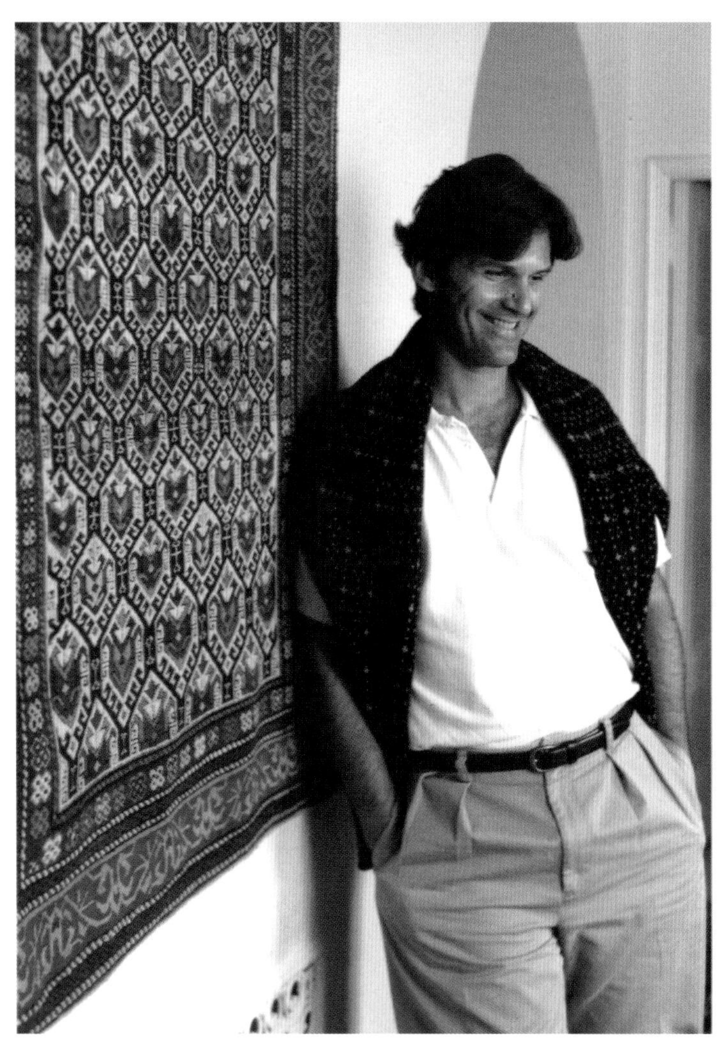
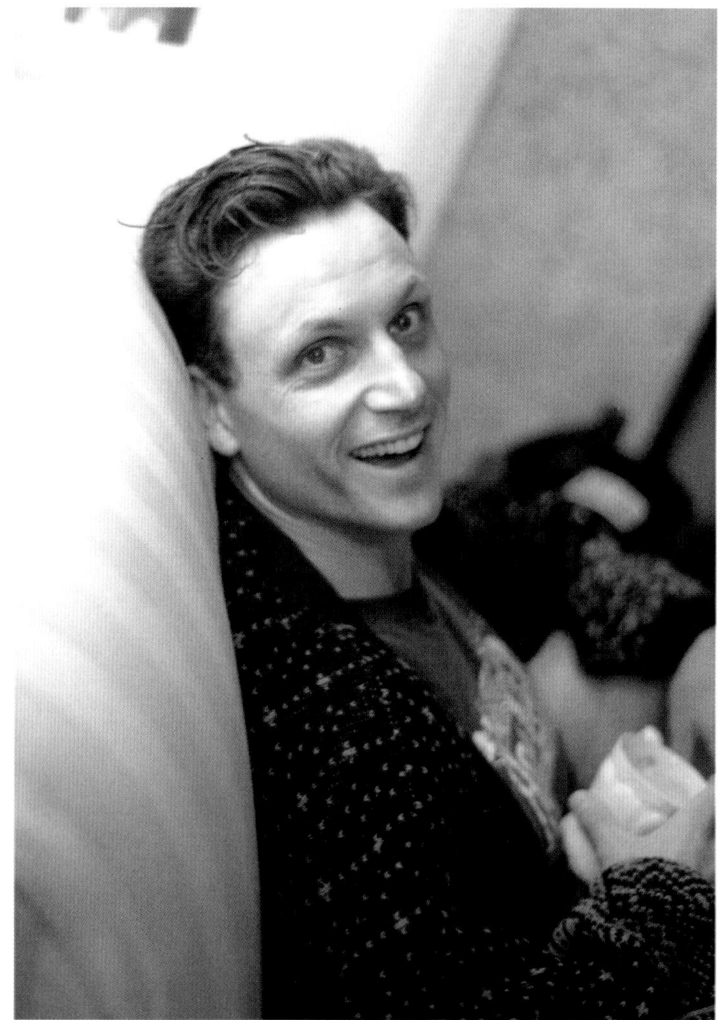
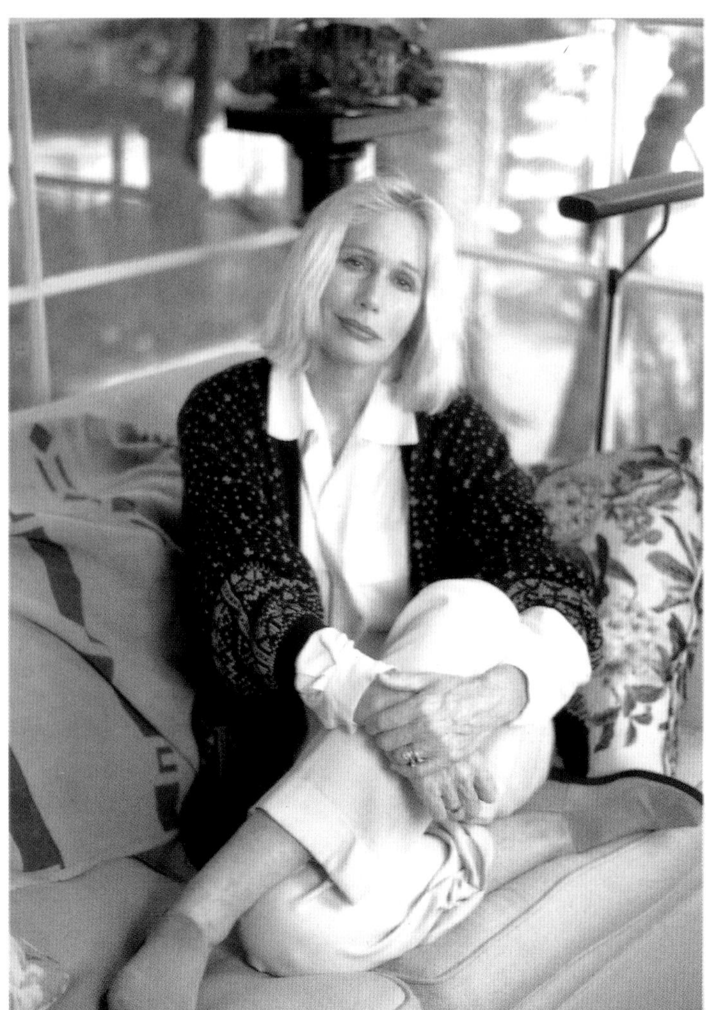
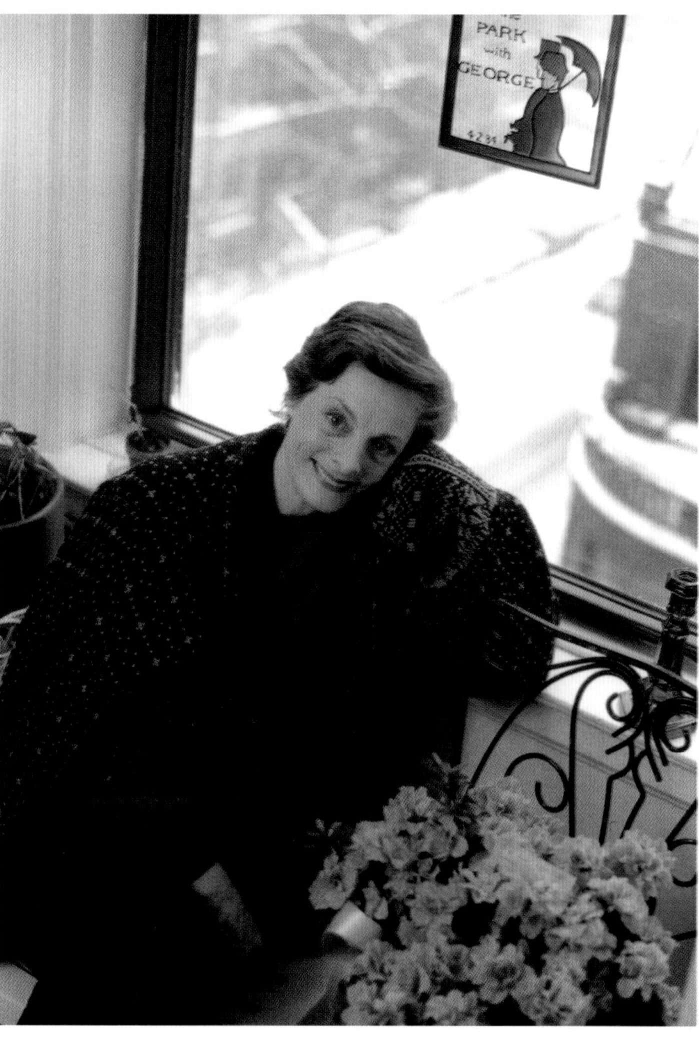
PARK
with
GEORGE

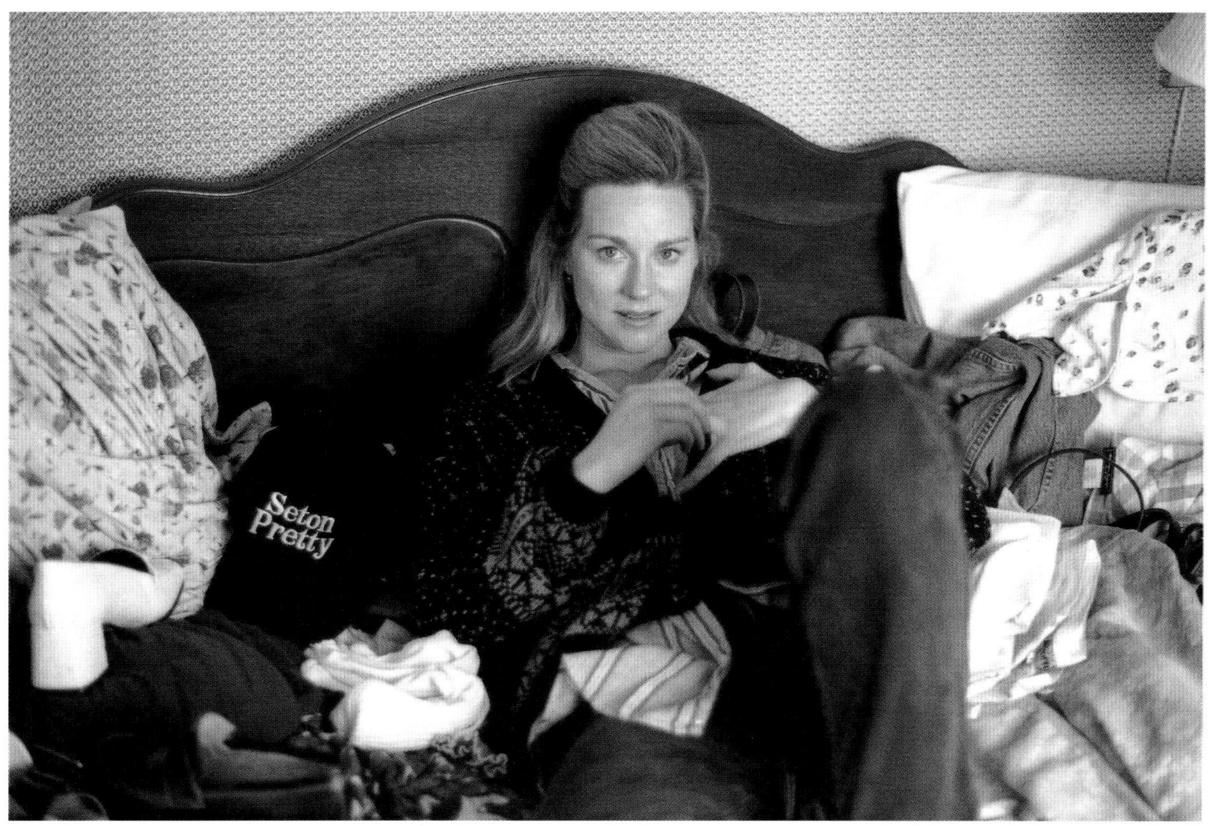

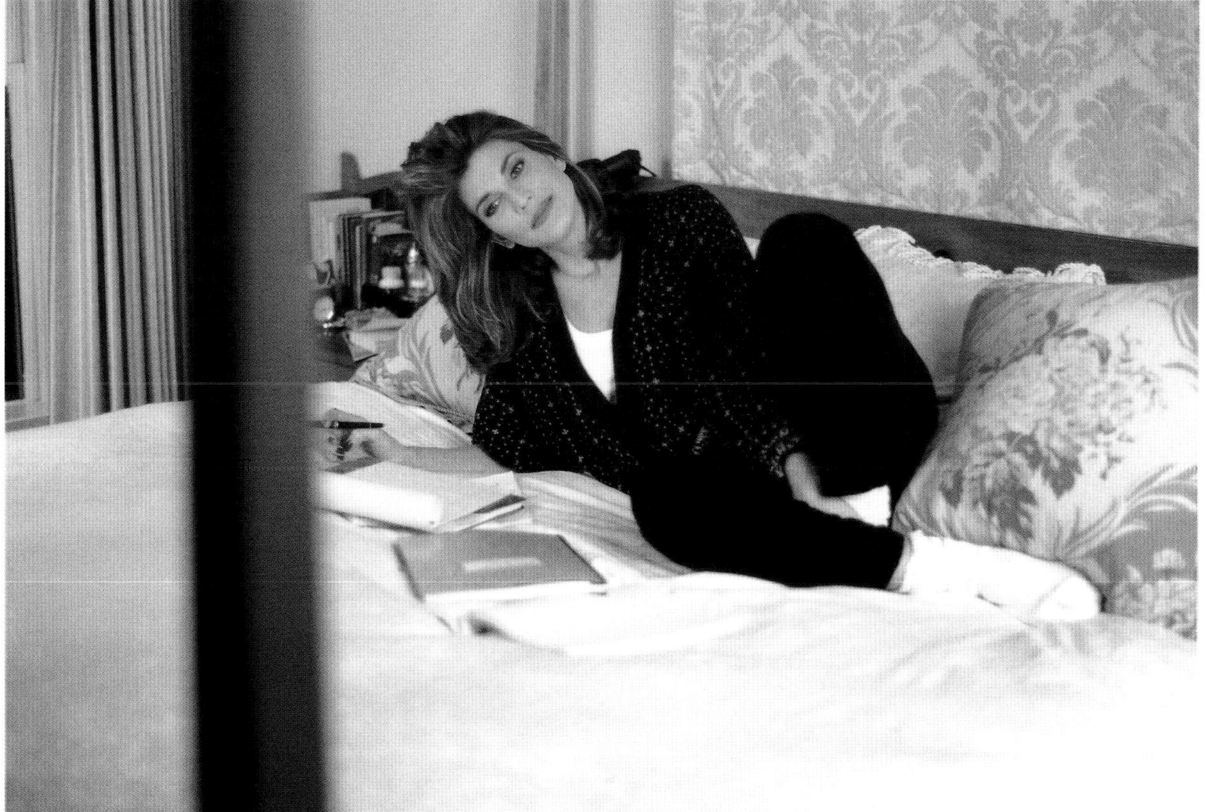

Laura Linney, Julie Moran

Opposite, clockwise from top left: DW Moffet, Tony Goldwyn, Dana Ivey, Sally Kellerman

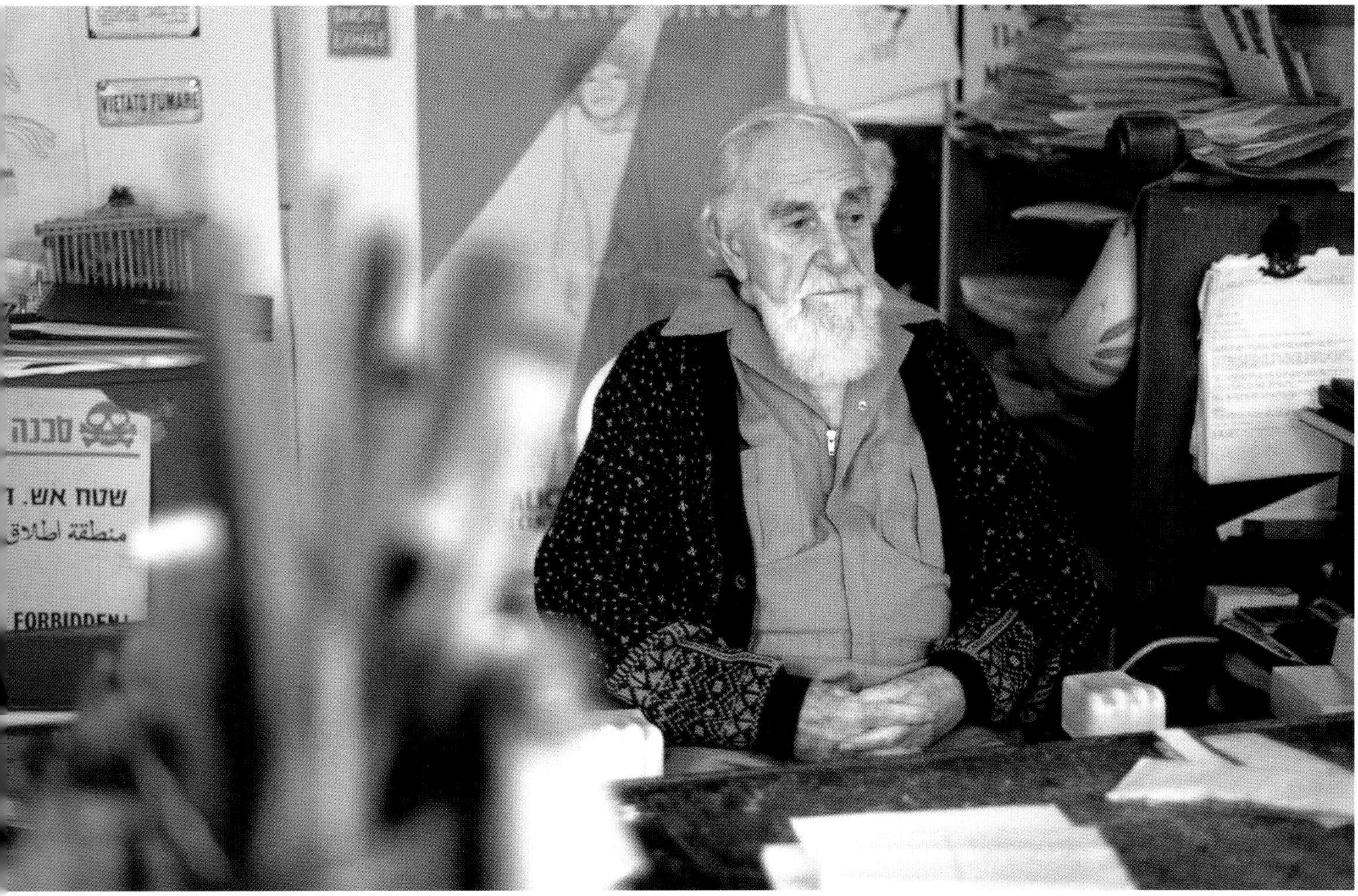

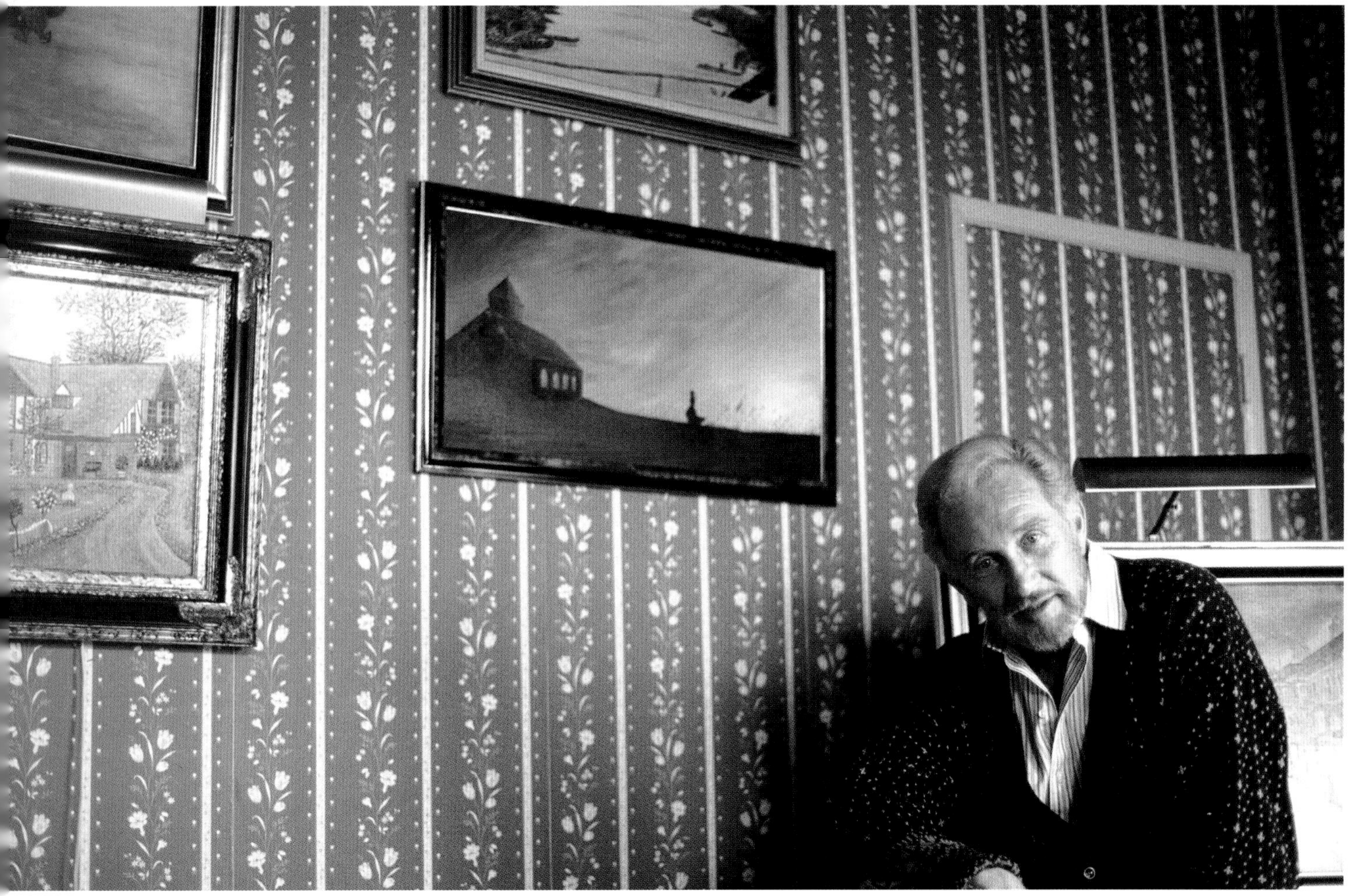

Al Hirschfeld, Roy Dotrice

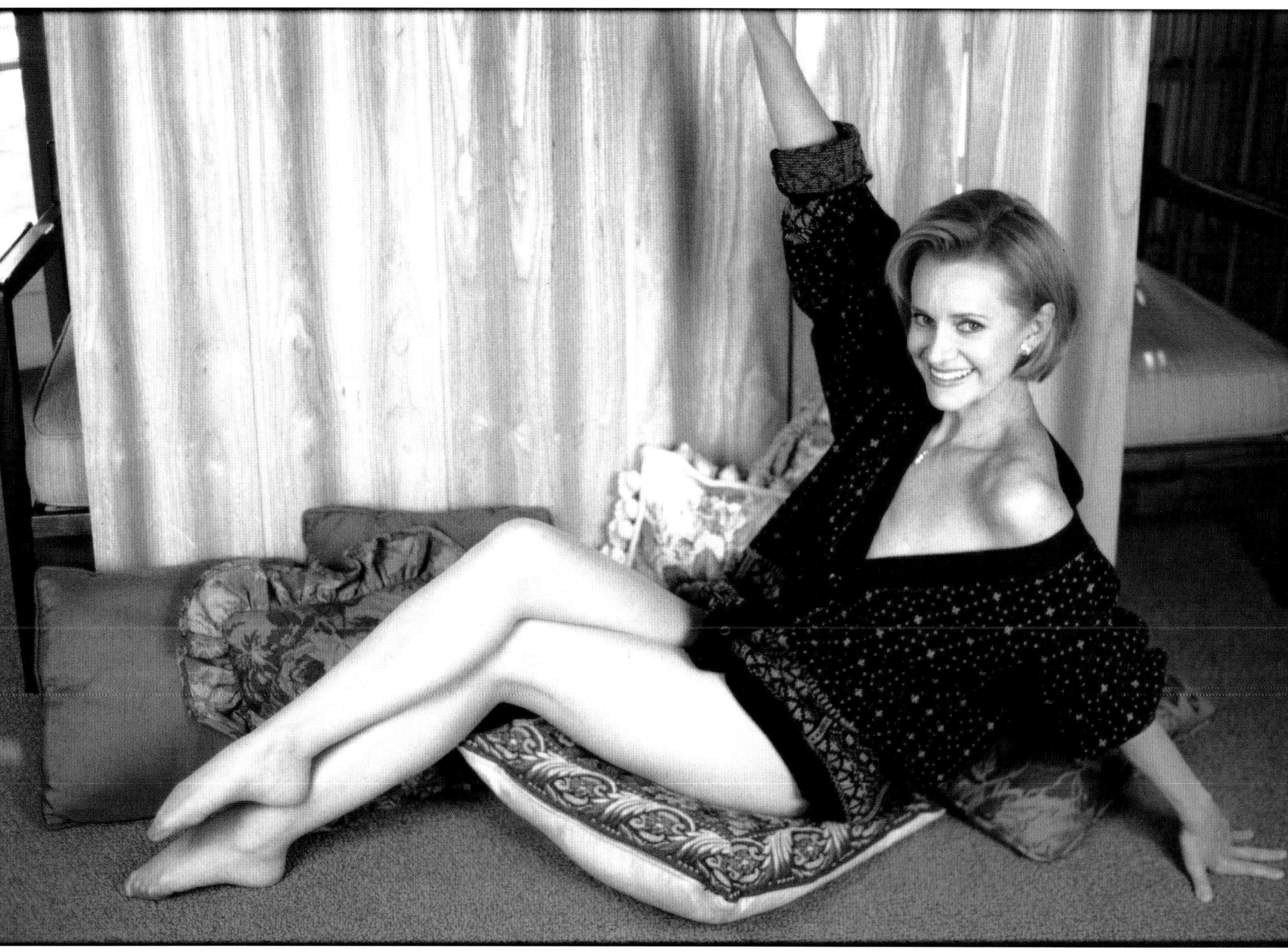

Swoosie Kurtz

I was very excited that Swoosie Kurtz was up for a little cheesecake when it came time to do her sweater picture. See, I know she is one of America's most distinguished actors, but there is a stigma attached to being a great actress and I personally wanted a chance to show off those gorgeous legs of hers—you know, remind the world what a sexy gal she is. All woman, through and through.

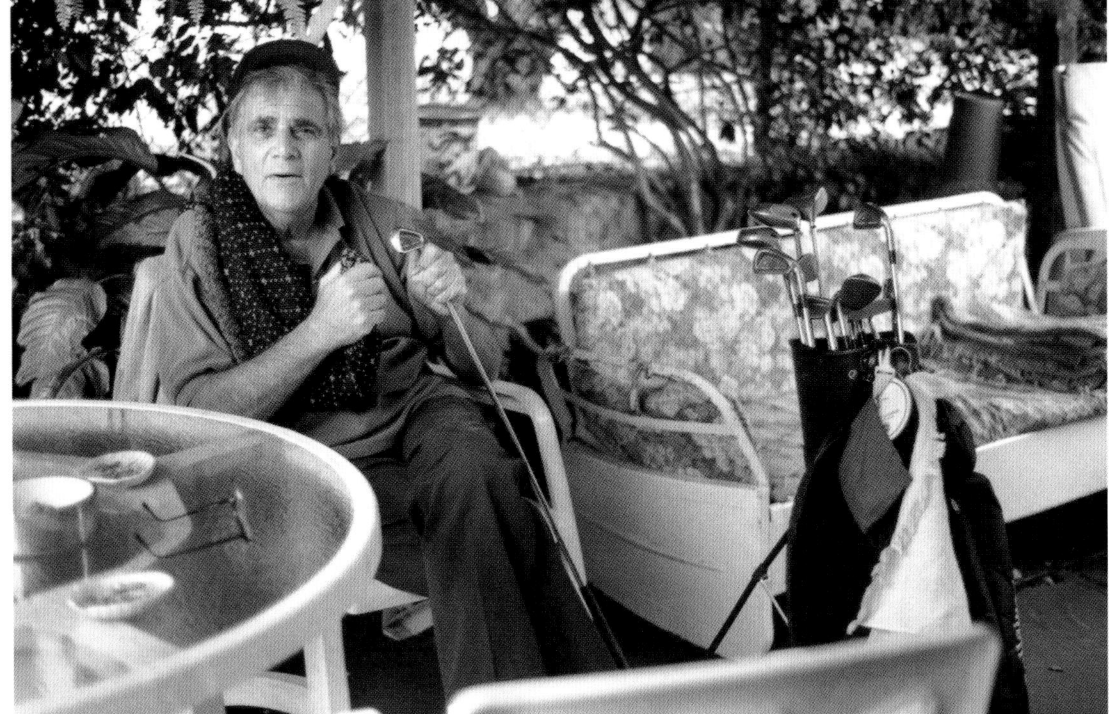

Alex Rocco
Doris Roberts
Alan Rachins

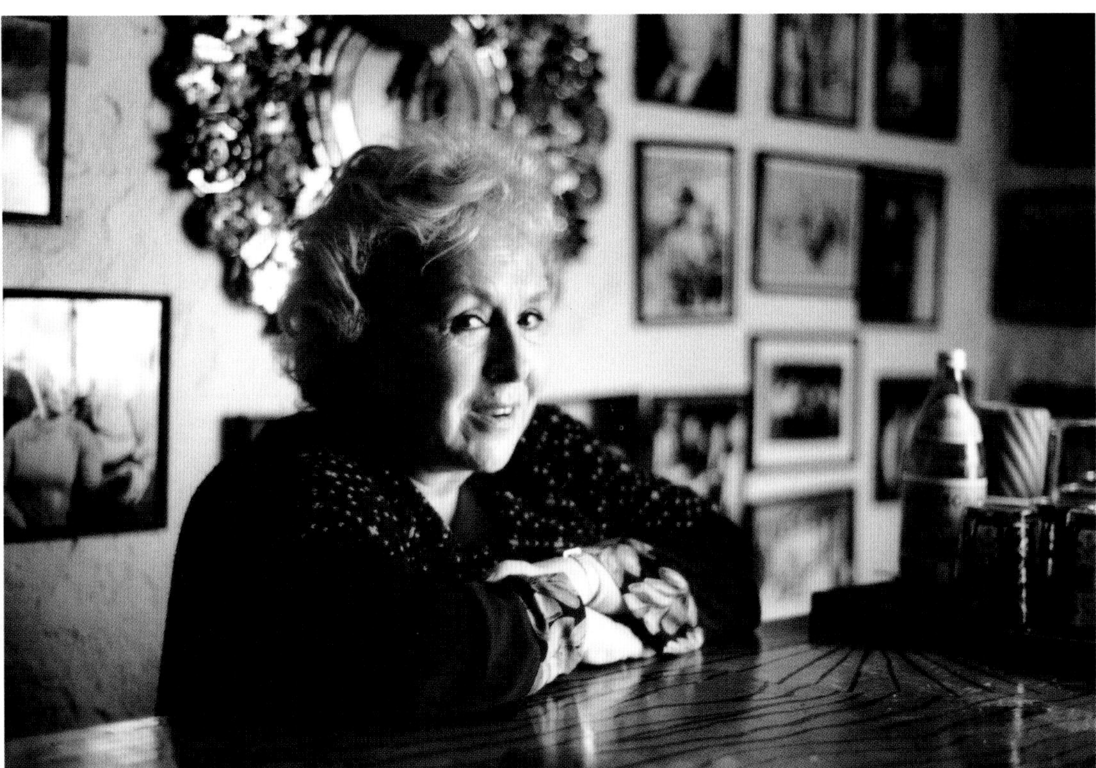

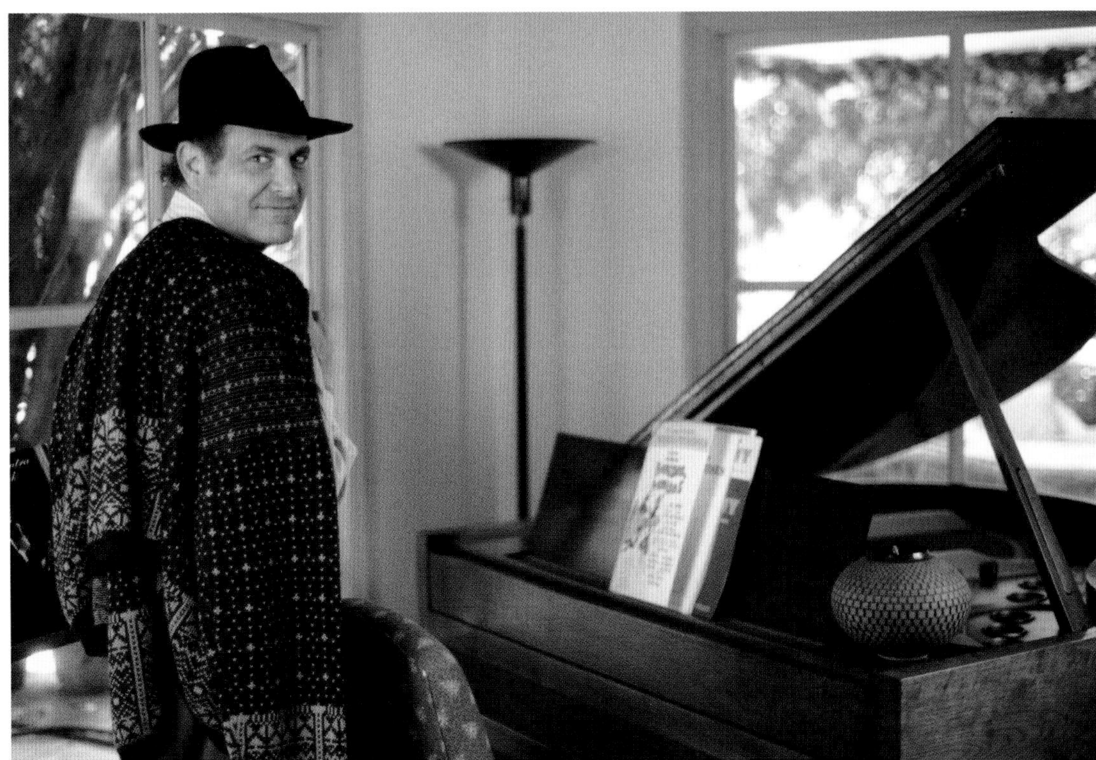

Clockwise from top left:
Charlotte Rae
Connie Stevens
Estelle Harris
Christina Pickles

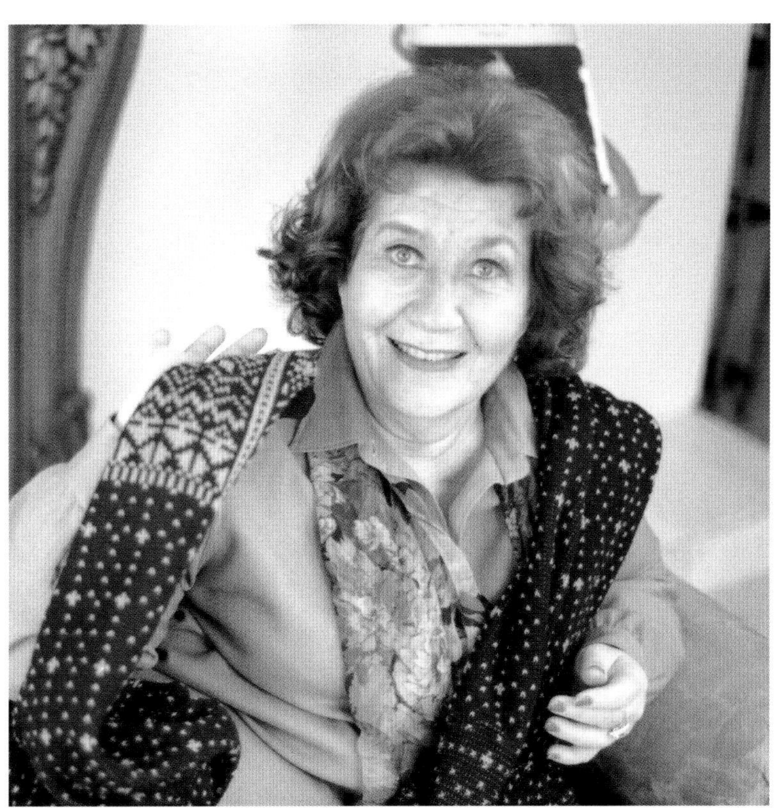

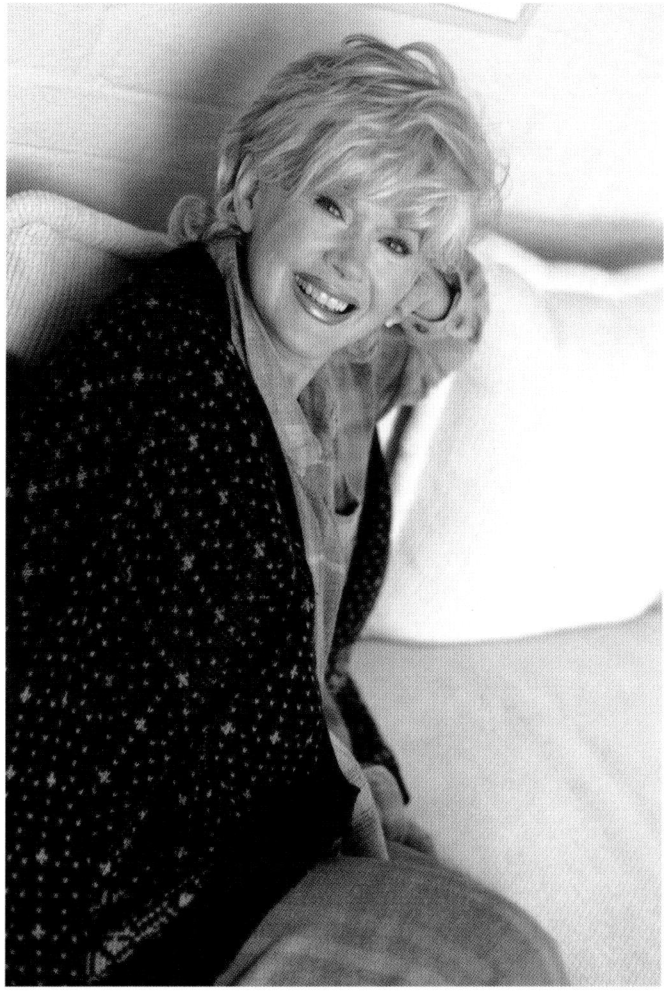

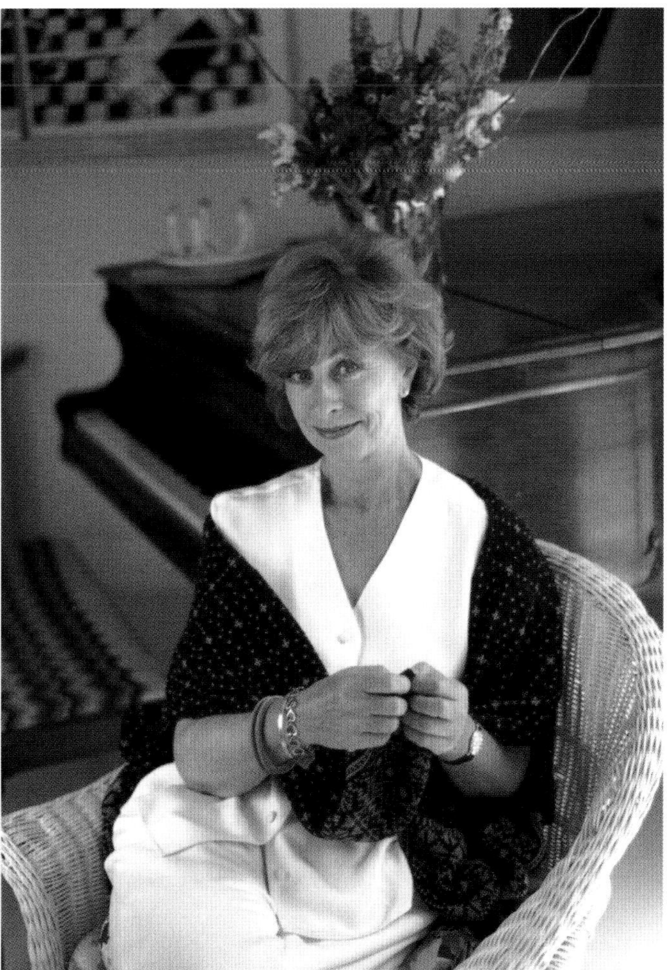

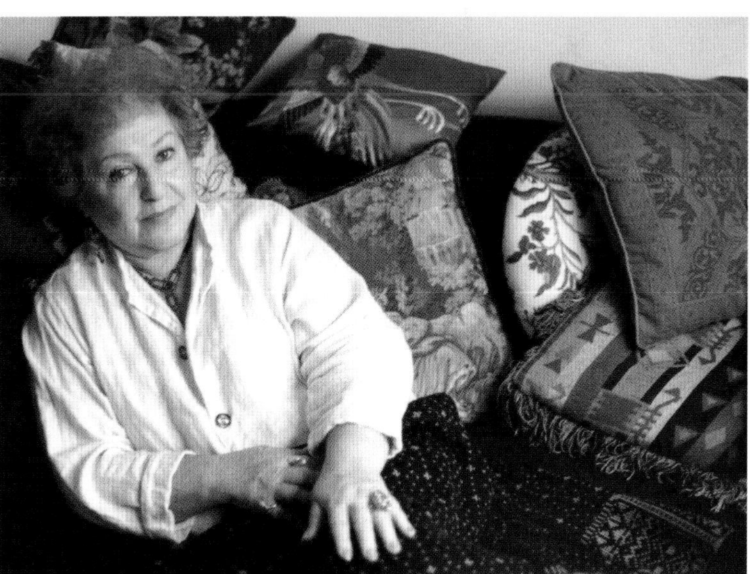

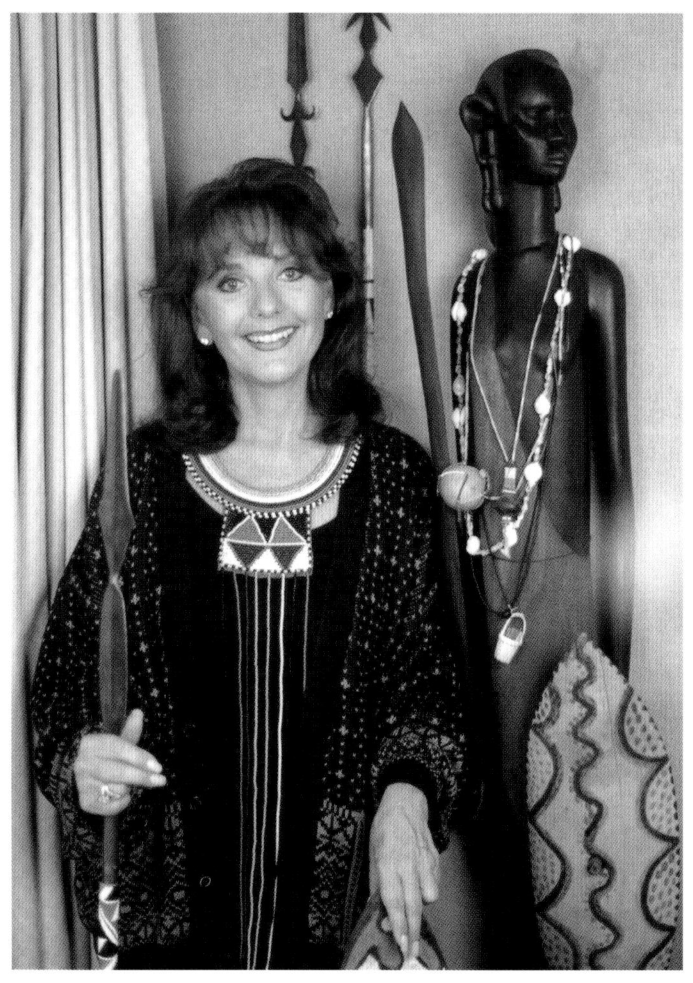
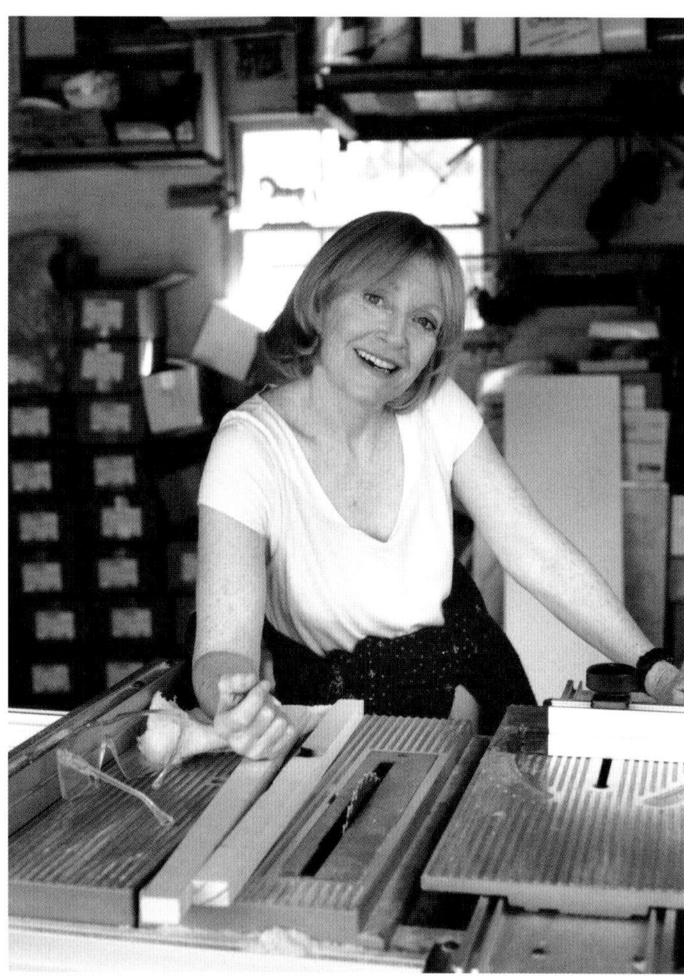

Dawn Wells, K Callan

Victoria Tennant, Heather McAdam

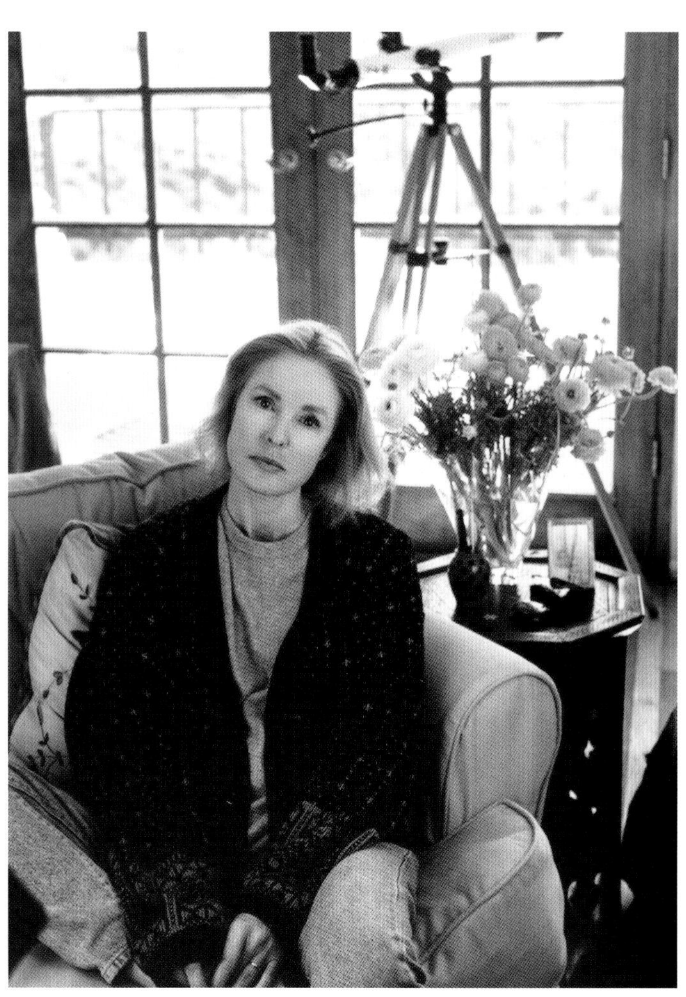
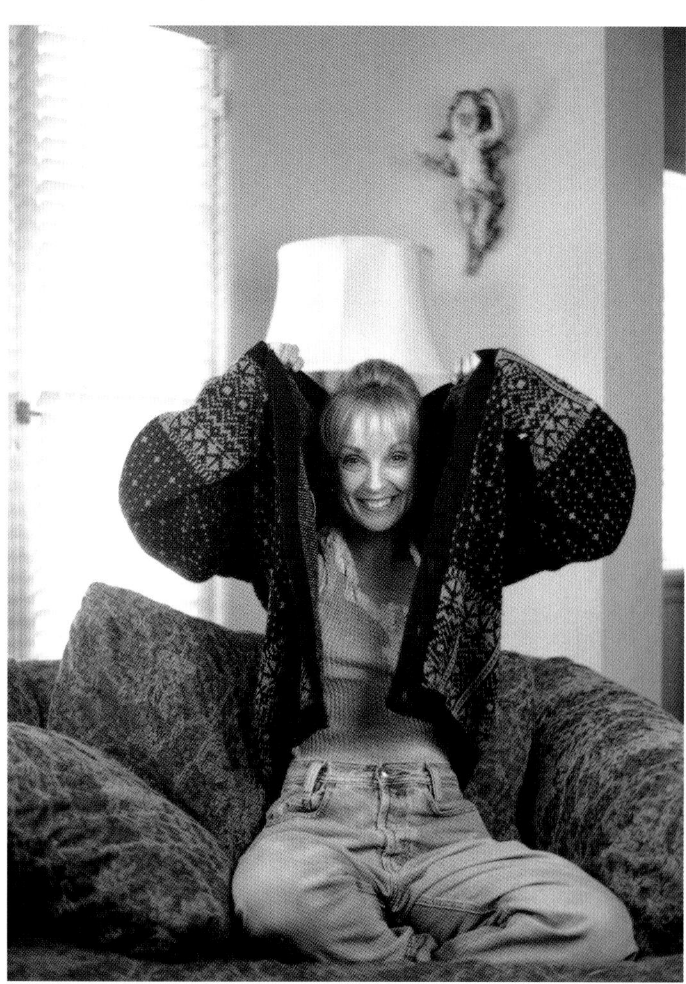

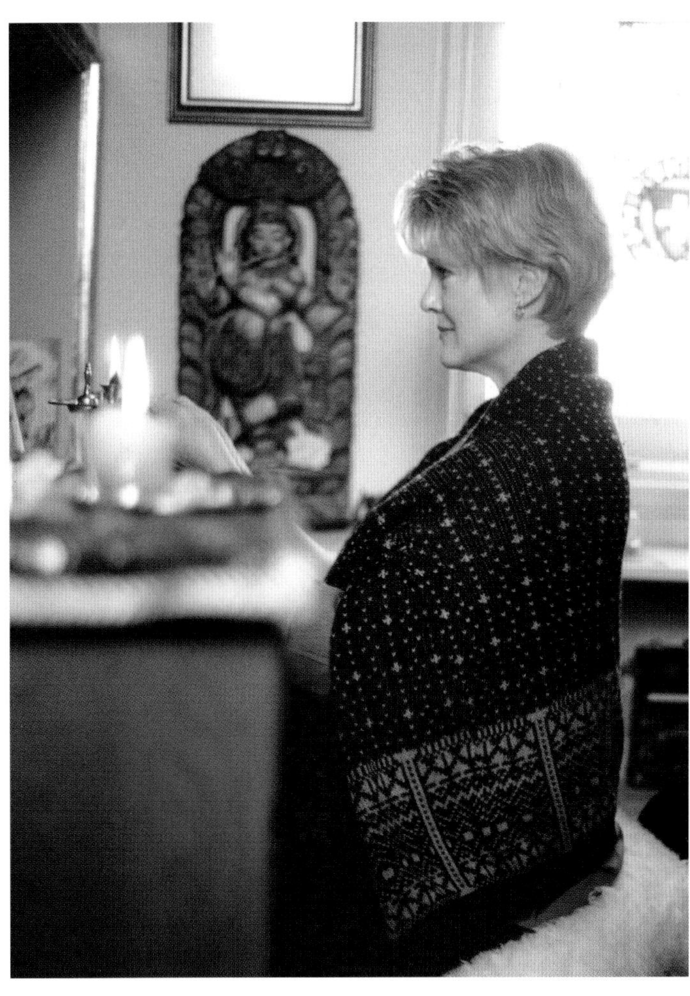

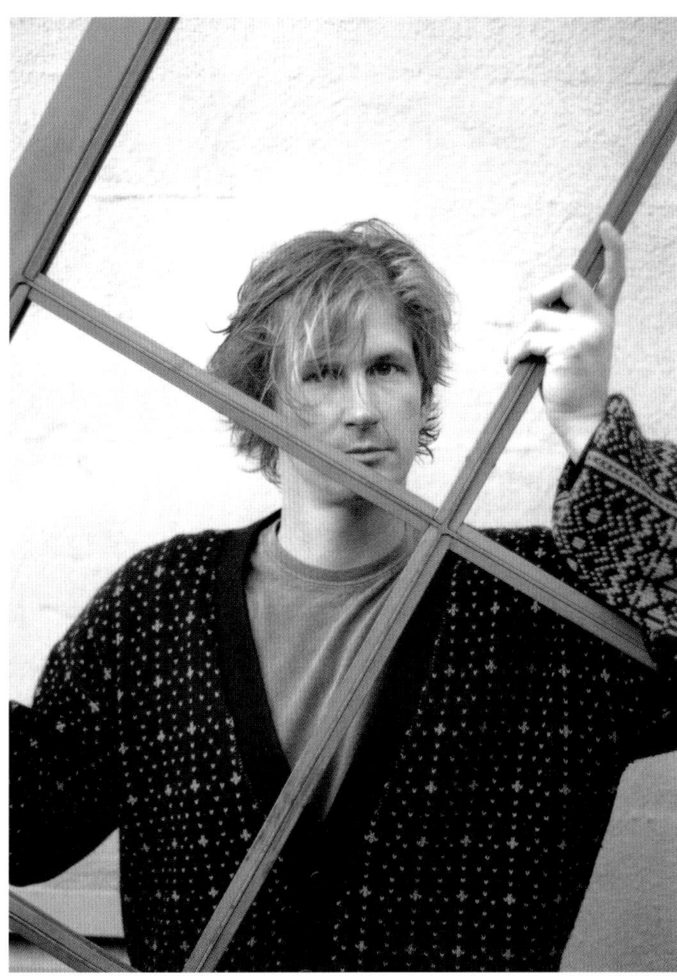

Gloria Loring, Bill Brochtrup
Michael Goorgian, Lorraine Toussaint

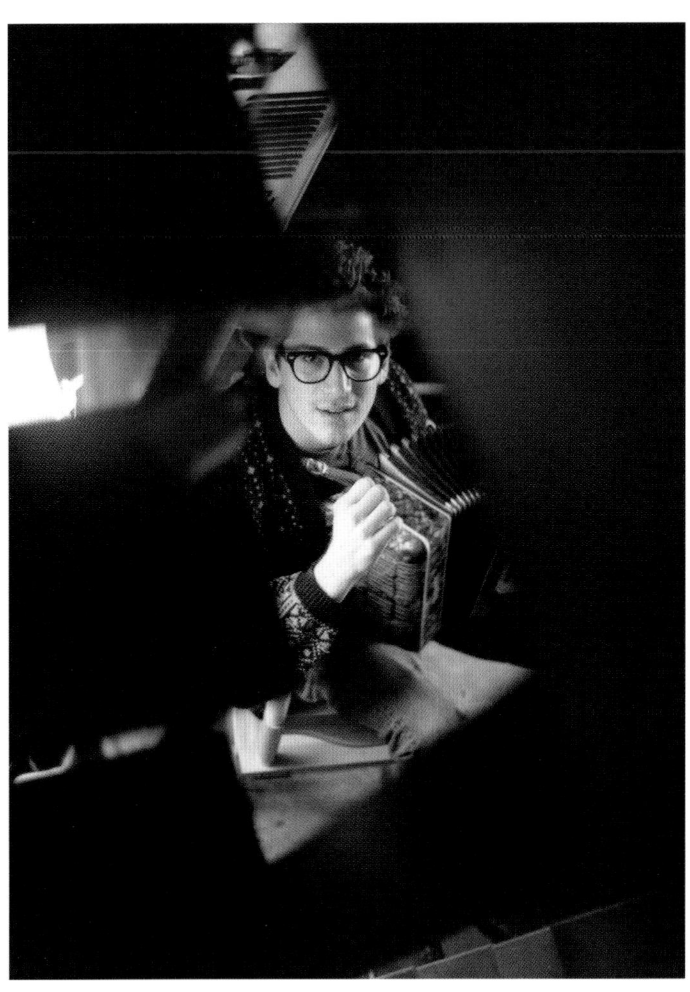

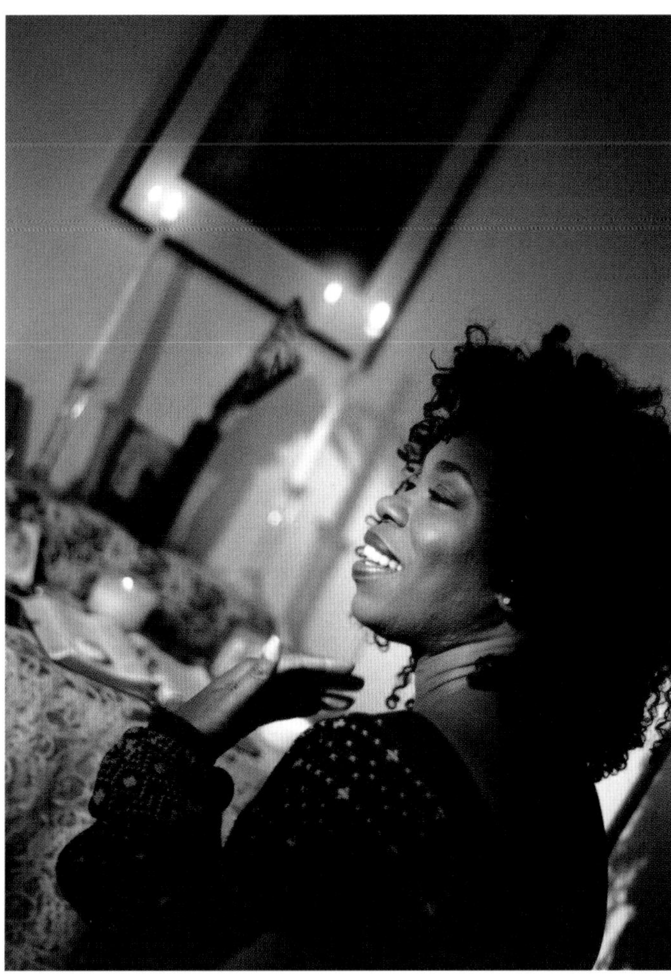

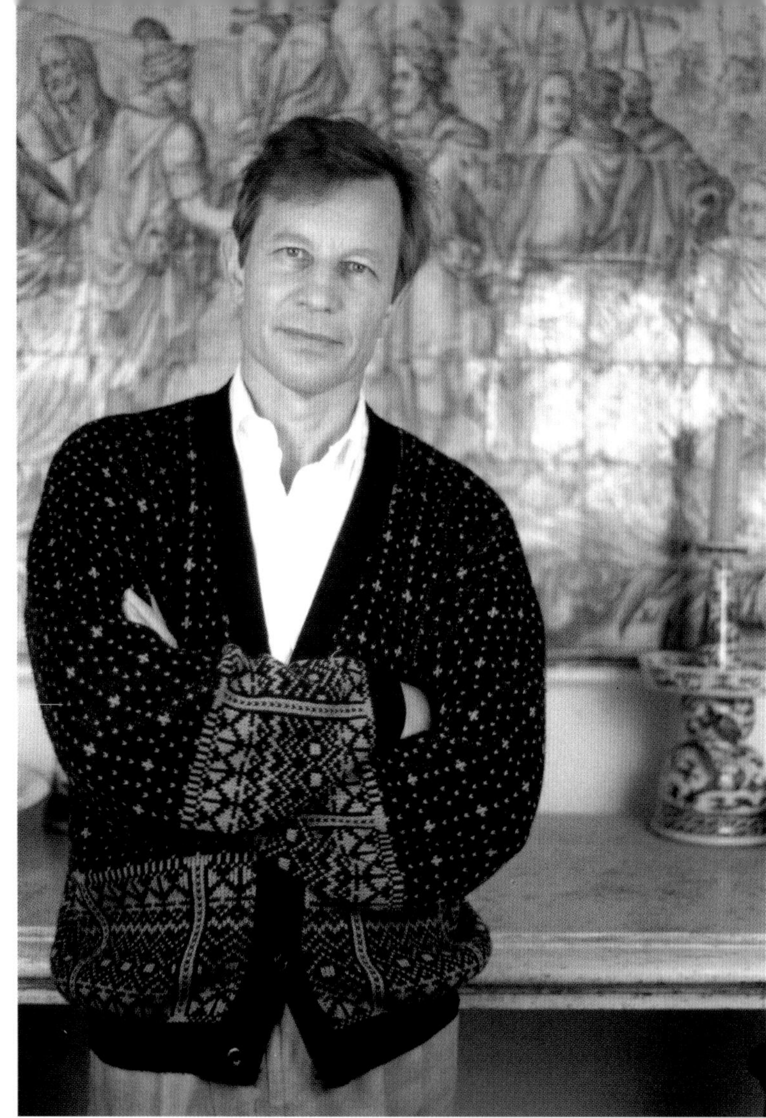

Michael York

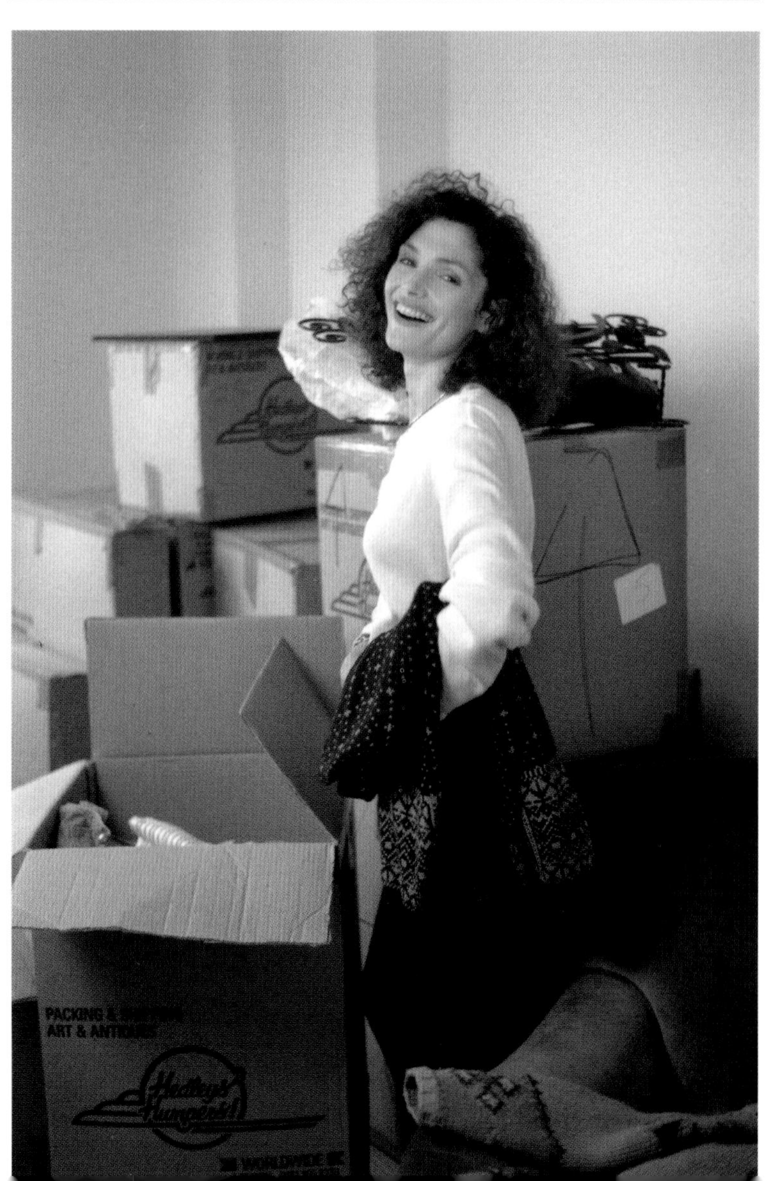

Mary Elizabeth Mastrantonio

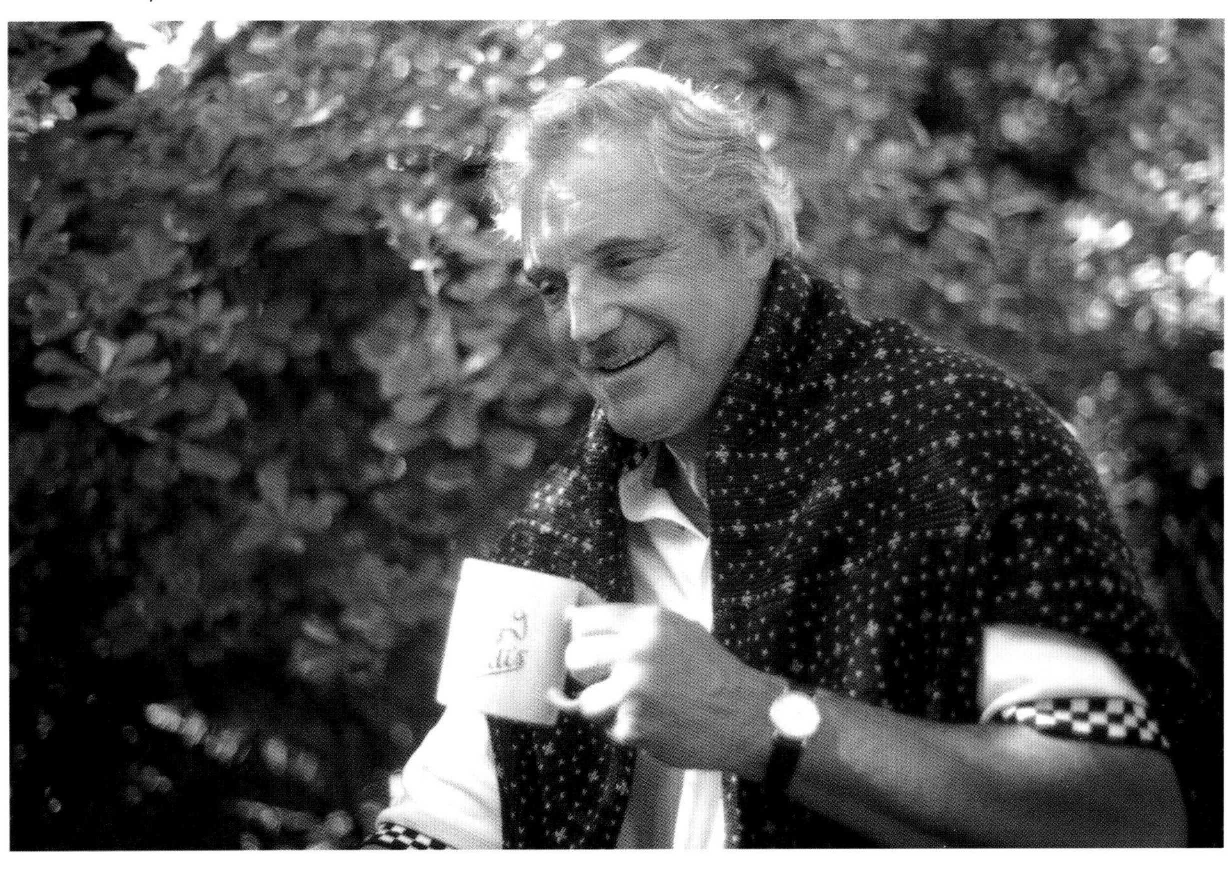

Hal Linden

Michele Lee

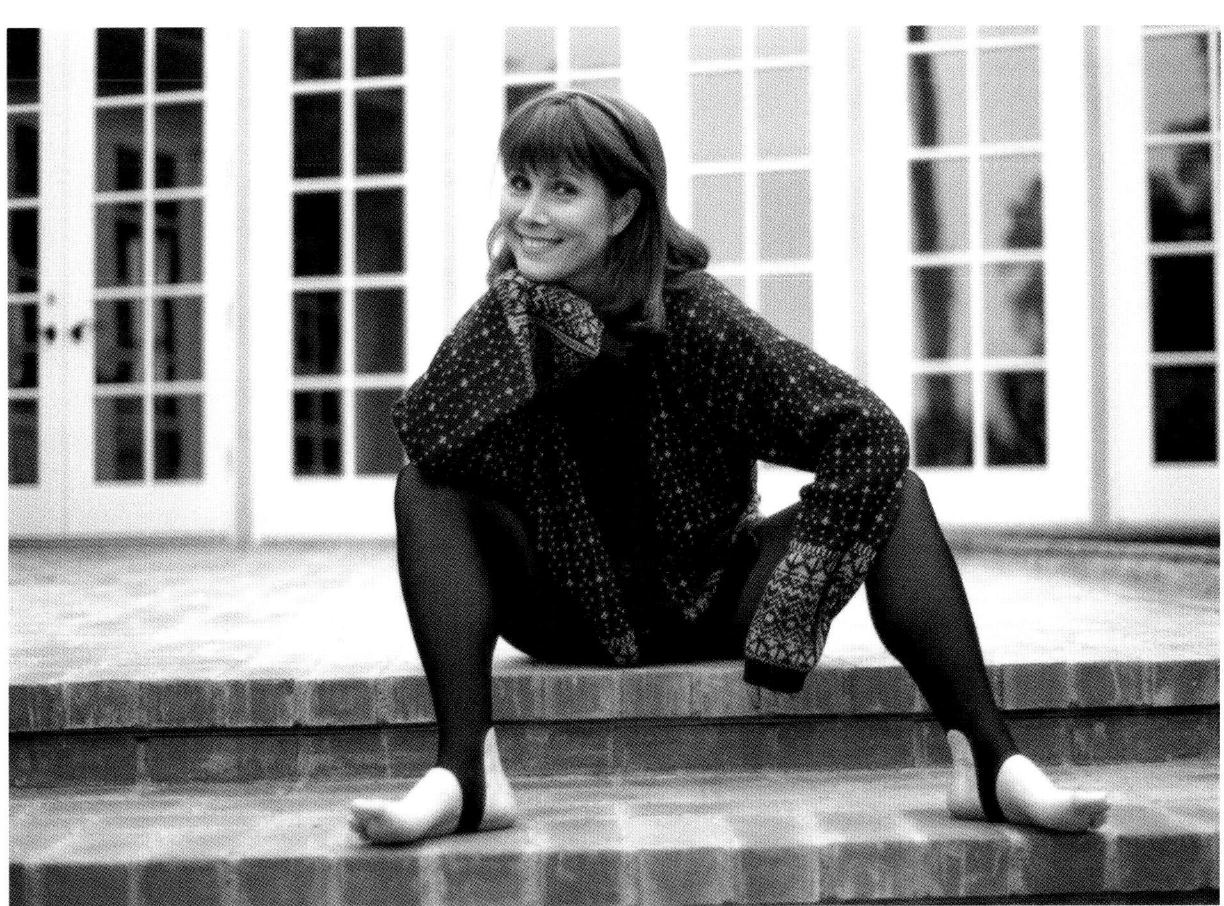

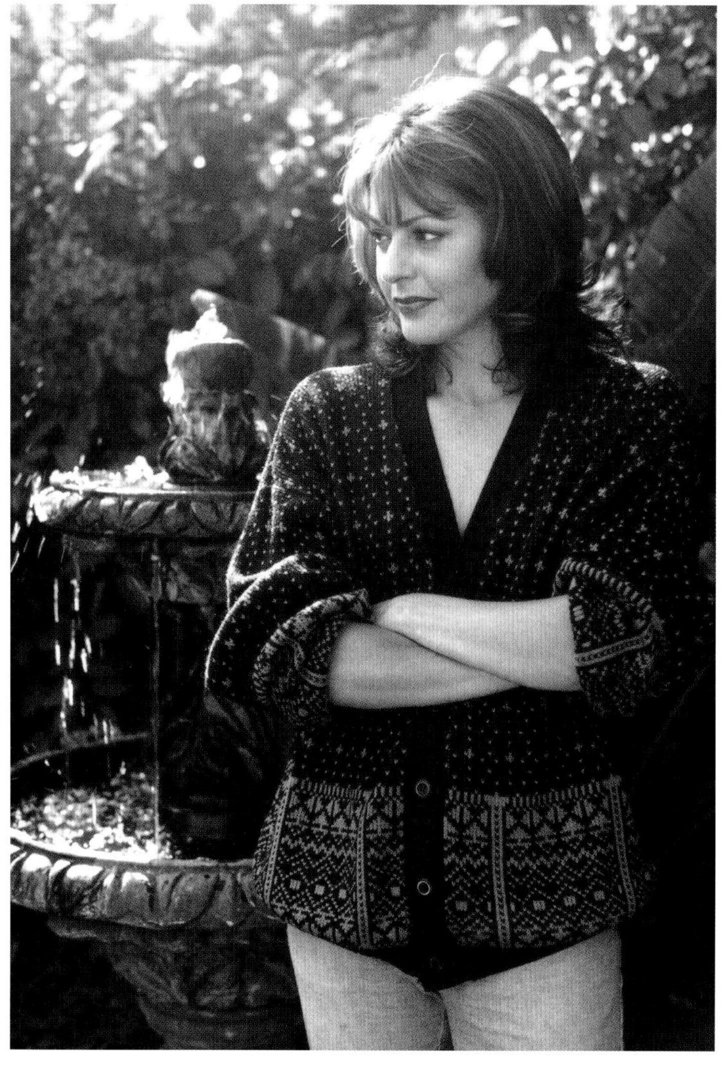

Jane Leeves

Jane Wyatt

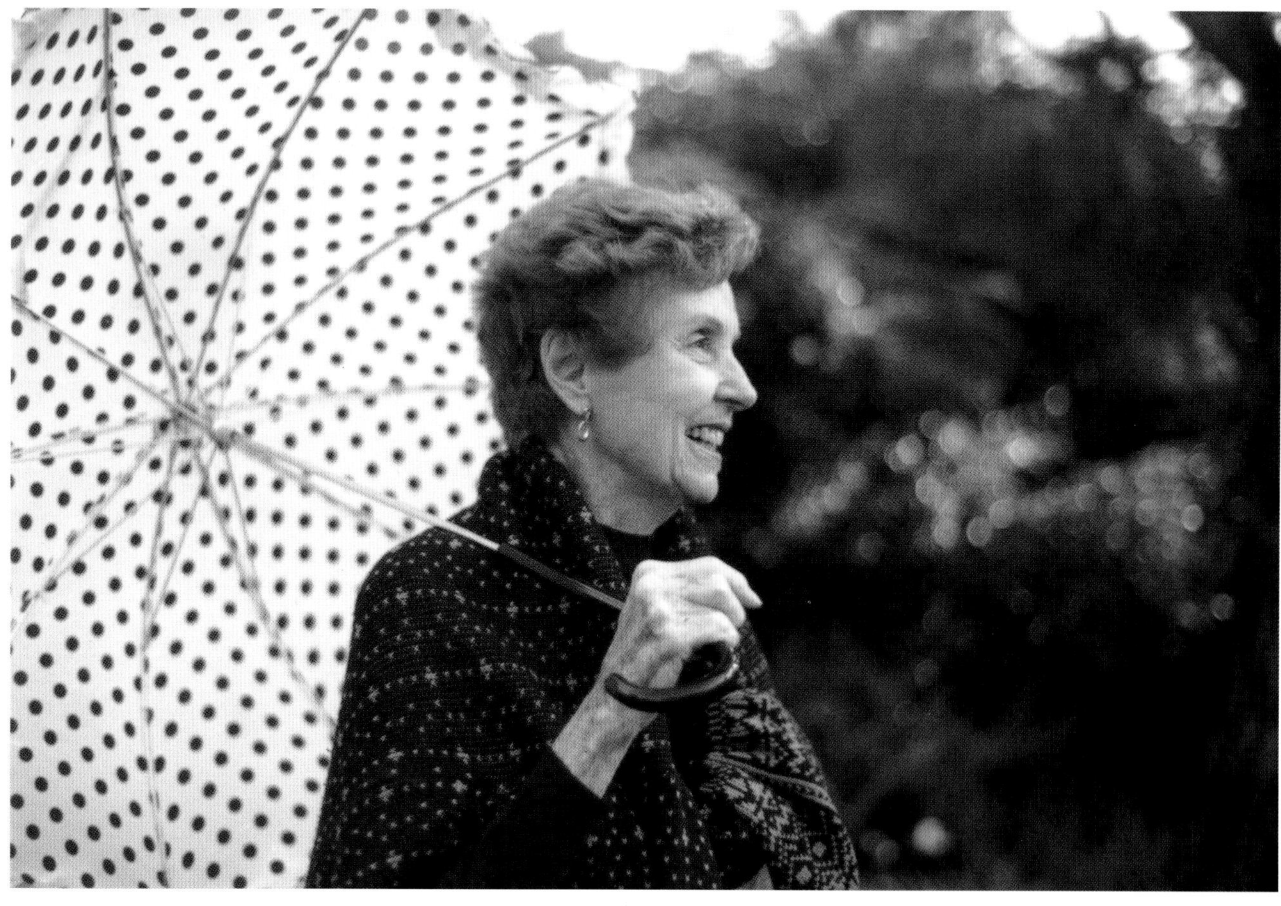

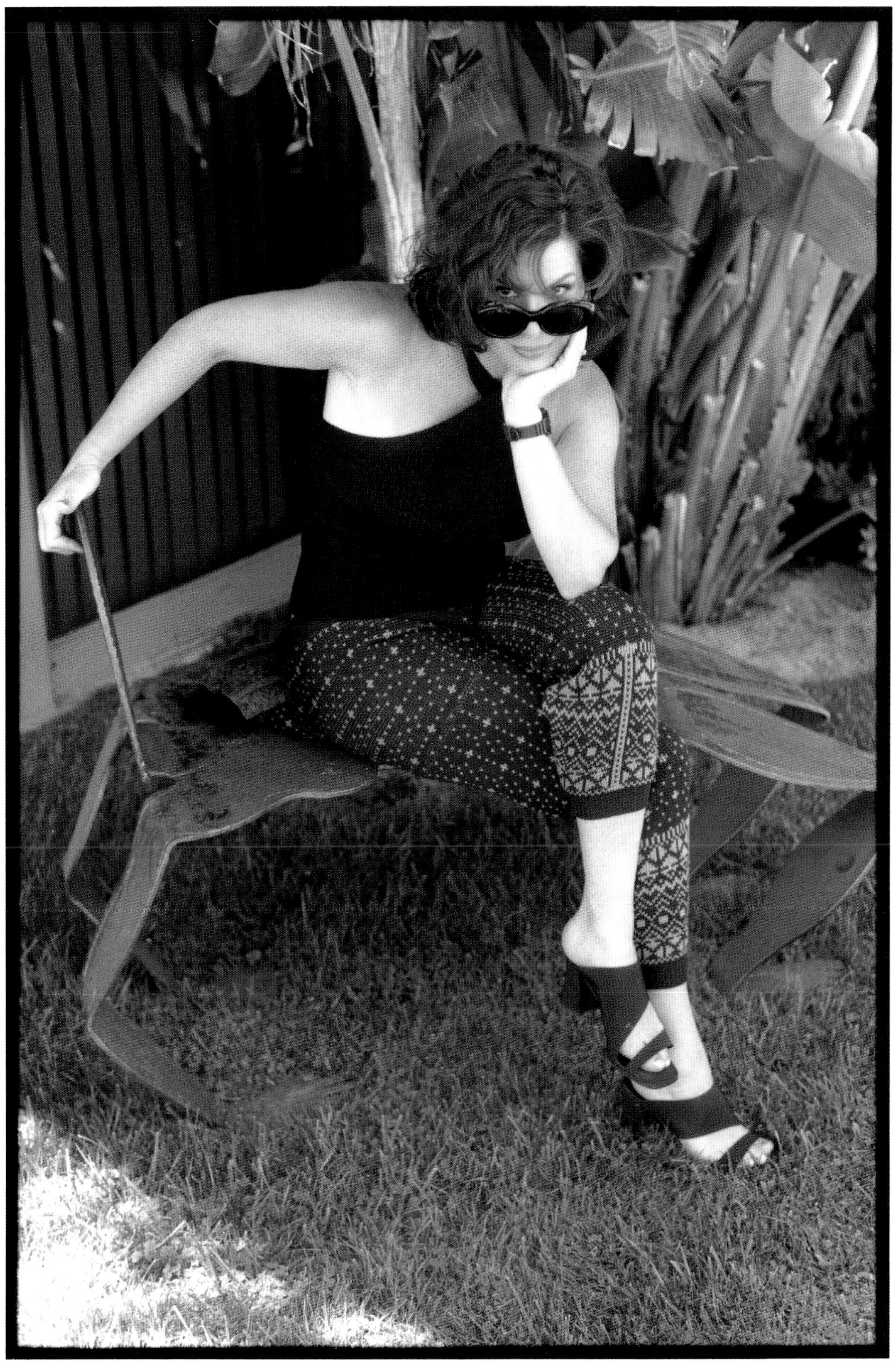

Marcia Gay Harden

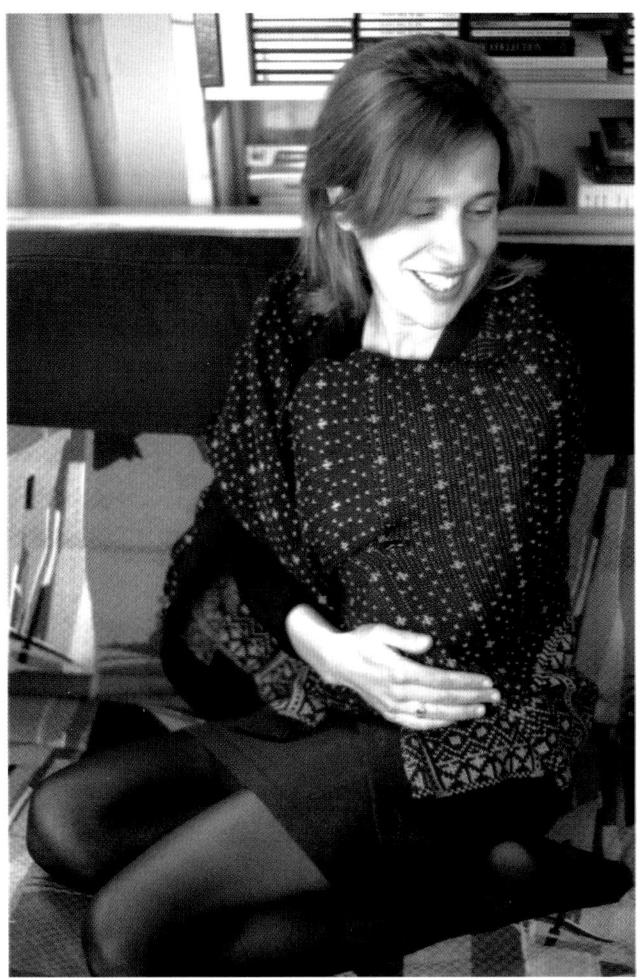

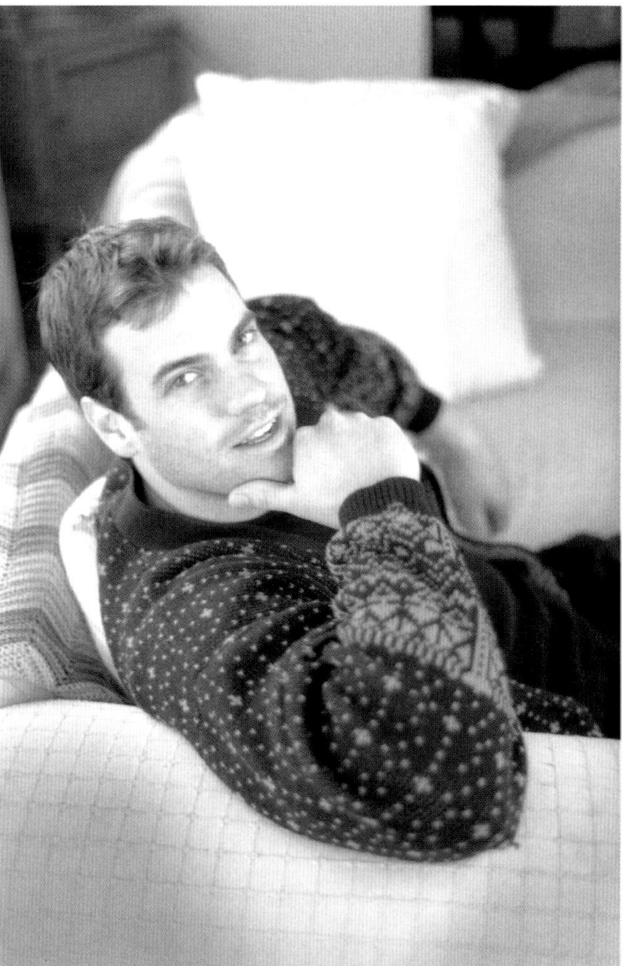

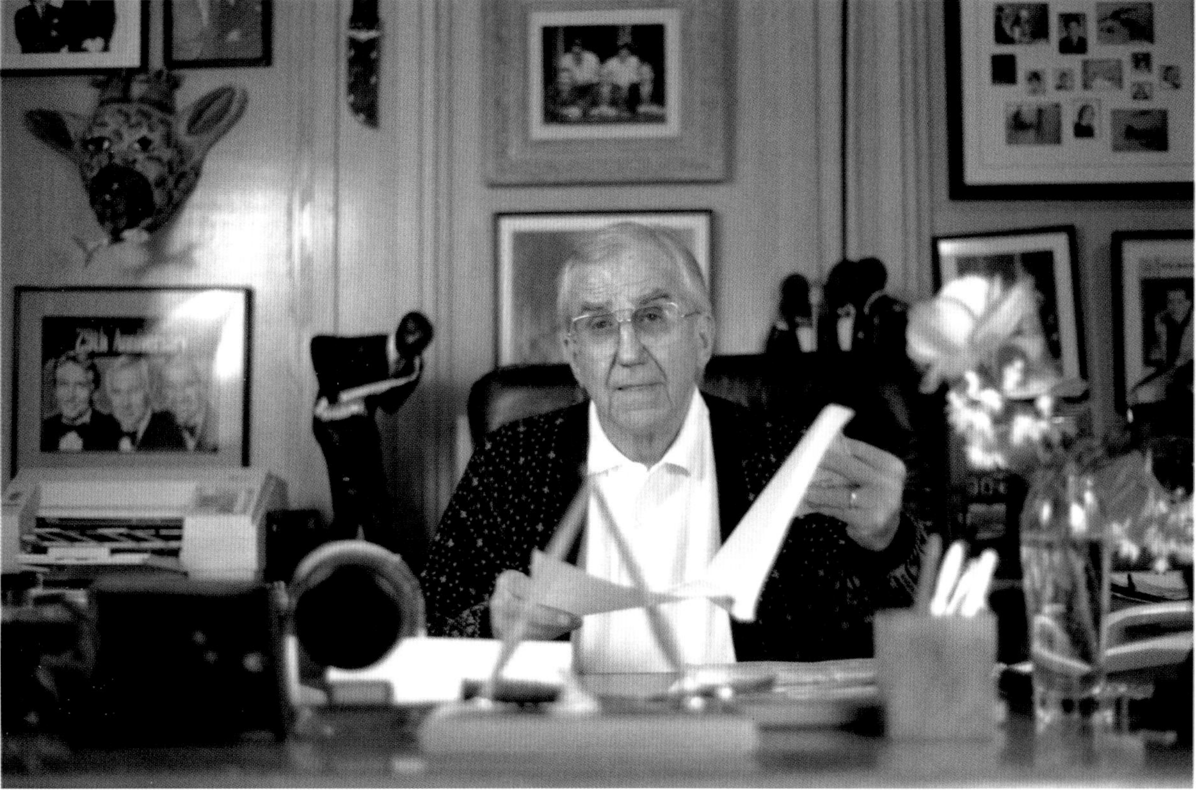

The picture of Ed McMahon (*bottom*) was shot at the desk in his office in his beautiful home; however, while you look at the pictures of Dana Reeve and Mitch Mullany (*top*), I must confess to you that these were taken not in their own homes, but in the homes of people who were strangers to them. I love these shots because they prove that if one is at home in one's own skin, one can be at home anywhere.

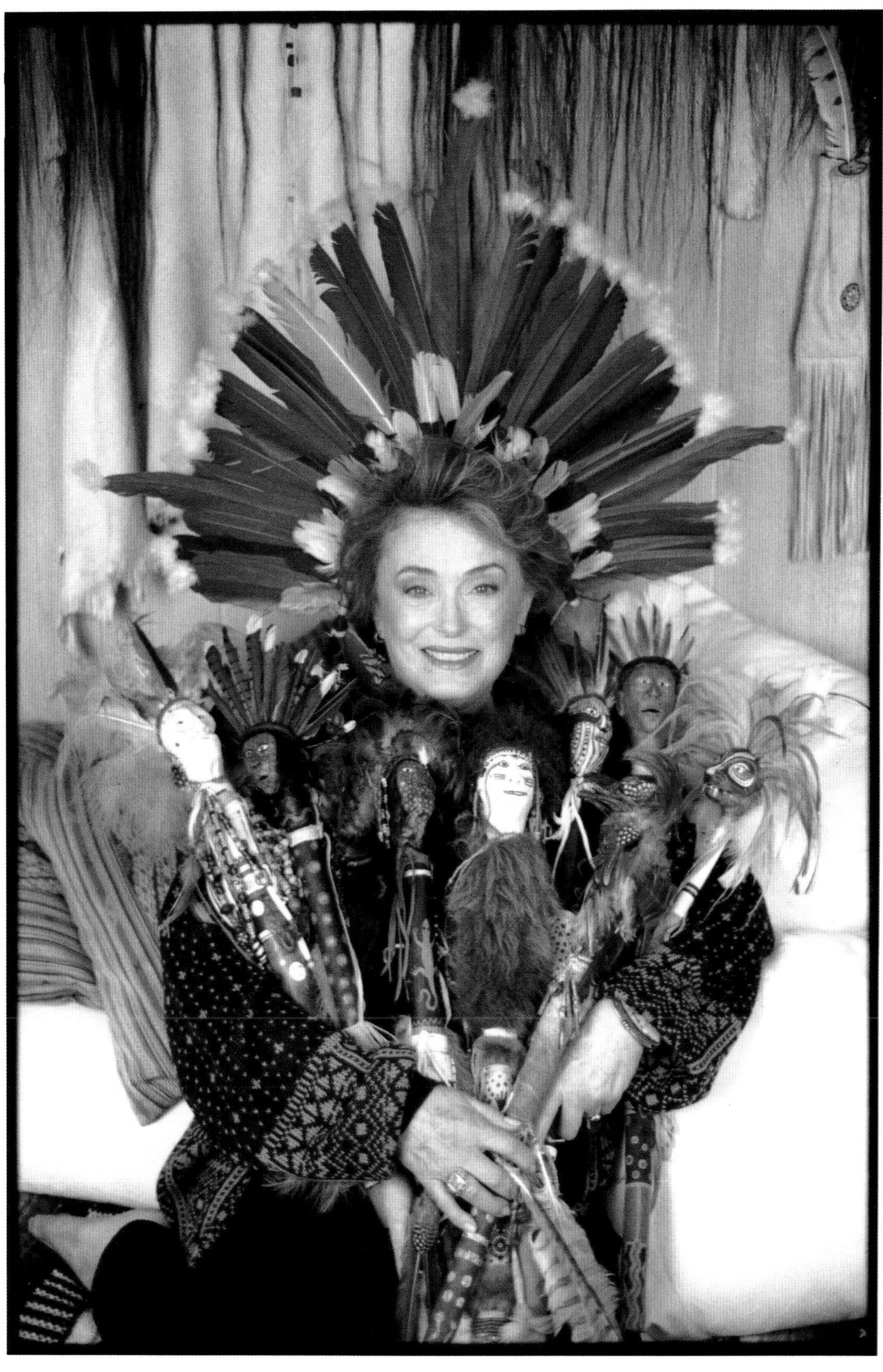

Rue McLanahan

You would never know it, given her famous Scottish-sounding names, but Rue McLanahan has Choctaw Indian in her heritage. I was very excited because I am part Cherokee and I love the history and the artwork of the Native Americans; clearly, so does Rue. Her home is filled with the artwork of her ancestors and we were like kids, running around the house, choosing the pieces that would be shown in the photo, cramming in as many as her arms would hold. Of course, the pieces we chose first were the ones that had already come loose from their places on the wall because of the last earthquake!

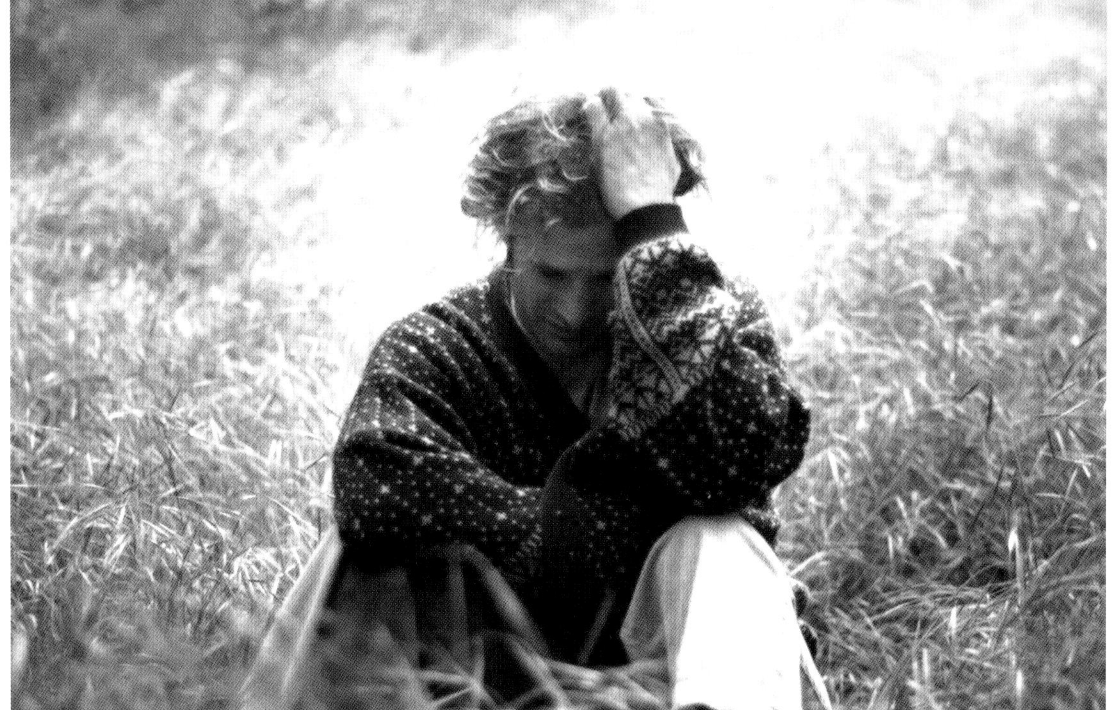

Kurt Deutsch

Bess Armstrong

Channon Roe

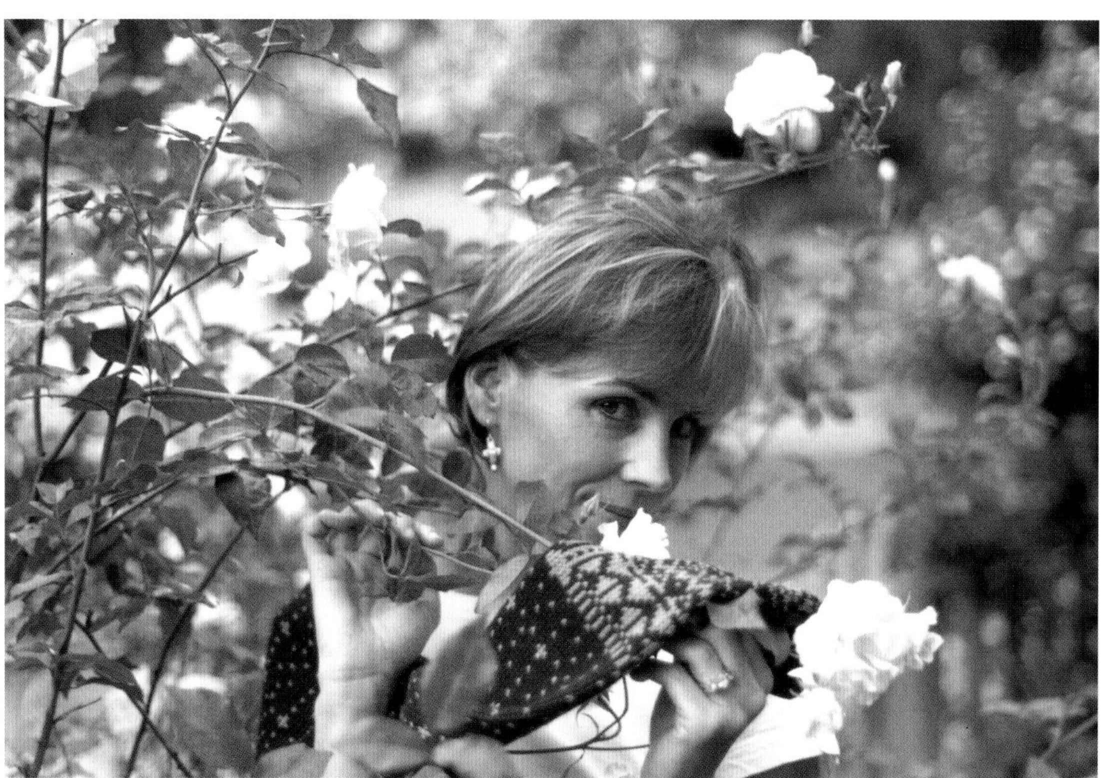

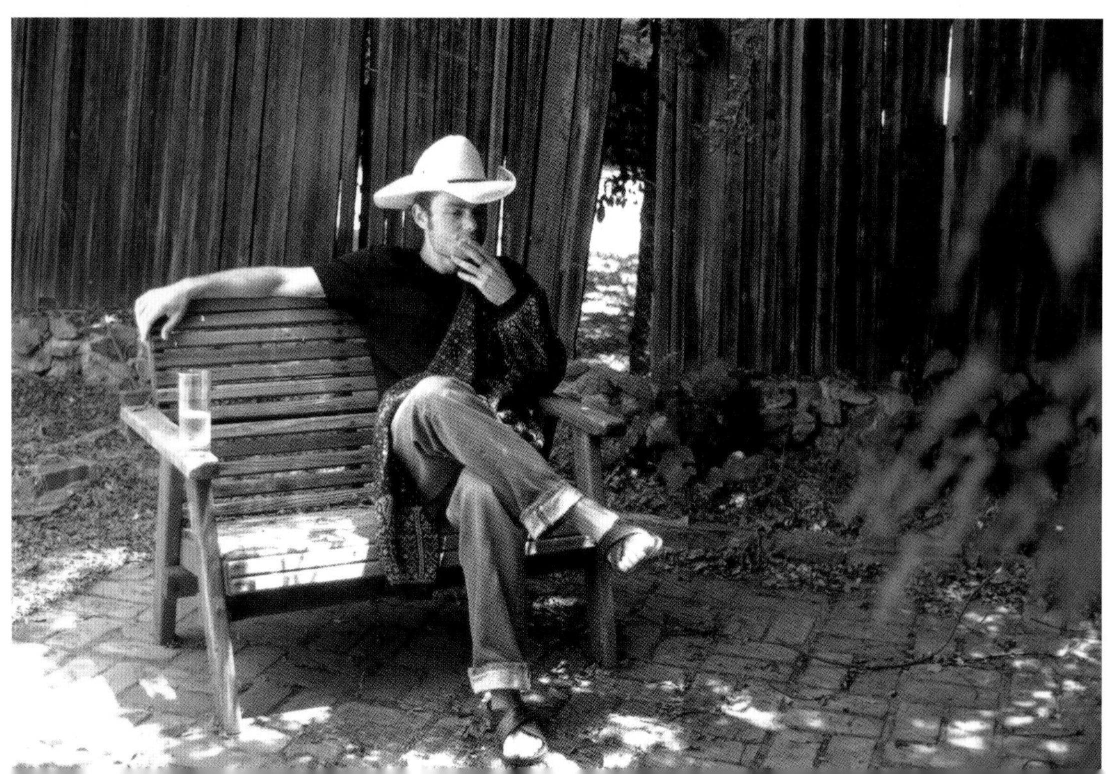

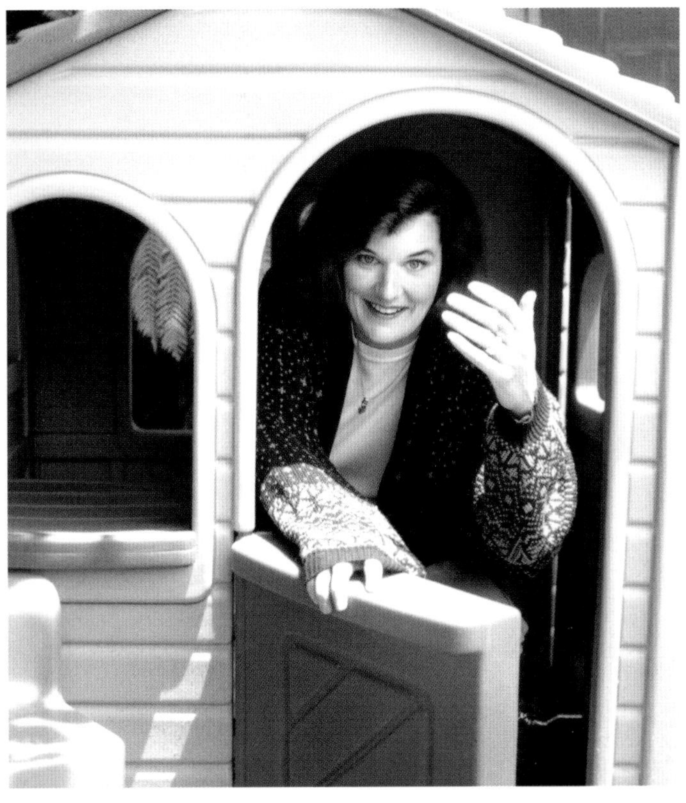

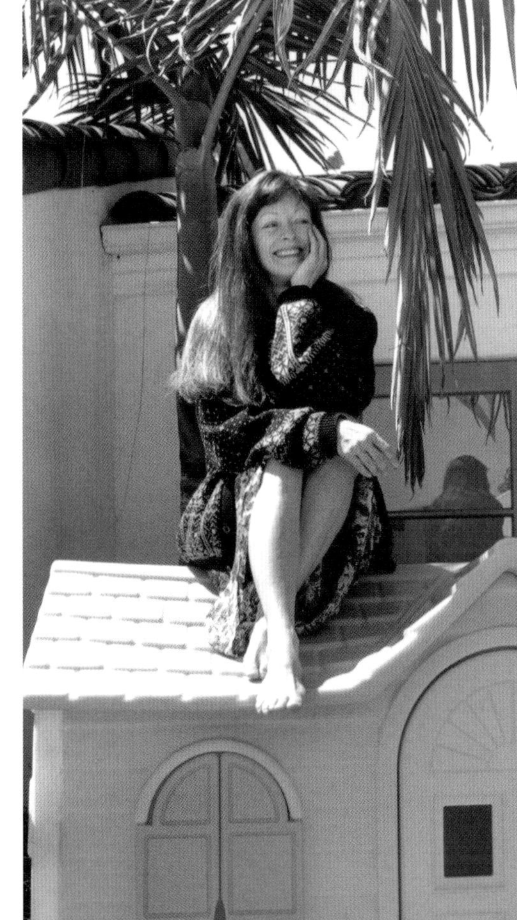

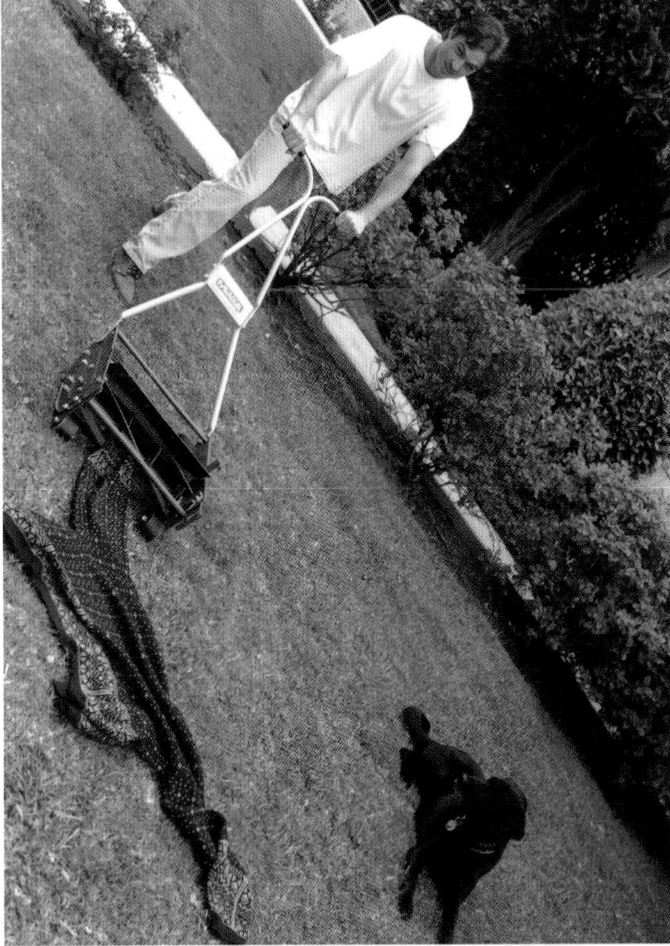

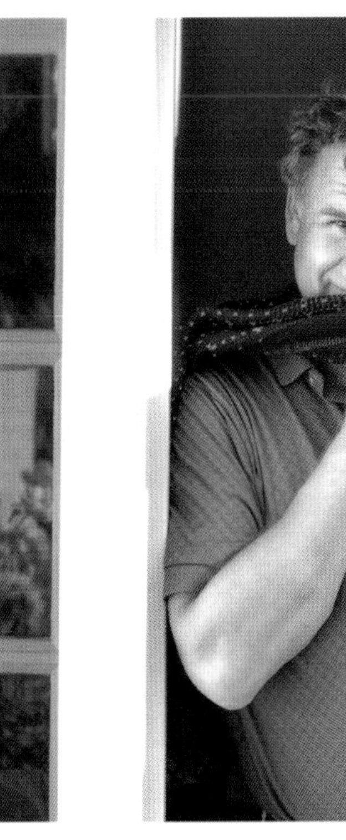

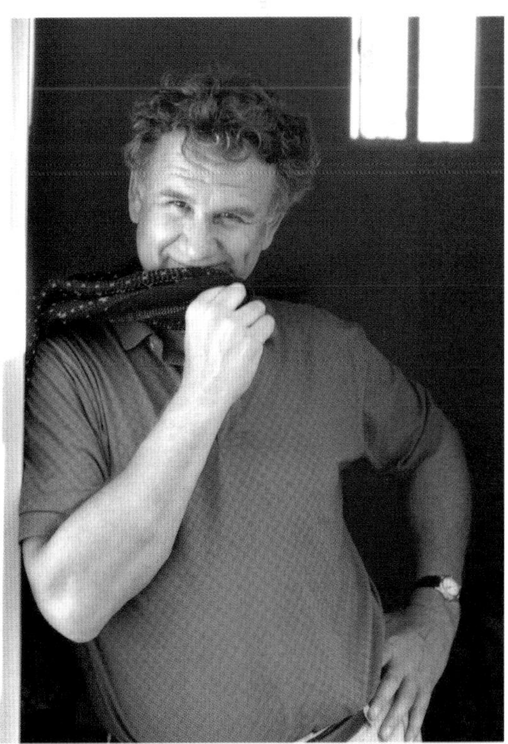

From left to right:

Paula Poundstone, Frances Fisher

Eric Close, Garrett Brown

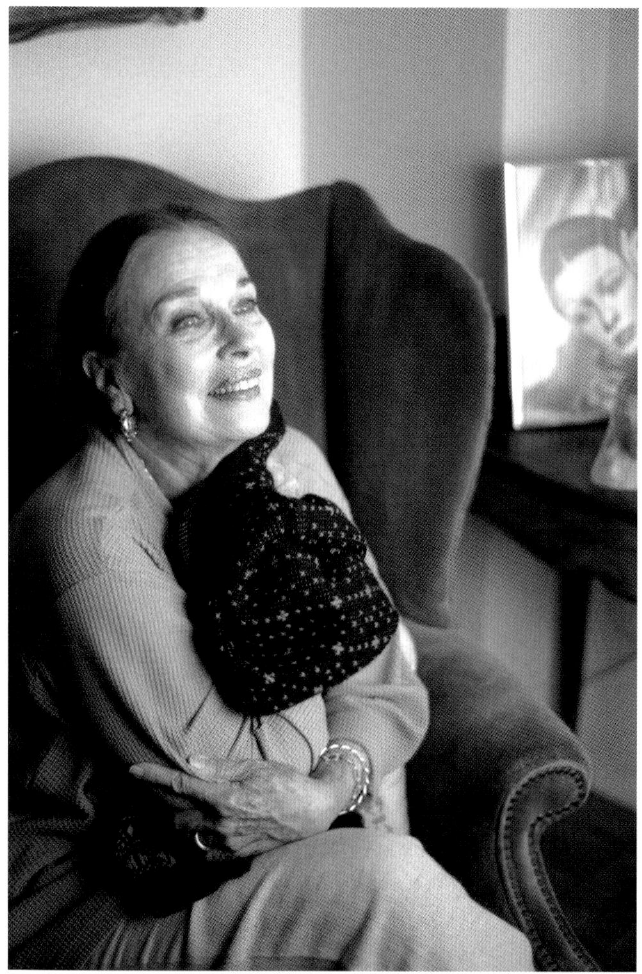

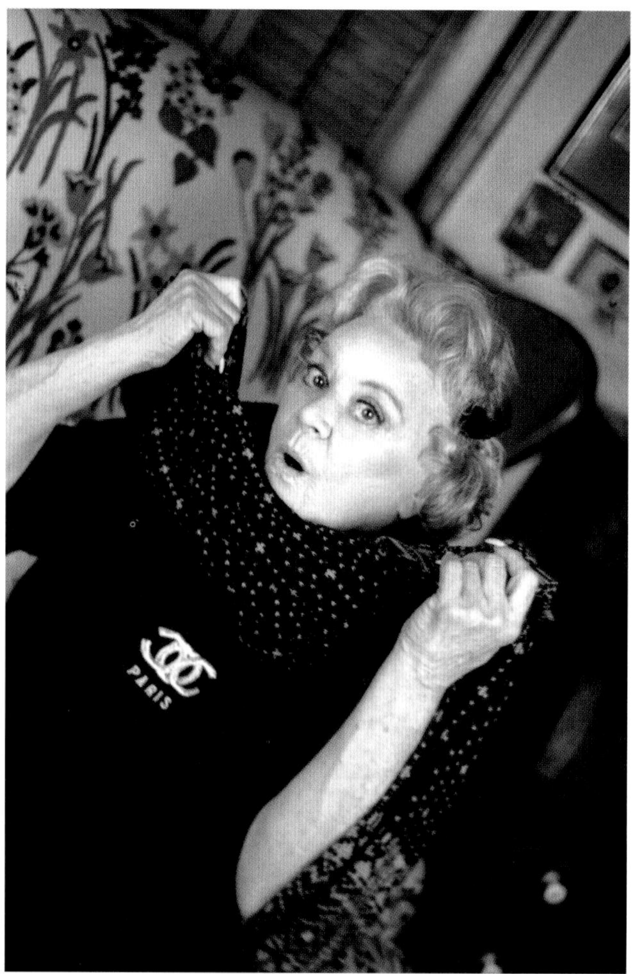

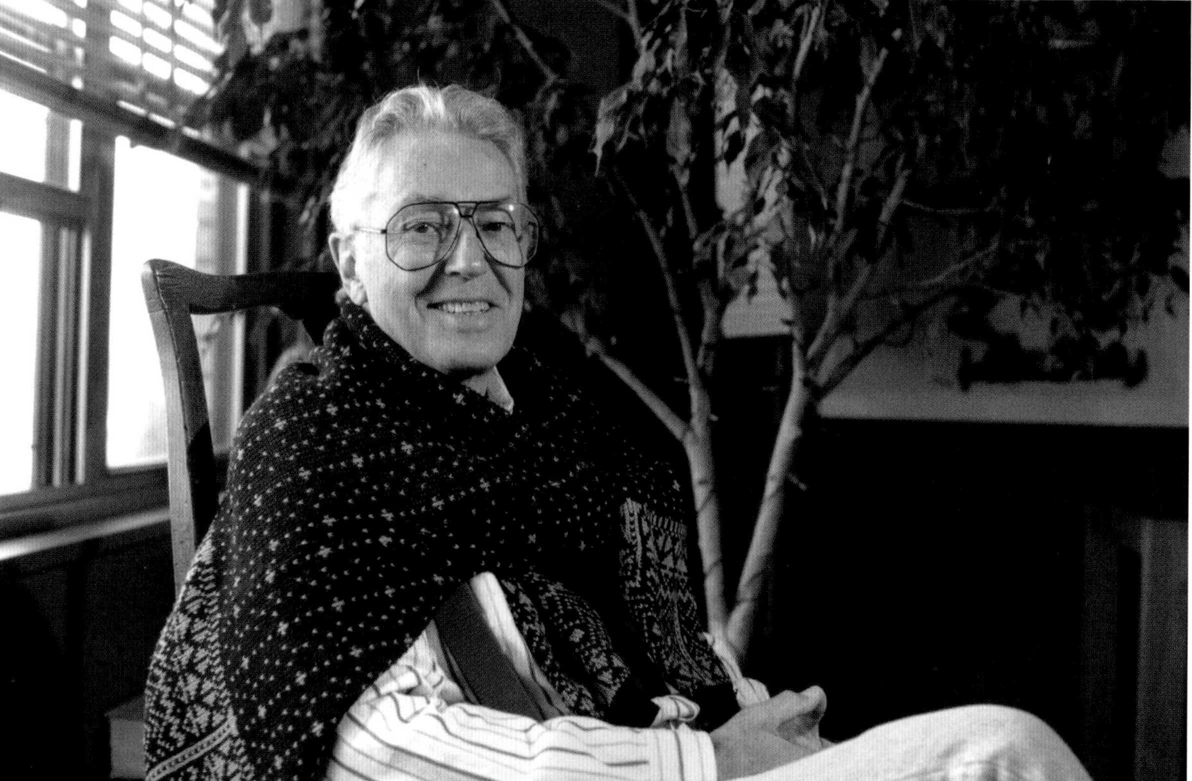

Clockwise from top left: Patricia Morrison, Rose Marie, Farley Granger

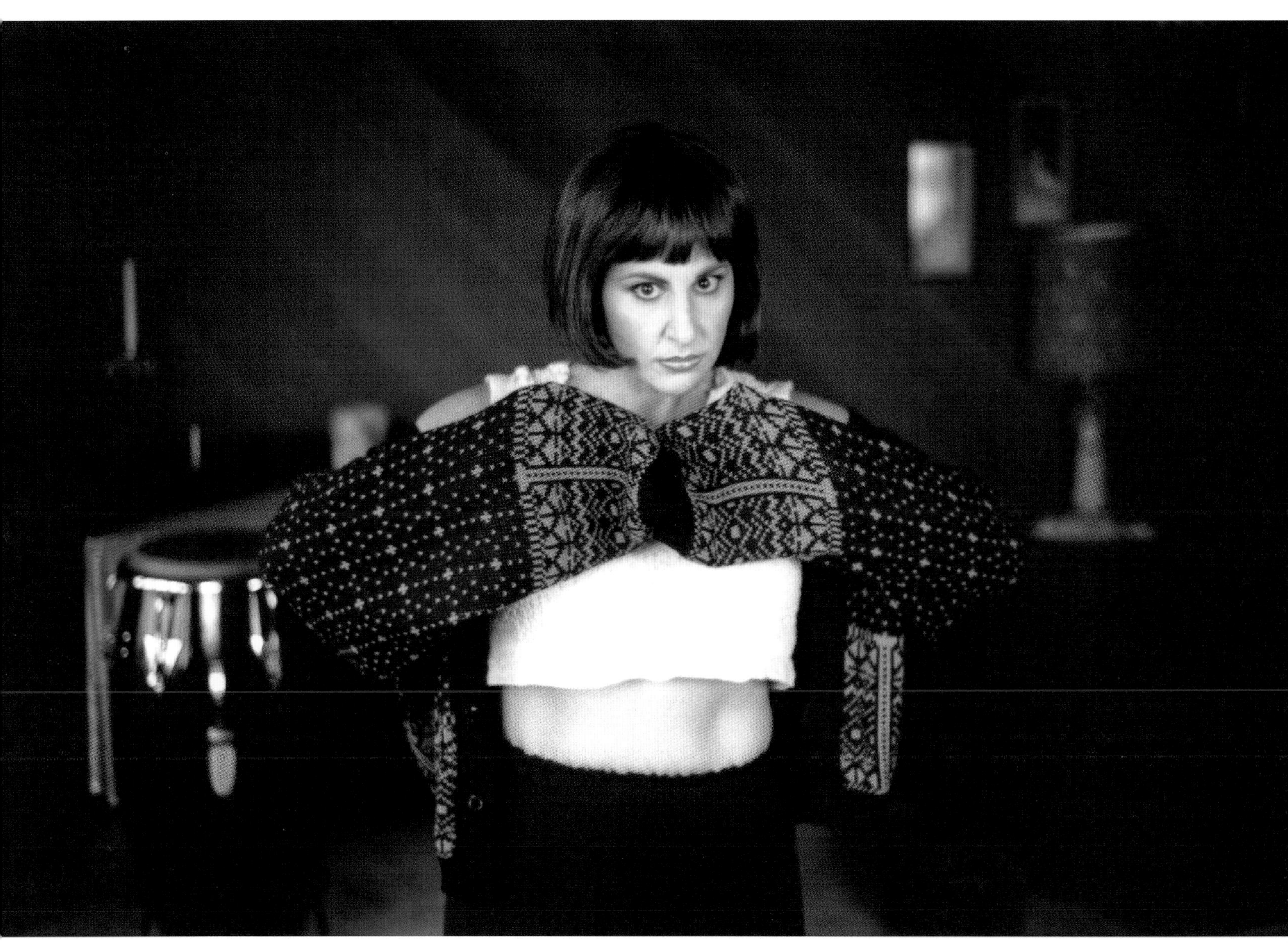

Kathy Najimy

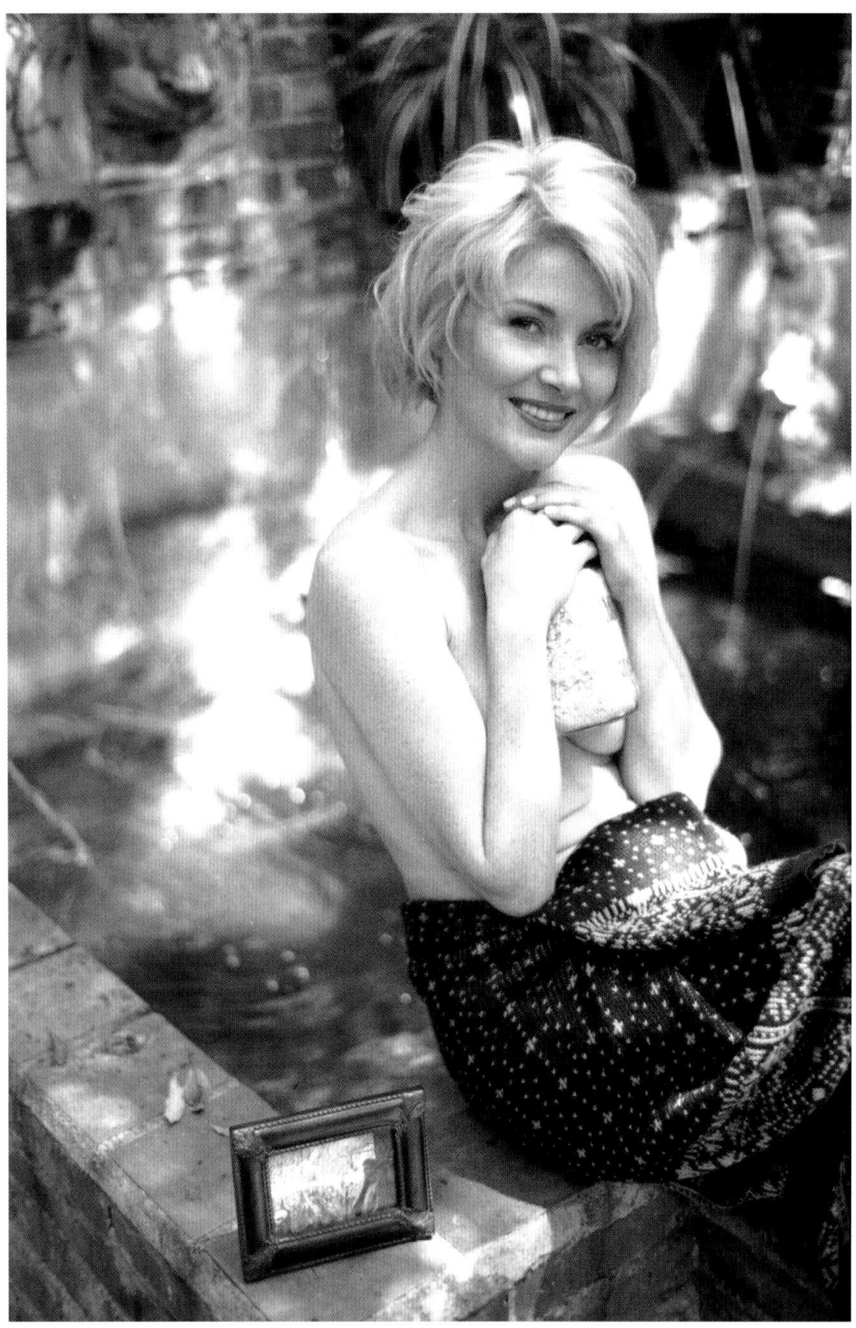

Beth Broderick

Beth Broderick is an AIDS activist. She has been involved with the fight from the very beginning, and I could not be more proud to know her and to have her in this collection. I was particularly moved when I arrived for the photo shoot and Beth told me that her best friend, Lance, had been lost in the crisis and that she wanted him in the photo with her. It was more, though, than the small framed photo of Lance that would sit on the fountain in her garden during the shoot; he would literally be cradled in her arms while we worked, for his ashes are kept lovingly in a mason jar in her home—always within arm's reach. It was an emotional shoot for me, but Beth lightened it when she told me that she had befriended this man when, late for an audition years ago, she ran out of her apartment and asked her next-door neighbor to help her unstick her broken zipper. This was the first time they had met, and when she returned home that night, there was a note on her door. Lance had gone to the movies that day and seen *Stealing Home*. The note declared that he had seen her in a movie that very day and thought she was marvelous and could they please be friends?

Friendships are made in a moment. Sometimes the moment is over before it has even started, but the wheels that it sets in motion have a momentum that is unending. How funny it is to think that a zipper set such a wheel on its path.

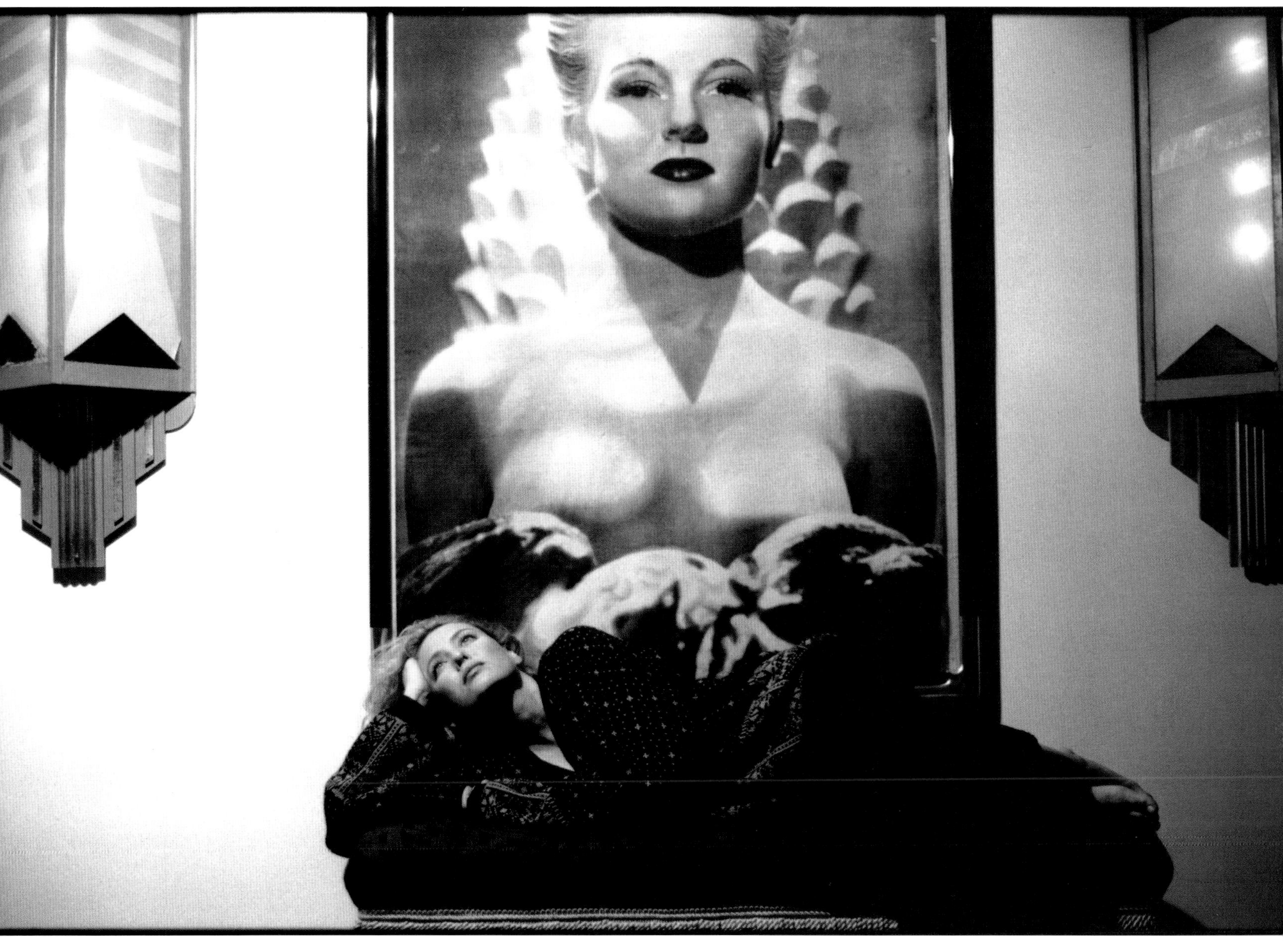

Virginia Madsen

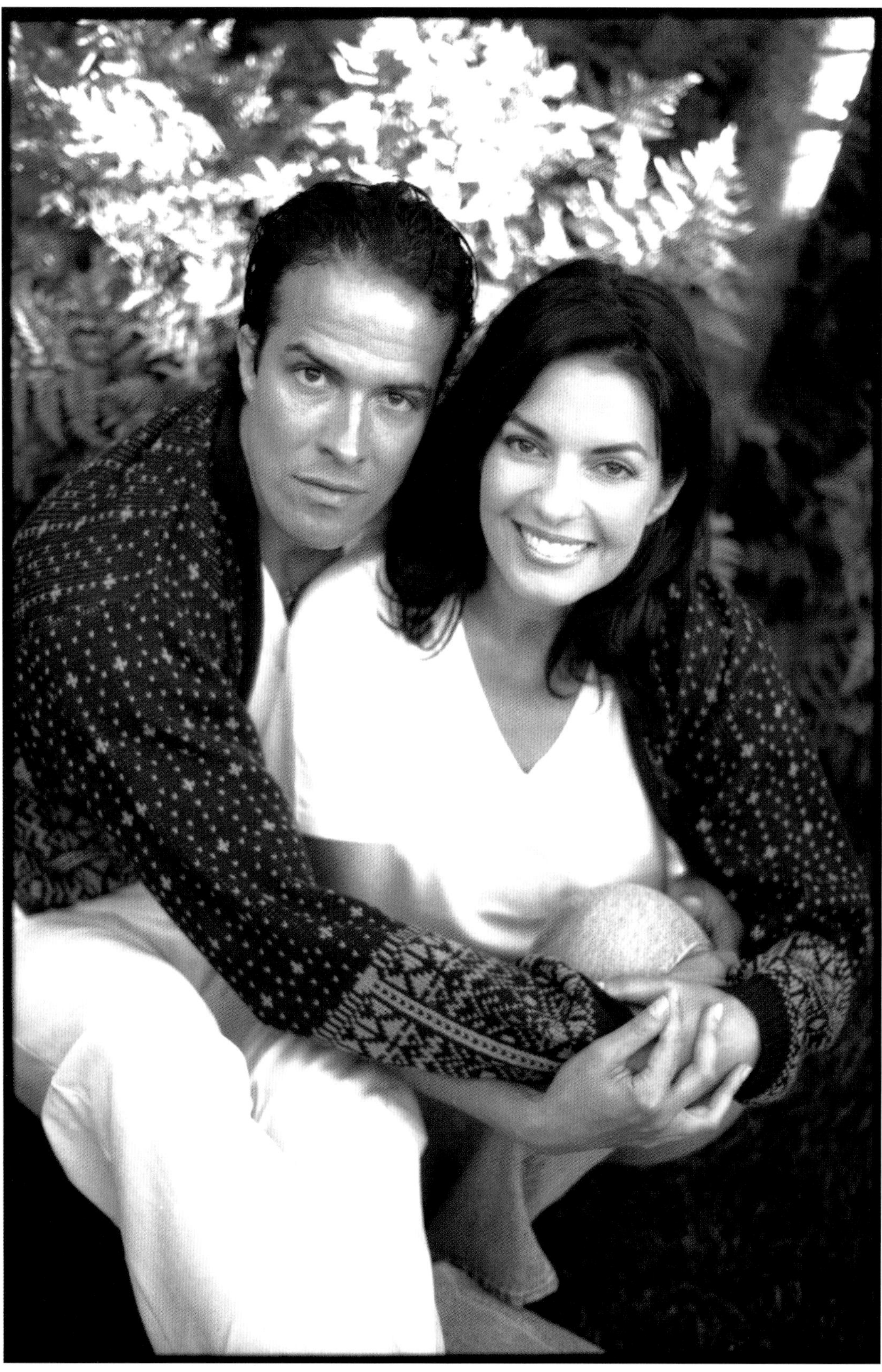

Brock Ward and sister, Sela

One of the philosophies from the TV show *Sisters* was that *parents die, children will leave, so do husbands and lovers but not your sisters. They're the only ones who know each other from cradle to grave.*

When Sela Ward is with Brock, it's clear to see there's no question about such devotion—just the sex of the sibling!

THE SWEATER OUT WEST— *in which the sweater goes Hollywood*

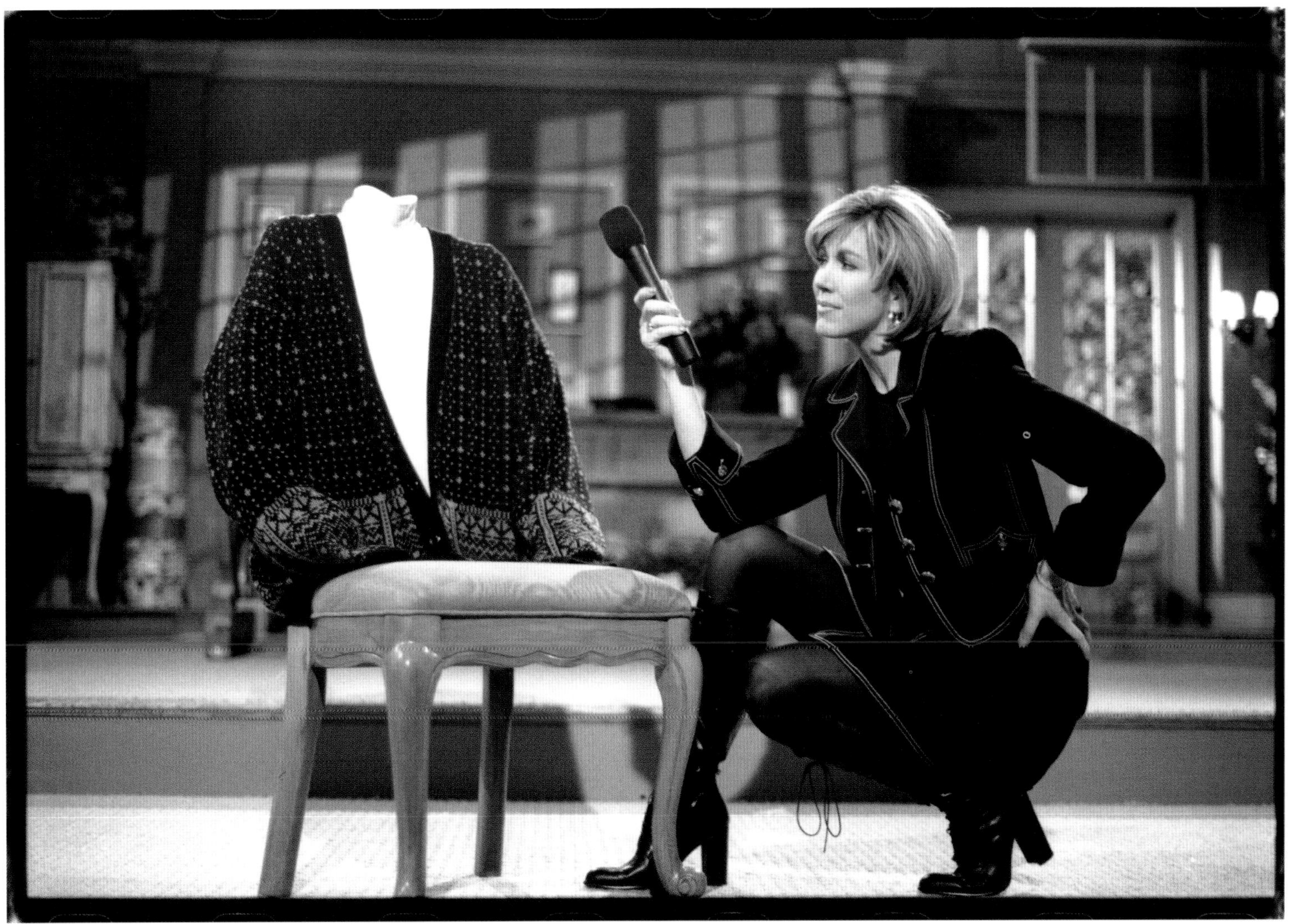

Leeza Gibbons

"Oh, sweatered one, you've been worn by so many people. If you could only talk, what would you say?"

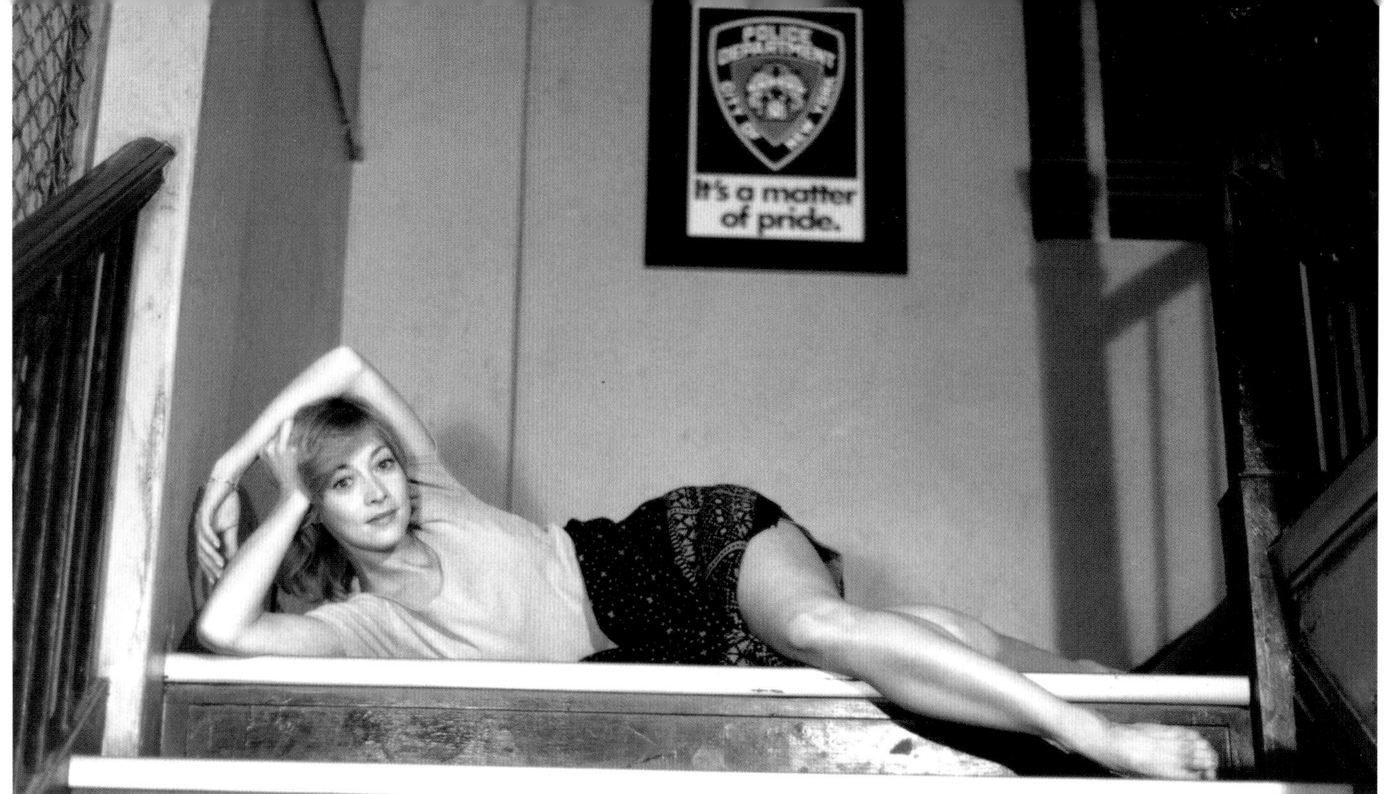
POLICE DEPARTMENT
It's a matter of pride.

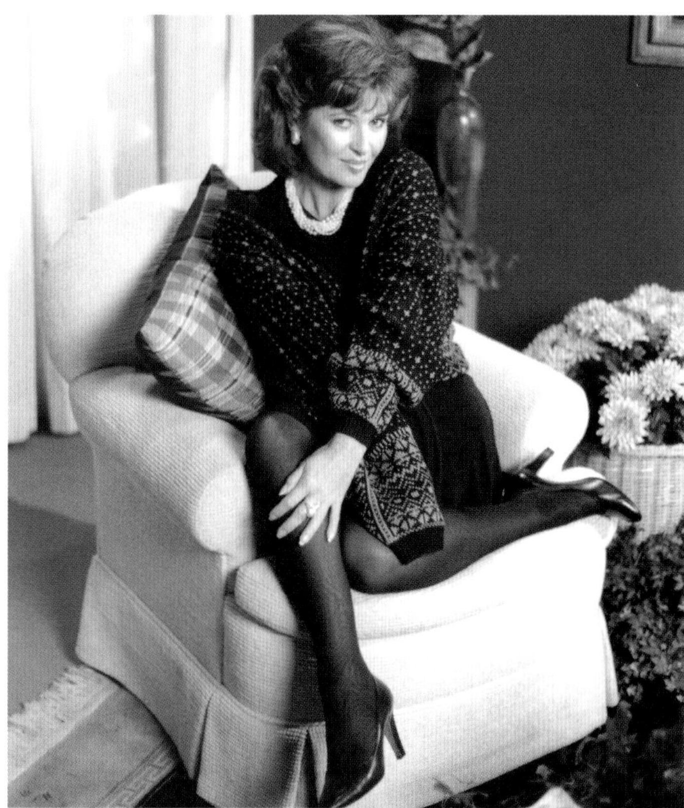

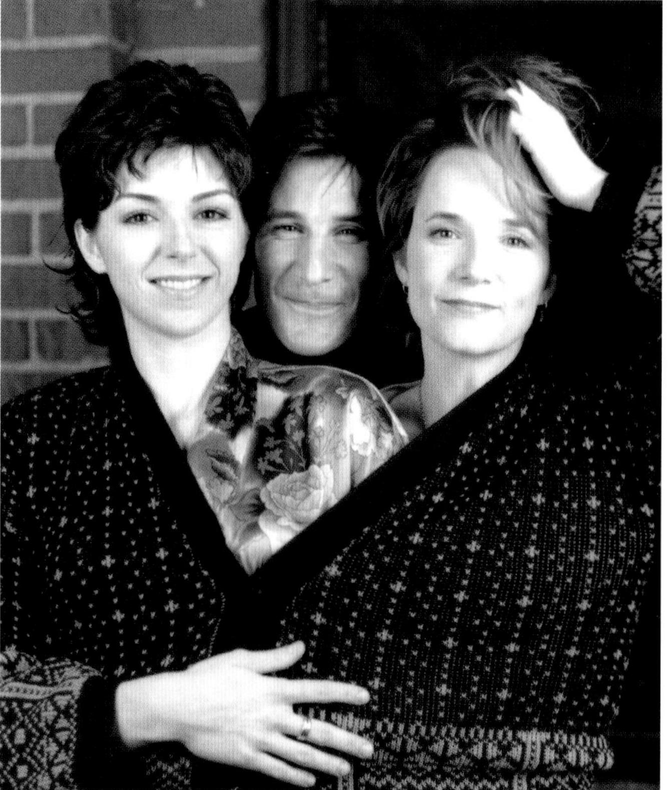

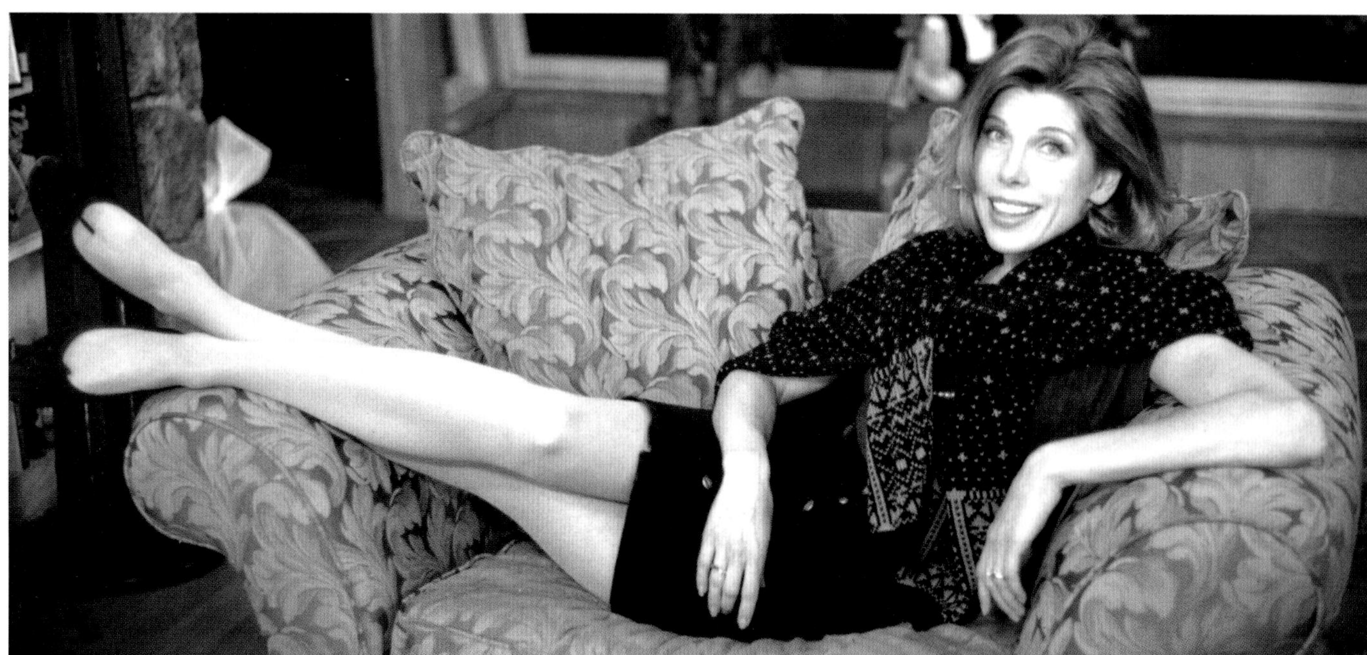

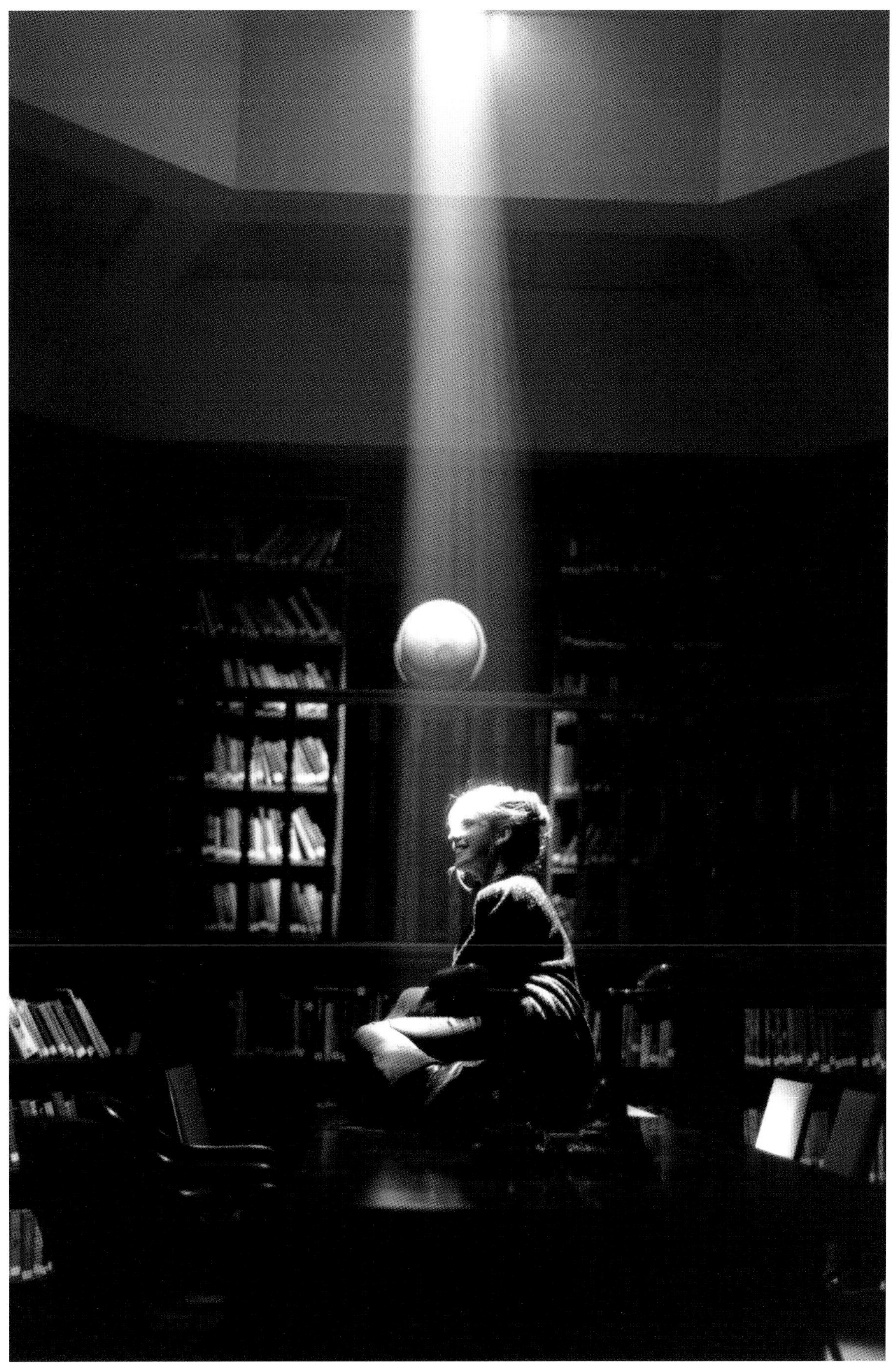

Sarah Michelle Gellar on the set of *Buffy the Vampire Slayer*

Opposite, clockwise from top: Sharon Lawrence on the set of *NYPD Blue*; Amy Pietz, Andy Lauer, and Lea Thompson on the set of *Caroline in the City*; Christine Baranski on the set of *Cybill*; Stephanie Beacham on the set of an infomercial

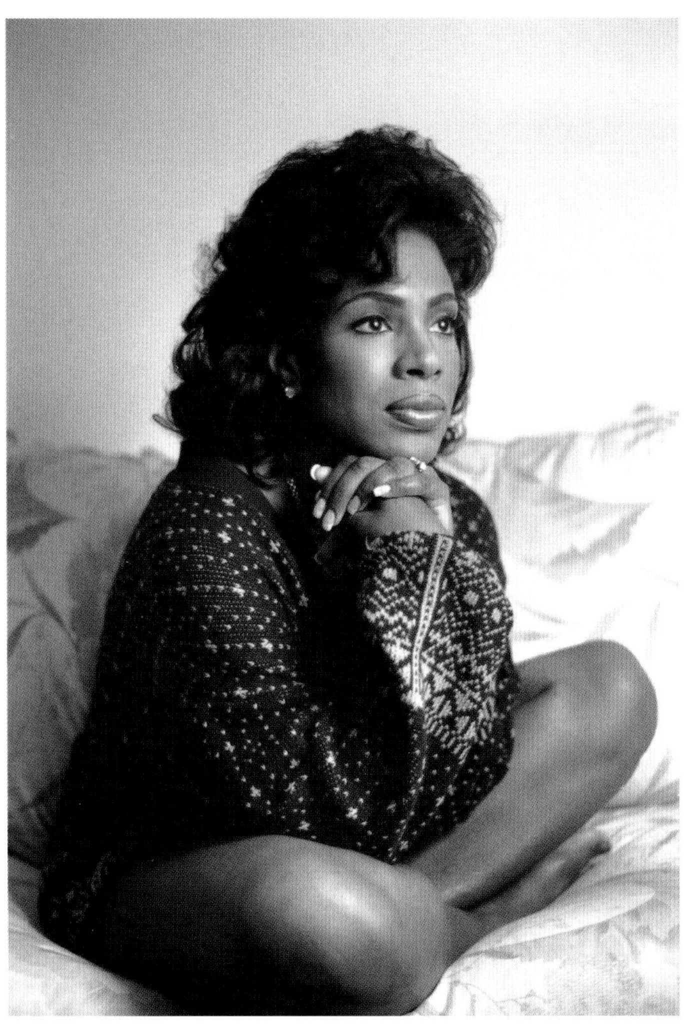

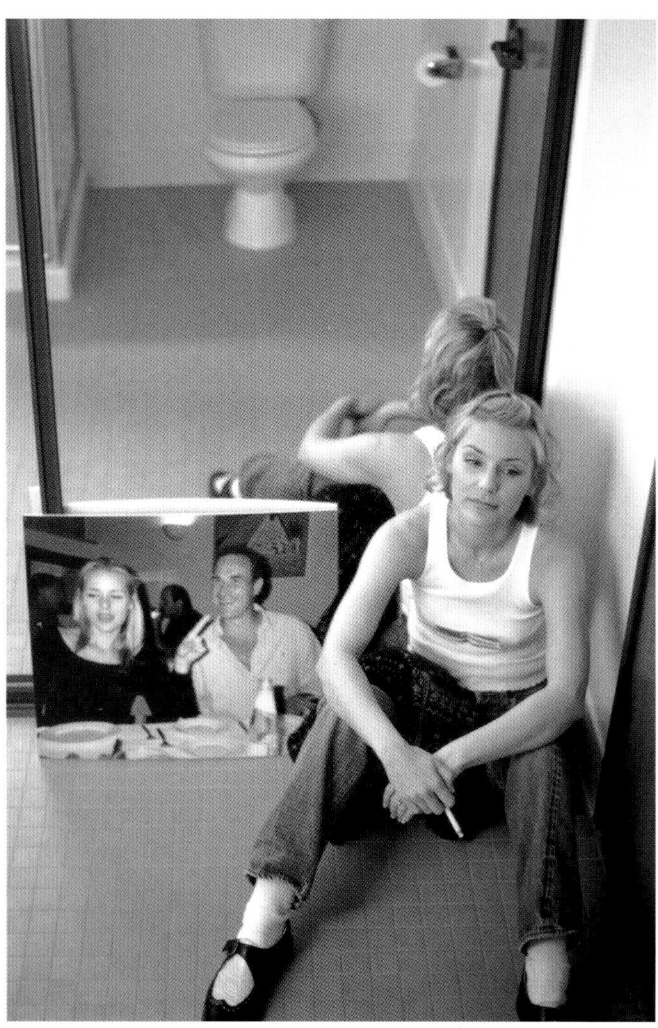

Sheryl Lee Ralph, DeeDee Pfeiffer

Peter Krause and Alicia Witt, Molly Hagan and Lightfield Lewis

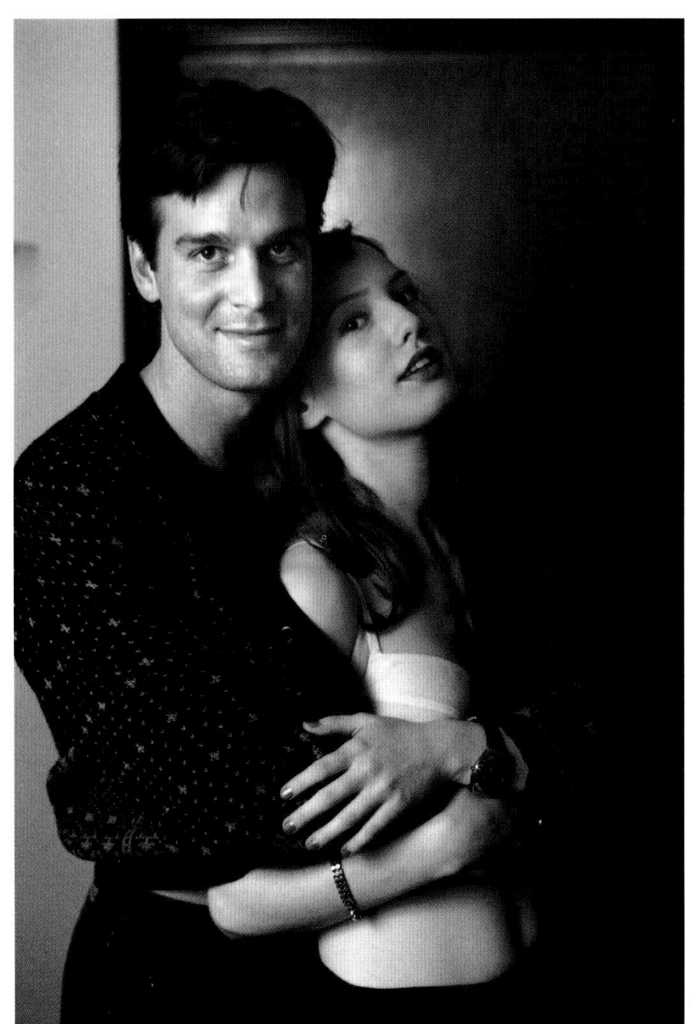

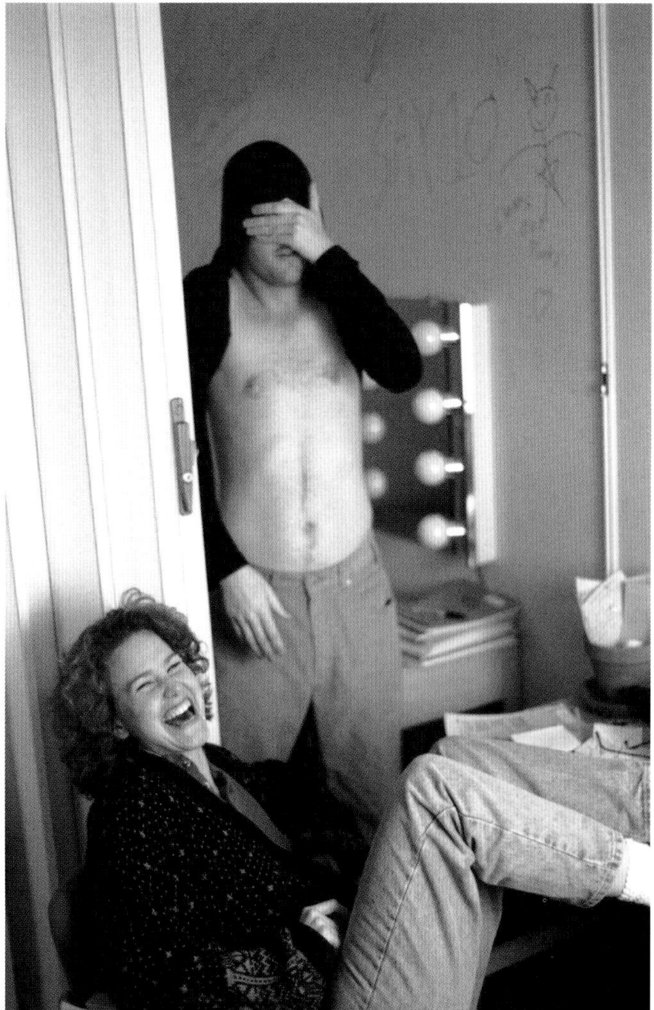

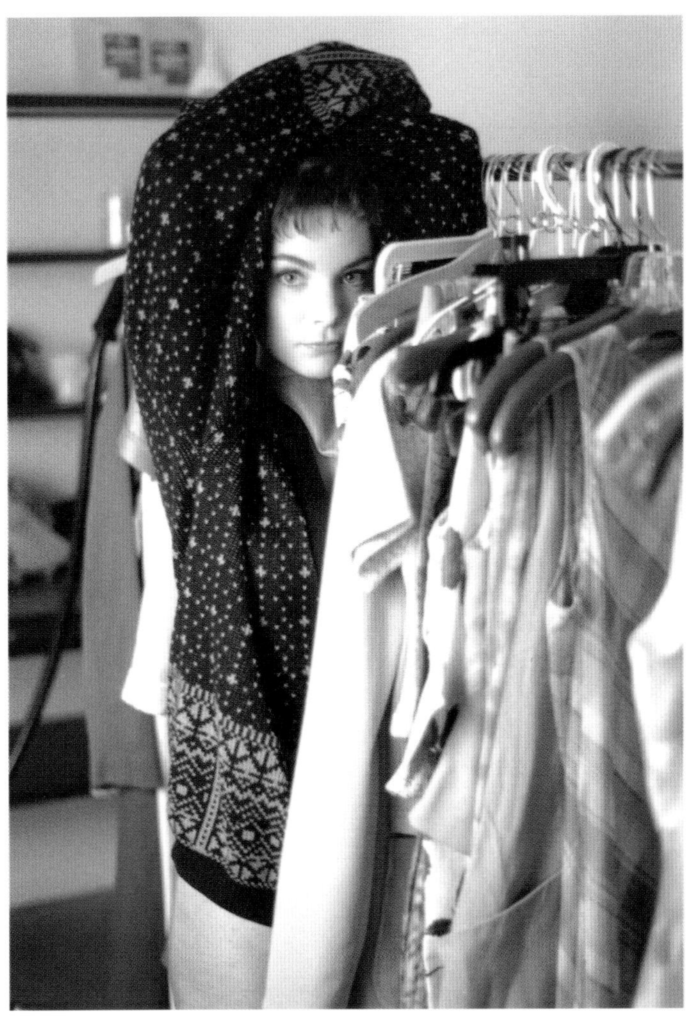

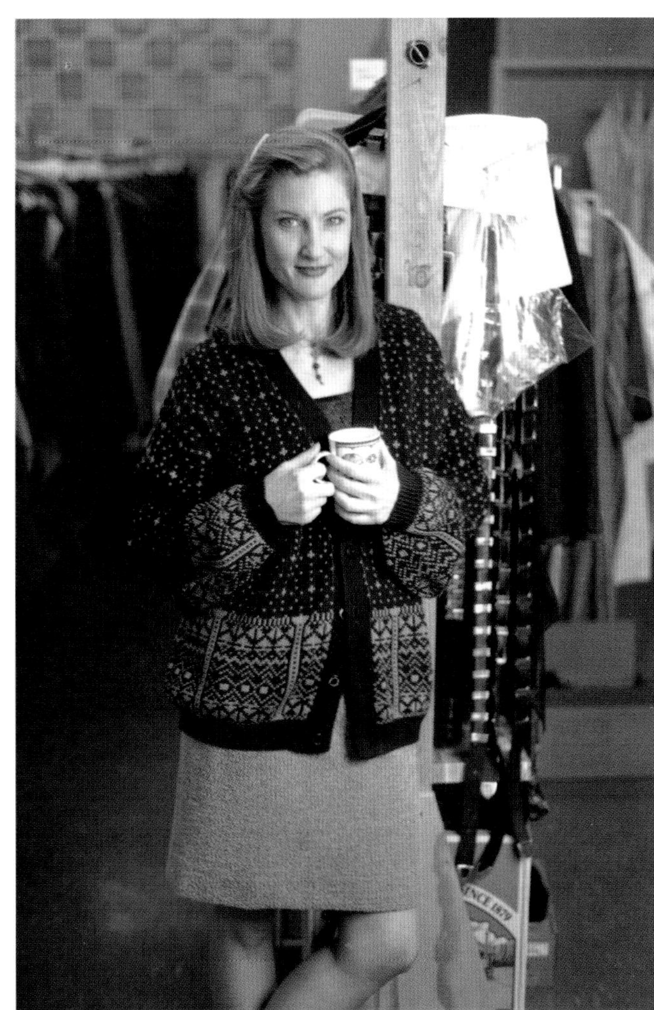

Kimberly Williams, Annette O'Toole
Jayne Brook, Melissa Joan Hart

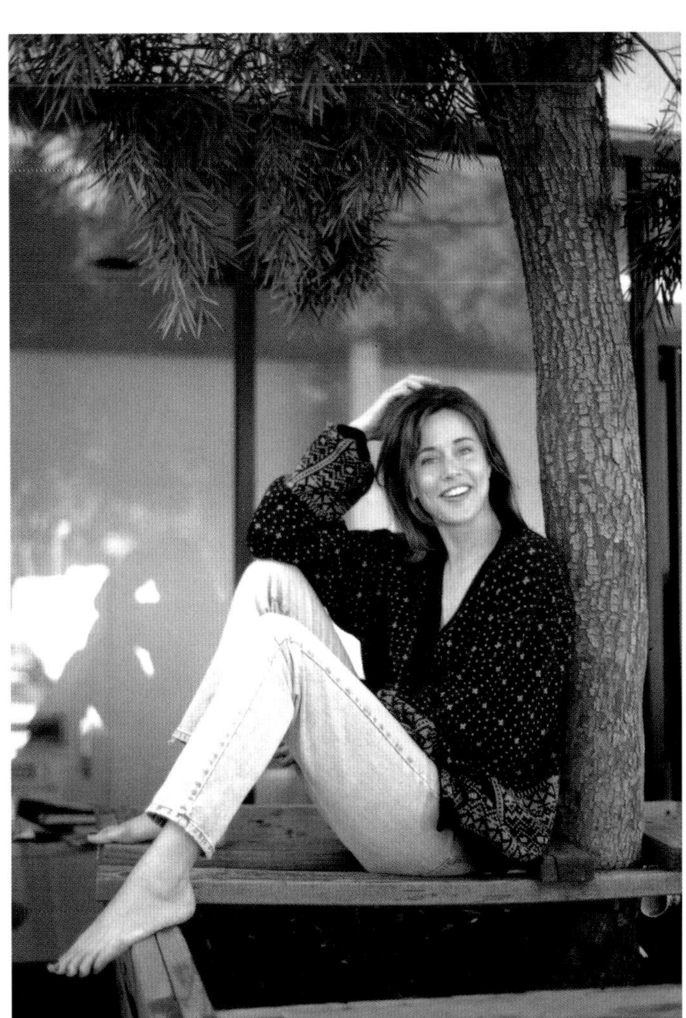

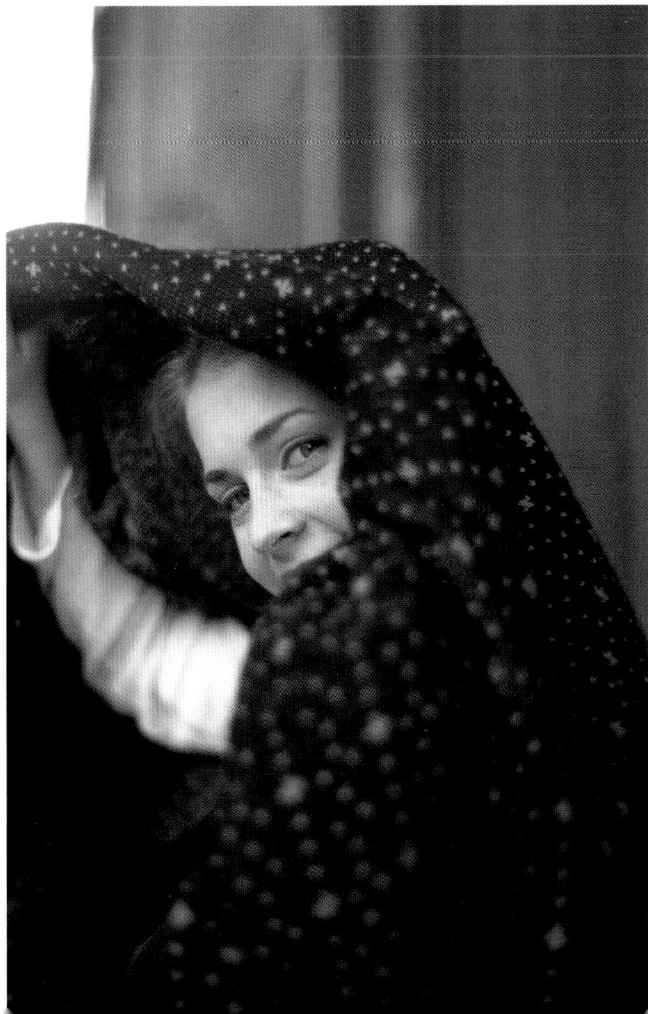

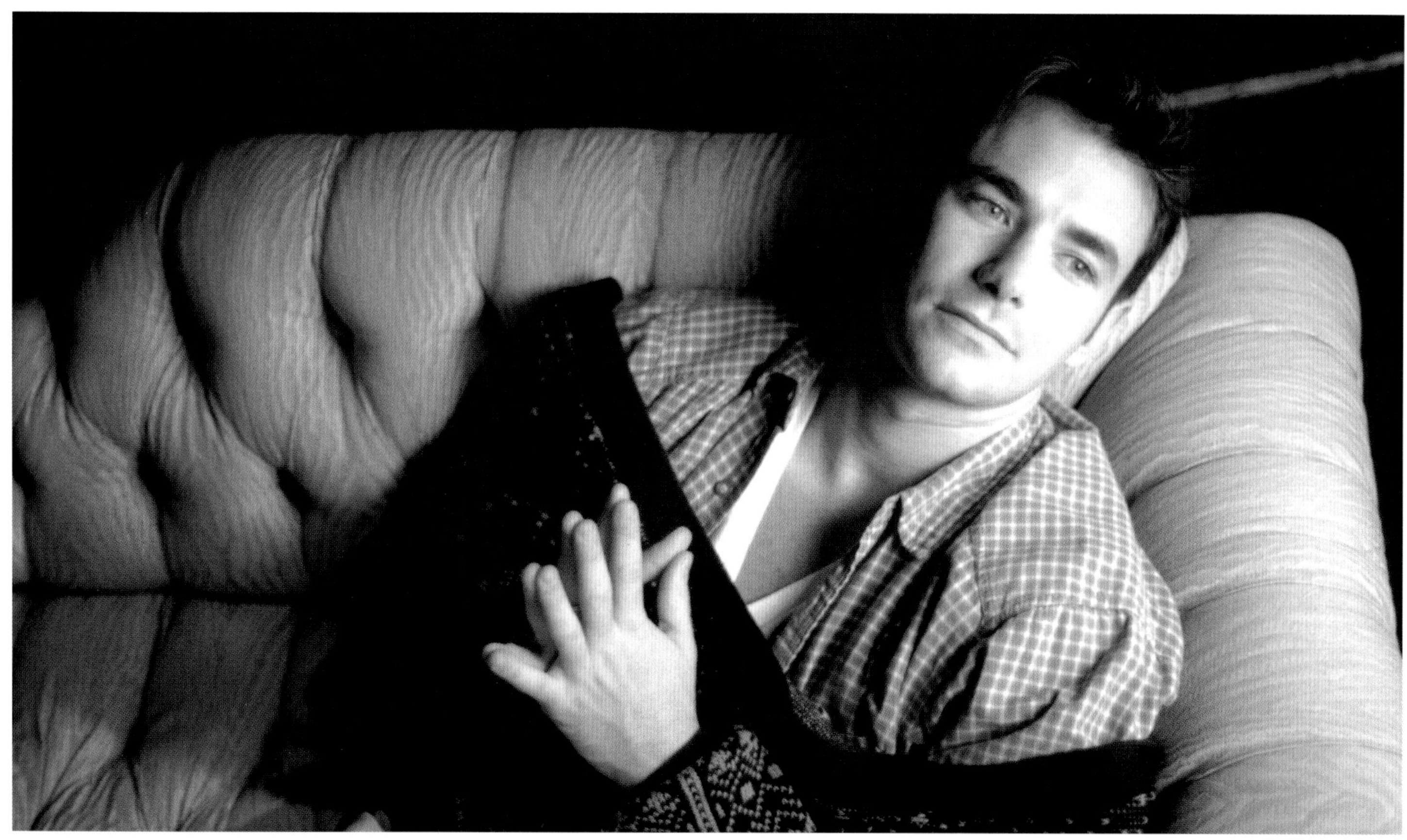

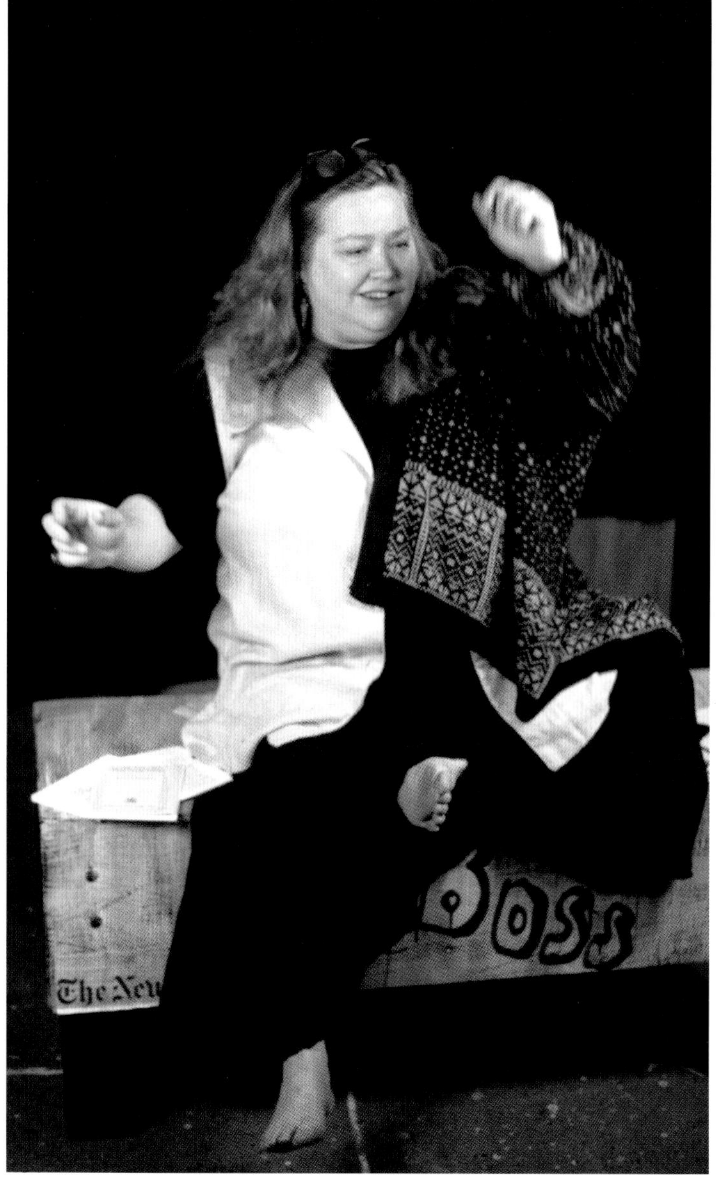
The New

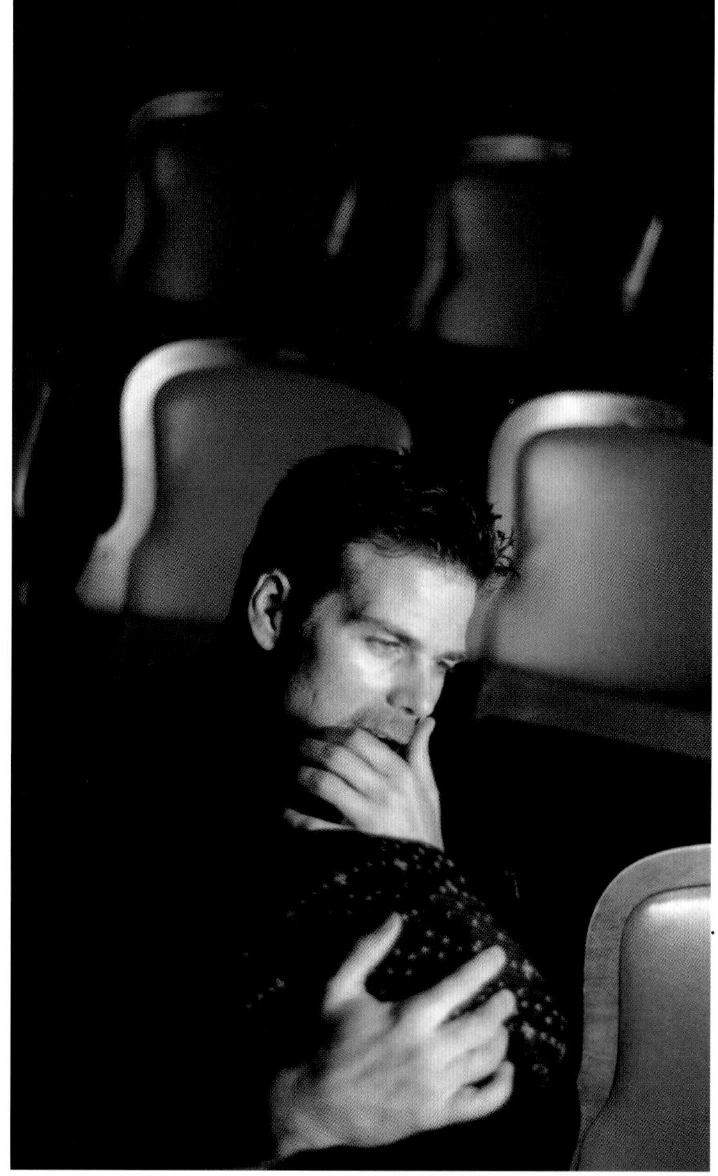

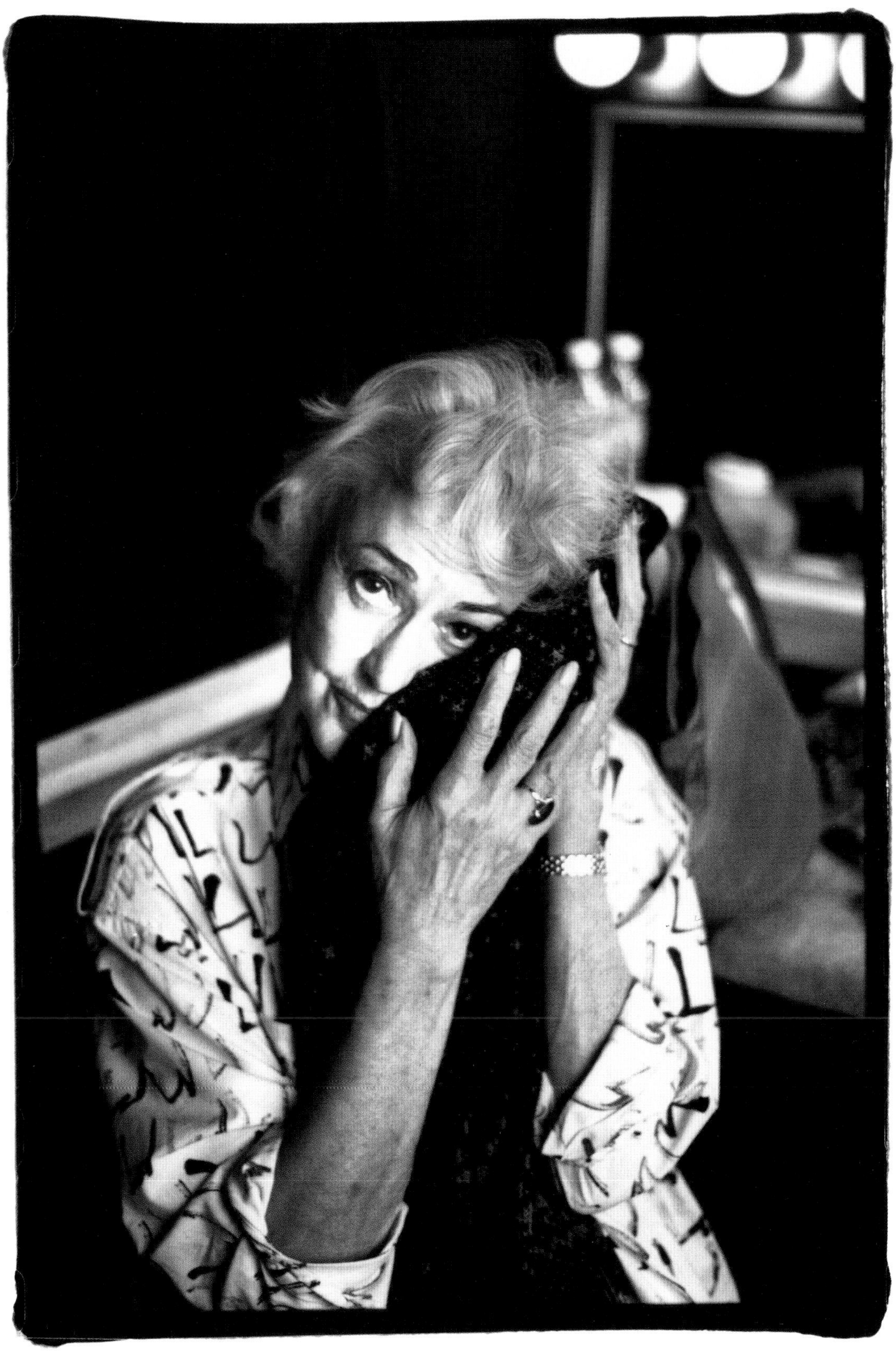

Bea Arthur

Even though Los Angeles is a film and TV town, there is a theatrical community where actors can have a chance to return to the stage, where they started. At any given time, film and TV stars can be found in small fifty-seat theaters or large elegant playhouses. It is fun for them and it provides an extraordinary chance for the public to see their favorite actors perform live. These are all pictures shot in some of those venues around Hollywood.

Opposite, clockwise from top: Larry Sullivan Jr., Bo Eason, Conchata Ferrell

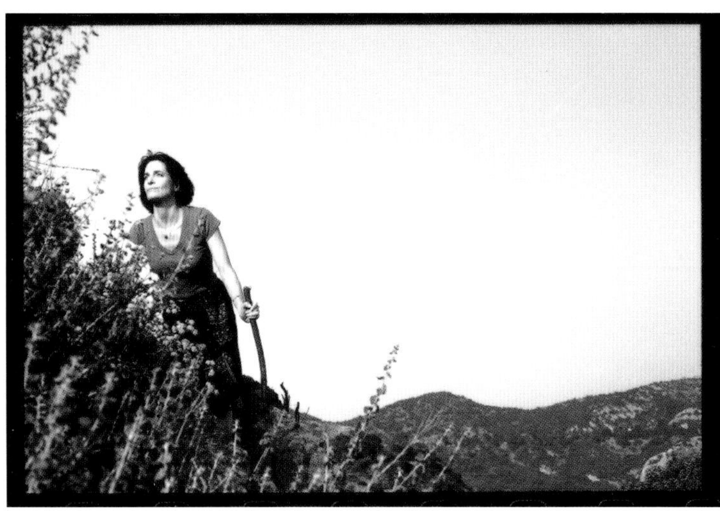

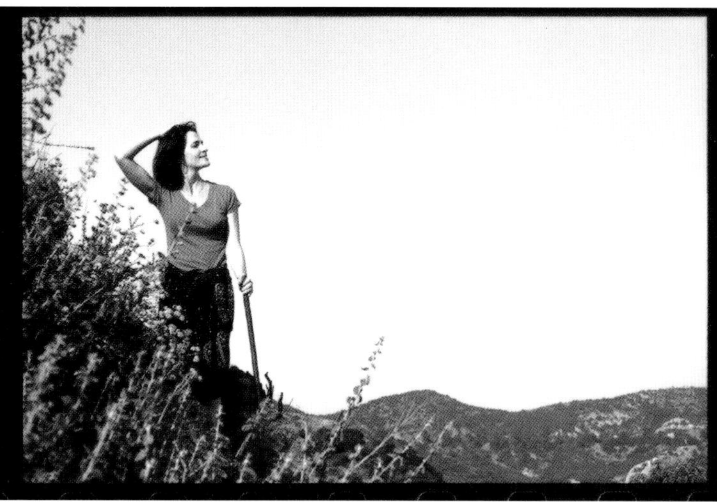

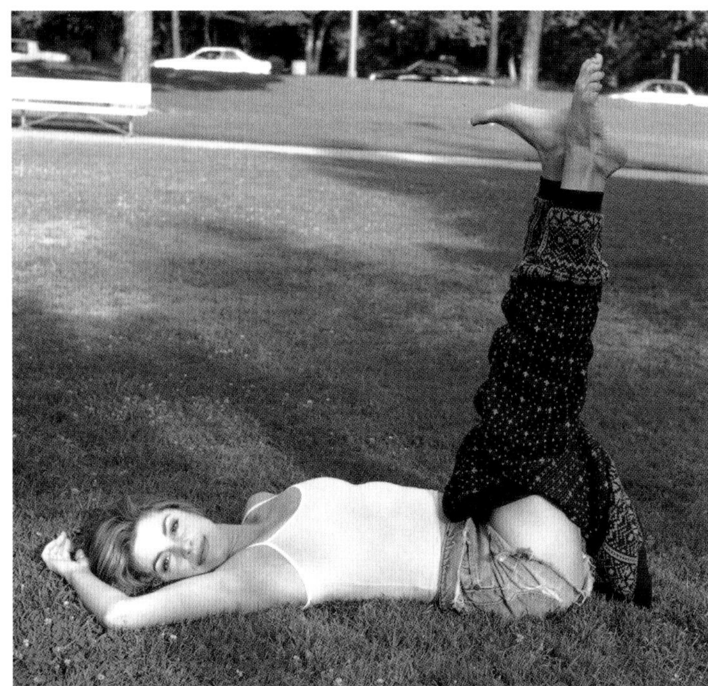

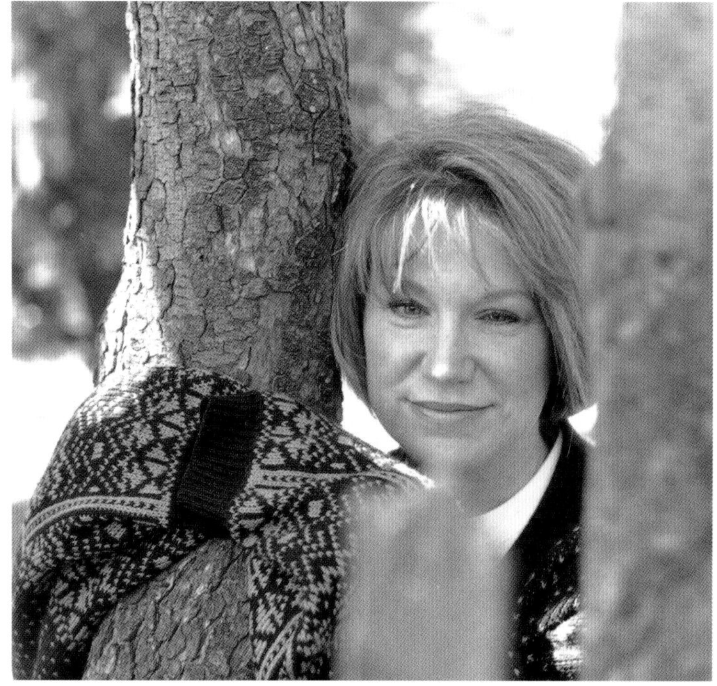

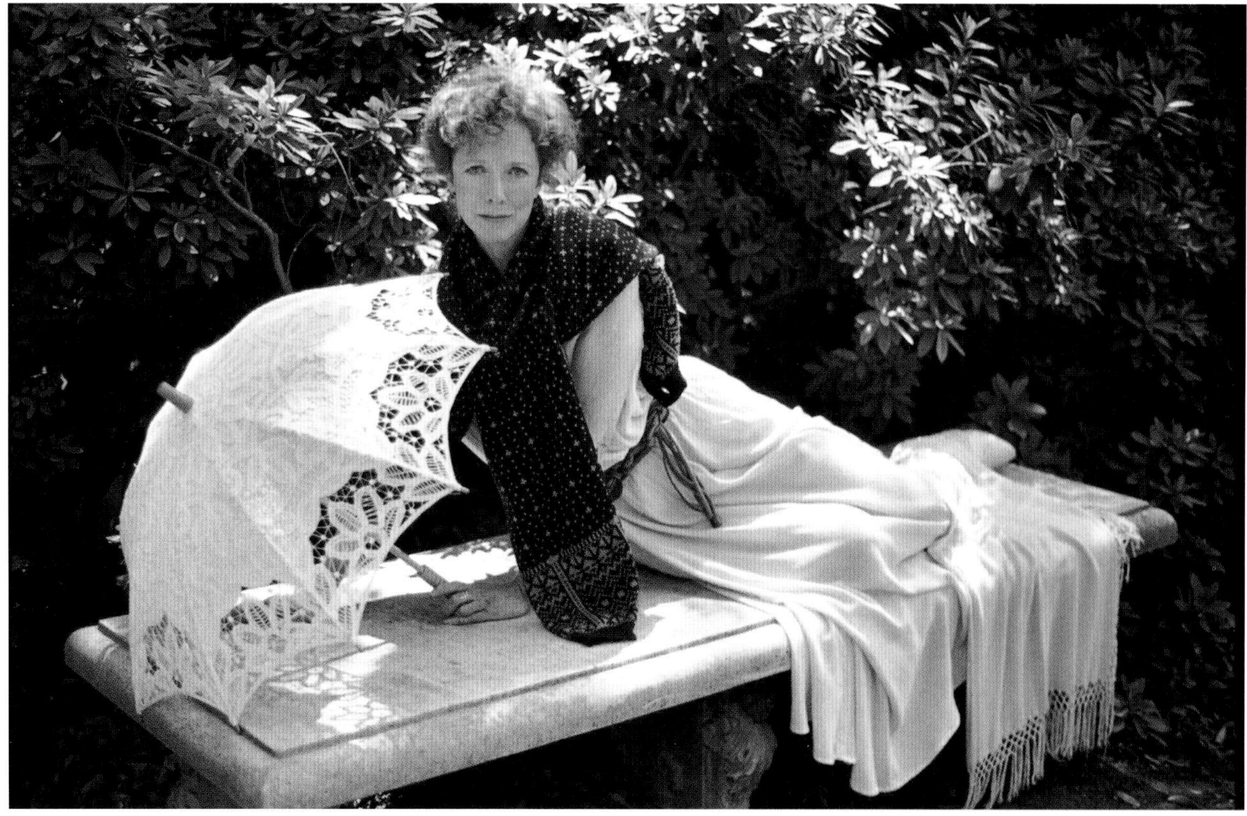

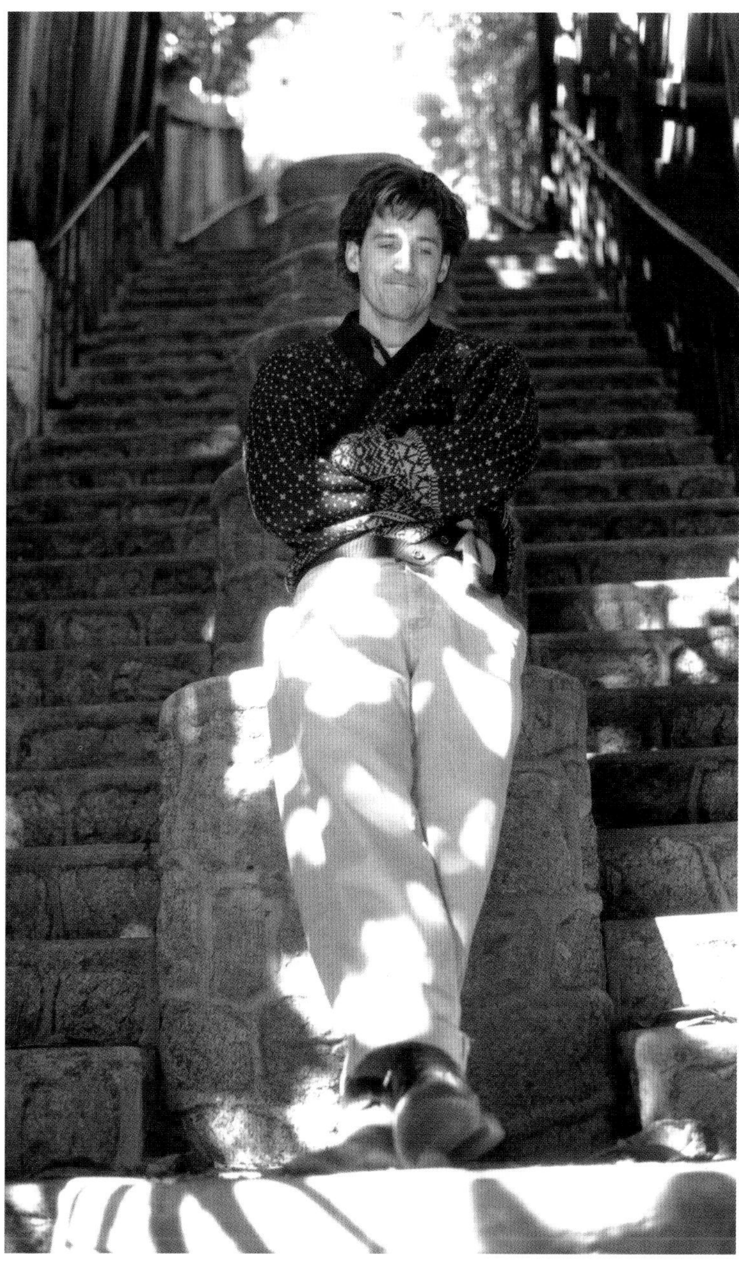

Opposite, clockwise from top left:

Sheila Kelley

Mary Kay Place

Barbara Babcock

Cynthia Gibb

This page:

Patrick Dempsey

Billy Campbell

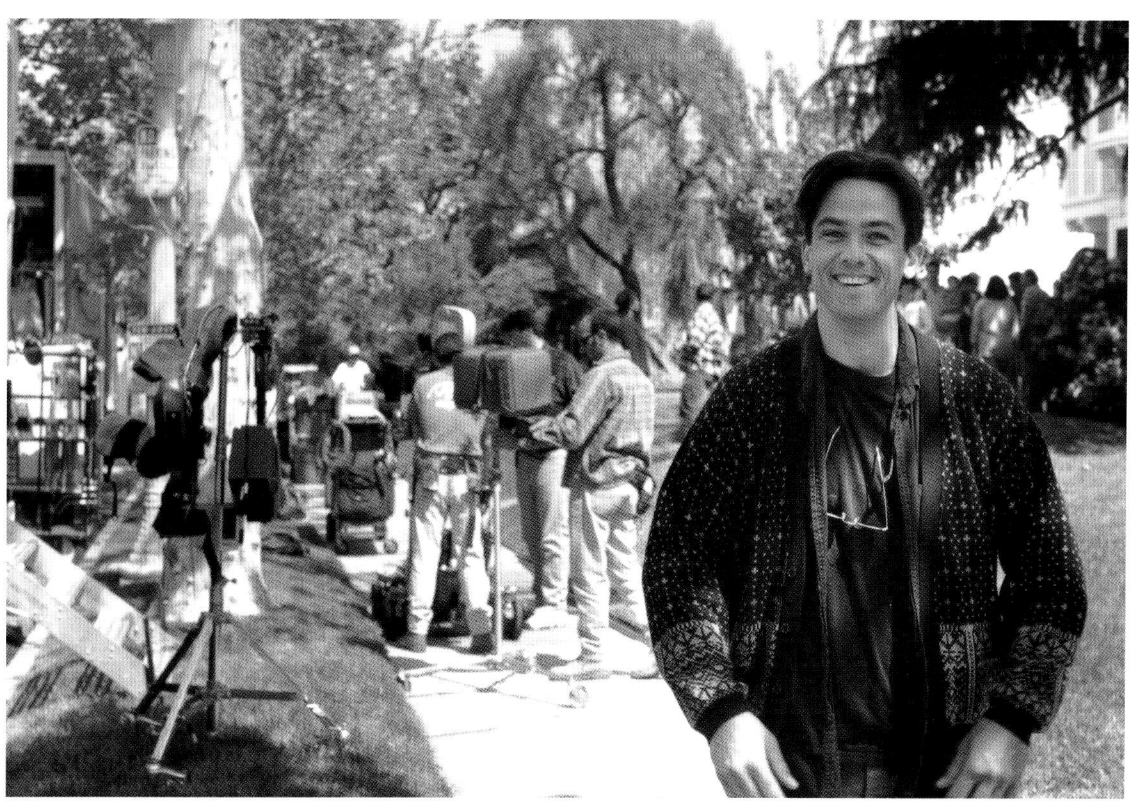

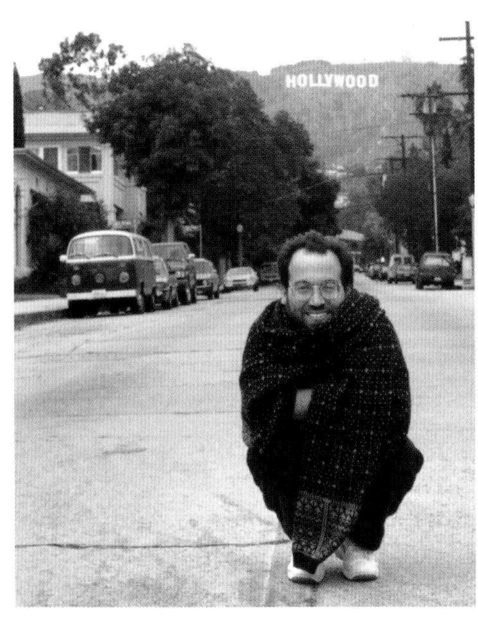
HOLLYWOOD

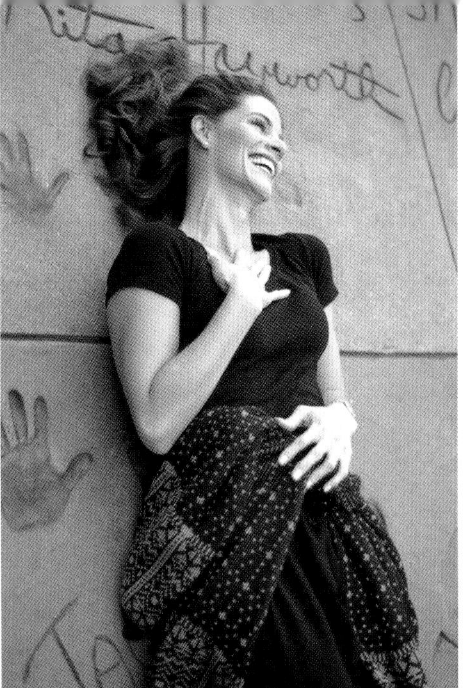
Rita Hayworth

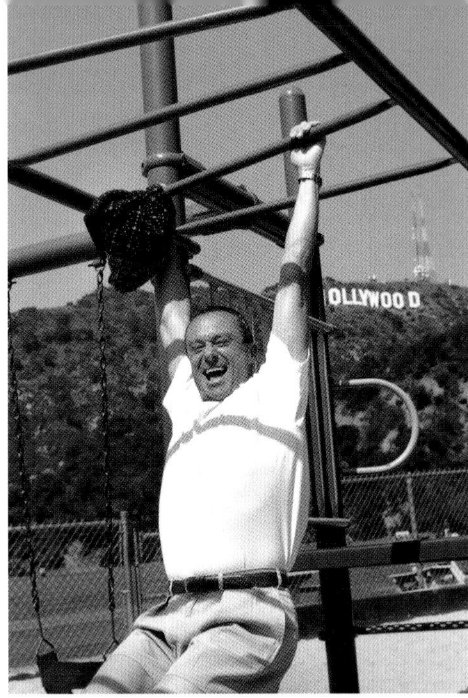

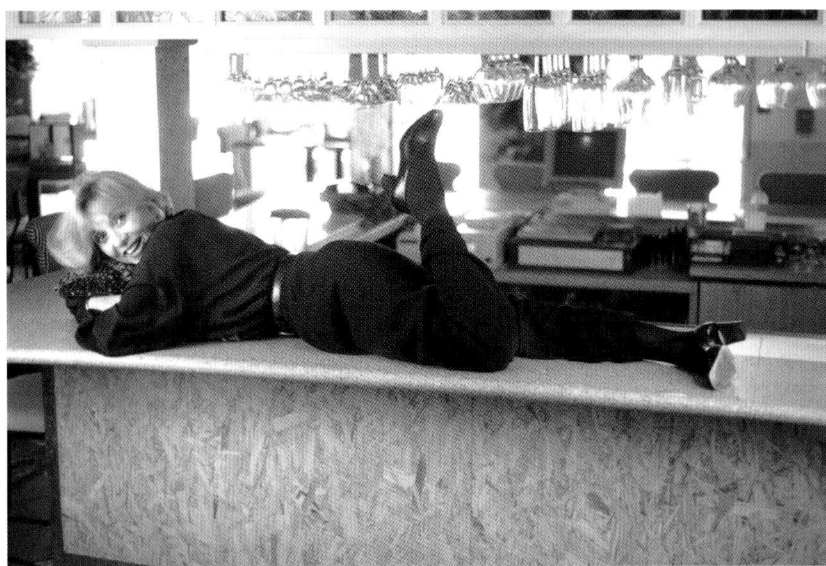

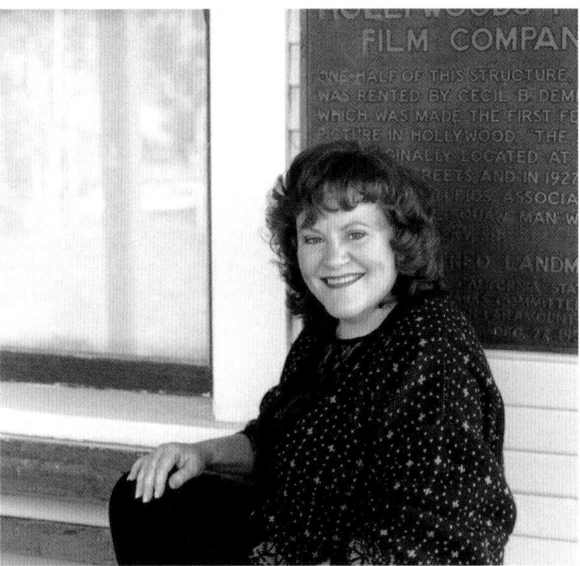
FILM COMPAN
ONE-HALF OF THIS STRUCTURE,
WAS RENTED BY CECIL B. DEM
WHICH WAS MADE THE FIRST FE

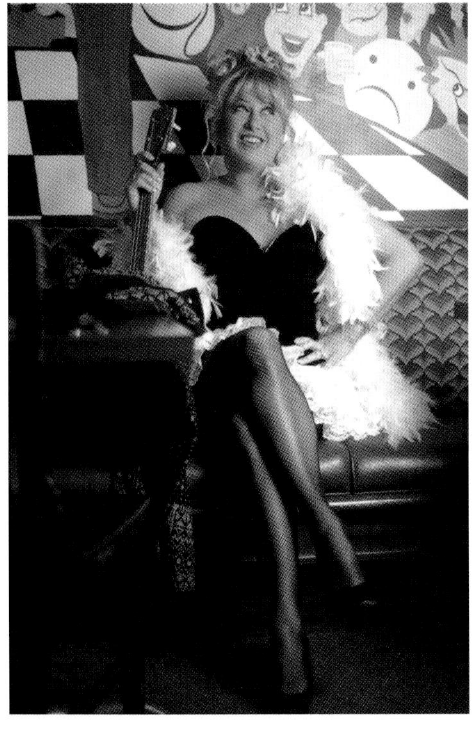

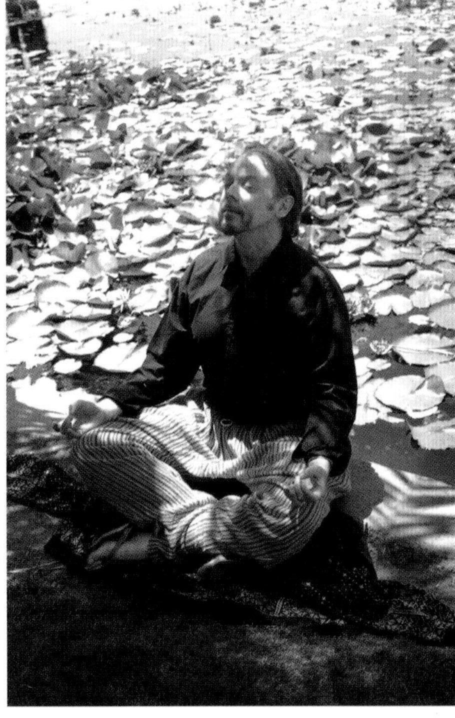

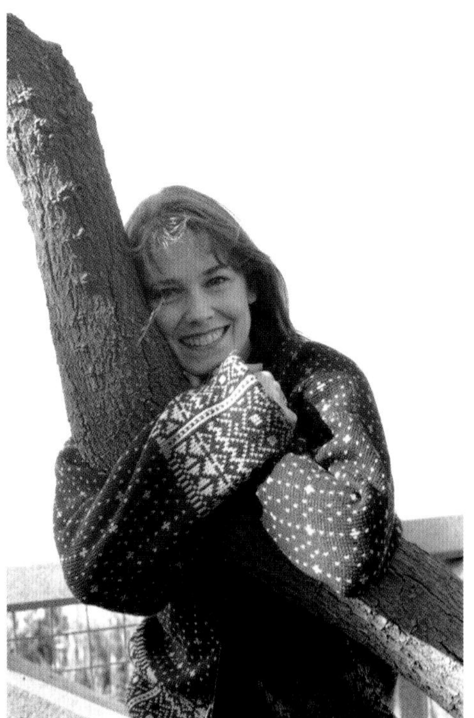

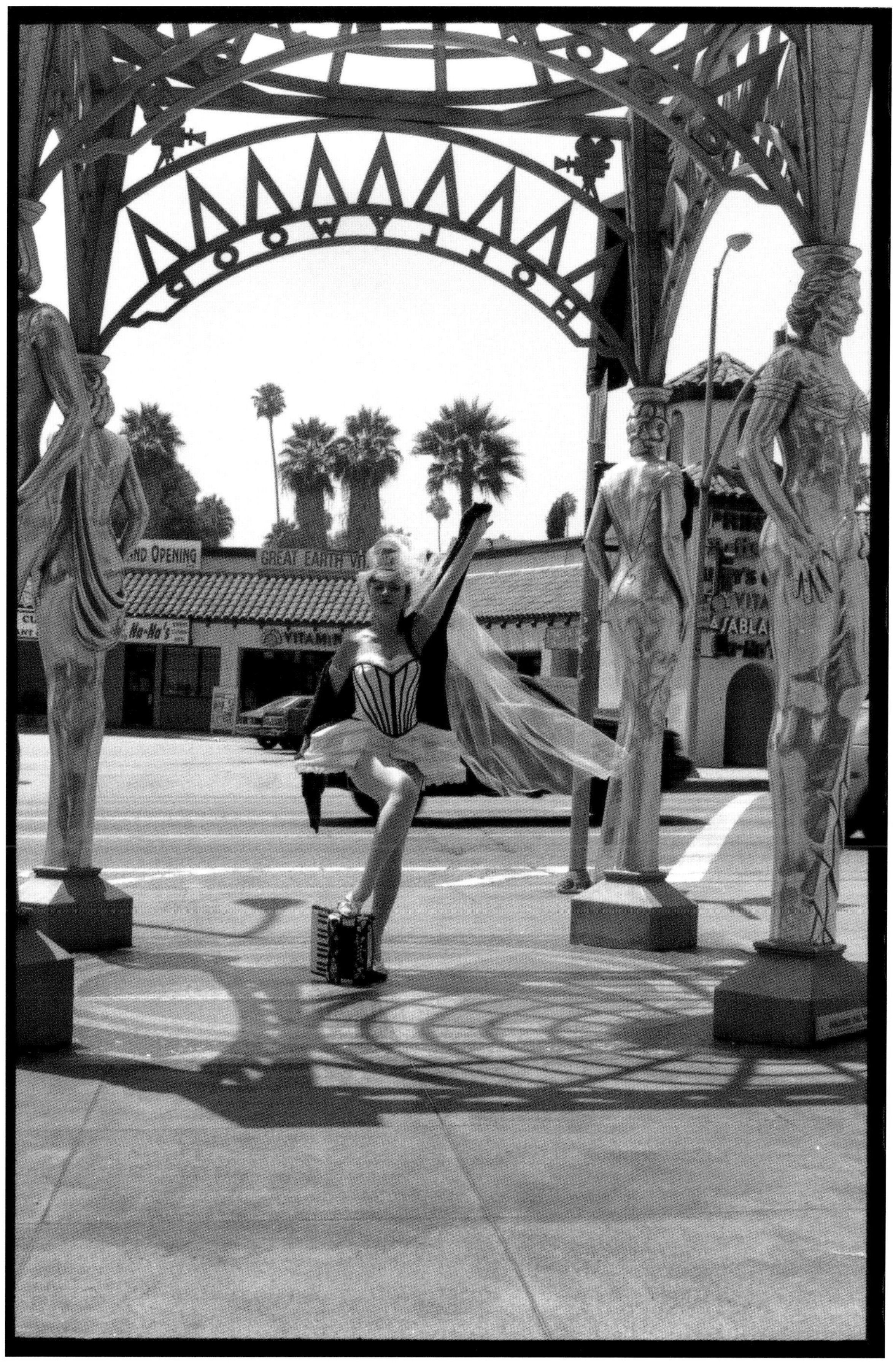

Judy Tenuta

Opposite, clockwise from top left: Danny Woodburn, Marcia Mitzman Gaven, Stanley Kamel, Edie McClurg, Isabel Glasser, Bud Cort, Victoria Jackson, Beverly Garland

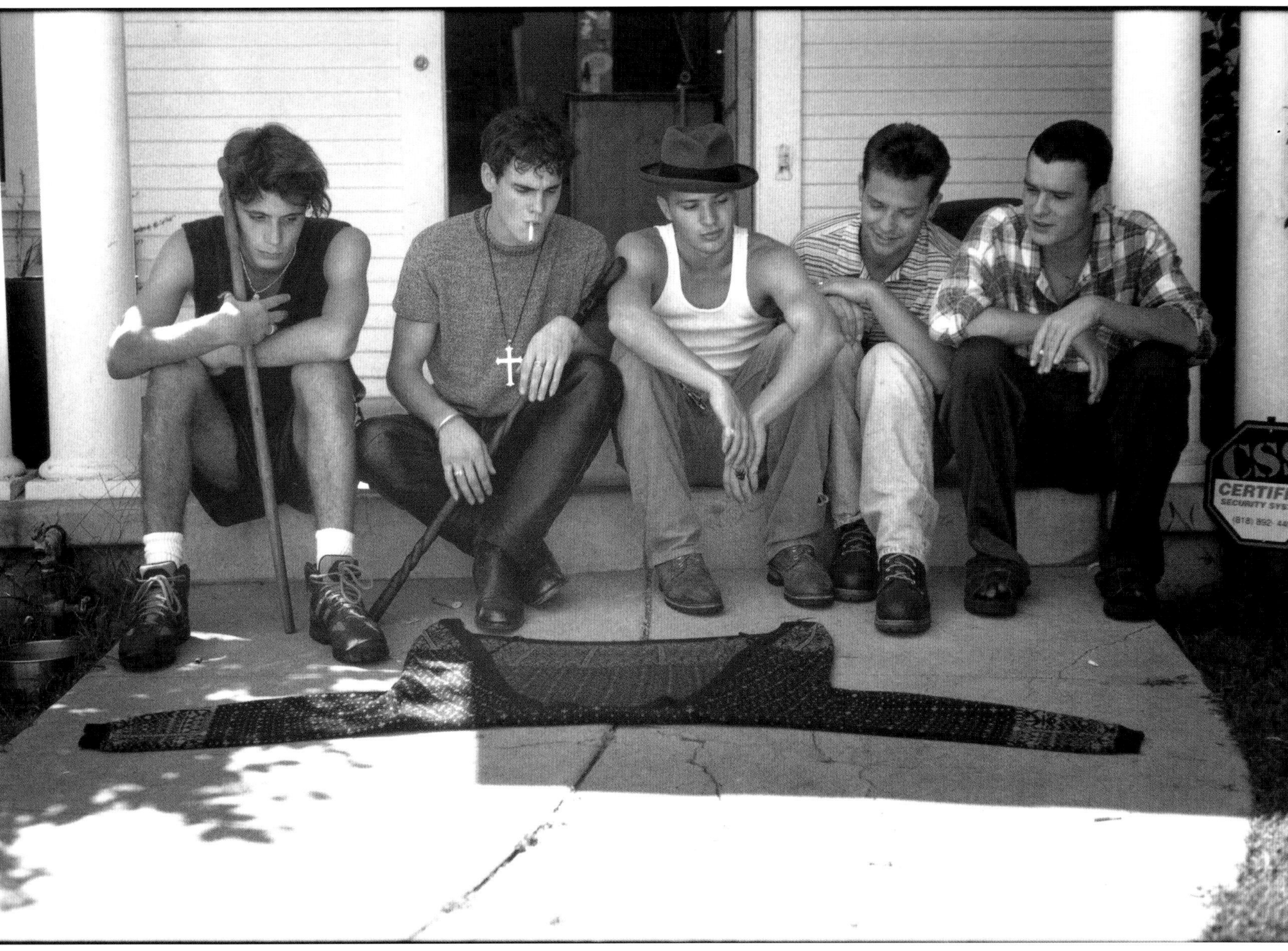

Jeremy Sisto, Eric Michael Cole, Ryan Phillippe, Josh Holland, Balthazar Getty

Jeremy Sisto and I had worked together and he suggested I do a photo of him and some friends he had made on a movie called *White Squall*. So it was arranged that I would arrive at the home of Balthazar Getty and shoot some of Hollywood's new stars. The five of them (one of whom didn't appear in the film but was one of the gang) formed a think tank about what to do with the sweater. Ideas bounced and Balthazar's dogs barked and noise came from the TV and the noise in my head became cacophony. Then I heard one of the voices say, quietly, "Let's sit on the porch . . . and put the sweater on the ground . . . and look at it." The others looked at one another thoughtfully, nodded their heads simultaneously, and in unison replied, "Cool."

And it was.

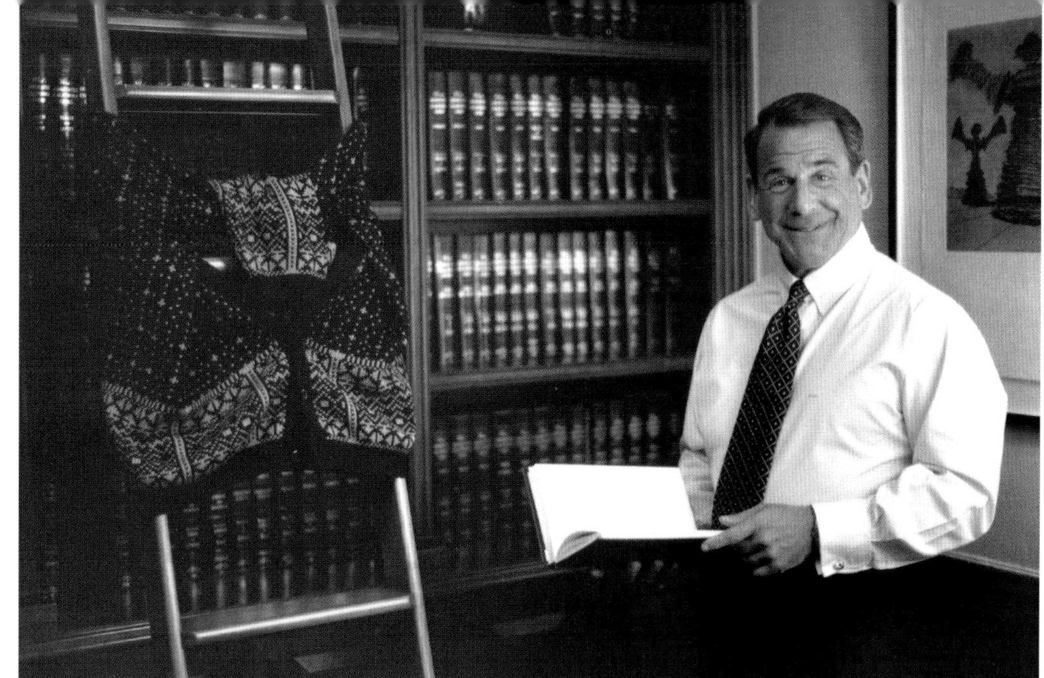

Clockwise from top:
Arthur Barens
Todd Newton
Nikki Haskell
Jill Novick

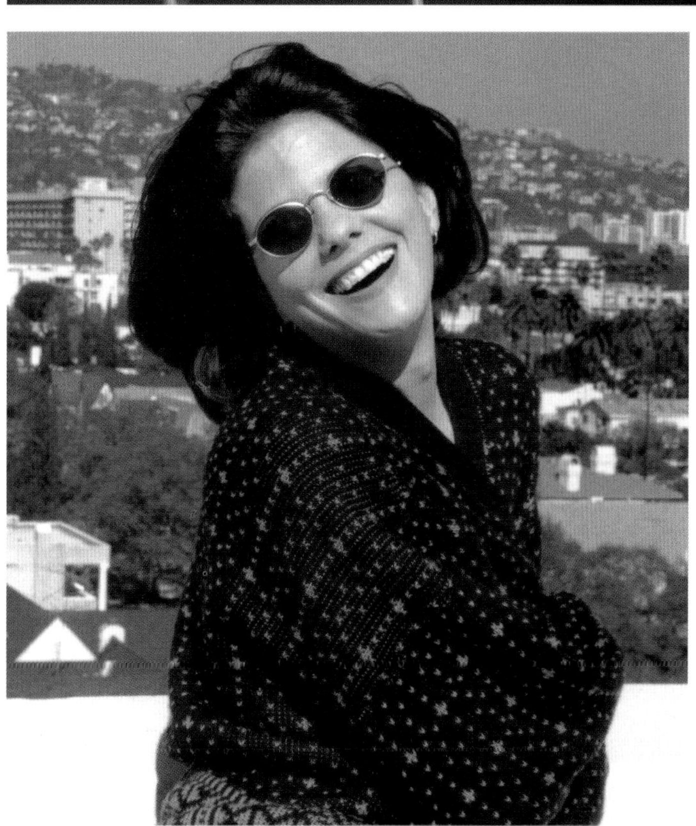

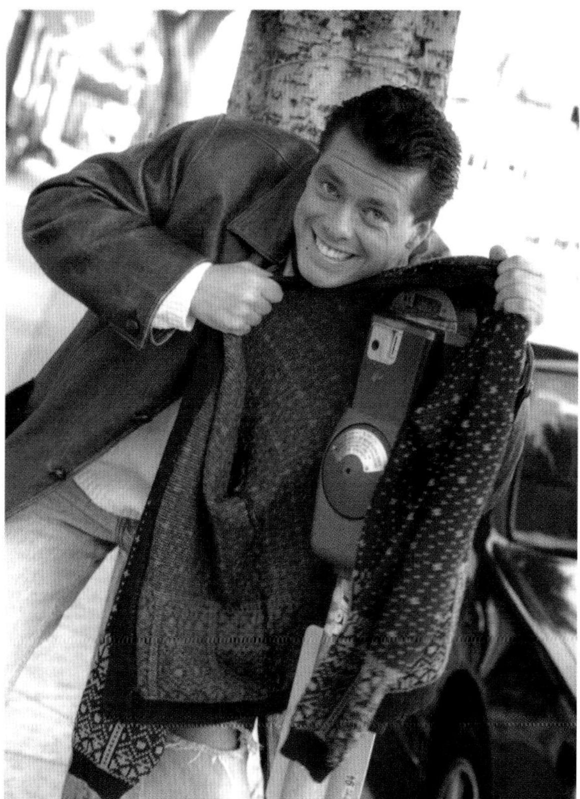

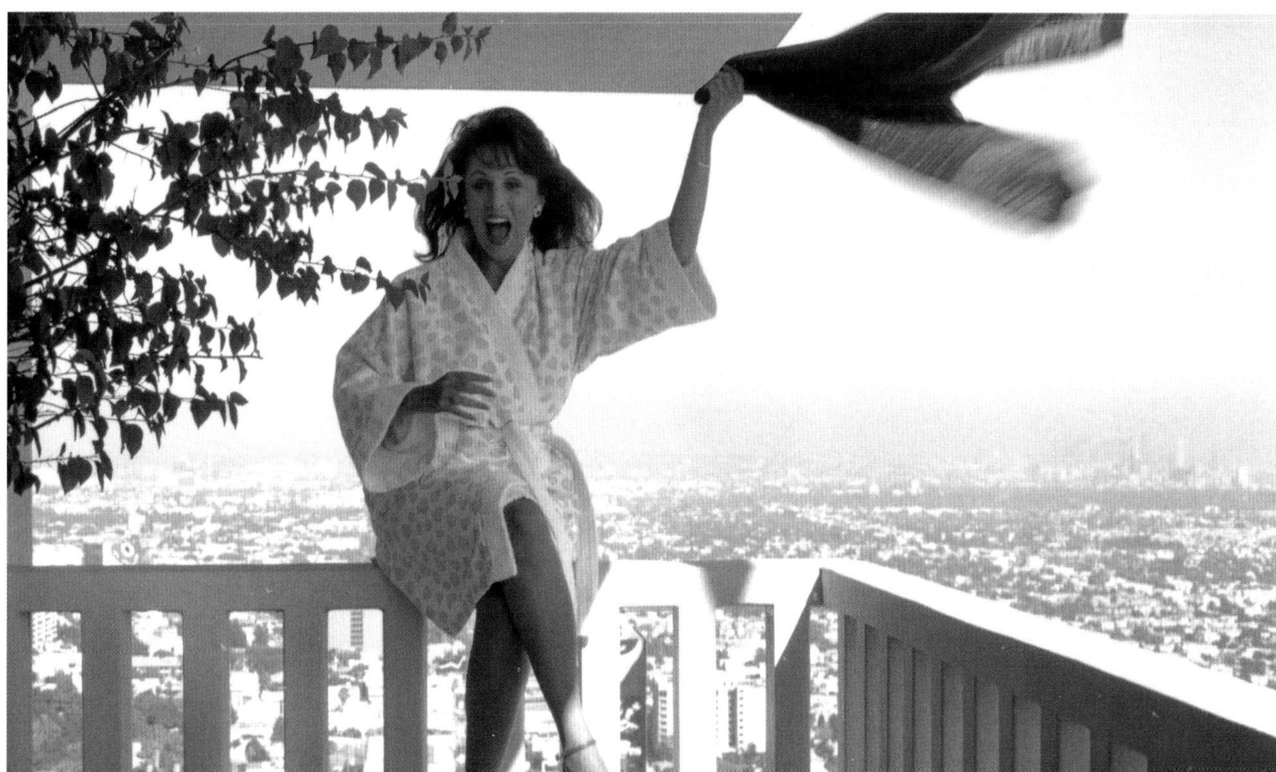

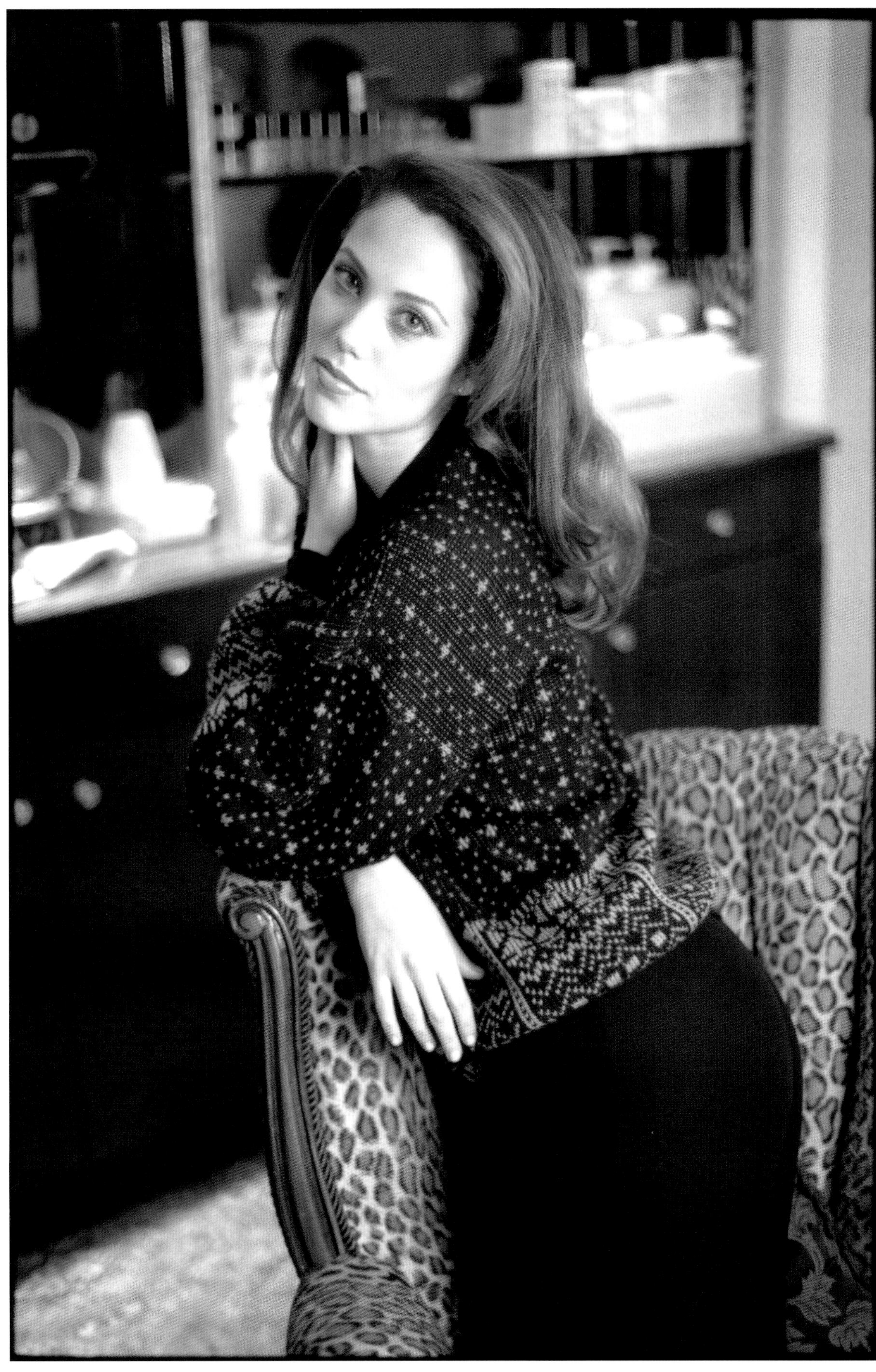

Elizabeth Berkley

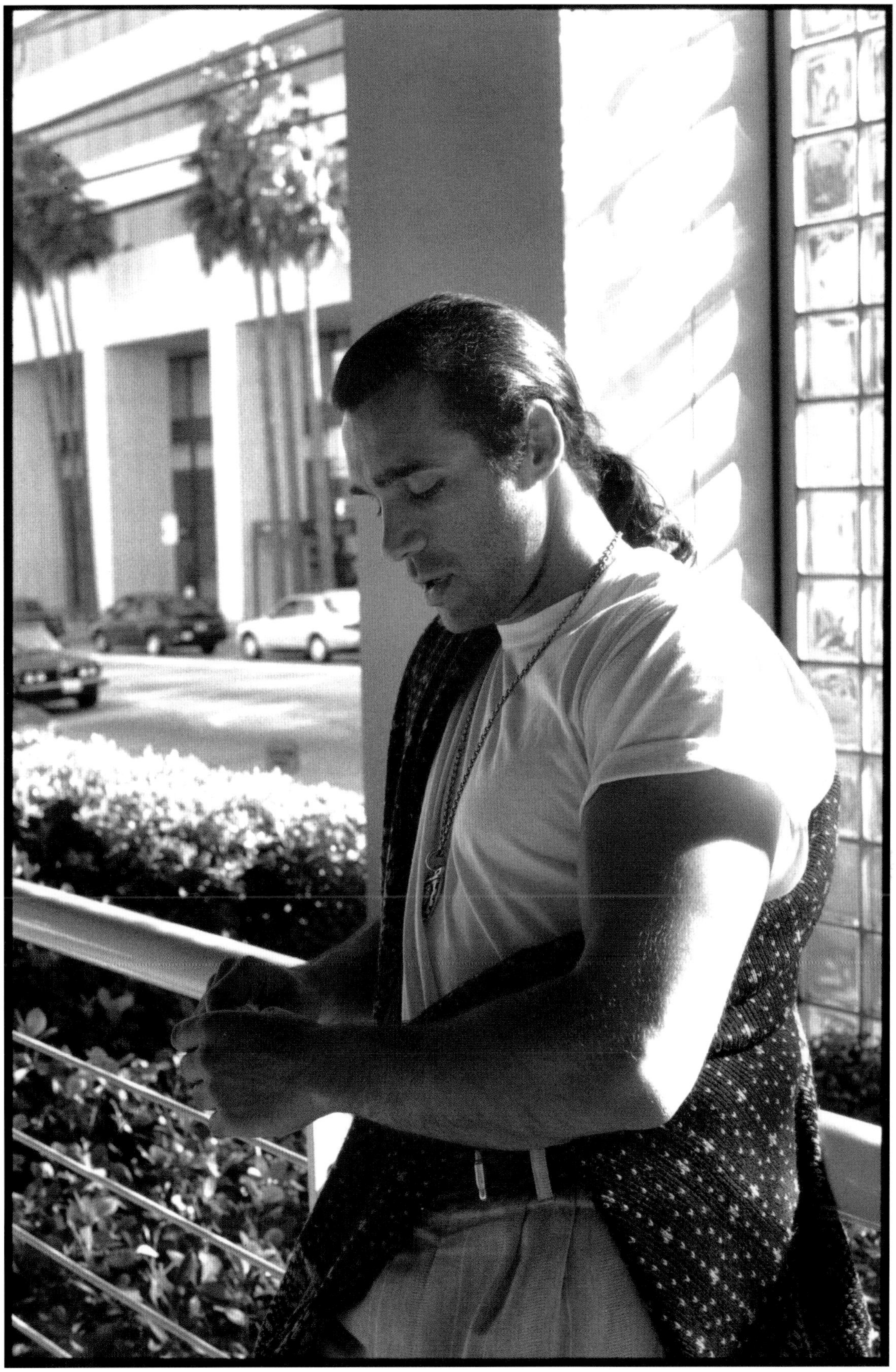

Adrian Paul

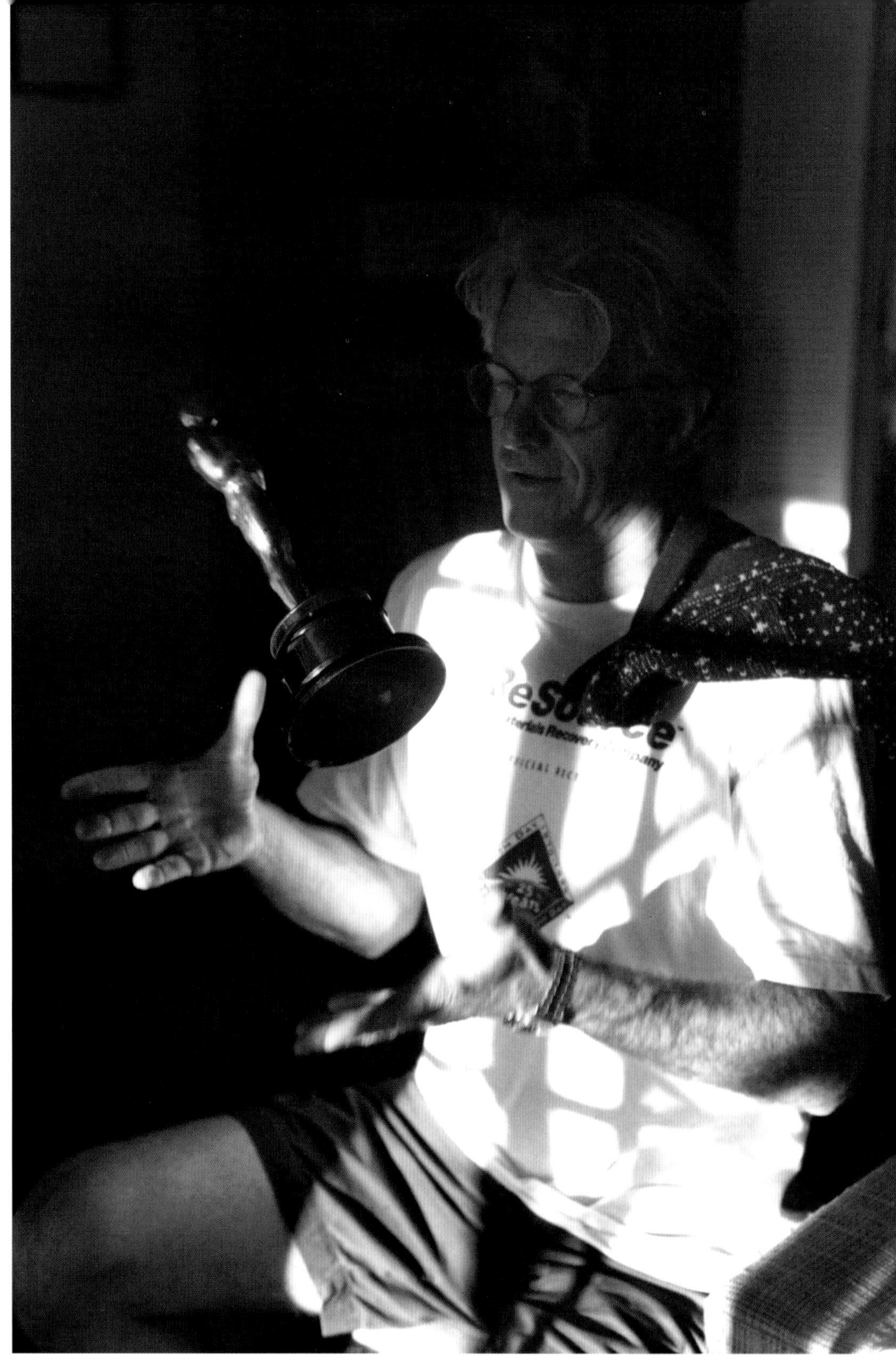

Ed Begley Jr.

Moments after photographing Ed Begley Jr. in his garden with his cat, Smokey, I spotted it on the mantel.

"I heard a story—can you tell me if it's true? I heard that when your dad won the Oscar for Sweet Bird of Youth, *he was so proud to be a working guy who made good that he had a case made to carry it with him so that when someone asked for a photo, he could reach in and pull out the statue to pose with. One time he sent you, as a child, to get the award and you dropped it and broke it. And the Academy sent over a new one."*

"Every single word."

Pat Dwyer is a huge fan of both Eds and of that story. So I asked Ed Jr. if he would do a special photo for Pat's birthday. Of course! I wanted to make a statement, though, of what I feel it must be like being the acting child of an acclaimed actor—so I had Ed sit in the shadow with the Gold Man in the light. At the last minute he said, *"Count to three."* I counted and suddenly Oscar was airborne! Sorry, Smokey, this had to be seen!

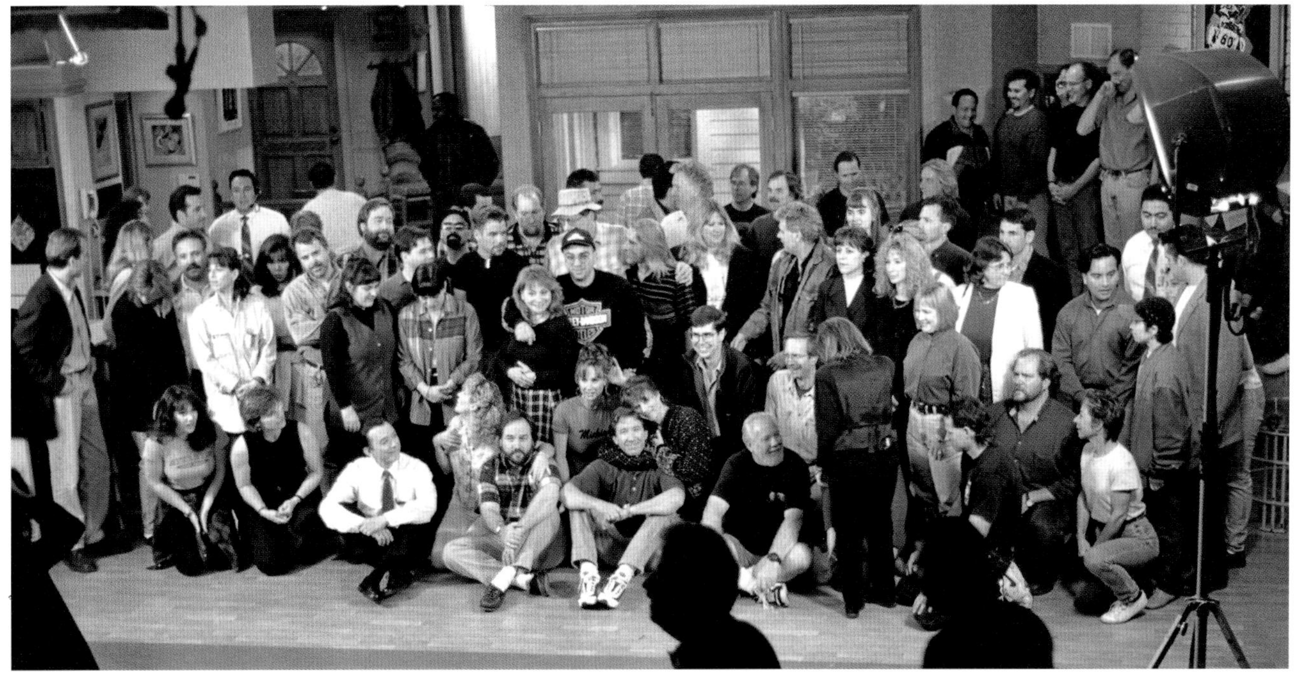

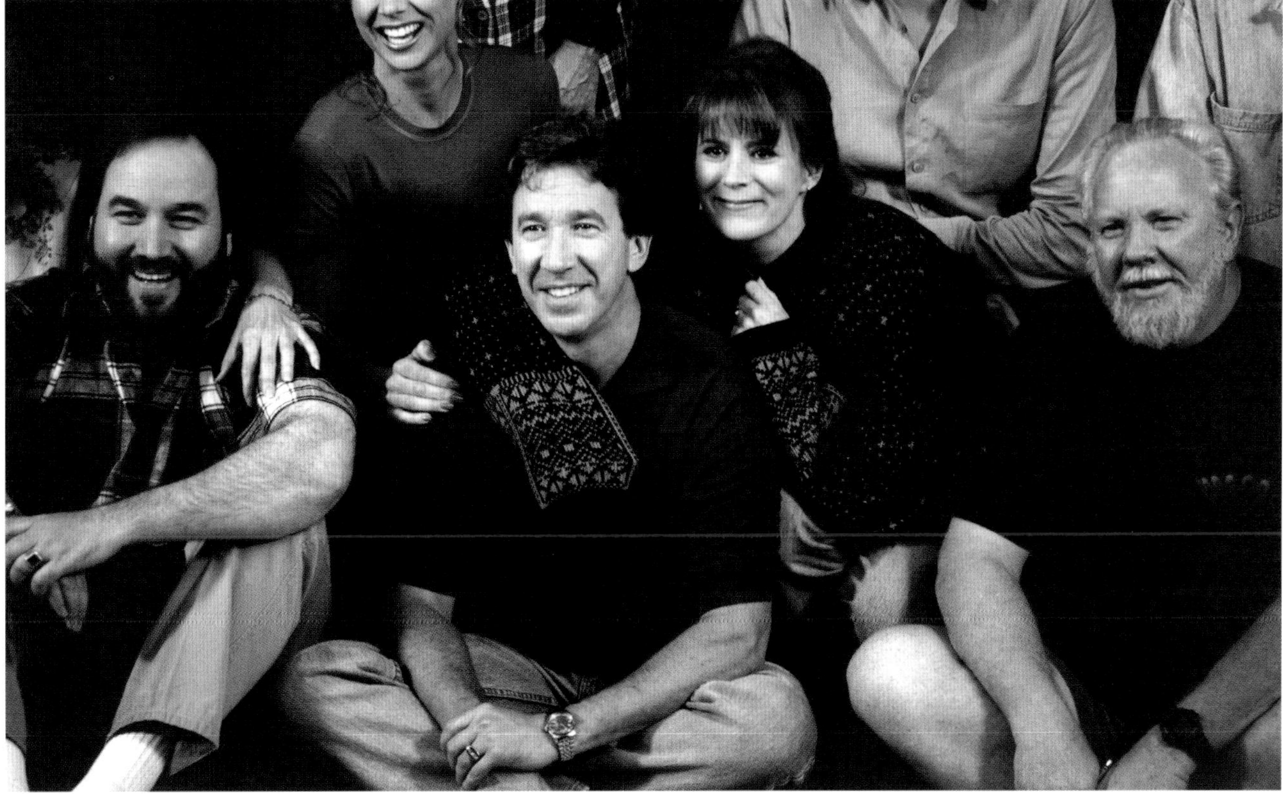

It was a defining moment. A Hollywood moment. Pat Richardson was going to wear the Sweater. It was the last day of filming before the season ended. Everyone in the cast and crew of *Home Improvement* was there. She wondered if I'd like to have the whole cast and crew in the shot. Tim Allen could not have been more gracious and loving or more generous in allowing me to crash their party. Clearly, the people who worked there all took their cue from him:

They made me feel like one of the family.

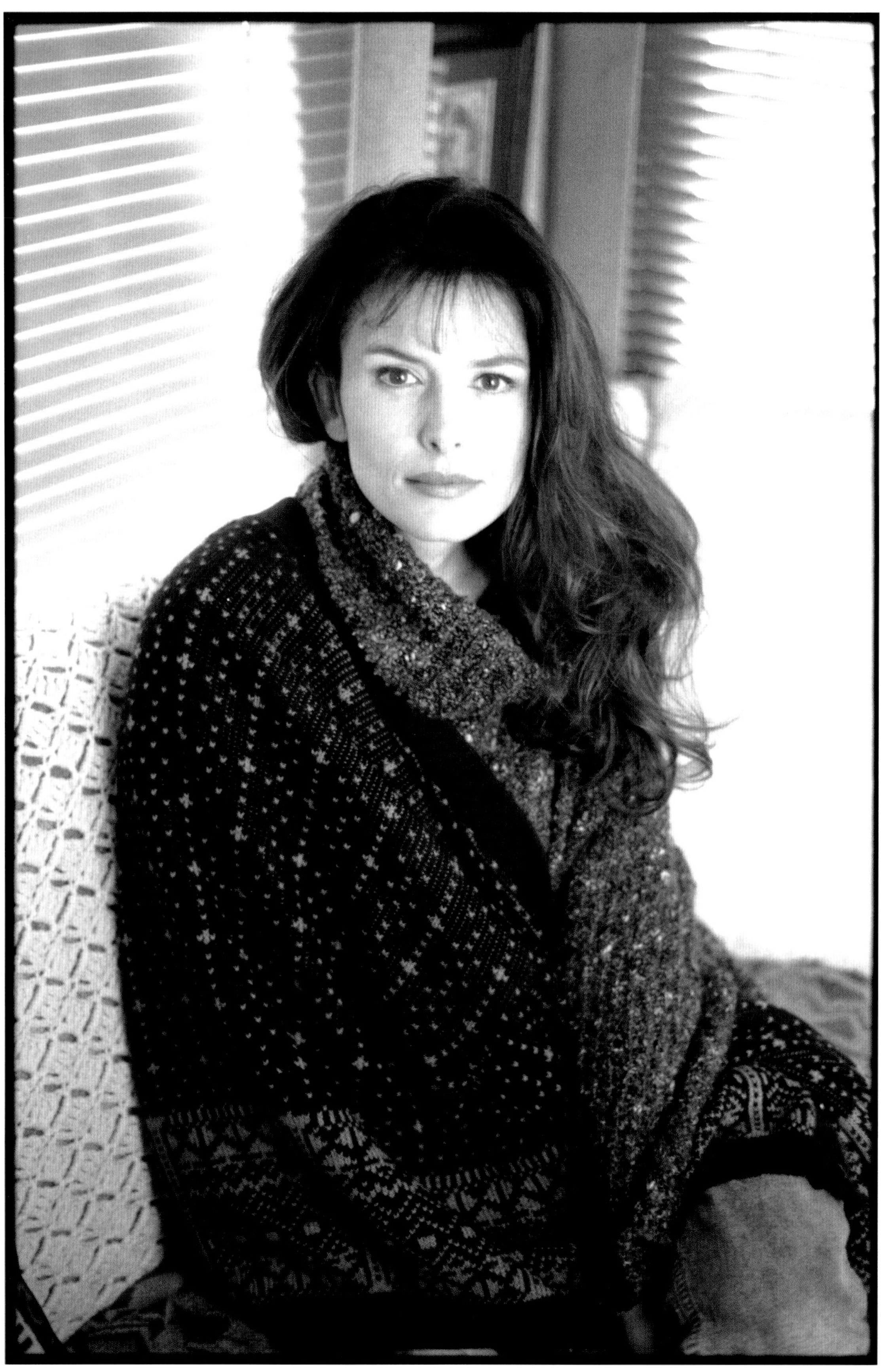

Roma Downey

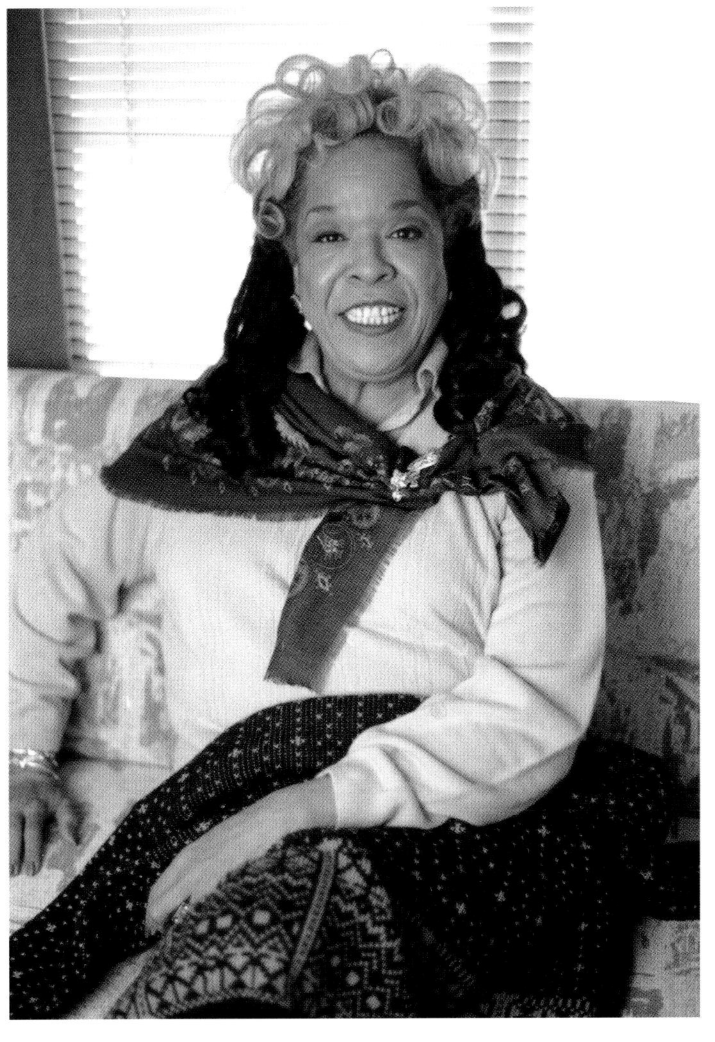

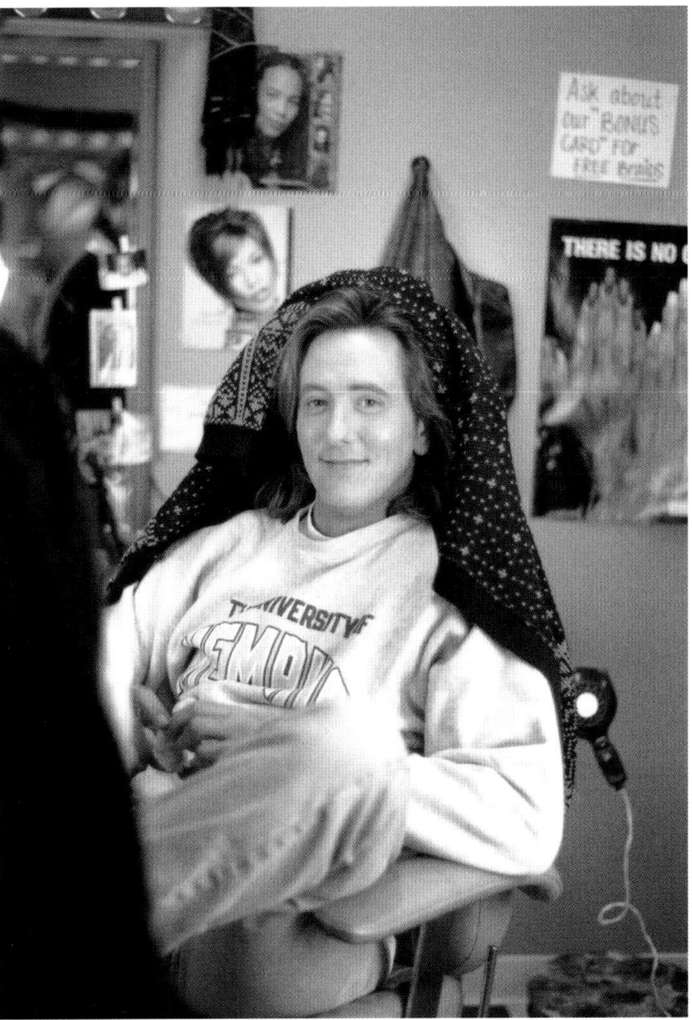

The casting director for *Touched by an Angel* and *Promised Land*, David Giella, spoke to the series creator, Martha Williamson, who afforded me the privilege of visiting the sets of her shows during shooting in Utah. Over the weekend I was given the opportunity to work with each of the show's stars (the photo of Celeste Holm had been previously shot in her New York home) and the guest stars. The episode was centered on an African American community and dealt with some weighty issues. In spite of the dramatic nature of the scenes they were shooting, the actors were friendly and generous, humorous and open-minded. It was an unforgettable experience and I was honored to be welcomed into their family. Why, after I accidentally left the sweater on the set, they even had one of the production team jump in his car and bring it to me at the airport. Now, *that* is what I call accommodating.

Della Reese
John Dye

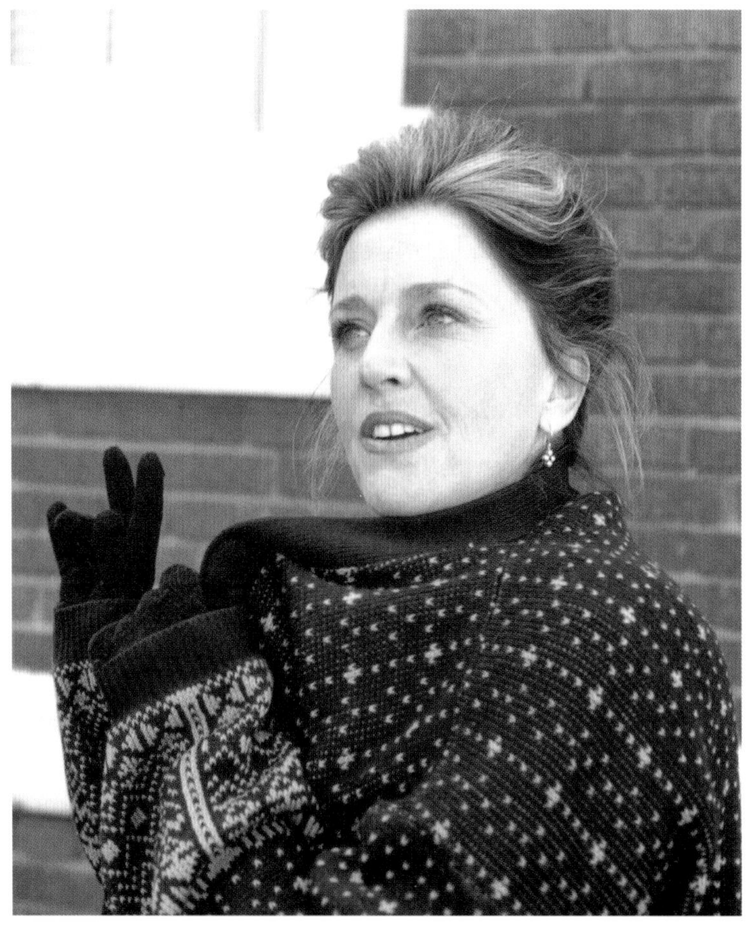

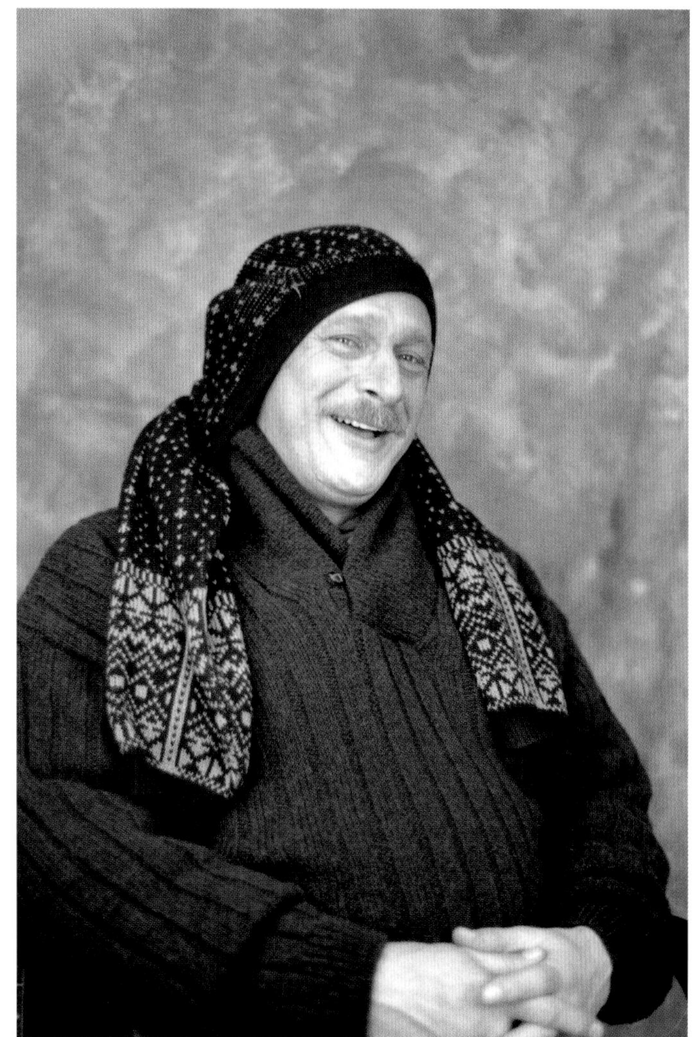

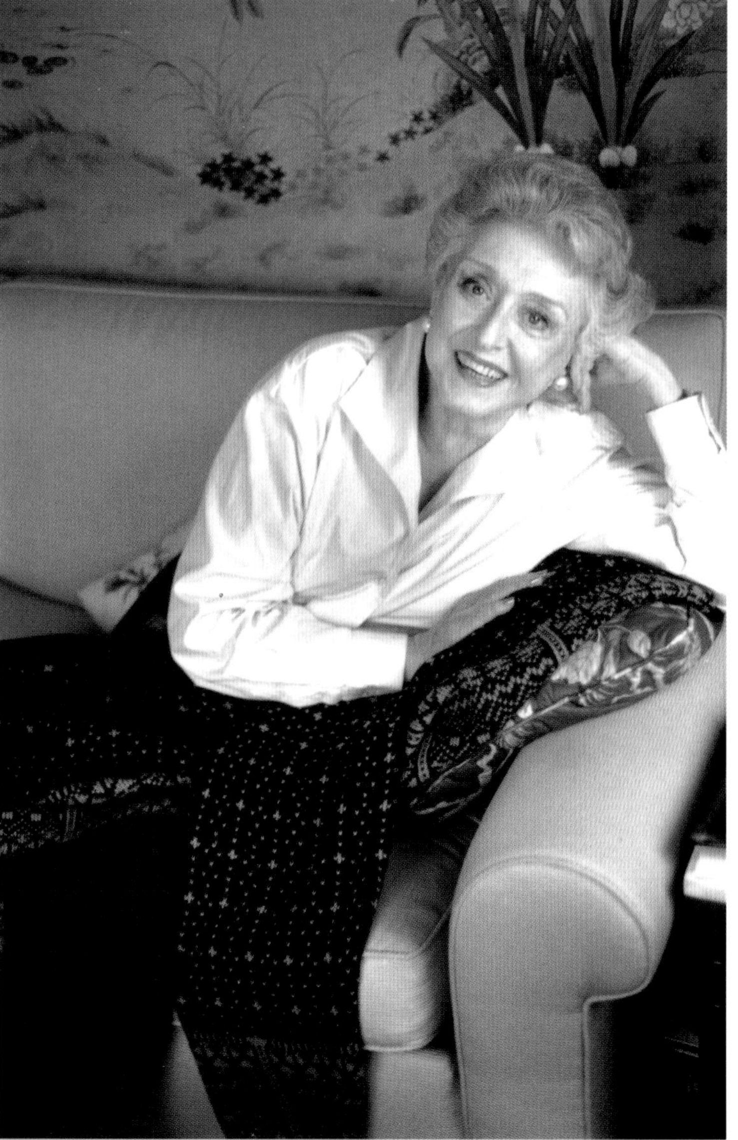

This page, clockwise from top left:

Wendy Phillips

Gerald McRaney

Celeste Holm

Opposite, clockwise from top left:

Sarah Schaub

Austin O'Brien

Martha Williamson

Eddie Carr

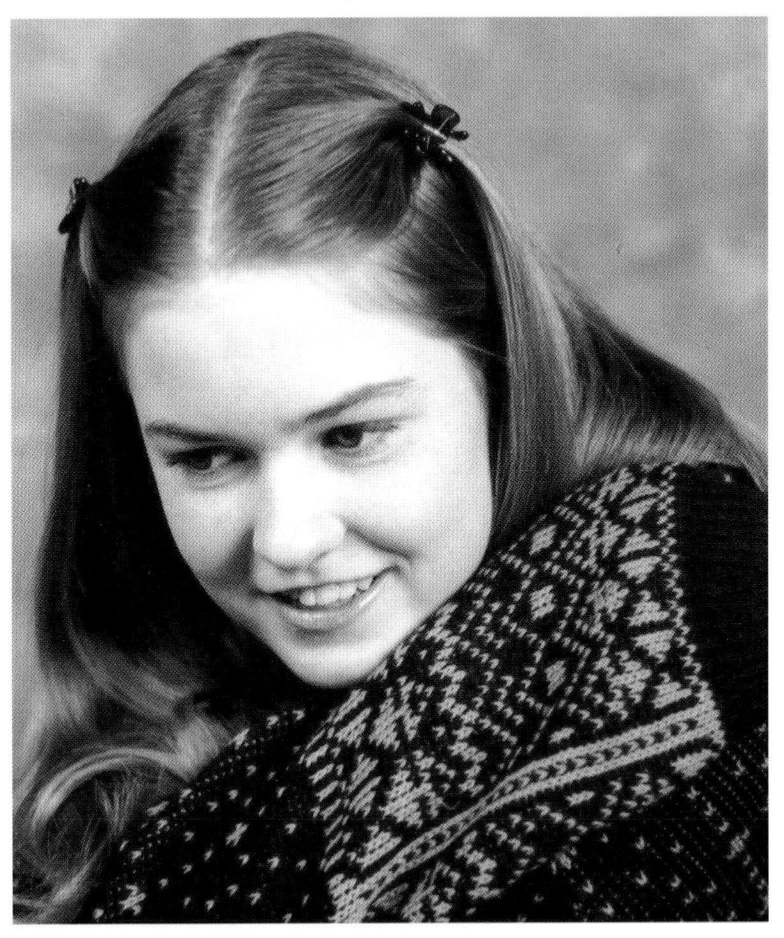
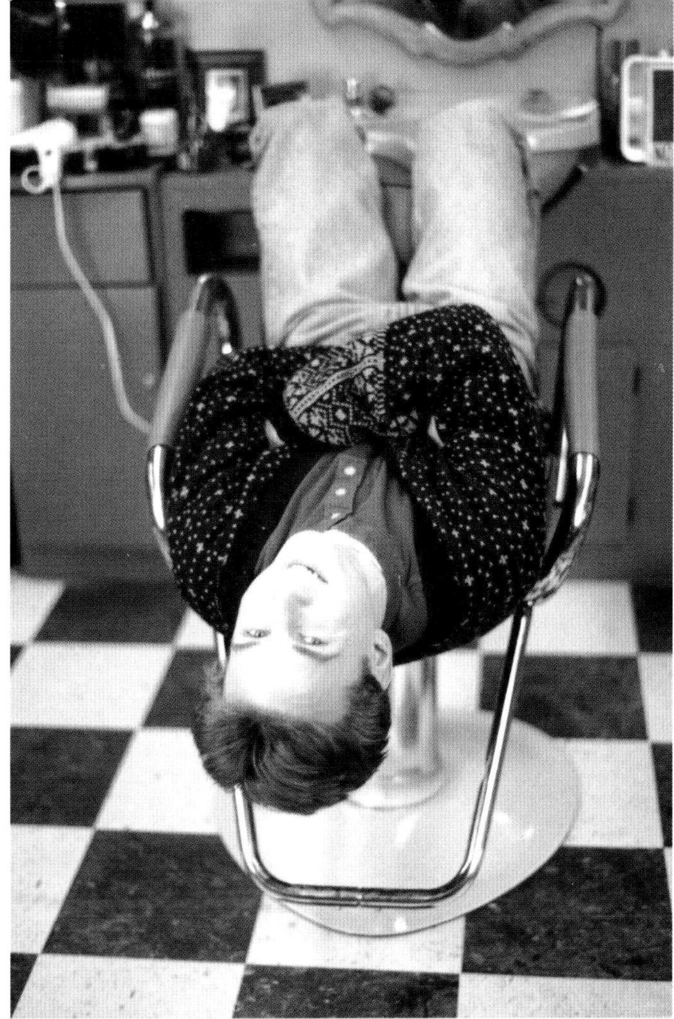
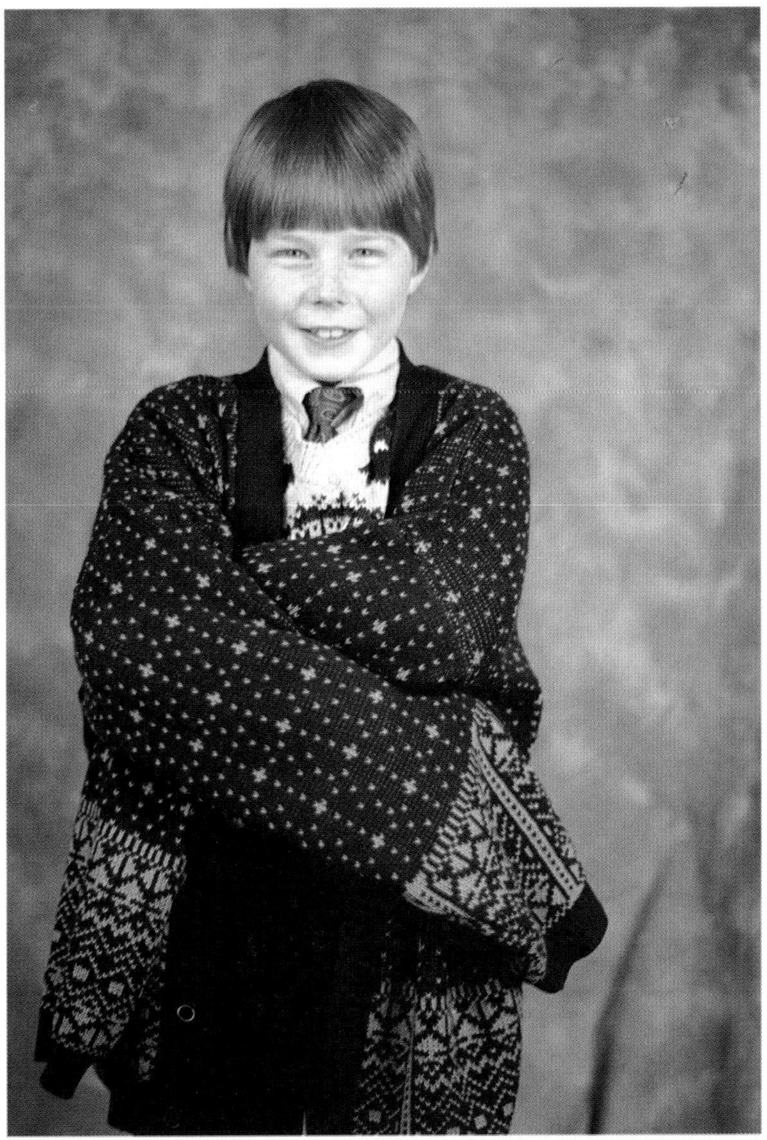
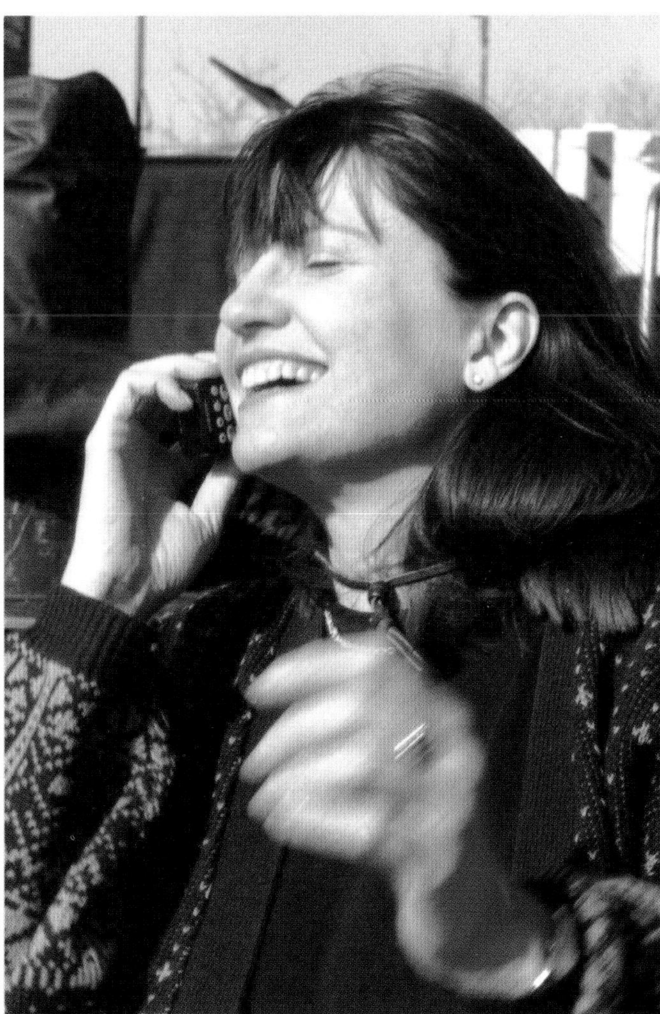

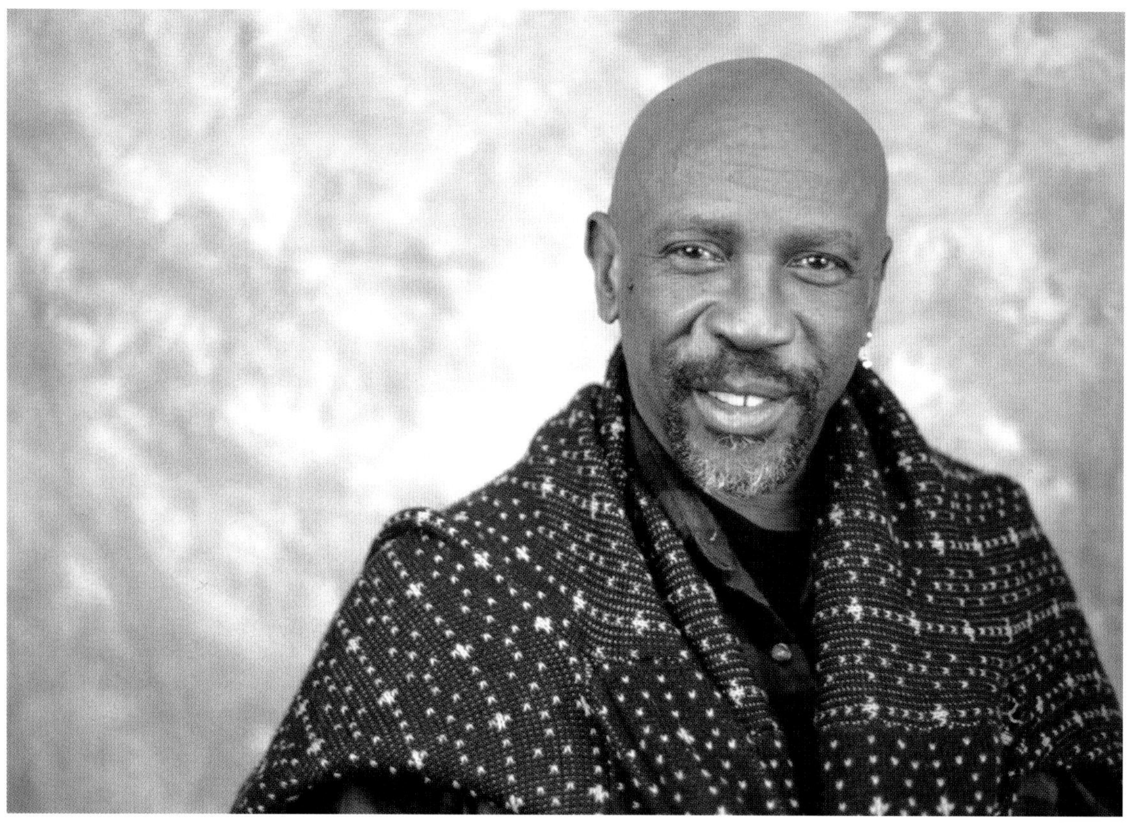

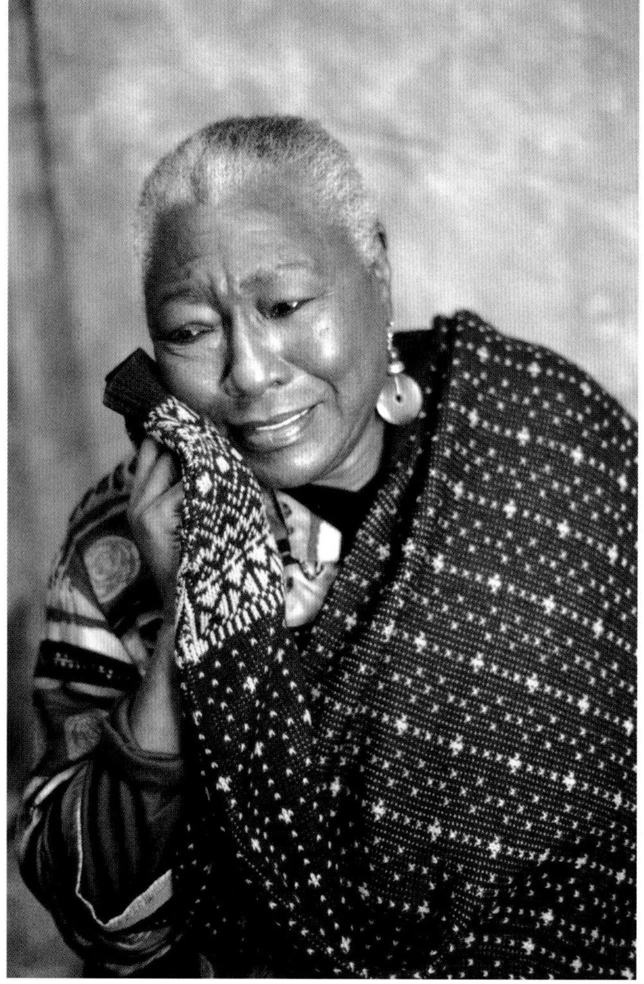

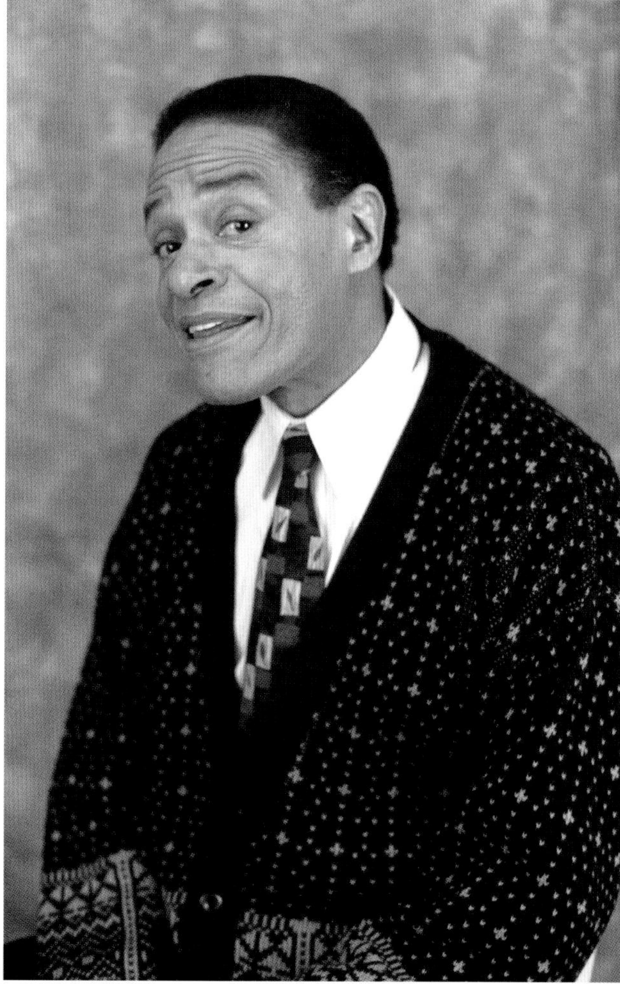

Clockwise: Louis Gossett Jr., Al Jarreau, Esther Rolle

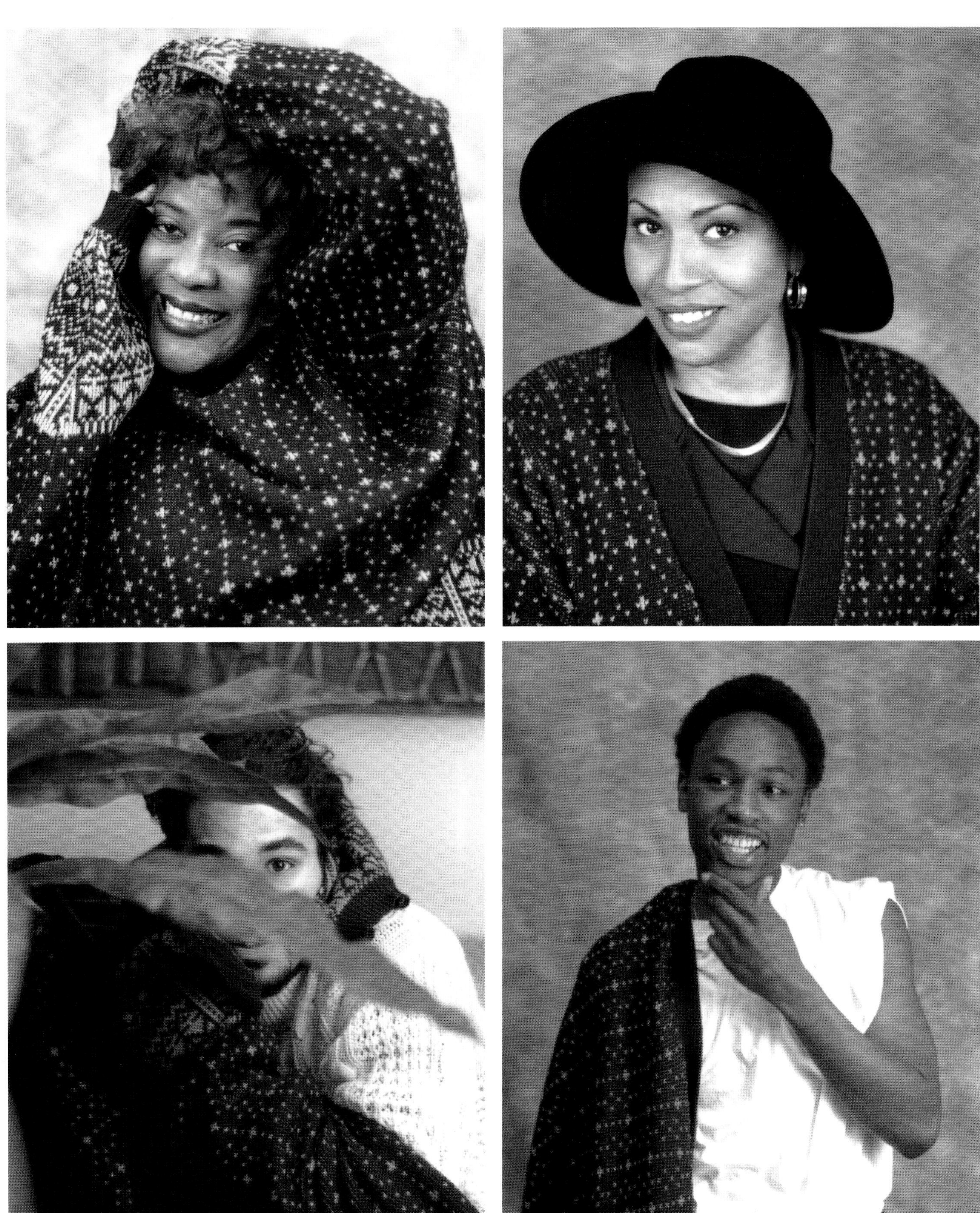

Clockwise from top left: Loretta Devine, Jenifer Lewis
Sean Nelson, John Oritz

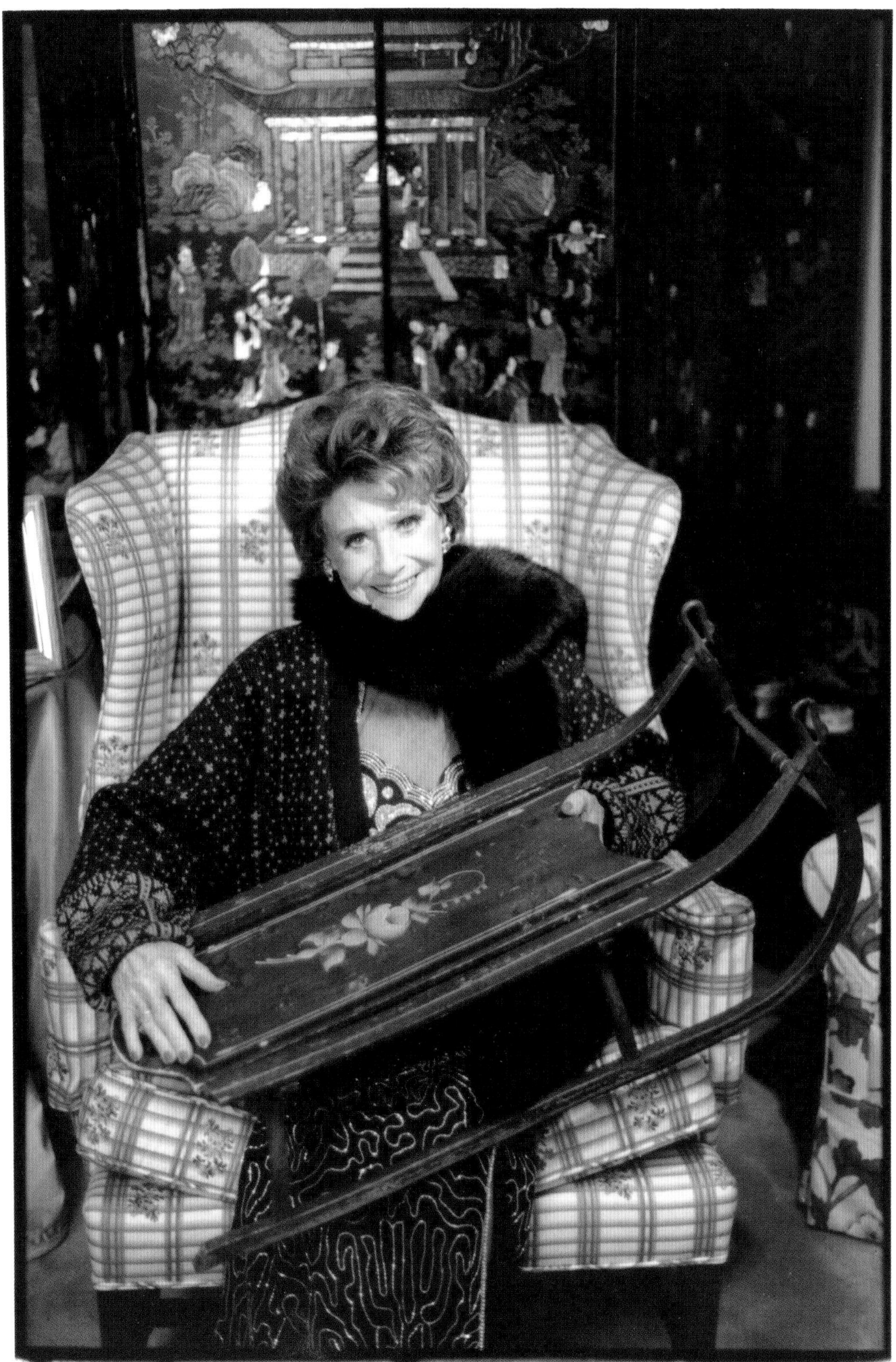

Ruth Warrick

She is soap opera royalty, having been the matriarch of *All My Children* for many a year. For me and Pat, though, she is Hollywood history, having appeared in *Citizen Kane*, what many consider the greatest American film ever made. We all talked about what she would do for her photo; she changed from a suit to an evening gown and fur; we tried a long shot in her elegant living room, showing the splendiferous decor. When Ruth Warrick brought out the rosebud sled, though, the decision was unanimous. Hollywood history.

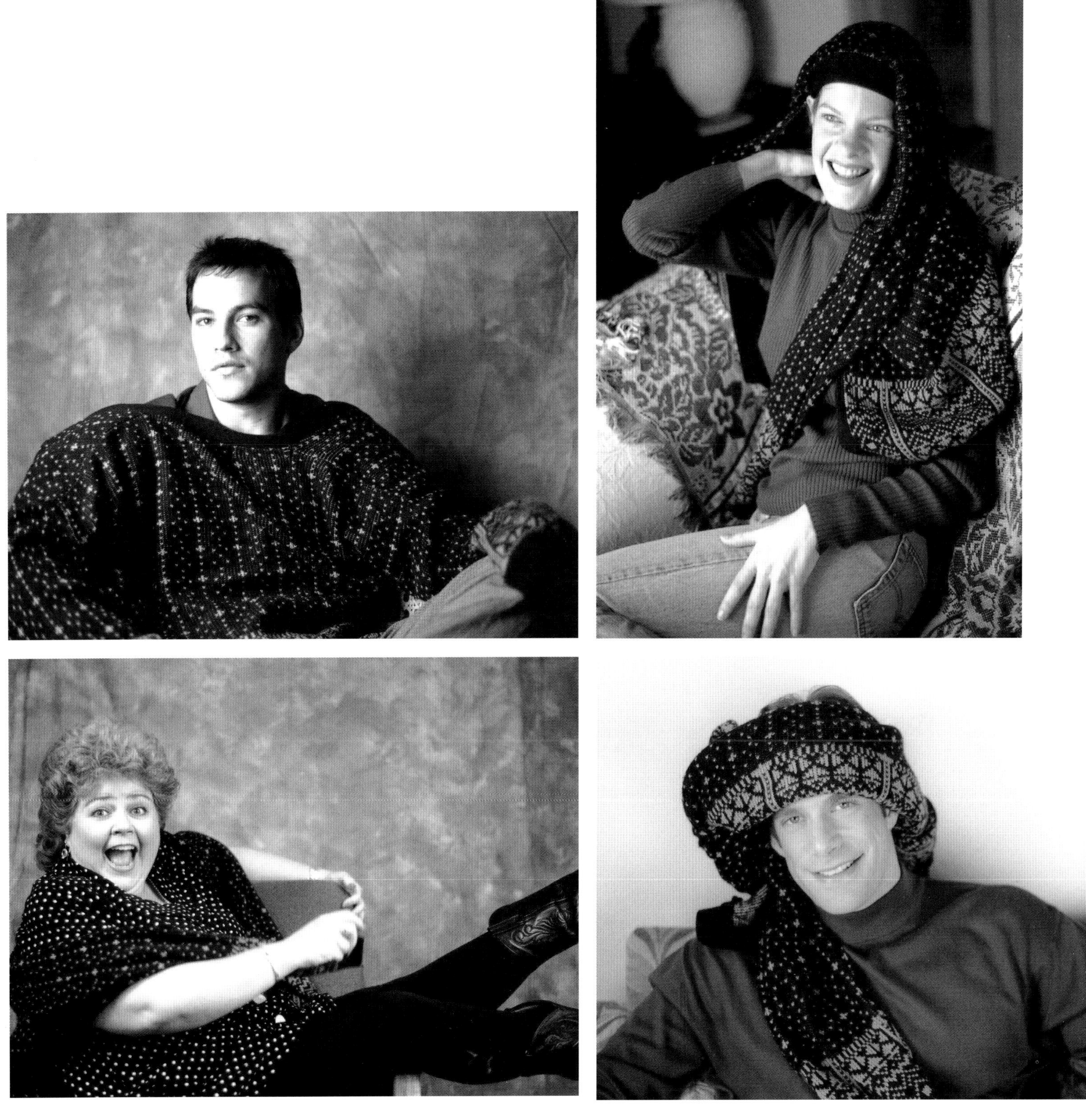

Clockwise from top left: Tyler Christopher, Michelle Stafford, Jason Brooks, Patrika Darbo

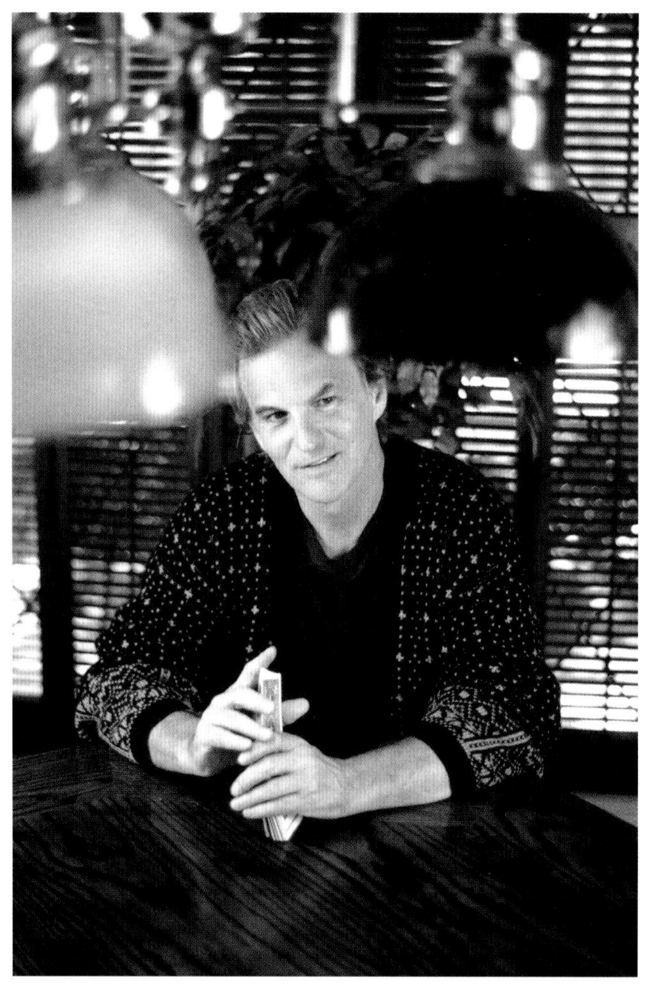

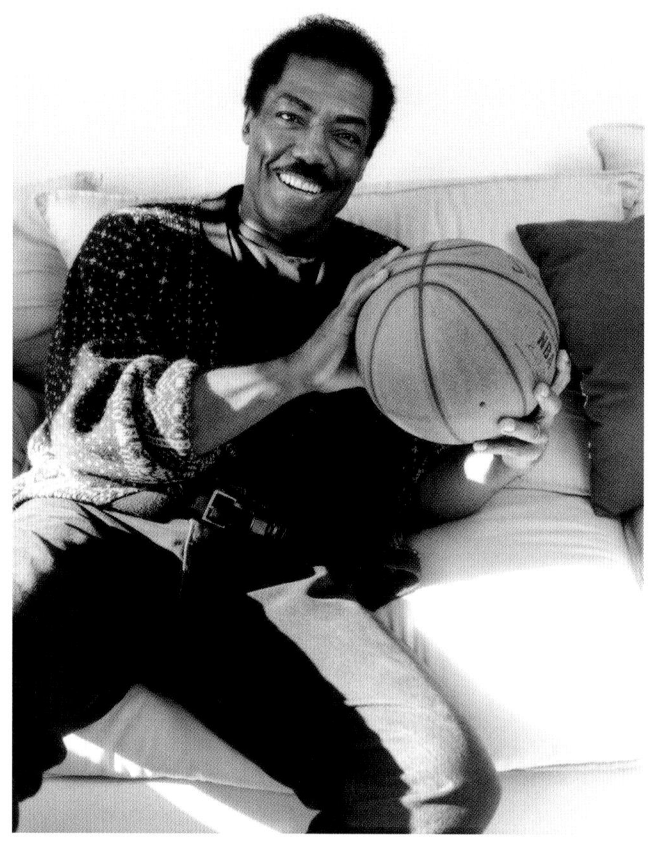

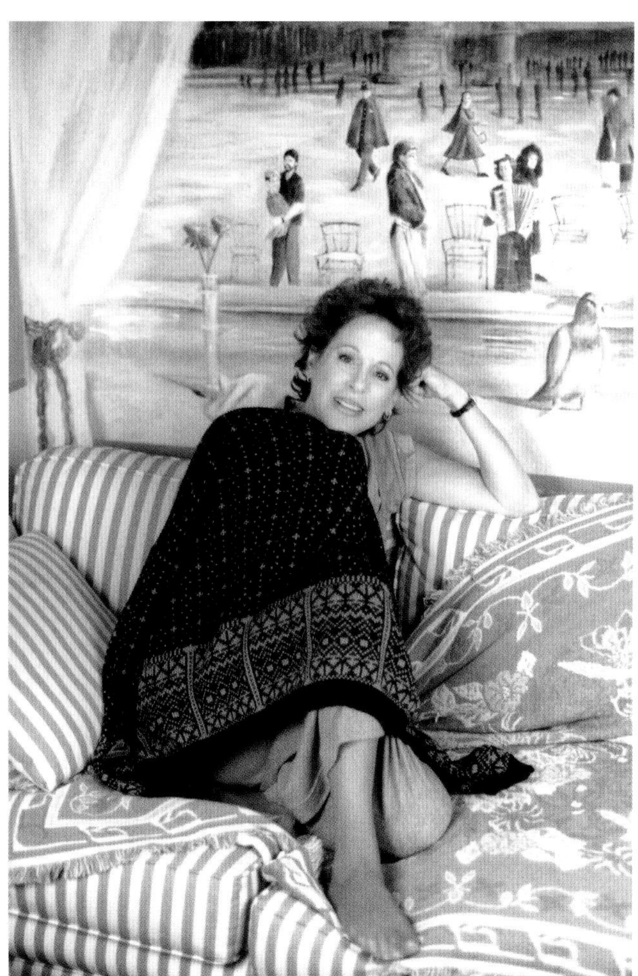

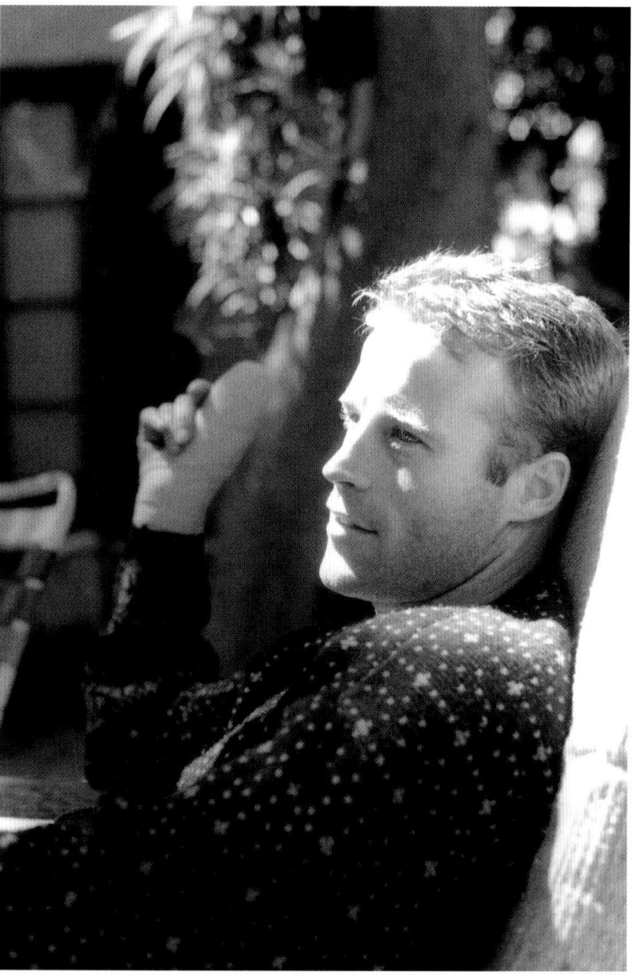

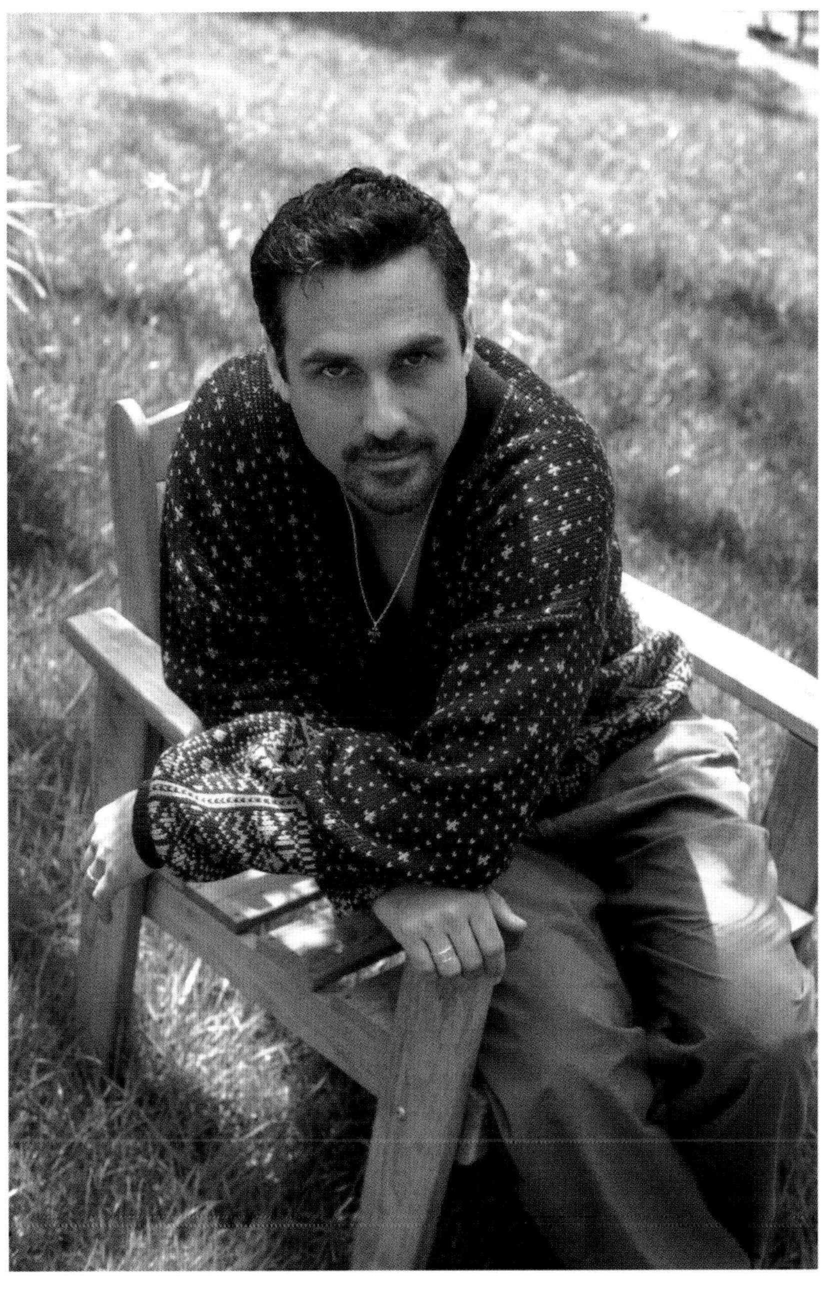

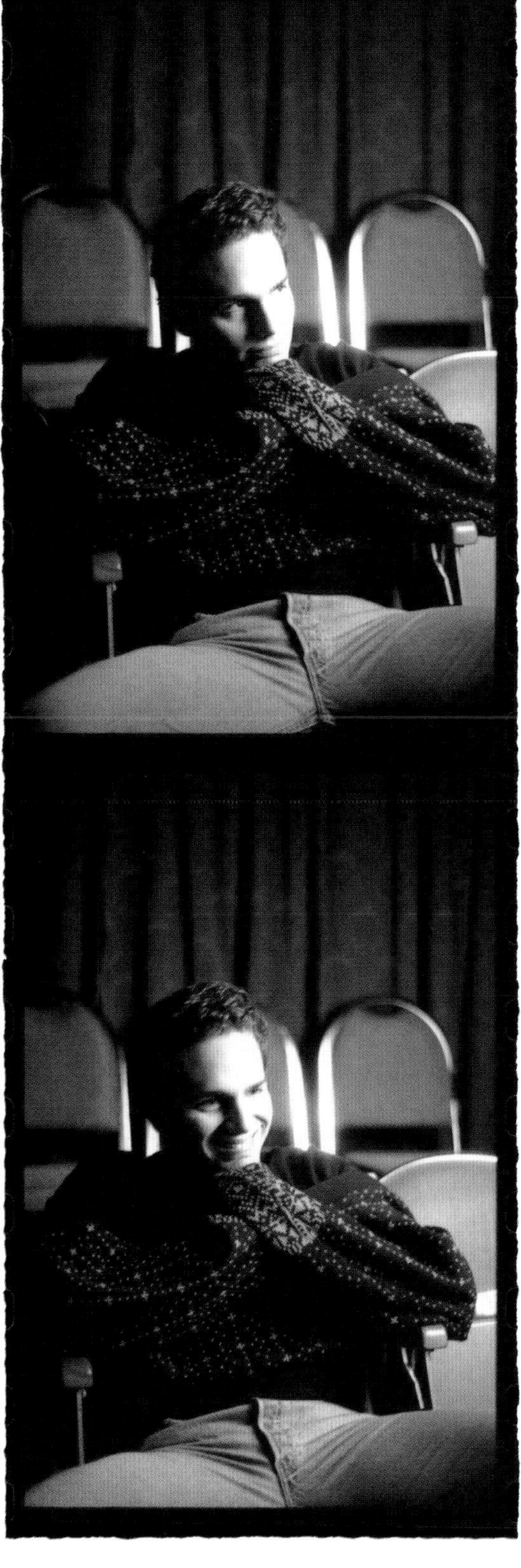

Opposite, clockwise from top left:
Josh Taylor
Jim Reynolds
Mark Valley
Louise Sorel

This page:
Maurice Benard
Right:
Paul Anthony Stewart

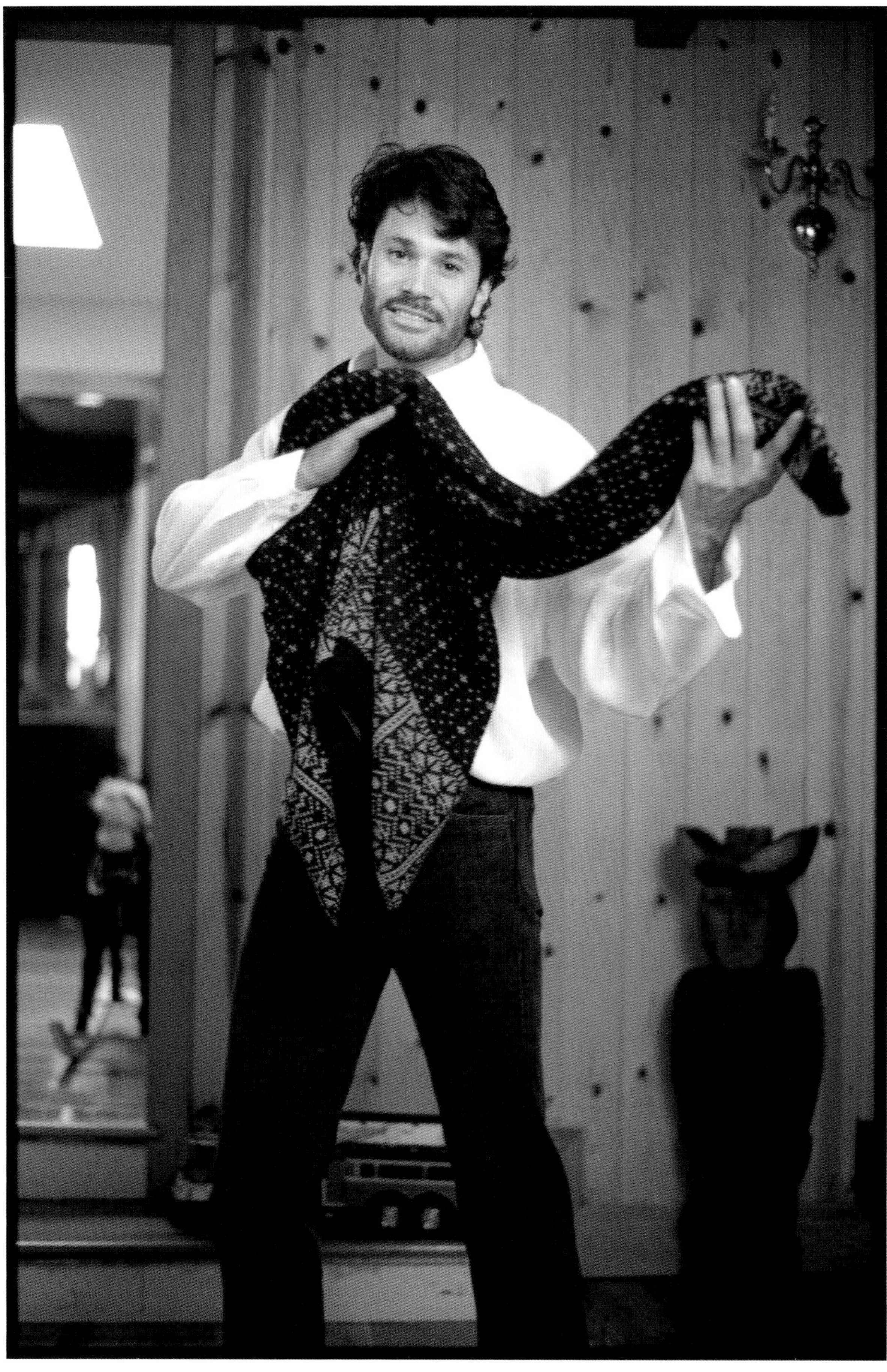

Peter Reckell

THE SWEATER AROUND THE GALAXY— *in which the sweater goes where no one has gone before*

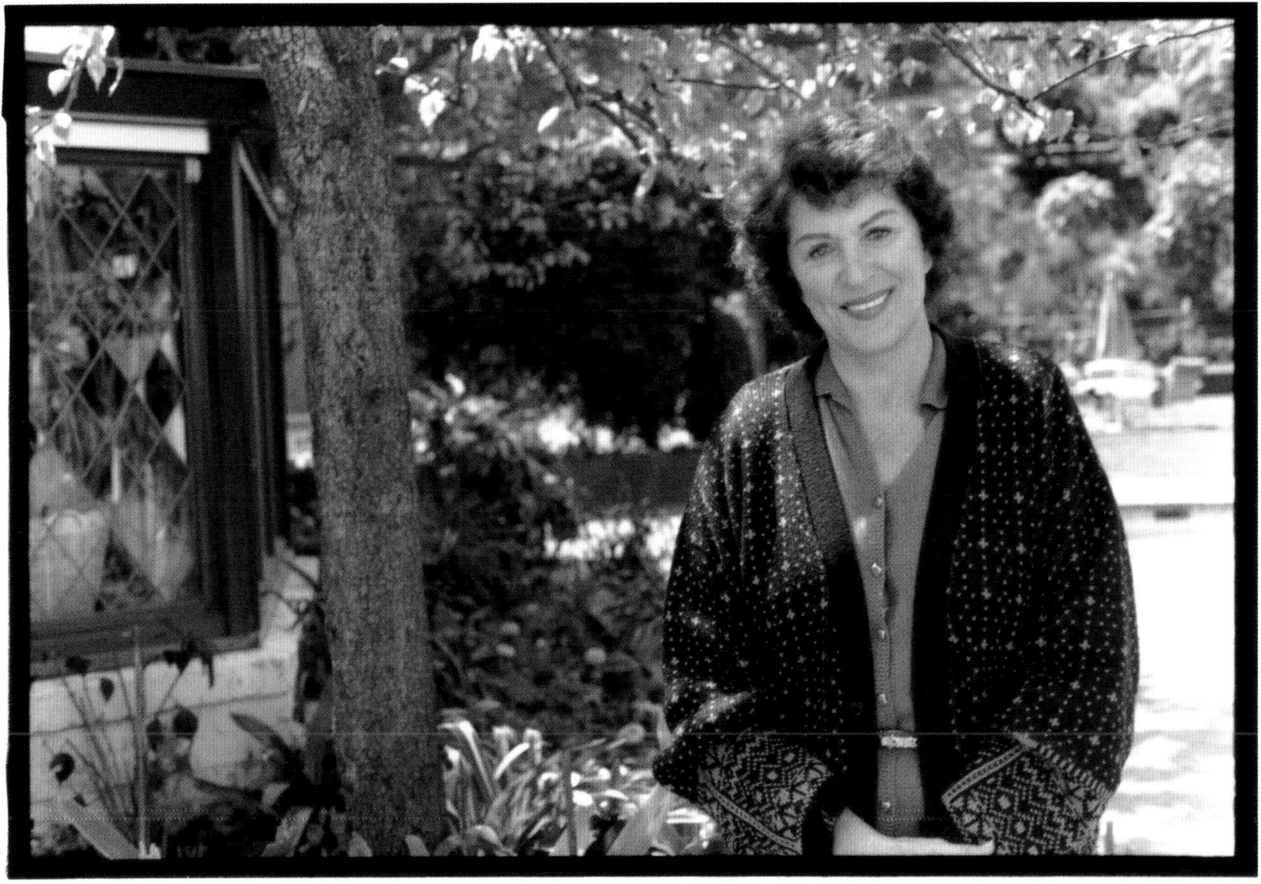

Majel Barrett Roddenberry

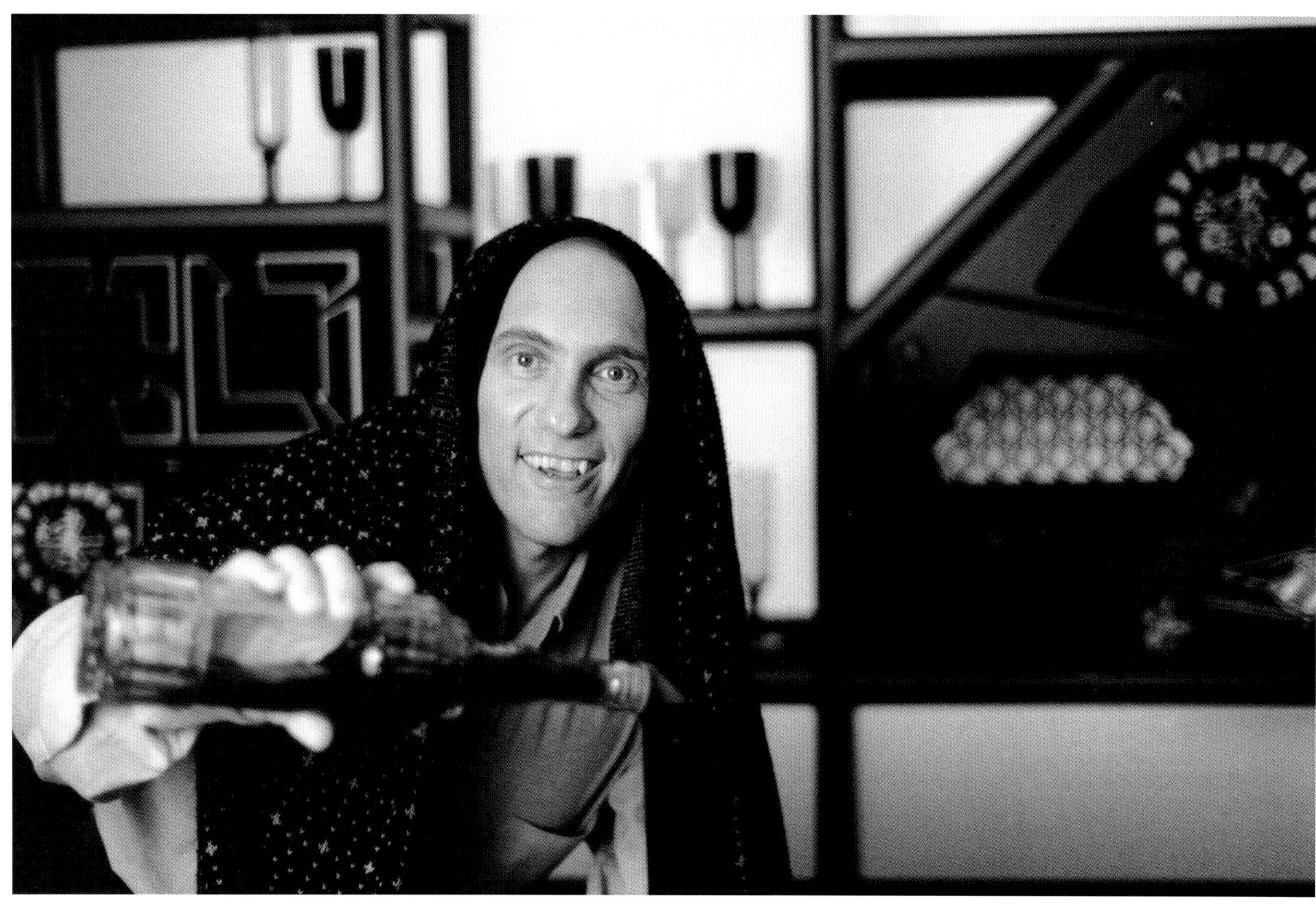

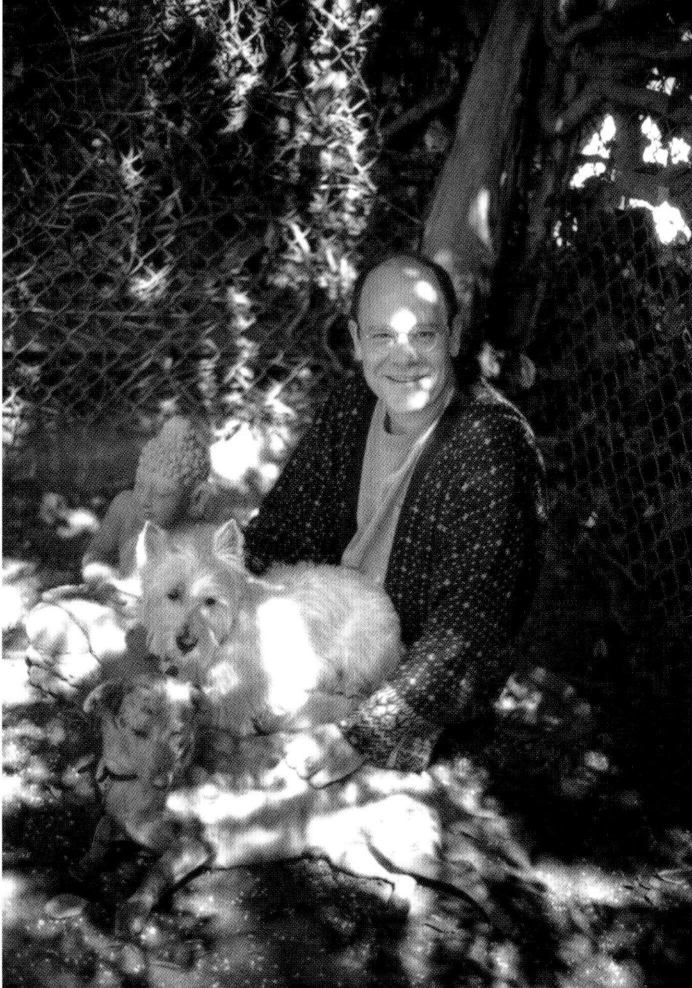

Armin Shimerman
Ethan Phillips

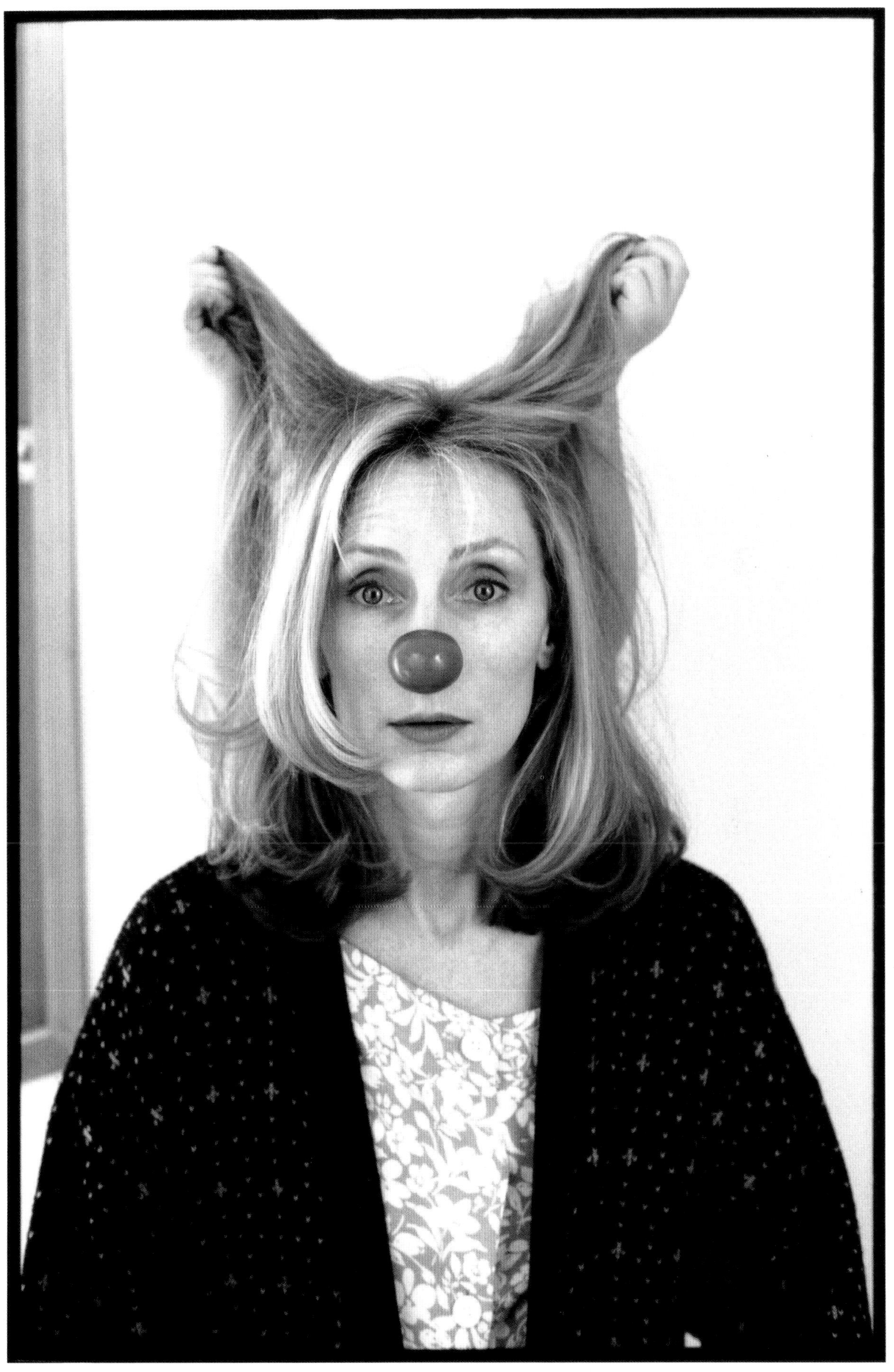

Gates McFadden

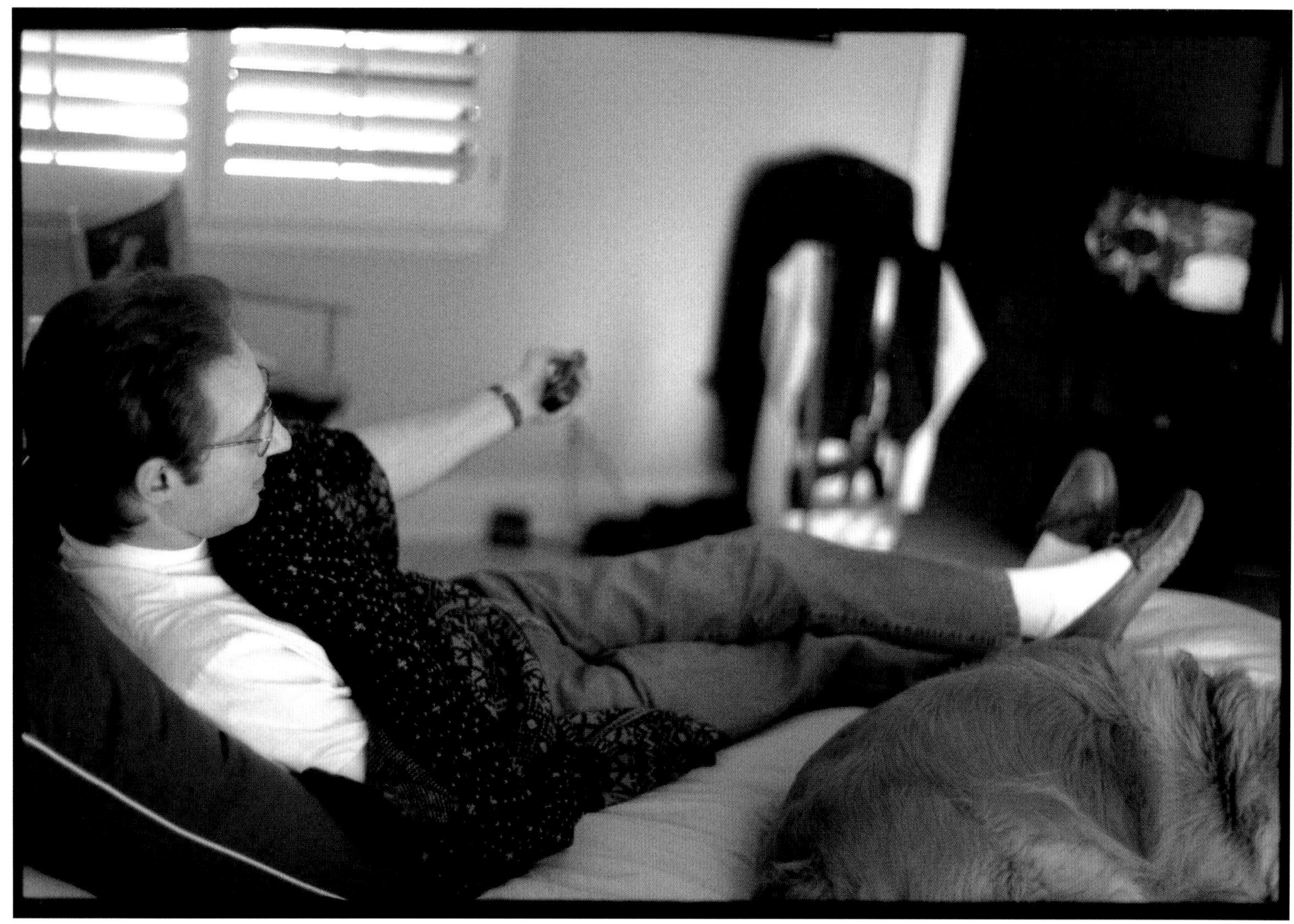

Brent Spiner

"For me, if I'm not on *TV, I'm watching it. It doesn't have to be anything in particular—it just has to move."*

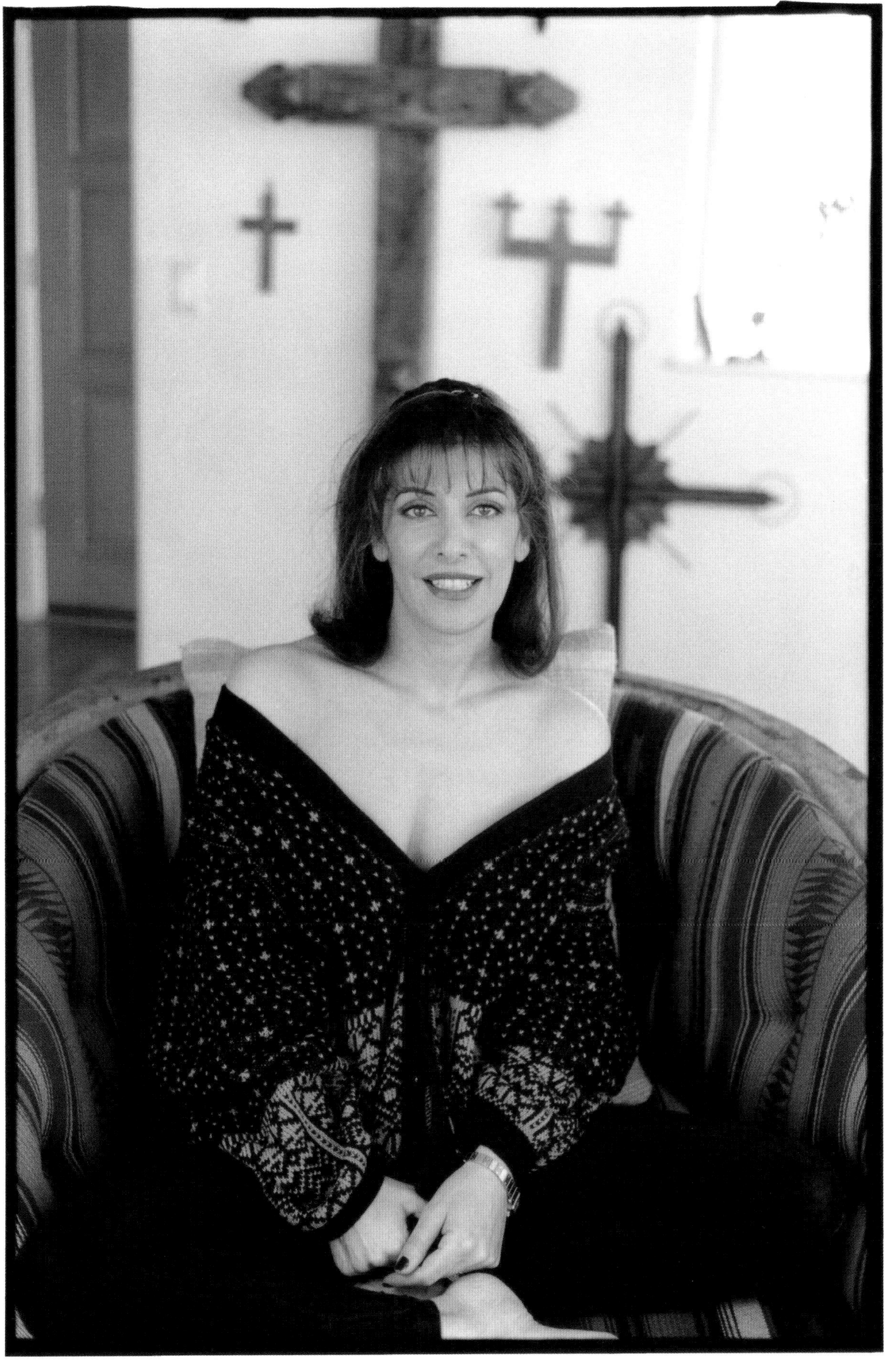

Marina Sirtis

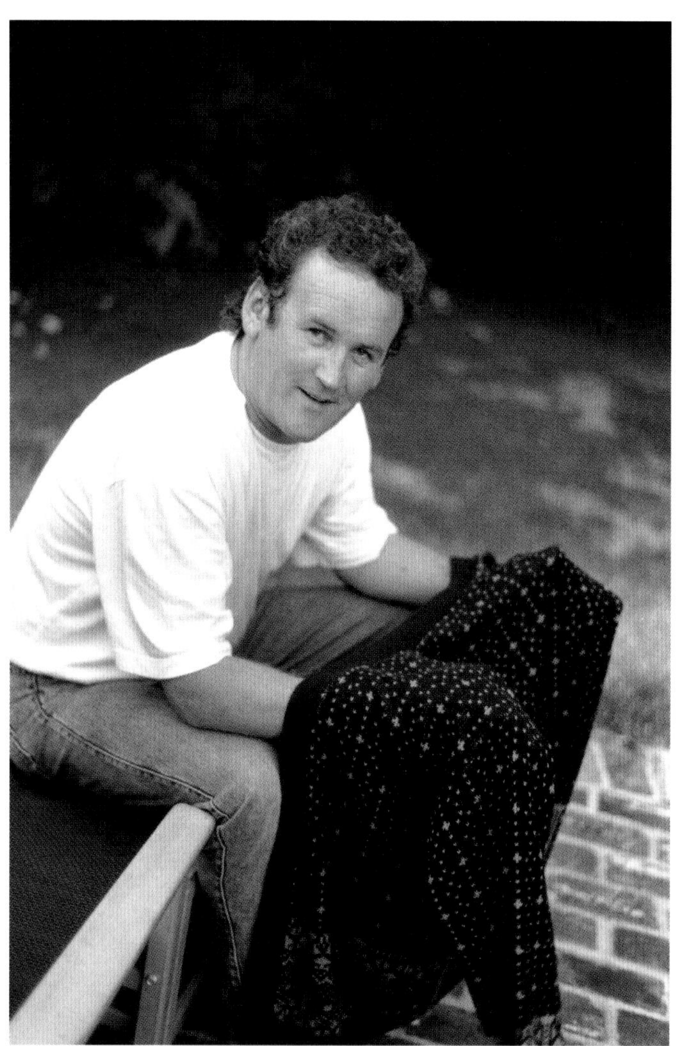

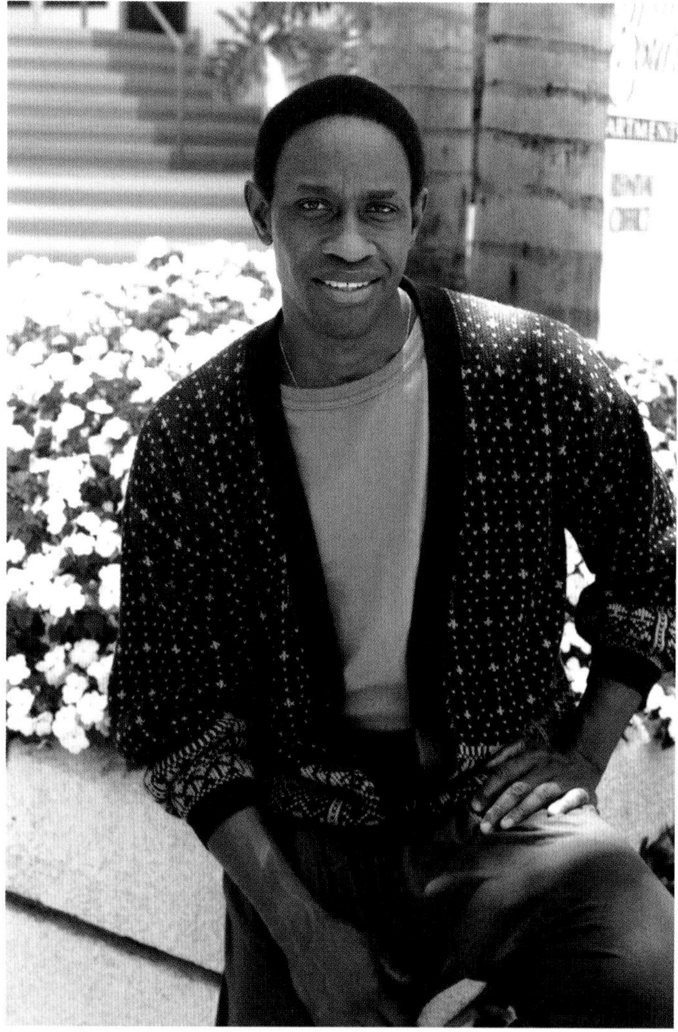

Colm Meaney

Tim Russ

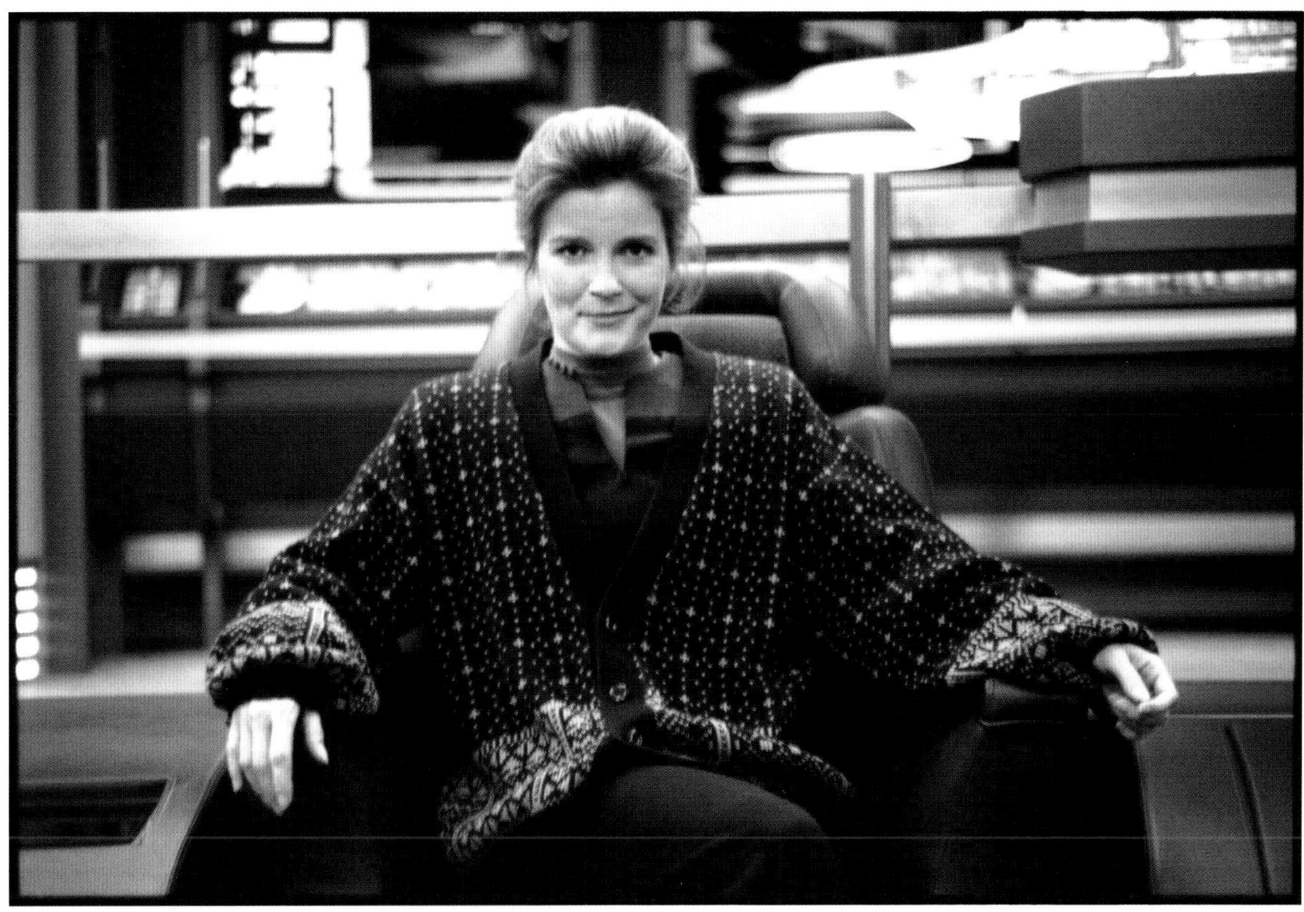

Kate Mulgrew

Invited to the set of *Star Trek: Voyager,* I had no idea that I would actually get to watch the filming of the season premiere. In the past, I had been on sets, in trailers, on the lots, everywhere but where I went on this particular day. A longtime fan of my personal favorite of all the Star Trek captains, I was excited enough to meet her, to shake her hand, to see how pretty she is in person, to learn what a real person she is. However, asked to wait and watch them shoot, I found myself so dazed that when after an hour someone yelled, "STEPHEN MOSHER!!!" I wasn't prepared.

"Yes?"

"You're up!"

A break in filming. I had been warned that I would have thirty seconds; I had not been told that I would be shooting on the bridge of *Voyager*. I handed the sweater to my captain, and as she gave me her full attention, talking to me, asking questions about the sweater and my work, I snapped as many photos as was possible until they called out that they were ready for the next scene. It was indeed thirty seconds, and my time with Kate Mulgrew was over.

And I had to come back to earth.

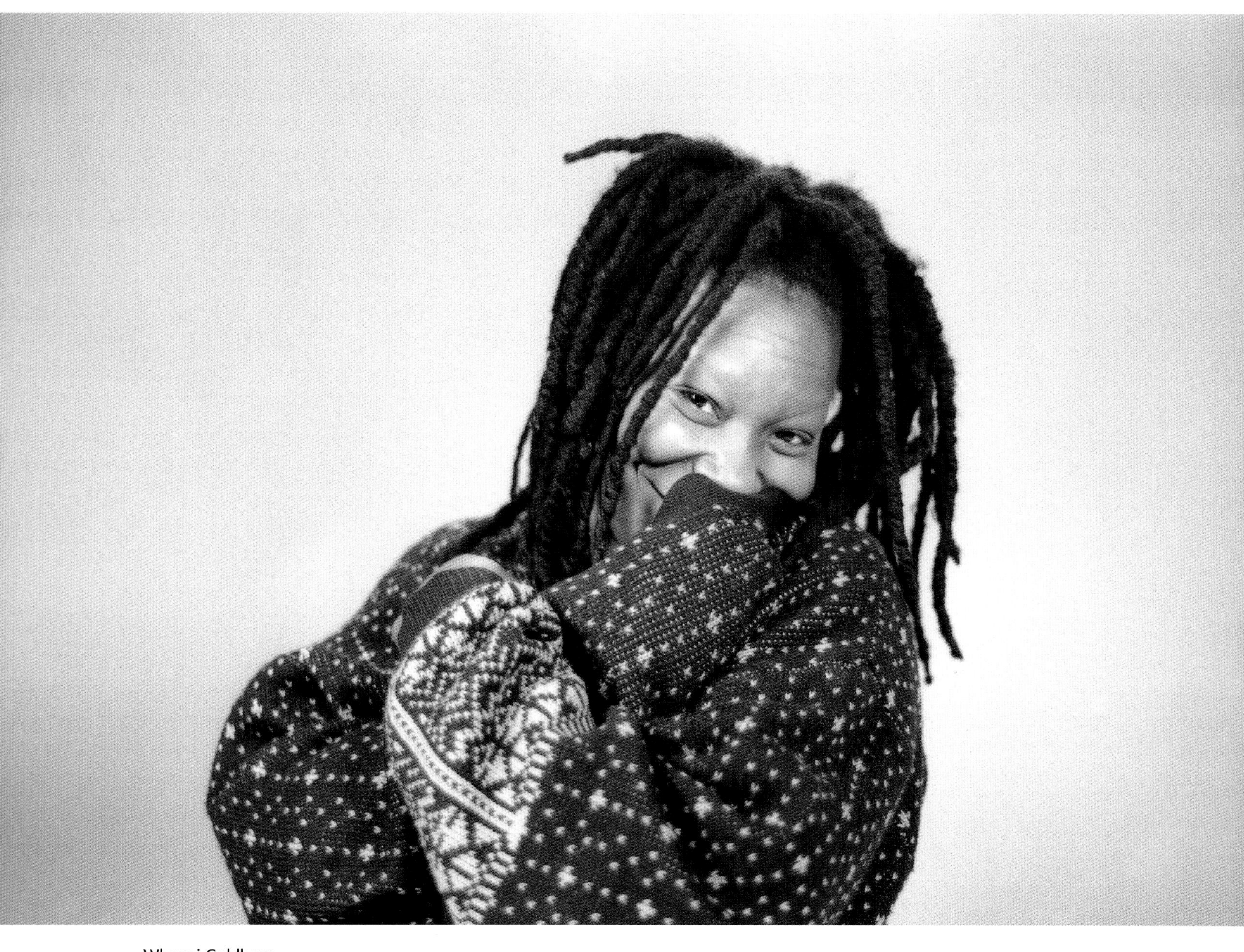

Whoopi Goldberg

So I sat down to choose the chapter into which I could place a photo of Whoopi Goldberg. The possibilities were endless. She is an actor, a producer, a singer, a comic, a commentator on social and political behavior, an awards show host, as well as the roles she plays in her personal life. I asked friends for help, and most often, the answer was *Star Trek*! I thought about Gainan, the unforgettable character she'd created. Warmth, wit, wisdom; mix in a little mystery and a lot of leadership qualities and utmost coolness: Whoopi and her character are almost the same person. And they both fit Gene Roddenberry's dream of the future.

So *Star Trek* it is.

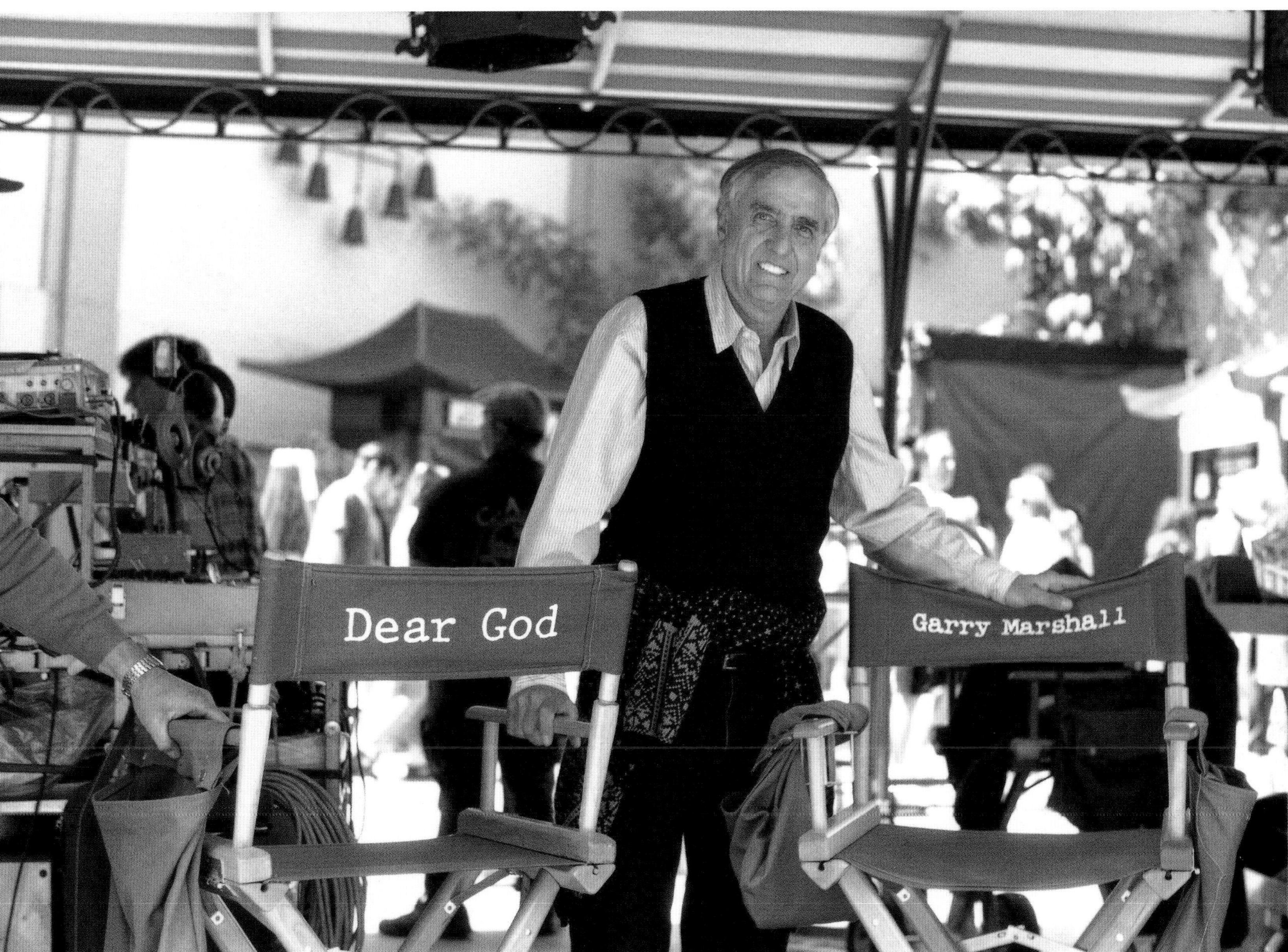

Garry Marshall

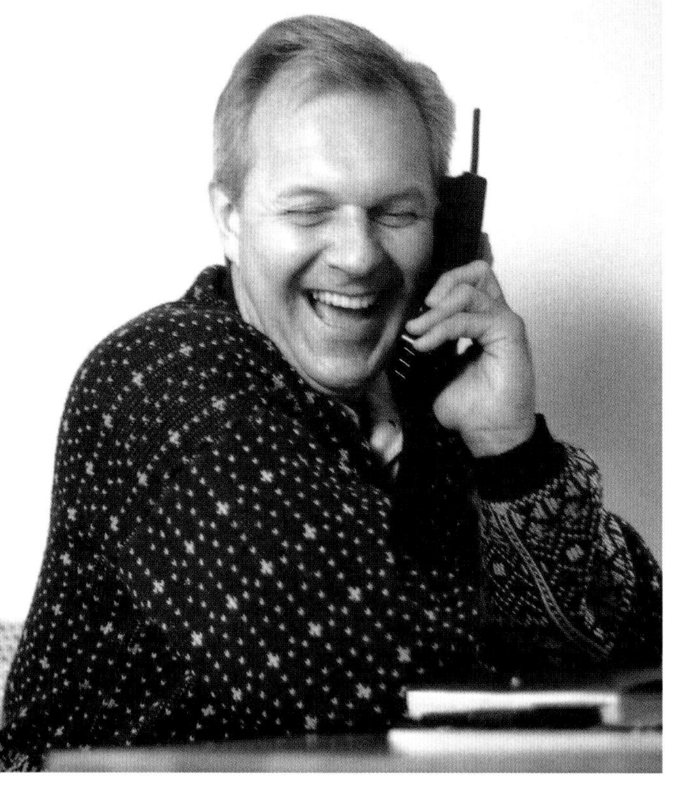

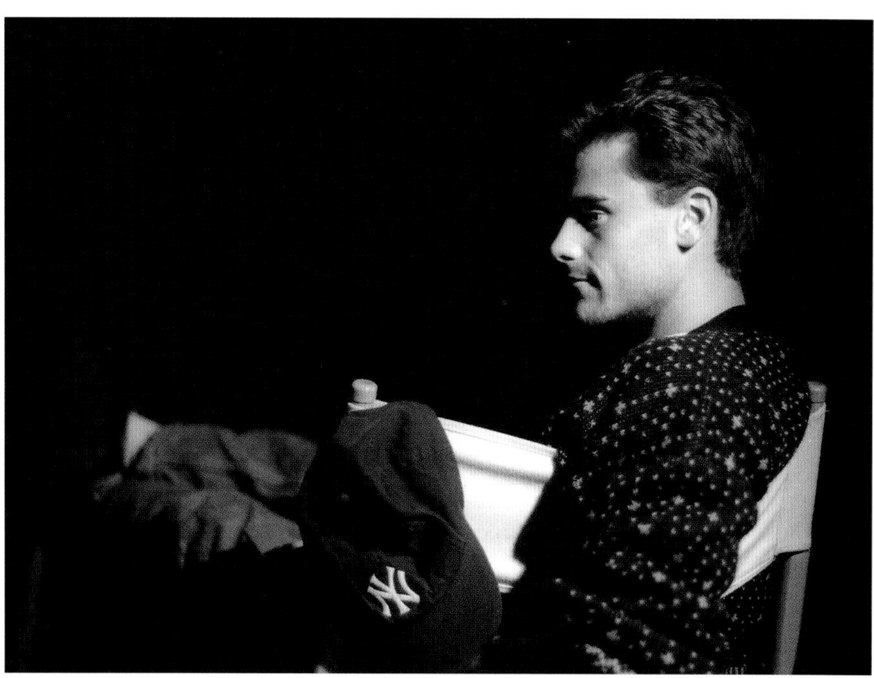

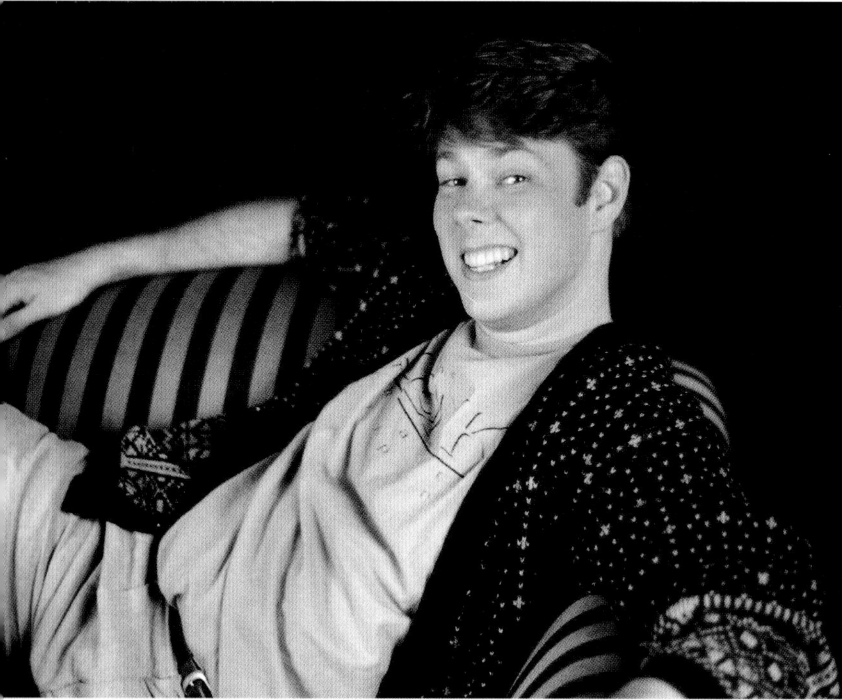

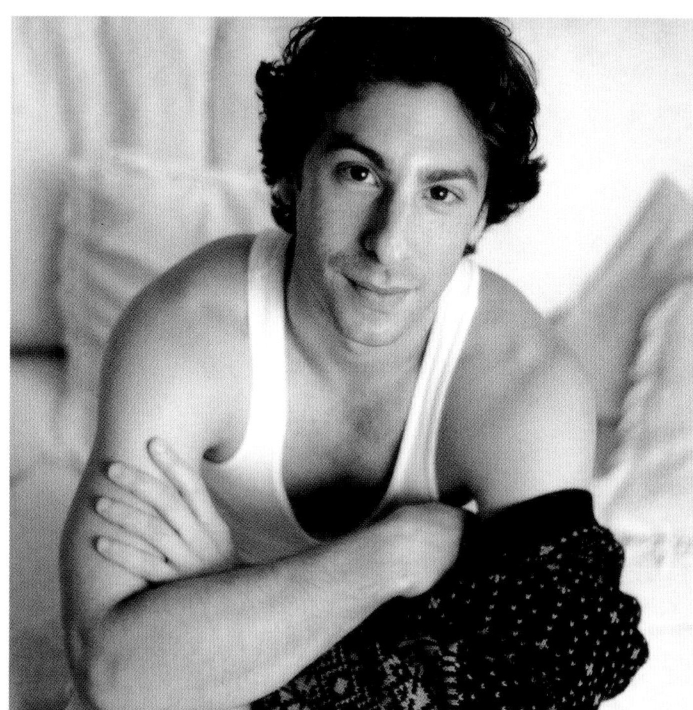

Clockwise from top left:

Walter Bobbie

Paul Etheredge

Jason Gould

Daniel Henning

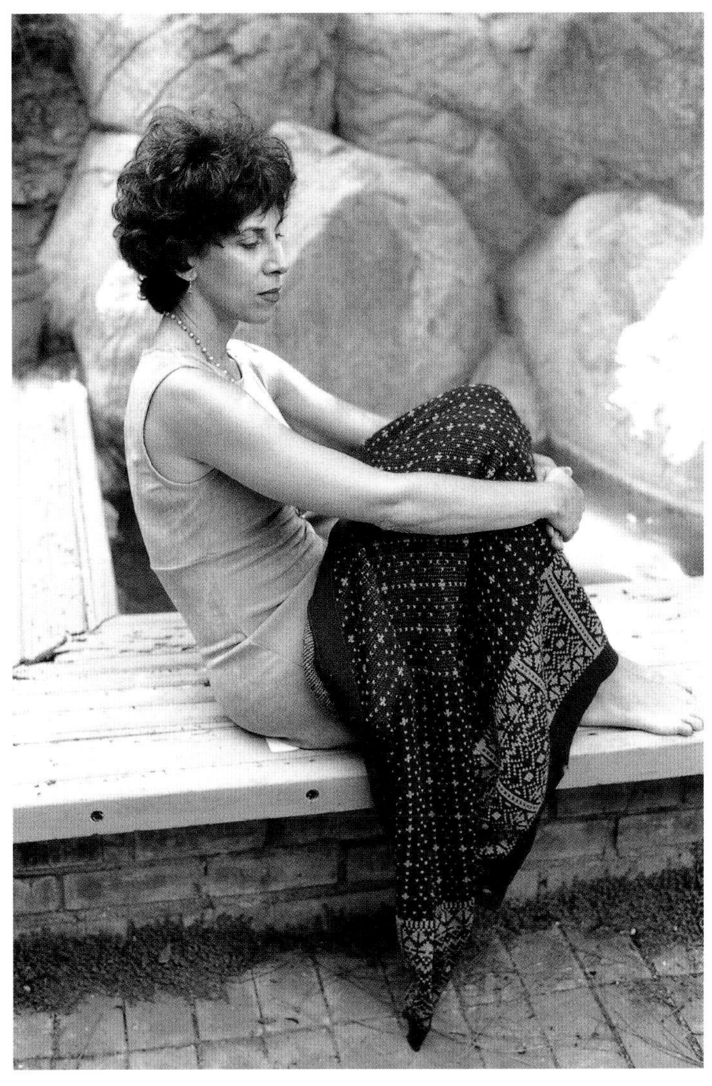

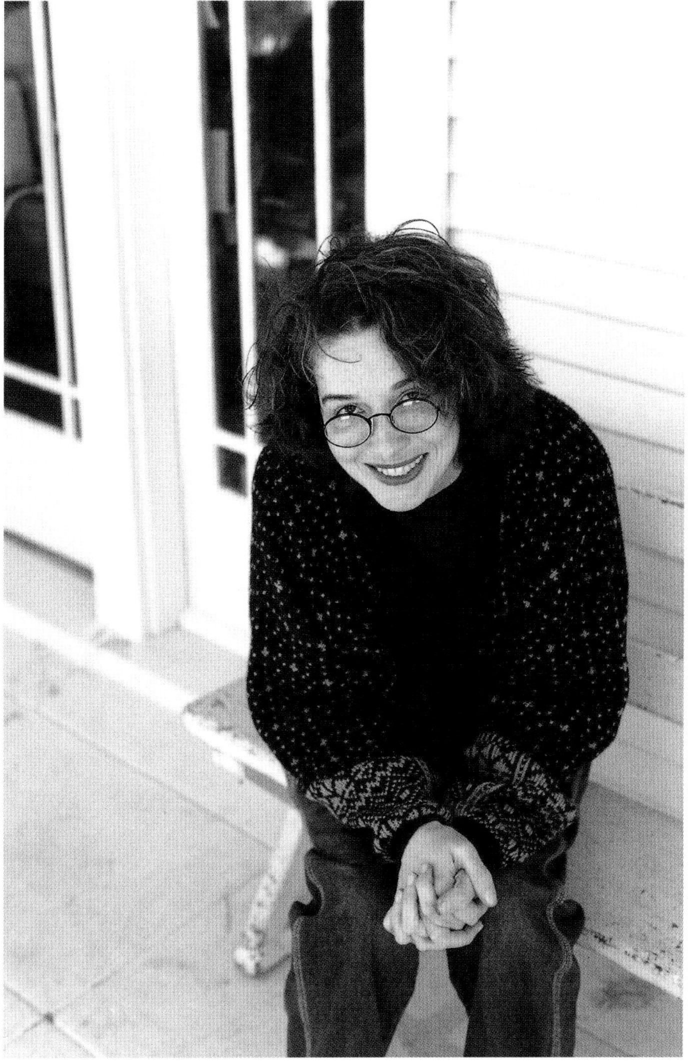

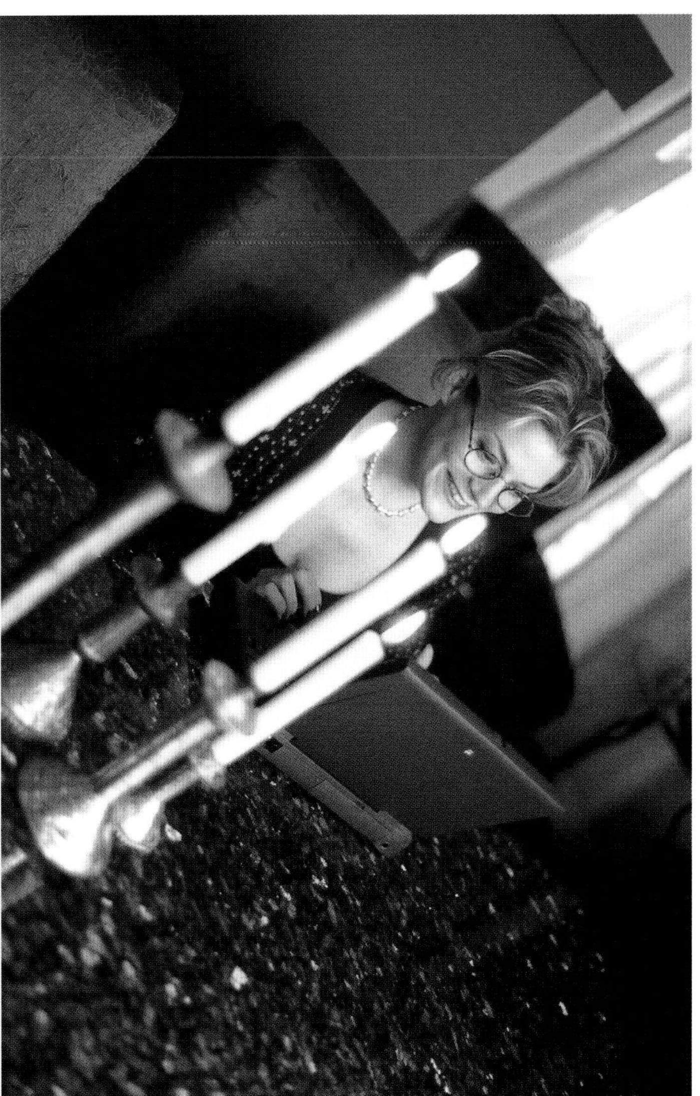

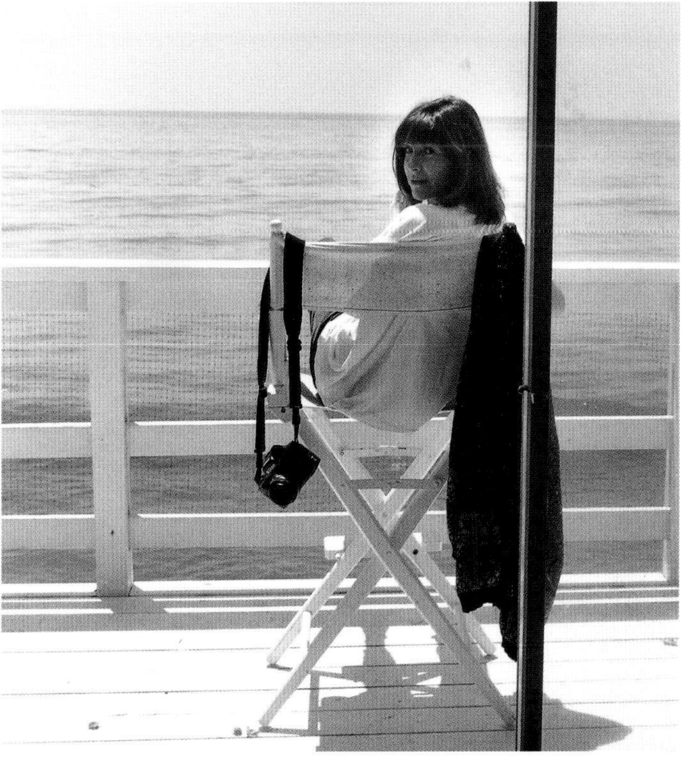

Clockwise from top left:

Anne De Salvo

Melanie Mayron

Dinah Manoff

Farrah Forke

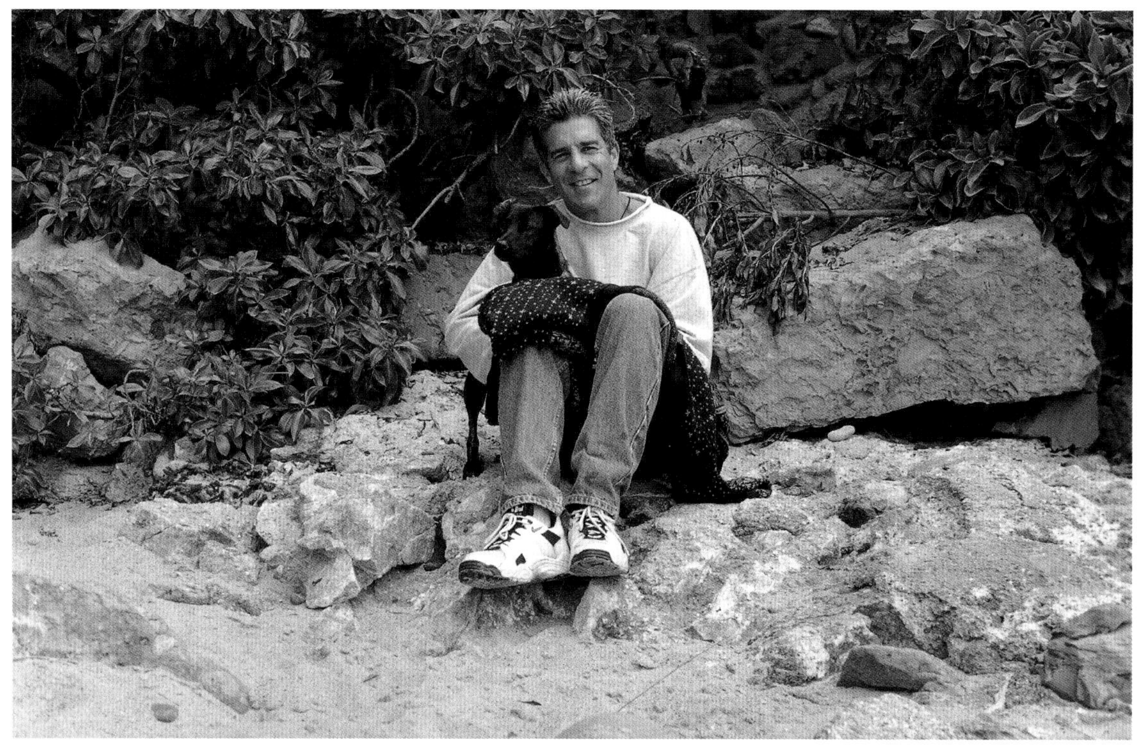

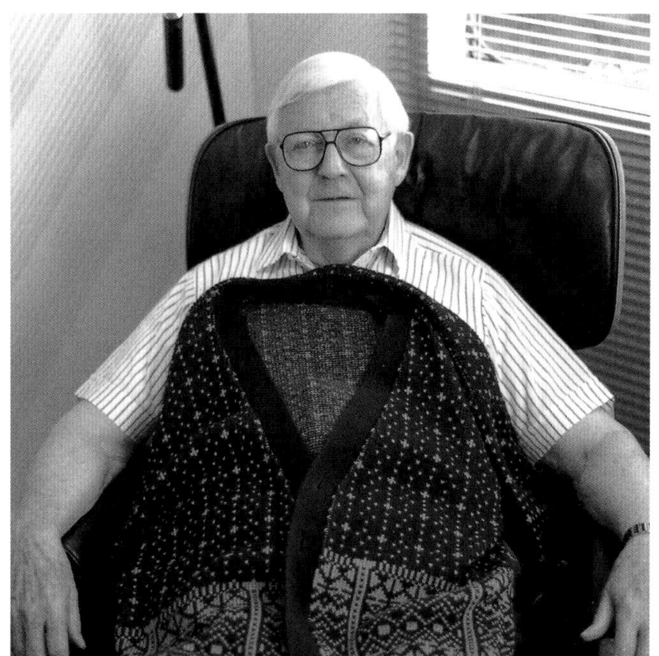

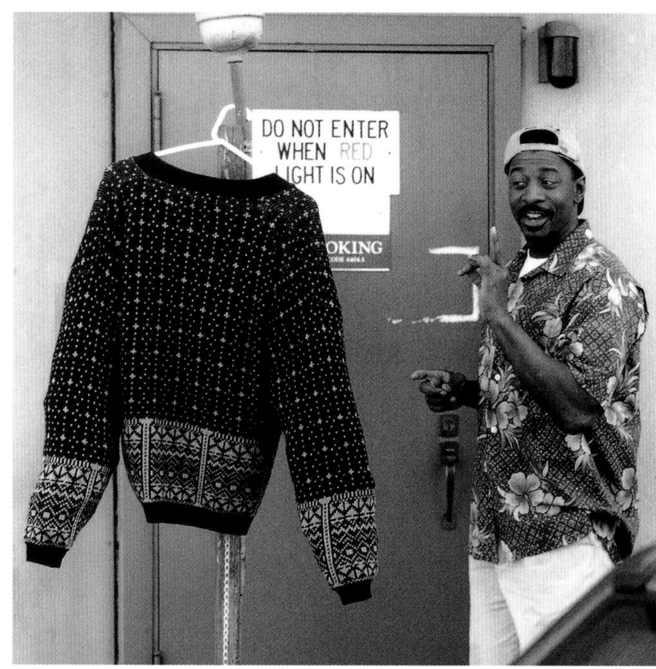

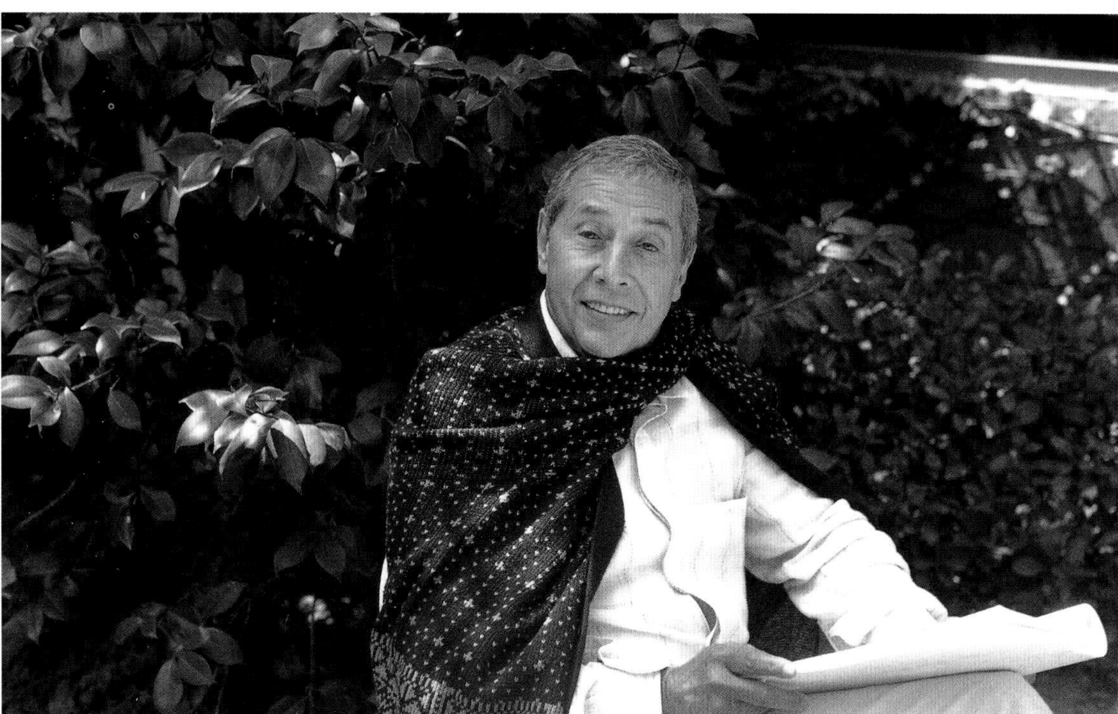

Clockwise from top:
Michael Lembeck
Robert Townsend
Mark Rydell
Robert Wise

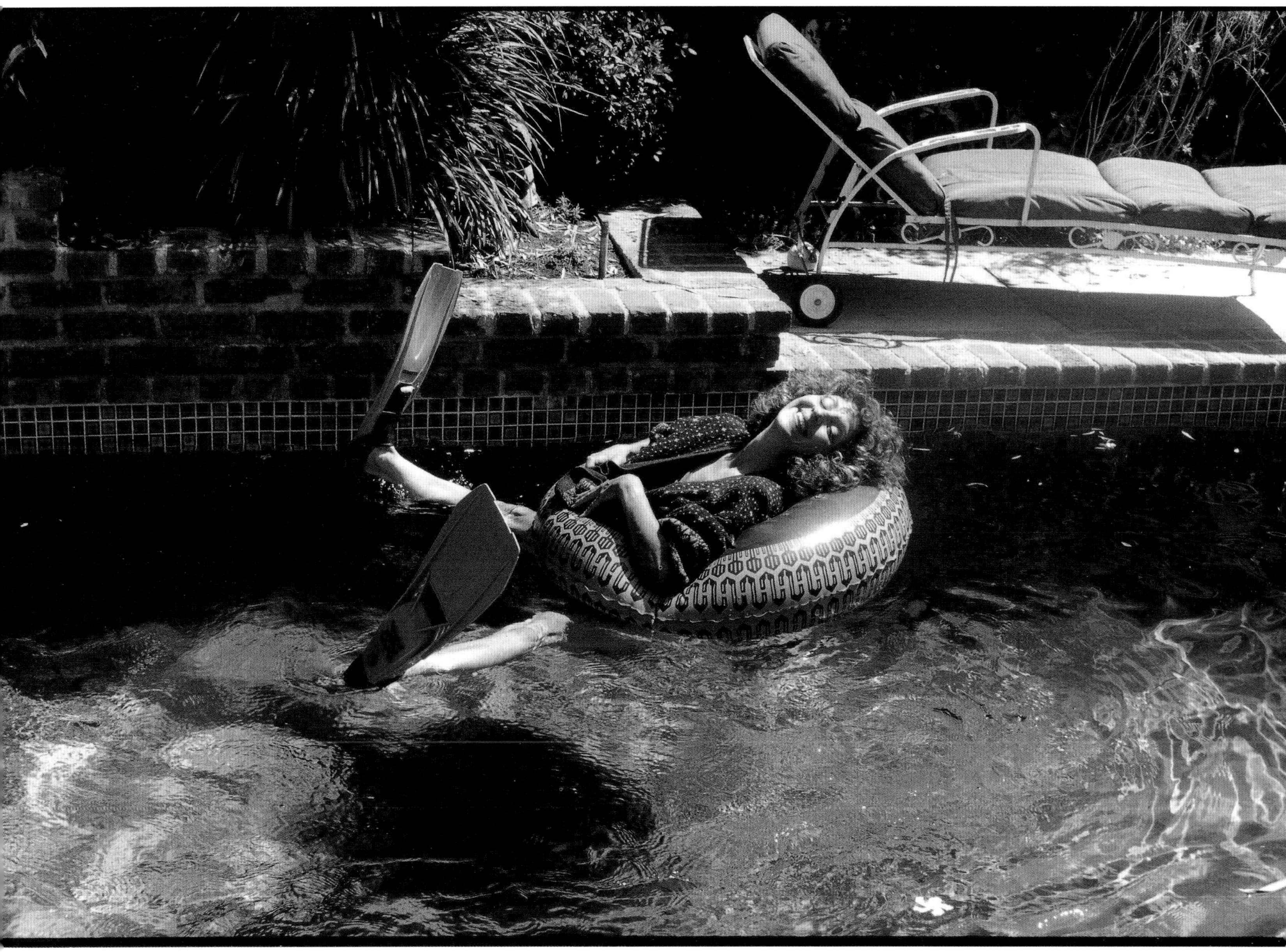

Andrea Martin

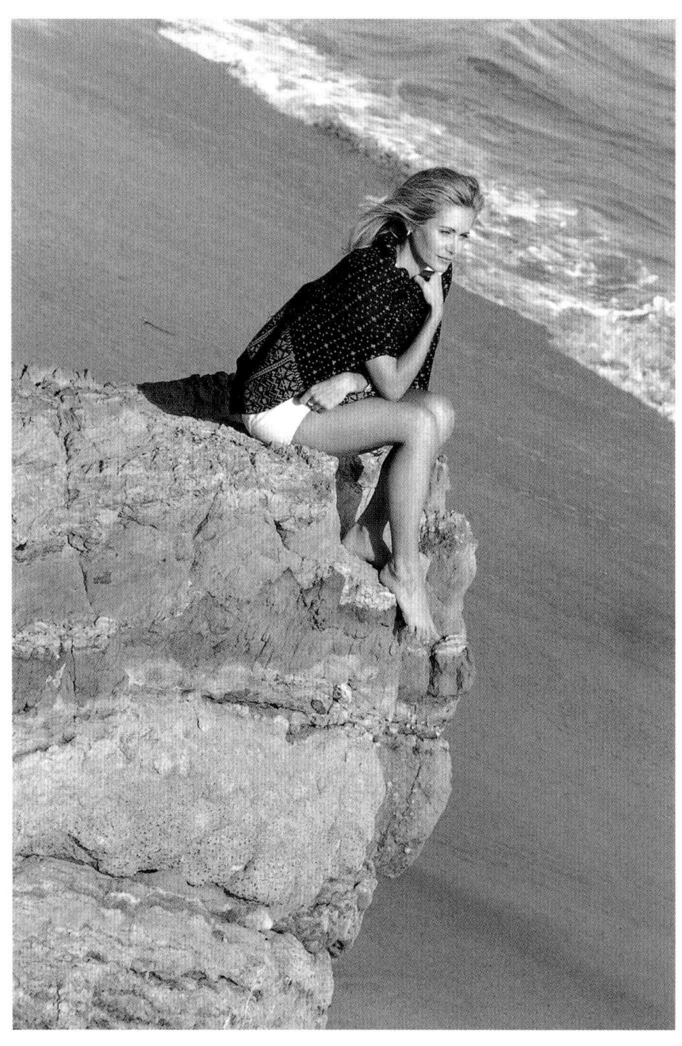

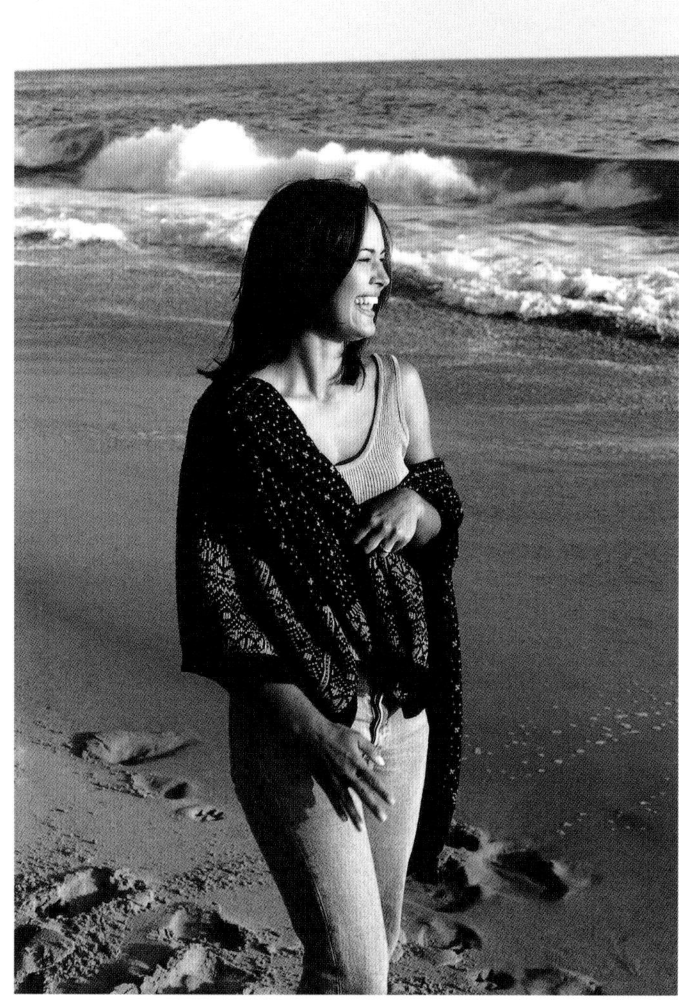

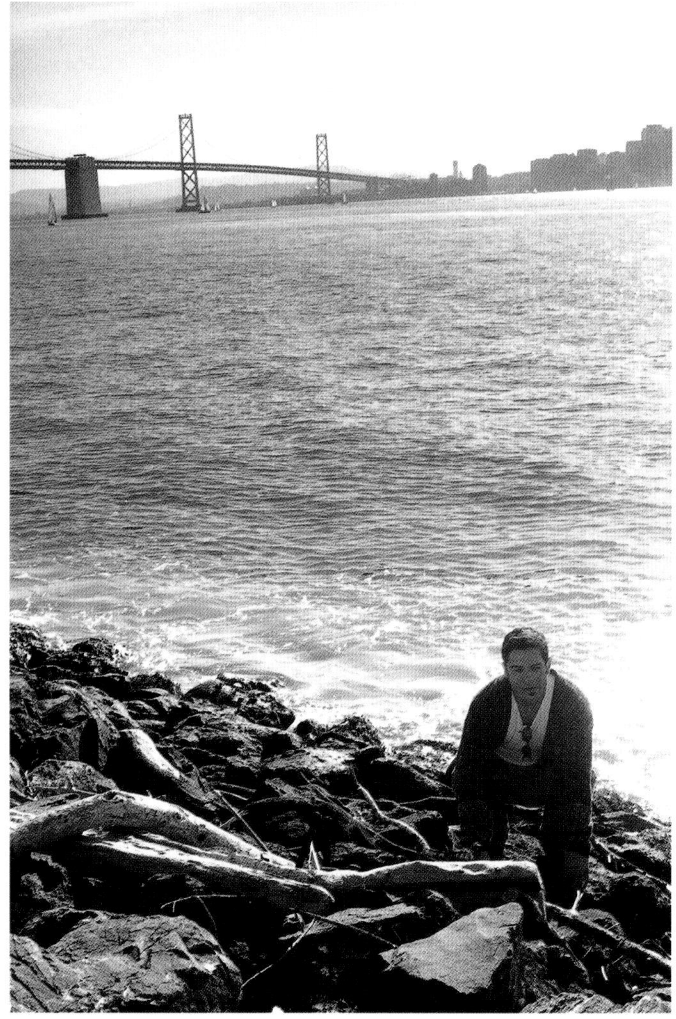

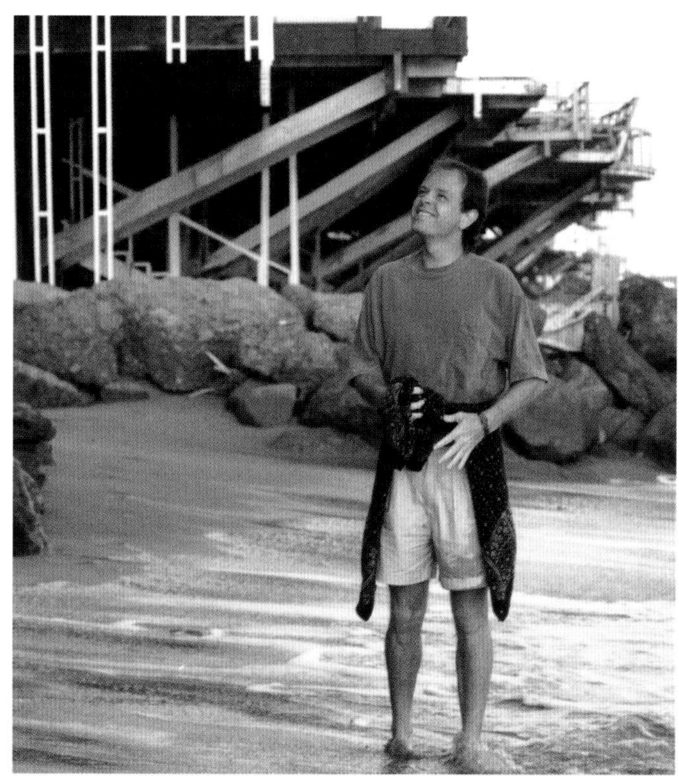

Clockwise from top left:

Heather Campbell

Sydney Penny

Dean Nolen

Jamie P. Gomez

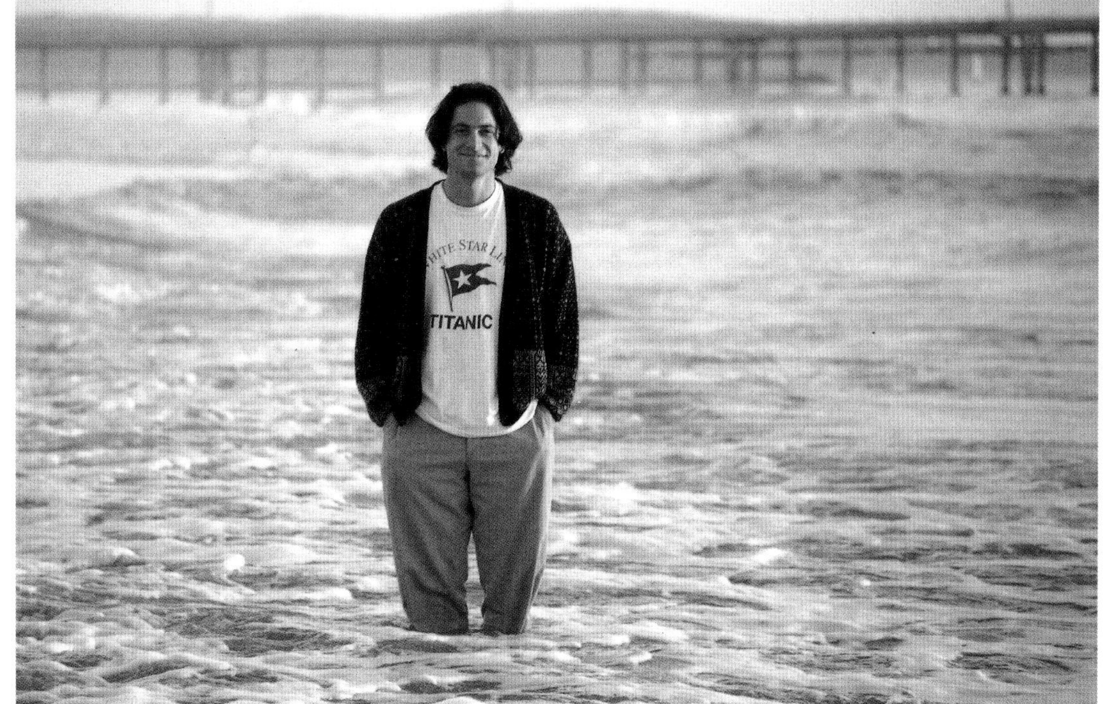

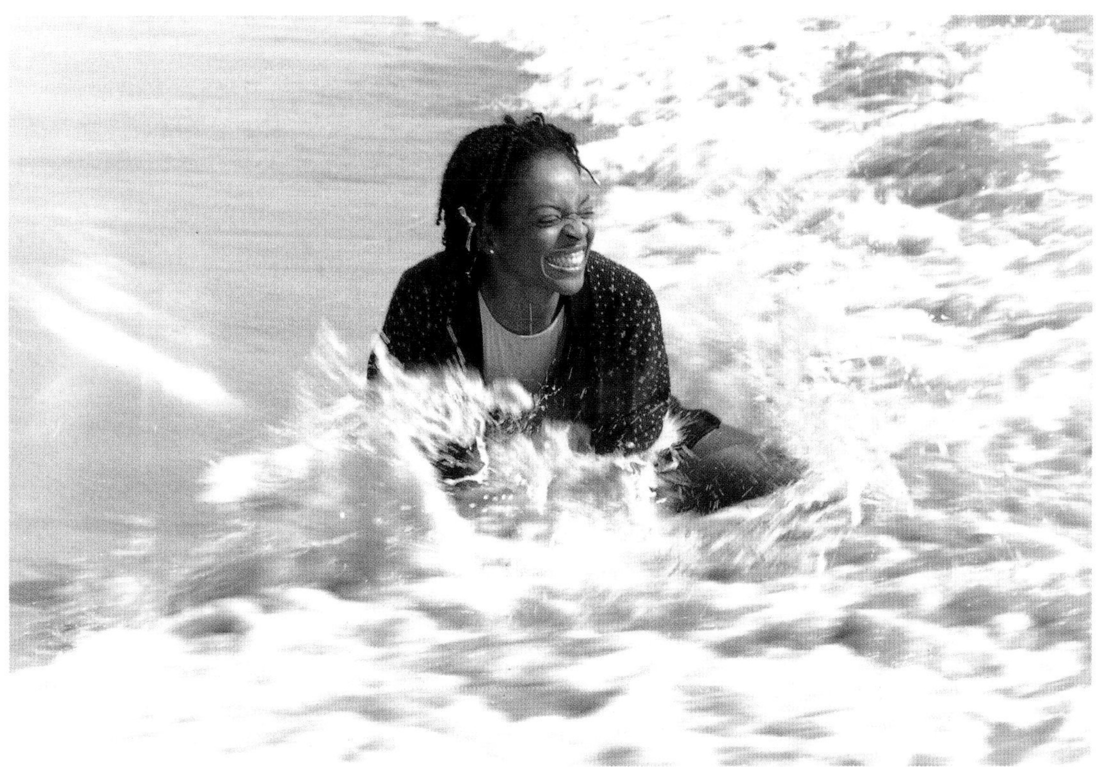

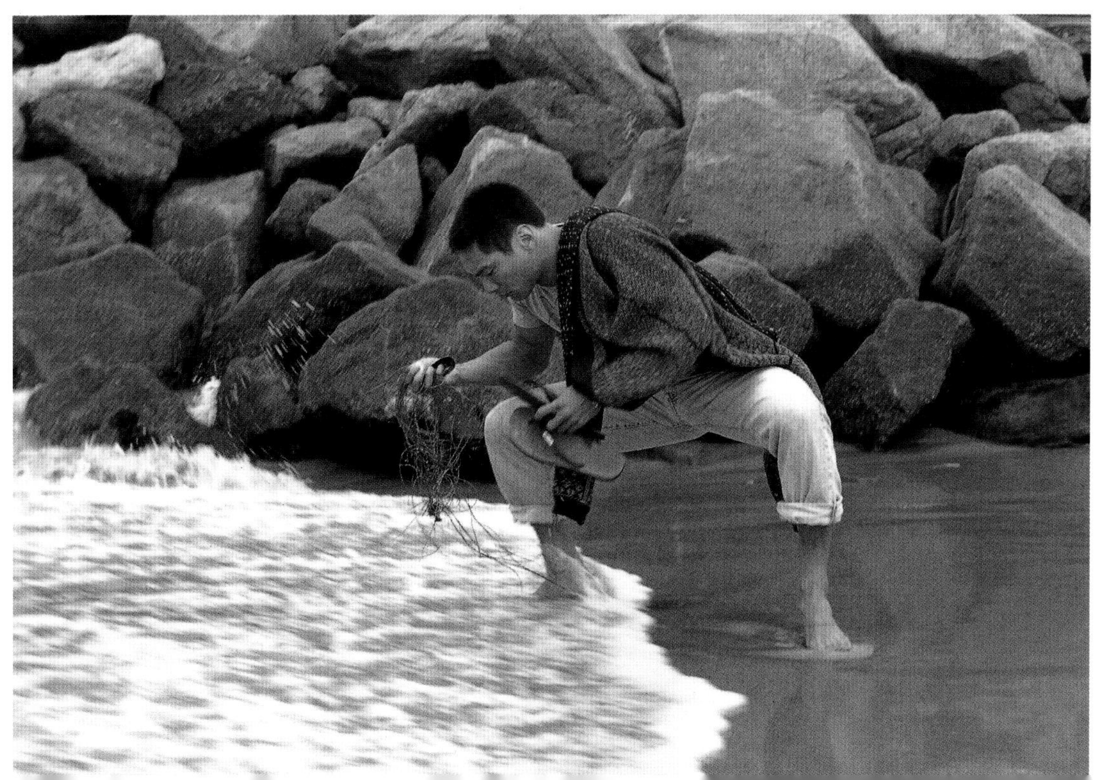

David Conrad

Tina Lifford

Jason Scott Lee

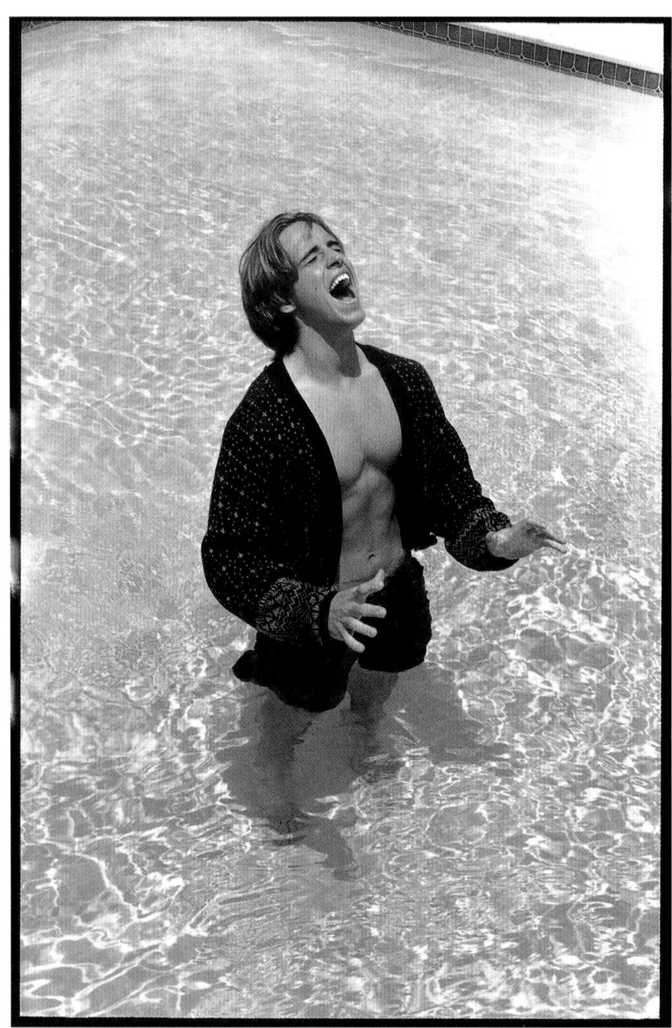

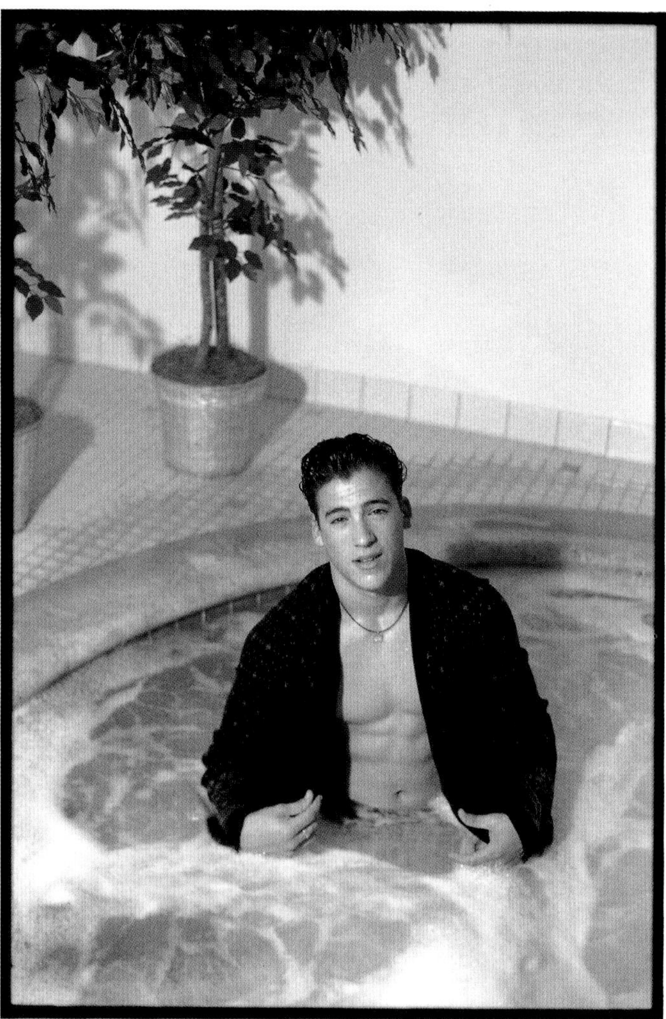

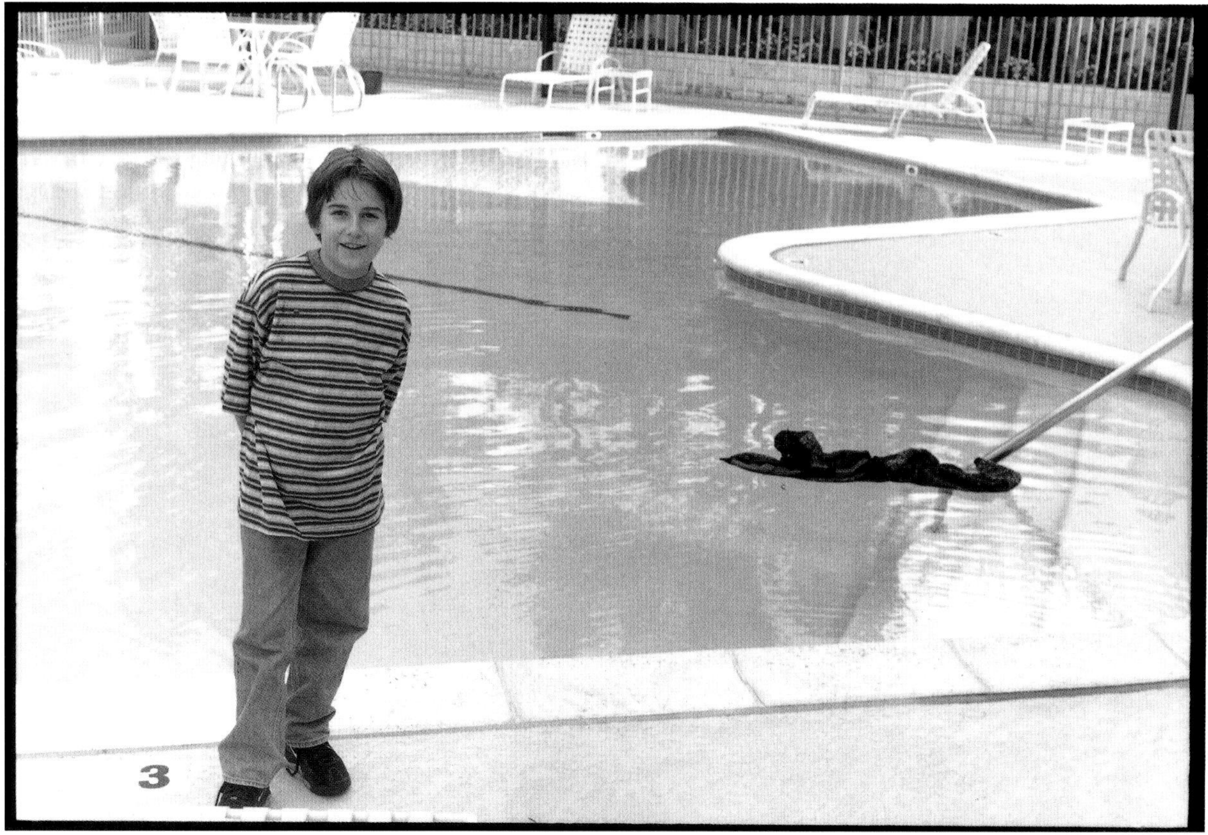

Will Horneff, Andrew Keegan, Miko Hughes

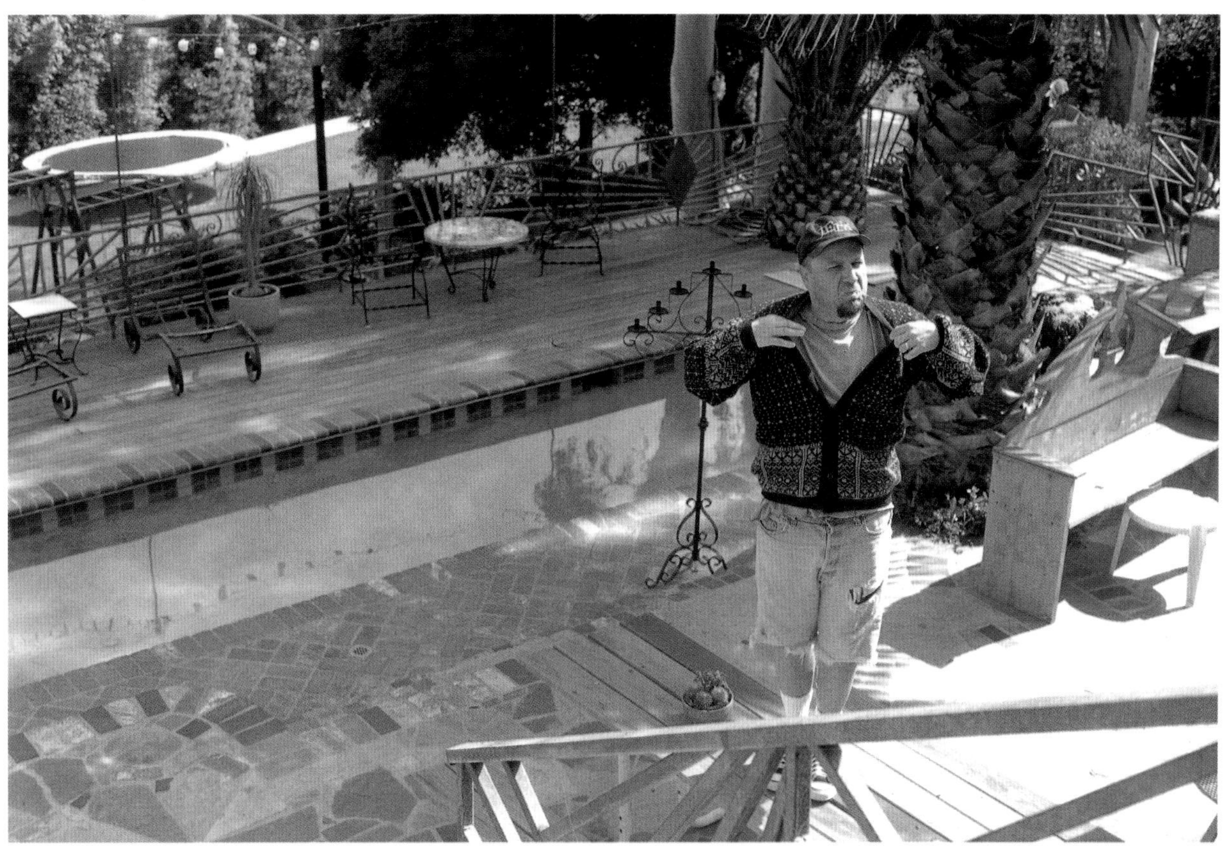

Bobcat Goldthwait

Cathy Moriarty

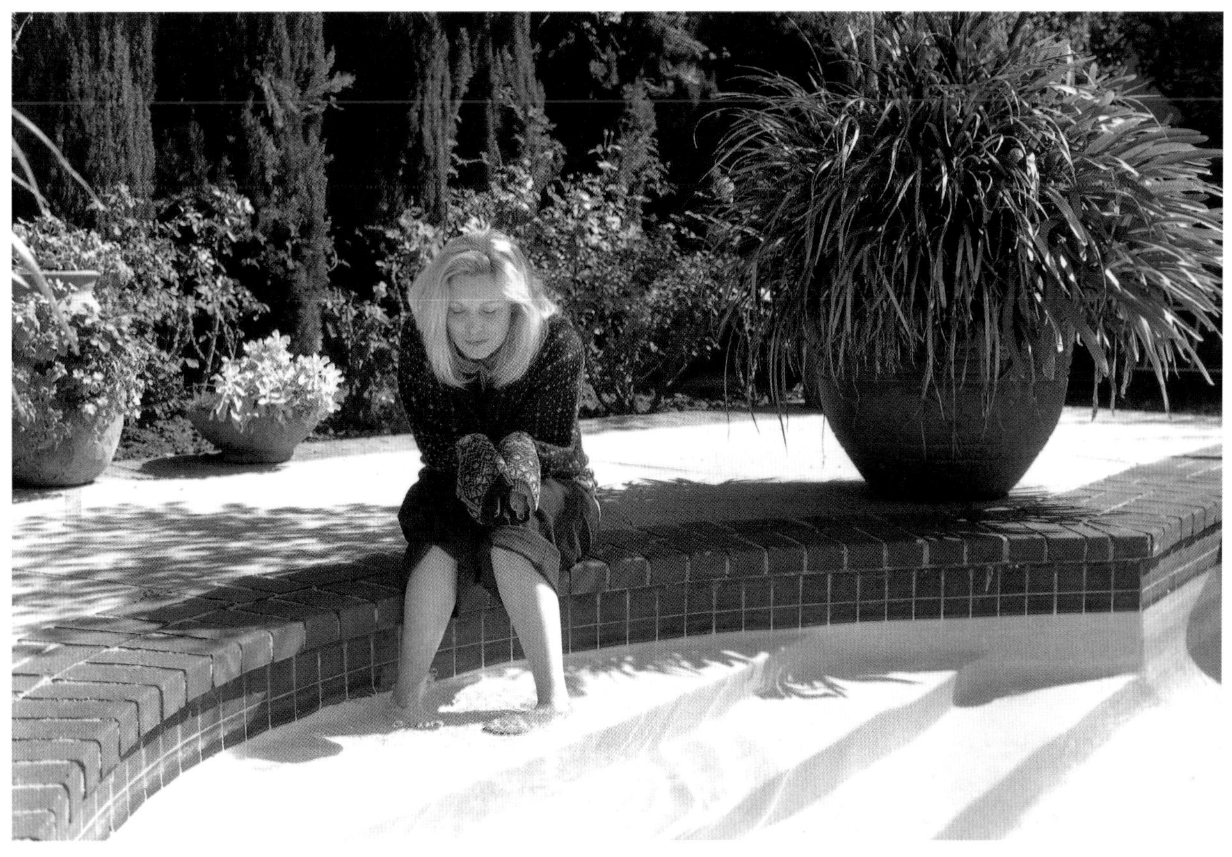

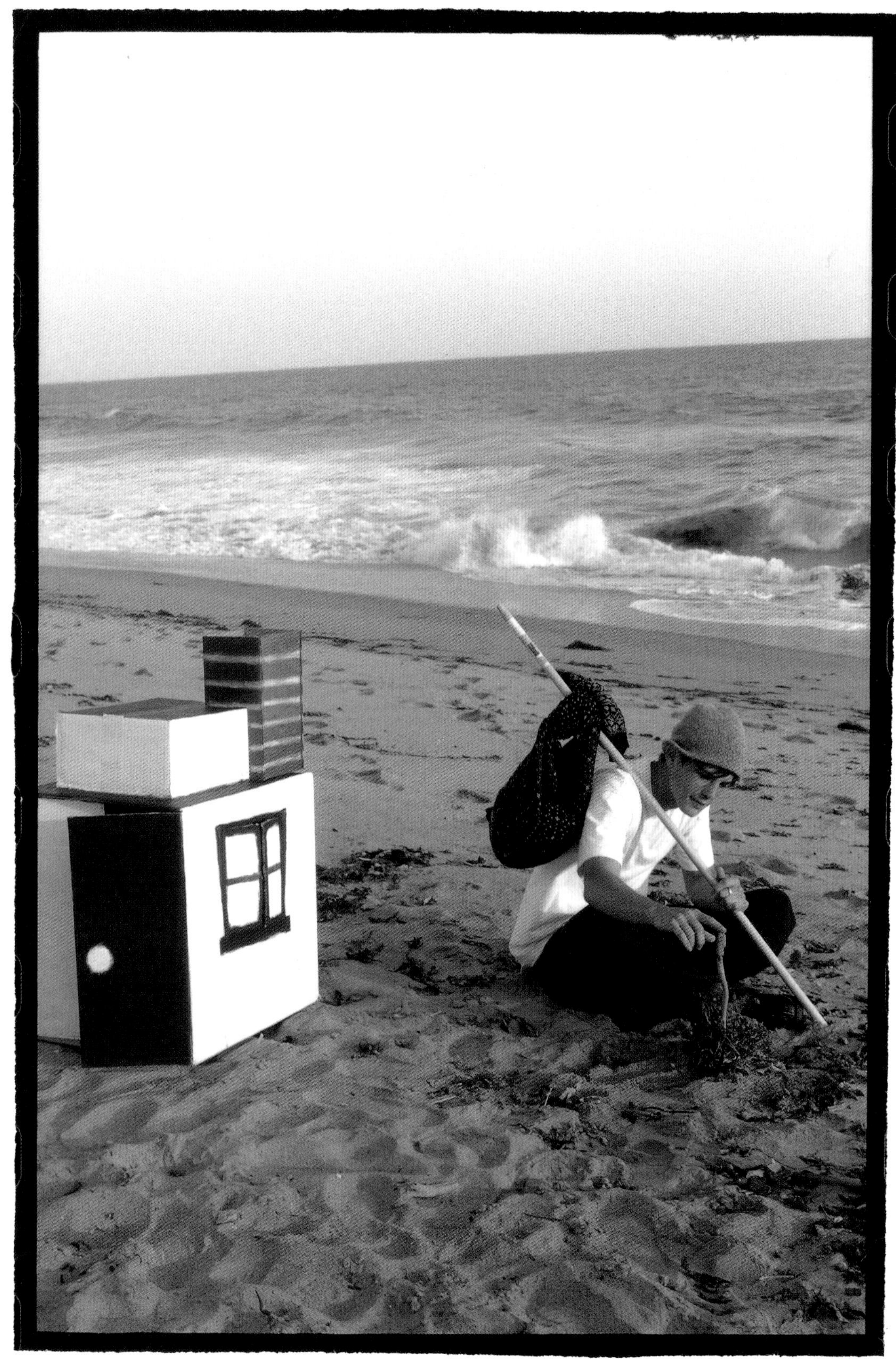

Josh Hartnett

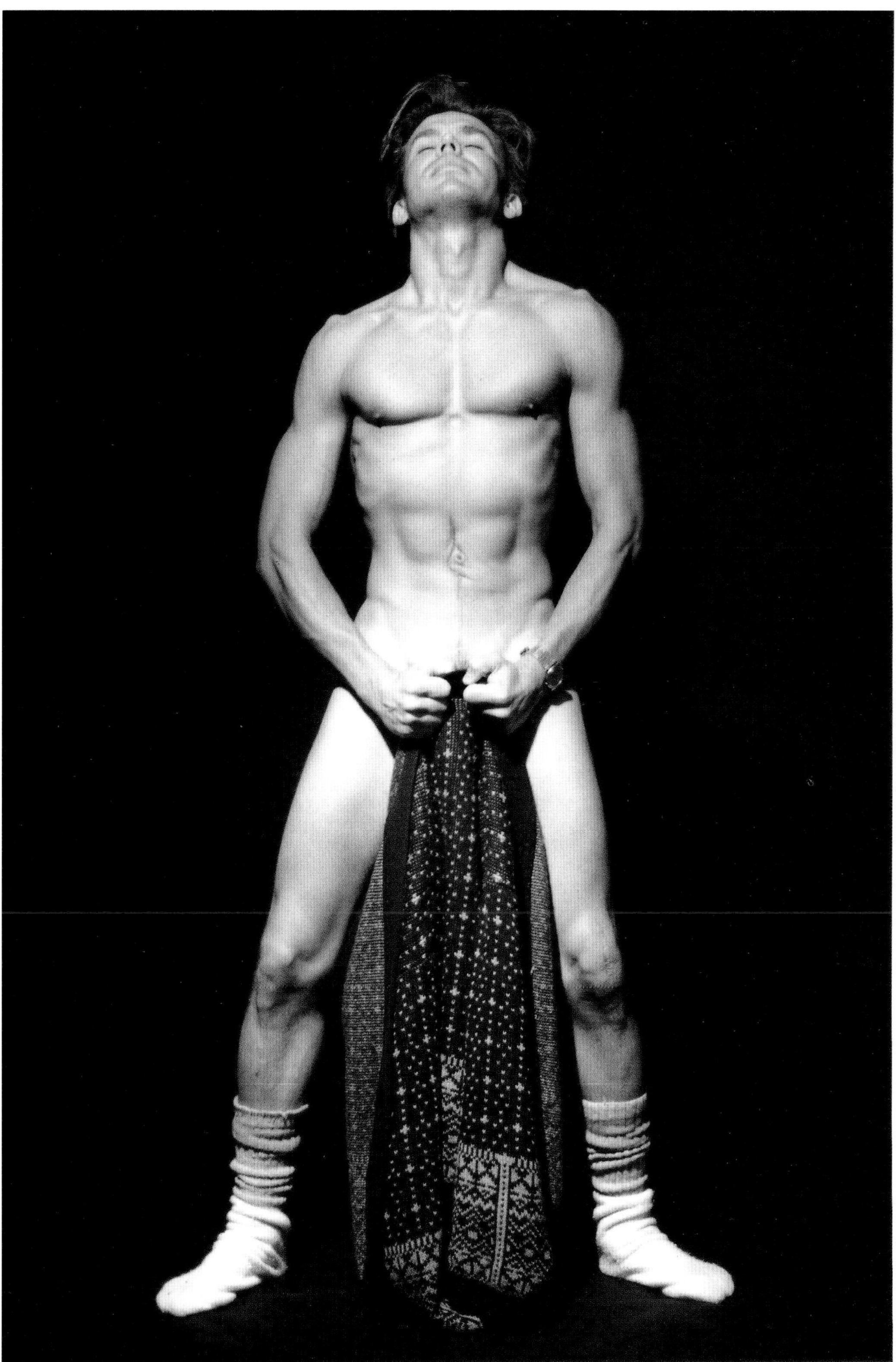

Dwight Sandell

Dwight Sandell had been in a terrible auto accident that kept him in and out of the hospital for about two years. The week before they were to take the pins out of his legs, he asked me to take this picture because there was no telling if he would ever walk again. I was happy to accommodate him and he was happy with the results.

He does, by the way, walk beautifully.

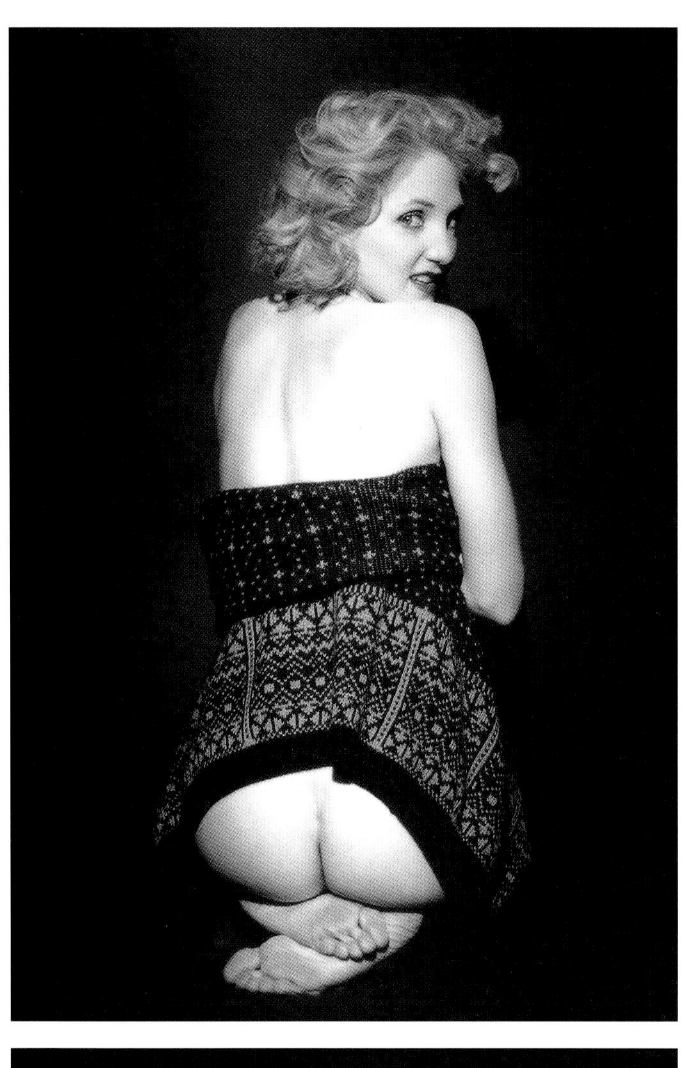
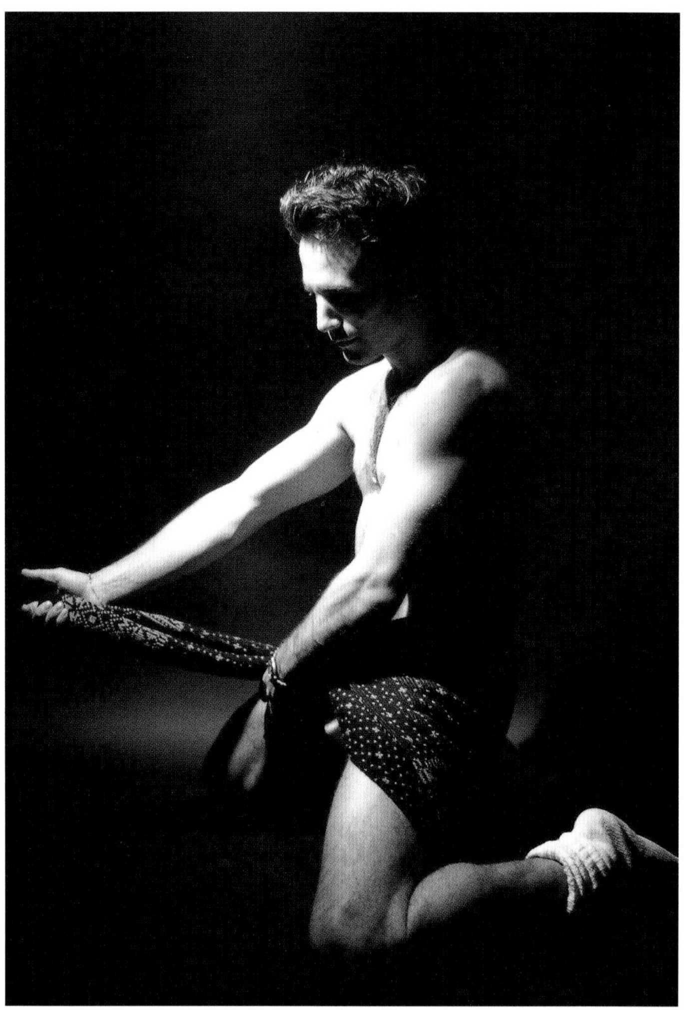
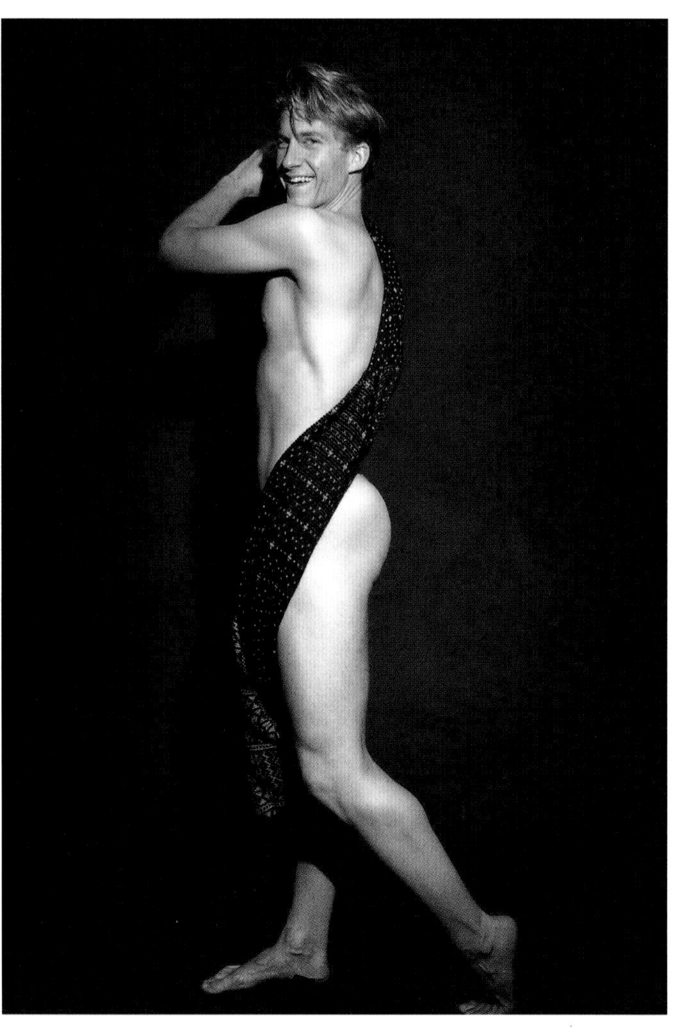
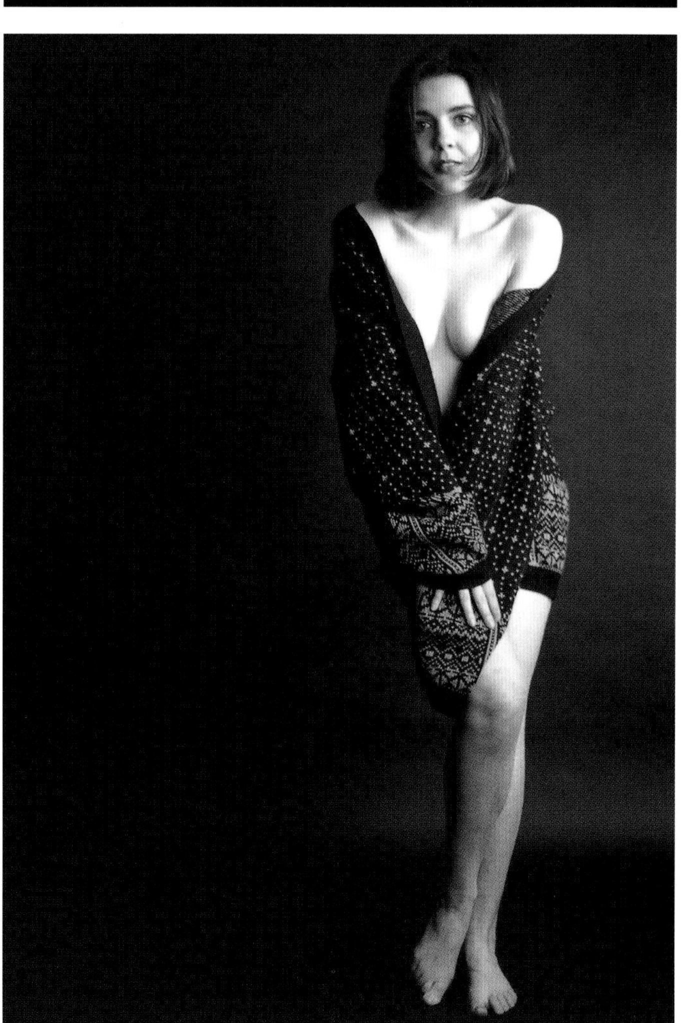

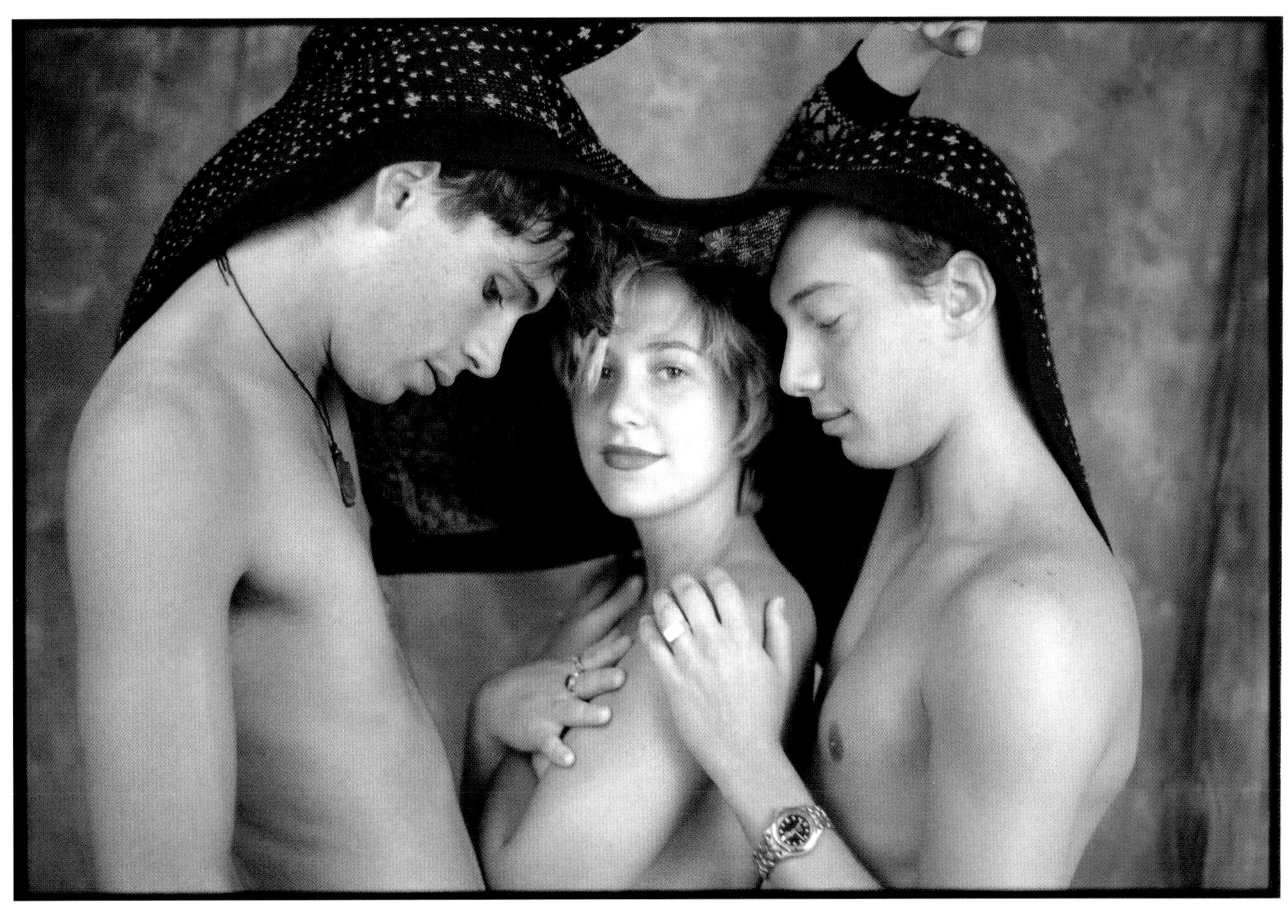

Opposite, clockwise from top left: Deb LaCoy, Peter Mastronardi, Laurelle Rethke, John Cantwell
This page: Jeremy Sisto, Marisa Ryan, Jonah Blechman; Devon Odessa

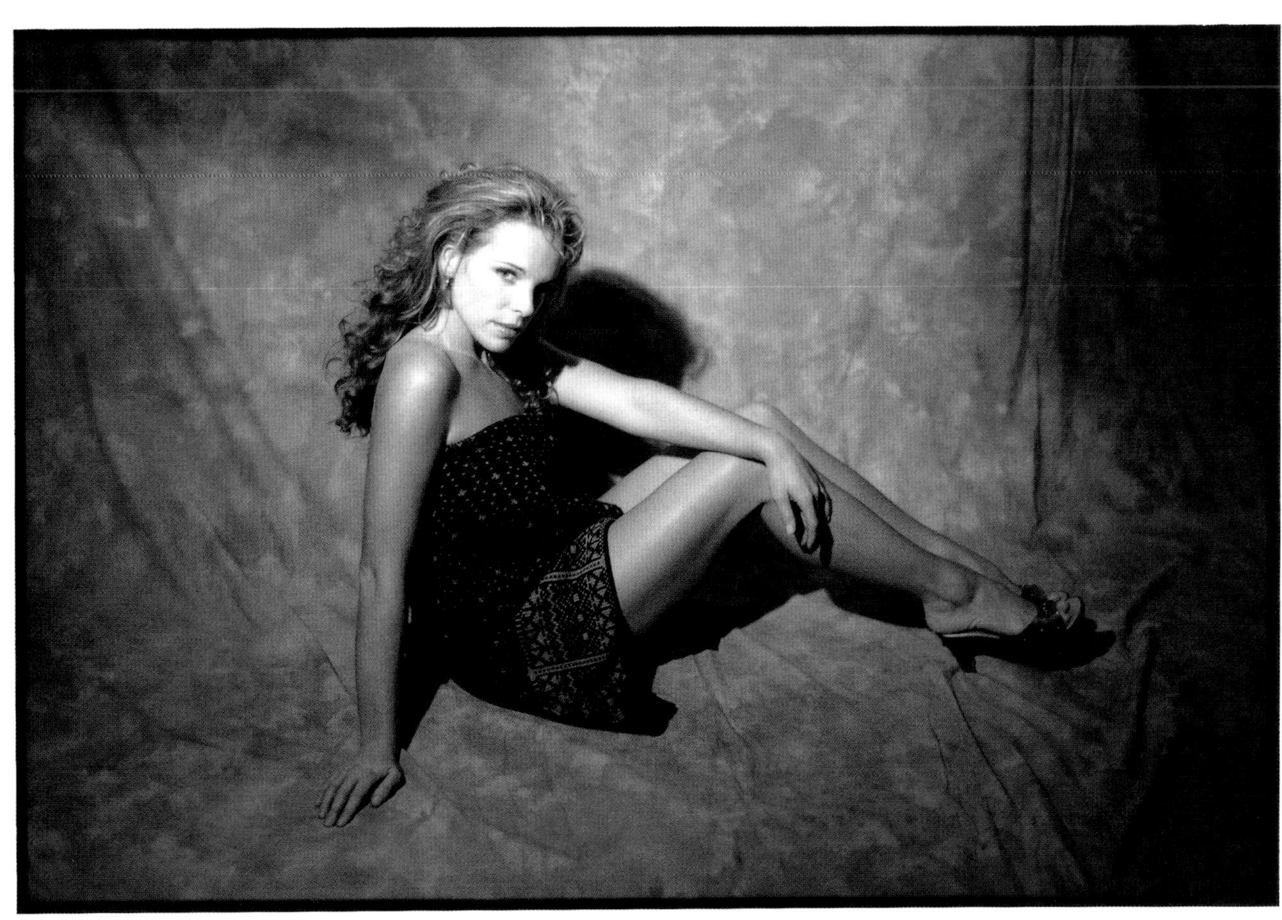

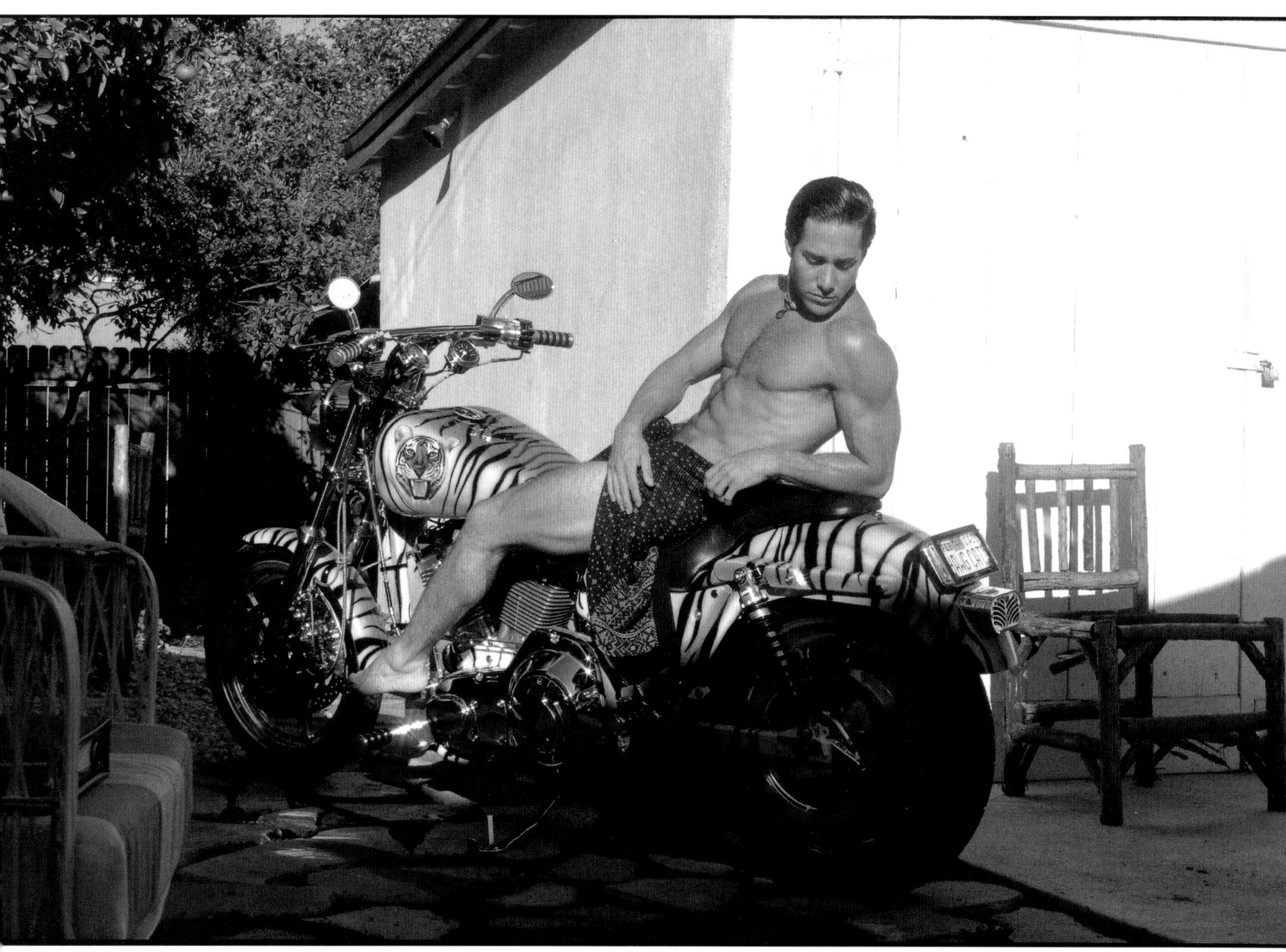

Tim Di Pri

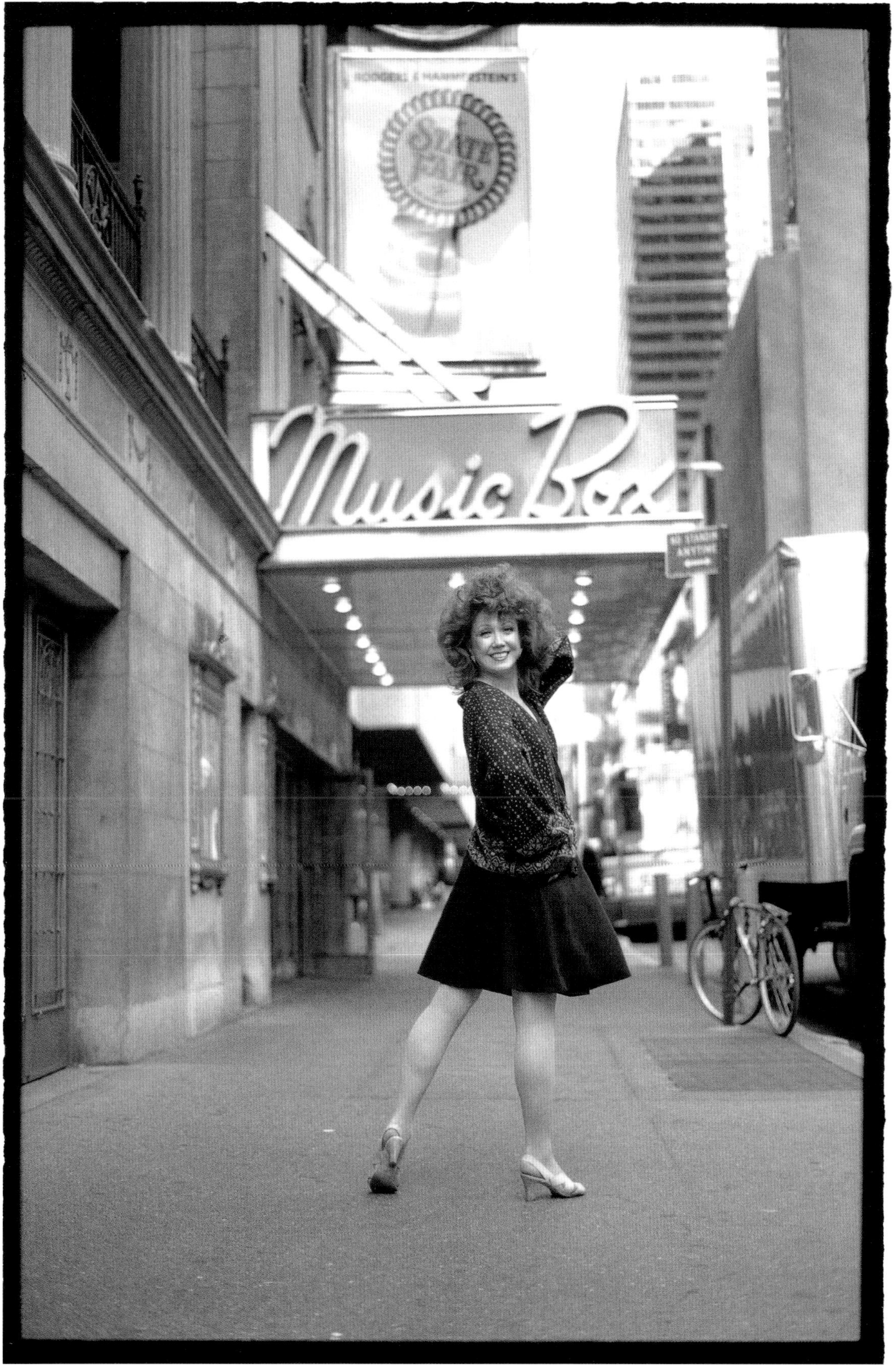

Donna McKechnie

There is only one Donna McKechnie and she is a singular sensation.

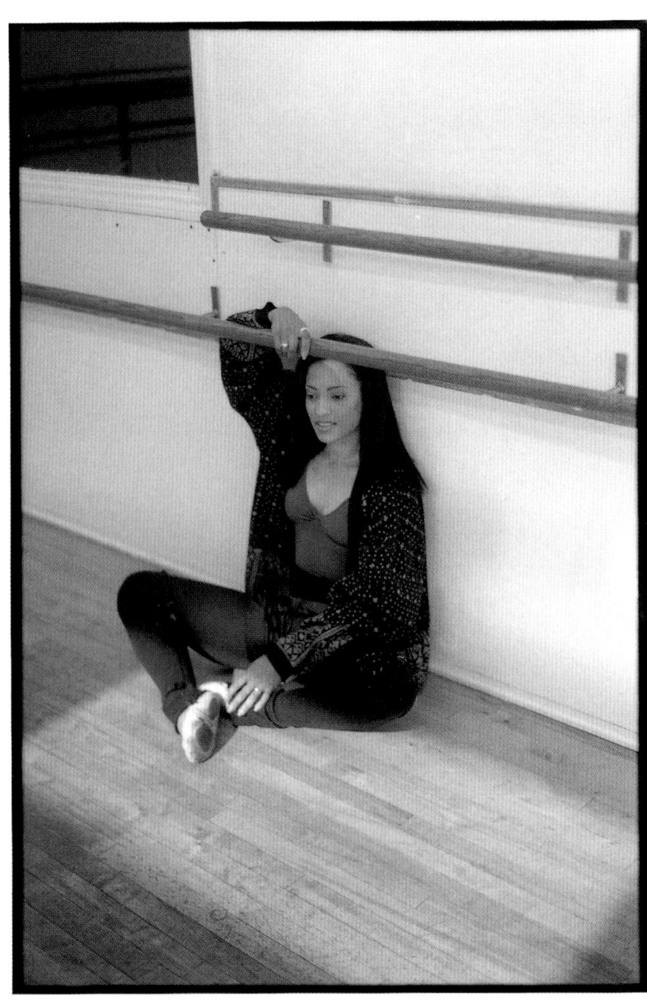

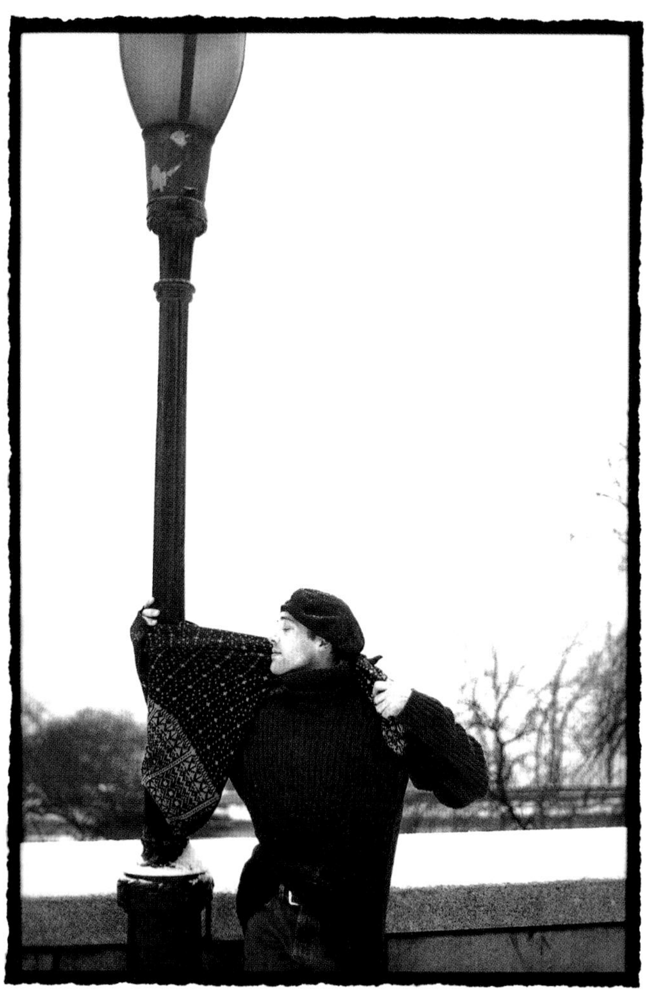

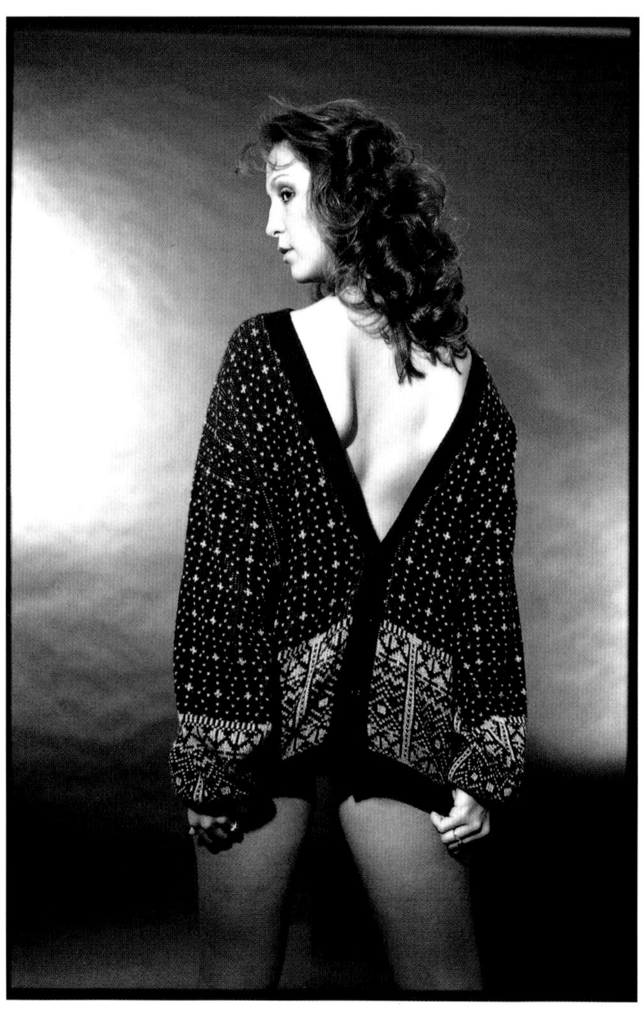

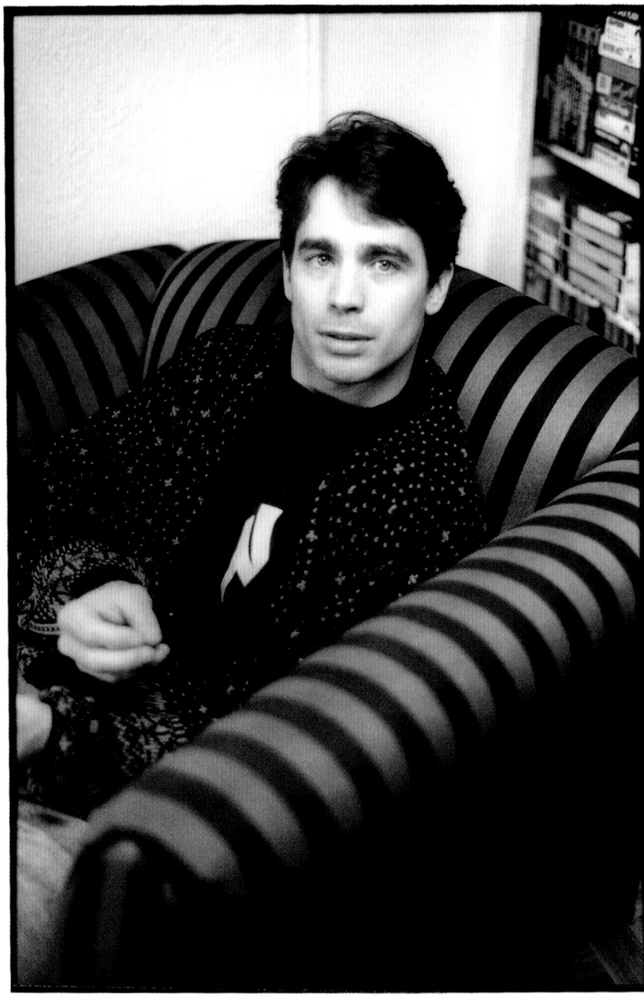

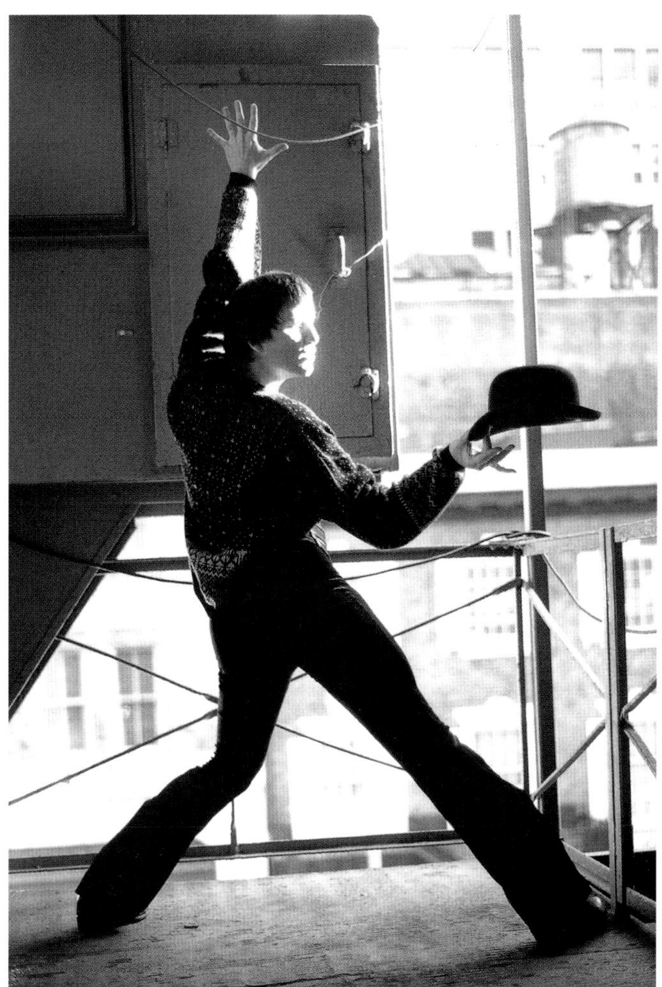

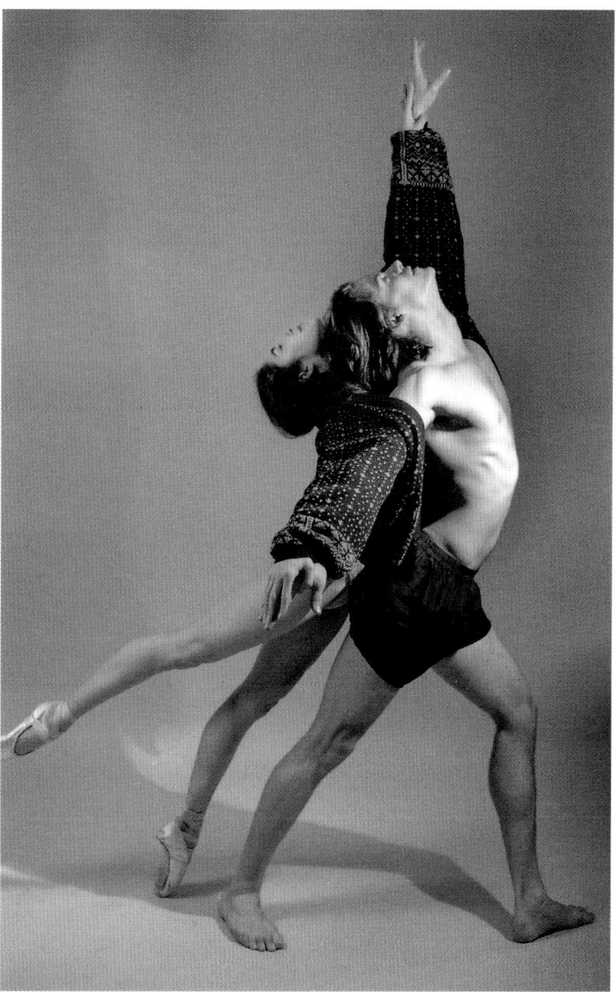

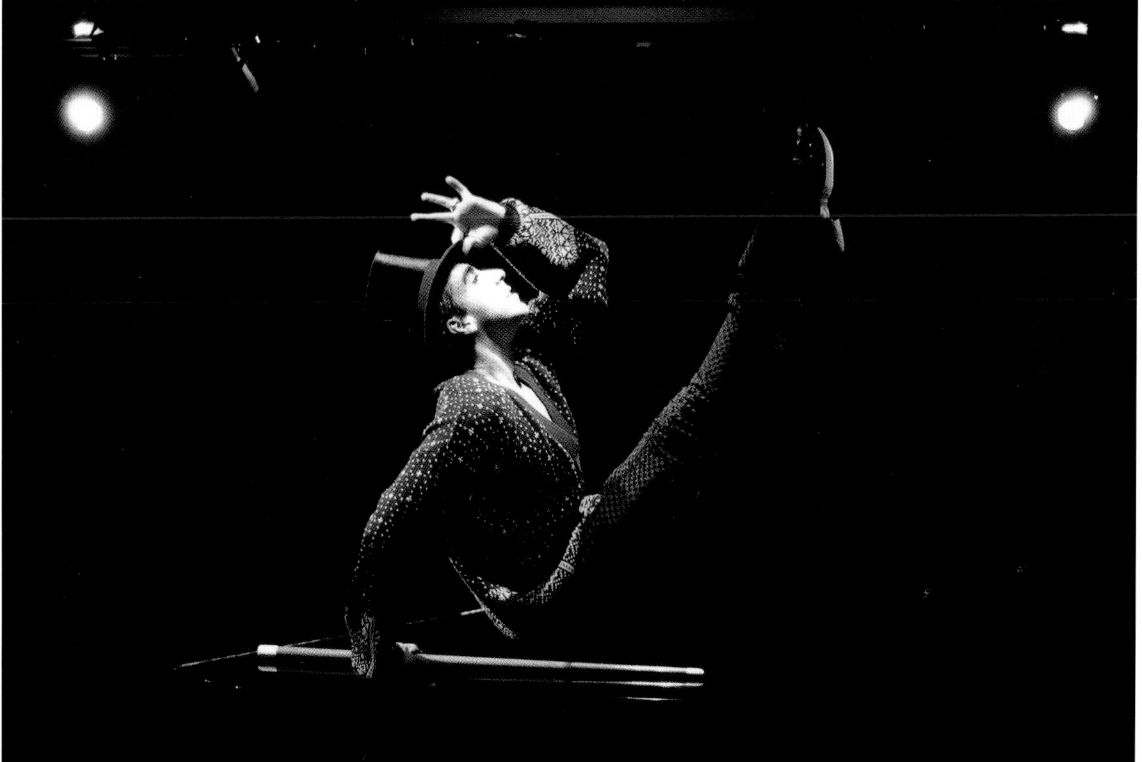

Opposite, clockwise from top left: Melissa De Sousa, Michael O'Donnell, Scott Wise, Marci Reid

This page, clockwise from top left:
Jim Borstelmann, Dana Stackpole and Jonathan Sharp, Rocker Verastique

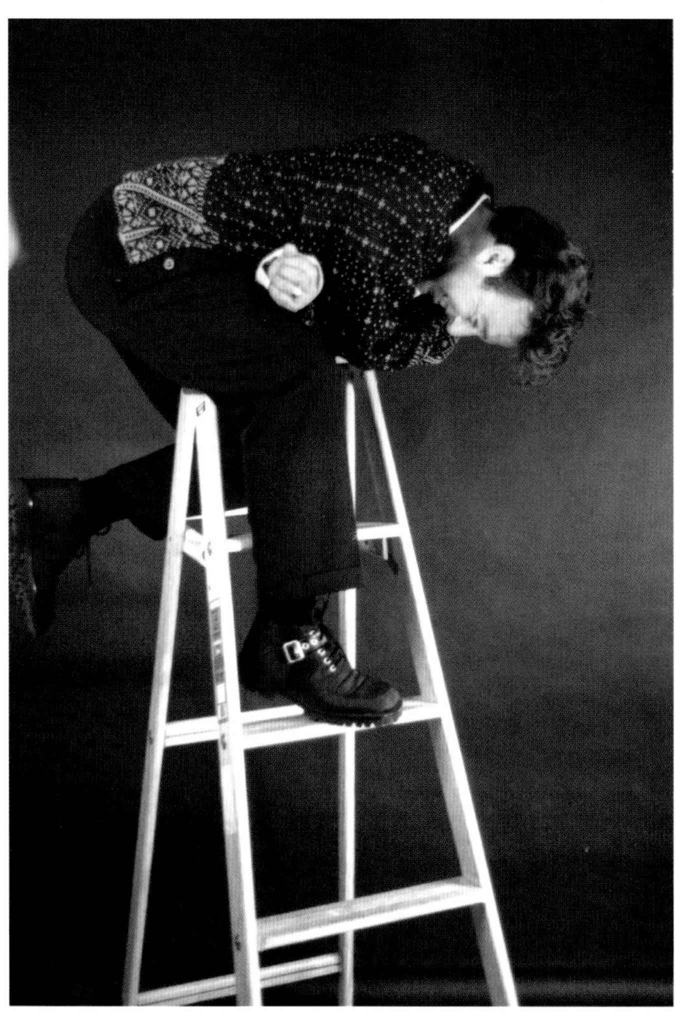

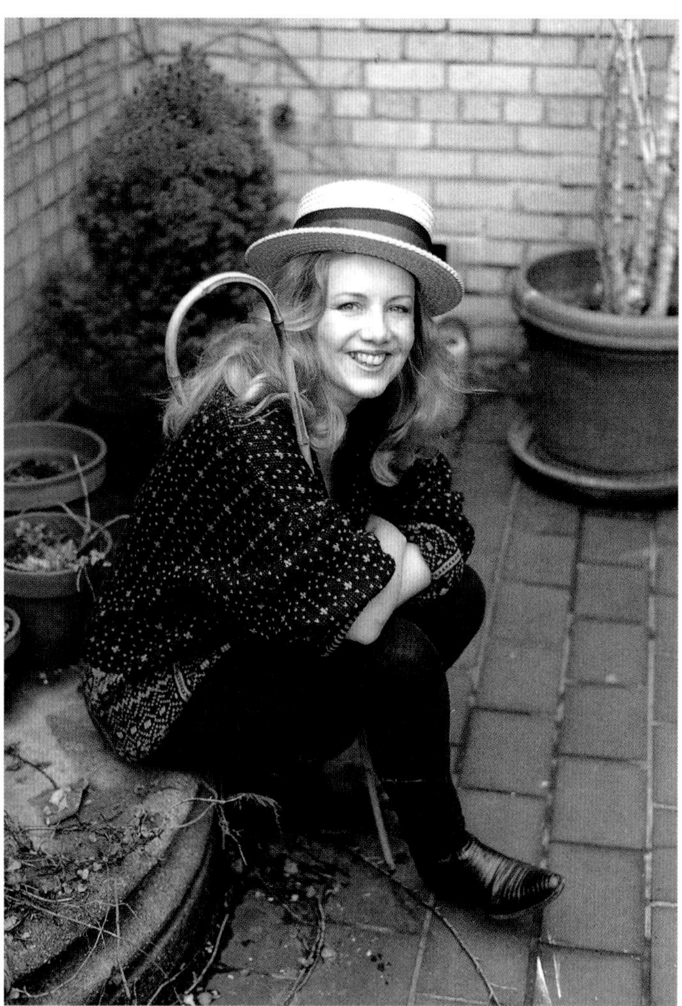

Wayne Cilento, Susan Stroman

Rob Marshall with the *Victor/Victoria* dancers

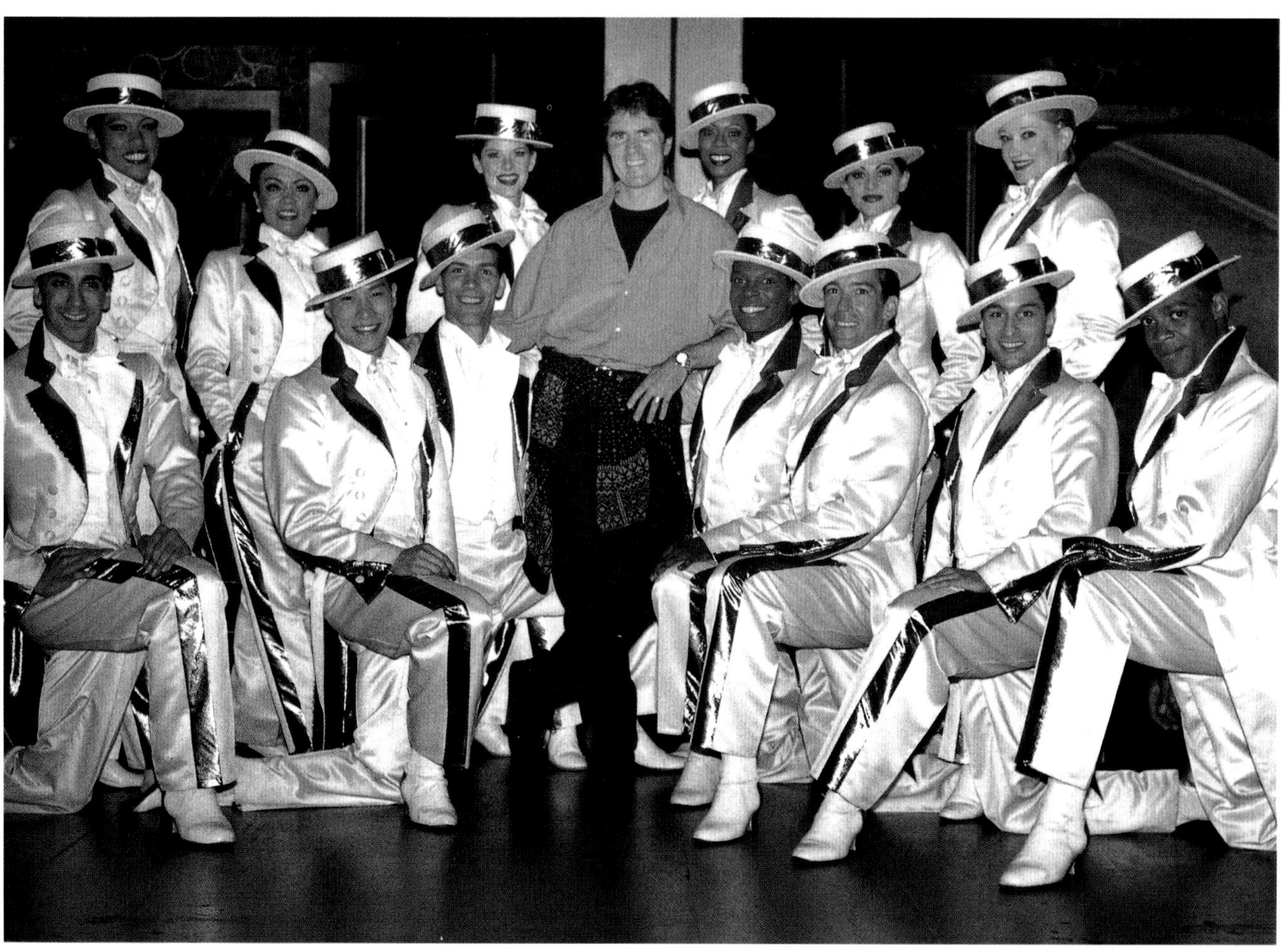

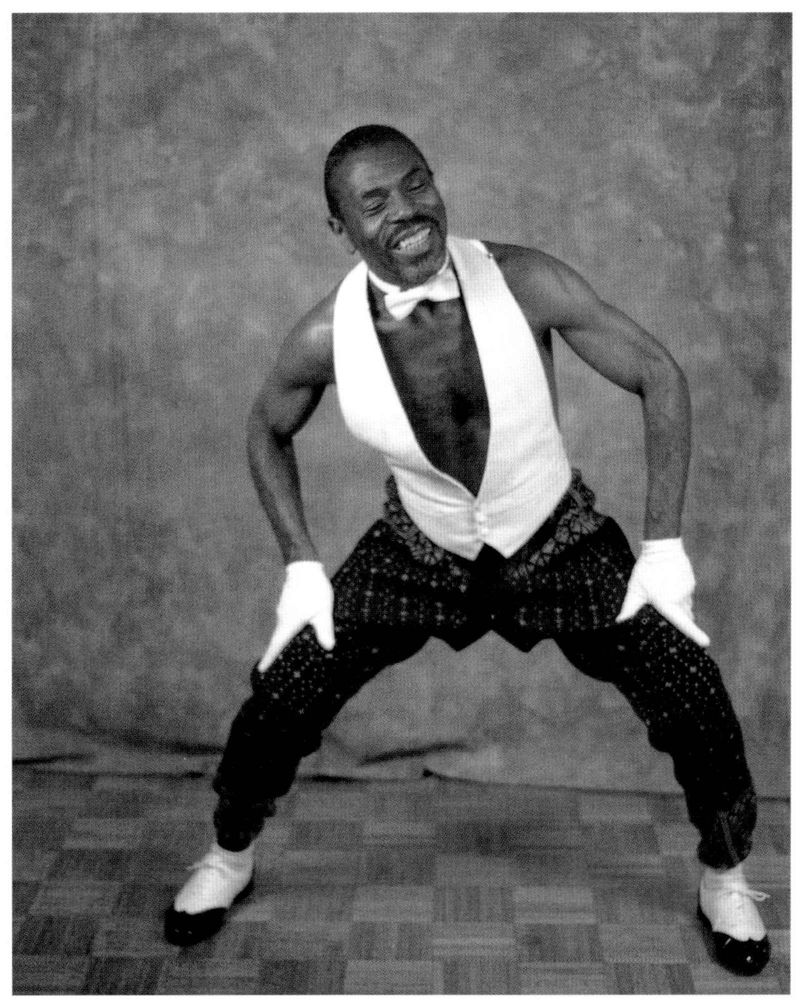

Andre De Shields

Karen Ziemba

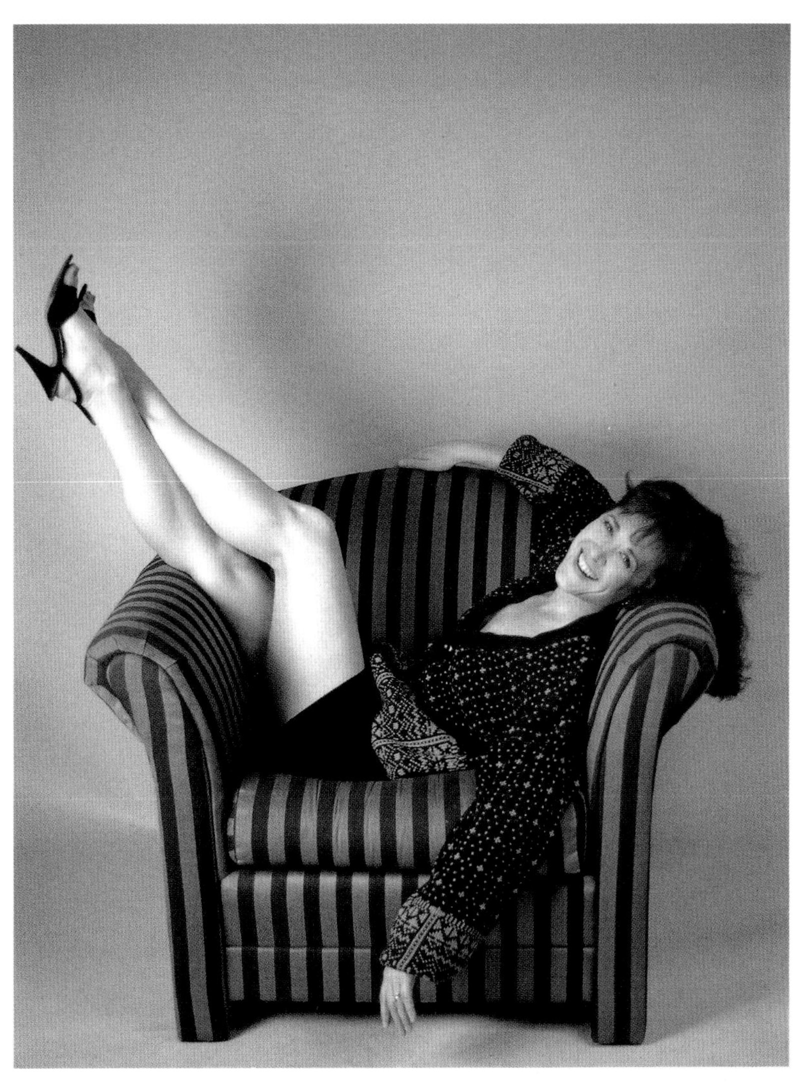

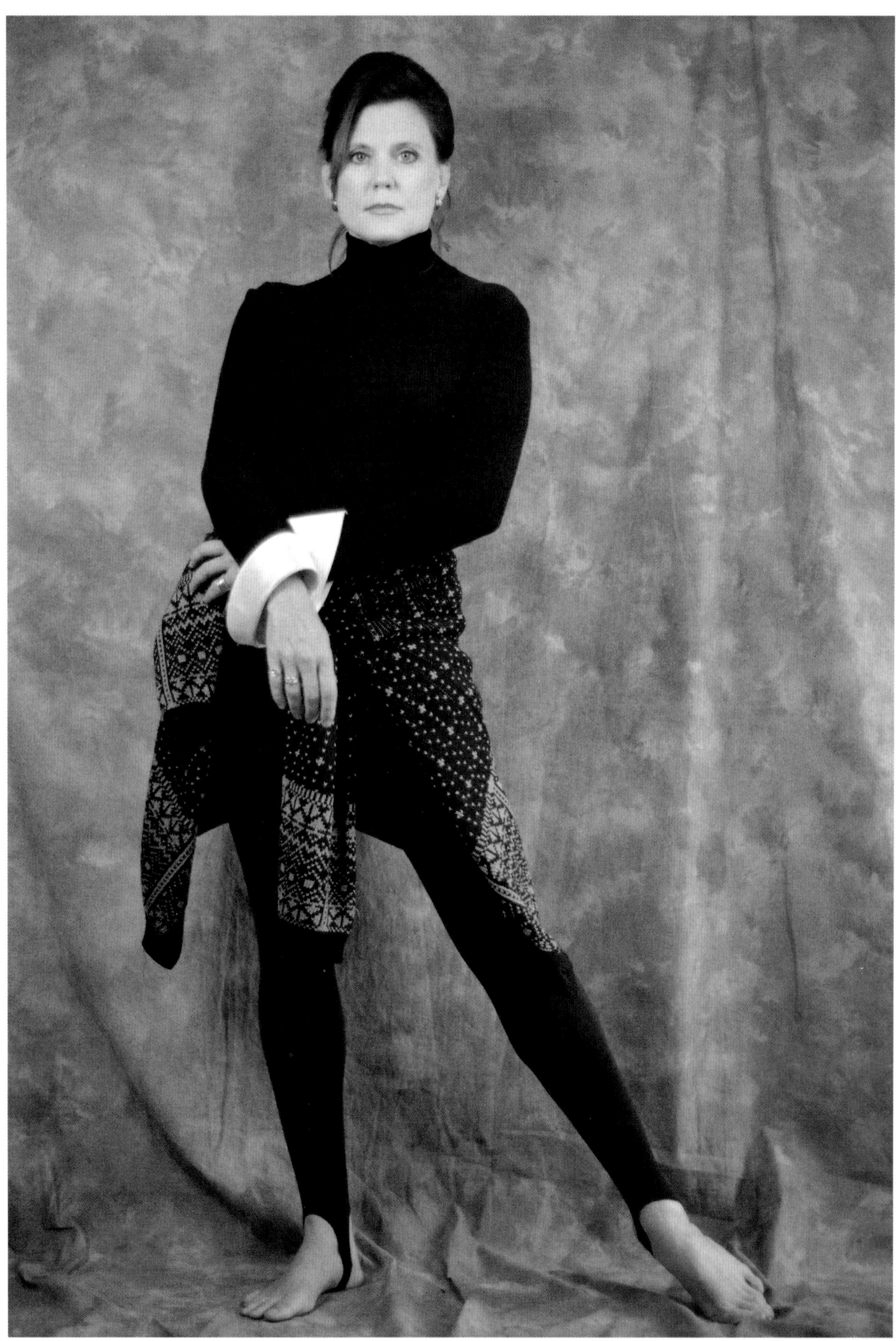

Miss Anne Reinking

THE SWEATER IN THE STUDIO

— in which the sweater watches the birdie

This is not a lie. First of all, I never believed for a moment that something this great could happen to me. When it did happen, it was a surreal moment that still feels like a dream. A lot went into making this happen, and when it did happen, we took all of our equipment to the ABC studios, where the lady was promoting her Broadway play *Moon Over Buffalo* on a popular morning talk show. We set up everything in a conference room, while watching her interview on the big screen television. They went to commercial, and maybe four minutes went by; my back turned to the doorway, I heard her voice. "Stephen?" It was as natural to hear that voice say my name as it would be to hear my mother or my best friend say it. I can still hear it in my head today. The great lady even took time out of our shoot to go above and beyond the call of duty to pose with one of her most ardent admirers. All I can say of my time with Miss Carol Burnett is this:

I'm so glad . . .

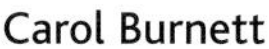

Carol Burnett

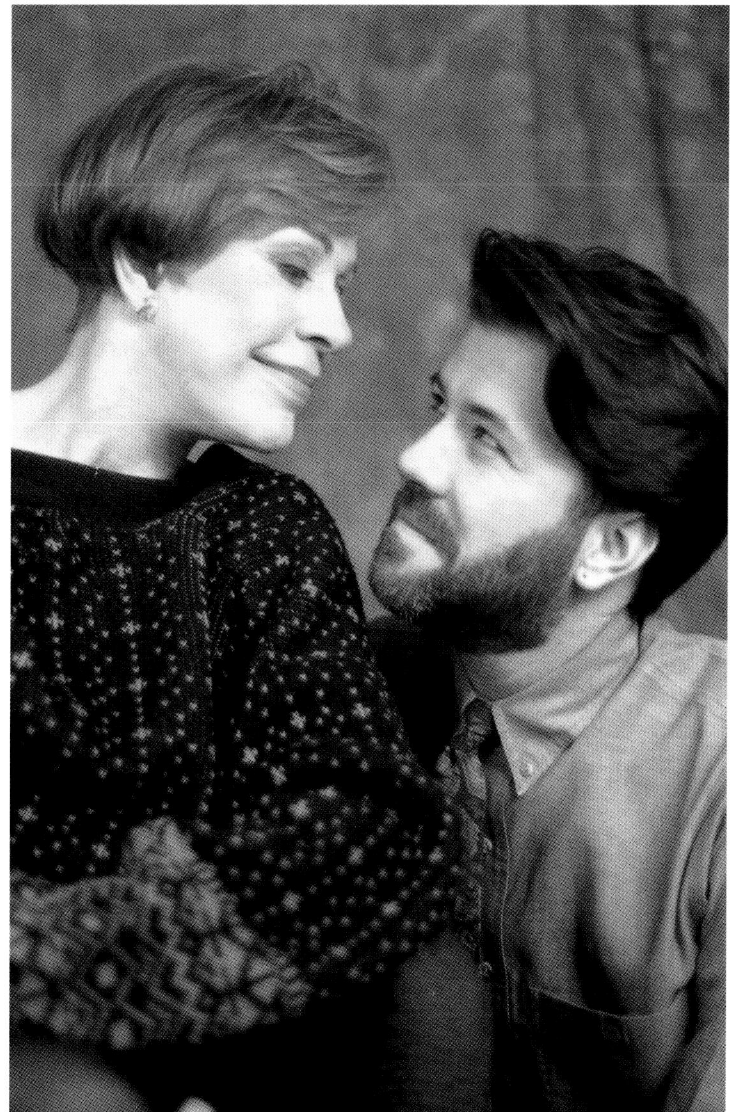

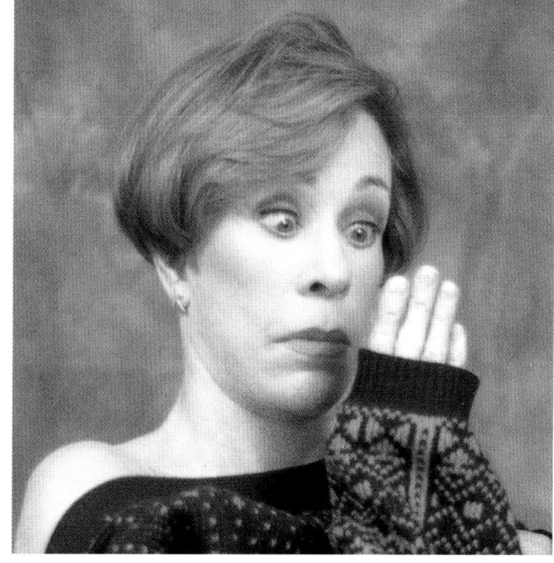

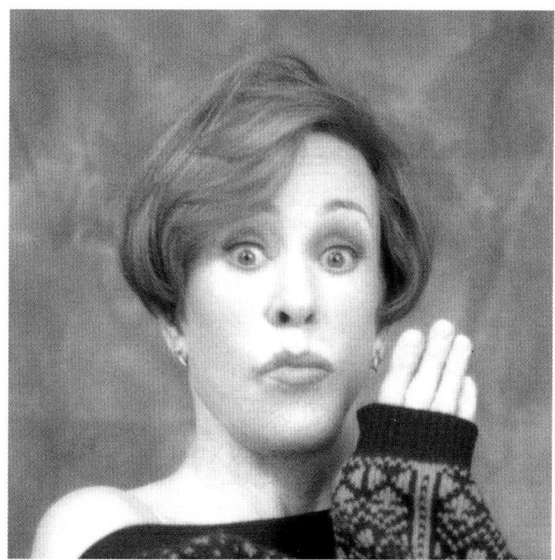

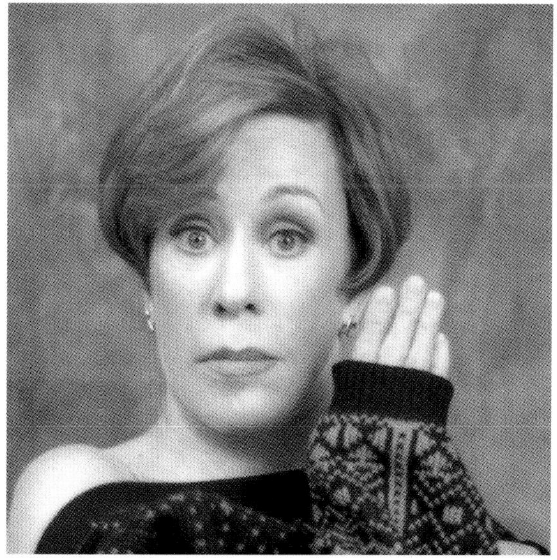

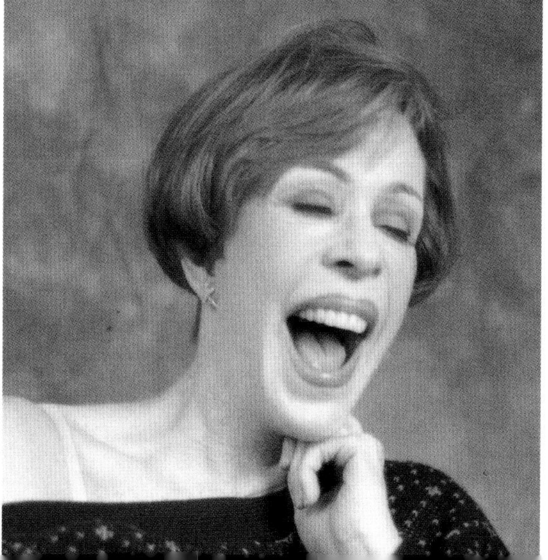

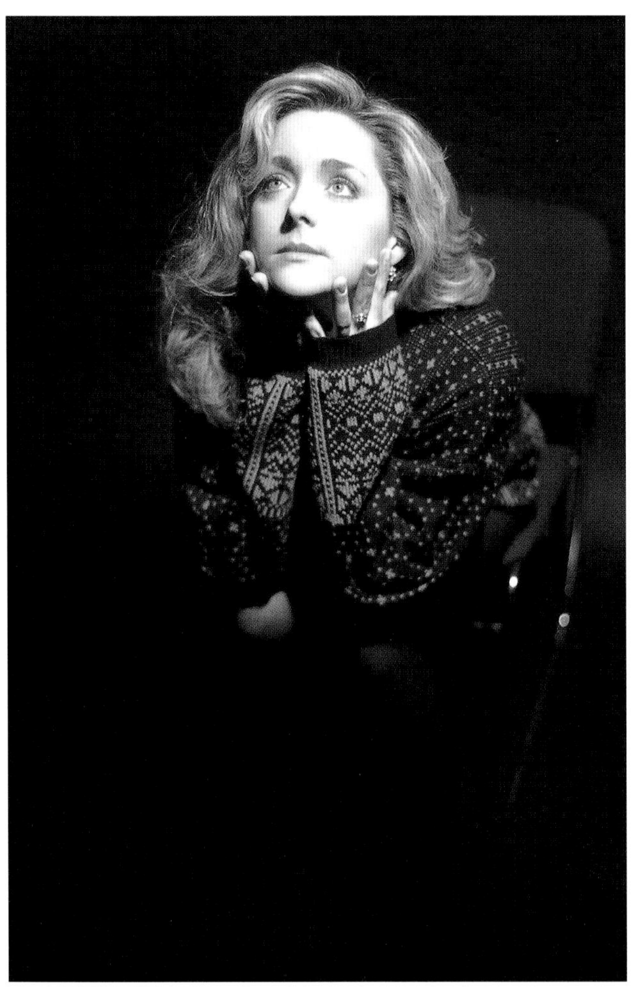

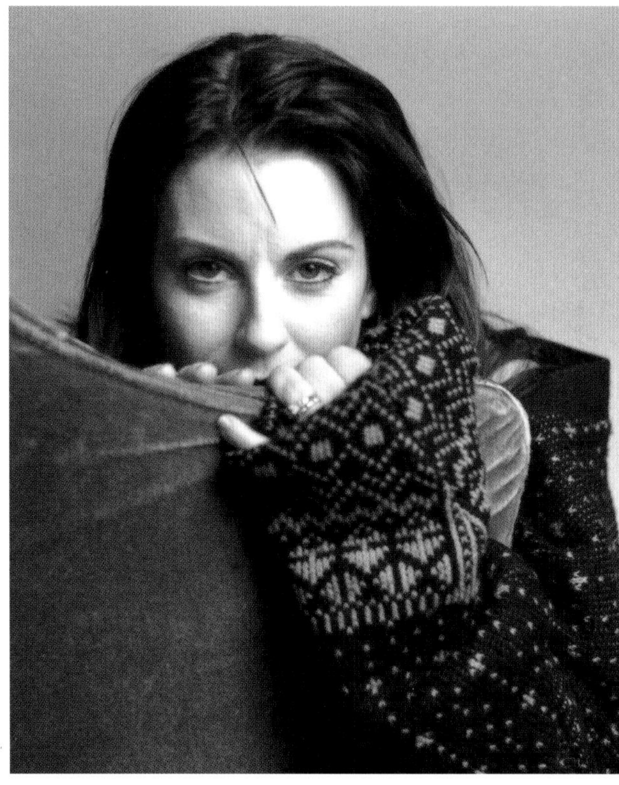

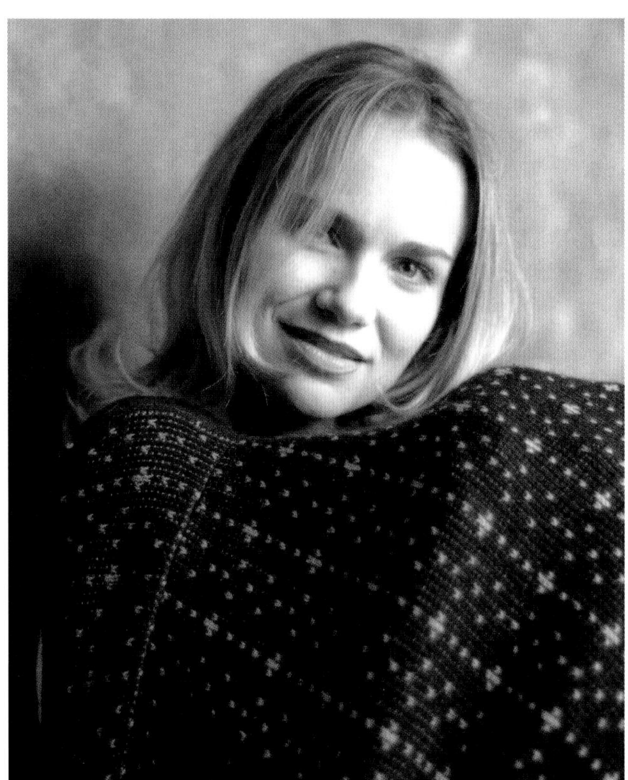

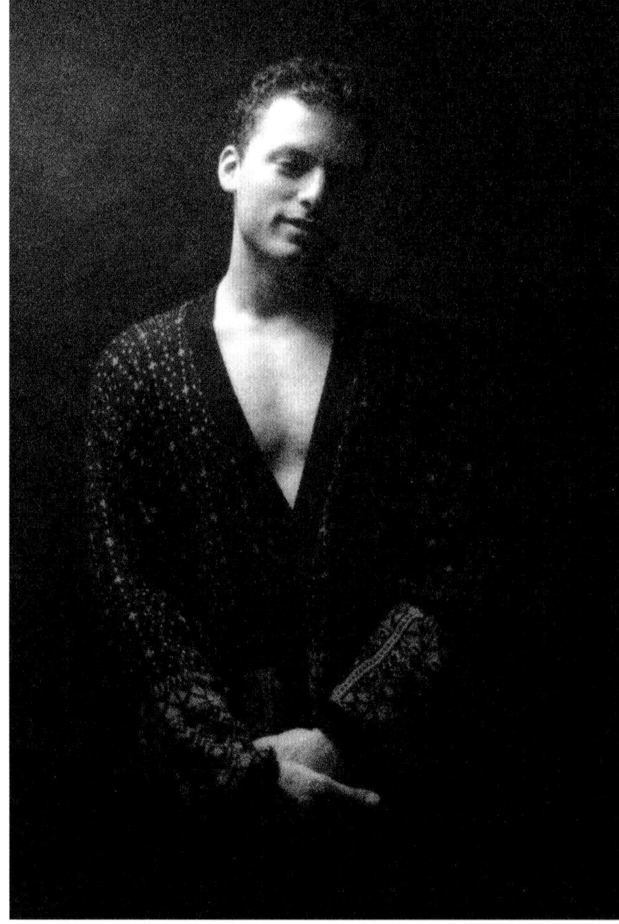

This page, clockwise from top left:
Jane Krakowski, Megan Mullally
Justin Kirk, Kristin Chenoweth

Opposite, clockwise from top left:
Charles Shaughnessy, Brad Dourif
Barbara Barrie, Valarie Rae Miller

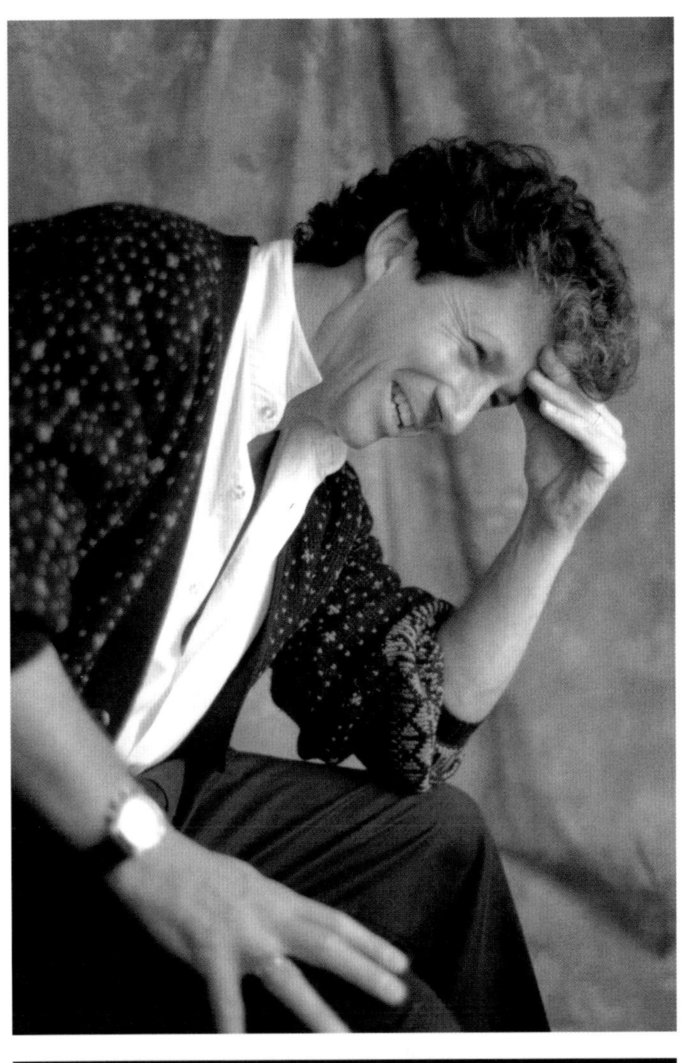
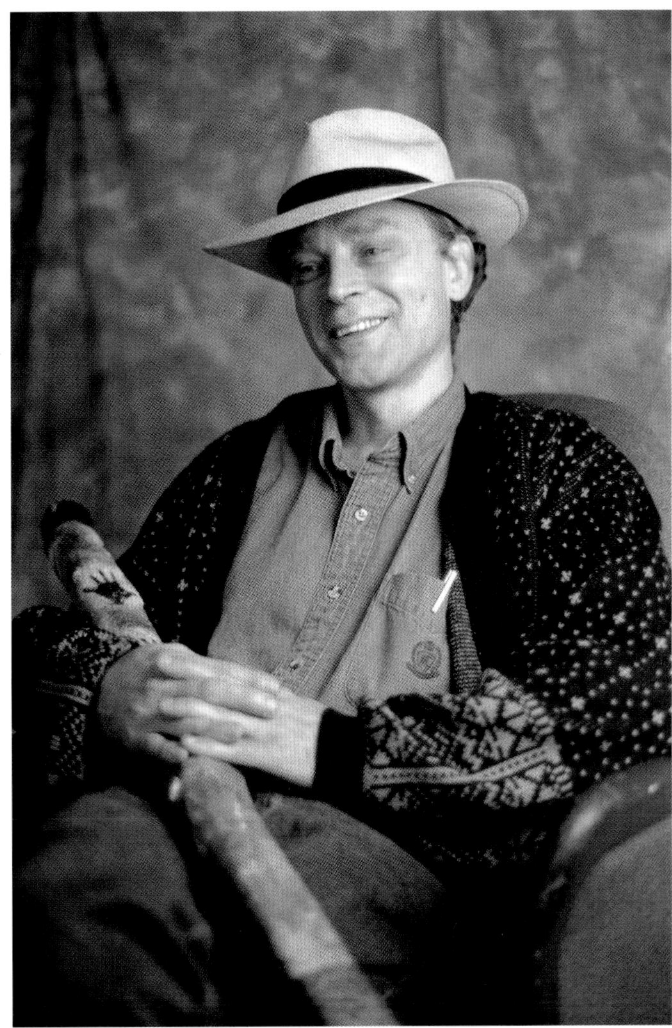
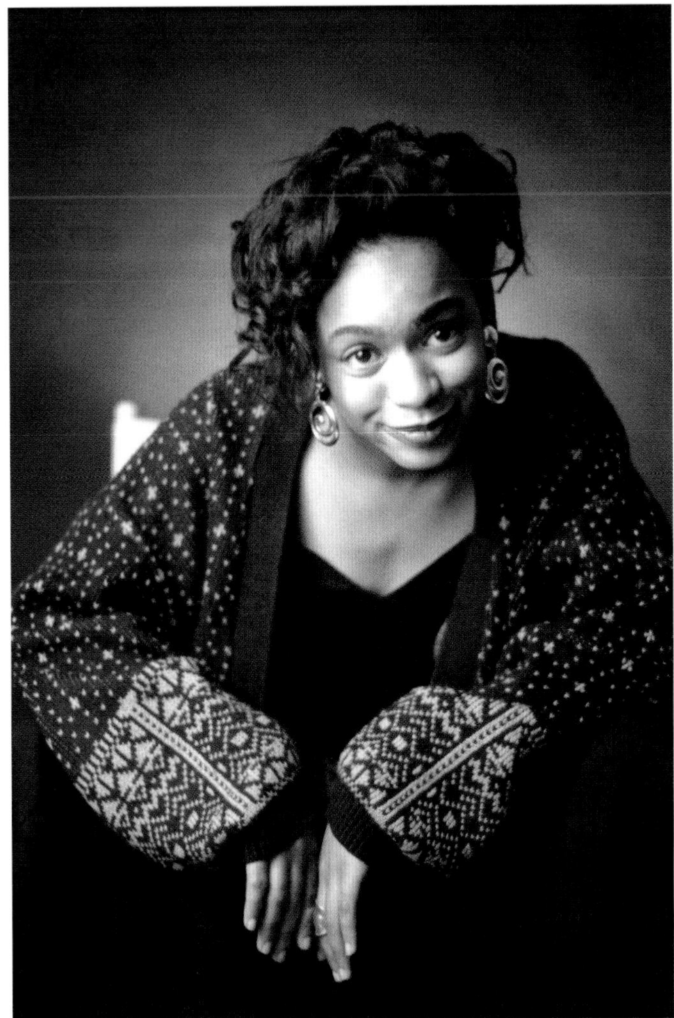
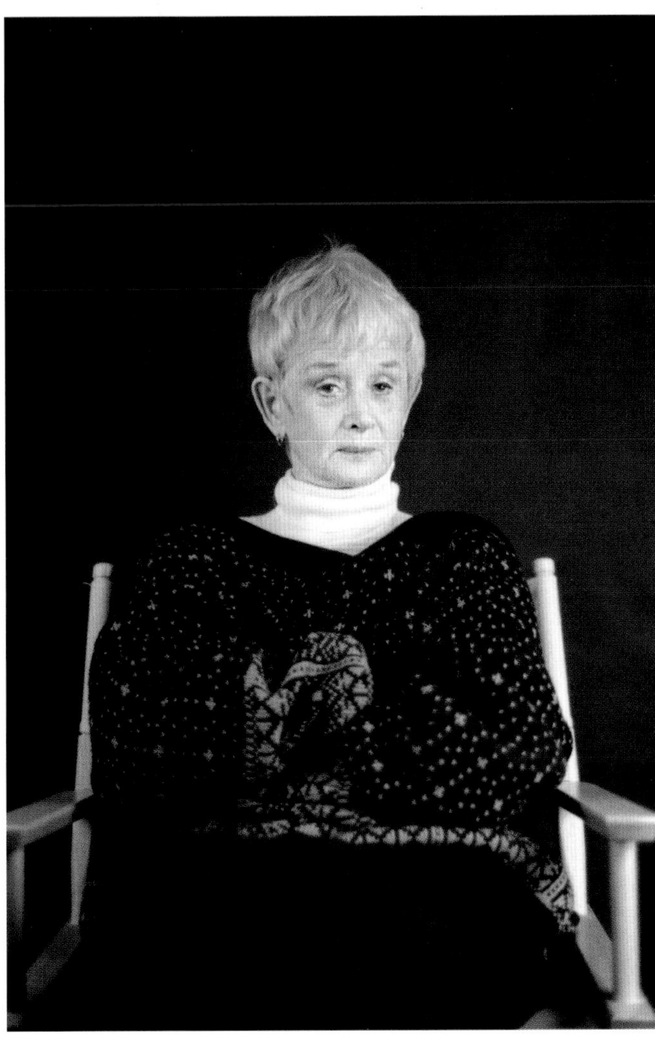

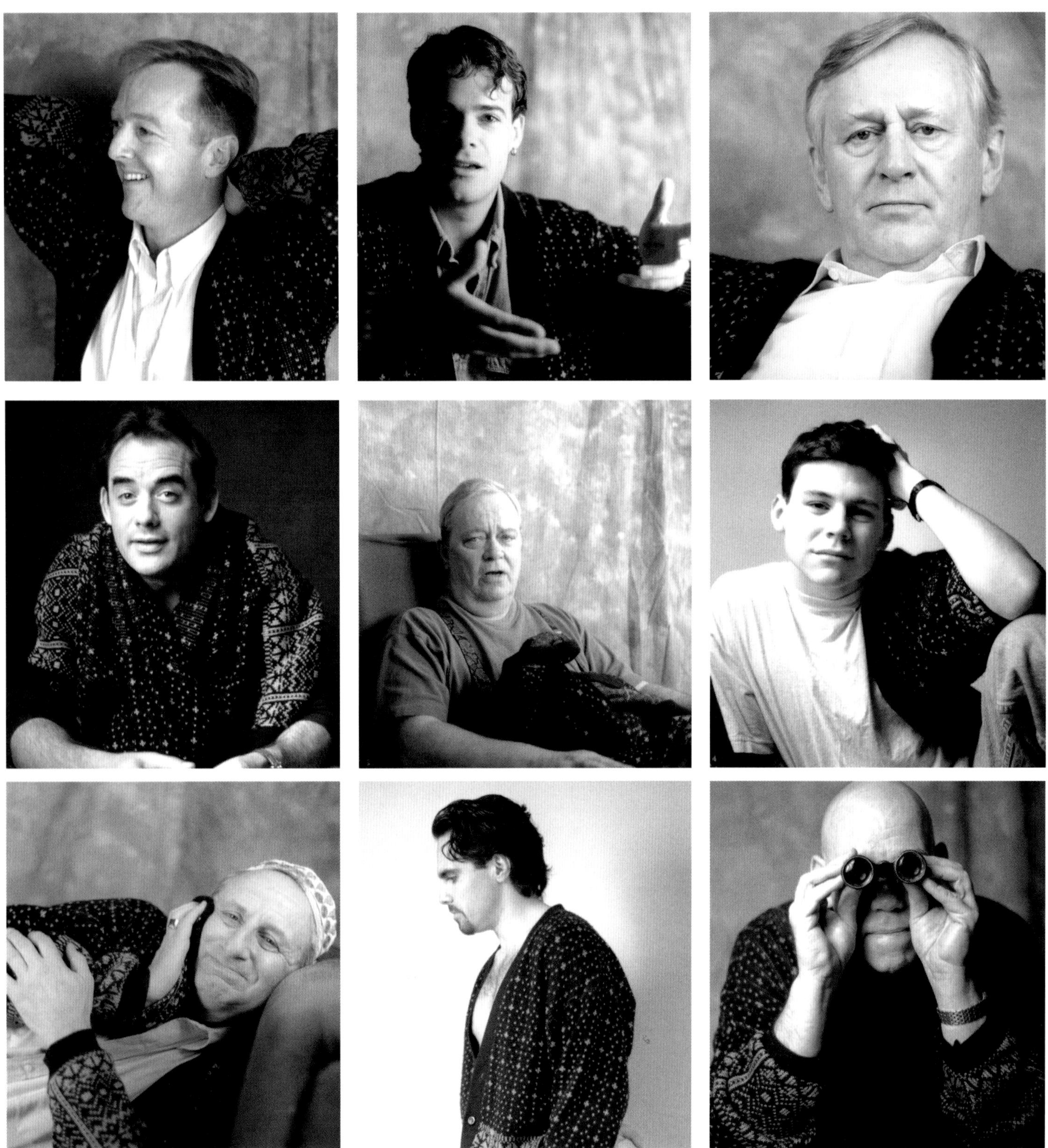

From left to right:
Edward Hibbert, Jim Ludwig, Len Cariou,
Tom Irwin, Eddie Jones, Blayne Weaver,
Steven Gilborn, Mario Cantone, Conrad John Schuck

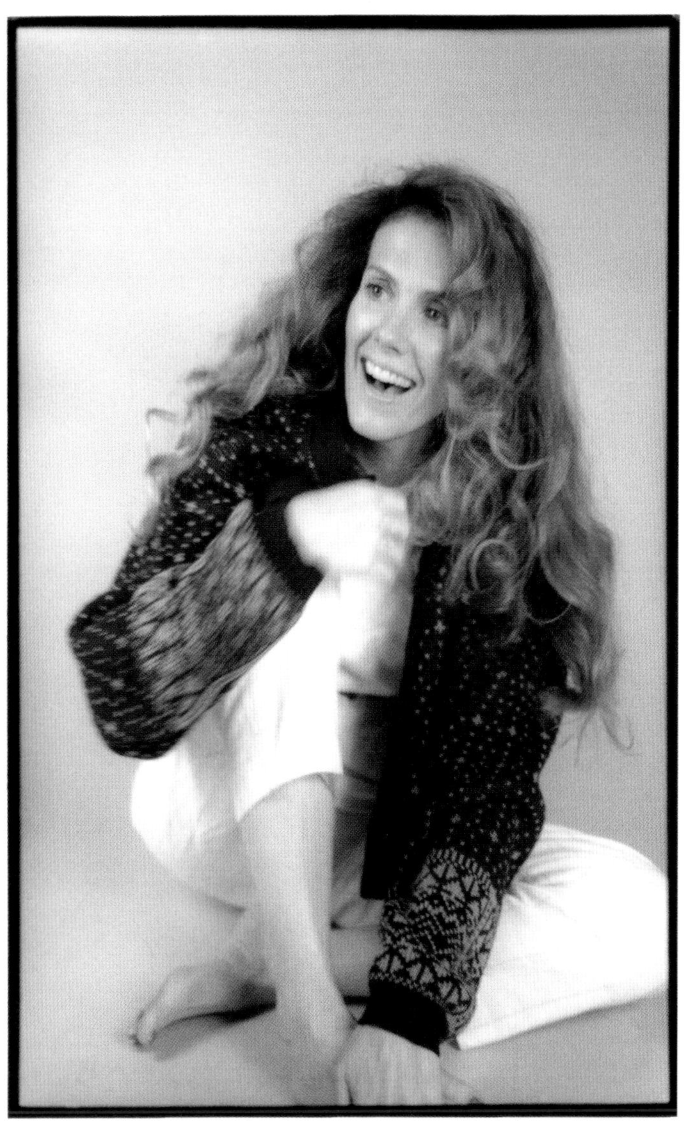

Julie Hagerty

Dee Wallace

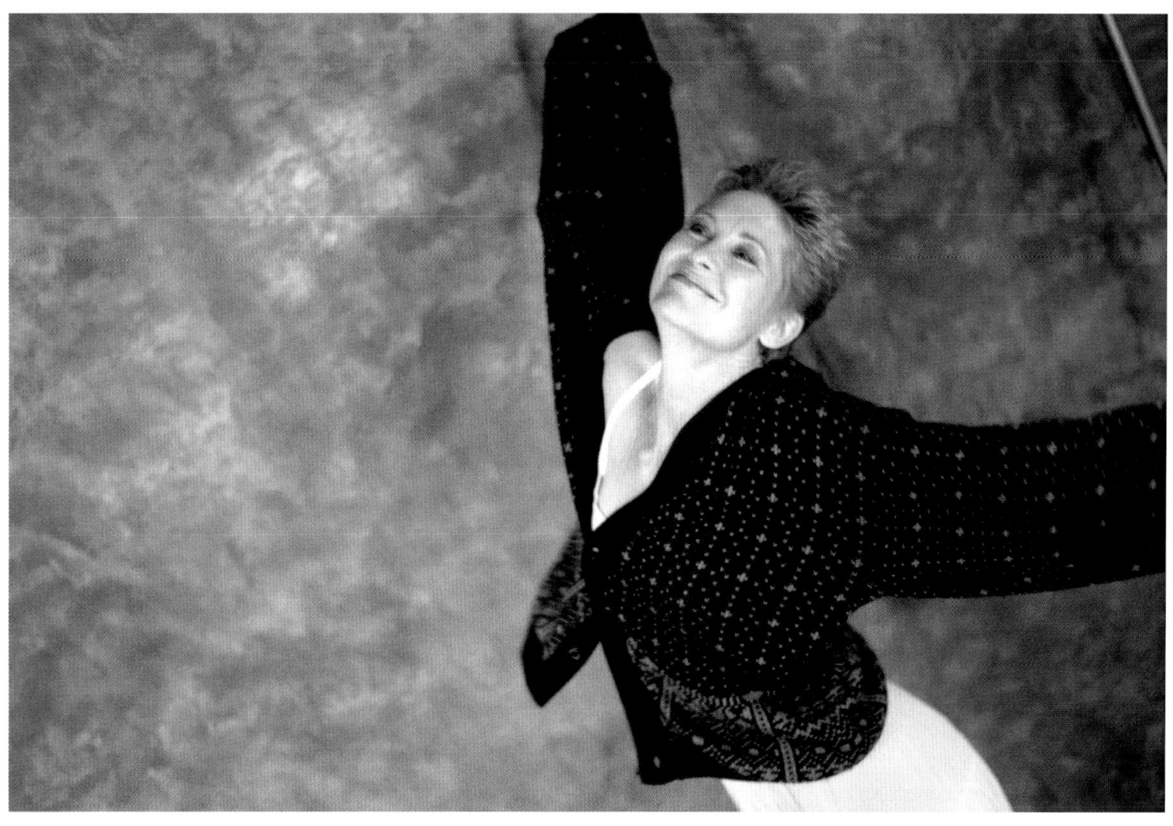

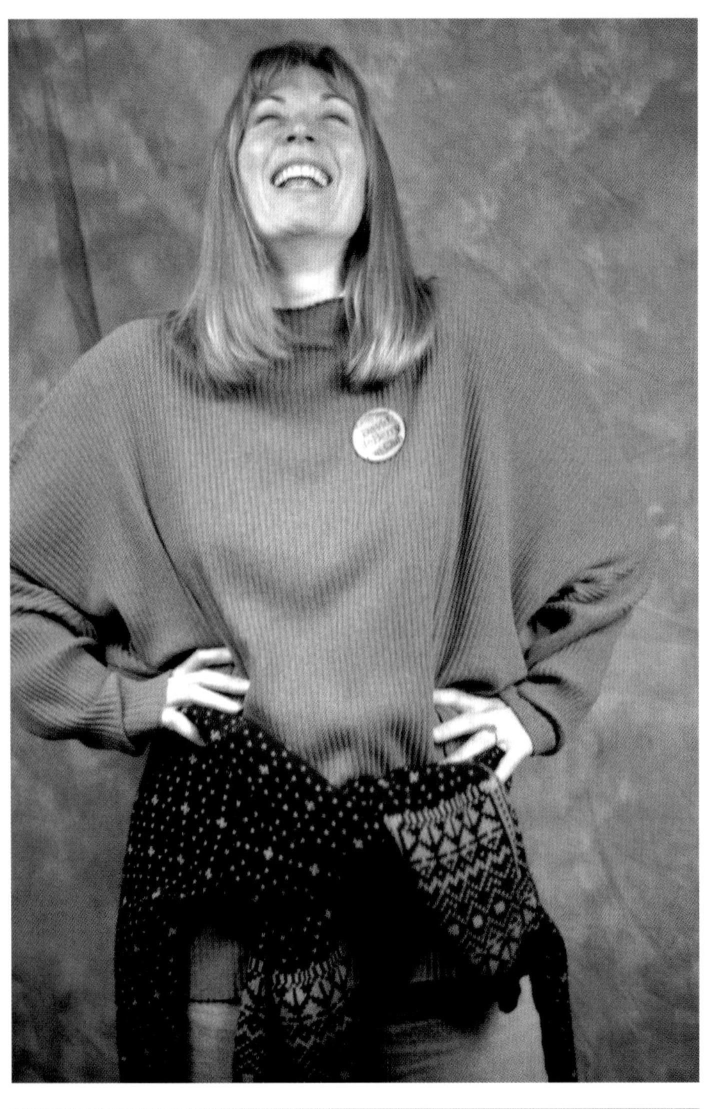

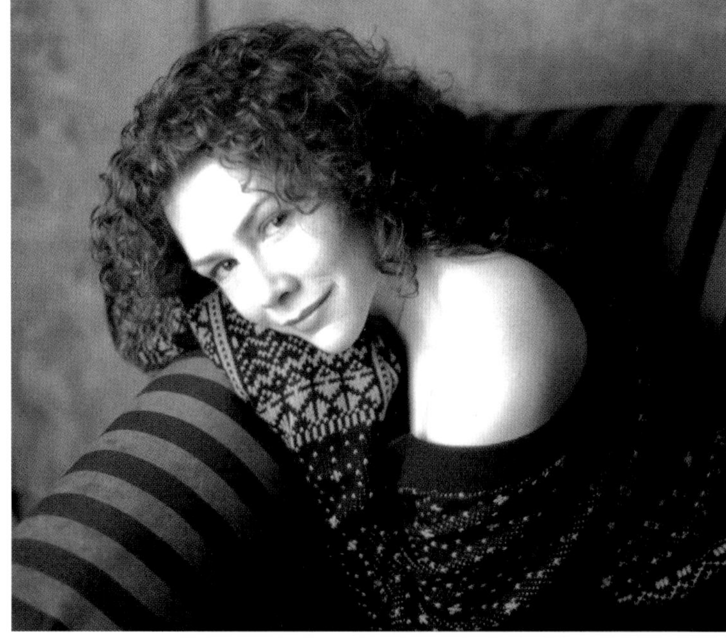

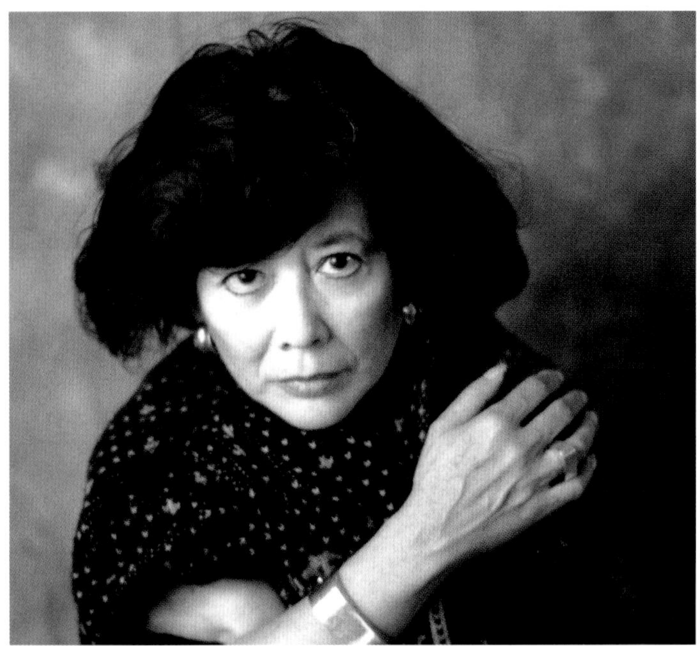

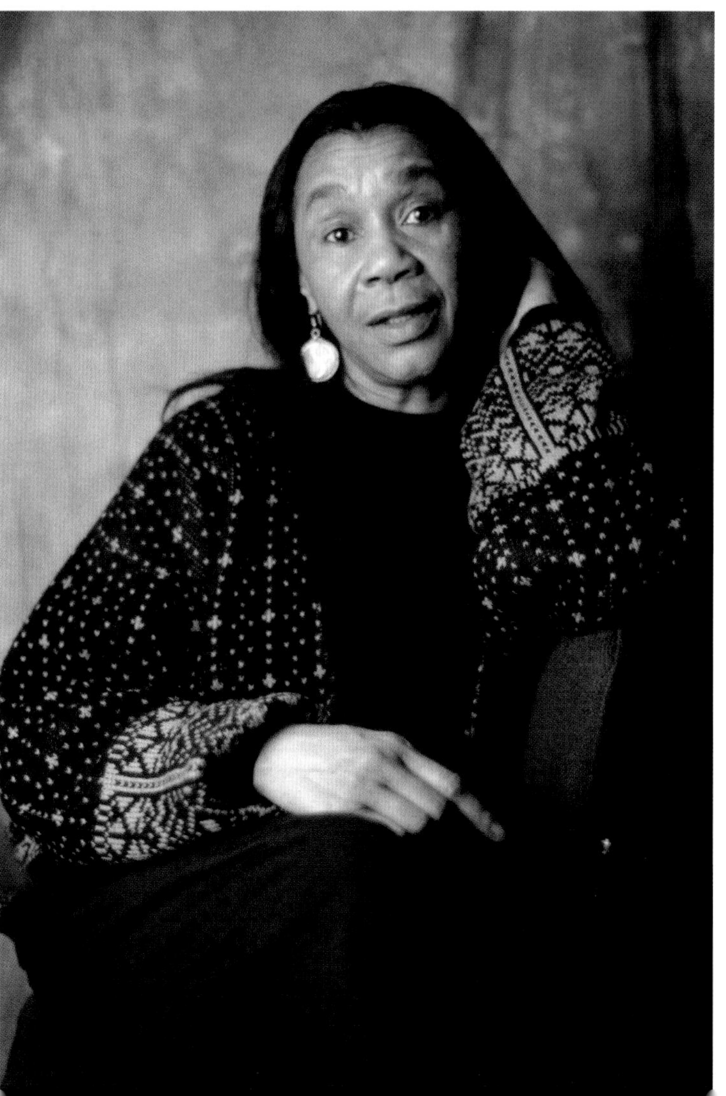

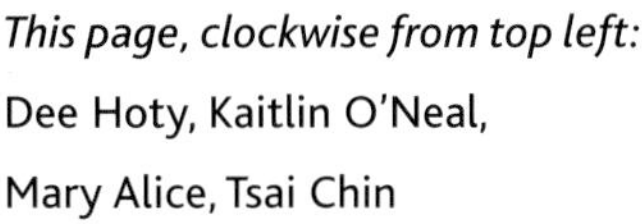

This page, clockwise from top left:
Dee Hoty, Kaitlin O'Neal,
Mary Alice, Tsai Chin

Oppposite, clockwise from top left:
Kim Hunter, Austin Pendleton,
Eli Wallach, Jane Connell

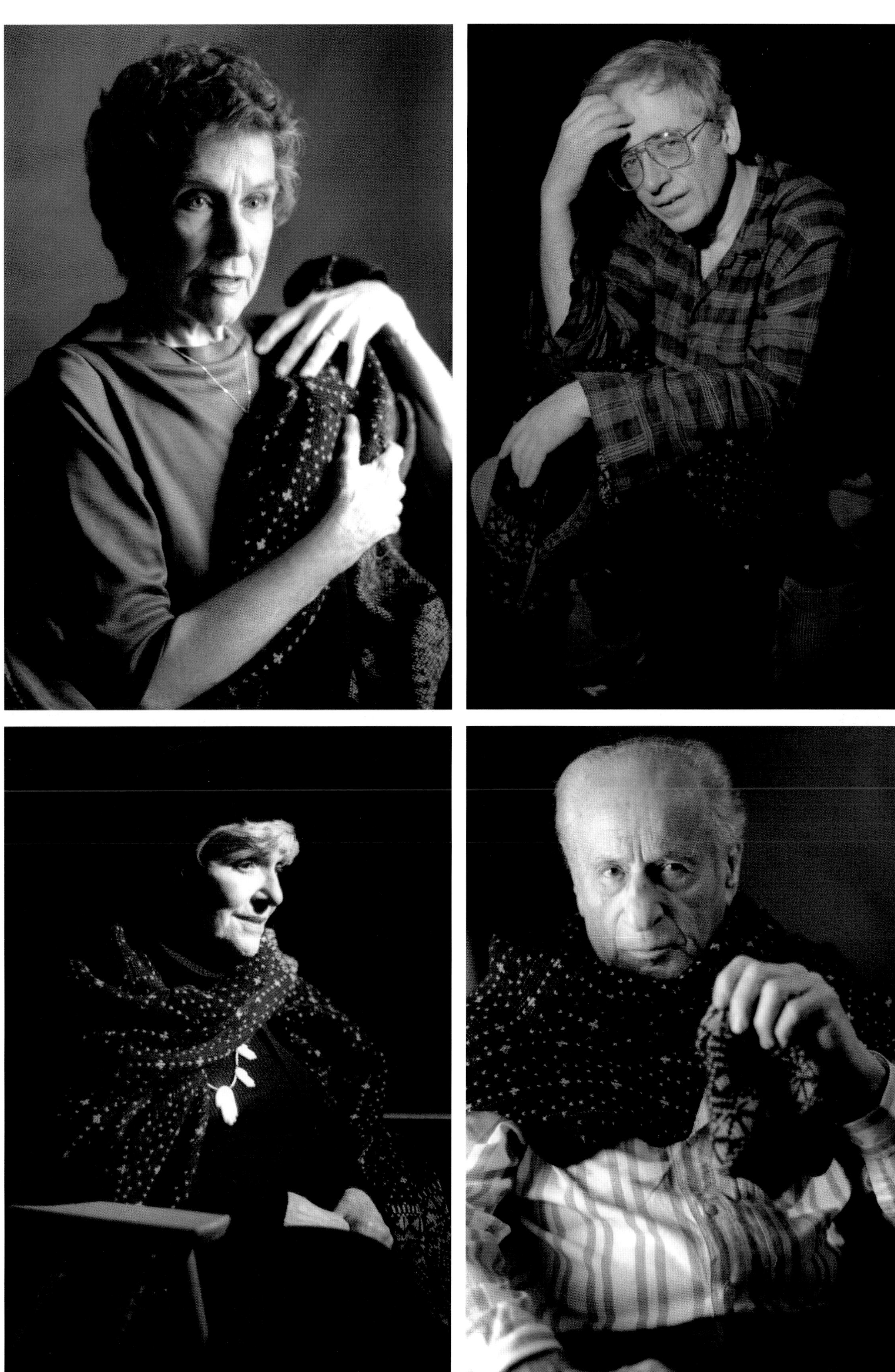

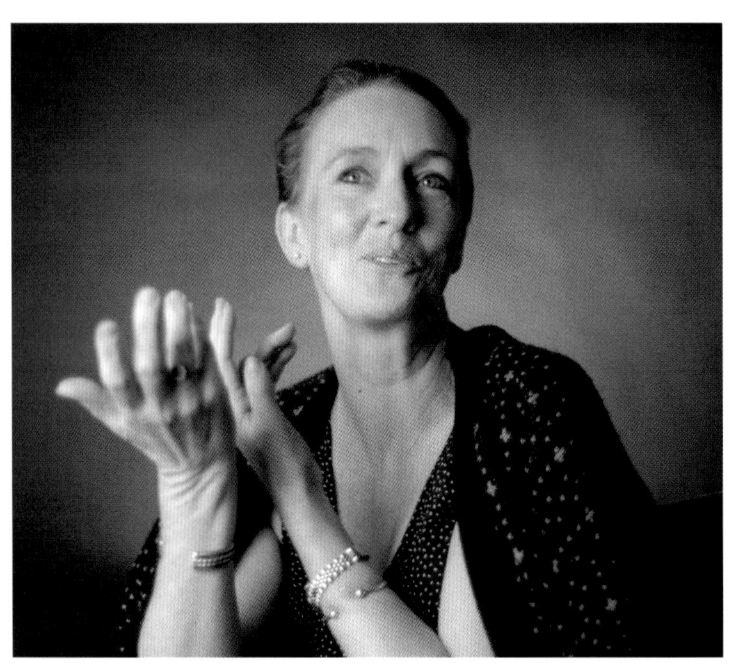

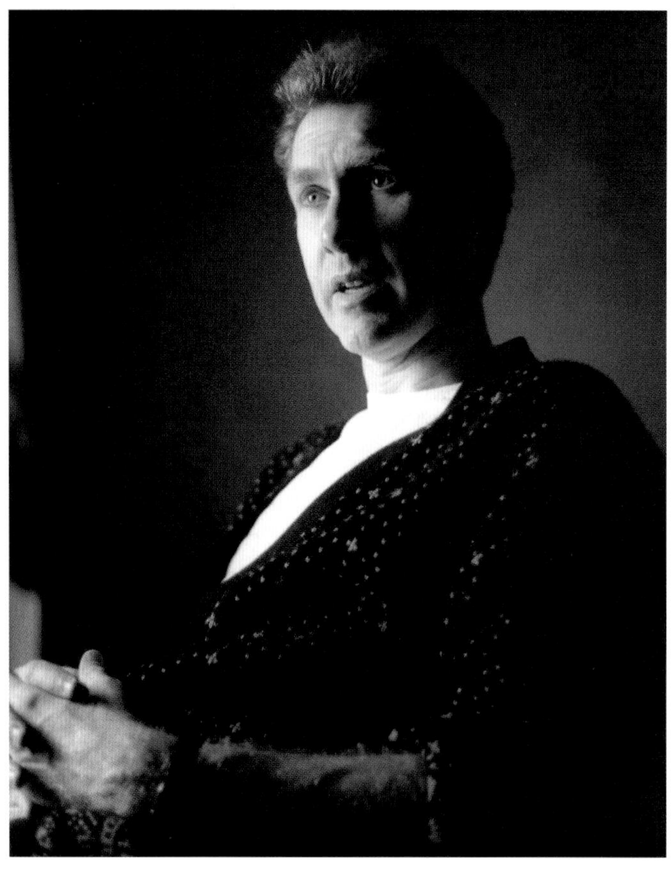

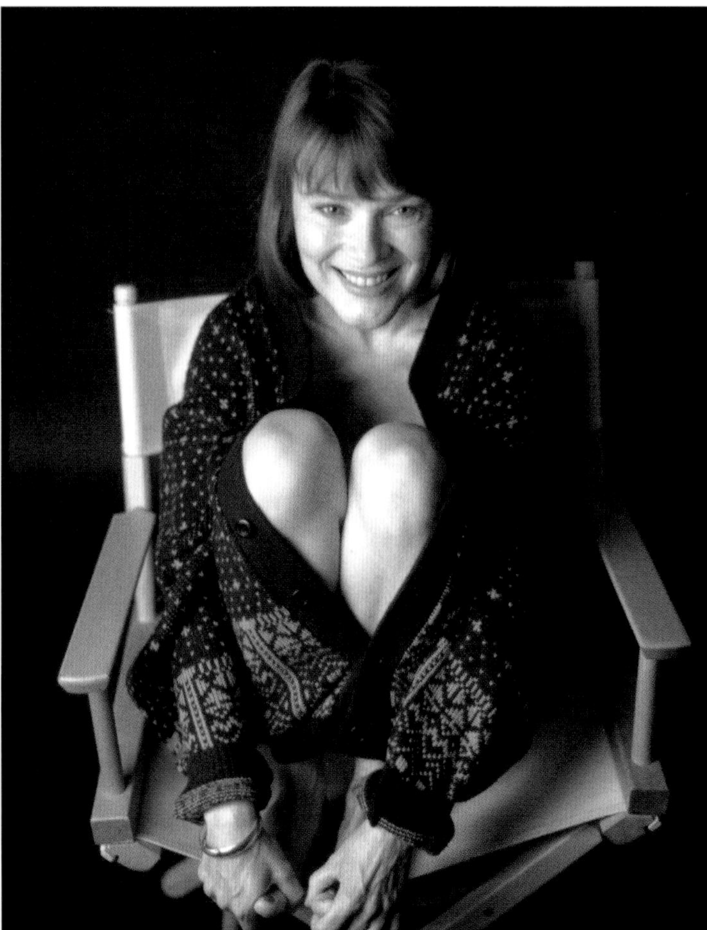

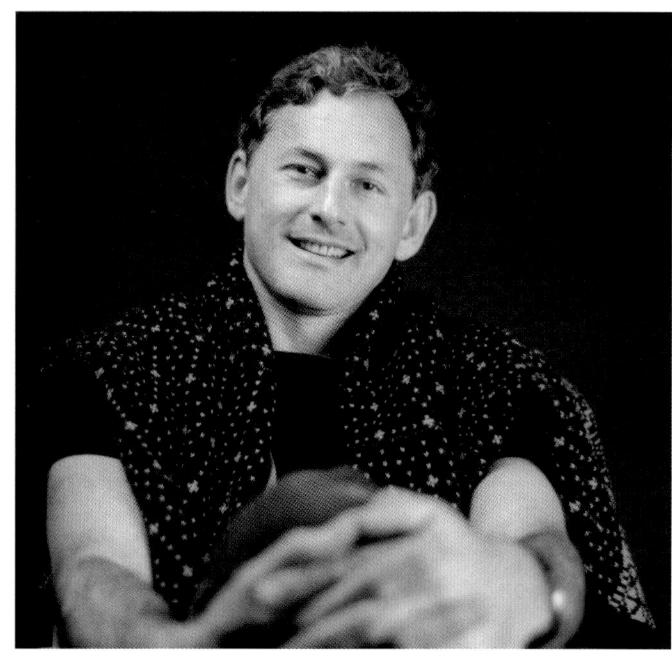

This page, clockwise from top left:
Kathleen Chalfant, Harry Groener,
Victor Garber, Maureen Moore

Opposite, clockwise from top left:
Bryan Cranston, Ken Page, Roger Rees, Kim Coles

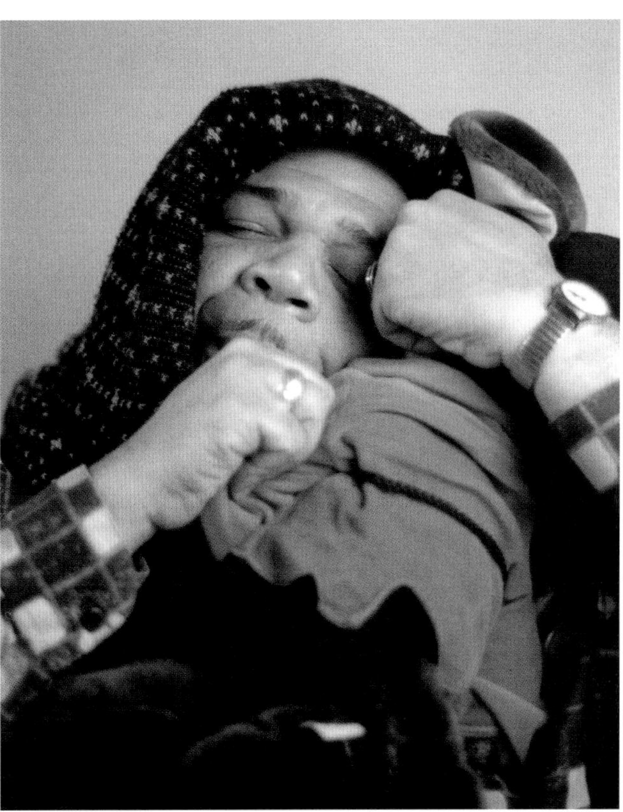

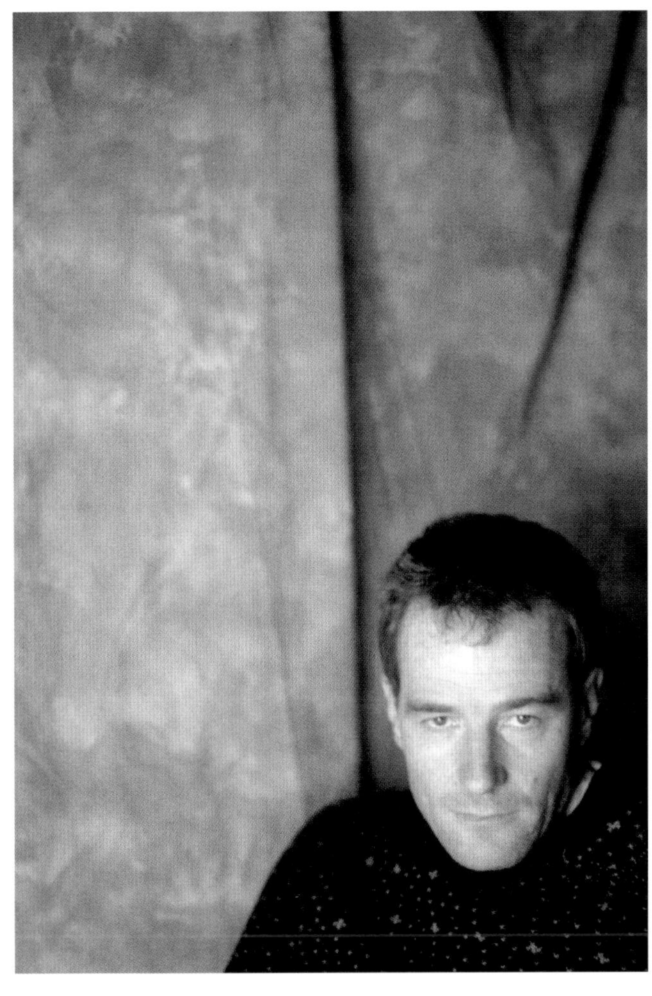

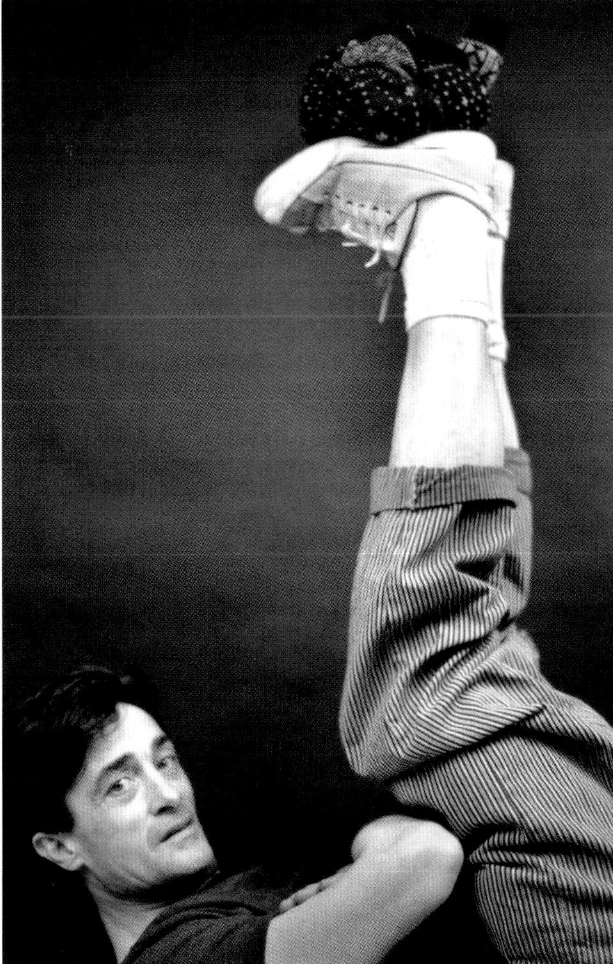

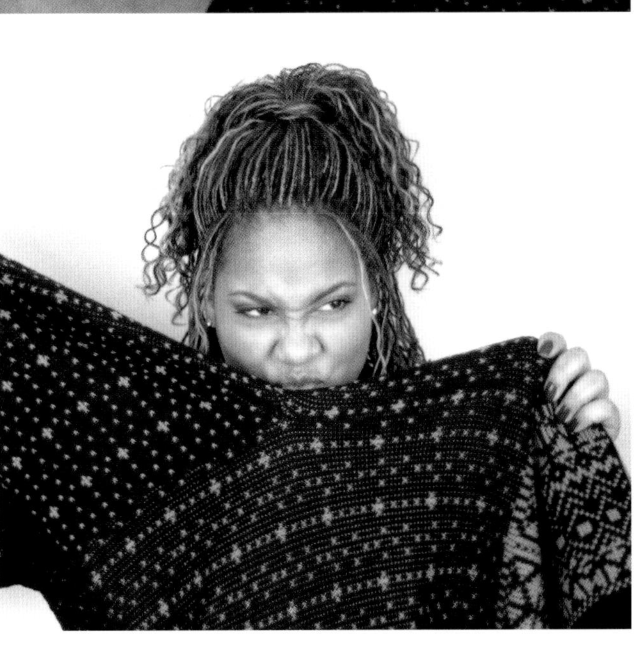

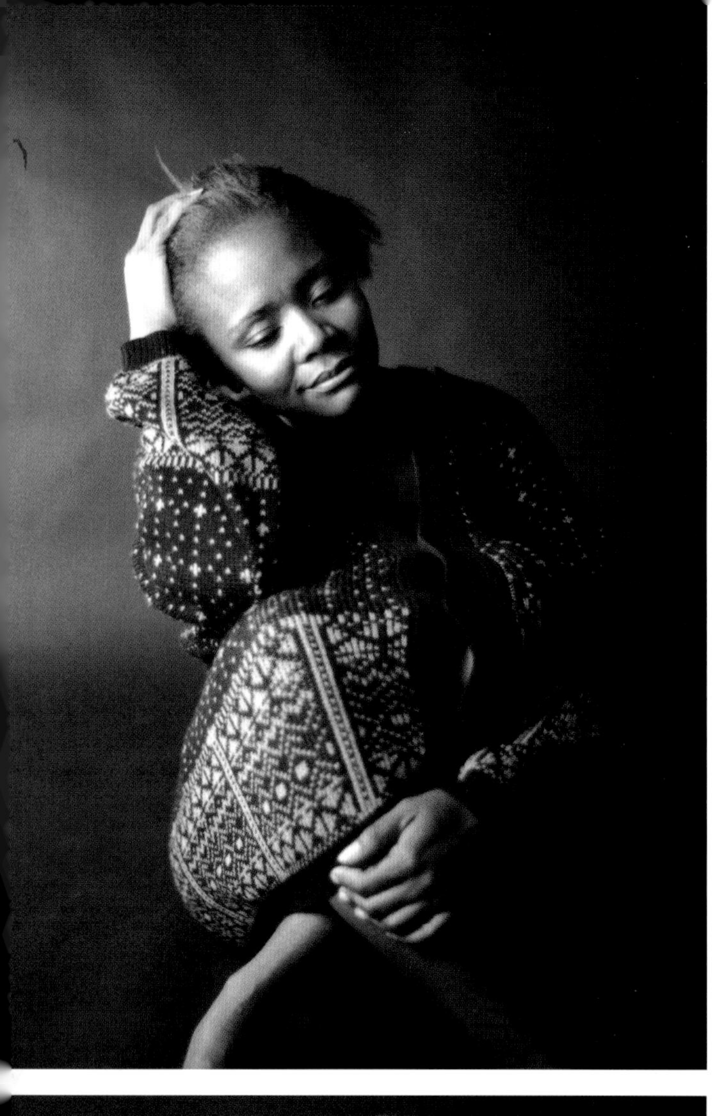

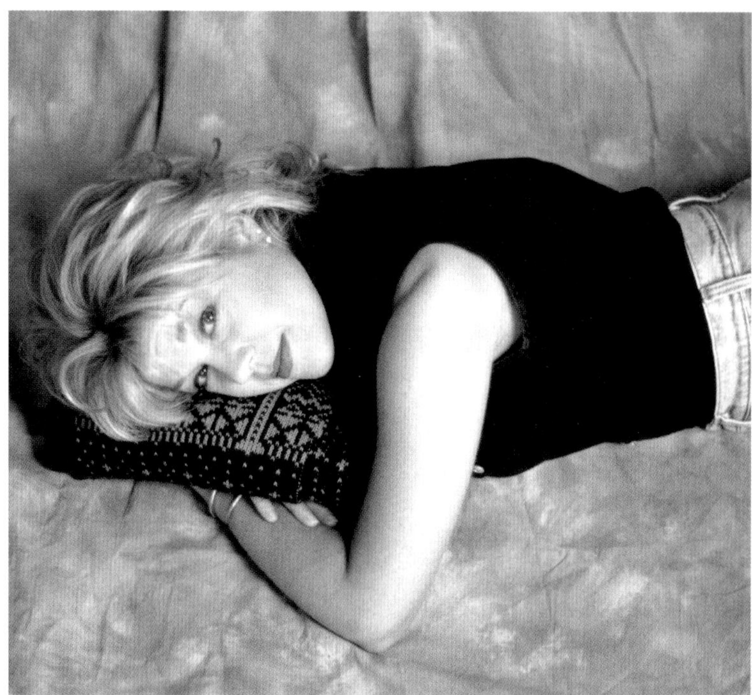

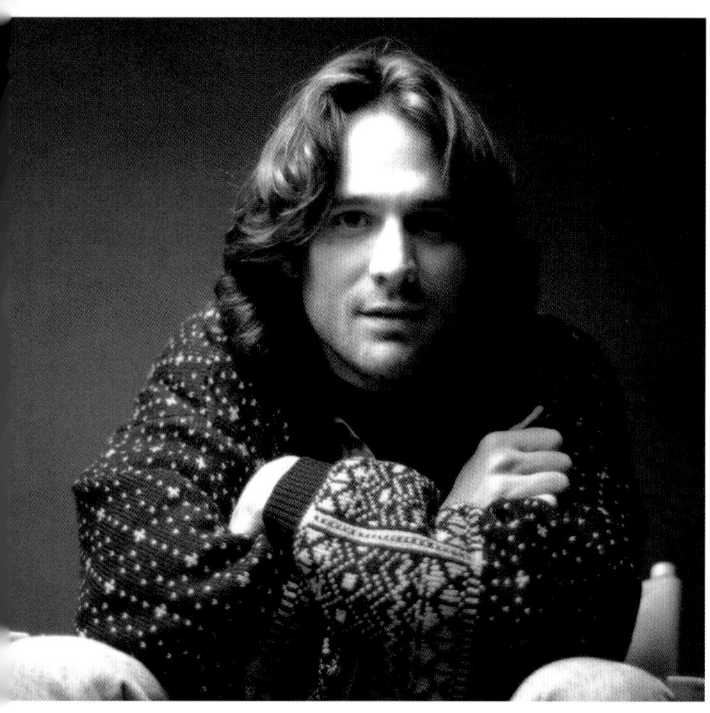

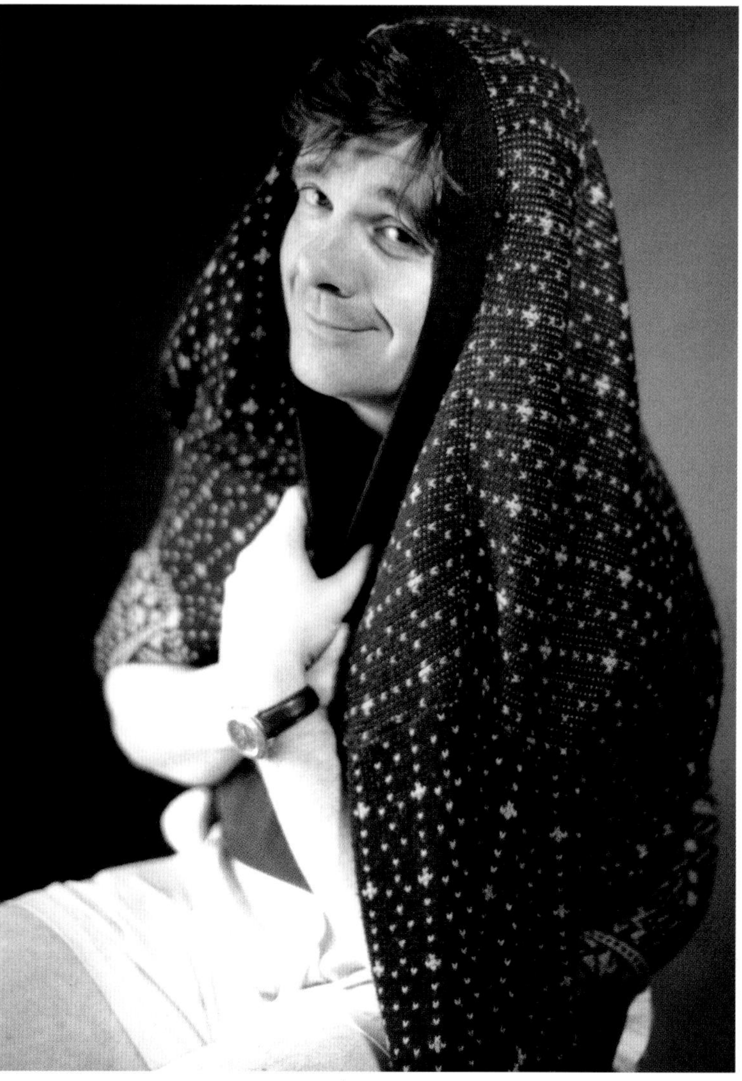

Clockwise from top left:

Tonya Pinkins

Stephanie Hodge

Nathan Lane

David Lee Smith

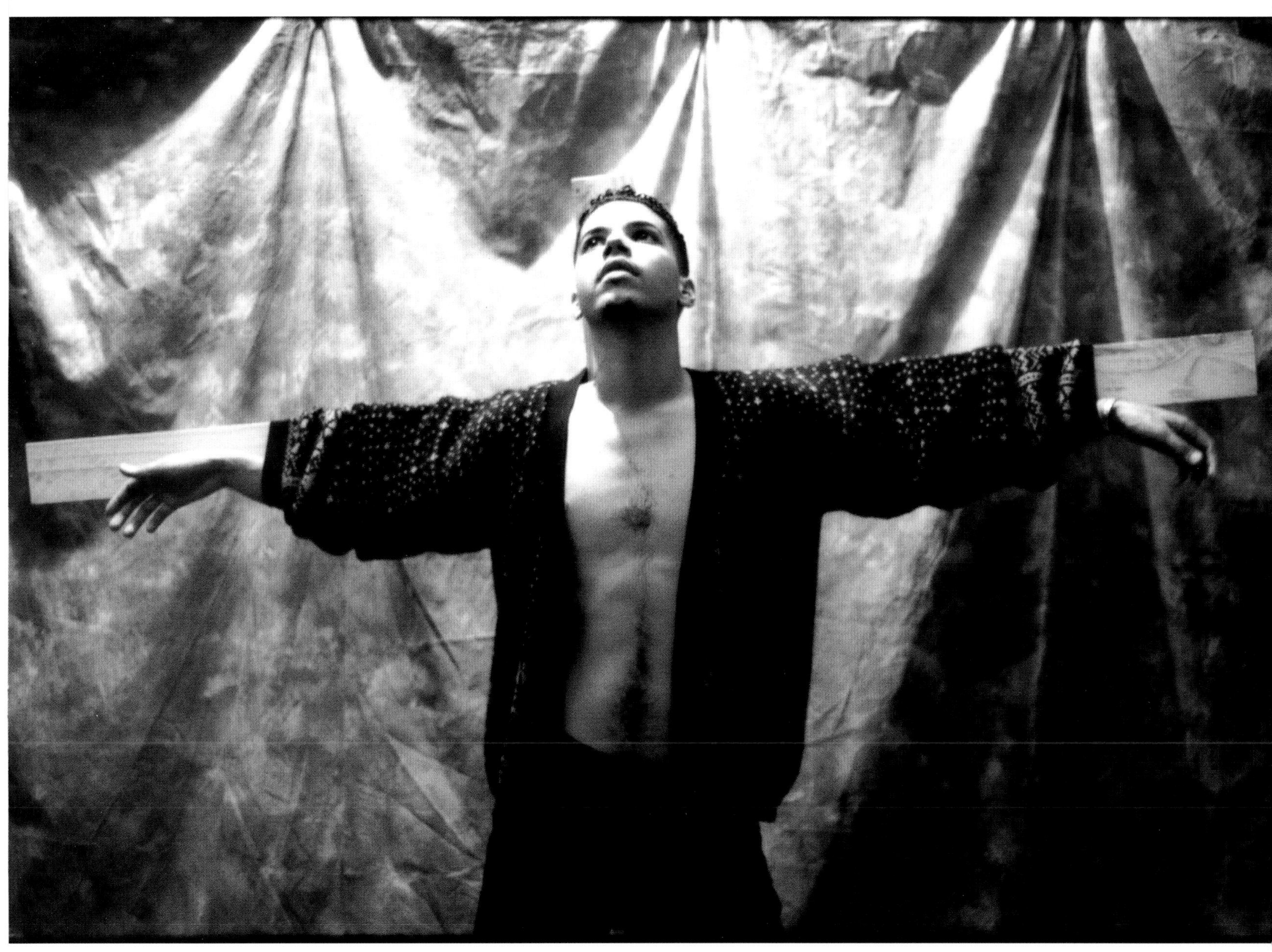

Wilson Cruz

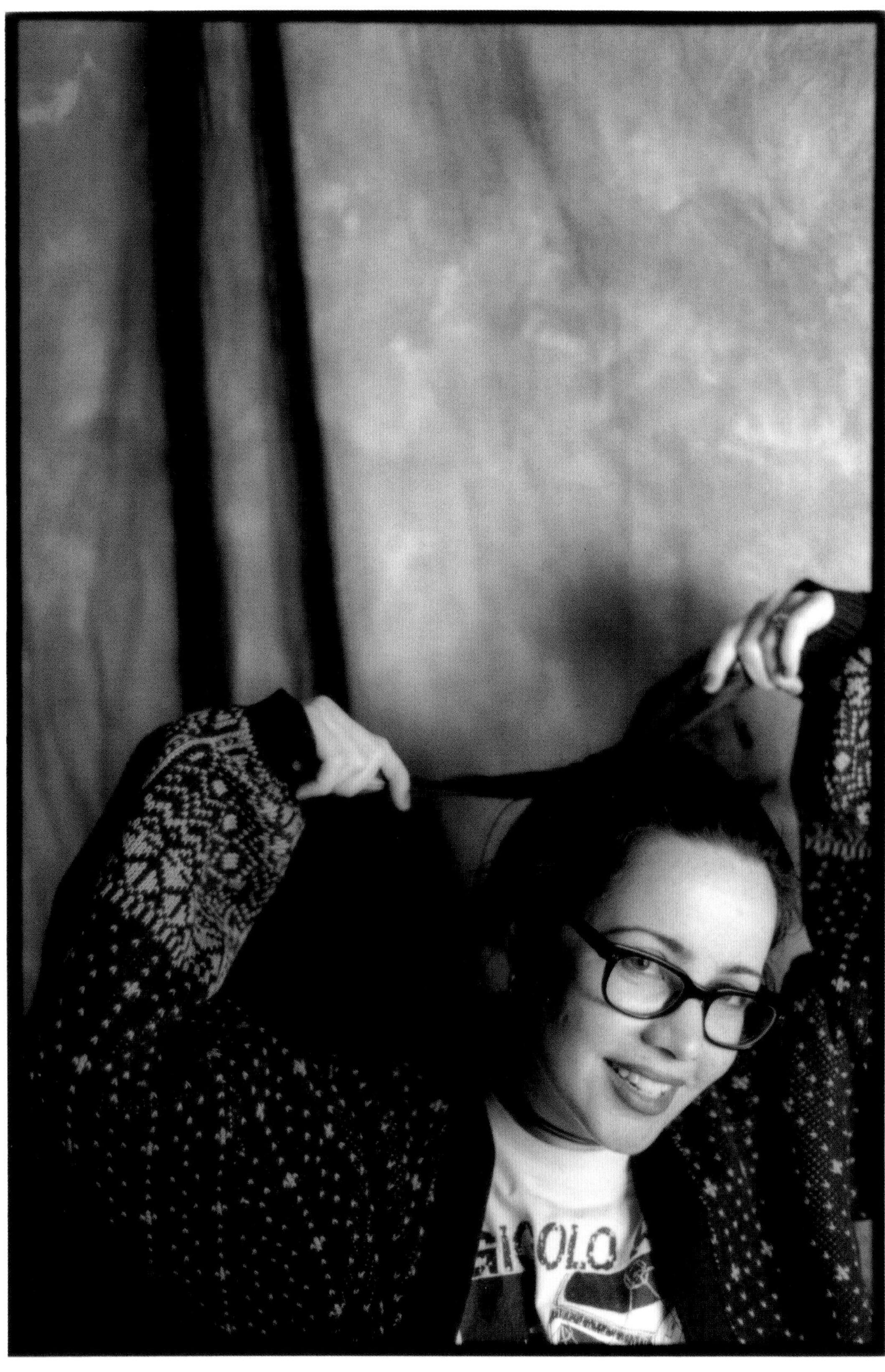

Janeane Garofalo

Pat was hurrying home from work to meet the great Janeane Garofalo but was running late. Our rapport was so good that the photo shoot was finished in no time at all and I was disappointed that Pat would miss the chance to say hello to one of the coolest people in the business. Proving herself the very coolest, she offered to hang out and wait awhile. Fifteen minutes later, though, the time was up; instead of saying good-bye, she asked from which direction he would be coming. Clueing in to her idea, I walked with her along the street until I saw Pat approaching and told her, "Here he is."

She walked toward him, saying hi and opening her arms for a hug.

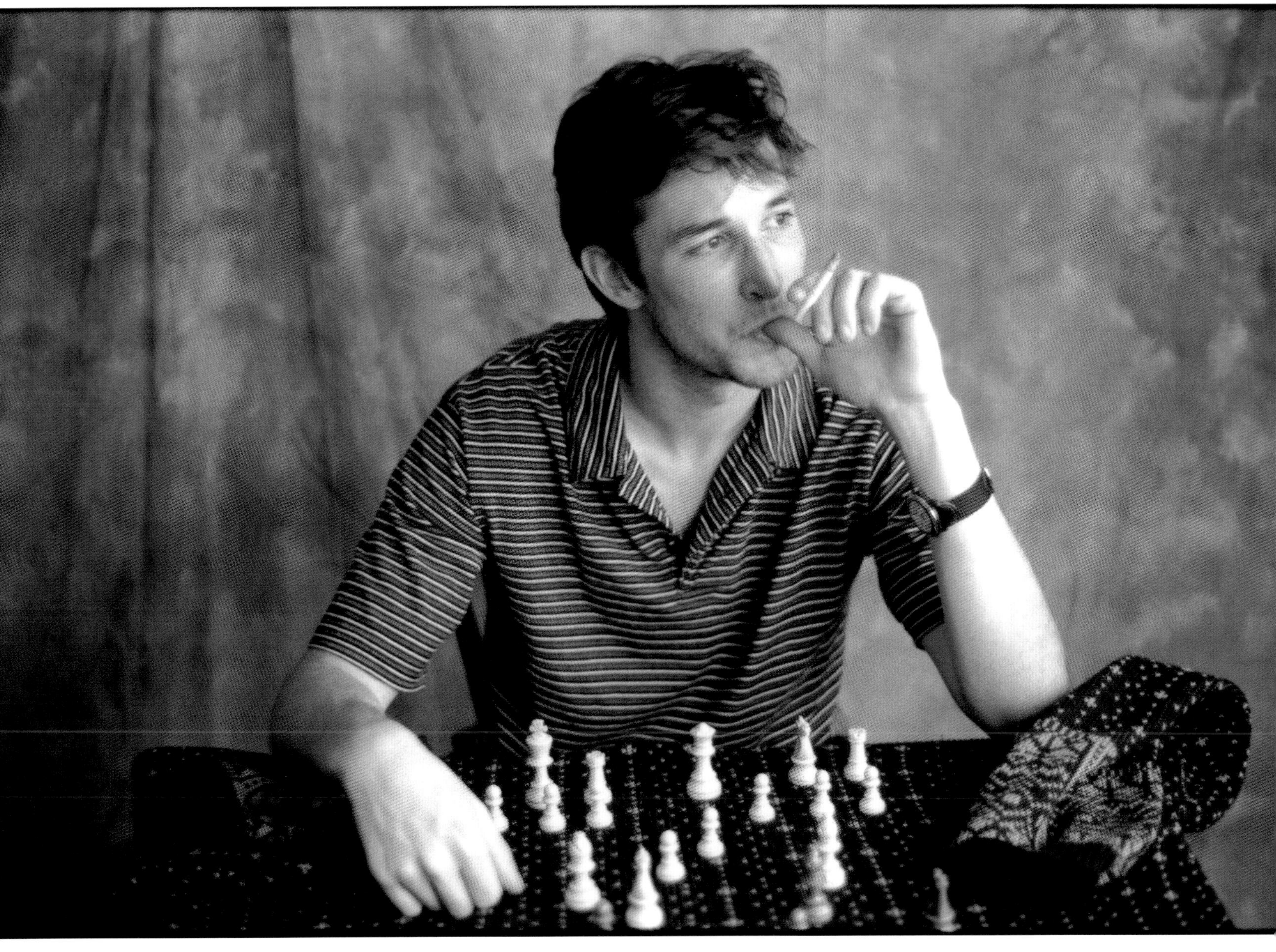

Noah Wyle

I work for the Blank Theatre Company in Los Angeles. The owners of the theater are Daniel Henning and Noah Wyle. My favorite Noah story is not about this shoot, but I am going to share it here. I arrived in Los Angeles, my flight having been delayed for hours, at three in the morning and missed my ritual of going directly from the airport to In N Out Burger. The next day Noah arrived two hours into the photo shoot, and during a break, he and I were having a gossip about my hateful flight and my disappointment at being in L.A. for ten hours and *not* having had an In N Out Burger! When my next shot was ready, I went back to work, and during the next break, I discovered Noah had left and I hadn't said good-bye.

Not so. He arrived back at the theater awhile later, In N Out in hand.

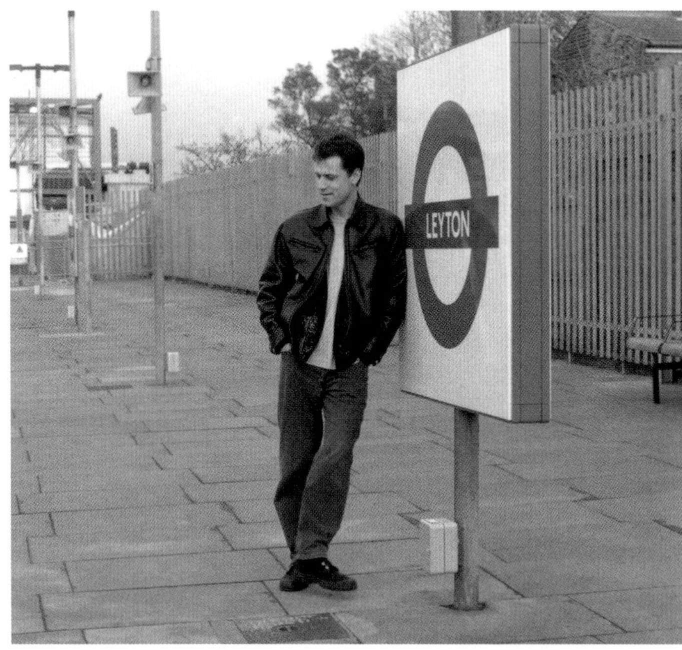

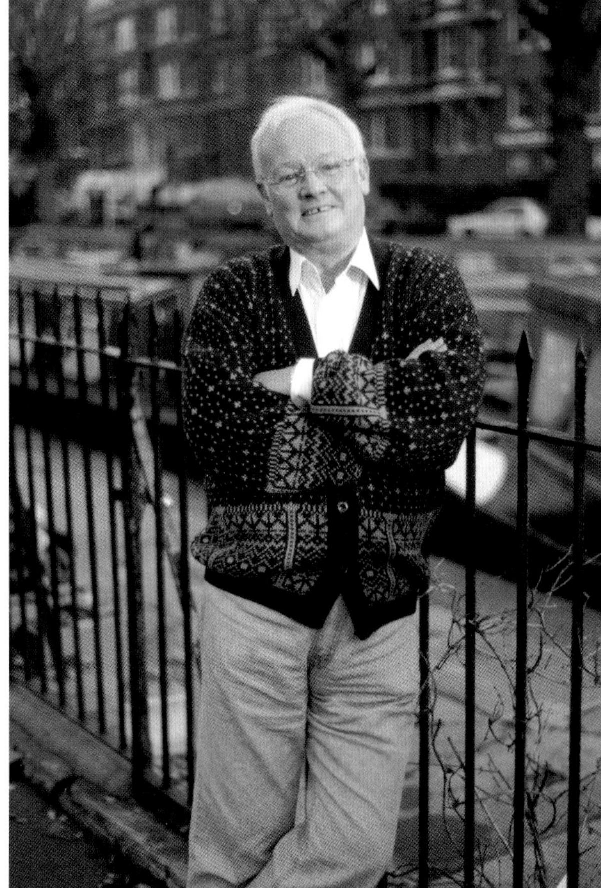

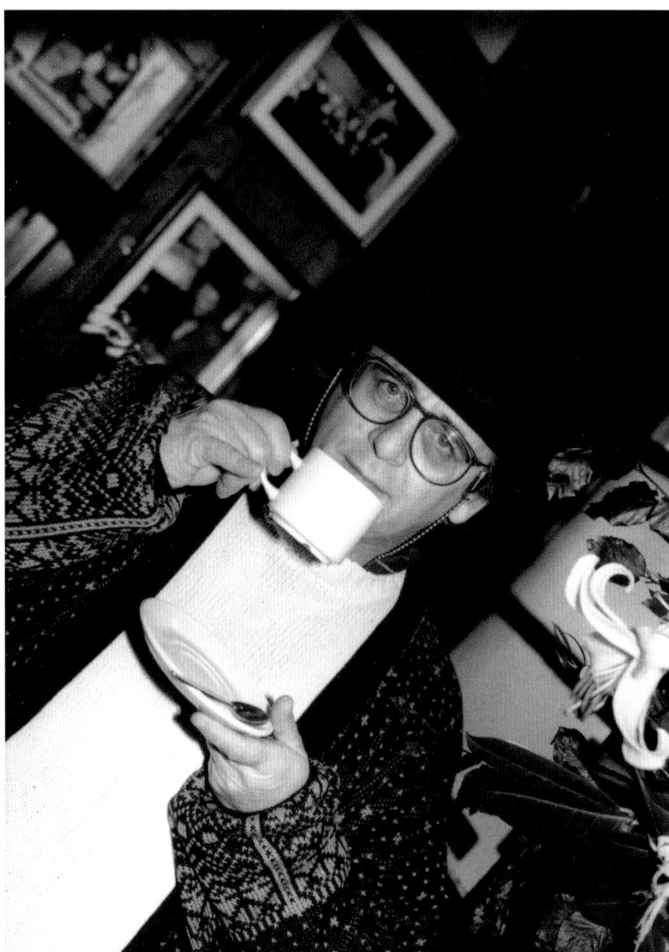

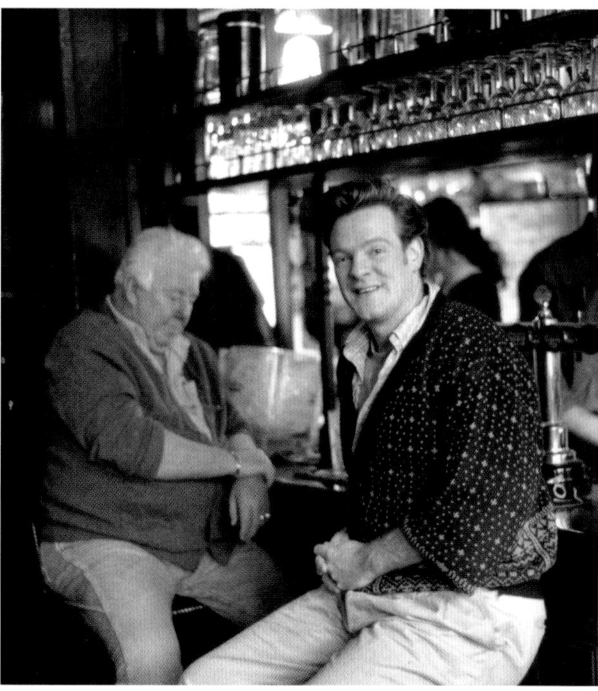

Clockwise from top left: Michael Grandage, John Inman, Chris Larkin, Sylvester McCoy

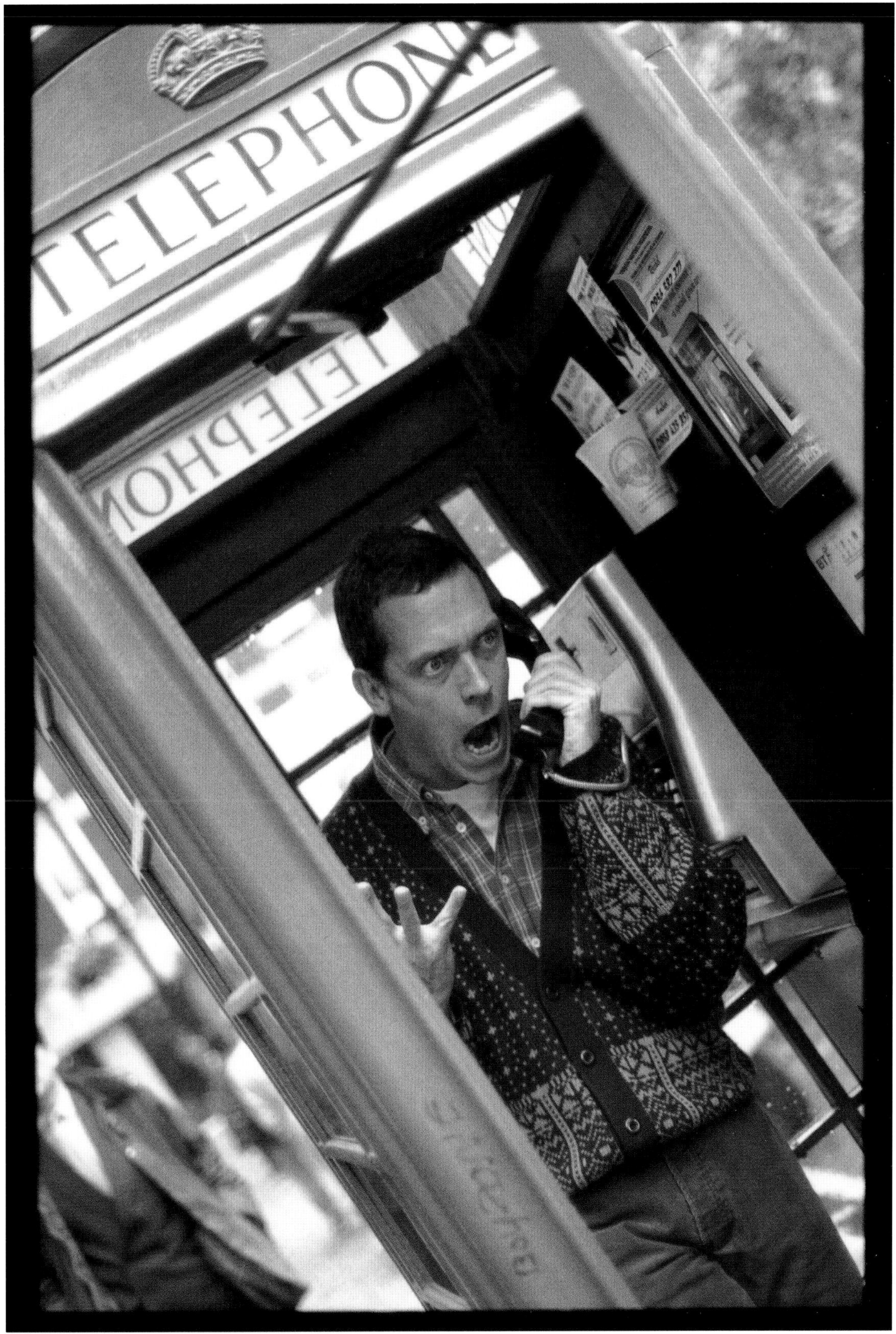

Hugh Laurie

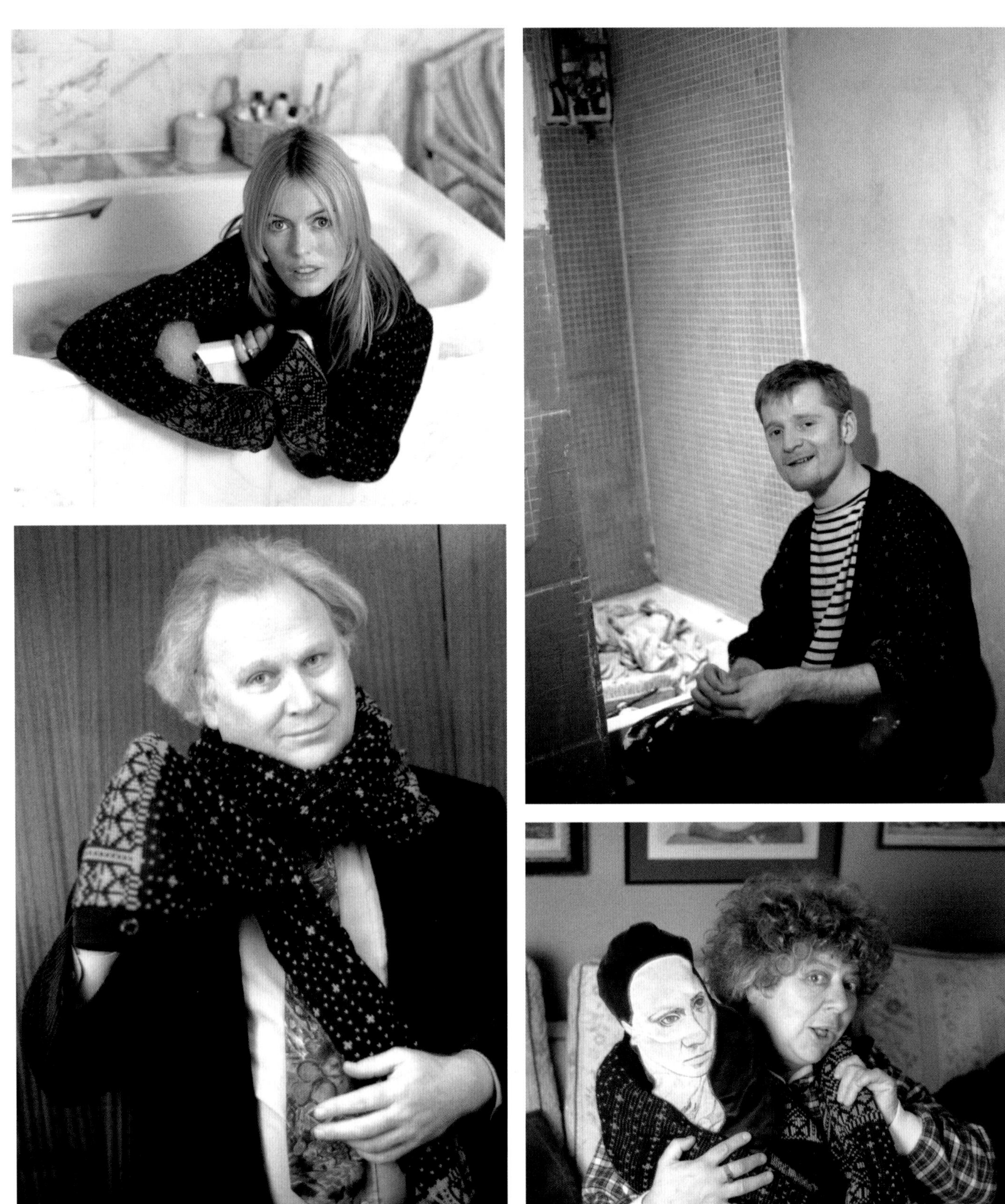

Clockwise from top left: Patsy Kensit, Christopher Oram, Miriam Margolyes, Colin Baker

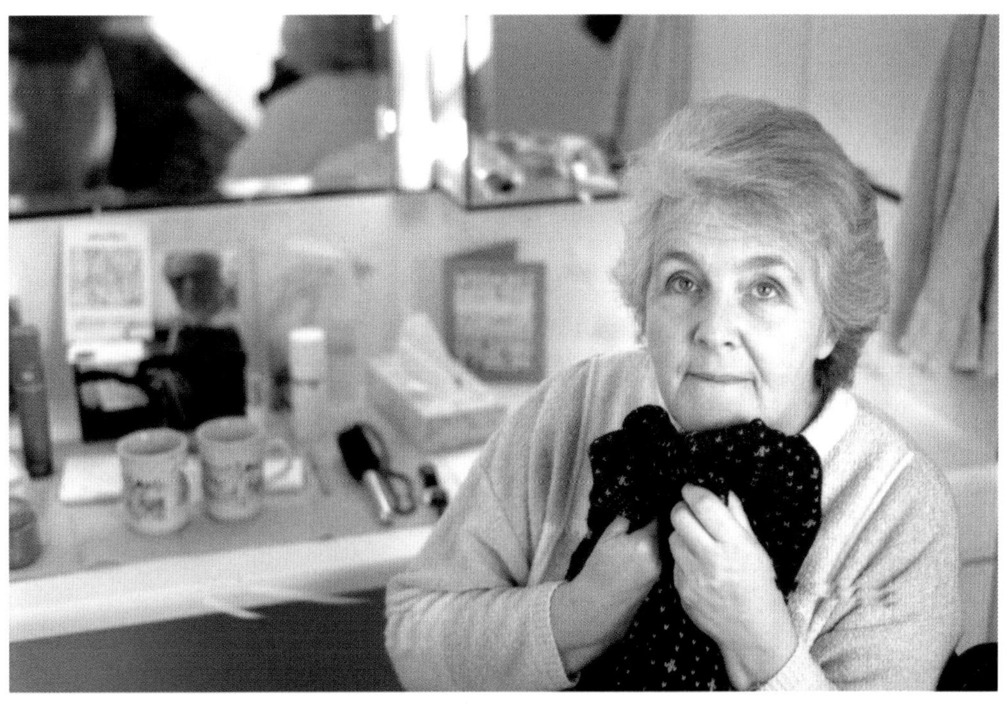

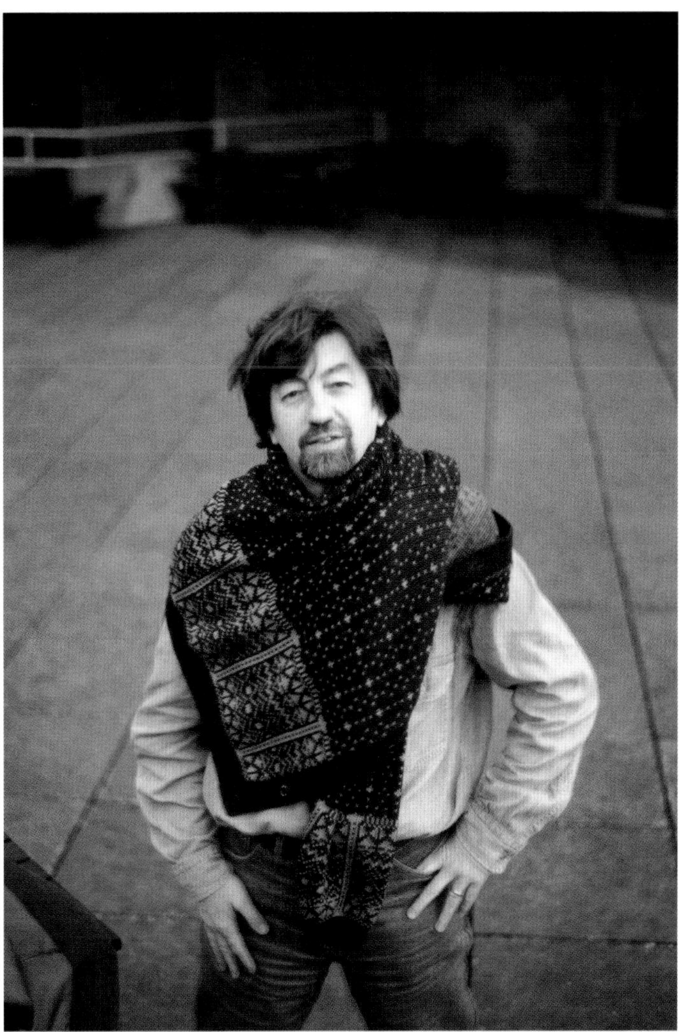

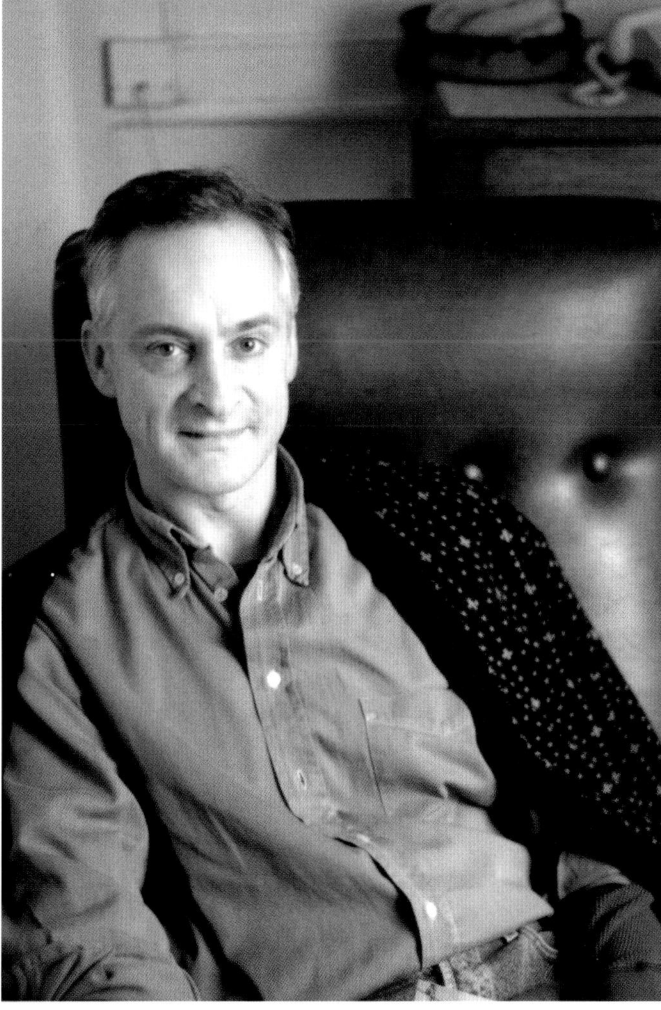

Clockwise: Stephanie Cole, Malcolm Sinclair, Trevor Nunn

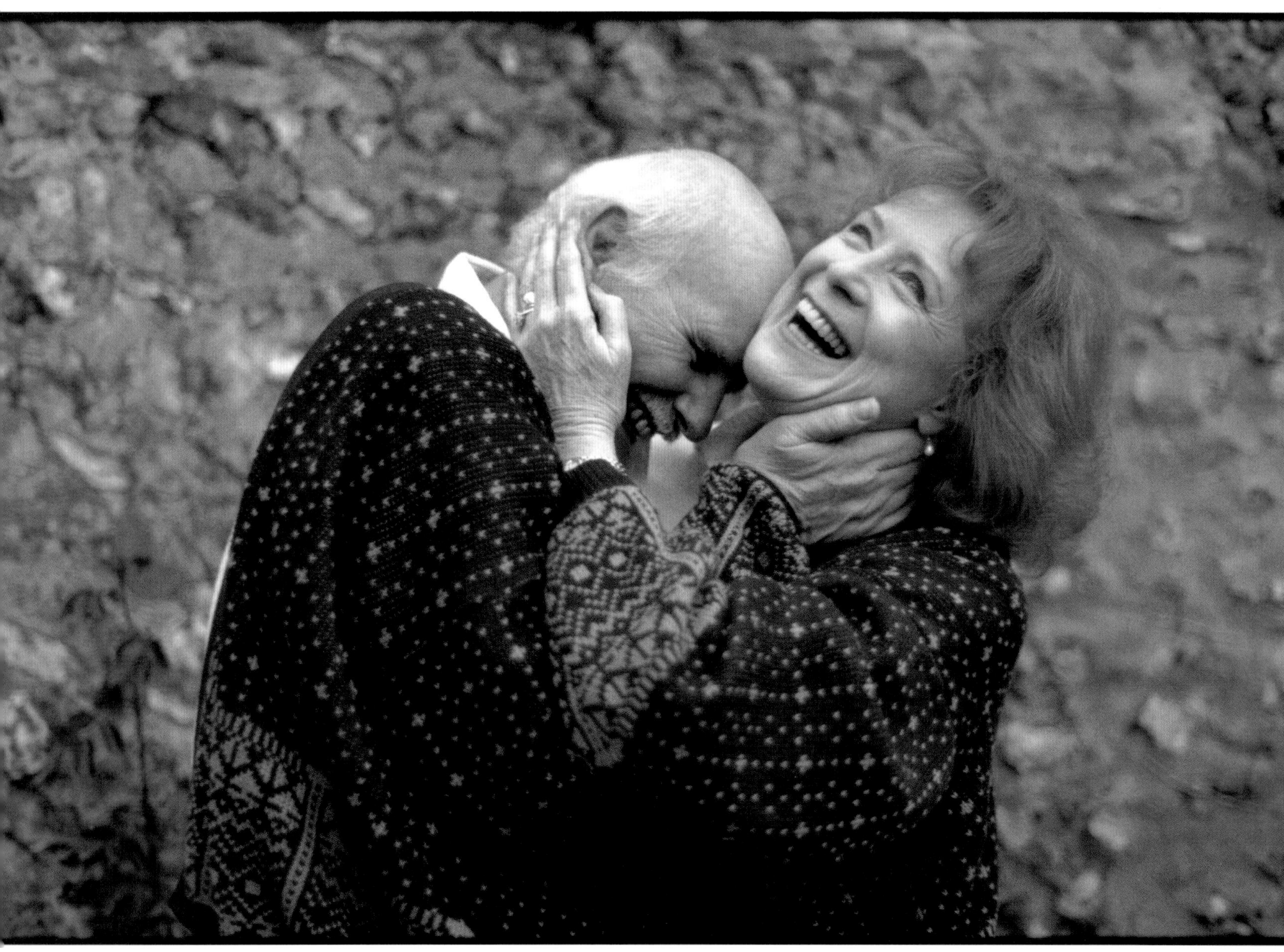

Tony Steedman and Judy Parfitt

In the garden of their home near Brighton, Judy Parfitt and Tony Steedman gave it a shot at being serious and romantic. Between shivering with the cold and getting the giggles, it simply wasn't to be. It didn't matter to me, though, because I have always thought that laughter between people in love is the height of romance. Judy and Tony are one of the most romantic couples I know.

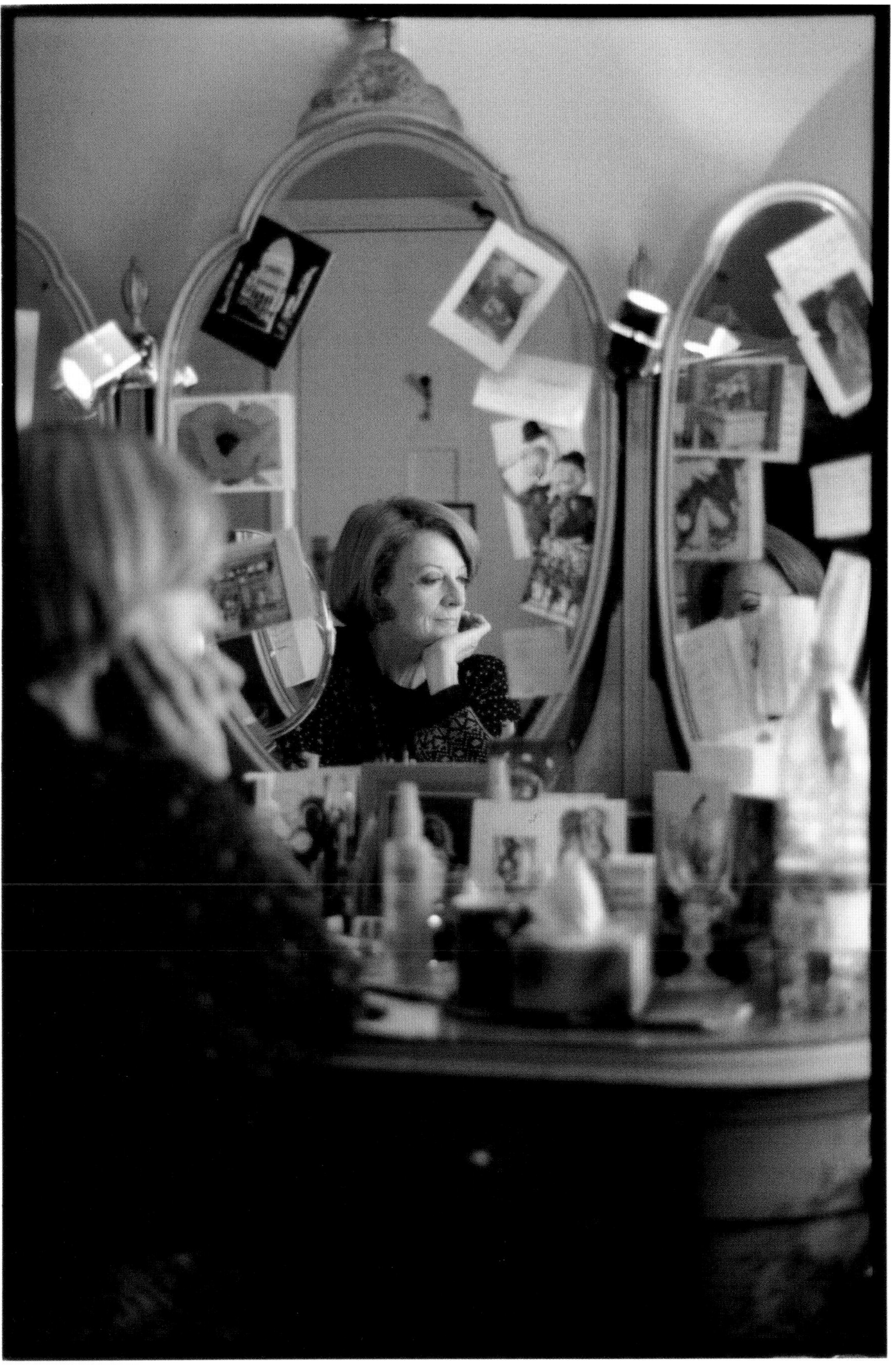

Maggie Smith

What the song says, Maggie Smith proves. *"There ain't nothin like a Dame."*

Someone once told me that I should use this book to show the journey the sweater has been on. It's been some journey, but there's a journey the sweater went on that I cannot show.

On May 4, 1998, I came out of an eleven-month depression. There's no need to go into detail; we all have them, and if we're lucky, they end. Mine did, and the next morning I got out of bed, showered, shaved, and got on with it.

On May 6, I had a morning photo shoot with singer/songwriter Gilles Chiasson in the boat basin off Riverside Drive in New York City. It was a lovely day and a good shoot and I found Gilles to be an artist filled with integrity and liberality. After we had finished our work, Gilles walked me to Broadway, where we said our good-byes. Happy for the first time in a long time, I decided to walk home. The sky wasn't incredibly blue but pretty and full of clouds, and in the spirit of hope, I was looking up.

I didn't notice when the sweater left me.

Taken? Possibly. Dropped? Probably. Gone? Absolutely. It was at the top of my bag, which was unzipped, and at some point during that thirty-block walk, the sweater went AWOL.

We went into a tailspin. Could we find it? Replace it? Should we tell? We began a search, and in the meantime, shoots were canceled until further notice. It looked bad for the recovery of my old pal. Some shoots with people I loved, artists committed to this project who deserved to be in the book, couldn't be rescheduled while we tried to find a replacement. What was I to do?

The answer came from a friend, who pointed out that all great stars have a stand-in.

Would people go for it? I'd no time to think. We took a sweater from my closet and began doing the shoots. Gingerly, we tested the waters with the new sweater. At first we didn't tell people that the sweater had been lost—it had been retired and the final chapter was a passing on of the torch. No one cared. All that mattered was the commitment to the project and to the cause.

After a while I began telling the awful truth.

Invitations to be in the book stopped going out. The final shots for the book would be the people who had accepted the invitation but not yet made it in front of the camera.

At the insistence of a friend, I spoke to a renowned psychic, well known for finding lost items. She assured me that the sweater was safe, hanging on the back of a chair in a refined but sparsely decorated apartment on the Upper West Side. The man who found it was a good-looking man in his twenties or thirties who actually knew someone in my circle of friends but who was unaware of what he had found. She assured me that one day, if I was willing to make the right sacrifice, the sweater would come back to me. A sacrifice—a reward? Possibly. Perhaps some assistance with a floundering career. I'd only to wait. I continue to wait.

I do view this loss as a sign from the universe that it was time to move on; and a sign from the sweater that it needed a rest. I promised the universe that if the sweater came back, I wouldn't make it work anymore.

So here they are—the very last picture of the sweater and the new sweater as it begins its job adorning the artists so special that its presence in my life was absolutely required.

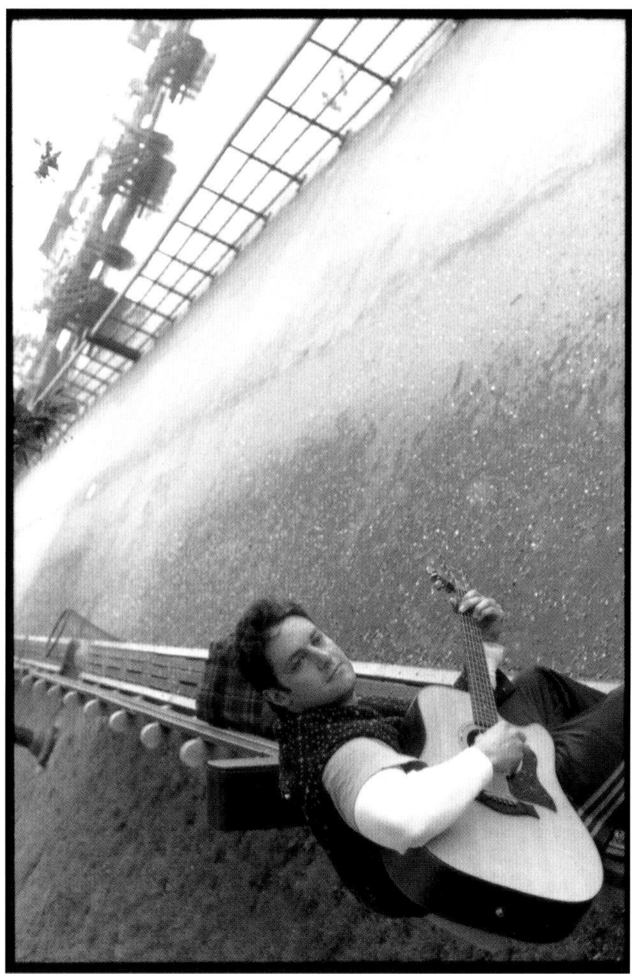

Gilles Chiasson
Riverside Drive boat basin

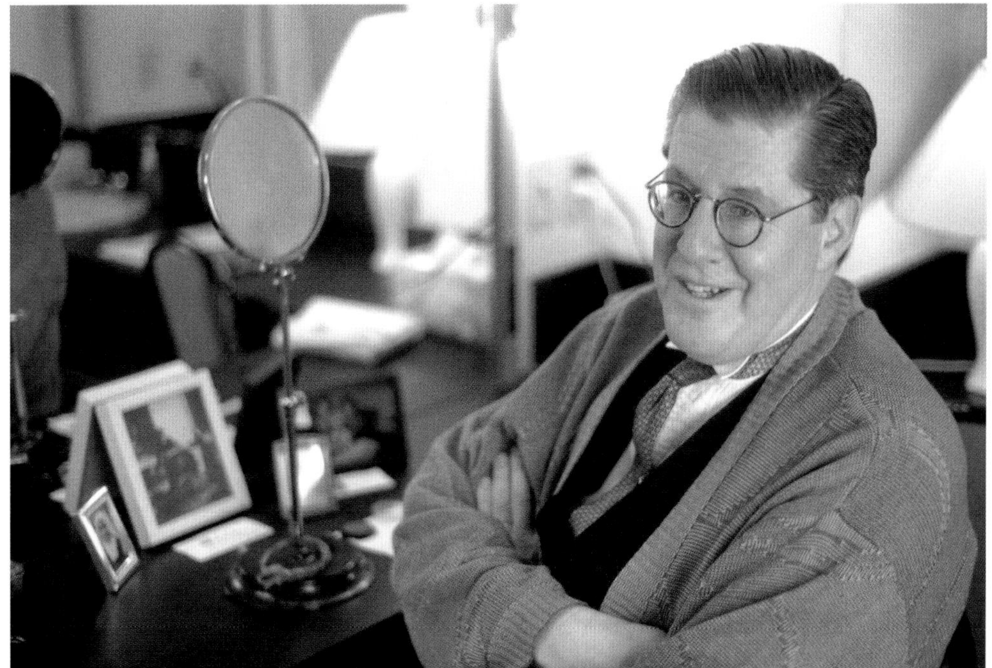

Edward Herrmann at the Roundabout Theater

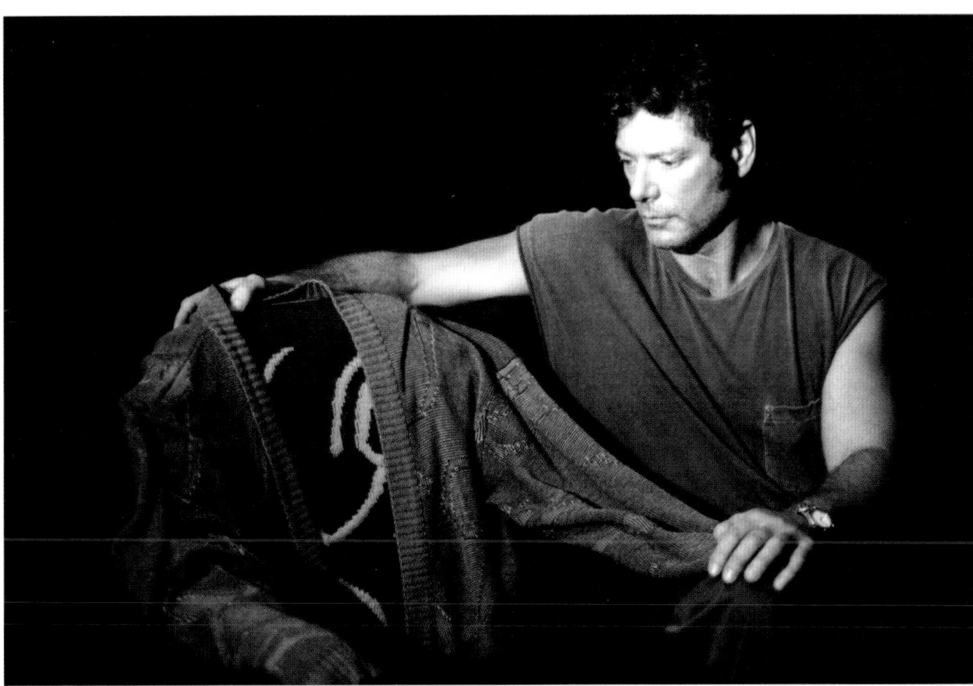

Stephen Lang at the Brooks Atkinson Theater

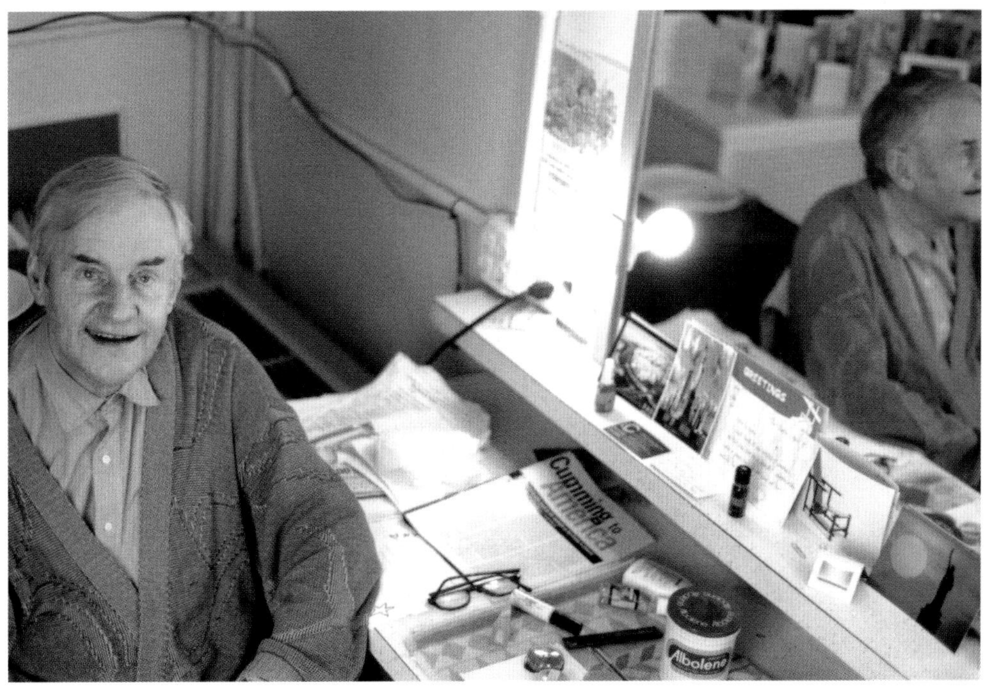

Richard Briers at the Golden Theater

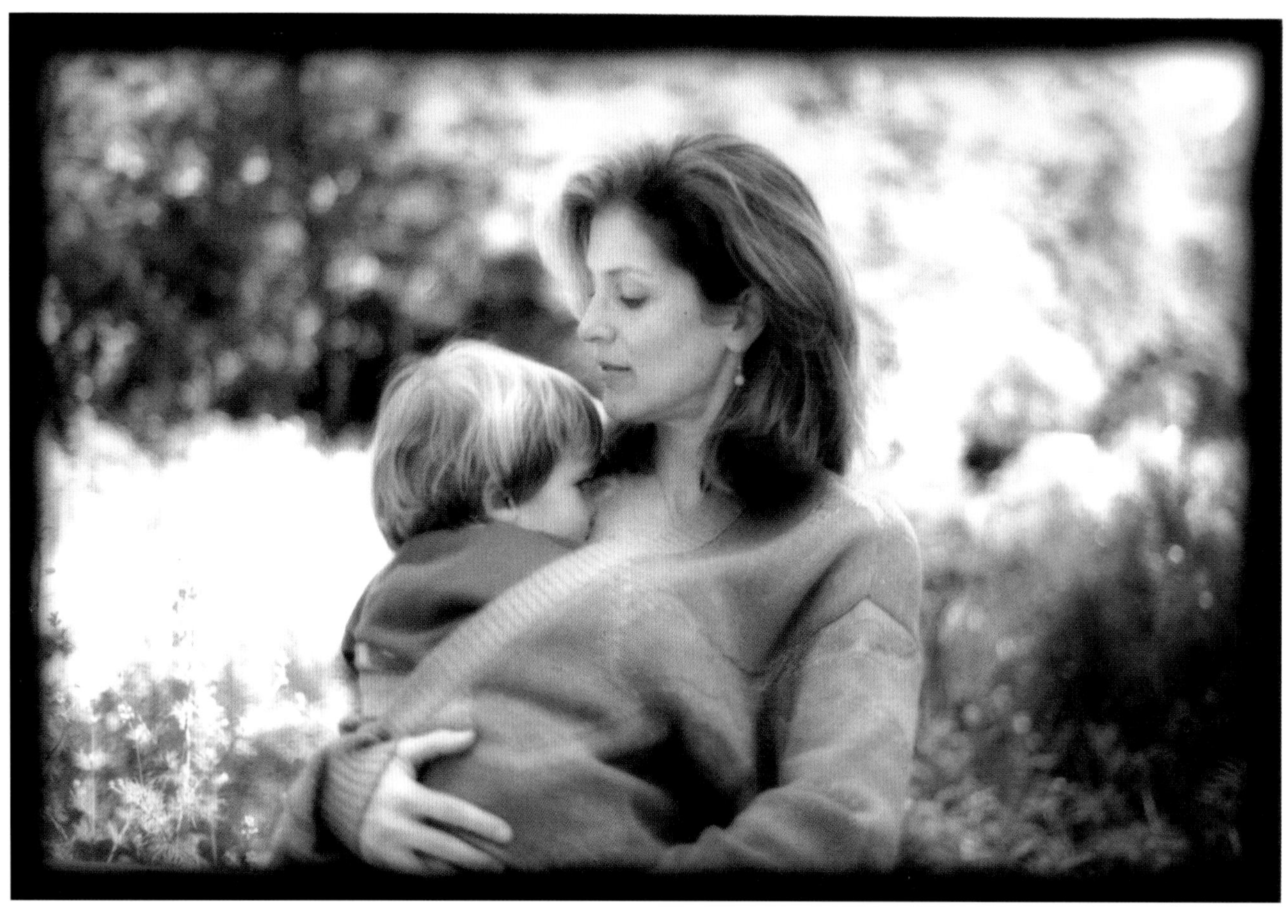

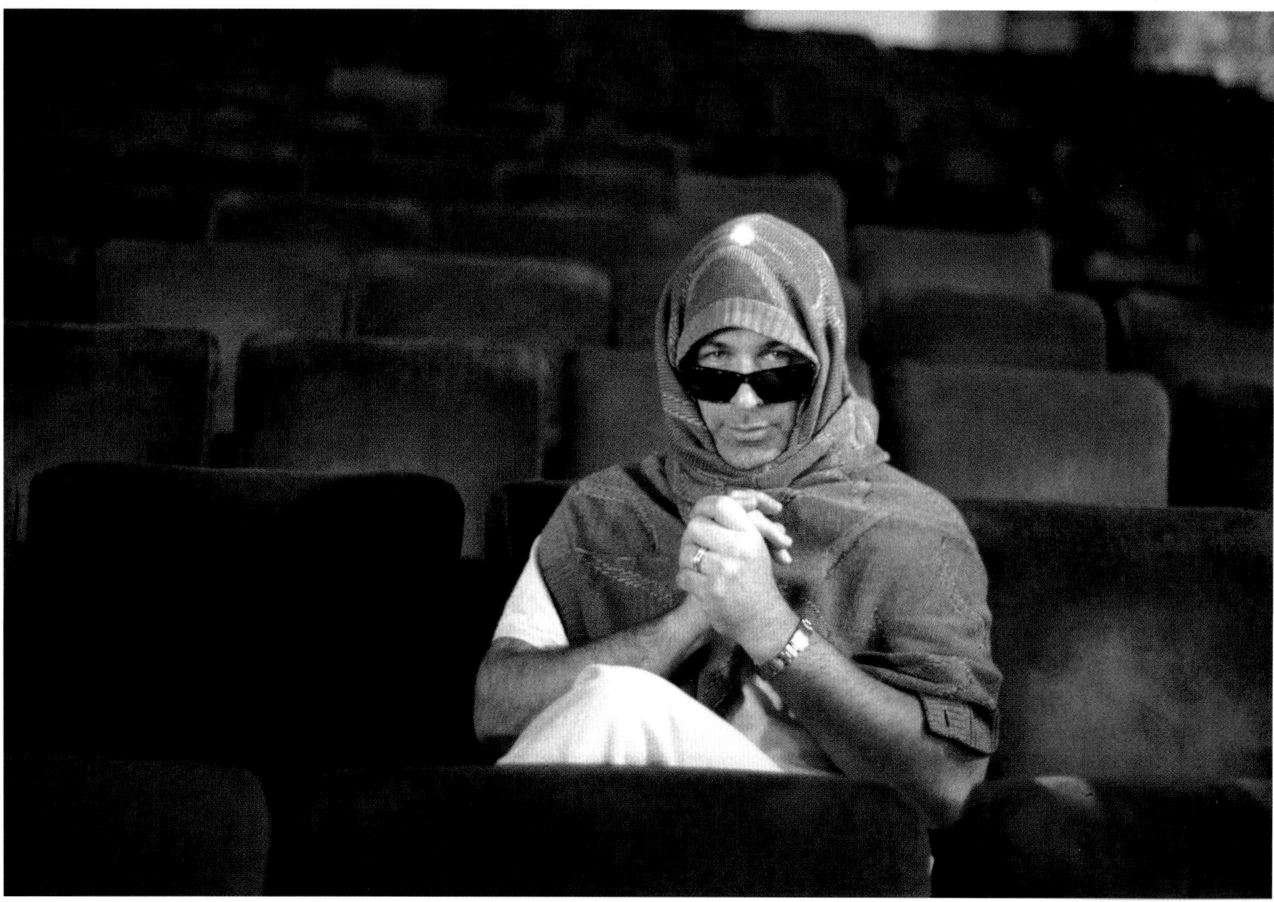

Patricia Kalember with Toby in Riverside Drive

Alec Baldwin at the Tony Awards rehearsal, Radio City Music Hall

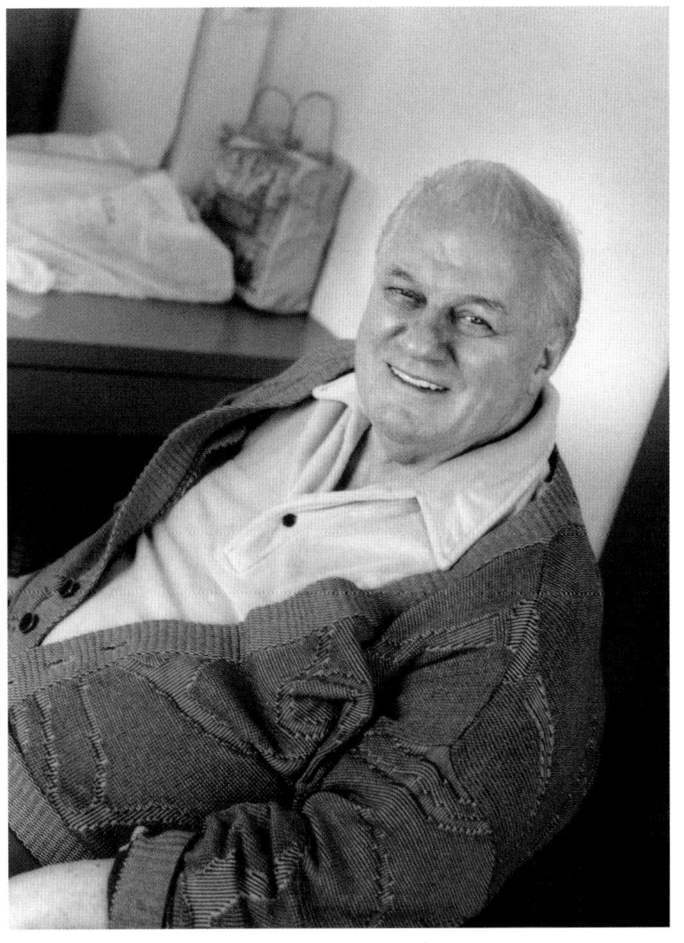

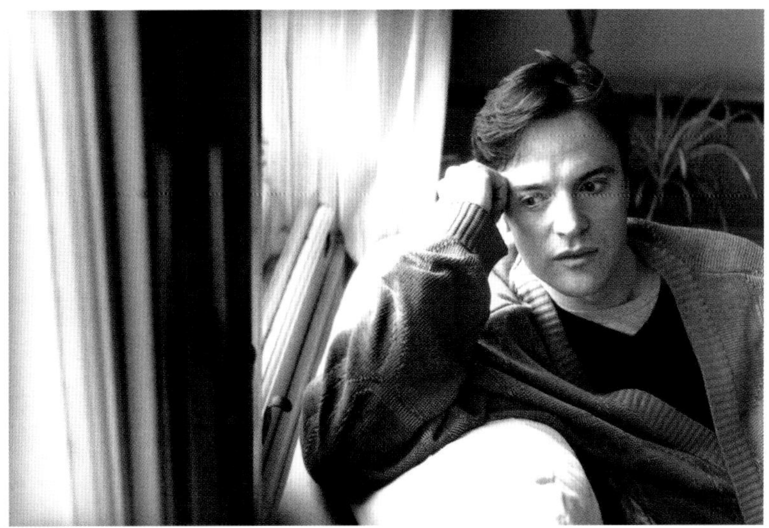

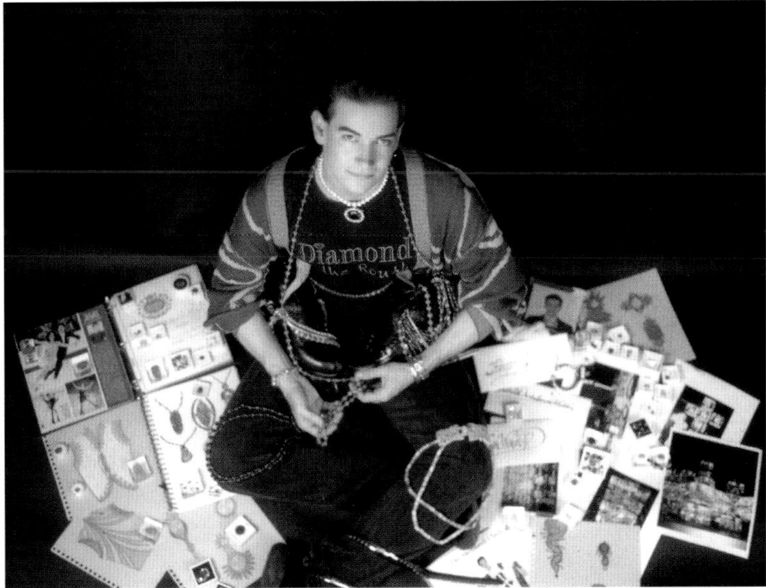

Clockwise from top left:

Charles Durning on the road with *The Gin Game*

Paul Rhys in West Norwood, London

Raven Snook in Hell's Kitchen, New York City

Shepherd Clark with his competition skates and new line of jewelry in New York City

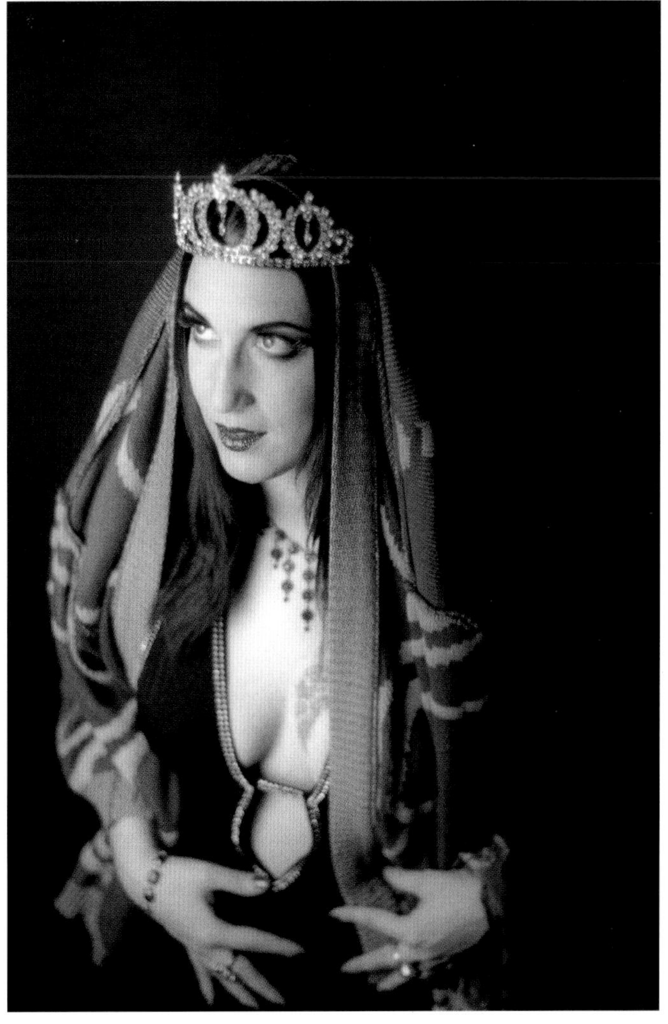

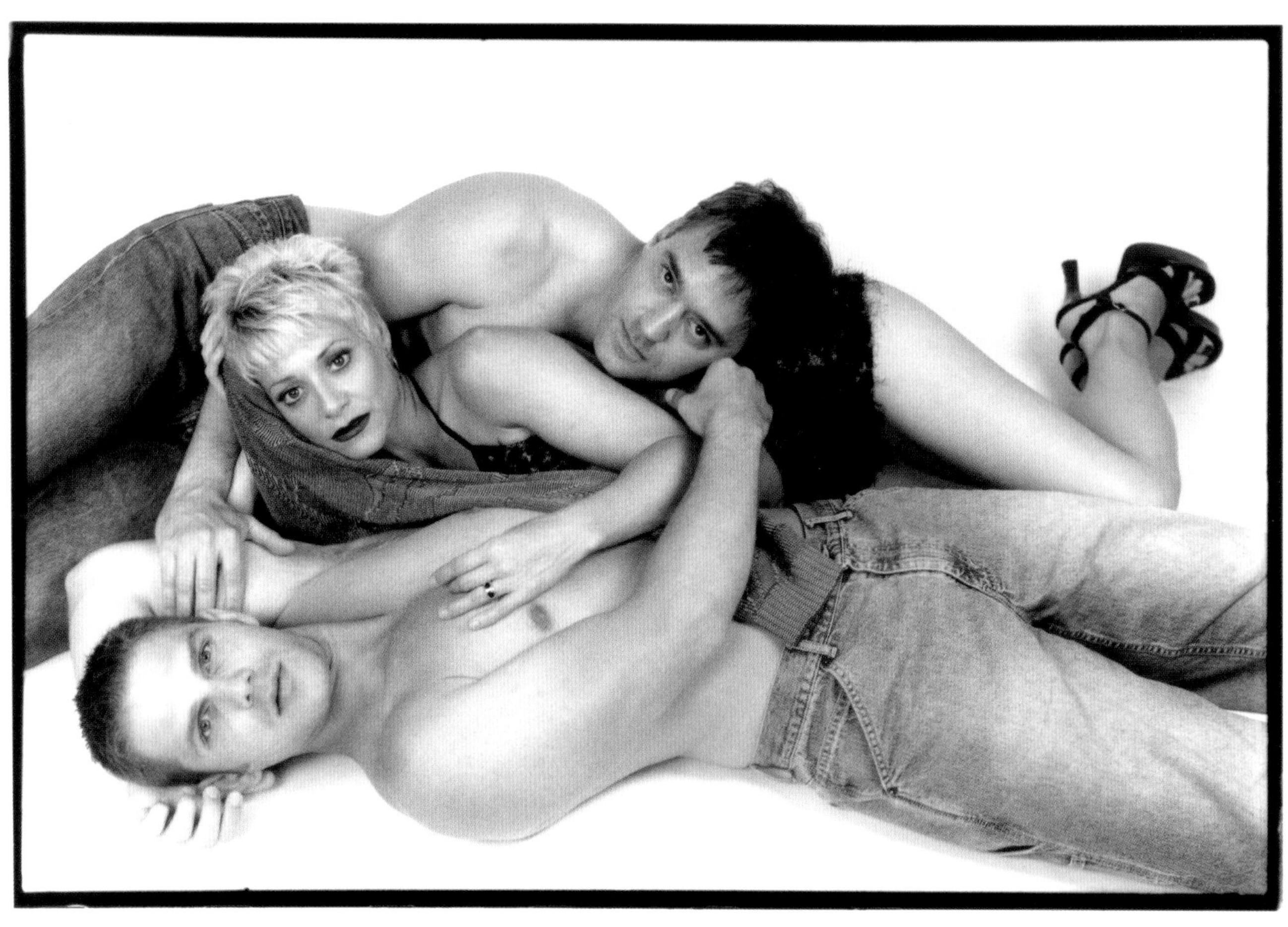

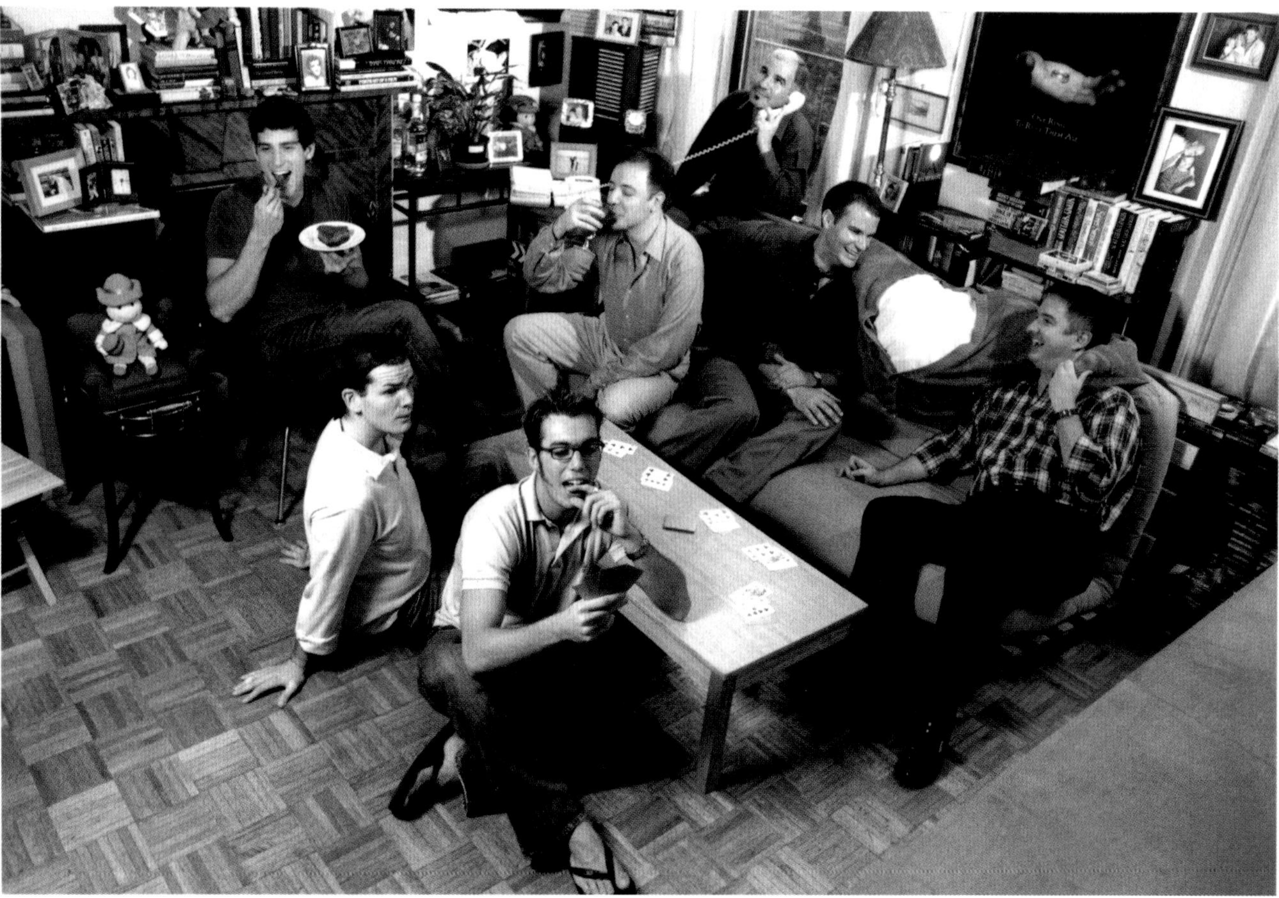

Top: AJ Triano, Jennifer Houston, and Mark Gilrain (*front to back*)

Bottom, clockwise from top left: Jonathan Chase, Michael Raymen, Mitchell Waters, Mark Ramsay, Paul J. Williams, Tim Dieterichs, Mark Addison

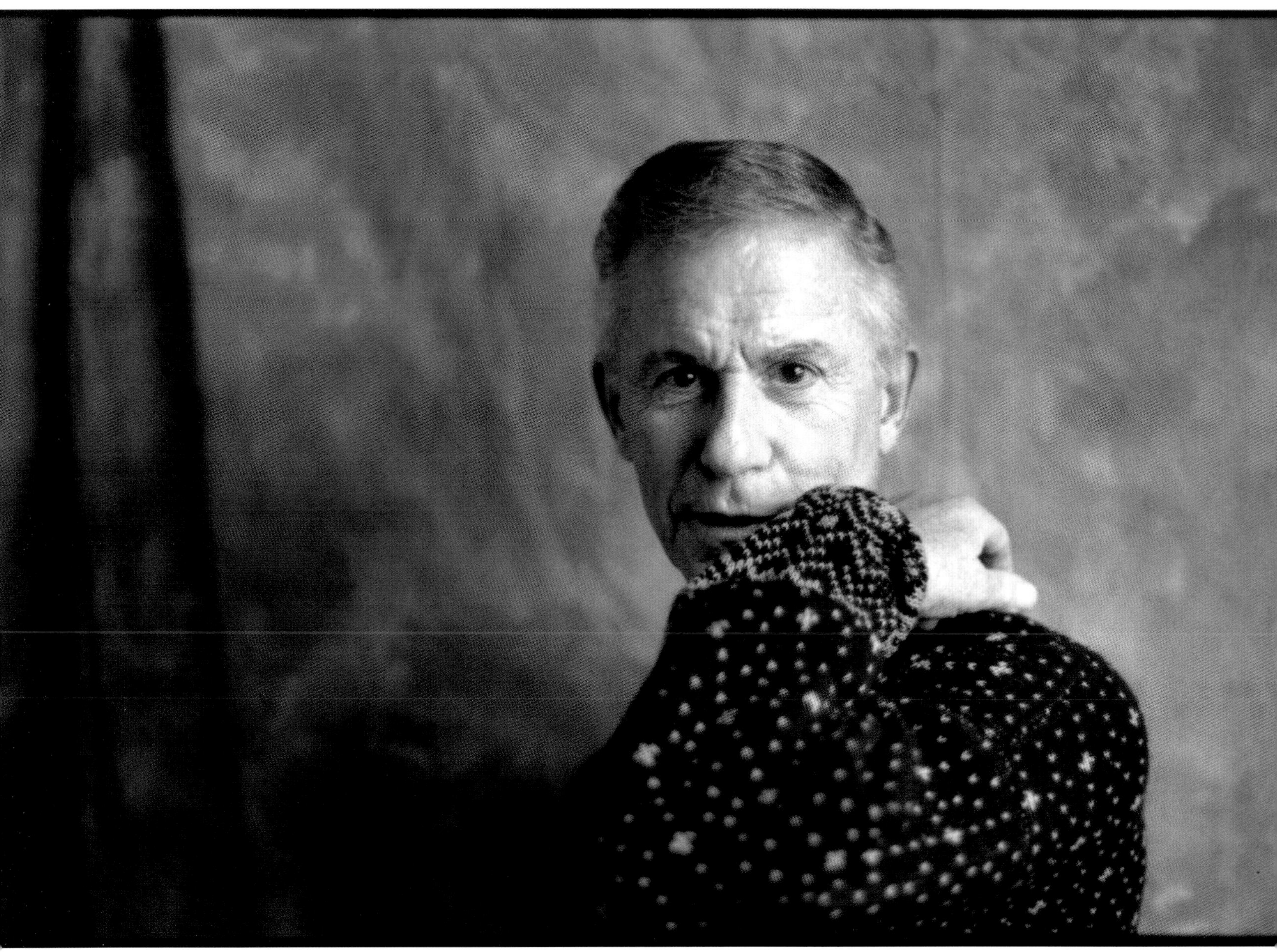

Roddy McDowall

I rarely work with other photographers—it's that intimidation thing. But when you're offered the opportunity to work with a favorite photographer who is also a favorite actor, you don't blink!

Interestingly, when I work, I frequently have one shoe and sock off—it's a personal thing. While working on this shoot, I looked down to see Roddy McDowall had one shoe off!
I didn't ask.

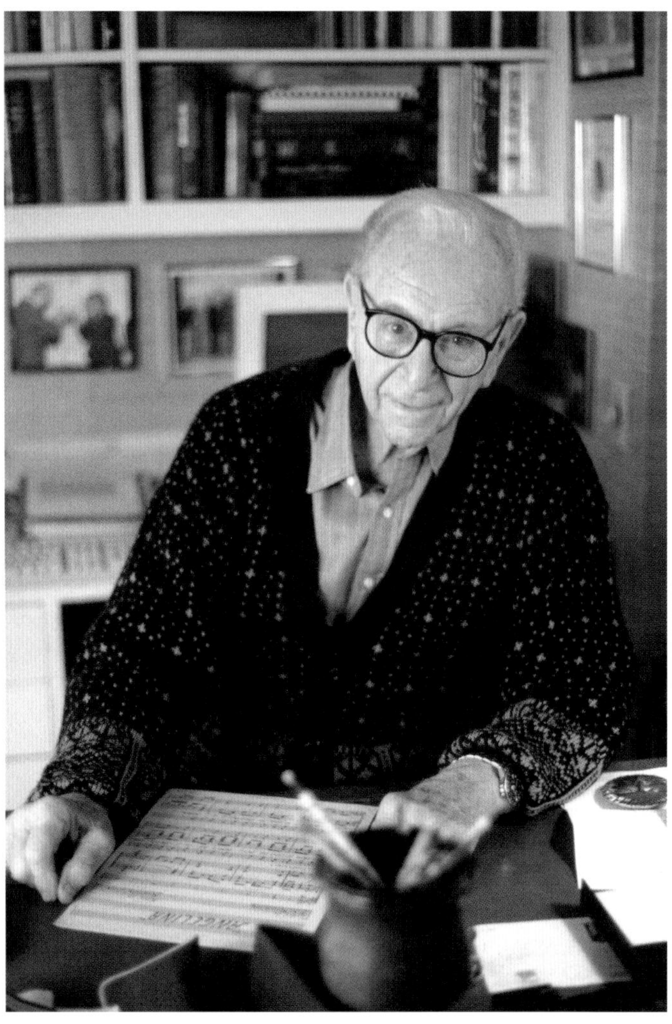

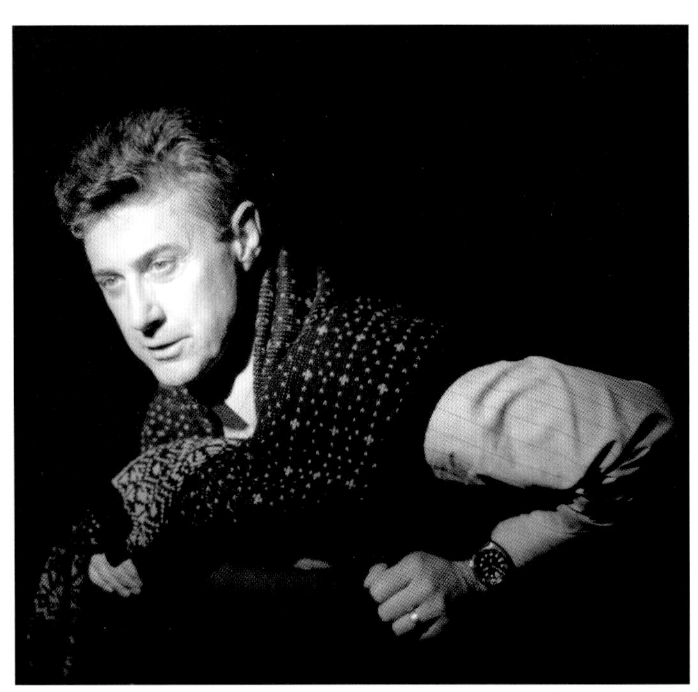

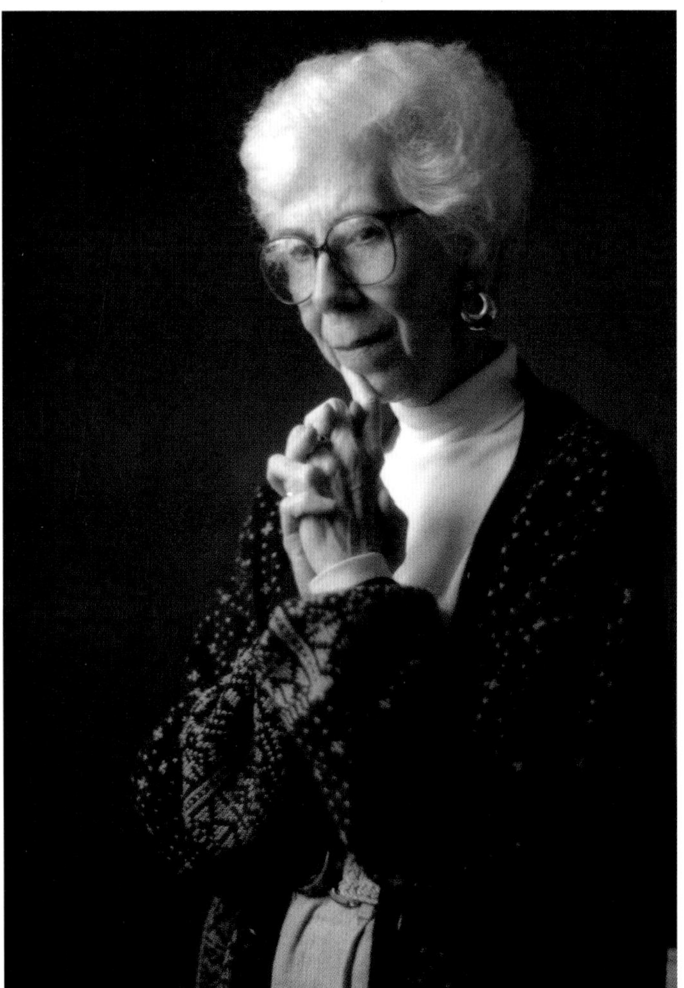

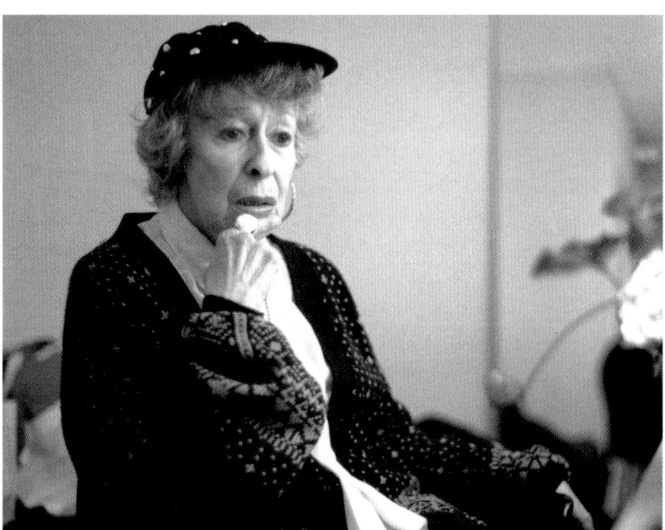

Clockwise from top left:

David Dukes

Burton Lane

Eileen Heckart

Portia Nelson

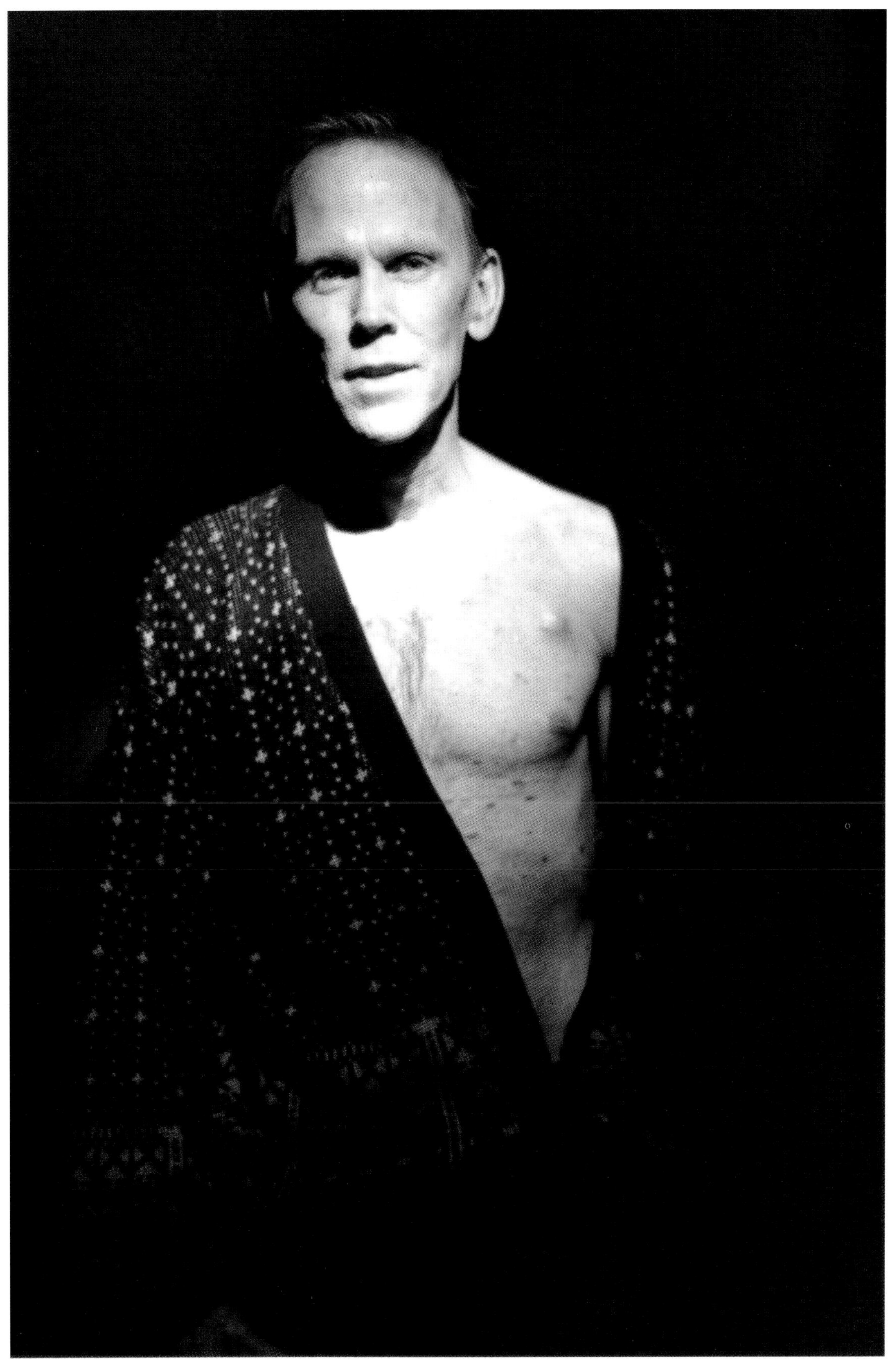

Bill Wright

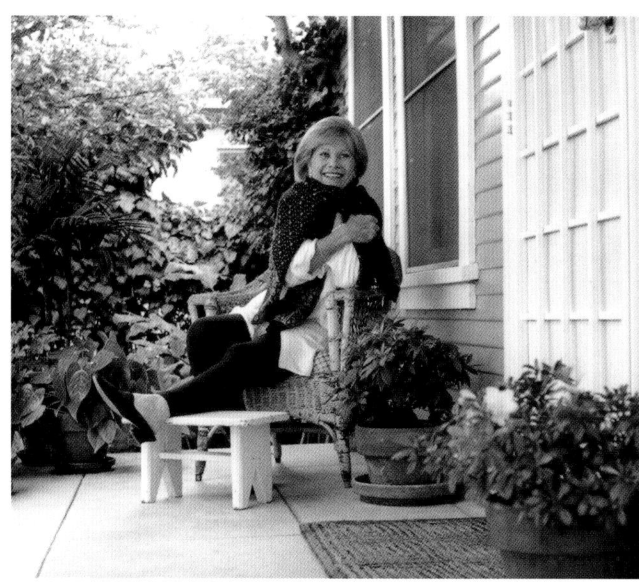

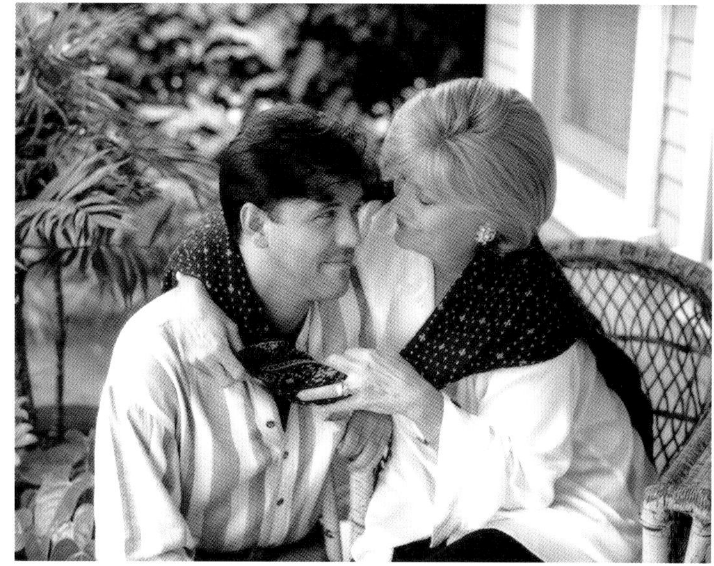

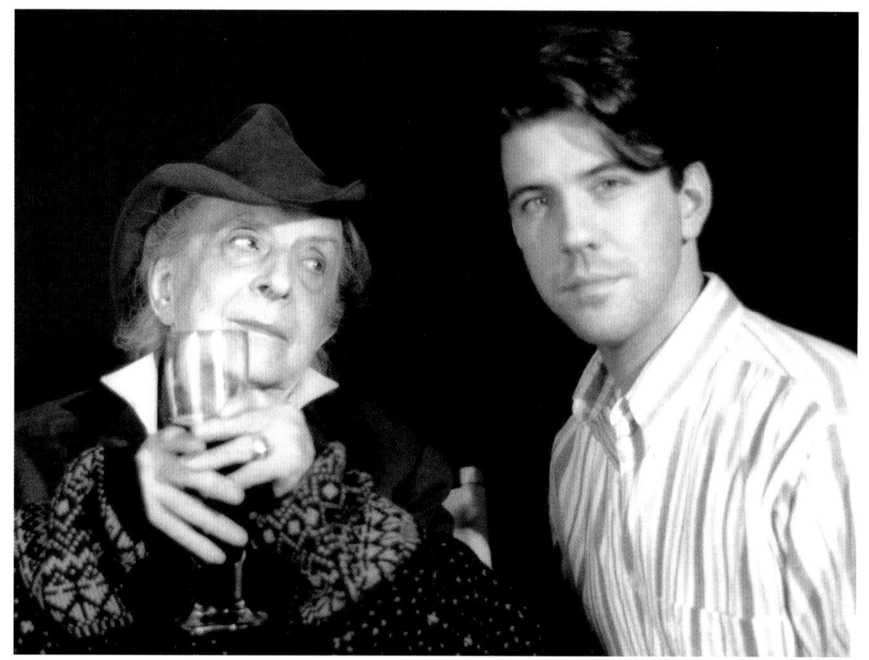

My greatest personal joy while working on this book has been making it possible for Pat to meet some of his personal heroes. He flew out to Los Angeles expressly to be with me on the day that I photographed his favorite actress, Bibi Besch (*above*). Bibi welcomed us into her home and embraced us and our admiration of her beauty and talent. During the afternoon, we shared stories and laughs and confidences, one of which was her admission to us that she was battling cancer. She was hale and hearty and ready to fight the fight. Sadly, a month later, the fight was over, and that afternoon remains one of the highlights, not of my career, but of our lives.

When the great personality and humorist Quentin Crisp (*right*) came for his photo shoot, we served him dinner and listened intently to each and every story. Every word, every joke, every platitude was a nugget of happiness for us, even though we had already read most of them in his books. I spent the evening listening to Mr. Crisp but watching Pat, who gazed lovingly at this wild and wonderful man who paved the way for so many. It was like watching a little boy with his granddaddy. For that experience, I will always be grateful.

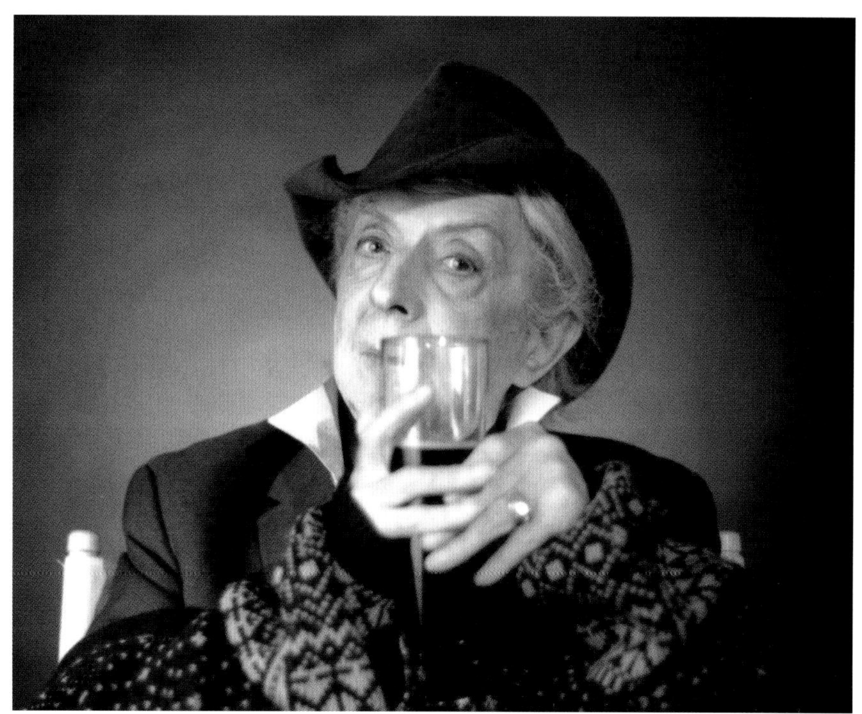

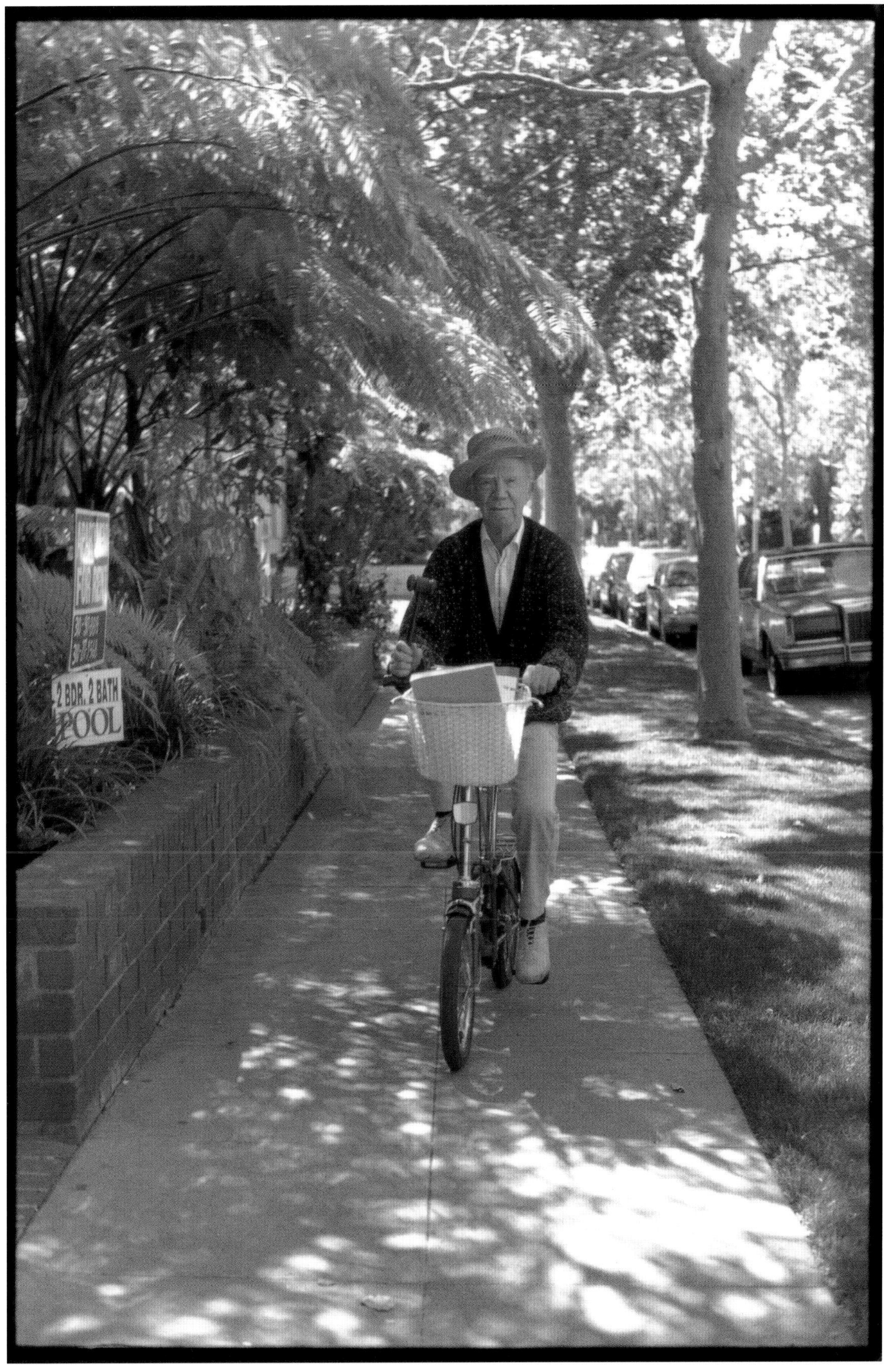

Mr. Ray Walston

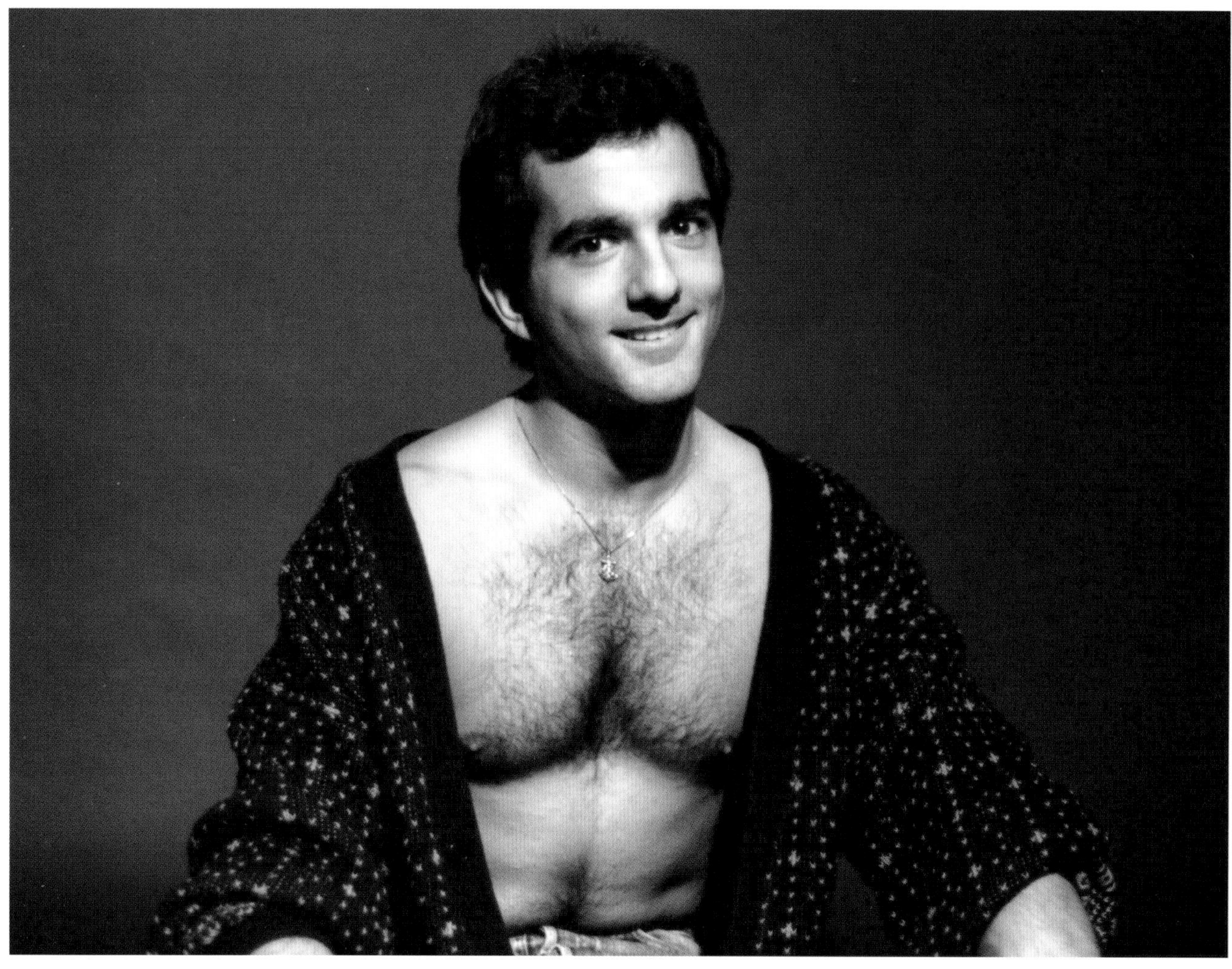

Gary Eddleman

This is my friend Gary Eddleman. He was quite possibly the most generous person I have ever known. The things he gave me ranged from the frivolous (videotapes) to the life-altering (driving lessons). Most important, he taught me some lessons that I'd like to share with you.

Gary waited too long to get an HIV test. When he tested positive, he waited too long to take his treatments seriously, skipping days' worth of medication and vitamins. One day we had a fight. We waited too long to make up. On July 17, 1994, Gary died. I loved him very much and I miss him. This is the lesson I learned:

If you haven't had an HIV test, get one.

If you test positive, get treatment.

If you care about someone, tell them.

If you have a fight, be the first to apologize, be the first to forgive.

Stop waiting. Time is running out.

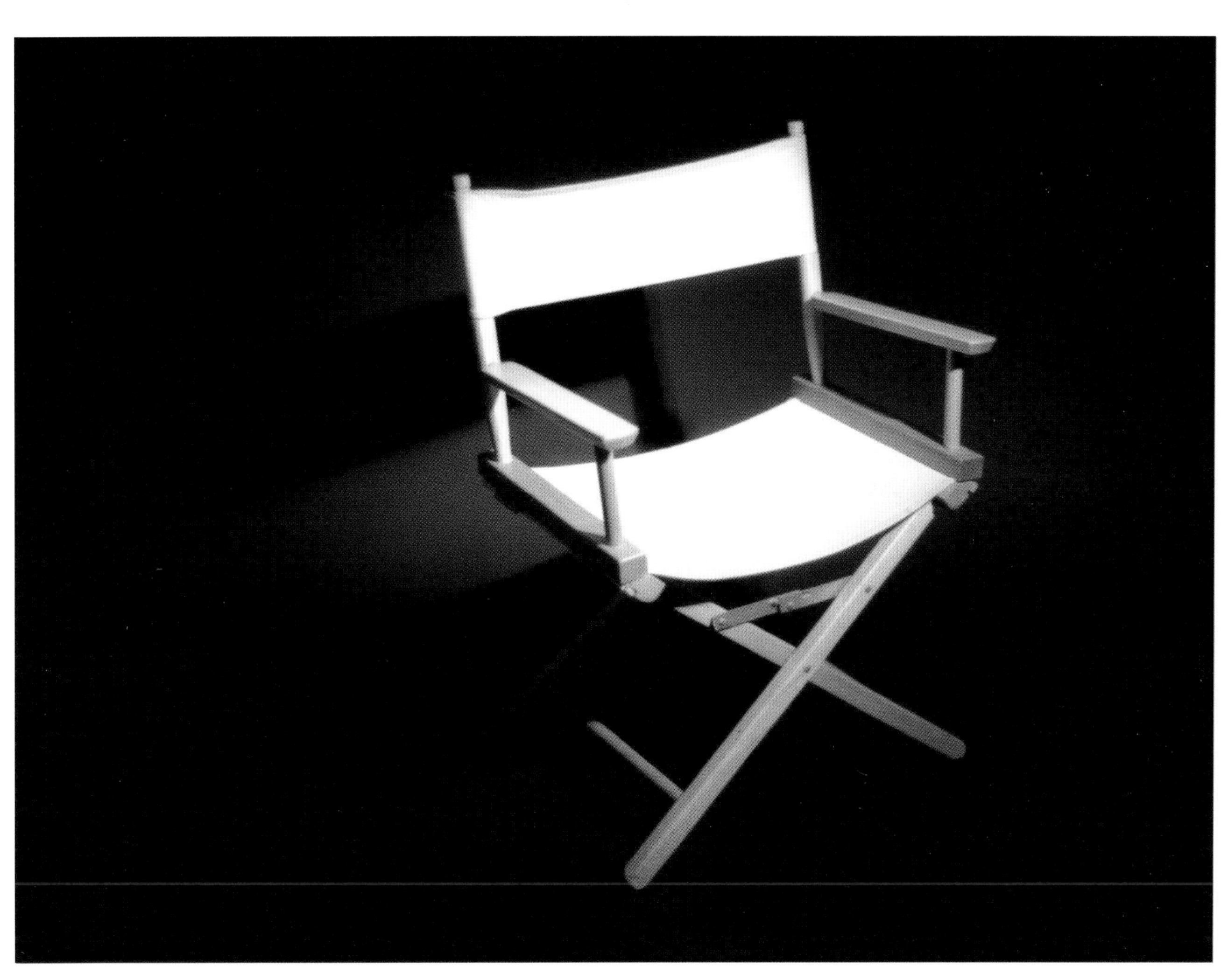

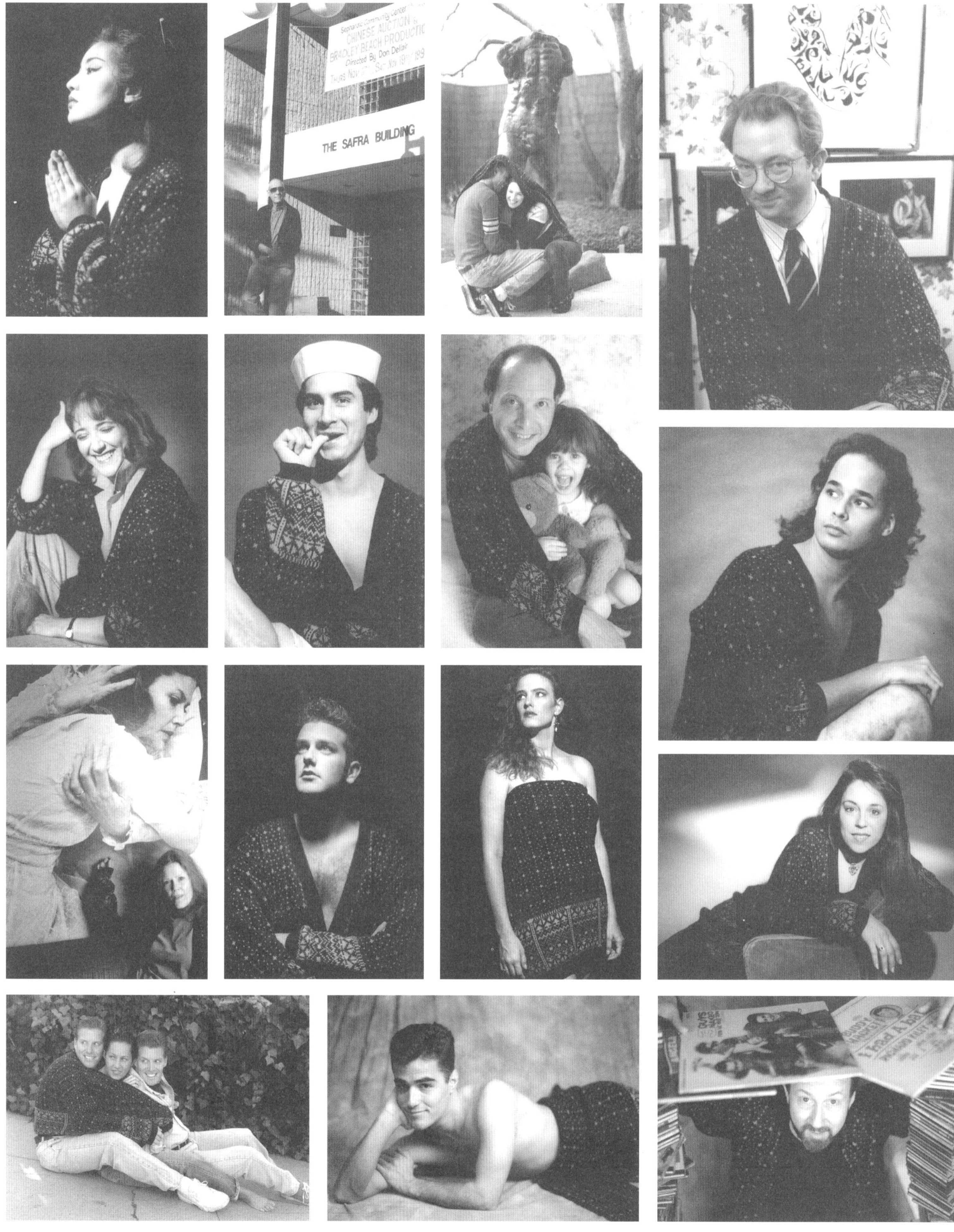
CHINESE AUCTION
THE SAFRA BUILDING